PILGRIMAGE IN GRAECO-ROMAN & EARLY CHRISTIAN ANTIQUITY

Pilgrimage in Graeco-Roman & Early Christian Antiquity
Seeing the Gods

Edited by
JAŚ ELSNER
and
IAN RUTHERFORD

OXFORD
UNIVERSITY PRESS

OXFORD

UNIVERSITY PRESS

Great Clarendon Street, Oxford OX2 6DP

Oxford University Press is a department of the University of Oxford.
It furthers the University's objective of excellence in research, scholarship,
and education by publishing worldwide in

Oxford New York

Auckland Cape Town Dar es Salaam Hong Kong Karachi
Kuala Lumpur Madrid Melbourne Mexico City Nairobi
New Delhi Shanghai Taipei Toronto

With offices in

Argentina Austria Brazil Chile Czech Republic France Greece
Guatemala Hungary Italy Japan Poland Portugal Singapore
South Korea Switzerland Thailand Turkey Ukraine Vietnam

Oxford is a registered trade mark of Oxford University Press
in the UK and in certain other countries

Published in the United States
by Oxford University Press Inc., New York

British Library Cataloguing in Publication Data

Data available

Library of Congress Cataloging in Publication Data

Data available

Typeset by SPI Publisher Services, Pondicherry, India
Printed in Great Britain
on acid-free paper by
Biddles Ltd., King's Lynn, Norfolk

ISBN 0–19–925079–0   978–0–19–925079–0

1 3 5 7 9 10 8 6 4 2

Acknowledgements

Many of the papers in this volume had their origin in a conference on pilgrimage (Seeing the Gods. Patterns of Pilgrimage in Graeco-Roman Antiquity) held at the University of Reading in July 2000. The editors would like to thank the University of Reading for providing facilities and the British Academy for a conference grant that helped to pay for the expenses of speakers. We would like to thank David Levenson, Barbara Kowalzig, and the Press's anonymous readers. Ian Rutherford would like to thank the University of Cincinnati for granting him a Tytus Fellowship in the spring of 2003, in the course of which some of the introduction was written.

Contents

PART II. PILGRIMAGE IN THE ROMAN EMPIRE

PART III. JEWISH AND CHRISTIAN PILGRIMAGE

List of Figures

CHAPTER 7

All images are reproduced by permission of the Deutsches Archäologisches Institut, Pergamon-Grabung.

CHAPTER 9

CHAPTER 10

CHAPTER 12

CHAPTER 14

CHAPTER 16

Abbreviations

GRBS	*Greek, Roman, and Byzantine Studies*
HThR	*Harvard Theological Review*
IC	*Inscriptiones Creticae*, ed. M. Guarducci, 4 vols. (1935–50)
IG	*Inscriptiones Graecae* (1873–)
IGLS	*Inscriptiones Graecae et Latinae Syriae*
JbAC	*Jahrbuch für Antike und Christentum*
JHS	*Journal of Hellenic Studies*
JPBC	J. Wilkinson (ed.), *Jerusalem Pilgrims before the Crusades* (Warminster, 1977)
JRA	*Journal of Roman Archaeology*
JRS	*Journal of Roman Studies*
LÄ	*Lexikon der Ägyptologie*, ed. W. Helck, E. Otto (Wiesbaden, 1972–92)
LF	Library of the Fathers, 43 vols. (Oxford, 1838–74)
LGS	J. de Prott and L. Ziehen, *Leges Graecorum Sacrae e Titulis Collectae* (Leipzig, 1896)
LIMC	*Lexicon Iconographicum Mythologiae Classicae* (Zurich, 1981–99).
LSAM	F. Sokolowski, *Lois sacrées d'Asie Mineur* (Paris, 1955)
LSCG	F. Sokolowski, *Lois sacrées des cités grecques* (Paris, 1969)
LSS	F. Sokolowski, *Lois sacrées des cités grecques*, suppl. (Paris, 1962)
NPNCF	Nicene and Post-Nicene Christian Fathers (Oxford, 1890–1900)
OGIS	W. Dittenberger, *Orientis Graecae Inscriptiones Selectae* (Hildesheim, 1960)
PCPS	*Proceedings of the Cambridge Philological Society*
PG	*Patrologia Graeca*, ed., J.-P. Migne (Paris, 1857–)
PIR² V	*Prosopographia Imperii Romani*, 2nd edn. by E. Groag, A. Stein, et al. (1933–)
PL	*Patrologia Latina*, ed., J.-P. Migne (Paris, 1844–)
PPTS	Palestine Pilgrims' Text Society (London)
PW	H. W. Parke and D. E. Wormell, *The Delphic Oracle*, 2 vols. (Oxford, 1956)
RE	Pauly-Wissowa, *Real-Encyclopädie der klassischen Altertumswissenschaft*
REA	*Revue des études anciennes*
REG	*Revue des études grecques*
REJ	*Revue des études juïves*
REL	*Revue des études latines*
RGVV	Religionsgeschictliche Versuche und Vorarbeiten, ed. A. Dieterich, R. Wünsch, L. Malten, O. Weinreich, L. Deubner (1903–)
RN	*Revue Numismatique*
SC	Sources Chrétiennes (Paris, 1942–)

SEG	*Supplementum Epigraphicum Graecum* (1923–)
SIG[3]	W. Dittenberger, *Sylloge Inscriptionum Graecarum* (Leipzig, 1915–24)
SIRIS	L. Vidman, *Sylloge Inscriptionum Religionis Isiacae et Serapiacae*, RGGV (Berlin, 1969)
ST	*Sacred Tales* (P. Aelius Aristides)
TAM	E. Kalinka et al., *Tituli Asiae Minoris* (1901–)
VChr	*Vigiliae Christianae*
YCS	*Yale Classical Studies*
ZPE	*Zeitschrift für Papyrologie and Epigraphik*

Contributors

MICHAEL ARNUSH is Associate Professor and Chair, Classics, Skidmore College

JAŚ ELSNER is Humphry Payne Senior Research Fellow in Classical Art and Archaeology at Corpus Christi College, Oxford

ANDREW FEAR is Lecturer in the Department of Classics and Ancient History at the University of Manchester

DAVID FRANKFURTER is Professor in the Department of History at the University of New Hampshire

MARCO GALLI is professore a contratto, Dipartimento di Scienze Storiche, Archeologiche e Anthropologiche dell' Antichità, Università degli studi, Roma 1 'La Sapienza'

WILLIAM HUTTON is Assistant Professor in the Department of Classical Studies at the College of William and Mary

BARBARA KOWALZIG is Caulkwell Fellow and Tutor in Ancient History at University College, Oxford

JANE LIGHTFOOT is Sherwood Fellow and Tutor in Classics at New College, Oxford

FRED NAIDEN is Assistant Professor of Classical Studies at Tulane University

ANDREA WILSON NIGHTINGALE is Professor of Classics and Comparative Literature at Stanford University

DAVID NOY is Lecturer in the Department of Classics at the University of Wales, Lampeter

ALEXIA PETSALIS-DIOMIDIS is Lecturer in Classical Archaelogy at Corpus Christi College, Oxford

WENDY PULLAN is Senior Lecturer in the Department of Architecture at the University of Cambridge and a Fellow of Clare College

IAN RUTHERFORD is Professor of Greek at Florida State University

SCOTT SCULLION is Fellow and Tutor in Classics at Worcester College, Oxford

SAROLTA TAKÁCS is Associate Professor of Classics at Rutgers University

GEORGE WILLIAMSON is working for Her Majesty's Government

Introduction

I. THE CONCEPT OF PILGRIMAGE
AND ITS PROBLEMS

The label pilgrimage does actual harm.

Fritz Graf[1]

Let us begin with the critical conceptual problem. This book has been put together on the following working assumption: a particular cluster of phenomena within religious practice, which have been labelled 'pilgrimage', can be identified to have existed both in Graeco-Roman antiquity and in ancient Christianity. This is the minimalist version of the assumption, based on the empirical range of subjects discussed by the various contributors. In fact the claim to examine pilgrimage at all implies a still bigger (or looser) working definition of the theme as a phenomenon susceptible to some generalization within the range of Christianity as a whole (both chronologically as well as across its regional and theological denominations) and—still more grandly— across other religions, in particular the so-called 'world religions' of Hinduism, Judaism, Buddhism, and Islam, as well as the polytheistic religions of antiquity. A big and loose definition of pilgrimage like this is common in a number of academic disciplines which have turned their attention to the various phenomena associated with it—one thinks immediately of anthropology and historical geography.[2]

---

[1] Graf (2002a), 195.

[2] For anthropology see for instance Morinis (1992a); Coleman and Elsner (1995). For geography, see Singh and Singh (1987); Bhardwaj and Rinschede (1988); Bhardwaj,

However, a number of distinguished scholars of ancient (Graeco-Roman and Egyptian) religion have been resistant to the term, for several cogent reasons.[3] The arguments adduced to insulate classical antiquity from pilgrimage include the looseness of applying a relatively vague terminology inevitably infected by Christian models, or models drawn from modern religion.[4] These models—it has been argued—may be applicable to some sites (such as mystery sanctuaries or some healing shrines) but not to others, just as the concept of 'pilgrim' may be applicable to some visitors to sanctuaries (seeking healing or spiritual advice) but not to others (such as official delegates known as *theōroi*, spectators at contests, participant athletes at panhellenic games and so on). For this line of scholarship, to apply the term pilgrimage to the multiple, varied, local, and highly differentiated cult practices and cult centres of antiquity is to cram a vast diversity into a uniform bed of Procrustes. Still worse, a generalizing and Christianizing label like pilgrimage—while it emphasizes continuity between antiquity and its successors—tends to elide important (perhaps constitutively essential) differences.

The impasse is about much more than terminology. It reflects profound disciplinary boundaries—especially the resistance among historians of ancient religion to the excessive Christianizing of their forebears.[5] This resistance, of course, is largely right. But it cannot help being ideological. That is, we may ask how much of the baby we throw out with the bathwater when we deny 'Christianity' to pre-Christian antiquity. Or to put this with less paradoxical or metaphorical grotesquery: in the move from numerous polytheisms to Christianity—a context that combined profound change with certain fundamental continuities in religion—the denial of the term pilgrimage (over-)emphasizes difference (and hence change), while its employment

Rinschede, and Sievers (1994); Park (1994), 145–85; Stoddard and Morinis (1997); and for geography as applied specifically to the ancient and medieval Mediterranean, see Horden and Purcell (2000), 445–9. Cf. Naquin and Yü (1992) on relationship between pilgrimage in the Chinese tradition and modern Western notions of pilgrimage.

[3] Not least Scott Scullion in this volume.
[4] See e.g. Siebert (1973), 52–3; Bernand (1988), 49; Graf (2002*a*), 194; Scheid (2000), 23 n. 18.
[5] For discussion of some 19th- and early 20th-cent. uses of 'Wallfahrten' and 'pèlerinages' for ancient religion in the likes of Curtius and Erman, see Bernand (1988), 50 and Graf (2002*a*), 194 n. 4.

(over-) emphasizes similarity and hence continuity. The pilgrimage problem is here a subset of the much bigger problem of continuity and change in religion between antiquity and Christendom. Since almost every observable practice of early Christian pilgrimage can be paralleled by, and was surely borrowed from, pre-Christian pagan (and Jewish) practices, it is surely absurd to deny all continuity.[6] Yet the idea that pilgrimage emerged *de novo*, with the rise of the Church is not uncommon.[7] Take the following extraordinary opinion advanced in a book published in 1988:

With Christianity we find at last an audience for the first-person travel account and a metaphysic in which private experience is valued and self-consciousness imperative. The new religion and the foreignness of its holy places together make a fertile ground for the development of an experiential kind of travel literature virtually unknown before Egeria's *peregrinatio*.[8]

The ignorance of classical traditions of sacred travel-writing (some of which are discussed in the essays of this book) is frankly shocking in what is presented as critical scholarship, though the judgement expressed here does not wholly misrepresent the ways ancient religions have been served by their historiography:[9] It is in part in resistance to this line of differentiation between the pagan and the early Christian worlds, that one might edge towards using the concept of pilgrimage (despite the problems).

But the difficulties are still more complex. Those who deny the validity of 'pilgrimage' for antiquity rarely trouble to define the term. One strategy, indeed, is to ignore it and all the manifestations of sacred mobility which pilgrimage implies in otherwise comprehensive accounts of, for example, Greek religion.[10] What scholars reject, in favour of the specific, nuanced, and subtle discussion of particular issues in

---

[6] In pilgrimage studies, the strongest assertion of continuity is Kötting (1950), 12–79.

[7] e.g. Campbell (1988), 7, 18, 20.

[8] Campbell (1988), 20.

[9] Cf. Parker (1996), 185: 'the individual motive is a habitual absentee from studies of Greek religion'.

[10] One thinks of Parker (1996), despite discussions of festivals (75–80) and of healing cults (174–87); or Parker (1985)—an excellent discussion of oracle consultation; or Price (1999) despite much discussion of festivals (25–46) and sacred centres (47–66). Likewise there is no mention of pilgrims or pilgrimage in Beard, North, and Price (1998) until the text moves to Christianity.

ancient religion, is a generalized 'straw man' infected with Christian presuppositions. The problem is well illustrated by the reactions to the suggestion that the second-century CE Greek travel writer, Pausanias, may be seen as a pilgrim.[11] One objection (clearly dependent on the importation of Christian notions of belief into the definition of pilgrimage) is that a pilgrim is one who must *believe in full* before embarking on a sacred journey—which would certainly distance not only Pausanias but also the rest of antiquity's religious authors (and not a negligible number of post-antique writers too) from characterization as pilgrims.[12] Yet belief is a term notoriously redefined by Christianity, and the notion of *full* belief is even harder to explain or substantiate historically, except in Christian theological terms. Another line of attack has been to argue that 'pilgrimage implies a journey by a devotee in pursuance of a primarily religious objective'—which is so purist a formulation of pilgrimage as to disqualify not only Pausanias but most other pilgrims in cultural contexts where the validity of the term has never been contested (such as Christianity or Islam).[13] If we are to use words like pilgrimage, we have to be careful to use them in ways that allow them at least some meaning in the contexts to which they are applied. As Horden and Purcell acutely remark in the course of their discussion of pilgrimage in the ancient and medieval Mediterranean:

The salient point about pilgrimage is that it need not always be a journey undertaken exclusively or even principally for religious reasons.[14]

The kind of Christianizing generalization for 'pilgrimage' so often assumed by ancient historians is not difficult to make since, from an anthropological view, pilgrimage has proved extremely difficult to

[11] The blame for this lies largely with the editors of this collection: see Elsner (1992) and Rutherford (2001*a*), now also Hutton in this volume.

[12] See Swain (1996), 342 n. 50.

[13] See Arafat (1996), 10–11 and n. 22, quote from p. 10. An insistence on this kind of purism in defining pilgrimage is common in writing on Christianity—see e.g. Kuelzer (2002), 152. But in fact the polarity of 'pilgrimage' and 'curiosity' (with all the non-sacred implications of that word), is as old as the earliest polemics on the subject. The classic Christian intervention is Gregory of Nyssa's 4th-cent. second epistle (*PG* 46.1009–16), with e.g. Coleman and Elsner (1995), 80–1, and Williams (1998), 94–131 for this text's continuing significance in the Reformation debate on pilgrimage. Generally on this issue, see Zacher (1976).

[14] Horden and Purcell (2000), 445.

define.[15] Victor and Edith Turner's grand attempt to present a general theory of pilgrimage in terms of a rejection of normal social structure and the celebration of a kind of socially undifferentiated state of 'communitas'—despite its hugely stimulating effect, the probable correctness of emphasizing the pilgrim's journey as a rite of passage and its success in combining some phenomenological aspects of pilgrim experience with objective outsider description—has proved impossible to sustain in the face of ethnographic data from the field.[16] In his much more minimalist attempt to provide a definition, Alan Morinis tries:

> Pilgrimage is a journey undertaken by a person in quest of a place or state that he or she believes to embody a sacred ideal.[17]

Even this—which might be accused of being so general as to be trivial— is open to question. While it rightly emphasizes the centrality of travel and eschews the necessity of a sacred centre as goal,[18] this characterization as it stands is probably too 'Protestant' in its emphasis on the individual. One might add 'or a group' to Morinis's 'person'. But what Morinis rightly emphasizes is the composite and varied nature of the journey, potentially including 'elements of mythology, ritual, belief, psychology, social roles, architecture, geography, literature, drama, art and spiritual concerns'.[19] It is extremely difficult, perhaps impossible to determine the boundaries between pilgrimage proper (if there is such a thing) and other kinds of travel such as tourism.[20] Indeed, one might say that for the religiously minded (or for those with a tendency to become so) any kind of journey has the potential to become pilgrimage.

One objection to all this discussion of pilgrimage is that it may be true, but is it so vague as to be hermeneutically useless? Here we run up

---

[15] The following contributors discuss the definition of pilgrimage: Kowalzig, p. 44; Scullion, *passim*; Nightingale, pp. 156–7; Williamson, pp. 220–3; Hutton, pp. 293–7; Lightfoot, p. 333; Galli, p. 262.

[16] See e.g. Turner (1973), and (1974*a*), Turner and Turner (1978), with summaries of the numerous critiques in Eade and Sallnow (1991) 4–5 and Coleman and Elsner (1991). For a sensitive assessment of the place of phenomenological experience in pilgrimage, see Harris (1999), xiii–xviii.

[17] Morinis (1992*b*), 4.

[18] On the particular early Christian model of pilgrimage as goal-less travel for the sake of God, see for instance Elsner and Rubiés (1999), 19–20.

[19] Morinis (1992*b*), 2.

[20] Morinis (1992*b*), 7. For antiquity specifically, see Horden and Purcell (2000), 445 and Rutherford (2001*a*).

against the problem of imagination in the study of religion. Imagination is extremely dangerous, of course, for without sufficient self-restraint, one can imagine anything (especially in matters of religion). But without imagination, our dry and dusty empirical data—the texts carefully culled to render a florilegium of religion-specific excerpts, the objects dug up, the topography, terrain, and remains of particular sites—are impossible to turn into a compelling picture. The problems of studying ancient religion (and here early Christianity must definitely be included) are numerous. As Fritz Graf has recently put it in the course of a discussion of sacrifice in antiquity, the weight of our sources is textual (which is to say biased in one way or another) while the archaeological evidence—even if it is less biased—is not only highly fragmentary but tends to represent not the normative but the aberrant. That is to say, at least in Graf's view, the archaeological data—always a particularist testimony to a specific site or set of sites—tends to emphasize the local eccentricities within the pattern of religion as a whole rather than what might be characterized as the general case.[21] To deal with these problems, historians of religion turn to comparative interdisciplinarity—drawing interpretative models from disciplines like ethnology or social anthropology.[22] Graf rightly objects that such models (apart from often being radically divergent if not mutually exclusive) tend not to offer detailed comparisons or comparanda but rather interpretative frames from elsewhere.

Pilgrimage firmly participates in this problematic. Its scholarly literature—spanning anthropology, history of religions, theology, history, archaeology, art history, and literary criticism—admits of no uniformity and no little contradiction. Moreover, apart from Victor Turner's much contested anthropological model of the 1970s, pilgrimage studies have hardly developed a suitable general theory that can be applied to anything. On the other hand the very diversity and rich ethnography of pilgrimage experience,[23] perhaps not susceptible to simple general-

---

[21] See Graf (2002*b*), 113–14. Here the archaeology of religion intersects with the anthropology of pilgrimage which tends also to reflect 'by definition exceptional practices, irregular journeys outside traditional social realms' (Morinis (1992*b*), 2). Further on the problems of ancient religion importing theoretical models from elsewhere (this time in relation to 'initiation'), see the acute discussion of Graf (2003).

[22] Further on some of the problems, see Brelich (1966), 67–70 and (1979), 230–55.

[23] The excellent site-specific studies of pilgrimage are numerous—for some recent examples (all Christian as it happens), see e.g. Tweed (1997), Frey (1998), Harris (1999),

ization or even to literary description and perhaps better caught in such media as anthropological film,[24] may itself prove a fruitful model for thinking with in relation to antiquity, if one thinks away any excessively (western) Christian elements (such as penitence, for instance). In part, the usefulness of pilgrimage as a comparative model to apply to antiquity lies in enlivening the surviving data with that extraordinary range of possibilities present in the lived and living practice of pilgrimage. Likewise, from a literary point of view, the typologies, tropes, and genres of pilgrimage-writing from outside antiquity may offer fruitful parallels to the ways ancient pilgrimage texts map sacred space into actual terrains and tie local landmarks to religious or mythological narratives.[25]

The extensive secondary literature of early Christian pilgrimage—much richer to be sure than that on Graeco-Roman pilgrimage—has colluded with the Classicists' doubts by regarding the emergence of Christian sacred travel as something radically new, whether it is presented as emerging from a general morass of pre-Christian activities,[26] or seen as essentially different.[27] This is a typical instance of the problem of 'uniqueness' in relation to Christianity which has dogged the historiography of ancient religion for centuries and which has effectively prevented comparison of Christian activities such as pilgrimage on an even or equal playing field with their pagan or Jewish counterparts.[28] It is worth endorsing, from our point of view, a point made forcefully and elegantly by Horden and Purcell:

What is absent from Greece and Rome is not sacred mobility in the broader sense, but a particular terminology and ideological consciousness that is characteristic of medieval Christendom (and, to an extent, of Islam). The pilgrim

Brading (2001). What this literature has not offered since Turner is any kind of attempt at generalization.

[24] e.g. for an outstanding anthropological documentary: J.-P. Urrusti, *El Pueblo Mexicano que Camina* (Istituto Nacional Indigneista, Mexico City, 1996).

[25] e.g. Williams (1998) and (1999); Coleman and Elsner (2002).

[26] See for instance Kötting (1950), 12–79; Maraval (1985), 52–5; MacCormack (1990); Taylor (1993), 48–85; Hunt (1999), 35–8; Talbot (2002), 153.

[27] The majority of the literature which makes no mention of any antecedents to Christian pilgrimage: e.g. Chitty (1966); Hunt (1982); Walker (1990); Wilken (1992); Davis (2001); Maraval (2002); Vikan (2003).

[28] See esp. Smith (1990), 37–46, 52–3.

ideology is a specialised outgrowth from less self conscious but no less wide-spread religiously motivated movements.[29]

Most fundamental is the long history of competitive self-differentiation between scholars of pre-Christian antiquity and scholars of the early Church—a series of complex self affirmations not only of different modes of scholarship but also of apparently different kinds of subject matter to be studied, as well as of different (sometimes subconscious) affiliations to 'Protestant' or 'Catholic' positions (even within Jewish or secularist scholarship).[30] Pilgrimage has been put firmly on the Christian side of this divide for the most part and that has happened to coincide nicely with the deeply secularizing tendency which has governed the writing of ancient history in relation to Greek and Roman religions throughout the second half of the twentieth century.[31] The problem of all this is that it denies the cult-centres of antiquity their rightful place at the centre of a vital network of religious activity whose meanings were not solely about politics or economics but also about subjectivity, culture, and individual as well as collective identity. The denial of pilgrimage contributes to the writing of these issues out of ancient religion and it specifically prevents the possibility of comparing phenomena which are not only parallel in terms of location, types of activity and respective social functions, but were also genealogically related in that the pilgrimage practices of antiquity were clearly ancestral to those inherited, borrowed, and adapted in the Christian and Islamic worlds.

Ultimately, the pilgrimage question puts us in the happy place of all being ideologically invested (whether we like it or not, whether we acknowledge this self consciously or not) whatever position we decide to uphold. If we deny pilgrimage to antiquity (or ignore it, which is simply a less explicit form of denial) we invest in one kind of model of ancient religion to suit our particular prejudices. If we affirm pilgrimage, then we invest equally in a different model, bringing with it a range of different problems. No position here is 'true' or 'right', 'objective', or 'neutral'. So it must be with the study of religion—especially religions

---

[29] Horden and Purcell (2000), 446.
[30] Smith (1990), 33–5, 43.
[31] For a passionate statement on this, which we wholly endorse, see Horden and Purcell (2000), 447.

whose ancestral relations to those who study them make investment or prejudice impossible to avoid. Pilgrimage is by no means unique as an ideological problem for the study of religion—recent scholarship has found itself fundamentally sceptical about such long-held certainties among ancient religious categories as initiation.[32] In the case of pilgrimage, we should find the ideological impasse liberating. For the question of whether we adopt the category or not, should not turn on issues of truth or an excess of refinement in matters of definition, but on whether it is *useful* and for what purpose. This is, we submit, both a pragmatic and a strategic matter. The concept of pilgrimage may indeed create wrong expectations in certain aspects of our assumptions about antique religion and the expectations it carries may indeed map only clumsily onto the range of evidence from antiquity, but it may also allow the opening for a discussion of other aspects of ancient religion than those usually stressed. These include some issues that have been wrongly suppressed for too long—questions of locality and space, of movement and identity, of individual and collective investments in religious ideals as embodied in material culture within the landscape. And, strategically, the employment of the concept allows the introduction of comparability between ancient religions and others, including their most direct successors, Christianity and Islam. Whatever choice we make about the adoption of the notion of pilgrimage, we will certainly be to some extent wrong. Its denial has for too long lost us the space it opens; its affirmation is certain to lead to excess (perhaps even in this volume!), especially if it is applied uncritically.[33] But, at least to us, it seems the right choice to take the risk with the category, and to try as hard as possible to be self-aware about the inevitable importation of modern investments.

II. TYPOLOGY OF ANCIENT PILGRIMAGE

The papers in this volume cover forms of pilgrimage in the Graeco-Roman period, roughly from the fifth century BCE till the maturing of

---

[32] See the essays in Dodd and Faraone (2003). Less sceptically, see also Burkert (2002).

[33] Here lies one of the major problems with Dillon (1997) which applies the terms 'pilgrims' and 'pilgrimage' systematically to ancient Greece without appearing to be aware of the difficulties and at no time attempting a definition or even discussion of the concept.

Christian pilgrimage in the 4th century CE. But it is as well to be aware that pilgrimage did not begin with the Greeks: as early as the third millennium BCE, in the land of Sumer, Gudea of Lagash recorded a journey he made from his home town to the sanctuary of the goddess Nanshe some distance away at Isin.[34] In Egypt too, although we have to wait for Greek historian Herodotus for unequivocal evidence for popular pilgrimage, there is reason to suppose that as early as the New Kingdom pilgrims attended the festival of Osiris at Abydos, and visited healing sanctuaries in the area of Deir-el-Bahari on the West bank of the Nile at Thebes.[35] In Anatolia in the second millennium BCE pilgrimage was a common feature of Hittite religion: the essential feature of the great festivals of the Hittite Kingdom was that members of the royal family journeyed from one sacred place to another, taking part in rituals and ceremonies on the way. And when the sacred city of Nerik was captured by Kaskan enemies, the main concern of the Hittites seems to have been that the transport of sacred offerings there would not be obstructed. Pilgrimage up mountains—which were important in Hittite religion— was common; one text records a sequence of songs performed by a chorus of girls as they ascend a mountain; another describes how the king, having made an ascent, offers food to a herd of stags.[36]

The sources for pilgrimage in Greece in the second millennium BCE are much less informative. For example, clay balls from Thebes seem to indicate that offerings were brought to the Theban capital from neighbouring settlements, including Karystos and Amarynthos.[37] However, for Mycenean Greece the nature of the evidence falls short of allowing us to establish any kind of adequate picture of religious practice.

---

[34] Gudea: Jacobsen (1987); Bottéro (1987); Ferrara (1973). And in Mesopotamia one god is thought to travel to visit another god, for example the journey of Nanna-Suen, tutelary god of the city of Ur, up river to the great cult centre at Nippur 150 miles to the north to visit his father Enlil, a journey recorded in an extraordinary poem: Penglase (1994).

[35] Egyptian pilgrimage: Volokhine (1998); Yoyotte (1960); Sadek (1987); Rutherford, this volume.

[36] Nerik: prayer of Arnuwandas and Asmu-Nikkal, Pritchard (1955), 1.400; Rutherford (forthcoming *a*); sequence of songs: Popko (1994); stags: Haas (1982), 58; mountains in general: Popko (1999).

[37] See Killen (1994), 67–88. A recently discovered Linear B tablet from Thebes has been taken to indicate that groups of ten men are sent to the Ptoia (po-to-a$_2$-ja-de), presumably a festival held on the Ptoion to the north, and the Teleia (te-re-ja-de), which may be a festival of Hera Teleia on Kithairon: see Aravantinos, Godart, and Sacconi (2001), 173–6, with 318–19, but their analysis has been treated with scepticism.

If we take as our scope the ancient Graeco-Roman world, from earliest times to the end of the fourth century CE, we find that the cluster of phenomena which may broadly be described as pilgrimage do not exist in just one form. Rather, there are a very large number of types, attested at different times and in different areas.[38] The sources are mostly literary and epigraphical, and it is important to remember that what we find attested represents only a tiny fraction of the total volume of pilgrimage (and possibly also a fraction of the types of pilgrimage) that actually happened. It may be helpful at the outset to provide a rough typology of these types.

Criteria for a typology of pilgrimage in the ancient world would have to include the following questions:[39]

The spatial relation between sanctuary and clientele, i.e. 'catchment area': are we talking about a region or the whole of the Greek world, or an even larger area?[40] Related to this is the question of whether the pilgrim returns at once to his own community, or is in transit somewhere else, making this what the French Egyptologist Yoyotte called a 'pèlerinage en passant'. Again, in some cases a pilgrim moves from sanctuary to sanctuary in an unlimited itinerary.

The identity of the pilgrims: are they ordinary people, or official representatives of a community, or members of a specific cult? do they include young people? do they include performers or artists? are they members of some profession, such as members of the koinon of the

---

[38] See Rutherford (2000*b*), and (2002); Dillon (1997).

[39] Morinis (1992*b*), 4–5 distinguishes six types: devotional pilgrimages, which have as their goal encounter with, and honouring of the shrine divinity, personage, or symbol; instrumental pilgrimages, which are undertaken to accomplish finite, worldly goals (e.g. cure from illness); normative pilgrimages, which occur as part of a ritual cycle, relating either to the life cycle, or annual calendrical celebrations; obligatory pilgrimages, such as the Muslim *hajj*; simple wandering, e.g. that of Basho, the Zen poet-pilgrim immortalized in his 17th-cent. anthology *The Narrow Road to the Deep North*; and finally initiatory pilgrimages. A different classification is suggested by Chelini and Branthomme, 462 ff.: (*a*) pèlerinages issues du nomadisme; (*b*) pèlerinages issues de la première installation dans les campagnes; (*c*) pèlerinages des villes fortes et dans métropoles; (*d*) pèlerinages de la décentralisation urbaine; (*e*) pèlerinages de renouvellement mythique; (*f*) pèlerinages à racines historiques (Christian and Islamic pilgrimages belong in this category). *a–d* are basically a developmental sequence, having to do with social and political circumstances; *e–f* are more like thematic categories.

[40] Cf. work on geography of pilgrimage in India, e.g. Bhardwaj (1973).

Asklepiadai of Kos and Knidos who are attested as visiting Delphi in the fourth century.[41]

Timetable: does the pilgrim visit the sanctuary once, or is it a regular practice? How long does the pilgrim stay at the sanctuary (in the limiting case the stay could be indefinite: cf. the case of Aelius Aristides discussed in Petsalis-Diomidis' paper, this volume)?

Activity at the sanctuary: is the purpose to attend a festival, to consult an oracle, to make a dedication, to seek physical healing, to undergo an initiation, to visit a place of religious or cultural significance, or perhaps something else?

Motivation: is the pilgrimage voluntary or mandatory, and, if mandatory, is it required by tradition, or by a religious code to which the pilgrim subscribed? or was it motivated by an oracle, or is it made in fulfilment of a vow?

In doing this, we will divide the typology into three sections, corresponding to forms of pilgrimage attested in classical and Hellenistic Greece, forms attested mostly in the Roman empire (both West and East), and Jewish and early Christian pilgrimage.

Classical and Hellenistic Greece

1 Theōria

The most conspicuous form of pilgrimage in classical Greece was the state-delegation, usually referred to as a *theōria*, a word that literally means 'watching' or 'spectacle', although it may have been falsely etymologized as related to the Greek *theos* ('god'). A *theōria* was made up of delegates or *theōroi* and led by an *arkhetheōros*. The significance of this terminology may be that delegates from one city do not share fully in a festival or ritual staged by the city that controls the sanctuary but witness it.[42] Little evidence survives about the experience of *theōroi* in transit between home-city and sanctuary, but we know that they

---

[41] e.g. the iron-workers of Deir-el-Bahari: Lajtar (1991). Judges make pilgrimages to the temple of Zeus Osogoa at Mylasa: Blümel (1987), 1 nn. 361–76.

[42] See Rutherford (2000*a*).

wore crowns to indicate their sacralised status (they were notionally inviolable), and that they travelled in special ships, called *theōrides*.[43]

1.1 *Festival* theōria.   City-states used to send *theōriai* to sanctuaries on the occasion of festivals there, liaising with the local authorities and with representatives from other cities. They would participate in rituals and sacrifices taking place at the sanctuary and, usually, arrange for a sacrifice to be performed on behalf of their own city. In the Hellenistic period such festivals were formally announced by delegates (also called *theōroi*) who travelled throughout the Greek world. Other festivals had a smaller catchment area, for example the festival on the island of Delos which had (at least once) drawn representatives from all over Ionia (see also §4, below). In general, the practice of sending delegations to the same sanctuary was a factor which expressed and fostered a degree of common identity among the cities involved, including panhellenic identity in the case of the national festivals. The official delegations to these festivals were no doubt accompanied by large numbers of private citizens who wanted to experience the festival.[44]

1.2 *Panhellenic* theōria *to athletic competitions*.   In the limiting case, some sanctuaries came to be panhellenic in scope, attracting delegations from all over Greece. These were the great festivals at Olympia, Delphi, Nemea, and the Isthmos, which were not only athletic competitions, but also religious occasions with great symbolic significance. In the case of the panhellenic athletic competitions it would be open to us to see the athletes themselves as pilgrims, especially since the athletic competition itself seems to have had a religious dimension.[45] At any rate, athletic competition and *theōria* were closely linked in so far as the *theōroi* sent out by the cities looked after the interests of athletes.[46]

---

[43] Crowns: Blech (1982), 366; Eur. *Hipp.* 806 ff.; Hesychius s.v. *theōrikos* (crowns on wagons); ships: Jordan (1975), 371 ff. Contrast the view of Scullion (below, p. 122).

[44] Generally see Dillon (1997), festival announcement: Boesch (1908); for *communitas*, see Kowalzig, this volume.

[45] Sansone (1988).

[46] On the cooperation of *theōroi* and athletes, see the inscription published by Ebert and Siegert (1999); Rutherford (2004*b*). On pilgrimage and Olympia, Des Bouvrie *(forthcoming)*.

1.3 Theōria *to a remote sanctuary independent of a festival.*   In some cases, a city-state might send a delegation to a remote sanctuary, even though there was no festival scheduled there. For example, the city of Thebes regularly sent a delegation bearing a dedication of a tripod to the oracle of Dodona.[47] Philostratus describes in his *Heroicus* a (possibly not wholly fictional) *theōria* regularly sent by Thessaly to honour the tomb of Achilles in the Troad.[48] On a grander scale, the Athenian *polis* dispatched a major delegation, the so-called Puthais, to Delphi, apparently making the choice to send it if, and only if, lightning was sighted in certain places; from documents recording enactments of this state pilgrimage in the late second century BCE and the early first, it emerges that the Puthais was a huge event, conveying many hundreds of Athenians to Delphi, including groups of singers (see further §14).[49]

2 Oracle Consultation

A common motivation for pilgrimage, at all periods of classical antiquity, was the consulting of oracles, ranging from major shrines such as Delphi, Dodona and the oracle of Ammon at the Siwa Oasis in Libya to numer-ous oracles with a narrower, regional appeal, such as the oracle at Korope in Thessaly (*LSCG* 83), or that of Trophonios near Lebadeia in Boeotia. Oracles also attracted pilgrims in the Roman period, for example, the oracle of Apollo at Claros, and the oracle of Alexander at Abonouteichus in Paphlagonia whose foundation Lucian parodied.[50] At all periods oracles could be consulted both in a public capacity by city-states (the representatives were called *theōroi* or *theopropoi*) or by private individ-uals. The best direct evidence for both forms comes from lead tablets found at Dodona, most of them still unpublished, dating between 500 and 250 BCE, which record oracular enquiries.[51]

The mode of consultation varied radically from site to site: in some cases it involved incubation (as at the Amphiareion at Oropos) or a rite of passage (as at the oracle of Trophonios); at the oracle of Ammon in Siwa Greek consultants may have used the normal Egyptian technique

---

[47] Proclus *Chrest.* 321b33; scholion on Dionysius Thrax 450. 19–20 Hilgard.
[48] Rutherford (2006).
[49] Boethius (1918).
[50] Trophonios: Schachter (1981), 4.83; Bonnechere (2003); Claros: Parke (1966); Alexander: Lucian, *Alex.*
[51] Parke (1966, 100, 259–273); Christidis, Dakaris, and Vokotopoulou (forthcoming).

of relying on the direction taken by the statue of the god when it was paraded outside the inner sanctum of the temple.[52] Some sites offered a range of approaches: at Delphi, for example, besides the familiar process of consulting the Pythian priestess via an intermediary (which was rarely available), it seems also to have been possible to make use of a lot oracle operating with fried beans.[53]

3 Amphictionies

An amphictiony is a special type of religious network in which a number of cities share control of a common sanctuary and send delegations to a common festival there. They existed in many ancient cultures, for example (probably) ancient Israel.[54] The most famous Greek instance was the Pulaian amphictiony in northern Greece, which had originally been based round the sanctuary of Demeter Pulaia at Anthela on the Malian Gulf, but later came to have control of Delphi as well; the Pulaia festival held yearly at Anthela was a famous festival in its own right. Other well-known amphictionies controlled Delos (at least at certain phases of its history) and the Panionion at Priene. A particularly well-documented case is the amphictiony around the sanctuary of Athene Ilias at Troy in the Hellenistic period, comprising cities in the Troad.[55]

Drawing a hard and fast distinction between festival *theōria* in the sense defined above (§1.1) and the operation of amphictionies would not be easy. Speaking generally, an amphictiony is a tighter organization, with a fixed number of members sharing control of the sanctuary and mandatory participation in the ritual or festival. *Theōria* implies a looser form of organization in which visiting delegations attend another community's ritual.

4 Dedication-Focused Pilgrimage

4.1 *The inventory-lists of Greek temples* attest the expensive dedications made there, and we may in general assume that a dedication

---

[52] Kuhlmann (1988), 127–36.
[53] *CID* 1.13, first published by Amandry (1939).
[54] See below, p. 27.
[55] The fundamental study of amphictionies in the ancient world is that of Tausend (1992). For the Delphic Amphictiony, the most complete recent study is Sanchez (2001). For the others, cf. bibliographical references in Kowalzig's paper.

implies a journey, albeit not always by the dedicator.[56] One case would be the ritual of the Hyperborean offerings, which mysteriously arrived in Delos every year after a long journey from the North.[57] Sometimes making a dedication was an incidental part of a visit to a sanctuary, but in other cases it was the main part. In some cases making a dedication was the main point of a journey: the Spartan king Agesilaos went to Delphi to dedicate a tithe of the booty from his campaign;[58] and Hyperides (4.24) describes how the Athenians sent a *theōria* to Dodona in order to provide the statue of Dione there with a new face and a new dress (they were rebuffed by the local authorities). In exceptional cases we find the inverse of dedication: the point of a journey from A to B is to fetch something from B, as, for example, a sacred ship is supposed to have gone every year from the island of Delos to the island of Lemnos to fetch sacred fire; so in the Hellenistic period a *theōria* from Ephesos seems to have fetched a sacred robe from Sardis.[59]

4.2 *Sending symbolic offerings in the context of power relations.*   A special type of dedication takes place in the context of a power-relation holding between a more powerful city and less powerful cities. A powerful city might require subordinate cities to send it token offerings on the occasion of festivals, as, for example, Athens required its subject allies to send *aparkhai* in the late fifth century BCE. Similarly, colonies were required to send symbolic offerings to their mother cities, as, for example, Athens required its colony Brea to send a phallos to the festival of Dionysus and an ox and a panoply to the Panathenaia.[60]

5 *Healing Pilgrimage*

From early times the Greeks associated healing with the god Asklepios. The comedian Aristophanes (fifth century BCE) already assumed that Athenians seeking healing would cross to the island of Aegina to visit the Asklepieion there. But healing-pilgrimage becomes much better attested

---

[56] On inventory-lists, see Linders (1987), 116 n. 4.

[57] Hyperborean Maidens: Bruneau (1970), 41.

[58] Xen. *Hell.* 4.3.22–3; dedication of a tithe from war: *IC* 1.viii.4; cf. Greeks after Salamis in Herodotus 8.12.1

[59] Lemnos: Philostratus, Heroicus 53.5 (= 67.8 De Lannoy); Ephesos: *IE* 2; cf. the inverse pilgrimage discussed by Noy, this volume.

[60] Aparkhai: *LSCG* 5; cf. *IG* 2.2.1672; Brea: *IG* 1.3.46.

from the fourth century and in the Hellenistic period. The best known early Asklepieia are at Epidauros and at Lebena in Crete; from the fourth century BCE there was a shrine of Asklepios in the temenos at Delphi, and we know that the guild of the Asklepiadai from Kos and Knidos visited around this time *(CID* 1.12); later the sanctuary of Zeus-Asclepios at Pergamon becomes important, as does the Asclepius-cult at Aigeai in Cilicia. Other deities were associated with healing pilgrimage as well: as early as the fourth century BCE Poseidon had the epithet 'Iatros' ('Doctor') on the Cycladic island of Tenos (the fact that Tinos is to this day a healing-shrine much visited by pilgrims is perhaps not unrelated).[61] Records of successful healing were sometimes displayed in special inscriptions or *iamata*, as at Epidauros and at Lebena. The typical healing-pilgrim represented himself as a suppliant (*hiketēs*), and underwent a process of incubation in the temple.[62]

In some cases, a healing-pilgrim might become a semi-permanent inhabitant of the healing-shrine, as Aristides did in Pergamon (Petsalis-Diomidis, Ch. 7 in this volume). The *enkatokhos* (permanent resident) was a common feature of Egyptian shrines as well.[63]

6 Initiation-Pilgrimage

For the most part, the experience of pilgrims at sanctuaries was doubly open: with a few exceptions anyone could take part,[64] and the rituals and festivals took place in the public space. However, a few sanctuaries offered their clientele a special sort of experience which represented an initiation into a secret rite, with the promise of salvation in this world or the next. The best known of these were the sanctuary of Demeter at Eleusis, probably from the sixth century BCE, and the sanctuary of the Great Gods on the island of Samothrace, attested mostly during the Hellenistic period. Candidates for initiation came from all over Greece to these sanctuaries, and they seem to have engaged in the ritual in an individual capacity, not as representatives of their city.[65] At Eleusis the

---

[61] Poseidon: Philochorus *FGrHist* 328 fr.176; for the modern tradition see Dubisch (1995).

[62] Krug (1984); Li Donnici (1995); Lebena: Guarducci (1934), Pergamon: Petsalis-Diomidis (2001) and this volume; Epidauros: Naiden, this volume.

[63] Thompson (1988), 216–24.

[64] Exceptions: Eleans at the Isthmian Games: Plut., *Mor.* 400e; Isinda at Panionia: Callim. *Aitia* fr. 78.

[65] Not 'brothers', despite Burkert (1986), 45.

ritual was extremely complex, requiring a preliminary initiation in the so-called 'Lesser Mysteries' near Athens, and participation in a mass-procession (itself a mini-pilgrimage) along the Sacred Way from Athens to Eleusis, and offering a second level of initiation (*epopteia* as well as the normal *muēsis*) for pilgrims who were willing to make a second trip. The content of the Mysteries remains elusive, but an enhanced existence after death is likely to have been a major focus.[66] For Samothrace we have much less information about the ritual, but we know that initiants received iron rings, and it seems likely that they were promised protection from the dangers of the sea.[67] Notice that Eleusis and Samothrace were also the venues for major festivals, which attracted pilgrims and *theōroi* and were more or less independent of the mystery-cult.

7 Local Pilgrimage

A great deal of movement for the sake of ritual goes on within the territory of a single city-state. In Attica, for example, members of individual demes came into Athens for festivals, and Athenians and others visited local sanctuaries such as that of Artemis at Brauron; to judge from a problematic passage of Aristophanes the Athenian state even sent an official *theōria* to Brauron.[68] Jennifer Larson describes evidence of pilgrimage to remote shrines of the nymphs in Attica.[69] In Menander's comedy *The Bad-Tempered Man* Sostratos complains about how his mother goes round the whole deme of Phyle sacrificing to gods every day (262–3); and these trips could apparently take her some distance south-east to the deme of Paiania (407–9). Ought we to class as pilgrimage comparatively short journeys—perhaps 20 or 30 miles, a journey of a day or two at most, and within the territory of a single *polis*? There is no clear answer, but certainly these were longer journeys than people would normally make in the course of their lives.

8 Oreibasia

Making pilgrimages up mountains was common in Greece, as it had been in Hittite Anatolia. In Euripides' drama the *Bacchae* (191–2) Teiresias and Kadmos make a pilgrimage up Mt. Kithairon to be in the company of the young Dionysos; old Kadmos wants to make the

---

[66] Mylonas (1961).   [67] Cole (1984).   [68] Ar. *Ach*. 713 ff.
[69] Larson (2001), 228–9.

journey in wagons but Teiresias insists that they walk, in order that they do the god more honour—a rare testimony to the importance of making the journey the hard way. In the comparatively real world of Pausanias' Greece, the women of Athens made a mountain-pilgrimage to Delphi every two years, performing dance at way-stations along the route, for example at Panopeus in Phokis. On Rhodes the three main cities each sent *theōriai* up to the mountain sanctuary of Zeus Atarburios, and in the *dēmos* of Antimacheia on Kos we hear of a *koinon* composed of people who journey together to the shrine of Zeus Huetios, presumably situated on a local mountain.[70] In the Roman empire, the sanctuary of Zeus Kasios on Mt. Kasion in north-east Syria was visited by Roman emperors.[71]

9 Pilgrimage to the Site of Battles

In many cultures battlefields become important cultural landmarks, and ancient Greece is no exception.[72] From the fourth century BCE one of the Athenian tribes, Aiantis, regularly sent a delegation bearing a sacrifice to a remote location on Mt. Kithairon to commemorate the Battle of Plataea in Boetia.[73] And we have independent evidence from the Hellenistic period that Plataea was the site of a festival which attracted delegates from Athens and Sparta.[74] Later on we know that the Athenian ephebes made mini-pilgrimages to sites of famous Athenian victories such as Marathon and the island of Salamis (see §10 below).[75] It is perhaps for a similar reason that Troy and the Troad, site of the greatest military campaign in Greek myth, became a centre for pilgrimage and

[70] Women of Athens: Paus. 10.4.3; Rhodes: Papachristodoulou (1999); Kos: Paton and Hicks (1891), 382. For mountain worship: cf. Herakleides 2.8 on the journey of the men of Demetrias/Pagasai to the top of Mt. Pelion, with Pfister (1951), ad loc, 208 ff and Buxton (1992), 10. Plato, *Laws* 1.624b, seems to have believed that Hom. *Od.* 19.179 said that king Minos visited Zeus on a Cretan mountain every 8 years (cf. Ps.Plato, *Minos*, 319e).

[71] Hadrian: SHA *Hadr.* 14.3; Dio 69.2.1 (see further p. 284 below); Julian: Amm. Marc. 22.14.4. For the cult in general see Koch (1993).

[72] Cf. Lloyd (1998).

[73] Kleidemos *FgrHist* 323F22 = Plut. *Sump. Prob.* 1.10, 628f11; id. *Aristides* 19.6.2.

[74] Schachter (1981–), 3.125–44. So too the Athenian orator Hyperides predicts in his *Epitaphios* (18), that people visiting the Pylaia would also visit the scene of the battle of Lamia nearby.

[75] Ephebes at Marathon and Salamis: Pélèkidis (1962).

tourism; the most famous early visitor was Alexander the Great (334 BCE), who performed religious rituals in honour of Greek heroes.[76]

10 Pilgrimage by Young People

A common pattern is for the focus of a pilgrimage to be children or adolescents. The Delphic Septerion festival seems to have required a young man to journey north to Thessaly where he underwent symbolic purification and gathered laurel, before returning to Delphi at the head of a *theōria*. Choruses of young people often accompanied *theōriai* to Delos or Delphi; for example, Herodotus talks of a group of a hundred young men sent to Delphi by the island of Chios. From the Hellenistic period we have evidence that the Athenian ephebes visited a number of sanctuaries within the territory of Attica, including the island of Salamis, where they celebrated the festival of Ajax (the Aianteia). In the Roman period, the sanctuary of Claros received hundreds of sacred delegations from towns, mostly in Asia Minor, and choruses of young men and women were central in these. It is possible that in some of these cases pilgrimage by young people to a sanctuary and back could be understood to amount to a sort of initiation-ritual.[77]

Most of these forms of pilgrimage are attested over a long period in ancient Greece, from the classical to the Roman periods. Some forms are much better attested in later periods (e.g. type 7) but, for the most part intestate religious practice in the Hellenistic and the classical periods seem to have a great deal in common.[78] Where there are changes, they are changes of emphasis alone. Thus Ptolemy Philadelphus appropriated the institution of panhellenic *theōria* when he founded the Ptolemaia-festival in Alexandria in honour of his father Ptolemy Soter, which attracted delegates from the Aegean and mainland Greece, who visited Alexandria to pay respects to the most powerful political force in the region.[79] This innovation implies a major shift: the scope of *theōria* has been expanded beyond gods to include deified mortals, a shift whose first intimations appeared a few decades earlier

---

[76] Alexander at Troy: Arrian, *Anab.*1.12.
[77] Septerion: Theopompus, *FGrHist* 115F80; Plut. *De Def. Or.* 15, 417e–418d; Chios: Herodotus 6.27 (see Kowalzig, this volume); ephebes: Pélèkidis (1962); Claros: Lane-Fox (1986), 178; initiation: Rutherford (2005).
[78] cf. e.g. Riggsby (1996), 14–15.
[79] Ptolemaia: Fraser (1972), 2. 380 n. 324.

when the Athenians sent *theōroi* to honour the Macedonian generals Antigonus and Demetrius (see Plutarch, *Demetrius* 11).[80] Another innovation is described in the following section.

11 Federal Pilgrimage

The nature of a religious network is coloured by the nature of the political relationship between the cities that make it up. In cases discussed above (§§2, 4) pilgrimage fosters a sense of communal identity among political communities which are more or less independent. But in other cases, the participants in a common festival are city-states which belong to a common political federation. This pattern, though perhaps not new, tends to be attested better in the Hellenistic period. A good example is the Boeotian Federation, which had several federal festivals, including the Pamboiotia held at Koroneia,[81] and perhaps also the Daidala festival held at Plataia where different communities presented ceremonial logs.[82] In some cases, it is very hard to determine whether we are dealing with a federal structure, an amphictionic structure, or something even looser. Take, for example, the case of the Khrusaoric League in Hellenistic Caria, whose members met at a festival at Stratonikaia; an inscription from the Carian city of Mylasa describes a delegate to Stratonikaia as an *ekklēsiastēs kai theōros*, an expression which covers the roles of political representative (which suggests a federal structure) and religious delegate (which suggests festival-*theōria*).[83]

12 Sacred Tourism

Another motivation may have been to see for oneself the sanctuary and the religious sights there, what one might call 'sacred tourism'. An early reference to this practice is Euripides' description of the hero Neoptolemus at Delphi, peacefully engaged in viewing (*thea*) the sanctuary (Eur. *Andr.* 1086–8). Some graffiti on the Memnonion at Abydos (see §15) state that the writer 'viewed' the place. In the Hellenistic period

---

[80] Plut. *Demetrius* 11. On this, see Scott (1928), 160–1; Habicht (1970). The envoys who visited Alexander at Babylon seem to have acted like *theōroi* honouring a god, but it looks as if they did not yet have the title (cf. Arrian, *Anabasis* 7. 23. 2): see Badian (1981); Boesch (1908), 7–8 n. 3.

[81] Schachter (1981–), 1. 123–6.

[82] Schachter (1981–), 1.245–50; Dillon (1997); Knoepfler (2001) suggests that the 14 logs involved come from seven 'divisions', not from cities.

[83] Blümel (1987), n. 101, line 15.

sacred tourism becomes better attested: thus, Callimachus composed a *propemptikon* (Iambus 6) for a friend who had gone to visit Olympia, describing in detail the celebrated statue of Zeus by Pheidias there.[84] So in a documentary papyrus from Egypt in the late second century BCE an official in Alexandria asks that certain sites in the Fayum, particularly the famous Labyrinth, be prepared for the visit of a Roman official (L. Memmius) who was coming there *for viewing* (*epi theōrian*). This sounds to a modern mentality like sightseeing, but it is worth observing that the preparations for the visit included materials for sacrifice.[85] 'Religious tourism', then, is perhaps not wholly distinguishable from pilgrimage, and the fact that the normal Greek for state-pilgrimage is precisely *theōria* seems to be a sign of a strong conceptual link between the two.

13 Pilgrimage by Poets and Musicians

In several cultures, some of the most conspicuous pilgrims are poets.[86] In Greece, poets had been visiting festivals since the time of Homer and Hesiod, and musical performance is an established part of *theōria* in the fifth century BCE. However, the Hellenistic period shows much richer evidence for poets and musicians visiting sanctuaries, the so-called 'wandering poets'. Honorific inscriptions from Delphi and other sanctuaries thank poets and musicians for their presence there. For example, in the late second century BCE Delphi honoured Kleodoros and Thrasuboulos of Phenea in Arcadia for performing lyric poetry and training the local chorus of boys (*SIG* 703). Many of these figures were members of the Artists of Dionysus, a professional organization which comes into being in the Hellenistic period.[87]

14 Pilgrimage in Graeco-Roman Egypt

14.1 *Native.* Herodotus (2.60) describes extensive pilgrimage in Lower Egypt in the fifth century BCE, though it is different in character

---

[84] Dawson (1950), 72, analysing the poem as a sort of tour-guide; contra Clayman (1980); also Kerkhecker (1999), 147–81.

[85] *P. Tebt.* 1, 33 (112 BCE); Foestmeyer (1989); Hohlwein (1940), 274; Malaise (1987), 63.

[86] Tamil: Peterson (1989); Basho: Shirane (1998), 223–30.

[87] Poets so honoured: Guarducci (1929).

from Greek *theōria* (Rutherford, Ch. 5 in this volume). To what extent pilgrimage is characteristic of earlier phases of Egyptian culture is uncertain, though some festivals probably drew visitors from a wide area, such as the festival of Osiris at Abydos.[88] By the Hellenistic period, it was certainly widespread: for example, a hieroglyphic stele from Buto in the Delta refers to a number of forms of pilgrimage in the region.[89] It has been suggested that the huge quantities of mummified animals we find deposited in many Egyptian sanctuaries—itself a late phenomenon—could represent in part dedications by Egyptian pilgrims.[90]

14.2 *Greek.* As early as the sixth century BCE soldiers, tourists, and pilgrims left graffiti in Greek and other languages on the walls of Egyptian monuments, such as the Memnonion at Abydos.[91] From the late Hellenistic period we find extensive pilgrimage-graffiti, characterized by several set formulas, particularly one in which the writer records *proskunema* or adoration before the deity of himself and his family or friends attested at the Memnonion, and at the temple of Isis at Philai, locations in Upper Egypt, where the conditions favoured preservation of monuments.[92] In visual representations pilgrims sometimes hold palm-branches, and their visits may sometimes be commemorated by images of feet.[93]

14.3 *Healing pilgrimage.* Both Egyptians and Greeks visited sanctuaries for the sake of healing. There was a popular healing-shrine at Deir el Bahari in Upper Egypt, a temple of Imhotep (identified by the Greeks with Asklepios) and Amenhotep, built into the mortuary temple of Queen Hatshepsut. Other parts of Deir-el-Bahari had been centres of healing pilgrimage from the period of the New Kingdom.[94] In the Roman period, we know of a healing shrine associated with the healing deity Piuris (a deified man, and thus given the title 'ḥsy') at Aïn-el-Labakha.[95]

---

[88] Rutherford (2003); Yoyotte (1960), 18 ff; Dunand (1997).
[89] Rutherford, this vol., pp. 137–9.
[90] Ray (1976), 143; Rutherford, this vol., pp. 144–6.
[91] For pilgrimage in Egypt in general, see Bernand (1988); for the Memnonion, see Rutherford (2003).
[92] Geraci (1971); Rehm (1940); Festugière (1970).
[93] Guarducci (1942–3); Takács this vol., p. 354 n. 4.
[94] Bataille (1951); New Kingdom material: Pinch (1993).
[95] Wagner (1996).

Pilgrimage in Egypt continued to evolve in the Roman period. For example, the articulate proskunema of a Roman soldier at Kalabsha in Nubia in the third century CE (Arthur Darby Nock's 'Vision of Mandaules Aion') suggests an intellectual and theological engagement characteristic of the period (cf. §16).[96] Again, from Philai we have evidence for official delegations making pilgrimages from Meroe in the fourth century CE, paying respects to the most significant Egyptian cult on their northern border (cf. §18. below).[97]

The Roman Empire

In Roman Italy pilgrimage seems to play a smaller part in Roman religion than in Greek, a fact perhaps partly to be explained by the fact that Rome tended to appropriate foreign deities by the process known as evocatio.[98] Nevertheless, many centres for pilgrimage are known: the official sanctuaries of the Alban Mount, locale for the *Feriae Latinae* and Lavinium;[99] other Latin centres were Lake Nemi, where there was a yearly festival of Diana; Fregellae, on the border between Samnite and Latin territory where there was a cult of Neptune and Aesculapius; and the grove of Helernus (Alernus) near the mouth of the Tiber.[100] If we exclude traditions of Roman consultation of the Delphic oracle,[101] Roman engagement with Greek sanctuaries begins in the late third century BCE with Marcellus' dedications at Samothrace and Rhodes; around the same period the tradition became established that the Roman Penates originated in Samothrace, and this may have encouraged Romans to go to Samothrace to seek

---

[96] Bernand (1969*a*), 576 n.166; Nock (1934); Totti (1985), n. 40.

[97] Török (1978); Rutherford (1998*b*).

[98] Evocatio: H. Versnel s.v., *DNP* 4.329 (1998); Belayche (1987), 146–8; early examples include the importation of Juno from Veii in Etrurua (Camillus in Livy 5.52.8 ff.); later examples are the importation of Asclepius from Epidauros in 292 BCE, of Venus Erycina from Sicily in 217 BCE, and of Magna Mater from Pessinus in 205 BCE.

[99] Alban Mount: Dionysius of Halicarnassus 4.21.2; Frayn (1993), 136–7; Lavinium: Belayche (1987), 143; Dionysius of Halicarnassus 2, 52, 3.

[100] Lake Nemi: Ovid, *Fasti* 3, 269–70; Fregellae: Strabo, 5, 3. 10; Frayn (1993), 139 ff; grove of Helernus: Ovid, *Fasti* 2. 67; 6. 105. For healing sanctuaries in the region, see Beard, North, and Price (1998), 1.12–13.

[101] Diod. Sic. *Hist.* 14. 98; Plut. *Camillus* 8; early Roman contact with Delphi: Gruen (1990), 9 with n. 18; Gagé (1955).

initiation.[102] From the period of the Punic Wars Rome also became interested, for territorial reasons, in the sanctuary of Herakles-Melqart at Cadiz (Fear, this volume).

The Roman Empire was characterized by a number of distinctive forms of pilgrimage:

15 Symbolic Pilgrimage by Roman Emperors

In the empire the most conspicuous pilgrimages are made by Roman Emperors: Vespasian's pilgrimage to the Sarapieion at Alexandria, Hadrian's unremitting journeys, which have been thought to be a model for the development of Christian pilgrimage, and later the pilgrimages of Julian to Pessinus and Mt. Kasion.[103] The model for this pattern may have been Alexander the Great's pilgrimage to the oracle of Ammon at the Siwa Oasis in Libya in 333/2 BCE.[104] Herodotus makes the journey of Persian King Xerxes through northern Greece resemble a pilgrimage in some respects (e.g. Hist. 7.197, where he hears the local story of Laphystian Zeus at Halus in Akhaia Phthiotis). Ultimately we may look to the Near East for this form: in 675 BCE Esarhaddon consulted Sin at Harran before embarking on a campaign against Egypt; in the third millennium BCE Gudea of Lagash recorded a journey he made from Lagash to the sanctuary of the goddess Nanshe at Isin. Among the Hittites we know that in the thirteenth century it was the custom for the king, sometimes accompanied by the queen, to visit towns to take part in festivals in honour of various deities.[105]

16 Intellectual Pilgrimage

In the period of the Second Sophistic, we find a common pattern in which members of the cultural and political elite visit traditional religious centres, often for the purpose of intellectual enlightenment. This is a complex form of activity, combining aspects of earlier forms of

---

[102] Romans at Samothrace: see Cole (1989); below, p. 66 Cicero's uncle: Clinton (2001); Romans at Eleusis: Clinton (1989).

[103] Vespasian: Henrichs (1966); Hadrian: Holum (1990); in general Halfmann (1986).

[104] Arrian 3.3.1–2; Strabo 17.143; Quintus Curtius, 4.7; Ps. Callisthenes, *Alexander Romance* 1.30.5.

[105] Esarhaddon and Sin: Green (1992), 36; Gudea: Jacobsen (1987); Hittites: Lebrun (1987).

pilgrimage with a self-conscious and even antiquarian attitude to cultural traditions that is characteristic of the age. Pausanias the Periegete may have been writing for readers of this sort; Apollonius of Tyana's philosophical journeys as described in Philostratus' *Life* resemble pilgrimages, as do those of Aelius Aristides round the healing shrines of north-west Asia Minor. There were earlier models here, for example Solon's philosophical *theōria* described by Herodotus, or the journeys of Greek philosophers, such as Pythagoras who is supposed to have visited Delos and the Idaean Cave on Crete.[106]

17 Pilgrimage and Cultural Nostalgia

In the new political reality of the Roman empire traditional forms of religious network may take on a radically different significance. For example, panhellenic *theōria* in the fifth century BCE was (among other things) an expression of shared religious and cultural traditions of participating states, and one of the most important principles of this activity was that every participating state was (at least notionally) an independent political unit; but in the Hellenistic and Roman period states were no longer independent in the way they once were, and the operation of religious networks served only to preserve or resuscitate Hellenic cultural traditions within a broader political structure. And in the early second century CE the emperor Hadrian established a new league in Athens based round the Panhellenion, a shrine linked to the temple of Zeus Olympios, all members of which sent delegates, the Panhellenes, who performed religious rites both at the Panhellenion and at Eleusis. Hadrian in fact reinvented the concept of panhellenism, situating its centre not in one of the traditional panhellenic sanctuaries, but in the most celebrated cultural centre of Greece.[107]

18 Ethnic Pilgrimage to a Mother Deity or Core Deity (particularly in the Near East)

In the Near East pilgrimage predates the coming of the Greeks and Romans (see §13). In the Hellenistic period, we find evidence of

---

[106] Pausanias: Elsner (1992); Apollonios: Elsner (1997*a*); Solon: Hdt. 1.23; Pythagoras: Diog. Laert. 8. 13 = Arist. fr. 489. Porph. *Vit. Pyth.* 17, 25.17 ff Nauck; Aristides: Galli and Petsalis-Diomidis, this vol.

[107] See Jones (1996); Spawforth (1999).

pilgrimage in the Phoenician world, for example Carthaginian pilgrims visiting their mother city, Tyre, or *hieronautai* ('sacred sailors') who set up statues of Tyre and Sidon at Delos in the fourth century BCE;[108] pilgrims came from Paphos in Cyprus to Sidon in the fourth to third centuries BCE.[109] Pilgrimage to the sanctuary of the Syrian Goddess at Hierapolis-Membij is described in detail by Lucian, and had a rather different character (Lightfoot, Ch. 12 in this volume).[110] Bronze medallions illustrating the three deities associated with the cult of Heliopolis-Baalbek (Zeus-Hadad, Aphrodite-Atargatis/Derketo and Mercury) have been found in other areas of Syria, perhaps distributed by returning pilgrims.[111]

One dossier of evidence from Roman Asia Minor which defies classification is that relating to the *Xenoi Tekmoreioi* of third-century CE Phrygia and Pisidia. The *Xenoi Tekmoreioi* seem to have been representatives of towns in the region who gathered at a central sanctuary or sanctuaries (apparently of Artemis; possibly also of Men Askaenos). Many questions relating to this organization remain unresolved, and it is quite impossible to say what sort of an organization it was.[112]

Jewish and Christian Pilgrimage

19 Jewish Pilgrimage

From the earliest stages in Israel's history, common Jewish political identity seems to have been articulated through the mechanism of participation in key sanctuaries in a quasi-amphictionic structure.[113] The Torah required of all Jews that they visit Jerusalem three times a year, and if this requirement was even partially fulfilled, pilgrimage must have been a major factor in Jerusalem's economy.[114] According to Philo of Alexandria, pilgrims came from the ends of the earth, and from all compass points (a surprising statement, since the diaspora had not yet taken place); this could be considered as a form of type

---

[108] Quint. Curt. 4.2.10; Polybius. 31.12.11–12; 2 Macc. 4:18–20; *hieronautai*: *ID* 46.
[109] Masson (1982).
[110] Lucian, *De Dea Syria*, 10 and 55–6.
[111] Hajjar (1977), 1, 177–8.
[112] See W. Ruge in *RE* 2.9, 158–70; Mitchell (1998), 12.
[113] See Chambers (1980), referring to Noth (1930).
[114] Exodos 23:17; cf. Josephus, *Ant.* 4.203; Goodman (1999).

§18.[115] At earlier times, though, there had been more religious centres in Israel, for example Shilo in Samuel.[116] For Jews in Egypt, however, it can be shown that pilgrimage destinations included not just Jerusalem, but also centres within Egypt, such as the synagogue at Alexandria, Onias' temple at Heliopolis, and other locations in the south.[117]

20 Christian Pilgrimage

Christian pilgrimage is richly attested, starting from the second century CE, and to begin with existing alongside traditions of pagan pilgrimage.[118] The principal forms of early Christian pilgrimage include the following.

20.1 Scriptural pilgrimage.   The paradigmatic early form of Christian pilgrimage is to the places celebrated by scripture.[119] This form of Christian pilgrimage probably started in the second century. The earliest recorded Christian to visit Palestine in order to see the sites associated with the life of Christ is a bishop of Sardis called Melito who visited both Jerusalem and places in Palestine.[120] Later we have the pilgrimages of Constantine's mother Helena in 312 (in the course of which the True Cross was supposed to have been discovered),[121] that of the Bordeaux Pilgrim in 333, the famous pilgrimage of Egeria, and that of Paula, recorded in a letter of Jerome (both late fourth century CE).[122]

---

[115] *On The Special Laws* 1.68–9; slightly later on, ibid. 1.78, Philo mentions *hieropompoi* who took first-fruits offerings to the Temple every year. In *De Prov.* 2 (216 Aucher; also in Loeb), Philo mentions a pilgrimage to Jerusalem that he himself had made (he stopped at Ascalon, and there observed flocks of birds).

[116] Kötting for Shilo: 58–9; 1 Samuel 1: 3–28.

[117] See the thorough study of Kerkeslager (1998).

[118] Lane-Fox (1986), 180.

[119] See Kötting (1950), 80–110 and (1988), 232–44, 305–7; Elsner and Rubiés (1999), 15–18.

[120] See Hunt (1999) for the most recent discussion in a long argument about origins. Melito: Kötting (1950), 84–5, his account is preserved in Eusebius, *Hist. Eccl.* 4.26.14. Other pre-Constantinian travellers to Palestine include: Clement: Kötting (1950), 85–6; *Stromata* 1.11.2; Origen: Kötting (1950), 86–8; Pionius: Kötting (1950), 88; *Martyrium Pionii* 4, 17 ff.; Alexander: Kötting (1950), 88–9; Eusebius, *Hist. Eccl.* 6.11.2.

[121] On Helena, see Hunt (1982), 28–49; Holum (1990); Drijvers (1992).

[122] Bordeaux Pilgrim: Leyerle (1994); Douglass (1996); Bowman (1999); Elsner (2000*a*). Egeria: Hunt (1982), 164–6; Smith (1987), 88–94; Campbell (1988), 20–33; Sivan (1988*a* and 1988*b*); Wilkinson (1981); Paula: Hunt (1982), 171–2.

20.2 Pilgrimage to the living saints. The second major phase of Christian pilgrimage is characterized by veneration of living saints and holy men.[123] While any one holy man had a relatively brief floruit, early Christianity provided a remarkable number of such 'athletes of Christ' in the rise of ascetic monasticism, along with a fundamental historiography-cum-panegyric in the form of saints' lives and their compendia.[124]

20.3 Relics. Hardly unconnected with the veneration of living saints was the worship of their dead remains—whether whole bodies or their fragments.[125] This is a radical Christian innovation by comparison with antique activity. The practice may have begun as early as Constantine,[126] or his son Constantius,[127] but it certainly took off in the second half of the fourth century under the patronage of the great Italian bishops Damasus of Rome and Ambrose of Milan.[128]

20.4 Icons and images. In addition to saints and relics, the first few Christian centuries saw the advent of a cult of images in which particular miraculous icons—often identified as palladia for their home cities—became significant objects for pilgrimage.[129]

Across the typology one might also see patterns whereby access to a specific or local sanctuary plugs the pilgrim into a wider network of collective experience. A few of them provided a context for an exhibition of the sort of communal identity that the Turners called *communitas* (see in particular §1.1 (festival-*theōria*), §3 (amphictionies), §14.1 (Egyptian), and perhaps §6 (initiation), and §11 (federal pilgrimage). In some

---

[123] See e.g. Brown (1971); Kötting (1988), 307–9; and now esp. Frank (2000*a*).

[124] With e.g. Hägg and Rousseau. (2000).

[125] The classic discussions are Delehaye (1912), 60–119; (1927), 196–207; (1930); and Brown (1981).

[126] e.g. the translation of Lucian of Antioch in 327 or 328 to Drepanum in Bithynia—the birthplace of Helena, which was renamed Helenopolis in her honour: *Chronicon Paschale* 1.527 Bonn, Maraval (1985), 367.

[127] There is a significant debate about whether Constantine or Constantius was responsible for the translations of relics to the imperial mausoleum in Constantinople. See Mango (1990*a* and *b*); Woods (1991).

[128] See Kötting (1988), 309–12. Damasus: Saghy (2000), with bibliography; Ambrose: Dassmann (1975), Clark (2001), 168–71 with bibliog.

[129] Fundamental are Kitzinger (1954), and now Belting (1994), 30–224.

cases, the *communitas* may be a reaction to the perceived threat of a ruling power, as in §18 (Near Eastern).[130] But *communitas* is not a universal feature of pilgrimage. In some forms the motivation is primarily the *ad hoc* needs of the pilgrim e.g. §2 (oracles), and §6 (healing), although some degree of communal feeling may present as well.[131] In other types the form of pilgrimage is used to provide a showcase for the power of a king or powerful state, as in the case of §15 (Roman Emperors; cf. also §4.2). There is also another dynamic, distinct from communitas but in some ways related to it: in some examples from our typology—perhaps the majority—pilgrimage serves as a mechanism by which the pilgrim comes into intimate contact with a shared cultural or religious tradition: this is particularly clear in type §9 (battlefields), type §12 (sacred tourism), and type §16 (intellectual pilgrimage in the Roman empire), where the shared identity accessed through pilgrimage is essentially the cultural and religious traditions of Hellenism; something analogous may be present in certain forms of Christian pilgrimage as well, e.g. §20.1 (scriptural pilgrimage) and §20.3 (relics).

III. DISCUSSION

This typology needs to be seen strategically. It is by no means meant to be comprehensive but rather suggestive—and additions of new categories or the elimination or conflation of categories are to be expected. The taxonomy has been largely constructed empirically, by identifying categories of activity and classifying them in a way that broadly charts a timeline. But this appearance of chronology is misleading at best. Take the kinds of *theōria* (state pilgrimage and festival pilgrimage) which constitute §1. These are apparent throughout the Greek-speaking world from archaic times to late antiquity. As a phenomenon of the Roman empire, they attest the continuation of earlier practices justifying and celebrating the city within a broader panhellenic structure. But pilgrimage as a celebration of civic identity at a time when city states were autonomous and independent (as they were, arguably, even under the Hellenistic mon-

---

[130] Cf. Lightfoot (this volume).   [131] Cf. Petsalis-Diomidis (this volume).

archies)[132] and what is apparently the same practice within the context of imperial control may be radically different in their meanings and implications. The issue is made still more complicated by the fact that our best source for all matters of Greek religion, Pausanias, was writing in the second century CE under the Roman empire. All too often modern scholars succumb to the temptation to which Pausanias was himself subject—taking the living evidence he reports so lovingly and vividly as offering a true picture of archaic and classical times as well as his own (cf. Hutton, Ch. 10 in this volume). That is certainly what he believed and wished to believe and what his informants generally thought. But it need not be true, and that should worry us. Effectively, one problem with religion and ritual and the persistent antiquarianism of their ideologies is that change (sometimes radical change) may be disguised by a fundamental rhetoric of continuity.

More problematic still—but most interesting—is the shifting nature of the categories in our typology. Those for pagan antiquity represent the empirical grouping of kinds of activity, emphasizing function. Those for Christianity are largely differentiated by the kind of material embodiment that offers a sacred goal for the pilgrim. This seems rather a significant shift. It reflects one aspect of the remarkable way that the early Church reshaped the structures of ancient religious experience while preserving many of their phenomena. Many of our pre-Christian categories in the typology—festival pilgrimage, healing pilgrimage, the consultation of a saint or shrine for advice and even prophecy, local pilgrimage, sacred tourism, inverse pilgrimage, oreibasia, imperial pilgrimage, intellectual pilgrimage, for instance—are attested within Christianity, but are restructured around newly constructed sacred goals. Aspects of all these forms of sacred mobility were offered by pilgrimage to the Holy Land or Mount Sinai, to holy men, to relics, and to icons—but it seems natural in respect of the social and cultural contexts of Christianity to regroup the categories of pilgrimage as we have. This is not simply a trivial reorganization of an arbitrary taxonomy: rather, it reveals the extent to which age-old social practices were transformed in what Michel Foucault once called the cultural *epistēmē*.[133]

---

[132] See Ma (2000), 10–11, 373–87.
[133] See Foucault (1970), xxii, 54, 74–5; (1974), 191–2.

We make no claim to totality in our typology—much might be added to our categories and much room for disagreement may exist, even among those who are persuaded that pilgrimage is an idea which deserves being entertained for antiquity. But at least they give a sense of the variety, richness and range of the phenomena which need to be accounted for, opening models of collective and individual activity. The diffusion and messiness, for what it is worth, is no more than that in modern ethnographies of pilgrimage—which is perhaps what one might have expected. The essays in this volume take different aspects within the very broad span of action and of time that is treated here, and subject them to much more detailed analysis than there is scope for in an introduction. Their authors do not all agree with us about pilgrimage—and show varying degrees of scepticism. We have not attempted to impose anything like a party-line, but have (for ease of reading but perhaps with insufficient imagination) assembled the chapters largely according to chronological principles. Some are more archaeological, others more text-dependent; some are more empirical, others more historiographic in scope; all attempt—from different perspectives and different areas of expertise— to bring to life a vital phenomenon in ancient religious life.

Not all, but most of these subtypes are touched on by the essays in this volume. The first six chapters (Part I) cover aspects of *theōria* and pilgrimage in classical and Hellenistic Greece. In Chapter 1 Barbara Kowalzig ('Mapping out *Communitas*') addresses the social and political significance of *theōria* within the context of amphictionies in the classical and Hellenistic period (cf. types §§2 and 4). The networks constituted by these organizations are, she argues, of immense importance in the social fabric of ancient Greece, and should be seen as cutting across other political groupings such as perceived ethnic allegiances. Choral performances at sanctuaries symbolize the social cohesion, the *communitas* (to use Turner's term) generated by these networks,

Fred Naiden's Chapter 2 ('*Hiketai* and *Theōroi* at Epidauros') explores an aspect of healing-pilgrimage (type §7) which is often neglected— supplication (Greek *hiketeia*). He analyses the relation between this andon the one hand other forms of supplication, and on the other hand *theōria*, which is primarily a matter of the activities of sacred delegates acting on behalf of their city-state, whereas *hiketeia* is usually conducted by individual suppliants making requests of the god on their own behalf. Naiden's thoughtful comparison helps to sharpen our understanding of both categories.

Michael Arnush ('Pilgrimage to the Oracle of Apollo at Delphi') surveys in Chapter 3 the history of consultation of the oracle of Apollo at Delphi (type §3). He shows that whereas the clientele of Delphi is largely public *theōriai* in the fifth century, consulting the oracle on political and international affairs, in the course of the fourth century public *theōriai* seem to be rarer, and private consultations are more important. Against the view that this is a consequence of religious scepticism, Arnush argues that oracle consultation remains common, at least at private level, and what happens is that Delphi becomes less frequently consulted on international matters, partly because the Athenians stop consulting Delphi, and partly because Alexander the Great shifts the focus a way to a broader range of oracles, including Didyma and Ammon.

In Chapter 4 Scott Scullion (' "Pilgrimage" and Greek Religion') challenges the appropriateness of the terminology of 'pilgrimage' to the phenomena of classical Greek religion. He argues that whereas the term 'pilgrimage' suggests sacred activity, a case can be made for sanctuary visitation belonging to the realm of the 'secular' rather than to the 'sacred'; that whereas the notion of pilgrimage implies that the journey is ritualized, there is little evidence of this in classical Greece (with the exception of Athenian *theōriai* to Delphi and Delos); that there is no Greek word corresponding to 'pilgrimage', and travel to sanctuaries by individuals was not treated by the Greeks as a general phenomenon but conceived and expressed distinctly as for example 'oracle consultation' or 'suppliancy' to healing shrines; and that students of ancient pilgrimage wrongly assume that the power of a god was conceived to be greater at regional and national sanctuaries than at local ones, whereas there is little evidence for this claim, or at least for such a simple model. Scullion makes the strongest possible case for his thesis, and the editors were happy to include his chapter, and to allow the reader to make up her own mind about the thesis. We should perhaps observe, however, that in our view, he is working with a notion of pilgrimage which is heavily coloured by medieval Christianity (e.g. pp. 125–6), and that the assumption that 'pilgrimage' has to belong to the 'sacred' (assuming we accept a clear-cut distinction between 'sacred' and 'secular') may be unreasonable, if, for example, the point of pilgrimage is precisely to move as much as possible from one realm to the other.

Ian Rutherford in Chapter 5 ('Down-Stream to the Cat-Goddess') takes as his subject Herodotus' account of contemporary pilgrimage by Egyptians to temples in the Egyptian Delta, particularly pilgrimage to the town of Boubastis where there was a celebrated temple of the goddess Bastet-Artemis (cf. type §16). As a source for Egyptian pilgrimage, at least before the Hellenistic and Roman periods, Herodotus' account is almost unique, native Egyptian sources, mostly from many centuries earlier, being almost entirely silent about it, as about all forms of popular religion. As Rutherford tries to show, Herodotus' reading of Egyptian pilgrimage seems to reflect his Greek frame of reference, not only in so far as he is most interested in aspects of Egyptian practice that are unusual from the Greek point of view, but also perhaps in that he tries in some respects to suggest parallels between Greek and Egyptian religion.

Chapter 6 by Andrea Wilson Nightingale ('The Philosopher at the Festival') examines the ways in which Greek philosophy makes use of the metaphor of religious pilgrimage. There was a strong terminological basis for this usage in so far as the technical term for philosophical contemplation was in Greek '*theōria*', the same word that we find used for sacred delegations to panhellenic festivals; this may even have been the origin of the philosophical term. Nightingale takes this further, and shows how the image of pilgrimage to a sanctuary followed by the return provides a structure for philosophical argument and philosophical literature.

The six chapters of Part II address various manifestations of pilgrimage in the context of Roman empire. Chapter 7, by Alexia Petsalis-Diomidis ('The Body in Space'), presents a vivid analysis of the experience of the healing pilgrim in the Roman Empire (type §7). Her focus is the Asklepieion at Pergamum which offers evidence of several types: architectural (the layout of the shrine), art-historical (dedications of body-parts), epigraphic (the illuminating Sacred Law), and literary (Aelius Aristides' *Sacred Tales*). From this evidence, she reconstructs an impression of the pilgrim's experience characterized by a tension between the control and order of communal ritual and the individual's experience of his illness and his encounter with the deity.

George Williamson in Chapter 8 ('Mucianus and a Touch of the Miraculous') examines the temple-visiting habits of C. Licinius Mucianus, a Roman governor in the age of Vespasian, and a writer of Republican history (cf. types §§14 and 15). The paper considers the functions and status of votives on display in sanctuaries, and asks what sort of response was evoked by the viewer who belonged to a polytheistic world in which belief was not really an appropriate criterion of religiosity, or indeed made an explicit matter of choice. The chapter argues that Mucianus' response—despite his not being a pilgrim in the official state sense—was more than an aesthetic sense of wonder, but rather a different sort of belief in the efficacy and reality of divine epiphany, as demonstrated both through miraculous happenings at certain sanctuaries, and also by the votives on display in others.

The theme of educated Romans visiting sanctuaries is continued in Chapter 9 by Marco Galli ('Pilgrimage as Elite *Habitus*'). Galli looks at the vogue for cultural pilgrimage among the ruling class, a vogue which developed during the Antonine Age, particularly in the eastern half of the empire. Among the centres for this activity he considers are major sanctuaries such as Delphi, the Asklepieion of Pergamon and the Artemision of Ephesos, sites of expensive dedications by members of the Roman elite, and also remote, rural sanctuaries of the sort established by Aelius Aristides and Herodes Atticus. Galli explores the reasons for this development, which may have included rivalry between elites belonging to different cities and a change in attitudes to religion in the Antonine Age.

In Chapter 10 William Hutton ('The Construction of Religious Space in Pausanias') examines the way Pausanias, the second-century CE author of the *Periēgēsis* of Greece, constructs a religious landscape, focusing on his account of Corinth. He starts from the observation that Pausanias faced a difficulty in trying to harmonize his description of Corinth with the rest of his Greek topography in so far as, having been destroyed by the Romans and refounded as a Roman colony, it was one of the most conspicuous emblems of Roman domination on the Greek mainland. Hutton shows how Pausanias solves the problem by employing a range of discursive strategies (exclusion, transformation, arrangement, and contextualization) whose culminative aim is to represent Corinth as far more Greek than it actually was.

Andrew Fear in Chapter 11 ('A Journey to the End of the World') looks at pilgrimage to the temple of Melqart-Herakles at Cadiz in southern Spain. This was a centre with a long history, originating in the Phoenician period, later of importance to Rome, and continuing to be important as a Christian centre. From the point of view of sacred geography it is highly unusual: located at the extremity of the Mediterranean West, but in terms of religious origin pointing back to the East.

Jane Lightfoot's Chapter 12 ('Pilgrims and Ethnographers') presents a close analysis of one of the most complete accounts of a pilgrimage in an ancient source, Lucian's account of extensive pilgrimage from areas in the Near East to the temple of the so-called Syrian Goddess at Hierapolis-Membij in northern Syria (type §17). And in Lucian's portrayal, this Syrian pilgrimage is significantly different from forms of pilgrimage indigenous to the Greek and Roman world (cf. Herodotus' account of Egyptian pilgrimage discussed in Chapter 5). This is another case (cf. again Chapter 5) in which literary evidence is our only source for pilgrimage, archaeological sources being more or less entirely unhelpful.

Moving from the Near East to Egypt, or at least Egyptian religion, we come to Chapter 13 by Sarolta Takács ('Divine and Human Feet: Records of Pilgrims Honouring Isis'), which explores evidence for pilgrimage in the context of Isiac religion which has spread from Egypt throughout the Roman empire. She focuses on two aspects in particular: on Isis' role as a healing deity (cf. also Chapter 7), and on a religious symbol often associated with pilgrimage, at least in the context of Egyptian religion: the footprint or foot.

Finally, Part III examines aspects of Jewish and Christian pilgrimage. Jewish pilgrimage to Jerusalem in the Hellenistic and Roman period is well established (cf. type §18), but David Noy's Chapter 14 ('Rabbi Aqiba Comes to Rome: A Jewish Pilgrimage in Reverse?'), which deals with the period after the Roman destruction of the temple in 70 CE, examines an unusual variation on the pattern. Noy takes as his theme the case of a group of prominent Jewish rabbis who visited Rome in 95 CE and addresses an instance of a general problem in studying the ancient world: how are we to interpret a journey by a given individual, especially one for which we have limited sources? In this case, should we think of the rabbis' journey as a diplomatic mission? Or as tourism? Or, in view of the presence of spoils from the Temple in Jerusalem in this period, as an unusual form of pilgrimage?

In Chapter 15 Wendy Pullan (' "Intermingled Until the End of Time": Ambiguity as a Central Condition of Early Christian Pilgrimage') proposes a new way of thinking about early Christian pilgrimage. The key to understanding it, she argues, is the Christian view of the terrestrial sojourn as a state of perpetual estrangement and journey, alienated from worldly concerns, on the way to but not yet arrived at the Heavenly City. The world that the early Christian pilgrim negotiated is thus one of paradoxes incurred by the shifting balance of immanent and transcendent; Augustine formulated this state of temporal ambiguity in his two cities, which on earth are 'intermingled until the end of time' (18.54).

Jaś Elsner's Chapter 16 ('Piety and Passion: Contest and Consensus in the Audiences for Early Christian Pilgrimage'), explores the general approaches to early Christian pilgrimage in the fourth and fifth centuries CE. While historians have generally taken the evidence to indicate a monolithic and united early Christian tradition (a reading of pilgrimage which flies in the face not only of contemporary anthropological doubts about consensus among pilgrims but also of the abundant fourth- and fifth-century evidence for religious and theological dispute), Elsner argues that The Holy Land was in fact a hotbed of theological dispute and accusations of heresy in this period, and the visiting pilgrims, coming from a very wide range of countries, and representing numerous Christianities, scarcely support the scholarly model of a harmonious ideal of pilgrimage practice in the most archetypal of Christian holy spots.

In Chapter 17 David Frankfurter ('Urban Shrine and Rural Saint in Fifth-Century Alexandria') examines the institution of pilgrimage-shrines in the context of relics of holy men in late-antique Egypt. He looks at two Alexandrian cults: that of the Three Hebrews, and that of Maracius of Tkow, who is assimilated to the established cult of John and Elisha; and he argues that these are best seen against the background of a tension between an official, biblical point of view, and a local Egyptian one focused on the relics of saints (roughly between our types §19 and §21).

The seventeen chapters take very different approaches, but we can detect in them a number of common themes. First, several contribute to the problem of definition and terminology: is the term 'pilgrimage' applicable to ancient practice (see Scullion in particular; also Williamson)? Do data from an ancient site which indicate that people visited a sanctuary also allow us to infer what sort of journey they made (see Fear; Takács)? and what are the precise spheres of application of the various ancient terms (in Greek and other languages) that are found in the context of pilgrimage (Naiden on *theōria* and *hiketeia*; Pullan on Hebrew terminology)?

Second, several contributors show an interest, derived in part from anthropological work, in the social significance of pilgrimage: either in so far as pilgrimage is a force that forges cohesion among participants (cf. e.g. Kowalzig) or, conversely, focusing on the different experience of classes of pilgrims with different social backgrounds (addressed with respect to the Pergamene Asclepieion by Petsalis-Diomidis; with respect to Jerusalem by Elsner; and to some extent with respect to pilgrimage in Egypt in Rutherford's piece). Hutton and Galli are also concerned with the social significance of pilgrimage for the elite groups that make it. And again in Coptic Egypt, as Frankfurter shows, popular pilgrimage to the tombs of local saints exists alongside, and in opposition to, official cults sanctioned by biblical authority.

Finally, a number of the papers address the complex relationship between pilgrimage and ancient literature. The first-person pilgrimage-narrative is not a genre well attested in Greek or Roman literature, at least before Egeria, although Aelius Aristides' *Sacred Tales* seem to come close to it (see the papers of Petsalis-Diomidis and Galli); and Williamson suggests that the fragments of Roman aristocrat Mucianus also suggest a first person narrative of sacred travel. However, many Greek authors describe pilgrimage, especially when it is happening in a foreign country, e.g. Herodotus (Rutherford), and Lucian (Lightfoot). The philosopher Plato makes use of Greek *theōria* as a symbol for philosophy (Nightingale). Equally, literature could shape pilgrimage, as Pausanias' *Periegesis* of Greece perhaps influenced the expectations of educated Greeks visiting religious sites (Hutton), or as the special concerns of Christian theology may have influenced early Christian pilgrimage (Pullan).[134]

[134] On pilgrimage literature in general, the reader is referred to Rutherford (1995), (1998*a*), and (2005*b*).

PART I

CLASSICAL AND HELLENISTIC PILGRIMAGE

1

Mapping out *Communitas*: Performances of *Theōria* in their Sacred and Political Context

Barbara Kowalzig

τὸ χωρίον μὲν γὰρ τσδ᾽ ἐστὶ πᾶν κύκλωι
Ὀλυμπία, τηνδὶ δὲ τὴν σκηνὴν ἐκεῖ
σκηνὴν ὁρᾶν θεωρικὴν νομίζετε.
εἶέν· τί οὖν ἐνταῦθα δρῶσιν αἱ πόλεις;
Ἐλευθέρι᾽ ἀφίκοντο θύσουσαί ποτε,   10
ὅτε τῶν φόρων ἐγένοντ᾽ ἐλεύθεραι σχεδόν.
κἄπειτ᾽ ἀπ᾽ ἐκείνης τῆς θυσίας διέφθορεν
αὐτὰς ξενίζουσ᾽ ἡμέραν ἐξ ἡμέρας
ἀβουλία κατέχουσα πολὺν ἤδη χρόνον.   15
γυναῖκε δ᾽ αὐτὰς δύο ταράττετόν τινε
ἀεὶ συνοῦσαι· Δημοκρατία θἀτέραι
ὄνομ᾽ ἐστί, τῇ δ᾽ Ἀριστοκρατία θἀτέραι
δι᾽ ἃς πεπαρωινήκασιν ἤδη πολλάκις

I would like to thank the two editors and Bonna Wescoat as well as audiences in Paris, Berkeley, Glasgow, and Rethymno for the helpful comments and suggestions on drafts of this paper; Erika Milburn for her help with the English text.

This place is all round, it is Olympia,
and there understand that you see the *skēnē*
housing the poleis' *theōria*-delegations.
Well then, what are the cities doing?
They had once come here to sacrifice in the festival of Freedom,
when they were just released from the tribute,
but since that sacrifice Indecision has been corrupting them
and has kept entertaining them day after day for a long time now.
A certain two women are harassing them with their
constant presence: Demokratia is the name of the one
Aristokratia that of the other, and
for their sake the cities have drunk themselves senseless many times.

(Heniokhos *PCG* fr. 5. 6–18)

The scene (*skēnē*, 'stage') of this fourth-century comic fragment is
Olympia, and is identified by a pun with the *skēnē* ('tent') hosting the
theōroi. The cities of Greece have assembled in a 'circular place' to
sacrifice, to celebrate their freedom from what may be an allusion to
the fifth-century imperial 'tribute' to Athens. But the celebrations have
somehow come to a halt: two enticing women, Aristocracy and Democracy, distract the cities, who are torn between attraction and obligation to the *khoros* of *poleis* of which they are a part. The ritual process is
delayed, causing, as it seems, perplexity on the dancing spot.

The extract comes from an unknown play of unknown content by a
poet barely known except for the rough period of his productivity in
the early fourth century BCE. Yet it presents a fascinating glimpse of
the workings and functions of classical *theōria*, as well as of its
perception. It gives us the fundamental idea that *theōria* is a communal activity, principally concerned with the creation and maintenance
of a community through shared ritual. In the case of unsuccessful or
abortive ritual the community it embraces would fall apart, and with
it that for which it stands; one defective member can easily upset the
social balance. Olympia itself performs in a role where it pools all the
associations *theōria* carries. Phlegon of Tralles reports, much later and
anachronistically, that the shine owed its final and lasting institution
to the attempt to 'restore the people of the Peloponnese to harmony
(ὁμόνοιαν) and peace (εἰρήνην)' as recurrent outbreaks of *stasis* beset the
area whenever worship of Zeus was temporarily abandoned.[1] Phlegon's

---

[1] Phlegon of Tralles *FGrH* 257 F 1.

Olympia is pristine and its catchment area limited, but it anticipates the shrine's later role just as Heniokhos expresses it for *theōria* more widely: theoric ritual was perceived as crucial for the social and political order between cities, and for the creation of a sense of communality among them. If the comedy's theoric community is presented as a—presumably dysfunctional—*khoros* this would lead the audience to expect a comic solution in which the plot's contradictions are dissolved in shared choral ritual.[2] The theoric *khoros* thus becomes a representation of a functioning theoric community, and a representation of harmony within Greece. Common ritual experience through song-dance is, the comedy would imply, an essential tool of working *theōria*.

It is this relationship between the practice of *theōria*, the nature of the community it embraces, and the ritual form it takes, that interests me here. Victor Turner, in a theory that has never lost its popular appeal, thought that ritual affords *communitas* as a way of dissolving social conflict temporarily and through the liminality of ritual. *Communitas* is also the notion of common identity, collective social values, and equality that he stipulated underlay the ritual of 'pilgrimage'.[3] While Turner's understanding of *communitas* might be accused of lacking complexity, the ritual experience shared between participants can nevertheless be shown to lie at the heart of *theōria*.

Theōria in Greece embraces a vast array of different religious activities, ranging from 'attending a religious festival' to tourism and philosophical reflection; most prominently, however, *theōria* acts through an institutional framework within the *polis*, or between *poleis* as a form of inter-state religion.[4] 'Seeing the Gods' (θεωρία cf. θεωρεῖν), a complicated and much-theorized interaction between viewer and what is viewed, is at the centre of the process by which any of these theoric activities assume meaning and receive function in a social context. *Theōria*, on whichever level it is enacted, is a ritual process, and hence

---

[2] Hunter (1979), 34–5 denies that the *khoros* is made up of individual cities, but cf. e.g. Aristophanes' *Islands*; Eupolis' *Poleis*. Cf. Rutherford (1998*b*).

[3] Turner (1974*c*). For his concept of 'communitas' cf. esp. (1969), (1974*b*), (1982).

[4] On the term '*theōria*' see now Nightingale in this volume; earlier discussions Koller (1958); Rausch (1982); Rutherford (2000*a*). On pilgrimage and 'viewing art' see e.g. Hunt (1982); Elsner (1992). Goldhill (1999), 5–8 discusses very briefly the range of meanings of '*theōros*'. Dillon's book on pilgrimage (1997) does not discuss the term.

has a performative quality to it; it is the ritual dimension from which all its significance emerges.[5]

I shall engage here with one particular set of performances of *theōria*. *Theōria* as a form of inter-state religion is essentially different from Christian 'pilgrimage' in that it involves the sending of public delegations, thus establishing a complicated network of exchange between cities through sanctuaries. The concrete shape this takes may vary, depending on every cult's role within the local and wider religious system: 'amphiktyonies' for example, tend to be considered local religious centres whose limited membership had both a share and an obligation in the running of the cult, while the abundant epigraphic record of the Hellenistic period gives us a taste of the vast organizational apparatus enveloping the process of *polis-theōria* at a grand, often panhellenic scale. But the distinction is blurred: the significant overlap between amphiktyony and *theōria* at prominent cult centres such as Olympia, Delphi, and Delos suggests that looking at the changing historical function of these cults through time might yield more than attempts at precise terminological definition.[6] In fact, as we shall see, even *theōria*'s Hellenistic complexity reveals features not so different from a practice as old as the Greek gods themselves: the creation, and constant re-recreation, of a community, on a scale from two cities to the entire Greek world, through participation in a shared cult that is perceived to be vital for the maintenance of social order.

This chapter attempts to explore the nature and workings of the social organization that lies behind broadly speaking 'theoric' cults, that is to say the vast number of cults in the Greek world frequented by several cities. It will emerge that theoric worshipping groups present an alternative form of social organization often complementing, but

[5] The relationship between 'performance' and '*theōria*' has certainly been identified, but not been extensively discussed: see briefly in Goldhill (1999), 5–8. For 'pilgrimage' it is implied by Turner (1974c).

[6] The overlap between amphiktyony and *theōria*: amphiktyonic decrees busy themselves with aspects of *theōria*: e.g. *CID* 1.10; a possible (likely?) supplement *theōros* occurs for a state delegation to the 'amphiktyonic' cult of Zeus Atabyrios on Rhodes: *SEG* 49 (1999), 1070. Demosthenes reproached Athens for not sending a *patrios theōria* to Delphi: D. 19.128. Cf. *H.Ap.* 535 ff. from where it is clear that Delphi expected to be maintained through the meat contributions of its theoric visitors. Heniokhos in our passage evidently thinks of Olympia as a panhellenic, theoric cult centre, Phlegon gives it the features of what is better known as an 'amphiktyony'.

quite as often competing with, political or other groupings; by virtue of this difference they function as a social tool within communities, fiercely exploiting what is not a peaceful, but in fact a highly conflictual, sense of *communitas*, projected into theoric ritual. The rather frequent appearance of the *khoros* especially in the more ancient record of *polis-theōria* is inherently related to the importance of ritual for *theōria*. Choral performance is one means by which theoric worshipping communities are forged, and through which they function. Indeed, I shall argue that chorality becomes a potent metaphor through which one could imagine, and exploit, forms of inter-*polis* contact. Chorality builds a framework through which to engage with *theōria*, and ultimately offers the key idea behind *polis-theōria*: the constant invocation of *communitas* in ritual lies at the heart of *theōria's* function in Greek culture.

I. THEORIC RITUAL BETWEEN COMPLIANCE AND DEFIANCE

Khoroi are ubiquitous in the literary talk of the early traditions on *theōria*:[7] for example, that of the Chians' 100-strong *khoros* of youths sent to Delphi, who tragically died in a thunderstorm. Only two dancers returned, something that, according to Herodotus, foretold much unhappiness to strike the island. Another touching story is that of the *khoros* from Sicilian Messene, which, on its way to Rhegion on the other side, perished on its journey through Skylla and Karybdis. Messene was founded by Anaxilas of Rhegion, and the choral tribute, performed κατὰ τὸ ἀρχαῖον, clearly manifests and maintains bonds with the mother city. The thirty-five adolescent victims and their aulete were glorified in bronze images at Olympia, as if to monumentalize the choral relation in the sanctuary that not only presented the archetype of *theōria*, but also specifically served the cities of southern Italy and Sicily. Eumelos of Corinth, much earlier, is supposed to have composed a *prosodion* for a *khoros* of the as yet free Messenians of the Peloponnese to take to Delos; this *theōria* is mentioned by Pausanias as immediately preceding the Spartan conquest, while the poem reappears in the

---

[7] Choral *polis-theōria* has only recently received the attention it deserves: Rutherford (2004*a*).

context of a festival celebrated annually by exiled Messenians at Nau-
paktos. In placing the theoric *khoros* at a critical point in Messenia's
history, the puzzling tradition illuminates an ancient relation between
the Peloponnese and the Aegean island world, which has left traces in a
period as late as the Athenian empire.[8]

That such stories have survived at all, and are thought to date back a
very long way, above all attests the horror felt at the death of the young.
But it also demonstrates the degree to which choral *polis-theōria* was
assumed to be an ancient practice, and a basic form of interaction and
mobility between places. Similarly, the fact that by and large stories of
the catastrophes, rather than of the regular, completed delegations
survive, suggests that a disturbed theoric relation caused great upset.
That a *theōria* could not work was unimaginable, a major disaster for
inter-*polis* contact, so much so that it was worth commemorating: the
stories function to disclaim responsibility, as if to pass the buck for a
long-standing relation being discontinued. If such disasters regularly
occur at sea, this simply confirms the notion that this sea-borne practice
is about what the sea itself enabled, that is contact. The well-known
honours that the Delphians conferred upon various poets for their
choral compositions is another testimony to suggest that the constant
flow of *khoroi* was something a sanctuary of *theōria* cared about, and so
presumably did the theoric community at large.[9]

The Greeks, then, seem to have taken *theōria* extremely seriously, and
the *khoros* stands out in many of the traditions that suggest *theōria*'s
importance in the first place. So much so that the *khoroi*, which are
generally not well attested epigraphically, feature in their connection to
state delegations in some sacred laws. One such example survives for the
Panionion at Mykale in western Asia Minor, which, as we know from
Herodotus and from its epigraphic dossier, functioned as a local—and

---

[8] Hdt. 6.23 (Chios); Paus. 5.25.2–4 (Rhegion); 4.4.1 (Messene). For Olympia as a
meeting place for Southern Italians see esp. Philipp (1994); a much-quoted example of
'inter-state' relations ratified by Zeus is the 6th-cent. treaty between Serdaioi and Sybaris
(ML 10). For Eumelos' prosodion, composed for a *theōria* led by a Phintas from Messene
see Paus. 4.4.1; 33.2. For Peloponnesians and notably Spartans on Delos in the 5th cent.
see now Prost (2001).

[9] See Sourvinou-Inwood (1995), *passim*, on attitudes towards the deaths of the
young. Kleokhares (230–225 BCE): *Sig.*[3] 450 = *FD* 3.2.78.4–6 = *SEG* 32 (1982),
540; Limenios: *Sig.*[3] 698A, C = *CA* 149–59 (129 BCE); anonymous Athenian: *Sig.*[3]
698B = *FD* 3. 47.19 = *CA* 141–8.

in this sense 'theoric'—cult centre for the so-called Ionian Dodekapolis. The cult regulation prescribes arrangements for what must be the fourth-century festival of the Panionia, providing insights into the mechanics of the cult's ritual group dynamics:

$$
\begin{aligned}
&[\tau\hat{\omega}\nu \; \delta\grave{\epsilon} \; \pi\acute{o}]\text{-} \\
&[\lambda\epsilon\omega\nu, \; \grave{\epsilon}]\grave{\alpha}\nu \; \mu\grave{\eta} \; \grave{\alpha}\pi\alpha\gamma\acute{\alpha}\gamma\eta\iota \; [\tau\iota\varsigma \; \tau\grave{\alpha} \; \acute{\iota}\epsilon\rho\epsilon\hat{\iota}\alpha, \; \grave{\epsilon}\kappa\gamma\rho\acute{\alpha}\phi]\text{-} \\
&[\epsilon\iota\nu \; \tau\grave{\eta}\nu] \; \pi\acute{o}\lambda\iota\nu \; \tau\grave{\eta}\nu \; \mu\grave{\eta} \; \grave{\alpha}\pi\acute{\alpha}[\gamma o\upsilon\sigma\alpha\nu \; \epsilon\grave{\iota}\varsigma \; \sigma\tau\acute{\eta}\lambda\eta\nu \; \acute{\epsilon}\xi\omega] \\
&[\tauο\hat{\upsilon} \; \Pi\alpha\nu\iota]\omega\nu\acute{\iota}o\upsilon, \; \mathring{\eta}\iota \; \tau\grave{\alpha} \; \acute{\iota}\epsilon\rho\epsilon\hat{\iota}\alpha \; \pi[\alpha\rho\acute{\iota}\sigma\tau\alpha\sigma\theta\alpha\iota \; \delta\epsilon\hat{\iota}] \\
&[\acute{\upsilon}\pi\grave{o} \; \tau\hat{\omega}\nu \; \grave{o}]\phi\epsilon\iota\lambda\acute{o}\nu\tau\omega\nu \cdot \; \mathring{\eta}\nu \; \delta\grave{\epsilon} \; \mu\grave{\eta} \; [\grave{\alpha}\pio\delta\hat{\omega}\iota, \; \kappa\omega\lambda\acute{\upsilon}\epsilon\iota\nu] \qquad 5 \\
&[\grave{\epsilon}\nu \; \tauο\hat{\iota}\varsigma] \; \grave{\epsilon}\pi\iotaο\hat{\upsilon}\sigma\iota \; \Pi\alpha\nu\iota\omega\nu\acute{\iota}o[\iota\varsigma \; \acute{\iota}\epsilon\rho\grave{\alpha} \; \pio\iota\epsilon\hat{\iota}\nu \cdot \; \theta\acute{\upsilon}]\text{-} \\
&[\epsilon\iota\nu \; \delta\grave{\epsilon}] \; \tau\hat{\omega}\iota \; \varDelta\iota\grave{\iota} \; \tau\hat{\omega}\iota \; Bο\upsilon\lambda\alpha[\acute{\iota}\omega\iota \; \tauο\hat{\iota}\varsigma \; \tau\epsilon \; \acute{\alpha}\lambda\lambdaο\iota\varsigma \; \theta\epsilon]\text{-} \\
&[ο\hat{\iota}\varsigma, \; ο\hat{\iota}\varsigma] \; \grave{\epsilon}\nu \; \chiο\rho\hat{\omega}\iota \; \theta\acute{\upsilon}\epsilon\iota\nu \; \delta\epsilon\hat{\iota} \; [\kappa\alpha\tau\grave{\alpha} \; \tau\grave{o}\nu \; \acute{\iota}\epsilon\rho\grave{o}\nu \; \nuό\muο\nu] \\
&[\pi\alpha\rho\acute{\epsilon}]\chi\epsilon\iota\nu \; \delta\grave{\epsilon} \; \tau\grave{\alpha} \; \acute{\iota}\epsilon\rho\grave{\alpha} \; \tau\grave{\eta}\nu \; [\pi\acute{o}\lambda\iota\nu \; \grave{\epsilon}\kappa\acute{\alpha}\sigma\tau\eta\nu \cdot \; \sigma\kappa\acute{\epsilon}\lambda]\text{-} \\
&[ο\varsigma \; \delta\acute{\epsilon}, \; \gamma\lambda\hat{\omega}]\sigma\sigma\alpha, \; \delta\acute{\epsilon}\rho\mu\alpha, \; \muο\hat{\iota}\rho\alpha, \; \pi[\lambda\epsilon\upsilon\rho\grave{o}\nu \; \tau\hat{\omega}\iota \; \acute{\iota}\epsilon\rho\epsilon\hat{\iota}] \qquad 10 \\
&[\kappa\alpha\grave{\iota} \; \tau\grave{\alpha}] \; \acute{\alpha}\lambda\lambda\alpha \; \grave{\epsilon}\pi' \; \acute{\iota}\sigma\eta\varsigma \; \tau\grave{\alpha} \; [\delta\grave{\epsilon} \; \tau\iota\theta\acute{\epsilon}\mu\epsilon\nu\alpha \; \grave{\epsilon}\pi\grave{\iota} \; \tau\rho\alpha\pi\acute{\epsilon}]\text{-} \\
&[\zeta\eta\iota] \; \mathring{\eta} \; \beta\omega\mu\hat{\omega}\iota \; \tau\hat{\omega}\iota \; \grave{\epsilon}\alpha\upsilon\tau[\hat{\omega}\iota \; \kappa\alpha\tau\epsilon\upsilon\chiο\mu\acute{\epsilon}\nu\omega\iota \cdot
\end{aligned}
$$

If [any of the cities] does not bring [victims, they must write up] the defau[lting] city [on a stele outside the Pani]onion, where victims [must be produced by the cities who] owe. If any of them fails [to produce them, it must be prevented from] making sacrifices at the next Panionia. [Sacrifice must be made] to Zeus Boulai[os and the other gods, to whom] sacrifice must be made in the *khoros* in accordance with the sacred law. [Each city must pro]duce victims. [Leg, ton]gue, hide, part (?), and [rib go to the priest and the rest (is divided)] equally. The parts [put on the table] and the altar go to the one who [makes a prayer] for himself. (tentative translation)

Sokolowski (1970), 11.4–15[10]

The law is concerned with participating members' contribution to the common festival. Sacred Laws often have a primary, practical function of guaranteeing the cult's continuity from a material point of view. It is, as we shall see, precisely in this interest in 'continuity' that the broader significance of the law lies, but this reaches beyond the pragmatics of festival organization to the reasons why the Greeks worried so much about their theoric relations being intercepted, and to *theōria*'s function in the landscape of social interaction in Greece.

---

[10] Note the rendering of this very difficult text in Hommel et al. (1967), 45–63.

The key lies in the unwarranted emphasis on the ritual role that each member state has to perform in a drawn-out process involving choral performance: 'sacrifices are to be made to Zeus Boulaios and the other gods, to whom sacrifice must be made ἐν χορῶι [in accordance with the sacred law]' (ll. 9–12), that is presumably accompanied by choral song.[11] '*Thysia* and *khoros*' appear regularly as a joint ritual commitment in literary texts, and the law here gives us an idea of what this might have looked like.[12] The remainder of the sentence, indicating that every individual city was to bring its own victim, implies that this procedure was unexcitedly repeated as many times as there were faithful cities. It is unclear whether the *khoros* was formed by representatives of all the participating cities or, more likely, this was a case of choral *polis-theōria*; but most relevant is the insistence itself that the sacrifice be made 'in the *khoros*': it suggests that the *khoros* was essential for the validity of the sacrifice, and that without the *khoros*, the sacrifice would have been void. The effect of the procedure relies on the potential that the putative choral song must have had in fostering the cult's *communitas* through every single performance. It is a law of ritual that the more repetitive—tedious—it becomes, the more powerful its inculcations, the more automatic the thinking that goes with it.[13]

The traditions of how the Panionion came about provide suggestions for what it was that had to be acted out regularly ἐν χορῶι, why choral performance might have been important in this cult. This is intrinsically related to the sanctuary's role in the creation and maintenance of an 'Ionian' identity of the Greeks in western Asia Minor. The Panionion has attracted much attention, but its actual *raison d'être* has remained curiously obscure. Of disputed age even in antiquity, it traditionally features as a 'meeting place' for the so-called Ionians of Asia, for them to share in ceremony what separated them from their barbarian cohabitants, neighbours, and overlords, a common 'ethnic' identity, manifested in language and religious traditions.[14] But there is not much evidence that many of these

---

[11] For the expression cf. *I. Tralles* 145.

[12] I discuss their joint appearance elsewhere: Kowalzig (2004), 49 ff.

[13] This point has been argued by Tambiah (1981).

[14] For the Panionion's archaeology see Hommel et al. (1967); for Ionians and the Panionion see e.g. Roebuck (1955); Huxley (1972); Emlyn-Jones (1980); Tausend

elements were truly shared. For example, those whom Herodotus labels 'Ionians' were, as he says himself in accordance with recent historical analysis, a mixed bunch of settlers from all over Greece, particularly the central Greek mainland.[15] Herodotus' definitions of what it means to be ethnically Ionian are a string of inherent contradictions: to give just one example, to identify Ionian cities on the grounds of a common festival, the Apatouria, quoting in the same breath two exceptions, does not make for consistency. That his account of Ionian communality constantly undermines itself—as if a rhetorical technique by which a conclusion develops through the narrative itself rather than through structured or formalized argument—might well give us pause.[16]

Just as revealing as the Herodotean attempt to forge 'ethnic' unity out of genuine diversity is how hard the cities' local traditions laboured to forge an Ionian legacy, and associated membership in the Panionion. Pausanias' account of the Ionians of Asia Minor, despite its anachronisms and doubtful historicity, gives, if nothing else, an idea of what issues were at stake. The twelve 'Ionian' cities frequenting the Panionion emerge from social conflict and the struggle for local power in a mixture of mutual help and aggressive intervention. Traditions only gradually developed into a network of relations expressed through a language of kinship designed to cover, and to configure to each other, its well-selected members, not least in the attempt to get to grips with those Greeks who were already in the East when the Ionians undertook their migration.[17]

The principal cities and rivals Miletos and Ephesos seem straight 'conquests' on the part of the 'Ionians' but their founders Neileus and

---

(1992), 70–4; Ragone (1996); Hall (2002), 67–73; Murray (1988), in relation to the Ionian revolt; Sakellariou (1958) is still the most comprehensive account on the traditions of the Ionian migration. The Parian Marble dates the institution very early, to 1087 or 1077 BCE; older scholarship tends to locate it between the 10th and the 8th cent.: Roebuck (1955), 32; Caspari (1915); Cook (1962), 34; Shipley (1987), 29–31 and Hall (2002), 67 f. favour a date in around the early 7th cent. On the traditions of the lists of member states see Moggi and Osanna (1994), *ad* 7.2 ff.

[15] Hdt. 1.146.1–2: 'Abantes from Euboia . . . Minyans from Orkhomenos, Kadmeians, Dryopes, Phokian refugees, Molossians, Pelasgians from Arkadia and Dorians from Epidauros'; cf. their origin from 'Akhaia' in the Peloponnese (1.145; 7.94). For the 'Aiolian' (= central Greek), substratum see now the concise analysis by Hall (2002), 69 ff.

[16] Hdt. 1.147.

[17] Paus. 7.2 ff.; see Moggi (1994), for a discussion.

Androklos, sons of Kodros, have strong Peloponnesian associations.[18] Then Androklos, king of Ephesos, is said to have conquered Samos from its 'Ionian' oikist, who in turn had imposed himself on the indigenous population. Of the original Samians, those who had not left for 'Samothrace' eventually reconquered the island from their refuge in mainland Anaia, leaving a serious question mark over Samos' 'Ionian' identity.[19] The same Androklos also 'helped' the Prieneans against Karians in the area; that said, the people of Priene are called both 'Ionians' and 'Thebans'.[20] The Ionians bound for Kolophon arranged themselves (συνεπολιτεύοντο) with the Greeks whom they found in situ, and took up the kingship; similarly the Teians got on well with the local Minyans from Orkhomenos, and in a later generation even received reinforcements from both non-Ionian Boiotia and possibly-by-then-'Ionian' Athens.[21] Meanwhile Erythrai's Ionian founder collected settlers from the other 'Ionian' cities to join as fellow oikists the pre-existing pool of Lycians, Karians, Pamphylians, and Kretans. Klazomenai is declared to house only a few Ionians, and for the most part people from Arkadia. The only Ionian presence amongst the Phokaians, themselves from Parnassos, were their oikists, while the city had been received 'by agreement' (κατὰ δὲ ὁμολογίαν) with Aeolian Kyme. And, Phokaia was not accepted at the Panionion 'before they had assumed Kodridai kings', who promptly came from Erythrai and Teos.[22] Altogether 'Aiolian' Smyrna, at some stage pleaded for

[18] Their father Kodros and his sons came from Messenian Pylos: Hdt. 1.147; 5.65; cf. Paus. 2.1 where 'Ionians' are distinct from 'Athenians'; there was no genos 'Kodridai' at Athens. Neileus' was the unrivalled sovereign of Miletos through its oldest history, recipient of cult and ancestor of a genos: Hdt. 9.97; Arist. fr. 556 Rose, Call. frr. 80–3; *Dian.* 226–7; Theocr. 28.3; Plut. *Mor.* 253f–54b; Polyaen. 8.35; *SDGI* 2.2.5501. Androklos has many royal namesakes in liberated Messenia's traditions: Paus. 4.4.4; 5.6; 15.7; 16.2; 17.9.

[19] Paus. 7.2.8–9; 4.2. On the identification of Anaia, an important refuge for exiled Samians in later centuries, see Fantasia (1986).

[20] Paus. 7.2.10. For the Boiotian stratum see also Hellan. *FGrH* 4 F 101; Str. 14.1.3; cf. Hdt. 1.146. Bias of Priene sometimes attracts Boiotian origins: Phanodikos *FGrH* 397 F 4; Paus. 10.24.1. For a discussion see Moggi and Osanna (2000), *ad* 7.2.76–8.

[21] Kolophon: Paus. 7.3.3, though cf. Mimn. fr. 9–10 W = Str. 14.1.3 for their putative 'Pylian' origin; for Teos see Paus. 7.3.6 and 2.3; 9.37.8; Pherek. *FGrH* 3 F 102; Str. 14.1.3 (cf. Hdt. 1.146 for the Minyan/Boiotian input into Ionia).

[22] Paus. 7.3.7–9. For the Kretan origins of Erythrai see also DS 5.769.1; 84/3; Kaibel no. 904. Str. 14.1.3 ignores this. For central Greek Phokians at Phokaia see Hdt. 1.146,

admittance to the Panionion.[23] Especially telling, finally, is Chios' turn to Ionian ethnicity. It was, strangely, Trojan Hektor, who, once he had expelled Euboian settlers, promoted Chios' participation in the Panionion gatherings, an initiative for which the 'Ionians' rewarded him with a tripod. But, Pausanias continues, the source for all of this, the fifth-century poet Ion of Chios, did not actually say 'why the Chians became Ionians' (τελοῦσιν ἐς ῎Ιωνας).[24]

The issues of social conflict inherent in this brief survey, and the ways in which they relate to social and political change in Asia Minor's distant past, are wide-ranging and deserve a separate treatment altogether—they involve not least a complicated relationship between the enigmatic traditional local 'kingships' (βασιλεῖαι) and the sixth-century Ionian aristocracy.[25] What matters for the present purposes is that the majority of Ionian cities became Ionian by adoption; that is to say that 'Ionia' was a social and political term, not geographical or ethnic, delineating the group of those who had mutually supported each other in carving out for themselves a comfortable position in the politically complex area which they 'agreed' to become Ionia; and which, perhaps, they newly invested with a social order we now associate with the Ionian nobles. Wherever this elite of Ionians had emerged from (whether real migrations or just a complicated social process which turned upside down the local hierarchies), it is clear that 'Ionians' were not initially in the majority. Similarly, the stipulations and recommendations by which cities were admitted to this exclusive group suggests that the Panionion's membership was socially crafted and had little to do with shared traditional forms of religious behaviour—apart from the compelling factor that participation in the cult would turn a new contact into tradition, itself a way of quietly forgetting the ethnic diversity of the past.[26]

for Peloponnesians cf. Nikolaos of Damaskus *FGrH* 90 F 51. Differing versions are found in Heracl. Pont. *FHG* 2 p. 223, fr. 35; St. Byz s.v.

[23] Paus. 7.5.1, circumstances known already from Hdt. 1.149 f.

[24] Paus. 7.4.8–10. Chios' participation in the cult at Mykale is described as συνθύειν, a word typically used for 'being a member of the theoric cult'. For the Euboian Abantids on Chios and in Ionia see Hdt. 1.146; Paus. 2.3; 5.22.3–4; Hippias of Eretria *FGrH* 421 F 1. Strabo 14.1.3 quotes 'Karians and Lelegians'.

[25] On kingship in Ionia see esp. Carlier (1983), 491–51; on the 'Ionian kings', magistrates, of the confederacy esp. 50–5 and Momigliano (1934).

[26] Panyassis' 6th-cent. epic on the 'Ktisis of Ionia' might well be a desperate attempt to knit together the populations of profoundly mixed Ionia, giving testimony to the fragile, rather than the firm configuration of 6th-cent. Ionia.

The Panionion's one surviving aetiology, its 'founding legend', helps in assessing the nature of this emerging set of theoric relationships. It suggests a system of mutual control rather than a proactive alliance, developing, just as Pausanias says, from local, partly inner-Greek conflict. It comes from a text as late as Vitruvius, as a little historical excursus orchestrating the emergence of the Ionian column order. Once the 'Ionians' had expelled the Karians and Lelegians, he says, they 'first of all built a temple to Panionian Apollo, as they had seen it in Akhaia'. Panionian Apollo is an anachronism, having become a 'Panionian' god by Vitruvius' time; but the reference to Poseidon at Helike in Akhaia, the putative ancestor of his cult at Mykale, makes it clear that the talk here is about the archaic Panionion.[27]

Somewhat surprising is the appearance among the Ionians of ancient Meli(t)e: Melie was once a city on the Mykale promontory, which, though perhaps Greek in part, had a strong Karian element.[28] This somehow moves the cult's origins close to another episode in the locality: the so-called Melian War, of possibly around 700 BCE, is one of those semi-mythical wars of the archaic age that obscurely but decisively set the scene for the shape of later Greece and not least for this reason survives the censorship of tradition. Two Hellenistic inscriptions authoritatively quote its outcome in order to settle a contemporary struggle over the division of land. A powerful city with probably a vast territory, Melie on the Mykalean promontory seems to have been a nuisance to the 'Ionians' who jointly contrived its destruction *propter adrogantiam civium*, as we learn from Vitruvius' passing reference, much in the same way as the prosperous city of Siris in socially fragmented southern Italy was erased by its jealous neighbours, striking up an 'Akhaian' identity. While Vitruvius portrays the foundation of the cult as the first 'collective' act of an already existing koinon of Ionians, it is more likely that shared interests emerged in targeting a common rival in the first place. In consequence, so the inscriptions tell us, Melie's

---

[27] Vitr. 4.1.3 ff. For Poseidon at Helike see *Il.* 8.200–4 (cf. 20.403–5); Str. 8.7.2; Paus. 7.24.5.

[28] Melie: Hekataios *FGrH* 1 F 11: πόλις Καρίας ἐθνικὸν Μελιεύς. A Κάριον φρούριον, possibly the ancient acropolis, is mentioned in *I. Priene* 37.9 ff, cf. Hommel et al. (1967), 79; 78 ff. for the mixed population of Melie, including a possible Boiotian stratum; Tausend (1992), 70–4.

territory was split up between its neighbours and opponents, Kolophon, Samos, Priene, and Miletos.[29]

The story gives us a fascinating glimpse of interacting poleis in the early Greek world and the role of religious institutions in it. The connection that arises between the partition of (enemy) territory and the establishment of common rites suggests that shared worship at the Panionion embraced a mutual agreement over possibly contentious land. While common cults and territorial agreements frequently go hand in hand in Greek history,[30] this need not mean that the problem with Melie only or necessarily lay with its land. Spread across the northern part of the Mykale promontory, this city was ideally positioned for example to control the Samian strait through which much sea traffic would have passed, and thus not least in a position to contribute to the myth of the Karian thalassocracy, dated by the Christian chronographers to the late eighth century.[31] Particularly in view of a sea-borne Melie, it cannot be a coincidence that the little we know of the archaic Panionion's actions concerns Poseidon's realm: it is explicitly by sea, and not by land, that his followers decide to fight *when* they fight concertedly in the 'Ionian revolt'. It may well have been their shared stake in Poseidon's territory that this consortium of cities was out to defend.[32]

Whatever the case may be, the invention and regular quotation of a shared tradition on how Melie's land was distributed seems to have had the function of maintaining and confirming the territorial status quo, and for this reason has also survived in Hellenistic epigraphy. It is all the more intriguing that this 'settlement' was in fact the beginning of a string of continuous territorial arguments and border conflicts unset-

[29] Vitr. 4.1.3 ff.; *I.Priene* 37, esp. 44 ff; 101 ff. (*c*.196 BCE; a Rhodian arbitration between Samos and Priene); *CIG* 2254 = Welles (1934), no. 7, 46–51 (Lysimachus' letter to the Samians (283/2BCE)). The most recent treatment is by Magnetto (1997), no. 20, 124–41 (cf. 44, 75), with extensive bibliography. On the Melian War see Hommel et al. (1967), 78–94 (where also an attempt at the city's history, including its territorial expansion, is made); Ragone (1986); Fantasia (1986); Tausend (1992), 70–4. How exactly the land was distributed after the war is unclear: Lenschau (1944), 233f; Shipley (1987), 31–7, with prior bibliography. For Siris' destruction see Iust. 20.2.3.

[30] The idea is to some degree implied in De Polignac (1994); cf. e.g. Artemis Limnatis at Paus. 4.4.1–3; Apollo Pythaieus at Asine (see below, Th. 5.53).

[31] Hommel et al. (1967), 93 imply this point, though their suggestion that Melian *hybris* might have lain in impeding powerful Miletos' ships from travelling through the strait is not convincing. Cf. Euseb. *Hieron.* 7.1.90.20.

[32] Hdt. 5.109; 6.7 ff.

tling the area for some time to come. The cities straight away seem to have sought to exchange their allotments, and the land continuously changed its owners, never to become stable again.[33] It is ironic that the documents surviving from the Hellenistic period adduce this arrangement as having brought about peace when really what it produced were intermittent wars. But the irony may unwittingly give us the clue to what the Panionion as a theoric cult centre was directed at: in constantly reminding its members of the putatively once-shared common interest, it emerges as an amphiktyonic cult centre configuring *poleis* in the area towards each other. The Panionion is not itself a source of power but regulates power relations amongst the member cities or the individuals who ruled them. The cult community formed an accurate representation of local social relations, allowing cities to keep a close check on one another. This would also clarify why cities were so keen to become part of the Panionion on the one hand, and were pushed into it by their potential rivals on the other, as reported by Pausanias for the cases of Chios, Phokaia, and Aiolian Smyrna. Membership meant being part of a comfortable arrangement where the god ensured that things remained as they were first set up; Poseidon at Mykale was the highly desired guarantor of peaceful relations in the neighbourhood.

But this also means that the way to keep members actively engaged is to nourish constantly the interest in the theoric community's self-preservation. Due to its concern with the maintenance of existing social relations, the Panionion is—as are other such associations—essentially a conservative institution, opposed to social change, and it is its apparent

---

[33] 'Exchange': *I. Priene* 37, esp. 57 ff.; cf. Hommel et al. (1957), 93–4; Tausend (1992), 71; the corrupt text at this point also quotes the contested local historian Maiandrios of Miletos. Samos and Priene continuously fought over their slots: see Tausend ibid. 74 ff. on this conflict (6th cent.?: Plut. *Mor.* 296a; Arist. fr. 576 Rose on the 'battle of the oak tree' and the arbitration by Bias of Priene's who tradition interestingly makes a Panionian visionist (Hdt. 1.170; DL 1.85). Cf. Piccirilli (1973), no. 4, 16–22 on this episode); Welles no. 7 (*c*.283 BCE); *I.Priene* 37 (*c*.196 BCE) present the resulting conflicts, for the arbitration of which the cities resort to the original land distribution after the Melian War (on which see most recently Magnetto (1997), nos. 20, 44, 75); continued into Roman times: *SC de Prienensibus* (136/5 BCE *I. Priene* 41; *Syll.* 688); decree regarding the Samian/Prienian border (*I. Priene* 42, shortly afterwards); see also *I. Priene* 37, 132, 151, 528. Cf. the war between Samos and Miletos over Priene in the 440s (Th. 1.115; DS 15.48.1? with Hornblower *ad loc*; Meiggs (1972), 428); oddly enough these two had originally been particularly good allies against the Karians: Val. Max. 1.5. On changing ownership of Anaia see Fantasia (1986); on the Samian possessions also Welles (1934), no. 7, 46–51; for Marathesion (*I. Priene* 37.58), cf. Str. 14.1.20.

invulnerability to change that is its greatest selling point. How this community sought to keep itself together in the attempt to foster continuity is paradoxically best understood through the testimonies to its fragmentation. The Panionion's members were famously all but loyal. The archaic institution, according to Herodotus, had constant problems of rallying the cities, who often preferred to be entertained by the Persian king rather than themselves to entertain the god.[34] The inscription with which we began, really concerned with the same problem, adds a little more information about the association's ethics. Despite obvious differences from the fourth century (for a start the Panionion had temporarily relocated to Ephesos at this point),[35] the sacred law reveals how focused the cult group was on maintaining a careful balance between attraction and obligation: 'if any city does not bring victims, [the defaulting city is to be written up on a stele outside] the Panionion where the victims must be produced by the cities who owe' (ll. 5 ff.). It then continues with a clause on such religious occasions in future, running along the lines of 'if anyone fails to [produce the victims, the city must be prevented from making sacrifice] at the next Panionia'. Such a culture of policing is not unknown; a similar regulation for the amphiktyony of Athena's cult at Ilion, called into existence in the aftermath of Alexander's death, sets out the penalties for disloyal cities. And one cannot avoid feeling reminded of Athenian imperial practice when cities' success or failure to comply were recorded in the Athenian tribute lists.[36]

The fact that cult places chose to set down such rules indicates that there were constant infringements, and that cities ruthlessly exploited the flexibility of the cultic networks which might have benefited them on another occasion. It is for this reason that the shared ritual—ἐν χορῶι—assumes such importance, because ritual alone, in constantly reaffirming the arrangements that the ritual sanctions in the first place, can afford the continuity that is the cult's greatest attraction. Cult groups' seemingly excessive concern about the sacred props for the

---

[34] Hdt. 1.141; 6.7 ff.

[35] On which see Hornblower (1982); Prandi (1989).

[36] *I. Ilion* nos. 5, 6, 10; the entire dossier are nos. 1–18. For a brief analysis of the cult see pp. xi–xv. Interestingly *kanephoroi* from the various participating cities performed in this cult: nos. 81–2; for the Lokrian (choral?), 'tribute' to Athena Ilias see *IG* ix i² 3. 706, with most recently Redfield (2003), esp. 85–150.

theoric ritual demonstrates how fundamental the constant invocation of *communitas*, the regular confirmation or recreation of the worshipping group through ritual, was to the community's working. The sacred tribute signified participation in the cult, and hence the validation of the arrangements for which it stood. The interest in the seamless continuity of these arrangements determines that in the continuity of the cult: because it was supposed to maintain the status quo of power relations, the disruption of the theoric landscape was a much-dreaded occurrence.

But by the same token, that Herodotus or the inscriptions go to the trouble of recording which city did or did not attend the meetings suggests in itself that accomplished or failed attendance was part of the phenomenon. The regularity and continuity, as well as membership, of the gathering were an ongoing problem, yet inbuilt into the structure: if exclusion from the next festival represents a valid penalty, the implication is that not being part of the worshipping community is utterly undesirable while it obviously constantly happened. The fact that cities' misbehaviour is made public points to the strengths and weaknesses of an arrangement that has enough of a shame-culture—and hence social cohesion—to hope this to be an effective measure; but is weak enough for this to be necessary in the first place. The maintenance of a careful balance between compliance and defiance may well have been part of the strategy to keep members on board, and to ensure the cult's continuity.

The Panionion, with its turbulent history and membership, thus provides a colourful instance of the importance of *polis-theōria*: it demonstrates that theoric cults are a form of social organization of its own. *Theōria* is a manner of political interaction, but not in the straightforward sense of, for example, a 'political alliance': it performs those functions that are difficult to fulfil by any institution of more directly sourced power in a multi-ethnic society characterized by constant and rapid social change. *Theōria* seems to react to that feature of ancient Greek culture continuously problematic as well as culturally prolific—this is a world of thriving contestation between *poleis* of roughly similar status and resources. It is for this reason, as our Olympic *khoros* had it in the first place, that archaic and classical Greeks were quite so concerned about *theōria*'s continuity—as a way to prevent *stasis*, and to grant 'harmony and peace' among perennial competitors.

2. DANCING FOR PEACE

The theme of peaceful relations generated through *theōria* and choral performance is indeed worth pursuing, not least because 'peace' occurs elsewhere as the theme of cult communities consisting of similarly powerful individuals. Bacchylides, for example, composed a paean for performance at the cult of Apollo Pythaieus at Asine in the Argolid, merging the cult's aetiological myth into a long description of a peace associated with ritual activity, as if this was what the cult was supposed to achieve. Similarly to the Panionion, the cult of Apollo Pythaieus, as far as we can tell, integrated considerable ethnic diversity among the cities of the Argolid in a shared cult in relation to territorial conflict, and irrespective of any political allegiances—and it is a peculiar coincidence that we seem to hear about the cult whenever the local balance was at risk.[37] But 'peace' was most visibly the common aim for the religious community which composed the spectacular Hymn to the Greatest Kouros (the so-called Hymn to Zeus) found inscribed in stone in the sanctuary of Zeus Diktaios at Palaikastro in Eastern Crete.[38] The hymn is generally believed to be a second-century CE copy of a fourth- or third-century BCE original. Why this sanctuary was established around the eighth century BCE we cannot know, given the oblivion adumbrating the lives of Crete's archaic cities, but instead may infer from the island's ferociously argumentative Hellenistic *poleis*. From epigraphic texts we know that there was a Zeus Diktaios at Itanos, perhaps at Dragmos, at Praisos and at Hierapytna.[39] Precisely these places are fiercely involved in continuing border conflicts over the territory reaching up to the

[37] Bach. fr. 4.56ff (mid-5th cent.); Th. 5.53 (418 BCE). I discuss the details of this argument in Kowalzig (forthcoming). See Barrett (1954), and Billot (1992).

[38] *IC* 2.2.2 (cf. *SEG* 28. 751). For this hymn see Murray (1908–9); Harrison (1908–9); Wilamowitz (1921), 499–502; West (1965); Bremer and Furley (2001), 65–76, and particularly the excellent analysis by Perlman (1995), who, at 163–5 also summarizes succinctly what is known about the archaeology of the sanctuary itself. For the religious context see now MacGillivray et al. (2000). Ancient references to the sanctuary of Zeus Diktaios: Str. 10.4.6 and 12 (located near Praisos).

[39] Str. 10.4.6; Itanos: *IC* 3 p. 89 no. 8; Praisos: p. 142 no. 7 A 15f (in a relatively safe supplement); Hierapytna: pp. 49–50 no. 5.11 f.; Dragmos *IC* 3.4.9. The sanctuaries at Palaikastro and Praisos yield very similar votive material, suggesting the same or similar clientele: Bosanquet (1908–9); (1939–40); Guarducci *IC* 3, p. 135.

sanctuary itself. Parts of their history survives, again epigraphically, in
the same way as the land division of the Mykale promontory, in a decree
trying to sort out the problem through external arbitration.[40]

It is from the choral hymn that we can infer the cult's mediating
role as preserving territorial and social integrity of the wider worshipping community.[41] The hymn, consisting of a refrain and six
strophes, presents the god's invocation to join the annual festival
(Refrain: Δίκταν ἐπ' ἐνιαυτὸν ἕρπε 'come to our yearly festival at
Dikte') and rejoice in the song (μολπή) by a *khoros* who, in the first
strophe, describes itself as standing around an altar singing to the
music of pipes. The myth of the Kretan birth of Zeus that follows
in stanzas 2 and 3 is fragmented, and numerous speculations have
been made, such as that of Jane Ellen Harrison suggesting that here
the *khoros* singers took on the role of the Kouretes who accompanied the
event of the birth.[42] What exactly the relationship between myth
and ritual is in this hymn cannot be known without supplying what
was not there. What can be said, however, is that the 'ritual moment'
is orchestrated as an epiphany of the 'Greatest Kouros' or Zeus directly
following the end of the mythical tale. The song means to project into
the present the world created by the mythical story: 'and mortal Justice
subdued [the community's men] . . . happiness-loving Peace' (st. 4,
καὶ βροτὸς Δίκα κατῆχε[. . .]ῆπε ζώι' ἀ φίλολοβος Εἰρήνα);   what
this entails in the present of the choristers follows as a list: the god is
summoned (st. 5 θόρε εἰς . . .) to fertilize herds, flocks, fields, private
homes. And then, in the last strophe, the Kouros is asked to care for
more specifically civic entities: 'our cities', 'ships', 'new citizens', and
'order' (θέμιν).[43]

Who really sang this hymn on a regular basis—a group of *poleis*,
whichever was the leading *polis* at the time, or representatives of *poleis*—
cannot be identified for certain, but it is interesting to note that the
hymn may presuppose a wider cult community who thought or wished

---

[40] *IC* III pp. 91 ff. no. 9 (112 BCE). A short concise synthesis of the territorial
wranglings through time is provided by Perlman (1995), 165.

[41] I use Guarducci's text as in *IC* 3.2.2; for strophe 5 see *ead.* (1974).

[42] See e.g. Harrison (1912), 1 ff.

[43] St. 6 [θόρε κὲς] πόληας ἀμῶν, θόρε κὲς ποντοπόρος νᾶας. θόρε κὲς ν[έος πο]λείτας
θόρεκὲς θέμιν κλ[ειτάν]. 'Leap into ('fertilize'), our cities, our ships, and our new citizens, and
renowned *themis.*'

itself integrated enough to pray for the social and military cohesion of individual cities as well as justice and peace for the ensemble of *poleis*. Was Zeus' *temenos* not so much a *polis*' border shrine waiting to defend some city's prerequisites, but rather one concerned with recognition, maintenance, and regular renewal of inter-state social and perhaps territorial definitions? The joint working of myth and ritual in the song give the illusion of shared justice, peace, and order, and the community chose to associate these with a deity they worshipped collectively in theoric *khoreia*.

Crete, as some have suggested, may well have been dotted with similar such mediating sanctuaries, as if their frequent occurrence reflected the number and degree of local conflicts;[44] cult regulations reflect, if not the failure of the system, certainly the continuing desire to recreate and rephrase old theoric relationships. What is more interesting, the persistence of the peace-dancers is visible on a different level, and this brings us into the more malleable spheres of 'theoric chorality' and the employment of the association of *theōria* and the *khoros* in a variety of social contexts. Unlike the cult communities considered so far who seek to keep distinct political and theoric community, Hellenistic Cretan *poleis*—as much as other contemporary Hellenistic communities—also exploited the slippery interface between the two when seeking to empower their volatile political alliances through shared cult activity. The stipulations of such treaties include mutual participation of the partner cities in each other's festivals, involving significant costs for sacrificial victims and, more excitingly, the instalment of a *khoros* or *thiasos*.[45] Despite the obvious differences in set-up, a sacrificial and choral 'tribute' seems to feature here as if inter-state relationships were modelled on theoric practice. That these arrangements are generally closely connected to what cities do with their 'graduating ephebes' supports this interpretation.[46] In fact, the often-observed coincidence between *theōroi* and ephebes confirms the view of theoric cults control-

[44] Chaniotis (1988), 32 ff. suggests, among other things, that many formerly independent—amphiktyonic—extra-urban shrines may have been usurped by individual cities in the course of Hellenistic *Landhunger*; the vast number of territorial arguments over sanctuaries' land might then well be a result of these appropriations.

[45] Chaniotis (1996a), nos. 5, 68–78 (*khoroi*); 27, 38f; 60 B 13; 61 A 44 (*thiasoi*).

[46] Both Chaniotis (1996a) and Perlman (1995) place the documents in the context of *ephēbeia*. For a relationship between *theōria* and ephebic initiation see Rutherford (2005).

ling power relations between their stubborn participants: pooling them
into a shared religious obligation labours the point that a working
theoric community rests on those members of the citizen body who
would be most involved in maintaining or disrupting what the theoric
cult seeks to integrate. It is not least for this reason that the ephebes'
appearance in a *khoros* is essential for the functioning of the different
types of inter-state obligations that have only been sketched here for
Hellenistic Crete.

3. *THEŌRIA* AND CHORALITY IN THE
MYSTERIES AT SAMOTHRACE

How intimately connected theoric, social, and 'choral' order were in the
minds of many Greeks emerges from the cultural productivity of this
relationship. The first clause of the Thucydidean Peace of Nikias of 421
BCE orders that 'with regard to the common shrines, whoever wishes to
sacrifice and travel there and receive oracles and to "see the gods"
(θεωρεῖν) should be safe to do so', implying that working *theōria* was
a premiss for, as much as attribute of, peaceful relations amongst the
Greeks.[47] Aristophanes' *Peace,* of just a little earlier in the year than the
Peace itself, brings home the intrinsic relation between this particular
settlement and *theōria*, when Θεωρία and 'Οπώρα ('harvest', or 'full-
fruit') appear as the two requisites of 'peace'.[48] The reception scene for
theōria (871 ff.) includes some striking overlaps with the rhetoric and
the rites of the Delia: the penteteric theoric festival pompously renewed
by the Athenians, on which Nikias himself might well have had an eye
in view of what would become his legendary *theōria* to Delos described
by Plutarch.[49] Not only does the suggestive joint performance of *theōria*

---

[47] Th. 5.18.
[48] The first of these two attractive women may well be more than the commentators'
generic 'festival' or 'holiday': e.g. Olson *ad* 523; Sommerstein *ad* 523 suitably calls
theōria 'showtime'.
[49] Cf. 876: *theōria's* attribute is πρωκτοπεντετηρίδα 'with a five-year-festival bottom'; 894 ff. an athletic competition and a horse race, items the Athenians had just
introduced at the Delia (Th. 3.104); an 'Ionian lamb' is sacrificed at 929 ff. The passage
is also jaded with references to other festivals, e.g. 872 (Brauronia). Nikias' *theōria*: Plut.
Nic. 5.3–8, for the date see Hornblower [comm.] 518 (421 or 417 BCE?); Parker (1996),
80–1.

and harvest in the logic of the play effect 'peace' but it also, by allowing the Athenians to be 'more affable' with their allies, highlights *theōria*'s function in inter-state relations (934 ff). It is unlikely to be a coincidence that Kratinos' *Deliades* of 422 BCE is another comic *khoros* of possible theoric content; the projection of the *Δηλιάδες*, Delian Apollo's *khoros* in myth and theoric ritual, onto the Athenian stage surely offered comment of some sort on Athens' theoric policies.[50] The heftiest subtext of all, however, comes from Eupolis' *Poleis*, also of 422 BCE: the comic *khoros* of allied cities attacks their compulsory sacred tribute to the City Dionysia as if, in handling the empire just as a theoric community, Athens had successfully led *theōria* ad absurdum when producing war through it instead of peace! Though this cannot be investigated in further detail here, the regularity with which peace, *theōria,* and the comic *khoros* appear in joint performance in this period should at least alert one to their shared associations. More plays survive to suggest that the theoric *khoros* had developed its own rhetorical potential, functioning as a kind of cultural metaphor through which to express inter-state relations.[51]

How powerful a means the association of *theōria* with chorality was for welding communities into a relationship becomes clear when we consider its role at another vaguely choral complex: that of the mysteries of the Megaloi Theoi at Samothrace in the Northern Aegean.[52] The mysteries present a whole set of different problems most of which cannot be dealt with here. Who these gods were, for example: Herodotus had already identified the Megaloi Theoi and the much more frequently appearing Kabeiroi,[53] a name not attested in Samothrace itself. For the purposes here it is enough to acknowledge that links to Samothrace were created between communities because of this identification.[54] To what degree initiates and *theōroi* were identical is

---

[50] For the Deliades see esp. *h.Ap.* 156 ff; Sim. 519 fr. 55; Eur. *HF* 687 ff.

[51] e.g. Epicharmus' *Thearoi*; Sophron's *Thamenai;* Aeschylus' *Isthmiastai*; Aristophanes' *Amphiaraos*; perhaps even *Lemnian Women,* and *Islands;* Euphron's *Theōroi.*

[52] The site is published in *Samothrace*; and a synthesis is provided in Lehmann and Lehmann (1959–98). Some relevant items of bibliography are Hemberg (1950); Cole (1984); (1989); Burkert (1993); and now Clinton (2003).

[53] Hdt. 2.51; cf. Stesimbrotos of Thasos *FGrH* 107 F 20; Mnaseas *apud Σ* AR 1.917. The ancient debate: Str. 10.3.19–21; cf. Hdt. 3.37? cf. Call. fr. 199. Burkert (1993), 181; Graf (1999*a*), 126–7; Cole (1984), 1–2.

[54] Burkert (1993) and Cole (1984) provide good discussions of the relevant texts.

another relevant question. There are long lists inscribed on stone for both these groups, who only occasionally coincide. The wider catchment area of both nevertheless seems specific enough to suppose that Samothrace's appeal spread mostly in the northern Aegean, Macedonia and Thrace and along the coast of western Asia Minor.[55] Evidence for the archaic and classical period is so scarce that for the moment we have to be content with the Hellenistic picture—which is, as I hope to show, highly interesting in terms of how chorality embraces the workings of theoric cults in a historical context. I will suggest that at this time, an association between *mystai* and *theōroi* is afforded by the shared ritual of choral dance; it is this association that turns Samothrace into a cult centre of competing political claims not unlike the ones already discussed. That the connection can be made at all may well be due to the association of *theōria* with chorality.

What went on at mystic initiations on Samothrace is a question much debated and frustratingly unsolved.[56] However, the Hall of the Choral Dancers, where, according to the most recent view, we have to assume that the initiation took place,[57] makes it abundantly clear that chorality was in some way central to this cult: a magnificent *khoros* of 800 female dancers projected onto the walls of this square fourth-century building surrounded the initiand in what has become the symbol of the Samothracian Gods. Ancient texts make suggestions about such choral foils in mystery cults. Dio Chrysostomus says apropos of the so-called enthronement ceremony that 'they have the initiands sit down, and they dance around them'. The passage is not itself linked to a locality (the author is concerned with the nature of the ritual experience, rather than with the initiating deity), but the universal association of the Megaloi Theoi with Korybants, in the context of whose rites an enthronement ceremony is attested, suggests the importance of the elements they share: secrecy and ecstatic dancing.[58] Whether and at what point a *thronōsis* might have occurred remains uncertain, but other structures suggest

[55] Cole (1984), 38 ff. for the lists of *mystai* and *theōroi*.

[56] See e.g. Hemberg (1950); Cole (1984), 26–37; Burkert (1993); Clinton (2003).

[57] With Clinton (2003), 61, who offers a general reassessment of what function the sanctuary's various buildings had in the process of mystic initiation.

[58] Dio Chr. *Or.* 12.33 f. (see Theiler (1982), F 368 for an attribution to Poseidonios); for the *thronōsis* rite of the Korybants cf. Pl. *Euthyd.* 277d; for the identification of the rites of Korybants and Megaloi Theoi see DS 3.55.9; Str. 10.3.19–21.

khoreutic presence. The so-called 'theatral area' at the sanctuary entrance, a fifth-century circular space, surrounded by five rows of steps
for onlookers to stand on, has been interpreted as a spot for dancing,[59]
not to mention the large later theatre carved into the rock, adjacent,
incidentally, to the Hall of the Choral Dancers. Last but not least, a
recently retrieved inscription suggests that, as in many other mystery
cults, there might have been a standing *khoros* of 'holy women'.[60]

It can indeed be argued that choral and mystic experience are closely
interlinked—but we must turn to myth for that association. It has
generally been suggested that the mystic rites 're-enact' or 'dramatize'
the wedding of Kadmos and Harmonia. Harmonia, one of the three
children of the local heroine Elektra, was abducted by Kadmos when he
passed the island on his migration from east to west; this event involved
a mythical search for the bride and culminated in a lavish wedding,
attended by all the gods. The choral element in the Samothracian
mysteries has been taken to represent their wedding song.[61] If this
hypothesis is correct, it is attractive to relate it to the Hall of Choral
Dancers: the association would present an excellent example of how
ritual works with diverse, often redundant, forms of visuality to create
ritual illusion. The similarities with Eleusinian Demeter's search for her
daughter and the subsequent wedding with Hades, as well as the fact
that the episode links Samothrace with Kadmeian Boiotia and through
the Boiotian Kabeiroi with other cults of this Aeolian legacy (Lemnos,
Imbros, and Pergamon all had prominent Kabeiria),[62] lends some
credibility to the couple's role in Samothracian mystic initiation.

Even though Kadmos and Harmonia themselves do not appear in the
oldest surviving traditions, the complex of myths of which they come to
form a part is the earliest attested in relation to Samothrace. It dates

---

[59] Clinton (2003), 62–4 suggests that a *thronōsis* ceremony might have taken place
here, with Nock (1941) as part of *myēsis*, the first stage in mystic initiation at Samothrace.
[60] Clinton and Karadima-Matsa (2002). For the theatral area see Lehmann (1998),
96–9; McCredie (1968), 216–34; (1979), 6–8. For the Hall of Choral Dancers see
Lehmann and Spittle (1982), 50–147; 273–6; 5–12 and 172–262 on the frieze.
[61] For the wedding see Ephor. *FGrH* 70 F 120; DS 5.48.4–50.1; cf. 4.2.1; Apollod.
3.4.2. Their role in the mystic rites was first suggested by Rubensohn (1892), 133 and
Kern (1919), 1428–9; cf. now Clinton (2003), 67 ff. Lehmann and Spittle (1982),
1.220–33; Lehmann (1998), 35 even thought to see a wedding dance in the frieze,
though cf. Rubensohn (1892), and Kern (1919).
[62] Cf. Hemberg (1950). It is worth noting that the earliest archaeological finds also
seem to relate to these places (ibid. 117).

back to the Homeric poems, and, in particular, the fragments surviving
from the *Catalogue of Women*:

```
ἐπ[                                                    1
κ[
να[
καὶ μα[
Ἠλέκτρ[η                                               5
γείναθ᾽ [ὑποδμηθεῖσα κελαινεφέϊ Κρονίωνι
Δάρδαν[ον
Ἠετίων[ά τε
ὅς ποτε Δ[ήμητρος πολυφόρβης ἐς λέχος ἦλθε.          10
καὶ τὸν μ[ὲν κατέπεφνε πατὴρ ἀνδρῶν τε θεῶν τε
Ἠετίωνα[ ἄνακτα βαλὼν ἀργῆτι κεραυνῶι,
οὕνεκα δ[ὴ Δήμητρι μίγη φιλότητι καὶ εὐνῆι.
αὐτὰρ Δα[ρδανος
ἐκ τοῦ Ἐρ[ιχθόνιος
Ἰλός [τ                                               15
νηϊ[
```

(Hes. fr. 177 MW; *P. Oxy.* 1359 fr. 2, ed. Grenfell–Hunt)

Electra [. . . submitted to the dark-clouded son of Kronos and bore] Dardanos
[and] Eetion [. . .] who once [came to the bed of Demeter, rich in food,] and
the latter, [lord] Eetion [was slain by the father of men and gods, shooting him
with a bright thunderbolt]because[he had intercourse with Demeter] But
Dardanos [ ] from whom Erikth[onios . . . and [Ilos].

Here we learn what later texts embellish with more detail: that the local
heroine Elektra had two children, Eetion/Iasion and Dardanos. Of these
Eetion got into trouble with Demeter, died and was thence related to
the mysteries; his brother Dardanos wandered to mainland Asia and
founded a string of cities there, including the one named after him.
When Harmonia joined the duo is unclear, though the association is
firm by the fifth century. This string of myths performs a prominent
function in the long history of the sanctuary, lending it significance and
continuity in the enquiry of why Samothracian *theōria* mattered.[63]

---

[63] For the myth cf. *Il.* 22.216 ff.; Kadmos and Harmonia first appear in Hellanikos
FGrH 4 F 23; [Skymn.] 679–93. The people in the Dardanelles may have claimed
descent from the Trojans: *Il.* 20.300–8, but cf. Horsfall (1987). For Eetion/Iasion's
relation to Demeter cf. *Od.* 5.125 f.; Hes. *Th.* 969 ff.; identification of Eetion/Iasion

A few remarkable pieces of evidence from the Hellenistic period demonstrate something of the place's mythical identity in these terms. Priene's second-century BCE epic poet Herodes was honoured by the city of Samothrace for having composed epics on the story of Kadmos and Harmonia, and of Dardanos. More interesting for Samothracian choral matters is an early second-century decree honouring the tragic poet Dymas from Iasos in Karia. He commemorated 'the greatest deeds of Dardanos' when he 'composed a history [lit. treatise] in the form of a drama' (πραγματείαν σ[υνέ]ταξεν ἐν δράματι τὰς μεγίστας τῶν Δαρ δάνου πράξεων μνημ[νεύων] ll. 18–20). The same Dymas, known as a *khorēgos* in his home city, also received citizenship at Samothrace. Iasians appear in the lists of *theōroi*, and indeed one of their delegates was honoured in a similar way to Dymas. That this decree, just as that for Herodes, was issued in the context of *theōria* to Samothrace cannot be proven but is extremely likely: it was to be entrusted to the first *theōroi* arriving from Iasos to take it back for erection in the poet's home city. Eetion's other name Iasion may itself be suggestive for an association of the city to the mystic island.[64]

The two poets bring together *theōria* and mystic cult through their works. Of particular interest here is the coincidence, and possibly even identity, of *theōroi* who came to see the Great Gods, and the 'choral poet': it means that performance of *khoroi* was part of the experience shared by attending *theōroi*, suggesting, creating, and maintaining relationships between them, and between individual cities and the sanctuary. The choral performances will have served the integration of the worshipping community. When looking further ahead in the history of Samothrace, it

in Hellanikos ibid. Another—possibly older—*hieros logos* may have been contained in the traditions related to two ithyphallic statues operative in the initiation: cf. e.g. Hdt. 2.51; Call. fr. 199 Pf.; Cic. *ND*. 3.56; Varro *LL* 5.58; Hippolytos, *Refutatio* 5.8.9, all discussed by Burkert (1993), 181–3; for the so-called 'Anaktoron' see Lehmann (1998), 56–61; Cole (1984), 12 f. Mnaseas' list of the Kabeiroi's names could also be related to this myth–ritual complex: *Σ* AR 1.917 (= Lewis (1959), no. 150). For the tradition that the Samothracian gods rescued worshippers from perils at sea see Ar. *Pax* 277; DL 6.59= Diagoras of Melos 36/7 Winiarczyk; Cic. *ND*. 3.89.

[64] *I. Priene* 68–9 (Herodes); *I. Iasos* 153 = *TGrF* 130 (Dymas' play); *I.Iasos* 160 (his *khorēgia*). For Iasian *theōroi* see *IG* 12.8.170e, 70–1 (2nd-cent. proxeny decree for two Iasian *theōroi*); *I. Iasos* 72 (3rd cent.; cf. now Habicht (1994)). On the two poets see briefly Cole (1984), 52–3. The issue of poets composing and travelling in a quasi-diplomatic role has been raised by Rutherford in an as yet unpublished paper, in which context the relationship between Iasion and Iasos is discussed.

is in fact the choral aspect of this mythical complex that seems to have been instrumental in tying a number of places to Samothrace in to a network of theoric relations. By the historical climate of the Hellenistic period, Samothrace had become the dancing floor for a worshipping community constantly redefining itself through a shared relation to Samothrace expressed in interacting myth and ritual and a form of chorality.

The key lies in understanding the significance of the associated myths in their local context, in particular the role of Dardanos, the missionary of the Samothracian mysteries. We remember from the *Catalogue of Women* that he had gone to Asia Minor where he founded Dardanos, whilst Troy—or Ilion—was established by his son Ilos.[65] Walter Burkert once put in poignant words what this tradition is directed at: 'this is a myth about Troy, and the mysteries.' In other words, this is a myth about non-Greeks who originate from Samothrace and who, significantly, seem irredeemably associated with the mystic rites, and their claims to the area surrounding them.[66]

It is of course their non-Greekness that later on becomes the selling point for the Samothracian gods—through these divinities the Romans construct their Trojan identity.[67] Less in the spotlight is the fact that the story of the contest over Samothrace's non-Greek past starts much earlier. Macedonians from Philip II onwards invested heavily in the mystic island and turned themselves into its rich supporters in what is often thought to be a desperate attempt to appropriate at least one prominent Greek sanctuary for themselves and their panhellenic aspirations alone.[68] However, there may be reason to think that Samothrace does not, or not only, help to prove that Macedonians 'truly' cared for

---

[65] For Dardanos in the Troad see e.g. Str. 13.1.25; Str. 7 frr. 49, 50.

[66] Burkert (1993), 179; for Ilos' grave at Ilion see already *Il.* 11.166.

[67] Burkert (1993), 187–8: the earliest texts mentioning the Roman Penates being Samothracians are Cassius Hemina fr. 6 (*HRR* 1.99 f.); Pomponius Atticus fr. 1 (*HRR* 2.6); Varro *ap.* Macrob. 3.4.7; DH 1.68.1–4; see Cole (1984), 100–3; (1989), 1580–96. For the Trojan legend appropriated by Rome see particularly Gruen (1992), 6–51 (though without a discussion of Samothrace).

[68] See Burkert (1993), 185: 'the motives of Philip are easy to guess. Samothrace was the only sanctuary of pan-Hellenic renown within his reach . . . While he was establishing his hold on Greece via Delphi and . . . Olympia, he did everything to raise "his" sanctuary in northern Greece to a comparable level.' See Cole (1984), 16 ff. for Macedonian building and other activity on Samothrace.

the Greeks. Rather, the island's mythical connotations served their ambiguous status between Greek and non-Greek and offered crucial capital in their attempt to link East and West.

It is chorality that appears to create these links. Philip II allegedly wooed his wife Olympias when they both met for initiation—which, we have to assume, took place in the predecessor of the Hall of Choral Dancers, the location where Kadmos and Harmonia were continually remarried and which Philip would later in his life adorn with images of dance. That Olympias, daughter of the Molossian king Neoptolemos and mother of Alexander, was famous for her love of ecstatic cults only fits the theory that somehow in this place the Macedonians welded the fragmented identities of their kingdom together through the shared experience of mystic dance.[69] If, in a late tradition, Alexander accused his father of having dallied about too long on Samothrace when he could have conquered Asia, this says something about the aspiring young king himself: the suggestion that Alexander himself did not care enough to attract the favour of the Samothracian gods, may well be a comment on his problematic 'politics of fusion'. Certainly, the enigmatic tradition makes more sense when related to the idea that Samothrace held significance for the meeting of East and West.[70]

From then onwards, Samothrace seems to have been part and parcel of how cities in the area related to each other; and interestingly, it is the mystic dance that features prominently in the way such connections are expressed, serving the cult community's constant redefinition. No doubt the island's potential for the royal houses of the north lay in its privileged link to Ilion, the city that carried all the legacy of Greek and non-Greek interaction; in fact Alexander himself marked the city and its Greek and Trojan gods in all sorts of ways with his appreciation,

---

[69] Philip and Olympias at Samothrace: Plut. *Alex.* 2.2; Himerius *Or.* 9.12 = Lewis (1959), no. 194; Olympias' inclination for ecstatic dancing: Athen. 13.560b–c. Both Philip II's (Hall of Choral Dancers) and Philip Arrhidaios' (a building at the theatral area: Lehmann (1998), 96–9) contributions to Samothrace's architecture are 'theatral', if not altogether choral. Other major buildings financed by the Macedonians are Arsinoe's rotunda (Fraser (1960), no. 10) and Ptolemy II's Propylaia (Fraser (1960), no. 11 and pp. 5–7). Arsinoe fled to Samothrace in 280 BCE: Iust. 24.3.9.

[70] Curt. Ruf. 8.1.26. In actual 'fact', the Samothracian Gods duly receive a spot amongst the Dodekatheion, the monumental precinct erected by Alexander in India to commemorate his army's easternmost advance (Arr. *An.* 5.29.1).

exploiting it for his own ambiguous identity.[71] It has been observed that Samothrace and Ilion featured among a number of places in Asia Minor selected to display royal decrees of the Seleucids from the early third century, as if no royal ideology could do without the two.[72] Ilion by that time had started to cultivate its links to Samothrace. As recent excavations have revealed, the so-called West Sanctuary, with excellent views across the sea to Samothrace, was restored in the course of the third century from the decay it had experienced following its first apex in the archaic period. One recently found votive inscription has been thought to identify the shrine as that of the 'Samothracian Gods', known for Ilion from two other dedications. Extensive building activity attests renewed interest in a cult place that now embraced a broader community of mystic gods: votive statuettes and reliefs showing Kybele, and possibly even Dardanos himself, suggest that 'Samothracian Gods' held a wider definition or was at least very inclusive.[73]

We need not look far to spot who was keen to link into this. The threads converge in a fascinating set of contemporary data, giving us an impression of the cult's potential in the landscape of social interaction in Hellenistic Greece. Just as Macedon used the shrine to weld piecemeal ethnicity into a whole, the place continued to forge communality in a deeply fragmented world, thus holding a key to power in the area. What emerges is a *koinē* of mystic dance, which brings together yet again theoric and mystic chorality in a common ritual, and, more significantly, which merges their two relevant associations: that *theōria* estab-

---

[71] Alexander honouring Ilion: Athena Ilias received a new temple: DS 18.4.5; Str. 13.1.26; cf. Plut. *Mor.* 343d; a tribe Alexandris: *CIG* 2.3615. Alexander honoured Greek heroes such as Ajax and Achilles (Arr. *An.* 1.11.7 ff.; Plut. *Al.* 15.4–5; Diod. 17.17.6–7; Iust. 11.5.12), but also Zeus Herkeios, expiating Priam's murder by Neoptolemos, whose blood Alexander carried through his mother (Arr. *An.* 1.11.8).

[72] Lawall (2003), 100, quoting Dittenberger (1903), 225.25–30; *I. Ilion* 45 (196 BCE); 63 (100 BCE) are published at both Samothrace and Ilion.

[73] This is the interesting conclusion drawn from a reassessment of the archaeology, including recent findings at the West Sanctuary: Lawall (2003). Increased building activity can be observed from the first quarter of the third century, and was particularly intense from the middle of the century onwards. The three references to the Samothracian Gods are *I. Ilion* nos. 44 (*c.*209–5 BCE), 63 (*c.*100 BCE); Cohen (1996) (*c.*100 BCE?). Note that Aristarkhe's dedication has been found at Sestos, but has been attributed to Ilion: see Robert and Robert (1964), 188–90, no. 272. Samothracian initiates from Ilion are represented in *IG* 12.8.206, 4–5; for Kabeiria in the Troad see Str. 10.3.21, on which most recently Graf (1999) (with further bibliography). For the presence of Kybele and Dardanos at the sanctuary see Lawall ibid. 95–9 (for their presence in the Troad cf. e.g. Lyc. 78–9; Str. 7, frr. 49; 50; DH 1.61.4; 68.4–69.1; DS 5.49.2 ff. and others).

lishes connections, while mystic cult is a particularly flexible social institution. As 'secrecy' is its most defining aspect, mystery cult lends itself to an exclusivity that is based on shared ritual activity alone, rather than common citizenship, putative ethnicity, or even gender.[74]

It is not a coincidence that the particular relevance of Samothrace crystallizes with the advent of the alien Romans, even if they were not necessarily the driving agent. More superficially, Philip V of Macedon's troublesome behaviour seems to prompt a role for Samothrace in cities' changing configurations. Already in 211 BCE the Roman commander Marcellus had commemorated his capture of Syracuse with a dedication to the Samothracian gods, as if to remind Philip V of Macedon, since 215 allied with Carthage, of Roman presence.[75] At around the same time, in *c.*209–205 BCE, Pergamene Aristarche, on behalf of Ptolemy IV and Arisinoe, made one of the three dedications to the Samothracian Gods at Ilion's sanctuary, a timely move when Pergamon, the Ptolemies and Ilion were all allied against Philip V of Macedon. Ilion and Pergamon were to become the *adscripti* in the Peace of Phoinike concluded between Rome and Philip V in 205 BCE. While Ilion at that time had already started to profit from Roman mediation in the East,[76] this is the same year that Kybele, a goddess the Pergamenes had started to prop up in the very recent past, travelled from Pergamon to Rome.[77]

Shared mystic experience of the 'Samothracian Gods' certainly identified this particular *communitas*, emerging as it was from a complex and ever-changing system of loyalties temporarily geared at warding off Philipp V. As if to confirm these notions, Diodorus curiously seems to feature its foundation myth when tracing the spread of the cult: Iasion, who 'was

[74] This is a point not much explored, though see Burkert (1993), 48 ff.

[75] Plut. *Marcellus* 30.6. See Cole (1989), 1570.

[76] The city was seemingly absolved from tribute, exacted by Seleukos II (?): Suet. *Claud.* 25.3, and granted tax immunity as well as two towns after Apamea (188 BCE): Liv. 38.39.10.

[77] Liv. 29.12.14 (Phoinike), prompting T. Quinctius Flamininus to boast descent from Aeneas in a dedication at Delphi: Plut. *Flam.* 12.6–7. Athena at Ilion thence became the starting point for future leading Romans in the area: Liv. 37.9.7 (C. Livius Salinator, 190 BCE); L. Scipio 37.37.103. Note Pergamon's lively interest in Kybele at the time, at Mamurt Kale (Philetairos' temple: Roller (1999), 210–12); at Kapikaya (Nohlen and Radt 1978); in Pergamon itself (Varro *LL.* 6.15; for its identifcation with a 3rd-cent. building see Radt (1999), 247–8). For Ilion's and Pergamon's mutual showings of sympathy see *I. Ilion* nos. 42; 121; ?43; Polyb. 5.78; Welles (1934), no. 62.

the first to initiate foreigners and thus made the initiations famous' (πρῶτοι ξένους μυῆσαι καὶ τὴν τελετὴν διὰ τοῦτο ἔνδοξον ποιῆσαι, DS 5.49) following the wedding between Kadmos and Harmonia, 'married Kybele and begat Korybas. And after Iasion had been removed into the circle of the gods, Dardanos and Kybele and Korybas conveyed to Asia the sacred rites of the Mother of the Gods and moved with them to Phrygia.' A number of ritual props are taken over from Samothrace, such as Korybas' aulos' journey to the mainland, in order to make the point about a wider religious association. Whatever the age of this tradition, it is attractive to think that the historical context just described had a role in preserving it.[78]

The intriguing conclusion must be that the language of community for this *communitas* is created through chorality and the joint associations between mystic and theoric dance. While the cluster of evidence for a short span of time is intriguing, it is possible, if not likely, that the *khoros* continued to integrate those happy to join the mystic rhythm of this new *koinē*. If Dymas' *Dardanos* was staged in the early second century BCE, perhaps just after his city of Iasos had been 'freed' from Antiokhos III in 190 BCE, in order to, as it were, join the mystic *khoros*, this just demonstrates how much potential there lies in the long-standing—particularly choral—associations of traditional Greek *theōria* in the complex mechanics of the Hellenistic world.[79]

The issue of long-term continuities in Greek *theōria* is indeed worth a few words in terms of a conclusion. While the practicalities of *theōria* can be tackled from multiple angles, I hope it has emerged that chorality provides access to a closer delineation of what *theōria* did for Greece. The reason for this lies no doubt in the role choral dance had for many Greeks: the *khoros* was a basic form of socialization, just as *theōria*; this

---

[78] In this context it is worth pointing out that an enigmatic structure on Samothrace has been interpreted as a heroon for Eetion and part of the desire to (re-)invent the island's mythical history in Hellenistic times: McCredie (1974).

[79] The city of Iasos is certainly embroiled in the triangle between Philip V, Antiokhos III, and Rome: see Ma (2000), 77; 85; 329–35; 247; *c.*197 BCE taken over by Antiokhos from Philip (for the date see ibid. 329–35, no. 26); contemporarily specifically named among the Greeks of Asia and Europe to be 'freed' from Philip according to the *SC* of 196 BCE (Polyb. 18.44, not necessarily directed against Antiokhos: ibid. 95); 191–190 BCE 'freed' from Antiokhos and passed over to Rome: Liv. 37.17.3–7 from which it also emerges that Iasian attitudes to Antiokhos are, despite Iasos' nominally free status, ambiguous.

may be why the *khoros* features in the actual practice and characterizes the ways in which *theōria* is imagined and recorded; and it may also be for this reason that 'theoric chorality' seems to function as a kind of metaphor for imagining all sorts of social relations. If the Greeks chose to highlight the *khoros* in theoric imagination, they also put into relief what I hope to have shown is the cornerstone in theoric practice and analysis: ritual and the community it creates lie at the basis of a healthy operation of Greek *theōria*.

I hope to have demonstrated that theoric cults feature a special form of social organization that performs a function highly relevant in the fragmented political and social landscape of the *polis*-world at large. Theoric cults are an alternative form of social negotiation and present a form of interaction between communities based on a—real or invented—consensus expressed in the worship of a common god. It is through the continuous ritual invocation of *communitas* that this consensus is re-established and reconfirmed, and that theoric ritual constantly redefines and reconfigures participants towards each other. In this way, it is a form of mutual social control, just as encapsulated in Phlegon's 'peace and harmony', designed to pacify the warring Peloponnesians. It is for this reason that the disruption of a theoric relationship or the defection of a member is deeply worrying, as it sets off the finely crafted power balance. Continuity and regularity are the most important prerequisites of *theōria*'s promise 'peace'.

Distinct from each other in principle, theoric and more strictly speaking 'political' groups are constantly intertwined in the real world, and the trick seems to lie precisely in playing off distinctness or overlap at specific moments. Theoric *khoroi* orchestrating political alliances are presumably the best example of the weaknesses of either arrangement, but also show that in principle the one may not necessarily be stronger than the other. How profoundly concerned Greek *theōria* is with the establishment and maintenance of a community is, finally, shown by the degree to which the world of theoric chorality comes to serve the integration of genuinely perceived diversity at Hellenistic Samothrace.

When looking at the many ways in which *theōria* seems to shape inter-state relations, it cannot be a coincidence that our initial two texts on Olympia's origin and function associate a form of 'harmony' with what tradition has chosen to place at the very creation of Greece's distinctive religious system. *Theōria* as a form of social interaction lies at the heart of Greek religion, basic to its mobility, and to social structure.

2

Hiketai and *Theōroi* at Epidauros

Fred Naiden

Like much of the vocabulary used in the field of Greek religion, the term 'pilgrim' is not of Greek origin.[1] The Greeks used two terms, *theōros* and the less common *hiketēs*, in particular, a *hiketēs* to a healing shrine such as Epidauros. This contribution to the study of pilgrims thus begins with a question, one not hitherto asked: why call both of these persons pilgrims? What, to be precise, do the two have in common?[2]

In the literal sense, the *theōros* watches, implying a spectacle, whereas the *hiketēs* arrives, implying some connection with those who receive him, such as *xenia*.[3] By extension, the *theōros* participates in the spectacle he sees, and becomes a festival-goer; by a further extension, he represents those who cannot attend, and becomes a delegate. In classical Greece, numerous *theōroi* were delegates sent by one *polis* or community to observe, and participate in, a festival in another. To watch, to go, to

---

[1] The root, *peregrinus*, means 'pilgrim' only in post-classical Latin. The classical meanings were not religious, and some of them were despective: *OLD* s.v. *peregrinus*, 2.

[2] Not asked, for example, by Rutherford (1995), 276, on *theōroi*, and Dillon (1997) on *hiketai*, or by any of the other writers on *hiketai* at Epidauros cited later in this essay. *Theōria* in brief: Rutherford loc. cit. *Hiketeia* in brief: Gould (1973), the most influential, gives the lead to Gödde (1998) and Chaniotis (1996*b*), both citing him; the *RE* article by Jessen is very brief. There is no article on *hiketeia* in *OCD*[3].

[3] For comments on the etymology of *theōria*, see Rutherford (2000*a*), 135–7; for the etymology of *hiketeia*, see Benveniste (1969), 2.254: '*hiketēs* doit bien être reconnu comme nom d'agent de la racine dont *hiko* est le présent thématique...le sens de "suppliant" s'explique par un usage de guerre connu dans l'épopée: celui qui, pressé par l'ennemi, veut être épargné, doit, pour avoir la vie sauve, toucher les genoux de son adversaire avant que l'autre au coeur même de la bataille l'ait blessé.' Similarly, Chantraine and Frisk s.v. *hiko*. *Hiketeia* into *xenia*: Herman 3.3 following Gould 90–4.

participate, and to represent form a characteristic complex recently identified by Ian Rutherford.

For *hiketēs*, the extension of meaning and the characteristic complex are quite different. The extension is that he who arrives makes a request of those to whom he has come, and that when they approve he and they initiate a relation such as *xenia*. The complex is one in which the *hiketēs* is not an observer, like the *theōros*, but a protagonist, a person acting on his own behalf. In addition, he is seldom a communal delegate.[4]

These distinctions suggest another, latent one. The *theōros* may be disinterested, not because of a want of belief, a concern that is irrelevant for this aspect of Greek religion, as for some others, but because the cult that he has come to witness is not his responsibility. The *hiketēs*, however, cannot be disinterested. Often his life is at stake. To save himself, he is often regarded as investing his action with magical power, what some scholars have called *Kontaktmagie*. This power binds him to the person approached, but also to the god of the shrine or ritual. A *theōros* is not a player in a game with such stakes, or such devices to secure success.[5]

This last, latent distinction has an unnoticed consequence. The *hiketēs* who comes to a healing shrine may be said to be a protagonist, and to do much else that other *hiketai* do, but he does not act with magical power. To the contrary: he submits to the power of the god. Hence some scholars who have studied *hiketai* have omitted those at healing shrines.[6] This is a consequence that scholars of pilgrimage have missed, and that should give them pause. They are using a term that scholars in a related speciality regard as problematic.

Before we answer our question, and say what the *theōros* and the *hiketēs* have in common, we should look more closely at the *hiketēs*, and ask who he is and what he does, both at healing shrines and elsewhere. We will find that the Asclepius of a healing shrine evaluates those who come to him, the same as the human beings who receive other *hiketai*.

---

[4] Oracle-seekers who are communal delegates are sometimes included among *hiketai* who are pilgrims, as in the editors' introduction to this book, but the term *hiketēs* is seldom used of them in the classical period, the one exception that I know of being Hdt. 7.71, where Athenian oracle-seekers are called *hiketai* only after they make the unusual decision to ask for a second oracle.

[5] *Kontaktmagie*: Kopperschmidt's introduction, followed implicitly by Gould and others as in n. 2 above.

[6] e.g. Gould (1973), Gödde (1998), and Giordano (1999).

In performing his evaluation, Asclepius follows conventions, or as they will be termed, fictions, that resemble conventions found in accounts of gods at oracular shrines. Finally, Asclepius deals with *theōroi*, not just *hiketai*, but *theōroi* of a special kind, sceptics. *Theōroi* and *hiketai* do have something in common, but something unsuspected, which we can trace in the *iamata*, or records of cures obtained by Greek pilgrims.

Like many topics in Classics, this one benefits from cross-cultural comparison. As will emerge from a brief glimpse at Latin American pilgrimage, persons resembling *theōroi* and *hiketai* need not be distinguished from one another. The Greek link between the two is not unique, whereas the narrative manner perhaps is.

In addressing Greek problems and Latin American comparanda, this chapter will not discuss the other term with which we began, 'pilgrim'. Originally medieval and Christian, it now covers a range of phenomena and cultures, and so the originally Christian characteristics of it, including penitence and reference to Scripture, have given way to overlapping definitions inspired by the phenomena and cultures being studied—in Classics, to definitions based on but not limited to an inter-communal journey to a public shrine, and thus reflecting the division of Greece into *poleis* through which the pilgrim passes on his way to a shrine administered according to local decrees.[7] These definitions accommodate an ample body of evidence, both for *theōroi* and their activity, *theōria*, and for *hiketai* and *hiketeia*.

LATIN AMERICAN HEALING PILGRIMAGE

In the town of Juazeiro do Norte, in north-eastern Brazil, pilgrims commemorate a miracle that took place there on the first Friday in March in 1888. When a priest, Padre Cícero, placed the host in the mouth of a mulatto laundress named Maria de Araújo, it grew red with blood, and a piece fell to the floor. Padre Cícero picked it up in an altar towel, and later placed it in a glass urn. The miracle recurred regularly until Ascension Day, word spread, and on 7 July, the feast of the Precious Blood, some 3,000 pilgrims set forth from Crato, some

---

[7] e.g. Rutherford (1995), 276 (sanctuary, long or difficult journey, religious aim); Dillon (1997), ch. 1 (journey, sacred purpose).

20 miles away, to Juazeiro, led by a curate whose sermon climaxed in the display of altar linens that he said bore the stains of Christ's blood.[8]

So began pilgrimage to Juazeiro, a practice comparable to Greek *theōria*, in that it includes a visit to a site where god is made manifest, and comparable, too, to practices elsewhere in the Catholic world. Approximately a million pilgrims come every year, mainly from north-eastern Brazil, and many take up permanent residence.

But as the later life of Padre Cícero shows, a practice like *hiketeia* also occurs. Perhaps it began when another priest who believed in the miracle swore to Padre Cícero that he would never betray him, and added that he hoped to go blind if he did. Then, when the authorities rejected the miracle, and he found it prudent to agree with them, he lost his sight. Padre Cícero had acquired power over the health of others, as shown by another story, heard in Juazeiro around 1980:

Once when Padre Cícero opened the church door, he found a mute boy inside. The Bishop asked him to make the boy speak. Padre Cícero then called the boy's name three times, asking him to tell everyone the identity of his mother and his father. The boy then told the crowd that his father was the Bishop and his mother the mother superior of the convent.[9]

This story suggests that Padre Cícero did not suffer any loss of popularity because of the refusal of the authorities to acknowledge the miracles of Juazeiro, and after his death the miracles continued. He is still working cures, one of the reasons that pilgrims choose to stay. If a prescription drug is effective, he receives the credit; if a pilgrim's health improves after leaving, his tea, brewed with stones from one of the town's streets, is responsible. Like Asclepius, Padre Cícero has become a heroic physician.

Some pilgrims come to Juazeiro for the sake of commemorating the miracle of the host, some for the sake of receiving the Padre's help, some for both, but in any event, a practice resembling *theōria* overlaps with a practice of making journeys to a healing shrine, one resembling *hiketeia*.

---

[8] What follows derives from Slater (1991), who gathered some 1,200 narratives relating to pilgrimage to Juazeiro between 1978 and 1981, her chief interest being not differing types of pilgrimage, as here, but the differences between oral and written versions.

[9] Quoted with incidental changes from Slater (1991), 178.

The pilgrims and their hosts do not draw a distinction between the two, using the term *romeiro* for both kinds of pilgrims. Nor is any distinction suggested by the colossal statue of Padre Cícero that looms over the church where the pilgrims come, the street of sacred stones, and the neighbourhoods full of pilgrims who have decided to live where prescription drugs are uncommonly effective.

Other faith healers have followings in north-eastern Brazil and elsewhere in Latin America. In Venezuela, pilgrimage to a healing shrine combines with visits to mediums, and not with *theōria* in the sense of festival-going; in the Peruvian Andes, the pilgrims are healed before they come, thanks to replicas of a famous cross erected about the same time as the original miracle in Juazeiro.[10] In these cases, the parallel with Asclepius is not as close, but there is still no distinction between two kinds of pilgrimage.

GREEK DISTINCTIONS REVISITED

If the activities of watching and seeking a cure commingle in Latin America, what of *hiketeia* and *theōria*? What, to begin with, do Greek sources mean when they repeatedly refer to those who come to a healing shrine as *hiketai*?[11]

The literal sense of *hiketēs*, which is one who arrives or approaches, appears in many familiar examples, such as Orestes' approaching Athena's statue in Aeschylus. It also appears in an example of *hiketeia* at Epidauros. This example concerns not the healing shrine, but the nearby temple of Apollo Maleatas.[12] The *hiketēs* is an Argive refugee, Callipus:

---

[10] Venezuela: Pollak-Eltz (1991); Peru: Vreeland (1991), 233 for the date of the discovery of the crosses, 1868, and 243 for replicas of the cross, though he also reports that cures are sought during the biannual festivals at which the cross is paraded.

[11] Nehrbass (1935), 55, citing *IG* iv² 1.121.4, 15, 20, 23, 34, 72, 90 for ἱκέτης, which is always followed by the phrase ποὶ τὸν θεόν. For examples of ἱκέτης elsewhere, see *IG* iv² 1.537.38, 2.1286.3, 1308, 1367; Paus. 10.32.12.

[12] Paus. 2.27.7, saying that it is atop Mount Cynortium, which is about half a mile away. Numerous inscriptions associate this temple and the shrine of Asclepius, e.g. *IG* iv² 1.127 (224 CE), as noted by Frazer ad loc.

Κάλλιπος Ἡικέτας
Εὐκλέος Ηυιὸς
τὸν Ἐπιδαύριον
παρ' Ἀπόλλονος
Πυθίο Ἀργεῖος
ἀρχὸς καὶ Φοικιάται[13]

Along with his household, the Argive leader Callipus, the son of Eucles, was a suppliant of the Epidaurians at the behest of Pythian Apollo.

Callipus has also been described as a 'landowner' accompanied by 'slaves', but in either event he has 'approached' a shrine, and has done so in phases, going first to an altar or statue and then to a public gathering where the Epidaurians voted to accept him.[14] So, too, with the *hiketēs* who comes to the shrine of Asclepius, and goes first to a place of sacrifice, then to a place of ablution, and finally to the place of incubation, the *abaton*.[15] A long trip may precede this approach, and Callipus took a long trip, too, so this is another common element.[16]

Yet another common element is contact, meaning physical contact, with the sacred. Benveniste said that this contact typically took the form of clasping the knees of a person or image, but earlier writers, beginning perhaps with Robertson Smith, argued that contact with the sacred did not have a typical form.[17] Instead there were numerous forms, the most important being the knee-clasp and contact with an altar or statue. This contact was the occasion for the *Kontaktmagie* that we have already mentioned as a motif of scholarship on *hiketeia*.

---

[13] *SEG* 26.449.

[14] For 'landowner,' see Klees (1975), 176–7; for background, Orlandos (1977), 104–5. 'Household' and 'slaves', the two translations of Φοικιάται, are both unsatisfactory. For an exiled citizen to mention his household is unusual, but if 'slaves' are to be significantly different from 'household members', Argive history must be adduced, as by Lambroudinakis (1998), who links this inscription to the battle of Sepeia.

[15] For the sequence of payment, ablution, sacrifice, and incubation, see Dillon (1994), 255 following Herzog (1931), 67.

[16] Longest: Epirus (n. 31) and Ceos (n. 39). The hardship of the journey was greater for women, but they come from Athens (4), Caphyiae (41), Ceos (39), Epirus (31), Lacedaemon (21), Messene (42), Pherai (25), and Troezen (23, 34). If the sick person is a temple attendant, the approach is so short that there is hardly any *hiketeia* (*IG* ii² 4514).

[17] Robertson Smith (1927), 148 n. 2; Nilsson (1967–74), 1.87; Kopperschmidt (1967) 11–12, using the term *Kontaktmagie*. Another possible line of descent: Robertson Smith to Onians, *The Origins of European Thought*, cited by Gould 77 n. 16, but Onians does not cite Roberston Smith.

Here again, Epidauros fits. Callipus no doubt clasped an altar or statue, and the *hiketai* in the *abaton* make contact in another way, by lying on holy ground. The holiness of the *abaton* emerges especially from Iamblichus' report that anything that fell to the ground had to be left undisturbed.[18]

At this juncture, however, the *hiketēs* who has come to the *abaton* behaves differently than other *hiketai*, including Callipus. They make requests of the persons approached, the supplicandi, but he makes a request of the god. He also expects a very different response—not a public, political response, as for Callipus, but an epiphany often mediated by a dream. The god comes to him, not the reverse, a switch that prevents him from being the protagonist in the usual sense and that, as noted, led scholars studying *hiketeia* to omit healing shrines.[19]

But we should not exaggerate these differences in regard to the request and response. The *hiketēs* at Epidauros also makes a request of the temple staff, which is to permit him to supplicate, and to judge from evidence from several shrines, they respond by imposing requirements that include not just the sacrifice and ablutions already mentioned, but also abstention from sex and from some kinds of food and drink for several days.[20] These ritualistic requirements resemble those imposed on suppliants who were polluted, especially murderers.[21] Nor were the Epidaurian *hiketai* exempt from other requirements. They were not to be atheists or victims of self-inflicted injuries.[22] Porphyry goes farther, and reports that a plaque at Epidauros said that suppliants must be pure of heart:

ἁγνὸν χρὴ ναοῖο θυώδεος ἐντὸς ἰόντα
ἔμμεναι· ἁγνεία δ' ἐστὶ φρονεῖν ὅσια.[23]

---

[18] *VP* 27, 126.

[19] Dismissed by Giordano (1999), 6.6. Omitted by Gould (1973); Gödde (1998); Chaniotis (1996*a*); Jessen (1913).

[20] For sacrifices, see cure no. 5, quoted below, and Paus. 2.27.1. Ablutions at Athens: Ar. *Plut.* 655–7. At Pergamon: Habicht (1969), 161.11–14. At Oropus: Philostr. *VA* 2.37. Edelstein (1945), 1.149 reasonably assumes that they were necessary at Epidauros also. Abstinence at Pergamon: Habicht 161.11–24. At Oropus: Sokolowski (1969), 69.43–7. For further details, see Dillon (1994), 244–6.

[21] For polluted suppliants who are murderers, see Parker (1983), ch. 4, though he does not expressly deal with supplication. There is no general treatment of murderers who supplicated, but for the case of Orestes, see Sidwell (1996).

[22] No atheists: Ael. fr. 89. No self-inflicted ills: Philostr. *Ep.* 18.

[23] Porph. *Abst.* 2.19; similarly, Clem. Al. *Strom.* 5.1.13.

A person entering the fragrant temple must be reverent. Reverence is having one's mind on holy things.

These were matters for the god, not the priests, and so the business of request and response was mixed. So, for that matter, was the request by and response to Callipus. The Epidaurians voted to accept him because he came παρ' Ἀπόλλονος 'at the behest' of the god and thus with the god's support. And we may add Orestes to the list, for a goddess interrogated him before presenting him to a human jury, and then broke a deadlock in the jury and voted to acquit him.[24]

We even know of a fictional case in which the god handled the responsibility for moral requirements, but apparently turned over the responsibility to the priests when the time came to take the unpleasant action of responding to a *hiketēs* who failed to meet these requirements. Philostratus says that a *hiketēs* of Asclepius at Aegae had committed incest. The god came to the priest of the shrine in a dream and told him, 'Let the man go away, and take all his possessions with him,' including some that he was going to dedicate to the god. The man was blind in one eye, so the god expressed his disapproval by adding, 'he does not deserve even to keep the other.'[25]

As I have argued elsewhere, studies of supplication have neglected this mixture, and in particular have neglected one important aspect of the god's role, the very one that Philostratus stresses. Asclepius may either give support or withhold it.[26] The fiction of Philostratus aside, this conclusion emerges from the Epidaurian *iamata*, the records of cures comprising the chief evidence for *hiketeia* at healing shrines.

THE *IAMATA* AS QUASILEGAL TEXTS

The Epidaurian *iamata* survive on two late fourth-century BCE stone stelae, or tablets, each about 1.7 metres tall and three-quarters of a metre

---

[24] Aesch. *Eu.* 436–42, resembling *anakrisis* by an Athenian magistrate, and thus internalizing the mixture of divine and human.

[25] *VA* 1.10: "ἀπίτω" ἔφη "ὁ δεῖνα τὰ ἑαυτοῦ ἔχων, ἄξιος γὰρ μηδὲ τὸν ἕτερον τῶν ὀφθαλμῶν ἔχειν."

[26] Naiden (2004), anticipated by Chaniotis (1996a), 84–5.

wide.[27] They were erected by the local Asclepieum, the most important shrine to that god anywhere in the vicinity, known as the Argolid, and perhaps anywhere in mainland Greece. Other shrines erected tablets, too, but unfortunately, only one other such tablet survives, from Lebena in Crete.[28] It contains only three intelligible cures, compared to forty-four from the two tablets found at Epidauros.[29]

Though we do not know exactly where any tablets of this kind stood, we can be sure that they occupied a prominent place in the shrine.[30] To judge from Pausanias, they were numerous as well as large, creating a memorable impression: a half dozen or more massive tablets, each containing dozens of records, or hundreds in all, on permanent display in a unified setting and uniform style.[31]

These stelae would present an official version of Asclepius' (or of his and his father's Apollo's) benefactions. We should note that this version more or less differs from any version that the *hiketēs* might leave in the shrine in the form of a thank-offering.[32] In addition, the two stelae from Epidauros differ somewhat from the other surviving one, from Lebena, which does not deal with the theme of the Asclepius' giving or withholding support. But with these reservations, we can not only trace this theme but learn why the god gives or withholds. The fragmentary *iama* no. 36 says that the god found that the *hiketēs* had committed *hybris*, and therefore rejected him.[33] Another *iama* reports that after a *hiketēs* named Hermo failed to bring a thank-offering, the god returned him to

[27] *IG* iv² 1.121–2, the text having been established by Herzog and accepted by Edelstein (1945), whose translations of several *iamata* I have consulted. The first stone: 1.71 by .76. The second: 1.69 by .74.

[28] *Iamata* commissioned at Lebena: *IC* 1.17.9. At Cos and Tricca: Str. 8.6.15. They no doubt existed elsewhere, e.g. Athens (other evidence of the cult of Asclepius gathered by Aleshire), Aegina (cult reported in Ar. *Vesp.* 121–3), Tithorea (Paus. 10.32.12), and especially Pergamon (the sources gathered by Remus, especially Aelius Aristides).

[29] *IC* 1.17.9. No tablets survive from Cos and Tricca.

[30] Information on the recovery of the Epidaurian stelae: Papachatze (1974–81), ad 2.27.3.

[31] Pausanias says that at Epidauros there once had been more than the six he saw (2.27.3), and Strabo loc. cit. says that the shrines at Cos and Tricca were full of them.

[32] Examples of these survive at Epidauros: *IG* ii² 4515 (2nd cent. CE), 1.125 (3rd cent. BCE), 1.126 (*c.* 160 CE). Also at Lebena: *IC* 17.17–18 (1st cent. BCE), (19, (1st–2nd cent. BCE) 24 (3rd cent. CE). One at Rome: *IG* xiv 966 (2nd cent. CE).

[33] τᾶς ὕβριος ποινὰς λαμβάνω[ν.

his original state of blindness, showing that he found him guilty of ingratitude.[34]

The god is passing judgement, and in these two cases, his judgement is to condemn. In other cases, it is to give aid:

> Νικάνωρ χωλός. τούτου καθημένου παῖς τις ὕπαρ τὸν
> σκίπωνα ἁρ–
> πάξας ἔφευγε· ὁ δὲ ἀστὰς ἐδίωκε καὶ ἐκ τούτου ὑγιὴς
> ἐγένετο.[35]

Nicanor, who was lame. When he sat down, a slave snatched his crutch and fled. He rose, pursued him, and so he became well.

In another case, the *hiketēs* is a victim of rejection, not wrongdoing, and the god helps him out of pity:

> Ἡραιεὺς Μυτιληναῖος· οὗτος οὐκ εἶχε ἐν τᾶι κεφαλᾶι
> τρίχας, ἐν δὲ τῶι γενείωι παμπόλλας· αἰσχυνόμενος δὲ
> [ὡς] καταγελάμενος ὑπ[ὸ]
> τῶν ἄλλων ἐνεκάθευδε. τὸν δὲ ὁ θεὸς χρίσας φαρμάκωι
> τὰν κεφαλὰν ἐπόησε
> τρίχας ῥίχας ἔχειν.[36]

Heraeus a Mytilenean. He had no hair on his head, but did have hair all over his chin. Ashamed because he was ridiculed by others, he slept (in the *Abaton*). The god anointed him with a drug and made him have hair on his head.

At still other times the *hiketēs* is the victim of circumstances, and the god once again takes pity on him. The soldier carries parts of a spear in his jaw, a wife cannot get pregnant or come to term.[37] Most pitiful of all is the blind man who dropped a *lekythos* and cannot find it.[38]

The ideal *hiketēs* is that most pitiful and innocent of human beings, a child, as emerges from two *iamata*, one where the god approves of a child's naivety and another in which a child sets an example. In the first case, the child offers to give dice as a thank-offering, and the god laughingly accepts the offer. In the second, the child sets an example for his father:

[34] no. 22; similarly, no. 47. For another view of this and related passages, see Dillon (1994) 252–4, seeing them as displays of power on the part of a god interested in the payment of thank-offerings.

[35] no. 16; also no. 13, where the god cures a victim of a mother-in-law's trickery.

[36] no. 19; other examples are discussed below.

[37] Soldier: nos. 12, 31, 32. Wives: nos. 1, 2, 25, 31, 34, 39, 42.

[38] An unnumbered *iama* at the end of *IG* iv² 1.123, beginning ἀνὴρ τυφλός.

παῖς ἄφωνος.

[οὗτος ἀφί]κετο εἰς τὸ ἱαρὸν ὑπὲρ φωνᾶς · ὡς δὲ
προεθύσατο καὶ
[ἐπόησε τὰ] νομιζόμενα, μετὰ τοῦτο ὁ παῖς ὁ τῶι θεῶι
πυρφορῶν
[ἐκέλετο, π]οὶ τὸμ πατέρα τὸν τοῦ παιδὸς ποτιβλέψας,
ὑποδέκεσ-
[θαι αὐτὸν ἐ]νιαυτοῦ, τυχόντα ἐφ᾽ ἃ πάρεστι, ἀποθυσεῖν
τὰ ἴατρα.
[ὁ δὲ παῖς ἐξ]απίνας "ὑποδέκομαι", ἔφα · ὁ δὲ πατὴρ
ἐκπλαγεὶς πάλιν
[ἐκέλετο αὐ]τὸν εἰπεῖν · ὁ δ᾽ ἔλεγε πάλιν · καὶ ἐκ τούτου
ὑγιὴς ἐγέ-
[νετο.³⁹

A boy who was dumb. He came to the shrine for his voice. Once the boy's father made the preliminary sacrifice and performed the usual rites, the temple slave who carries the fire for the god then looked at the boy's father and asked him to promise to make a thank-offering for the cure in a year's time, provided that he found what he had come for. Suddenly the boy said 'I promise'. Stunned, the father asked him to speak again. He did, and so he became well.

The boy's eagerness makes the process of incubation unnecessary.

In several instances, the god makes his judgement plain by way of contrast between two *iamata*. One will describe his response to the innocent, the next to the guilty. Once reproved, the guilty party may learn the error of his ways, and thus obtain the god's help, making for a new contrast: first the simple tale of the good, next the twofold tale of the reformed. To help the reader notice these contrasts, there is a thematic or symbolic link between the two cases.

There are three pairs of these contrasting *iamata*, nos. 6 and 7, 8 and 9, and 10 and 11. The first pair contrasts two *hiketai*, one of whom is good, and gives thanks promptly, the other of whom is wicked, and gives thanks belatedly. The link is double, first, a thematic link, which is the involvement of the second *hiketēs* in a dedication to be made by the first one, and second, a symbolic link, which is the headband, or *tainia*, worn by both *hiketai*. The first *hiketēs*, the good one, is named Pandarus, and the second, wicked one is named Echedorus:

³⁹ The dice: no. 8. The dumb boy: no. 5.

Ἐχέδωρος … λαβὼν πὰρ [Παν]—
[δάρου χρήματα], ὥστ᾽ ἀνθέμεν τῶι θεῶι εἰς Ἐπίδαυρον ὑπὲρ
αὐ[τοῦ],
[οὐκ] ἀπεδίδου ταῦτα· ἐγκαθεύδων δὲ ὄψιν εἶδε· ἐδόκει οἱ
ὁ θε[ὸς]
ἐπιστὰς ἐπερωτῆν νιν, εἰ ἔχοι τινὰ χρήματα πὰρ Πανδάρου
ἐ[ξ Εὐ]—
θηνᾶν ἄνθεμα εἰς τὸ ἱαρόν· αὐτὸς δ᾽ οὐ φάμεν λελαβήκειν
οὐθὲ[ν]
τοιοῦτον παρ᾽ αὐτοῦ· ἀλλ᾽ αἴ κα ὑγιῆ νιν ποήσαι, ἀνθησεῖν   60
οἱ εἰκό—
να γραψάμενος·

Echedorus. After receiving money from Pandarus for an offering to the god at Epidauros on Pandarus' behalf, he did not spend the money. In his sleep he saw a dream. It seemed to him that the god stood before him and asked him whether he had any money from Pandarus of Euthenae for a dedication for the shrine. He said he had not got any such thing from Pandarus, but if the god made him well, he would inscribe and dedicate an image.

As it happens, Echedorus is 'unwell' because he has tattoos, and Pandarus had tattoos also, so the god responds this way: first, he takes Pandarus' tattoos and puts them on the headband. Then

μετὰ δὲ τοῦτο τὸν θεὸν τὰν τοῦ Πανδάρου ταινί—
αν περιδῆσαι περὶ τὰ στίγματά οὗ καὶ κέλεσθαί νιν, ἐπεί κα ἐξ—
έλθηι ἐκ τοῦ ἀβάτου, ἀφελόμενον τὰν ταινίαν ἀπονίψασθαι τὸ
πρόσωπον ἀπὸ τᾶς κράνας καὶ ἐγκατοπτρίξασθαι εἰς τὸ ὕδωρ.

the god bound (Echedorus') tattoos with Pandarus' headband and asked (Echedorus) to leave the *abaton* and remove the headband, wash his face in the well, and look in the water.

Echedorus no doubt was hoping for the best:

ἀ-
μέρας δὲ γενομένας ἐξελθὼν ἐκ τοῦ ἀβάτου τὰν ταινίαν   65
ἀφήλετο,
τὰ γράμματα οὐκ ἔχουσαν · ἐγκαθιδὼν δὲ εἰς τὸ ὕδωρ ἑώρη
τὸ αὐτοῦ
πρόσωπον ποὶ τοῖς ἰδίοις στίγμασιν καὶ τὰ τοῦ Πανδ <ά>ρου
γρά[μ]—
ματα λελαβηκός.[40]

---

[40] no. 7.

At dawn he left the *abaton* and removed the headband and it no longer had the tattoos on it. When he looked in the water he saw his face. In addition to his own tattoos, he had those of Pandarus also.[41]

Since Echedorus kept Pandarus' money, he gets Pandarus' tattoos. The punishment fits the crime.

The second pair contrasts the naiveté of the boy who offers dice to the god with the naivety of a blind man who believes that god can restore sight to a missing eye. Both are innocent and pitiable, both naive, both rewarded. So far, the god wants gratitude and money. But the third pair of *iamata* shows his support for other, broader values. The first story is about belief, the same as the story of the blind man, but it has complications that make it worth quoting in full:

κώθων. σκευοφόρος εἰ[ς τὸ] ἱαρ[ὸν] ἕρπων, ἐπεὶ ἐγένετο
   περὶ τὸ δε—
καστάδιον, κατέπετε · [ὡς δὲ] ἀνέστα, ἀνῶιξε τὸν γυλιὸν   80
   κα[ὶ ἐ]πεσκό—
πει τὰ συντετριμμένα σκ[ε]ύη · ὡς δ᾽ εἶδε τὸν κώθωνα
   κατε[αγ]ότα,
ἐξ οὗ ὁ δεσπότας εἴθιστο [π]ίνειν, ἐλυπεῖτο καὶ συνετίθει
   [τὰ] ὄ—
στρακα καθιζόμενος.

The cup. When a porter came to the shrine, he fell after he reached the tenth stade. When he rose, he opened his bag and saw that the contents had been crushed. When he saw that the cup that his master liked to drink from was broken, he grieved, and sat down and tried to put together the pieces.

Enter a sceptical passer-by, and after the sceptic, the god:

ὁδο[ι]πόρος οὖν τις ἰδὼν αὐτόν · "τί, ὦ ἄθλιε, " [ἔ]—
φα, "συντίθησι τὸν κώθωνα [μά]ταν; τοῦτον γὰρ οὐδέ κα
   ὁ ἐν Ἐπιδαύ—
ρωι Ἀσκλαπιὸς ὑγιῆ ποῆσαι δύναιτο." ἀκούσας ταῦτα   85
   ὁ παῖς συν—
θεὶς τὰ ὄστρακα εἰς τὸν γυλιὸν ἦρπε εἰς τὸ ἱερόν· ἐπεὶ
   δ᾽ ἀφίκε—
το, ἀνῶιξε τὸν γυλιὸν καὶ ἐξαιρεῖ ὑγιῆ τὸν κώθωνα
   γεγενημέ—

[41] 'Tattoo': Jones (1987), 144.

νον καὶ τῶι δεσπόται ἡρμάνευσε τὰ πραχθέντα καὶ
λεχθέντα ὡ—
5 δὲ ἄκουσ᾽, ἀνέθηκε τῶι θεῶι τὸγ κώθωνα.

When a passer-by saw him, he said, 'You wretch, why are you trying to put it together? Not even the Asclepius of Epidauros could make it whole.' After he heard that the slave put the pieces in the bag and went into the shrine. After arriving, he opened the bag and removed the cup, which had been made whole, and told his master what had been said and done; and after the master heard the story, he dedicated the cup to the god.

Asclepius has confounded the sceptic, and thanks to the cup and the *iama*, he will continue to confound sceptics.

The next story is about another value, respect for holy things. It has a link to the preceding story, as in previous examples of pairs of *iamata*, but the link does not take the form of an object, such as the headband, or of a theme, such as naiveté, but instead of an action, falling. Like the porter, a man named Aeschines falls.[42] While *hiketai* slept and encountered the god in their dreams, he climbed a tree overlooking the *abaton*, spied on them, and fell to the ground, blinding himself. Later, he returns to the shrine and supplicates the god, καθικετεύσας τὸν θεὸν, an unsurprising phrase, but used in only one other *iama*, the one in which the god punishes a *hiketēs* for *hybris*.[43] This phrase is reserved for wrongdoers who make repeated or intense entreaties when seeking to reinstate themselves in the god's good graces.[44]

These two-part morality tales constitute only a minority of the *iamata*, and even if the other tales of the guilty and the innocent are added, especially those of wives unable to bear children, the total is 21, or less than half of the intelligible.[45] But none of the other *iamata* present a *hiketēs* who is any way reprehensible, and so they tend to justify Porphyry's claim that a suppliant had to have a 'pure heart', provided that purity is practical and modest: fulfilment of ritualistic

---

[42] no. 10: κατέπετε no. 11: Ἀισχίνας . καταπετῶν.

[43] no. 36: καθικετεύσας τὸν θεόν, the same phrase.

[44] The sense given in *LSJ* s.v. καθικετεύω, but without citing the Epidaurian *iamata*; the word does not appear in *iamata* from Lebena.

[45] i.e., six two-part tales and fifteen tales of innocence, listed in nn. 26–30 above, including seven women. Well-preserved: nos. 1–48, plus two more *iamata* at the very end of *IG* iv² 1.123, one beginning Δαμοσθένης and the other ἀνὴρ τυφλὸς. Nos. 35, 38, 40, 45 may or may not have moralizing material that has not been preserved.

requirements; no disqualifying circumstances, such as being responsible for one's illness, or if one is responsible, like Aeschines and Hermo, being willing to pray for the god's succour; and, at best, proof of one's innocence through a show of gratitude.

But the best proof that the god passes judgement is the dumb boy of *iama* no. 5. As we have seen, the god cures him immediately, making entry into the *abaton* superfluous. In this case, morality trumps ritual; generally speaking, they are both important. So, though it is too much to say that the *iamata* are legal texts, they are quasi-legal. They deal in judgement, reward, and punishment.

THE FICTION OF SUCCESS

Only one of the forty-four *hiketai*, Echedorus, fails to obtain a cure. The fact that many other *hiketai* were not cured goes unacknowledged, or finds its way into stories that prove that a cure may be delayed, but is sure to come in the god's own time. The *iamata* present a fiction of success.

Sostrata of Pherae, for example, failed to obtain either a cure or a dream.[46] So the god makes a tardy appearance:

$$\Sigma\omega\sigma\tau\rho\acute{a}\tau a\ \Phi\epsilon\rho a\acute{\iota}[a\ \pi a\rho]-$$
εκύησε. α[ὖ]τα ἐμ παντὶ ἐοῦσα φοράδαν εἰς τὸ ἱαρὸν ἀφικομένα
    ἐνε[κά]—
θευδε. ὡς δὲ οὐθὲν ἐνύπνιον ἐναργ[έ]ς ἑώρη, πάλιν οἴκαδε
    ἀπεκομίζ[ε]—
το. μετὰ δὲ τοῦτο συμβολῆσαί τις περὶ Κόρνους αὐτᾶι καὶ
    τοῖς ἑ[πομέ]—
νοις ἔδοξε τὰν ὄψιν εὐπρεπὴς ἀνήρ...[47]   30

Sostrata of Pherai miscarried. When she was in very poor condition, she came to the shrine and slept (in the *abaton*). When she had no clear dream, she returned home. Later, it seemed to her that someone met her and her party at Kornoi, a handsome man,...

---

[46] The only such case in the *iamata*, but see Pl. *Curc.* 216–73.

[47] no. 25. παρ]εκύησε: Fraenkel, *IG* iv 952. θηρι'] | ἐκύησε ζῶια ἐκύησε Herzog (1931), 80–2. The supplements of Fraenkel and Herzog both mean that her pregnancy was abnormal, as is said at the start of *iamata* nos. 1 and 2. Φεραι[ᾶτις ἐκύησε: Scullion (2000) 120.

The stranger is the god, who promptly effects a cure.

The mention of Kornoi suggests that it has some potential for becoming a new cult centre, as happens in another case that also begins unsuccessfully:

> [Θ]έρσανδρος Ἁλικὸς φθίσιν. οὗτος, ὡς ἐγκαθεύδων
> [οὐ]δεμίαν ὄψιν
> [ἑ]ώρη, ἐφ᾿ ἁμάξας [ἄμπαλ]ιν ἀπεκομίζετο εἰς Ἁλιεῖς,

Thersander of Halieis, who had consumption. When he slept (in the *abaton*) and saw no dream, he returned to Halieis by wagon, ...

This time, the god makes a tardy appearance in the form of a snake:

>   δράκων δέ τις
> [τ]ῶν ἱαρῶν ἐπὶ τ[ᾶς ἁμ]άξας καθιδρυμένος ἦς, τὸ πο[λ]ὺ
> τᾶς ὁδοῦ περιη—
> [λι]γμένος περ[ὶ τ]ὸν ἄξονα διετέλεσε. μολόντων δ᾿ [α]ὐ[τ]ῶν
> εἰς Ἁλιεῖς
> [κα]ὶ τοῦ Θερσ[ά]νδρου κατακλιθέντος οἴ[κο]ι, ὁ δράκων
> ἀπὸ τᾶς ἁμά—
> [ξα]ς καταβὰ[ς τ]ὸν Θέρσανδρον ἰάσατο.

A snake from among those at the shrine had entered his wagon and stayed wound around the axle for most of the trip. When they came to Halieis and Thersander was lying down at home, the snake descended from the wagon and cured Thersander.

The god has waited so long that the miracle no longer seems to be the work of Epidauros:

> [ἀγγε]λ[λ]ούσας τὸ γεγενημένον καὶ διαπορ[ουμένας]
> περὶ τοῦ ὄφι—
> [ος, πό]τερον εἰς Ἐπίδαυρον ἀποκομίζωντι [ἢ αὐτὸν κα]τὰ
> χώραν ἐῶν—
> [τι, ἔ]δοξε τᾶι πόλι εἰς Δελφοὺς ἀποστεῖλα[ι χρησομέ]νους ...[48]

The community of Halieis heard the news and after debating whether to return the snake to Epidauros or let him stay there, voted to send a mission to Delphi to obtain a prophecy, ...

---

[48] no. 33.

Unsurprisingly, the oracle satisfies both the supporters of a new shrine and the supporters of Epidauros, for it advises Halieis to build a temple for the snake but to send an offering to what is now the mother shrine.[49]

Besides leading to cures in unexpected places, the fiction of success leads to cures in seemingly impossible conditions. Asclepius removes spearpoints from the jaw, forehead, and lungs (nos. 12, 30, 32), cuts open the eyes, belly, and chest (nos. 4, 27, 13), and even decapitates pilgrims or restores a head decapitated by someone else (nos. 21, 23). In one case the patient even objects to the risks, and resists treatment:

> ἀνὴρ ἐ[ντὸ]ς τᾶς κοιλίας ἕλκος ἔχων. οὗ—
> τος ἐγκαθεύδων ἐν[ύπνιο]ν εἶδε · ἐδόκ[ε]ι αὐτῶι ὁ θεὸς
> ποιτάξαι τοῖς
> ἑπομένοις ὑπηρέτα[ις συλ]λαβόντας αὐτὸν ἴσχειν, ὅπως   40
> τάμηι οὐ τὰν
> κοιλίαν · αὐτὸς δὲ φεύ[γει]ν, τοὺς δὲ συλλαβόντας νιν
> ποιδῆσαι ποὶ ῥό—
> πτον · μετὰ δὲ τοῦτο τὸν [Ἀσ]κλαπιὸν ἀνσχίσσαντα τὰγ
> κοιλίαν ἐκτα—
> μεῖν τὸ ἕλκος καὶ συρρά[ψαι] πάλιν, καὶ λυθῆμεν ἐκ τῶν
> δεσμῶν· καὶ ἐ—
> κ τούτου ὑγιὴς ἐξῆ[λθ]ε, τὸ δὲ δάπεδον ἐν τῶι ἀβάτωι
> αἵματος κατά—
> πλεον ἦς.   45

A man with an ulcer in his gut. He slept (in the *abaton*) and saw a dream. It seemed to him that the god ordered his attendants to seize and hold him so that he could cut open his guts. He fled, but they seized him and bound him to the table. Later, Asclepius split his guts and cut out the ulcer and sewed him up again, and he was freed from his bonds. And so he left a well man, but the floor of the *abaton* was full of blood.

The sequel shows that the patient was right. He leaves cured, but 'the floor of the *abaton* was full of blood'. He should have perished, or at least suffered, yet he does neither.

In such cases, the fiction of success modulates into one of narrowly averted failure. Between them, the two fictions account for many

---

[49] For the 'colonization' of Pergamon and Cyrene by the Epidaurian Aesculapium, see Paus. 2.26.8–9. Among temples to Asclepius, only Epidauros is reported to have 'colonies'.

cases, and rejection of the guilty accounts for the rest. Nothing mean-
ingless can happen: this, not the cure, is the miracle wrought at
Epidauros.[50]

ORACULAR FICTIONS

The fictions of success and near failure also appear in accounts of
oracular responses. Fontenrose's study of Greek oracles, unpersuasive
in its attempt to show that oracular ambiguity occurs only in literary
texts, did the service of listing the many oracular replies that showed that
a god always foretold the future—the fiction of success—and sometimes did so while making incredible or incomprehensible predictions—the fiction of near failure.[51] To cite but one example: suffering
from an incurable wound, Telephus is told that the person who
wounded him will heal him, or that he will be healed if the wounder
becomes a physician. The incredible prediction proves true.[52]

According to Fontenrose, these oracles have several features: a salutation, a restatement of the question asked by the consultant, an
assertion of the authority of the oracle, a conditional or unconditional
message in the form of a command, warning, or prediction, and an
explanatory comment.[53] Most of these features have counterparts in one
or more *iamata*. The god greets Sostrata on her way back from Epidauros, a salutation; he shows Echedorus what is wrong, a restatement
of the matter at hand, if not of a question; and the god's priest tells the
dumb boy's father to make a thank-offering, a command. Conditional
messages are missing, but they appear in a kind of text that bridges the
gap between *iamata* and oracles, oracles spoken by Asclepius. None of
these come from Epidauros during the classical period, but some come
from other temples of Asclepius later. Philostratus furnishes an example,

---

[50] Other interpretations of the miracles: faith-healing (Edelstein 1945 1.142–5);
credulity of the *hiketai* (Dillon (1994), 258 and (1997), ch. 1); quackery (Wilamovitz
(1886), 37). Further references: Edelstein (1945), 2.143 with n. 10.

[51] Fontenrose (1978) 21 presents a table of 'ambiguous commands, . . . prohibi-
tions . . . [and] predictions' and 'conditioned predictions', all appearing in sources that
he characterizes as 'legendary' rather than 'historical'.

[52] First version: schol. Ar. *Nub.* 9–19. Second: Lib. *Decl.* 5.9, schol. Dem. 18.72.

[53] Fortenrose (1978), 177–9.

ἥκων δὲ ἐς τὸ Πέργαμον, ὅτε δὴ τὰ ἄρθρα ἐνόσει, κατέδαρθε μὲν ἐν τῶι ἱερῶι, ἐπιστάντος δὲ αὐτῶι τοῦ Ἀσκληπιοῦ καὶ προειπόντος ἀπέχεσθαι ψυχροῦ ποτοῦ . . . [54]

When he [Polemo] came to Pergamon he was sick in his joints. As he slept in the temple, Asclepius appeared to him and told him not to drink anything cold.

The conditional message takes the form of a prescription, and as it happens, the patient refuses to accept it.

The *iamata*, in contrast, do not report prescriptions. Whether or not this feature distinguishes Epidauros during the classical period from other times and places, including Philostratus' Pergamon, it does place the *iamata* at one end of a spectrum. At Epidauros' end, the god can be a heroic physician, scanting conditions; at the other end, at Pergamon, he can be unheroic, imposing the same conditions as a human physician would. But even when unheroic, he functions as before. If the patient follows his prescription, he is always cured, and the fiction of success is at work.

In the light of Asclepiadic and other oracles, the fiction of success cannot be considered aberrant. It is one more illustration of a type of ritual discourse studied outside Classics by Mary Douglas and Jonathan Z. Smith. It moulds and predicts, making ritual a force for order.

EPIDAURIAN *THEŌROI*

Now that we have re-examined *hiketeia*, does it resemble *theōria*? If we define *theōria* as festival-going, the approach and some kind of contact are common elements, but the request for help and the passing of judgement are not. Neither are the fictions of success and near failure. *Theōroi* do fail in some mythic cases, but in reality, *theōroi* who were official delegates received protection, and were usually able to complete their missions. [55]

But if we define *theōria* as 'watching', that is, 'watching for a mani-festation of a god', the two do overlap in the person of the sceptics who

---

[54] *VS* 1.25.4. Other conditional oracles about healing: Aristid. *Or.* 50.17, *IG* iv² 1.125, 126, xiv 966, *IC* 17.17–19.

[55] Mythic troubles: Rutherford (1995). Privileged status: a garlanded ship gave Athenian *theōroi* safe passage to Delos (Pl. *Phaed.* 58a–b, Hesych. s.v. θεωρικός). Official delegates who fail: DS 14.109.3 and other examples at Rutherford (1995), 278–9.

challenge the god to display his powers. They appear in *iamata* nos. 3, 4, 9–11, and 47; their presence is implied in nos. 12–14 and 30.

Some of these *iamata* deal with the vagaries of perception. In no. 9, the sceptics fail to realize that even a man with impaired eyesight can have a vision, an ὄψις. In no. 11, the sceptic who climbs the tree and spies on the *abaton* is attempting to observe what happens in a dream. Other *iamata* pre-empt scepticism by referring to proof that the cure occurred.[56] We have noticed, for example, that the miraculously restored cup is dedicated to the god, and thus can offer permanent, public proof of his power. But the piece of evidence need not take the form of a dedication. In no. 14, a *hiketēs* who has recovered his strength moves a rock to the front of the *abaton*, where it remains.

Most of this evidence is unprepossessing. According to the *iamata*, however, this is no drawback. As the first one says, referring to the *iamata* themselves, οὐ μέγε-[θο]ς πίνακος θαυμαστέον, ἀλλὰ τὸ θεῖον, 'the size of the record is not to be wondered at, but its godliness'. Epidauros has its own kind of seeing, its own *theōria*, one that rejects the common criterion of size, and also the related criteria of rarity and costliness. It thus breaks with the tradition exemplified by Herodotus, in which size, rarity, and costliness are common features of objects and phenomena called 'wonders', or *thaumata*.[57] Instead it conforms with a traditon beginning with Hesiod.[58] The most impressive dedication mentioned in the *iamata*, a silver pig, is modest compared to what either Herodotus or Pausanias report.

Besides having their own visual priorities, the *iamata* on one occasion offer an implicit rebuke to the alternatives of size, rarity, and costliness. The last *iama* about sceptics, no. 47, reports that a fishmonger promised to make a dedication to Asclepius, but failed to keep his promise. The god assailed him in broad daylight in a public place, the market of Tegea, sending a horde of mosquitoes that 'wound

---

[56] nos. 12–15. Comparable to nos. 12: 30. Comparable to no. 15: *IG* iv² 1.125 (*c*.160 CE).

[57] A recent treatment of this aspect of Herodotus: Thomas (2000) ch. 5, stressing Herodotus' scepticism, which does not extend to healing shrines.

[58] Hes. *Op.* 336 (as best one can), Eur. fr 327, 946, Isoc. 2.20, Men. fr. 683 Koerte, Theophrastus fr. 152 Wimmer. Hdt. 1.50.1 takes a middle view, criticizing Croesus not for costly dedications, but for using them to 'purchase' Apollo's good will. For these citations, and others from philosophers, see Parker (1996), 119 n. 48.

his body'.[59] This infestation prompts the only use of the word *theōria* in the *iamata*, and also the only use of any word derived from the root, **the(a)*. *Theōria* can be public without being official.

A MODE OF NARRATIVE

The revision of *theōria* is a narrative convention accompanying several others: pairs and strings of tales, repetition of motifs, and the fictions of success and near failure. Together they constitute a manner of storytelling, to which we may add another salient feature, the relation of text to reader. Besides being *about* the *hiketēs*, the *iamata* are *for* him, and they are *for* him as a *hiketēs*, not a visitor.[60] Since this feature does not appear in other records of *hiketeia*, including oracles, or in records of *theōria*, whence does it derive? Most of the surviving *iamata* date from the fourth century, when the Greeks had been codifying their laws for several hundred years. Literacy and legal concepts have spread—how far and how deeply remain controversial—but they have spread far enough so that a pan-Hellenic shrine can rely on a religious equivalent of the countless depositions processed in law courts.[61] Even if we assume that most visitors could not read the *iamata*, temple staff and others could assist them.[62] And we can be sure that what they learn from the documents, albeit indirectly, is central to their visit. The *iamata* are virtual advertisements, answering several obvious complaints about the product—its slow operation, its unreliability, and its cost.

The role of documents also distinguishes Epidauros from some non-Greek forms of pilgrimage, like healing pilgrimage in Brazil. Otherwise,

---

[59] ἐ[τίτρω]σκον τὸ σῶμα.

[60] Similarly, Dibelius (1933), 170–2, though he stresses the shrine's control over the image that it presents of the suppliants. A different interpretation of this feature: Dillon (1997), dealing with the evolution of Greek religion.

[61] As explained by Mirhady (1996), depositions replaced oral testimony in Attic courts in the early 4th cent. We do not know when or whether this happened in Epidauros or other places.

[62] Holding that those able to read would be very few, approximately 5–10 per cent: Harris (1989), esp. 90, where he argues that the illiterate would be impressed by records like the *iamata* but does not conclude that they would be likely to ask others for help. A different view, stressing the interaction of literacy and illiteracy: Thomas (1992), esp. 150–6. A third view, seeing literacy spreading in the 4th cent. BCE, but only in Athens: Robb (1994), ch. 8

the two are similar: the heroic physician, the embarrassed sceptics, the punished wrongdoers. Not that this kind of pilgrimage does not generate records, including verse chapbooks celebrating the miracles of Juazeiro and similar in content to the *iamata*. But these chapbooks do not take the form of standardized, authorized testimony, and they are not sold or displayed in a shrine. In short, they are not official publications. If they are to be called documents, they deserve this name only insofar as they attest to a tradition of storytelling. The same goes for the inscriptions found at the bottom of Mexican *retablos*, ex-voto paintings that sometimes commemorate cures effected by Jesus, the Virgin, San Rafael, and others. These are the work of artists serving an individual or a community, and are influenced rather than composed by the personnel of the churches where some of them are displayed. Another difference is that the inscription is always a caption, whereas the *iamata* are separate from and usually independent of any dedication.[63]

For healing pilgrimage dependent on documents, we must look not to cross-cultural comparisons, but to the opening scene of the novel *Daphnis and Chloe*. Here the author, Longus, tells how *hiketai*, or pilgrims, come to look at a picture, and thus double as *theōroi*.[64] This doubleness shows some similarity between Longus and Epidaurian cult, but on closer examination, two things distinguish this scene from Epidauros: first, since the *hiketai* seek a cure for love-sickness, their sufferings are psychological, not physical; and second, they are looking at a picture, not a document, something that does come into being later, when Longus makes the picture the subject of his novel. And there is a third, subtle difference: in *Daphnis and Chloe*, *hiketai* may read this document and obtain a cure at the same time. Reading and cure have fused. The *iamata*, in contrast, do not provide for such a fusion. After reading, the pilgrim must go to the *abaton*. To suggest that reading can pre-empt this task, or that reading itself is oneiric, a dream beheld with the mind's eye, is a conceit imputable to the novelist, but not an assumption operative in cult. There is more than one way to reject the immediate, visible world, and Longus chooses one, the healing word, while the *iamata* choose another, the healing vision.

---

[63] An example of a *retablo* commemorating a cure: Giffords (1991) no. 74, an 1842 ex-voto to the Lord of Chalma after recovery from a 'gran afflicción' mentioned in the brief inscription.

[64] θέαμα and ἱκέται who behold it: *Proem* 1. Document as cure: *Proem* 2.

This chapter should end on a cautionary note. It has regarded *hiketēs* and *theōros* as religious terms, but the *iamata* do not distinguish between religious terms and those that are medical. Pilgrimage was also a trip to the specialist, the *hiketēs* was also an out-of-town patient, and the *theōros* was also a sceptical customer. If we forget this aspect, we will be allowing ourselves our own kind of fiction, a fiction of religion in the abstract. Pilgrimage is often urgent; at Epidauros, it was often desperate.

3

Pilgrimage to the Oracle of Apollo at Delphi:

Patterns of Public and Private Consultation

Michael Arnush

I. INTRODUCTION

[Croesus] at once made inquiries of the Greek and Libyan oracles, sending messengers separately to Delphi, to Abae in Phocis, and to Dodona, while others were despatched to Amphiaraus and Trophonius, and others to Branchidae in the Milesian country. These are the Greek oracles to which Croesus sent for divination: and he told others to go inquire of Ammon in Libya. His intent in sending was to test the knowledge of the oracles, so that, if they were found to know the truth, he might send again and ask if he should undertake an expedition against the Persians . . . When [those] who had been sent to various places came bringing their oracles, Croesus then unfolded and examined all the writings. Some of them in no way satisfied him. But when he read the Delphian message, he acknowledged it with worship and welcome, considering Delphi as the only true place of divination, because it had discovered what he himself had done.[1]

This famous Herodotean account of how Croesus came to consult the oracle of Apollo at Delphi is one of our earliest indications of the reliability and fame of the oracle in antiquity. Indeed, the Delphic

I wish to thank the participants in the *Seeing the Gods* conference, including Celeste Lovette for a useful bibliography on Didyma, and Ian Rutherford in particular, for helpful suggestions throughout this paper. All errors are, of course, my own.

[1] Hdt. 1.46, 48, tr. A. D. Godley, in Perseus, http://www.perseus.tufts.edu/cgi-bin/ptext?doc= Perseus %3Atext%3A1999.01.0126 &layout=&loc=1.46.1, accessed May 2002.

oracle was renowned throughout the Mediterranean world from the Greek archaic age to the Roman imperial period. No other oracle—not Dodona, not Ammon, nor Didyma—could match the reputation of Delphi, the 'omphalos' of the world and the most reliable and respected of all oracular seats. By the end of the classical age, however, the pilgrimage to Delphi was a mundane and inconsequential event, no longer on the grand political scale but reduced to queries about mules, marriages, and money.

This chapter focuses specifically on the period when public consultation of the oracle—that is, the dispatch of state representatives to Delphi on matters of national or international importance—decreased substantially, and on the diminishing significance of the oracle in the fourth century BCE, when the world of the *polis* is sometimes thought to have been drawing to a close.

In previous scholarship two major explanations have been given for the demise of the Delphi oracle:

1. Its demise coincides closely with that of the autonomous *polis*,[2] and as the Greek world shifted from the age of colonization, religious organization, and political and military conquest to personal rule and the lack of significant debate, the oracle was no longer essential to decision-making in *poleis*. The *polis* divorced itself from oracular consultation for political purposes as its influence diminished.

2. Changes in the political fortunes of the Delphic oracle must also be viewed in light of changing attitudes towards chresmology. Thucydidean scepticism and the sophistic rejection of traditional beliefs have been discussed extensively by Flacelière and Parker,[3] among others, and they have maintained that this led to an increasing reluctance to consult oracles.

I propose that it was not just these factors that contributed to Delphi's waning influence, but a sequence of events over the course of more than a century that set the stage for the political marginalization of the oracle and thus eliminated the presence of politically motivated pilgrims.

---

[2] Morgan (1989), 36.
[3] See e.g. Parker (1985), 323, on the emerging role of rhetoric and human deliberation in political decisions, and their substitution for public divination; cf. Flacelière (1965).

II. PUBLIC AND PRIVATE PILGRIMAGE IN THE FOURTH CENTURY BCE

For all of its history Delphi attracted both public delegations (*theōriai*) representing their city-states and private individuals, motivated by a desire either to consult the oracle, or to attend festivals, and to perform sacrifices.[4] Our evidence for public delegations tends to be better, since they are well represented in the epigraphic record. Private consultants may in some cases have accompanied public delegations from their cities.[5] It seems likely that both public delegations and private consultants made use of the same institutions:

1. Consultants liaised with a Delphic proxenos assigned to their *polis*, and the same proxenos probably dealt with both public and private consultants.[6]

2. Delphi awarded privileges, such as *promanteia* (priority in order of consultation) to some city-states, and it seems likely that both state delegations and private citizens from the city in question could make use of these.[7]

3. Both public delegations and private consultants presumably consulted the oracle at the same time, i.e., on the one day of the year the oracle was open.[8]

4. Consultants of both types probably enjoyed a guarantee of inviolability in their journey to and from the sanctuary.[9]

---

[4] On the term *theōria*, see Introduction, pp. 12–13.

[5] Cf. *CID* 1.7.

[6] Dillon (1997), 154–5 and n. 23.

[7] For corporate awards of *promanteia*, see Pouilloux (1952). The most well-known and prominently displayed award of *promanteia* was to the Chians, inscribed on their gift to the Delphic sanctuary, the altar before the Temple to Apollo. See *FD* 3.3.213. For a 4th-cent. BCE renewal of *promanteia* for citizens of Thourii, which raised political difficulties with the Tarantines, see Roux (1990).

[8] Originally the 7th day (the day of Apollo's birthday) of Bysios, the 8th month of the Delphic year, falling roughly in March and concurrent with the spring meeting of the Delphic Amphiktyony. Dillon (1997), 153–4; Roux (1979), 3.

[9] Dillon (1997), 28; cf. Thuc. 4.118.1–2 and 5.18.2 for the Delphic award of *asylia* after the Peace of Nikias in 421 BCE.

5. Consultants of both types had to pay taxes in the form of a sacrifice
   and a special type of cake (the *pelanos*) in order to gain access to the
   oracle. There does, however, seem to have been a considerable
   difference in the taxes public delegates and individual pilgrims paid
   to consult the oracle.[10]

Against the background of these similarities it must be recognized that
public delegates and private individuals probably consulted the oracle for
different reasons. For the state, according to Catherine Morgan in a piece
on divination at the Apolline oracles of Delphi and Didyma,

> Oracles . . . enable community authorities to use divine sanction to achieve a
> consensus of opinion over difficult, often unprecedented, and potentially
> divisive decisions. They commonly [sanction] already formulated decisions
> on problems concerning the past or present conduct of the community; oracles
> do not bestow overall divine authority upon particular rulers, nor do they
> predict the future.[11]

Greek oracles did not intervene directly in the politics of an individual
polis, but rather provided sanction for actions already considered at
home, selected and then proposed to the oracle by the consultant.[12]
The oracle was most significant at the time of state formation, colonization, and religious institutionalization in the eighth and seventh
centuries BCE.[13] However, a visit to Delphi might not only resolve an
issue that had divided the decision-makers, but it could also be used as
leverage against other *poleis*.[14] This does not mean that each public
consultation had political overtones beyond the confines of the *polis*, but
oracles that confirmed a *polis'* authority could be used as a political
weapon when necessary.[15] The most obvious context for consulting the
oracle publicly was that of war, to seek sanction for a campaign or for a
radical course of action to reverse a series of losses.[16] Public consultation

---

[10] Eur. *Ion* 226–9; Dillon (1997), 167–8 and n. 87, citing Amandry (1939) 184 ll. 6–
8 with 185–219; *BCH* 68/9 (1944/5), 411–16.

[11] Morgan (1989), 17.

[12] Morgan (1990), 176; contra, Snodgrass (1986), 53–4.

[13] Flacelière (1965); Parker (1985), 298–326.

[14] Parker (1985), 303 and n. 21.

[15] Plut. *Mor.* 435d–e attributes to the oracle benefactions 'in wars and the founding of
cities and in plagues and the failure of crops'.

[16] Parker (1985), 308; cf. 318, where he argues that the Pythia's power was so limited
that she could not realistically influence the outcome of military campaigns.

was usually not intended to settle the internal political or juridical affairs of a *polis*, unless the issues involved religious matters.[17]

For individual consultants at Delphi, we have much less information. But it is probably legitimate to appeal to the much more abundant data from Dodona, in the form of the lead tablets, which show that the prime motivation was to seek advice on mundane courses of action such as marriages, expenditures, business ventures, and travel.[18]

III. ACCESS FOR ATHENIAN DELEGATIONS

Access to the sanctuary for pilgrims, and the fact that Delphi always figured as a political and a financial prize, means that the sanctuary was vulnerable to seizure and pillage. Here, then, let us examine those times in Delphi's history when travel to the sanctuary may have been difficult and dangerous, and investigate what the obstacles were to a successful public consultation—both the purely physical obstacles, such as war, as well as political obstacles, such as a predisposition on the part of the oracle towards one 'faction' or another. I will suggest that a sequence of obstacles that stretch from the Peloponnesian War to Alexander of Macedon's rule contributed substantially to the diminishing importance of international, political pilgrimage to the oracle.

There are instances earlier than the Peloponnesian War that illustrate both the dangers inherent in visiting the sanctuary and the tendency by the oracle to support a particular political faction—typically, an individual *polis*—in times of strife. By the middle of the fifth century BCE Delphi had on numerous occasions fallen prey to a particular power and supported that power in political acts. These included the First Sacred War in the sixth century, when the Amphiktyony wrested control of the sanctuary away from the port of Krisa; the Alkmaeonid bribe of helping to rebuild the Temple of Apollo in the late sixth century, which led to the Spartan-assisted overthrow of the Athenian Peisistratid tyrannical

---

[17] The main exception, of course, is the presentation of the *rhetra* to Sparta by Apollo: Parker (1985), 310–11; Tyrt. fr. 4; Nilsson (1967–74).

[18] For private consultations at Delphi, see Fontenrose (1978); contrast the case of Dodona, where we have a large number of lead tablets, to be edited by Christidis, Dakaris, and Vokotopoulou (forthcoming).

family; and the anti-Hellenic stance of the oracle and the Persian occupation of Delphi in 480 BCE, which did little to deter the Greeks from expressing their gratitude to the oracle with dedications like the serpent-column and the Athenian stoa after the conclusion of the war.[19]

The tradition that Sparta liberated Delphi from Phocian control in the 450s indicates continued competition between the major powers to secure the oracle's support.[20] Delphi responded to the Spartan intervention by declaring herself openly at the onset of the Peloponnesian War. The Spartans asked the oracle if it would be better for them to wage war against the Athenians, and the startlingly direct response was that the Spartans would be victorious if they fought 'with all of their strength' for they would receive assistance from the god Apollo himself; the Spartans subsequently marshalled troops at the sanctuary.[21] This amounts to a stark declaration of partisanship by the oracle, and is very likely to be a direct expression of gratitude to Sparta for her earlier efforts to separate Delphi from Phocian control.

Did this mean that Delphi was unavailable to Athenian pilgrims during the war? To a great extent, probably so; Athenian state pilgrim-ages consulted Dodona and the oracle of Ammon at Siwa during the War,[22] probably because Delphi was in Spartan hands and hence not always accessible. Yet, Athenian envoys did inquire at Delphi about whether to restore the Delians to Delos in the year of the Peace of Nikias, 421 BCE, although this was motivated as much by religious as by political reasons;[23] Argos, an Athenian ally, made a dedication in 414;[24] and on more than one occasion Athenian pilgrims consulted the oracle

---

[19] First Sacred War: Davies (1994); Alkmaionid Bribe: Hdt. 5.55 ff; anti-Hellenic sentiment: e.g. the oracle to the Cretans, Hdt. 7.169, and the oracle to the Athenians, Hdt. 7.139–42.

[20] Thuc. 1.112.5. Parker (1985), 325; cf. Meiggs (1972), 418–20. On the question of the interpretation of *IG* 1.3.9 (= *IG* 1.2.26), which has been taken to be a fragment of an alliance between Athens and the Amphiktyony, see Roux (1979), 44–6 and 239–41; Sanchez (2001), 109–11; Lefèvre (1998), 66 n. 303, 159 n. 38.

[21] Fontenrose H5 (PW137) in 431 BCE; Thuc. 1.118.3, 123.1; 2.54.4; 3.101.1; cf. 121.3. At 2.8.2 Thucydides notes the activity of *chrēsmologoi* at the outbreak of the war; see also Hornblower (1992), 193–4.

[22] Lloyd-Jones (1976), 70; Parker (1985), 308–9 and n. 99.

[23] Fontenrose H8 (PW162); Thuc. 5.32.1; Parker (1985), 308 and n. 38.

[24] Lloyd-Jones (1976); for other dedications during the Peloponnesian War, see Parker (1985), 325 and n. 98.

about other religious matters.[25] The Athenians then maintain a presence at the sanctuary for nearly all of the war only on religious affairs, and this, coupled with the two stipulations in Thucydides (in the armistice of 423 and again in the Peace of Nikias in 421) that access to Delphi be guaranteed,[26] suggests that the shrine had been virtually inaccessible—at least for political consultations—during the Archidamian War.[27] Delphic partisanship had made an Athenian consultation difficult, but did not prevent the Athenians from seeking to restore access to the oracle in a treaty negotiation. Partisanship then was viewed as a temporary, perhaps even a necessary outcome of war, and did not in and of itself tarnish Delphi's reputation sufficiently to dissuade the Athenians from consulting the oracle there.

From 404 to 371 Sparta, which had had a long association with the Delphic oracle, assumed the pre-eminent position among *poleis* in Greece, and no evidence suggests that the support she had had from Delphi in 431 had waned by the battle of Leuktra. In this period we hear of fewer public pilgrimages, and in fact after the battle in 371 consultations of a military nature seem to die out rather quickly. Parker interprets this disinterest as a reflection of a social reality expressed by Xenophon in the Hellenica that 'ancestral custom forbad consulting oracles about wars against other Greek states'.[28] I would suggest that other factors contributed as well.

The earthquake of 373 BCE surely brought to a halt operations at the sanctuary, at least temporarily; we hear little of the earthquake and its repercussions from the literary sources, but we do know from the epigraphic evidence that the rebuilding (which took 40 years) got underway with the help of the Amphiktyony, indicating a continuing desire on the part of the Greeks to secure and stabilize the oracle.[29] We

---

[25] Fontenrose H9 (PW164) and H10 (PW165), during the period 421–415 BCE. For Athenians seeking permission from the Boeotians to consult the Delphic oracle during the war, see Ar. *Birds* 188–9 and *passim* for oracular activity during the war at Delphi, Dodona, and Siwah.

[26] See supra n. 9.

[27] Hornblower (1992), 194 characterizes Athens' status at Delphi (and at Olympia) as 'unloved, but not actually locked out', a generous assessment of the difficulties evidenced by the language of the treaties in 423 and 421.

[28] 3.2.22; Parker (1985), 303 and 309.

[29] See Davies (2001), esp. 213 ff. As Davies indicates (214 and nn. 22–3), the oracle may have ceased to function from the earthquake in 373/2 until Apollo's sanction of Philip of Macedon's treaty with the Chalkidike in 357/6, a considerably lengthy religious privation for pilgrims and an economic hardship for Delphians.

should expect nothing less than a concerted effort by the community of Greeks to maintain one of the oldest and most venerated of all shrines, even if Delphi had begun to lose her relevance in the political sphere. So, although the temple may have been out of service, the severe damage to the sanctuary did not prevent the oracle from operating altogether: in 370 the Delphians themselves consulted the god in the face of the threat of Jason of Pherae, who intended to preside over the Pythian Games and perhaps despoil the sanctuary;[30] and in 356 Philip of Macedon and the Chalkidike sought an oracle confirming the merits of their alliance.[31]

The next significant event at the sanctuary was more devastating than the physical damage wrought by natural causes: the Phocians occupied Delphi for a decade, from 356 to 346, during which they plundered the sanctuary in order to pay the mercenaries in their employ and compelled the Pythia to side with them.[32] In this Third Sacred War, pilgrimage was more severely affected, this time by a despoilment which subsidized the ensuing war against the Amphiktyony. Presumably, citizens of the communities represented on the Amphiktyony— which means virtually every Greek, for the Amphiktyony was a council of twenty-four representatives chosen from the various Greek *ethnē*— could not gain access as pilgrims to the shrine safely,[33] except for those allied with the Phocians—notably, the Athenians. I think this incident had wide-ranging implications for the role of the oracle in the political fortunes of the Greeks, and contributed significantly to the diminishing importance of the oracle in international affairs.

Phocian occupation did not prevent pilgrimage entirely, for we know that Athens consulted the oracle in 352/1 BCE in hopes of deciding whether to lease sacred land in Eleusis.[34] Flacelière[35] and Amandry[36] argue correctly that a religious issue of such paramount importance still required the participation of Pythian Apollo; I would just add that even if this incident did represent a political consultation rather than an exclusively religious one, Athens as a Phocian ally would be expected to

[30] Fontenrose H17 (PW256); Xen. *Hell.* 6.4.30.
[31] Fontenrose H19 (PW260); Tod 158 = *SIG*³ 633; see supra n. 29
[32] Flacelière (1965), 71.
[33] Dillon (1997), 51 and n.95. For thorough studies of the Amphiktyony see Busolt and Swoboda (1926), 1292 ff், and Sànchez (2001).
[34] Fontenrose H21 (PW262); *IG* 22.204 = *SIG*³ 204.
[35] Flacelière (1965), 69–70.
[36] Amandry (1950), 151–3.

have access to Delphi at this point. By this period, however, virtually all of the various types of political pilgrimages disappear from the historical record: treaties, arbitration, military decisions and alliances no longer seek or receive affirmation from Apollo at Delphi.

IV. THE IMPACT OF ALEXANDER

When the Third Sacred War came to a close because of the intervention of Philip of Macedon, resulting in his (and later Alexander's) assumption of the presidency of the Delphic Amphiktyony, Delphic partisanship passed from a Greek *ethnos* to the Macedonian kingdom. The account of Alexander's confrontation with the Pythia—at which he accosted her on a day when she was not prophesying, and she declared him *anikētos* or invincible[37]—even if exaggerated, nonetheless supports the view that Delphi was now under the influence of the Macedonian monarchy.

When soon thereafter Alexander conquered Miletos and re-established democratic rule in the city, he revived the dormant oracle at Didyma[38] *c.* 334 BCE. We have seen that he made a visit to Delphi and received the Pythia's critical assessment; from then on he ignored the Delphic oracle. Why did he now restore the defunct oracle of Didyma and resort to it and later to Zeus Ammon in Siwah? Because these two oracles were situated in the eastern half of the Mediterranean, in what was now the heart of Alexander's empire, and were seats of divination in 'liberated' Asia Minor and Egypt, where local sanction and affirmation of his godhead were essential to gaining and preserving the respect and admiration of the local communities.

As Morgan points out, at first Alexander stressed the panhellenic nature of his campaign, a campaign to avenge the damage wrought by

---

[37] Plut. *Alex.* 14.6–7 relates an incident when Alexander of Macedon came to Delphi to consult the oracle, but he wished to consult the oracle on a day when it was inauspicious and contrary to law; cf. Dillon (1997), 154 and DS 16.25.3 for a similar incident with Philomelos the Phocian. See also Arnush (2002), 153–63.

[38] Callisthenes, historian of Alexander, *FGH* 124 F14; cf. Strabo 17.1.43. The Apollo oracle at Didyma remained silent from the destruction of the temple in 494 until Alexander's victory at the Granicus and subsequent seizure of Miletos: Hdt. 6.18–21; Parke (1985), 35 ff.; Fontenrose (1988), 12–13 and n. 19 (choosing 494 BCE over 479).

Xerxes in 480 BCE, so co-opting Delphi might have been essential at first.[39] Although perhaps in Alexander's own eyes he was the legitimate heir to his father's presidency of the League of Corinth, and to Greece's need for vengeance against the Persians for Xerxes' invasion 150 years earlier, to the Greeks—at least to Demosthenes and the Athenians—he offered no better than the continuation of a tyrannical regime, and will have sought sanction to legitimize his claim. Soon, as his attention shifted eastward, his relationship with mainland Greece became poorly defined and regulated; instead, Didyma and, to a lesser extent, Siwah, became oracular centres available and more attractive to the Macedonian monarch and his successors.

It should come as no surprise, then, that the oracular assessment of Alexander's divinity came not from Delphi but from Siwah in Egypt—not only because it was politically expedient for the new Macedonian-cum-Egyptian pharoah to receive divine sanction in Egypt, but just as importantly because a Delphic proclamation was no longer import-ant—to the Greeks, to the Egyptians or to the Macedonian monarch for that matter.[40]

Morgan's work on Didyma strengthens considerably my argument that it was Delphi in particular, not oracles in general, that no longer played a role in political matters. Where Delphic oracles now focused on 'marriages, mules and money', the oracle at Didyma entertained a multitude of questions from the citizens of Miletos dealing with local and interstate politics[41]; it was essential in helping Miletos to carve out a relationship with the Seleucid (and other) dynasties,[42] and in sanction-ing political, religious, and economic decisions.[43] But by the Roman

---

[39] Morgan (1989), 29.

[40] Callisthenes and later sources certainly characterize the consultation at Ammon as divine sanction, but it was an expression of divine will over an already formulated decision. Alexander surely already assumed himself to be of divine parentage; then, his earlier consultation at Delphi, a non-oracular divination, if you will, was not a prediction of his invincibility in the coming Asian campaign, but instead—at least to Plutarch and, if the story is true, to Alexander also—the recognition of what Alexander already knew, presumably predicated on his performances at Chaironeia and against the Maedi. He was invincible in those campaigns, and would be again in Asia.

[41] Morgan (1989), 31; Fontenrose, (1988), 16 ff.

[42] Morgan (1989), 37; Parke (1985), 44–6, 57–8.

[43] Fontenrose (1988), 105. For oracles of probable authenticity in the period 331 BCE—363 CE that addressed issues of political concern, see the Catalogue of Didymaean Responses in Fontenrose (1988), esp. nos. 4–13, 33, 41–3; Parke (1985), 59–64.

period, Didyma too lost her political relevance, as Rome chose other avenues to formulate and/or resolve issues.[44]

Delphi, since it was not like Didyma in being under the control of one state, managed to maintain its political popularity from around 750 to 350 BCE, a remarkable run for a religious institution. It emerged during a time of considerable transition in religious organization and political authority, and survived attacks upon Greek traditional modes of organization during the Persian Wars and the national strife of the Peloponnesian War, and only really began to succumb to external pressures as a result of the decade-long presence of the Phocians during the Third Sacred War.

This sequence of events—from Spartan influence in 431 BCE until Macedonian control in the 320s—amounted to a series of fatal blows to Delphi's prestige as an instigator, arbiter, and mediator of political affairs in Greece, for effectively over the course of a century Delphi was either closely aligned with the Spartans, severely damaged by the earthquake, occupied by the Phocians, or in the hands of the Macedonians. With the oracle under first Phocian and then Macedonian control for over thirty years, the sanctuary pillaged and the tenor of the times already inclined away from public consultation, it comes as no surprise that the oracle virtually ceased to play a role in Greek political affairs. Athenian embassies on political missions had steered clear of Delphi for nearly 150 years, and an aversion to consulting Delphi on political matters was so ingrained in the Athenian psyche that other more viable options substituted for, and eventually replaced, the Delphic oracle.

That Athens consulted Dodona rather than Delphi in the years after the Third Sacred War[45] lends credence to this position, and so when Demosthenes accused Delphi of Philippizing in 339 BCE,[46] his comments reflect a political reality that decades of partisanship had, in the end, marginalized Delphi's political relevance.[47]

---

[44] For the role of the oracles at Didyma and Klaros during the Imperial period, at the expense of Delphi, see Fontenrose (1988), 22–3. Throughout the Hellenistic age, the Didymaean oracle served primarily the needs of Milesian citizens: Fontenrose (1988), 104–5. See also Parke (1985), 64–8 and chs. 5–6 (Didyma), 7–8 (Klaros).

[45] Lloyd-Jones (1976), 70.

[46] Aeschines 3.130; cf. Parker (1985), 316, 325.

[47] Parker (1985), Appendix, 324–6, considers this act of bribery a fairly isolated case, and although he does cite some instances of oracular trustworthiness, the number of

V. THE AETOLIAN PERIOD

This pattern of decline is sustained during the period of Aetolian domination in third and second centuries BCE, when there is little evidence for political consultation at Delphi. Awards of collective *promanteia* ('priority in consultation') and individual *proxenia* both suggest Delphi's diminished importance. Pouilloux's study of group-*promanteia* reveals that such awards peaked in the fourth century and declined significantly during the Hellenistic period, while awards of *promanteia* to individuals continued unabated.[48] The decrease in communal grants of *promanteia* may well reflect the increasing irrelevance of state-sponsored consultation of the oracle.

One significant exception to this trend would seem to be the Matrophanes Decree of 211 BCE, in which the city of Delphi, in response to the presence of Matrophanes of Sardis, whom it describes as '*theopropos* and ambassador', proclaims that it is appointing itself *proxenos* for Sardis, and that it undertakes in this role to sacrifice on his behalf (a highly anomalous procedure, since the role of *proxenos* would normally have been held by a citizen of Delphi). *Prima facie* this looks like evidence for a state delegation consulting the oracle, but, tellingly, the decree justifies the anomalous arrangement on the grounds that 'men of Sardis have not been able to come to the oracle for a long time'. Neither Sardis nor the Sardians, then, had been regularly consulting Delphi in recent history, despite the conspicuous precedence for a Sardian consultation in Croesus' overture to Delphi centuries before.[49]

Awards to private citizens—of *promanteia*, *proxenia* and so on—are also significant for a different reason. If Delphi continued to have political importance in this period, we would expect that many of the awards would come from states with political significance, but this is not so. Of the four hundred individuals so honoured with *proxenia* in the third century BCE, during the period of the Aitolian protectorate, only thirteen are Aitolians, six of whom receive *proxenia* prior to the Aitolian

incidents of Delphic partisan politics he lists undermines his argument that there was no pattern to Delphic biases.

[48] Pouilloux (1952), 484–513, esp. 488–92. On awards of *promanteia* at the oracle at Didyma, see Fontenrose (1988), 105.

[49] *SIG* 548; see Pouilloux (1974). See supra p. 97 and n.1

defeat of the Gauls in 279, and the remainder appear sporadically over the course of the rest of the century.[50] That only 3 per cent of those honoured are Aitolians—at a time when Aitolia comes to dominate the Amphiktyony, when the festival of the Soteria celebrated a political and military victory for the Greeks at Delphi and presumably had its individual heroes who were well-deserving of being singled out with gestures of *proxenia* and other honours, and when we should expect to see the strongest connection between political influence and subsequent honorifics—indicates that the political tenor of the times had no significant connection on awards given to visitors to the sanctuary.[51] In fact, the overall *proxenia* corpus from this period does little to guide us: among these same four hundred honorands, individuals from seven *poleis* receive one-third of the awards, and while some of the *poleis* that predominate seem logical—Athens, Thebes, and Aitolia—others appear with some frequency but little explanation.[52] The Pythian Games may have continued for centuries, but the oracle's role in Greek political affairs had come to a halt. Similarly, awards of *promanteia* to private citizens, whose frequency did not abate in the Hellenistic age as did the communal awards, were made to citizens from disparate *poleis* with no particular political import or influence.[53]

---

[50] 300–279: *FD* 3.1.142 (295/4?); 3.1.145 (293/2?); 3.1.149, 150 (282/1?); 1.143, 144 (280/79?); 279–200: *FD* 3.1.198; *SIG*[3] 417 (273/2); *GDI* 2595 (268/7); *GDI* 2590 (261/0?); *FD* 3.1.199; *FD* 3.1.147, 148 (237/6?). *SIG*[3] 418A (272/1) is for an individual residing in Aitolia. The dates are from Flacelière (1937), App. II, and many remain in some doubt, but all of these texts can be dated with confidence to the 3rd cent. BCE.

[51] The case of Chios substantiates this interpretation. Chios joins the Amphiktyonic Council mid-3rd cent. (Flacelière (1937), App. II.55, dates this to 243/2; Scholten (2000), App. Table A3, assigns the entrance of Chios to the Council to 251/0[?] or 247/6[?]), while only four of the seven Chiotes honoured with *proxenia* in the 3rd cent. BCE receive their awards after Chios' inclusion on the Council; the earliest occurs as much as a decade afterwards—*SIG3* 447, which dates to the late 240s or 230s.

[52] The seven *poleis* most heavily represented are Athens (37), Megara (28), Thebes (13), Megalopolis (13), Aitolia (13), Pellana (11), and Rhodes (11). That all but two of these *poleis* had erected treasuries or other major monuments at Delphi (some as recently as the Rhodian chariot of *c*.304 and the Aitolian stoa of *c*.279) may indicate that awards of proxeny are based on long-standing relationships between the sanctuary and its greatest benefactors. But how to explain the relatively high frequency of awards of *proxenia* to citizens of Megalopolis or Pellana, whose *poleis* had not left an indelible mark at Delphi to date?

[53] For example, there are 15 awards to Keians, 28 to Megarians, 12 to Pellanians, 14 to Megapolitans, and 10 to Thebans.

When in 279 BCE the Aitolians saved Delphi from the invading Gauls, and established their dominance over the sanctuary for the next century, such an act of occupation prompted virtually no response from the community of Greek *poleis* and Hellenistic monarchies. The Delphic oracle was no longer relevant on the international stage as a political player. The defeat of the Gauls may have prompted the establishment of the penteteric festival of the Soteria, reorganized in the mid-third century, to celebrate in ways akin to the Pythian Games, but the epigraphic record reveals no sudden influx of politically motivated consultations of the oracle, even though the festival found its origins in a political event. The great festivals of Delphi attracted large numbers of *theōroi*, pilgrims, and other visitors, perhaps on an even greater scale than in the classical period, and the oracle continued to be consulted by private citizens, but now almost exclusively for 'marriages, money and mules'. Delphi had, then, by the early third century, already ceased to attract visitors to settle diplomatic affairs, and not even the creation of another panhellenic festival could prevent its increasing irrelevance.

CONCLUSION

What we see at Delphi is not the decline of oracular consultation on personal matters, but the gradual marginalization of oracular prophecy in international and political affairs. Recall the second-century BCE inscription providing *proxenoi* for citizens of 135 cities;[54] private pilgrimage remained popular well into the Hellenistic period. Only in Plutarch's day 300 years later, when he tells us there is one Pythia instead of three,[55] do we have clear evidence that interest in private consultation finally waned.

---

[54] *SIG*³ 585.
[55] Plut. *Mor.* 414b.

4

'Pilgrimage' and Greek Religion:

Sacred and Secular in the Pagan *Polis*

Scott Scullion

A recent monograph and several journal articles as well as some of the contributions to the present volume are devoted to the study of 'pilgrimage' among pagan Greeks, and so it seems likely that this new subfield is here to stay. Nevertheless—and thanks to the open-mindedness of the editors—I shall here argue that the term and concept 'pilgrimage' are misleading rather than illuminating in their application to Greek practice, and should therefore be used, if at all, only with explicit and thorough qualification.

At bottom, my objections are two: that the word 'pilgrimage' elicits associations appropriate to the 'world religions' but inappropriate in fundamental ways to Greek paganism, and that, partly because this failure to register fundamental differences encourages other kinds of vague generalization, students of Greek 'pilgrimage' tend both to confuse distinct sacred practices one with another and to interpret essentially secular practices as sacred.

These objections are based on certain premises about the nature of Greek religion, and in particular on the view, widely rejected nowadays, that the Greeks clearly distinguished secular from sacred, which need at least to be made clear, though they cannot here be justified in adequate detail. By way of placing in its broader context the detailed discussion of 'pilgrimage' that follows, I therefore turn first to these general matters.

SACRED AND SECULAR IN THE GREEK *POLIS*

It is widely taken for granted these days that, as Bruit Zaidman and
Schmitt Pantel put it in their introductory book on Greek religion, 'in
the world of the Greek cities the opposition between the sacred and the
profane—which we assume to be fundamental in the area of religion—
was either blurred or utterly irrelevant'. Burkert, by contrast, speaks in
Greek Religion of a distinction between sacred and profane, noting that
'it is presupposed that the sacred does not constitute the entire world
and does not lay infinite claims on men'.[1] Burkert's discussion is careful
and thorough, and it seems difficult to do justice to the Greek material
without employing this distinction, as the hedging of Bruit Zaidman
and Schmitt Pantel perhaps suggests. Anthropologists and latterly Hellenists have made heavy weather of the sacred/profane dichotomy
largely on the basis of the exaggerated formulation of it in a single
famous passage of Durkheim:

> Whether simple or complex, all known religious beliefs display a common
> feature: They presuppose a classification of the real or ideal things that men
> conceive of into two classes—two opposite genera—that are widely designated
> by two distinct terms, which the words *profane* and *sacred* translate fairly well.
> The division of the world into two domains, one containing all that is sacred
> and the other all that is profane—such is the distinctive trait of religious
> thought.[2]

In this form, as an absolute dichotomy of mutually exclusive things, the
distinction has proved of marginal utility at best. It is obviously unnecessary, however, to operate the distinction in these Durkheimian
terms, and so curious that the Hellenists who have recently called it into
question take Durkheim's extreme formulation as their point of reference; in practice, anthropologists and historians of religion seem to find
a non-absolute distinction of sacred from profane indispensable.[3]

---

[1] Bruit Zaidman and Schmitt Pantel (1992), 8; Burkert (1985), 269–70.
[2] Durkheim (1912), 34; note however that Durkheim himself speaks of the process
by which things can pass from one realm to the other (36–7).
[3] Connor (1988) uses the Durkheim passage as his epigraph, but is aware that it does
not represent the state of the art (cf. however his remarks at 184); he also allows that the
distinction is in certain contexts useful. Bremmer (1998), on the other hand, directs his
criticism at the dichotomy as defined by Durkheim. He notes, e.g., that 'in their

The Greeks made both a conceptual and a linguistic distinction between sacred and profane. Jan Bremmer has recently concluded otherwise, noting that the Greeks 'split up "the sacred" into a number of words' and claiming that they 'had not developed a term for "the profane" '.[4] Yet even this strictly lexical argument cannot stand. The fact that Greek—like many other languages, including English—has a specialized vocabulary for differentiated aspects of the sacred clearly does not preclude its having a distinction between the sacred and the profane, and it *does* have a vocabulary of 'the profane'. There is first of all the common phrase τὰ ἱερὰ καὶ τὰ ὅσια 'sacred matters and secular (or profane) matters', terms which were also applied to distinct categories of business before the Athenian *boulē*.[5] ὅσια 'profane', varies in this polar pairing with ἴδια or δημόσια, 'private' or 'public',[6] and inscriptions contain such oppositions as τὰ θῖνα καὶ τὰ ἀντρόπινα, 'sacred and human', and τὰ θῖνα καὶ τὰ πολιτικά, 'sacred and political', which

Durkheimian meaning the terms "the sacred" and "the holy" are still absent from the most recent edition of the *Oxford English Dictionary*' (30), and largely on this basis speaks of the distinction as originating or being redefined and as 'invented' (in inverted commas) around 1900 (31). Of these three descriptions, only 'redefinition' seems at all justified; a distinction between 'holy' and 'profane', in a sense not radically dissimilar to Durkheim's, has been familiar to speakers of English since well before 1900, e.g. from such biblical passages as Ezekiel 22:26, Hebr. 10:29 and, conceptually rather than verbally, but certainly famously, Mark 12:17 (Caesar's things and God's). Bremmer presents his own arguments as supplementing those with which Goody (1961) and Evans-Pritchard (1965) 'wiped the floor with' Durkheim. Both of these writers have a tendency to conflate the distinction of sacred and profane with that of supernatural and natural: Goody (1961), 156 speaks explicitly of 'the sacred-profane, supernatural-natural dichotomy', and Evans-Pritchard (1965), 65 uses as an argument for the intermingling of sacred and profane evidence from his field work for a lack of distinction in sickness between 'physical symptoms' and 'spiritual intervention'. This conflation was certainly not intended by Durkheim, yet it is the supernatural-natural dichotomy that is the principal target of both Goody and Evans-Pritchard, both of whom themselves employ a general (non-Durkheimian in the sense of non-absolute) distinction of sacred from profane or religious from secular (or 'non-religious'): see Goody (1961), 159, who makes a basic and terminological distinction between ceremonials 'which celebrate mystical powers' and those 'which have an exclusively secular significance'; Evans-Pritchard (1965), 111–12, cf. 8. This general sort of sacred/profane distinction is endlessly recurrent and probably indispensable in religious studies; in Goody (1997), e.g., an important cross-cultural study of ambivalence about representation, Goody often traces the source of the ambivalence to concerns about the distinction of sacred from secular: see 99–100, 138–42, 150, and esp. 258–9 (cf. 249 for appropriate qualification).

[4] Bremmer (1998), 30.
[5] Connor (1988) collects most of the passages. Agenda of the *boulē*: *Ath. Pol.* 43.4.
[6] e.g. Solon 4.12 West and Hdt. 8.109.

makes it clear that in such contexts τὰ ὅσια are profane or secular things, even though this is a semantic specialization of what is by origin a sacral term.[7] English 'profane' comes from the Latin word meaning etymologically what is 'away from' or 'outside the temple', and the words 'secular' and 'lay' are also etymologically opposed to religious terms: the secular is the temporal as opposed to the eternal, and the lay is the λαικός as opposed to the κληρικός, what belongs to the people rather than the clerics. None of this constitutes an argument that either the Greeks or speakers of English are confused about the distinction between sacred and secular; it merely reflects the unsurprising fact that the secular is originally defined by contrast with the sacred.

What do we moderns mean by 'the profane'? In a narrower, technical sense the term more often than not signifies what is offensive from a religious point of view ('profanity' in the sense of blasphemous speech, for example). In the general sense, however, 'profane' or the more frequent 'secular' indicates (as in Burkert's formulation) what is *neutral* in respect of the sacred or not under religious authority. I see no justification for the assumption that the Greeks could not conceive of such a religiously neutral realm, though Greeks like moderns will have had various attitudes about whether, under what circumstances, and to what degree certain matters in the 'secular' realm might also be of religious significance. Even among moderns, surely, the concept of the 'secular' need not imply hostility to religion or commitment to some such cause as Weberian 'rationalization' or 'modernization'.[8]

In an influential article, W. R. Connor recognizes the existence of the Greek distinction, speaking of 'two separate but co-ordinated realms'. He argues, however, that the co-ordination of sacred with profane is more important than the distinction between them, insisting (in rather vague language) that the linguistic collocation ἱερὰ καί ὅσια 'is an indicator of a much deeper and more recurrent way of looking at the *polis*', 'an expression of a deeper structure'. Connor's points that in the Greek *polis* sacred and secular are often closely coordinated and that it is regarded as important that both flourish are valid but hardly surprising; the word 'deeper', however, suggests that the distinction is somehow

---

[7] Inscriptions: *IC* IV 72.x (*Leg.Gort.*), *SIG*³ 526.29, 35. Other passages and further bibliography are collected by Connor (1988), 162 nn. 4–5.

[8] See esp. Weber (1925); ch. 2 on Weber in Habermas (1981) is the most comprehensive and acute discussion.

superficial or trivial. Connor seems inclined to privilege the sacred realm and to regard the secular as a subset of it, but to my mind his evidence does not justify this conclusion.[9]

Let me offer two examples of the Greek distinction in action, one fairly technical, the other more general. The first is highly relevant to the issue of Greek 'pilgrimage'. 'Profane' literally means what is 'in front of' the temple, and this corresponds to the fact that in the Roman as in the Greek world prominent sanctuaries have both a sacred inner precinct, often walled off, and a surrounding, non-sacred area where visitors to festivals would be put up.[10] Aischylos in *Suppliants* (501) refers to such a secondary area as a βέβηλον ἄλσος, a 'profane grove', literally 'treadable' as opposed to the untreadable ἄβατον or sacred precinct. Ulrich Sinn has recently claimed that inner precinct and surrounding facilities are equally sacred, but his evidence is thin and unpersuasive.[11] Let us note for future reference that cultural and athletic facilities—dancing-grounds, theatres and *stadia*—are as a rule situated in the non-sacred area of the sanctuary. The temples and altars of a sanctuary were within the walls of the inner precinct, and so the sacrificial rituals would take place there. The topography of the Greek sanctuary is thus a very concrete manifestation of the distinction between sacred ritual events on the one hand and non-sacred or at most very vaguely sacred cultural and athletic events on the other.

---

[9] Connor (1988), 177, 176. Connor writes at one point of 'the sacred and the ostensibly secular' (171), which again seems based rather on predilection than on evidence. Connor's very schematic comparison (173–4) of the relationship between Agora (secular) and Akropolis (sacred) is based on a false dichotomy: the Agora is hardly an exclusively secular 'space'.

[10] See e.g. Tomlinson (1976), 19.

[11] Sinn (1993), 165–6, who offers two pieces of evidence: (1) Pindar's description of Herakles' foundation of the sanctuary at Olympia (*Ol.* 10.43–49), where Herakles is said to have marked off the 'hallowed grove' of the Altis (the inner, sacred precinct) and then to have 'established (θῆκε) the plain all round as a resting-place for the banquet'. There is no implication here that the 'plain all round' is sacred space, as the Altis explicitly is. Sinn translates θῆκε as 'set apart'; this may be the basis of his argument, but if so the verb does not justify it. 2) Votive offerings, which 'according to Greek sacred law...could be deposited only inside the sanctuary', were discarded in wells in the outer area at Olympia. The votives were sealed in the wells together with cooking-refuse, so apparently this votive-trash was conveniently dumped with other trash; this hardly constitutes compelling or sufficient evidence for Sinn's general claim.

My second example comes from Robert Parker's comprehensive study of the use of Greek oracles by Greek states. Oracles are constantly consulted on cultic matters, though more often than not, on these matters as on all others, what was sought from and provided by the oracle was confirmation of decisions already taken by the state. But, as Parker puts it, 'There is one very significant reserved area about which oracles were almost never consulted in the historical period: the internal politics, legislation, and jurisdiction of the state.'[12] The state thus avoids being hampered or even much influenced in its secular business by the one kind of religious institution, the panhellenic, that is not, like the *polis* cults, under its direct control. Even the practice of oracle consultation, then, reflects not only a clear distinction between sacred and secular, but a manifest subordination of sacred to secular.

Even those who suppose that the Greeks lacked a thoroughgoing distinction between secular and sacred would still have to face up to the question whether the Greeks tended to see things in general in what to us would seem more 'sacred' or more 'secular' terms. The present tendency is to assume the former, but this is merely an assumption, and there are good reasons for regarding the opposite conclusion as closer to the truth.

It seems to me helpful here to draw on anthropological models and parallels. Clifford Geertz applies to his analysis of Balinese society a model of polar types of religion derived from Weber. 'Traditional religions', says Geertz,

consist of a multitude of very concretely defined and only loosely ordered sacred entities, an untidy collection of fussy ritual acts and vivid animistic images which are able to involve themselves in an independent, segmental and immediate manner with almost any sort of actual event. Such systems (for, despite their lack of formal regularity, they are systems) meet the perennial concerns of religion . . .—evil, suffering, frustration, bafflement and so on—piecemeal. They attack them opportunistically as they arise in each particular instance . . . employing one or another weapon chosen, on grounds of symbolic appropriateness, from their cluttered arsenal of myth and magic.

What Weber called 'rationalized religions', on the other hand, 'disenchant' the world by drawing the diffused sacral powers of the traditional

---

[12] Parker (1985), 90 (in the reprint).

religion together into a centralized, comprehensive conceptual system that is more abstract and logically coherent.[13] Weber regarded the earlier forms of Greek religion as 'traditional' in this sense, and saw 'Greek rationalism', that is Greek philosophy, as its 'rationalized' successor. Philosophy is not religion, and Greek religion in its 'traditional' form continued not only to operate in the old way but to be the dominant cultural model for most Greeks well into the Hellenistic period. There are serious problems with this and other aspects of Weber's model, but the basic polarity, as developed by Geertz, seems to me illuminating for our understanding of the Greeks.

We still do not reckon adequately with the fact that Greek paganism, unlike any modern international religion, is a very radically non-centralized conglomerate, fitting very well into the category of 'traditional' religions. Modern scholars, under the influence of 'rationalized' religious traditions, still tend to look for overarching and co-ordinated meanings in Greek religion and to overlook its diffuse nature and piecemeal functionality. Can we get any sense of the lived reality of their traditional religion for ordinary Greeks? Referring to the detailed ritual prescriptions of the decree of the religious club of the Salaminioi, J. K. Davies remarks: 'It is a fair guess that for most people most of the time such rituals and sacrifices formed the central core of religious observance, unaffected by the meanings of myths, the complications of a polytheistic theology, or the awkward challenges of rationalism and scepticism.'[14] To many of those working on Greek cultural history today this would sound antediluvian, but Davies's instinct is strikingly

---

[13] Geertz (1973), 172; the whole of ch. 7, ' "Internal Conversion" in Contemporary Bali' is relevant; cf. also ch. 6, 'Ritual and Social Change: A Javanese Example'. These particular essays attempt an analysis of the dynamics of social change, an issue difficult to deal with on the model of 'culture' as an all-embracing (and in many ways reified) whole, which tends to obscure on principle socio-economic and personal factors. Geertz's commitment to this sort of model—though in a far more cautious and qualified form (see e.g. Geertz (1973), 10–11, 20, 407–8) than it takes in the work of many of those he has influenced—comes out in this quotation in his emphasis on traditional religion as a 'system', an inheritance from the social-scientific theory (and organizational model for the social sciences) of Talcott Parsons. Habermas (1981), ch. 7 analyses Parsons's theories, bringing out in particular the fundamental problems with his attempt to combine an action-theoretical with a systems-theoretical model, an attempt which opened the way to a cultural-determinist approach. For critical appraisal of Geertz's model of 'culture', its intellectual antecedents and development, and his method of cultural analysis see Kuper (1999), ch. 2–3.

[14] Davies (1993), 171.

confirmed by Geertz's fieldwork in Bali. Balinese religion is, or was when Geertz studied it in the 1950s, very much of the 'traditional' type. 'Beyond a minimal level', he says,

> there is almost no interest in doctrine, or generalized interpretation of what is going on, at all. The stress is on orthopraxy, not orthodoxy—what is crucial is that each ritual detail should be correct and in place. . . . But the conceptual side is of much less moment: the worshippers usually don't even know who the gods in the temples are, are uninterested in the meaning of the rich symbolism, and are indifferent to what others may or may not believe. You can believe virtually anything you want to actually, including that the whole thing is rather a bore, and even say so. But if you do not perform the ritual duties for which you are responsible you will be totally ostracized.[15]

Sokrates, we remember, counters the accusation that he is impious by pointing out that he regularly performed his ritual duties, and ends his life by making sure that the cock he owes Asklepios is sacrificed. As has often been observed, Sokrates' ritual rather than doctrinal model of piety was in normal circumstances—not, that is, in the context of an intensely political trial—the operative one.[16]

The problem of the sacred/profane dichotomy can profitably be reconsidered in these terms. In the modern West the ideology of the secular state can conflict fundamentally with the claims of what are, by comparison with 'traditional' religions, highly 'rationalized' and centralized modern religions. In pagan religion there was never anything remotely like the kind of thoroughgoing rationalization that marks the modern Church, and so the conditions requiring a confrontation between it and the secular state were simply not present. The unsystematical structure of traditional Greek religion means first that there is plenty of room for an autonomous realm of the secular, and secondly that where there is disjunction between secular concerns and sacred traditions the former can be met largely through accretions, reshufflings and shifts of meaning that reshape the sacred tradition rather than through general ideological opposition that rejects it. In pagan terms, the sacred normally coexists comfortably with the secular: an unproblematized ritual tradition, taken very much for granted, can accompany unproblematically a wide range of social, political, and cultural ideologies. The relationship between sacred and secular never needs to

---

[15] Geertz (1973), 177.   [16] See e.g. Burkert (1985), 274–5.

be worked out in a *systematic* way, and so is equally easy whether they are operating independently or in combination.[17] A residual tendency to conceive paganism on the model of a modern 'rationalized' religion continues to distort our understanding of the distinction between sacred and profane in the Greek world.

PILGRIMAGE AND THE GREEKS

We are now in a position to consider the topic of Greek 'pilgrimage' in an adequately broad context, and to turn from airy generalities to the very earthy personification of Theoria in Aristophanes' *Peace*.[18] Theoria's name, which literally means 'viewing', is the term for an institution of the Greek *polis*; she personifies the delegations sent by city-states to international, especially panhellenic festivals, or what we are now asked to call 'state pilgrimage', and she can I think help us see where the pilgrimage model goes wrong.

Peace was produced in the year 421 BCE, probably only a few days before the swearing of the peace of Nikias. Our hero Trygaios rides a dung-beetle to Zeus' palace in the sky to question him about the war, only to discover that in their anger with the Greeks the gods have decamped, leaving Polemos, personified war, in residence. Polemos has shut Peace up in a cave, but Trygaios with other Greeks frees her. Peace is represented by a statue, but turns out to be accompanied by two female attendants, Opora or 'Harvest' and Theoria. Trygaios takes them back to Athens, where he restores Theoria to the *boulē* (the Athenian Council), inaugurates the cult-image of Peace with sacrifices, and marries Opora.

Everything to do with Theoria in this play is profoundly—or perhaps I should say superficially—sexual. Commentators have generally taken the view that Theoria represents the pleasure of individuals in 'shows' of all kinds rather than specifically that of official delegates to international festivals, but a number of sexual jokes in the play reinforce the natural

---

[17] Sanctuary-asylum was perhaps the most persistent cause of conflict between sacred and secular. Chaniotis (1996*b*) gives a thorough account of the various Greek strategies for limiting and getting round the right of asylum; practical progress in this respect might be accompanied by protestations of devotion to the priority of sacred custom, which I am less inclined than Chaniotis to take at face value.

[18] See also Rutherford (1998*b*), 141–5.

inference that it is attendance at *international* festivals that is primarily affected by the war. When the Greeks begin celebrating Peace before they have actually hauled her out of the cave, Trygaios tells them that there will be plenty of time later: πλεῖν, μένειν, κινεῖν, καθεύδειν, εἰς πανηγύρεις θεωρεῖν 'to favour sailing or to refuse, to have a shag or take a snooze, to go on delegations to the festivals' (341–2). Πανηγύρεις are international festivals, and in that context the verb θεωρεῖν, 'go on a *theōriā*', must refer primarily to official *polis* delegations. Such delegations seem to have consisted largely of members of the *boulē*, and were almost certainly appointed by it. Aristophanes stresses the link between Theoria and the *boulē*, to whom she used to belong and to whom she is to be returned (713–15). So too the sexual adventures Trygaios's slave thinks of when he meets Theoria are connected with festivals: he asks 'is this the Theoria we used to bang to Brauron?', observes 'that's quite a quadrennial keester she's got there', and is soon 'staking out a spot for my erection—of a tent—at the Isthmian Games' (872–80). Brauron may be chosen because of the connection of the cult of Artemis there with young girls, and the Isthmia for a pun on ἰσθμός, 'narrow passage', in a sexual sense, but the reference to the penteteric or four-year cycle of major festivals cannot be explained in this way and must be introduced for its own sake. Trygaios then takes Theoria toward the βουλευτικόν, the section of the theatre auditorium where members of the *boulē* sat, has her strip naked, and as he returns her to them jokes that they can now hold an athletic contest—consisting, needless to say, of sexual events. He concludes with a joke, which turns on the last word, ἐκεχειρία which is a technical term for truces such as the Ὀλυμπιακὴ ἐκεχειρία declared for the holding of panhellenic festivals—that is for the sending of delegations, θεωρίαι by the *boulē*— but which literally means 'hands off'. Translating freely to bring out the joke:

Chairmen, receive Theoria. Look how enthusiastically the chairman welcomed her—clearly a 'hands-on approach' there! Wouldn't have been like that though if you'd had to introduce some business without a bribe—in that case I'd have found you upholding the festival truce—keeping your hands off![19]

---

[19] Aristoph. *Peace* 905–8: Θέασ᾽ ὡς προθύμως ὁ πρύτανις παρεδέξατο. Ἀλλ᾽ οὐκ ἄν, εἴ τι προῖκα προσαγαγεῖν σ᾽ ἔδει, ἀλλ᾽ ηὗρον ἄν σ᾽ ὑπέχοντα τὴν ἐκεχειρίαν. On this passage, see Rutherford (1998*b*), 144–5.

All of this presents us with something of a conundrum. In Aristophanes, Theoria is clearly a goodtime girl, associated with festivals, shows, and games and above all with sexual congress, which was of course subject to strict purity restrictions in Greek sanctuaries and cultic practice.[20] All Greek festivals had a religious component, but Theoria apparently has nothing to do with religious activity as such. This coheres with the fact that the noun θεωρός becomes a standard Greek term for 'ambassador', a political or secular rather than a sacred role. So far so good, and the translators seem to catch the spirit of the thing by calling Theoria 'Holiday' or 'Showtime'. But now along come the students of pilgrimage to tell us that in the context of festivals *theōria* is a technical term of Greek religion. Ian Rutherford suggests that in this context *theōria* should be translated as 'state pilgrimage', and in general points to the family of words sharing the root θεα- as the Greek equivalent of our 'pilgrimage' terms.[21] Is the Theoria of Aristophanes' play, then, henceforth to be known in English as 'Pilgrimage'? Perhaps no one would go that far, but is the portrayal of Theoria in the play a distortion of reality, ignoring for comic purposes the fact that *theōria* was essentially a religious institution belonging to the anthropological category of 'pilgrimage'? It seems a little odd that Aristophanes should so clearly mark as secular a real religious institution while marking as religious what was an invented cult, the actual cult of Peace at Athens not being founded until 375 BCE.[22] I suggest that, though of course exaggeratedly sexual, the personification of *theōria* in the play corresponds in essentials to the general conception of the institution, and is in fact excellent evidence that the problem lies rather in the notion that Greeks practised 'pilgrimage'.

Is there anything in classical Greek religion it makes sense to call 'pilgrimage'? Before attempting to answer this question we really ought to have a clear idea what the English term itself refers to. This is a contentious issue, and there's the risk that 'pilgrimage' may go the way of a perfectly good word like 'initiation', which has been made to mean so much that it ends up meaning very little. Perhaps I can simply say that Simon Coleman and Jaś Elsner make out a good case for a functional

---

[20] See Parker (1983), 74–9.
[21] Rutherford (2000a), 133–6.
[22] See Parker (1996), 229–30 with n. 45.

definition of pilgrimage as the widespread phenomenon of sacred travel.[23] They speak of the 'sacred centre' as the goal of pilgrimage, but their phrase 'sacred travel' suggests that the journey itself is a sacred activity, and they show that it has been regarded as such in Hindu, Buddhist, Christian, and Muslim tradition.[24] The pilgrim is etymologically a *peregrinus*, a 'foreigner', and though some pilgrims never enter foreign territory in a political sense, both technical and metaphorical usage of the term shows that they do so in a religious or spiritual sense by leaving behind the ordinary round of life in their familiar cultural and social setting. In all the great living religions, pilgrims have a special status, usually visibly marked, from the time they set out from home, and are both literal and spiritual journeymen.

This central aspect of pilgrimage is completely missing in Greece. It is true that attendance at panhellenic festivals was facilitated by truces, and that these are always called 'sacred truces',[25] but there is nothing markedly sacred about the terminology employed to distinguish them from other Greek truces, and like other truces they were often broken. Indeed, disputes between the Eleians and the Spartans in 399 BCE and the Eleians and the Arkadians in 364, which were ostensibly over such truces and the control of the festival at Olympia, led in both cases to battles fought in the sanctuary itself, spectacular offences from a religious point of view which prove that secular rather than sacred motives were at play.[26]

So far as our evidence goes, neither official delegates nor private wayfarers to Greek sanctuaries and festivals were distinguished by any special attire. We do know of three or four fully ritualized processions between sacred sites, of which the Pythian *theōria* of the Athenians to Delphi, subject of a classic study by Boëthius, is the best known. But Boëthius regarded these few processions as constituting a distinctive group, pointing out that they probably originated in actual transfer-

---

[23] Coleman and Elsner (1995), 6, 206–8.

[24] Coleman and Elsner (1995), 141, 149–53; 186–95; 88–9; 58–61.

[25] See e.g. Dillon (1997), 1–8.

[26] 399 BCE: Xen. *Hell.* 3.2.23–31; Paus. 3.8.3–6, 6.2.2–3; Diod. 14.17.4–12, 14.34.1. 364 BCE: Xen. *Hell.* 7.4.12–32; Diod. 15.78.1–3. A not dissimilar (if less spectacular) readiness to subordinate sacred to secular was institutionalized in the Hellenistic period in the granting of *asylia* to cities. These grants were sought essentially as a matter of civic honour, since the 'sacred' guarantee of territorial inviolability they offered was routinely ignored; see Rigsby (1996), 22–9.

ences of cult, and that they were certainly regarded as commemorating or re-enacting journeys made by the god Apollo himself.[27] In his study of 'The Types of Procession in Greek Cult', Nilsson too treats these processions as exceptional. In all other cases there is the 'big difference' between Greek *theōria* and pilgrimage that 'the manifestations of piety which give Christian pilgrimage its character are missing: the group expedition as such has no religious significance', 'it represents nothing more than the travel itself, and the main action'—participation in the sacrificial rites of the festival—'only takes place after its arrival' at the festival site.[28] The 'sacred travel' characteristic of other religious traditions is then absent from Greek paganism.

Am I just being captious here? Are people whisked to Rome or Lourdes by jet not 'pilgrims' nonetheless? My own sense is that the efficiency of modern transport can be reconciled with the notion of 'making a pilgrimage' only because such pilgrims still come to the sacred site from afar, and in their own way mark, or at any rate conceive, the journey itself as sacred. Certainly we would not describe as a 'pilgrim' someone walking a short distance to a faith-healing session at the local conventicle. This is not mere quibbling over linguistic usage. We all ought nowadays to be sound on the lexical method and proof against the dangers of *Geistesgeschichte*, but we know too that language is a primary medium of ideology, and 'pilgrimage' is a word heavy-laden with ideological burdens. And after all it is probably significant that the Greek language lacks an equivalent term, a fact which at any rate coheres with our observations about the Greek practices themselves.

As we noted earlier, Rutherford argues that the Greek for 'pilgrimage' is *theōria*, which he acknowledges is applied only to 'state pilgrimage'. This word and its congeners share the root sense of 'viewing', and Rutherford concludes that 'the prestige-activity of watching the panhellenic games was the dominant paradigm for other forms of sacred visitation', which he compares in a general way with the Hindu tradition of *darshan* or 'sacred contemplation'. Going a step further, he suggests that when people went off κατὰ θέαν, usually translated 'sightseeing', 'many of the places to be visited ... were religious centres, so we might rather translate: "sacred sightseeing" '.[29]

---

[27] Boëthius (1918), 34–8.   [28] Nilsson (1916), 167–8.
[29] Rutherford (2000*a*), 133; 146; 135.

Rutherford's possible but not necessary conclusions seem dubious. The hypothesis that 'watching the panhellenic games was the dominant paradigm for other forms of sacred visitation' is probably right, but I would neutralize the loaded phrase 'sacred visitation' and say simply 'paradigm for other forms of official *theōria*'. The idea of being a spectator is basic to the whole word-group, but *theōria* is often used of straightforwardly secular sightseeing and gawking, and its usage in this sense in the *iamata* or inscribed cure-testimonials from Asklepios' healing sanctuary at Epidauros makes it very hard to sustain the argument that *theōria* is sacral terminology. In one *iama* it is said of the sufferer that 'looking at (θεωρῶν) the votive tablets in the sanctuary he disbelieved the cures and scoffed at the inscriptions'.[30] One gets no sense that this is either an ironic juxtaposition or a quite inappropriate use of θεωρεῖν in what is a religious text *par excellence*; the god cures this man and teasingly names him Ἄπιστος, 'The Doubter', but anyone who knows these texts would find it oversubtle to suggest that the participle θεωρῶν is a kind of ironic, proleptic allusion to the man's access of faith. There is a very similar use of the noun *theōria* in another *iama*, where a crowd gawks at the 'spectacle' of Amphimnastos the fishmonger's burning fish, struck by lightning because he had failed to deliver the promised tithe of his profits to Asklepios.[31]

Now just as there is nothing sacred about the 'viewing' in these cultic inscriptions, so too we have no warrant for assuming that the *theōria* that consists in 'watching the panhellenic games' is a sacred activity. There is no reason to conclude that everything a delegate did at a festival was *ipso facto* 'sacred', and no reason to attach that adjective to every term connected with festivals. Most of the 'watching' at festivals was done not in the sacred inner sanctuary but in theatres and stadia outside it. It seems tolerably clear that θεωροί are basically *polis*-delegates sent to festivals to show the flag and enjoy the show; that they participated as well in cultic rituals such as συνθυσία or 'co-sacrifice' is also true; but

---

[30] *IG* IV² 1.121.23–5: θεωρῶν δὲ τοὺς ἐν τῶι ἱαρῶι πίνακας ἀπίστει τοῖς ἰάμα-σιν καὶ ὑποδιέσυρε τὰ ἐπιγράμμα[τ]α. For vision in the context of the Epidaurian Iamata, see Naiden's paper (above).

[31] *SEG* 22 (1967) 280. 21–9, lines 25–6: ὄχλου δὲ πολλοῦ περιστάντος εἰσ τὰν θεωρίαν. *SEG* reproduces the important but overly bold re-edition by Peek (1963) of *IG* IV² 1. 123.21–9; a more sober edition by R. Merkelbach is added as an appendix to Dillon (1994). There is however no doubt about the text of this clause.

calling this combination of activities 'sacred contemplation' or 'pilgrimage' is really very arbitrary. As for the notion of 'sacred sightseeing', there appears to me to be far more of sightseeing in festivals than of sacredness in sightseeing.[32] I objected earlier to the phrase 'sacred truces', and in all these cases insistent use of words like 'sacred' and 'pilgrimage' to translate terms that are not drawn from the rich fund of Greek sacral language finds little or no justification in our evidence for the practices they refer to. It is in this regard that our consideration of the sacred/secular dichotomy provides the necessary contextualization of the 'pilgrimage' issue. Far too often nowadays the truism that in Greece sacred and secular tend to be linked turns into a sort of omnisacralization that borders on the absurd, as though all those attending a panhellenic festival considered themselves pilgrims on a sacred mission—jetsetters jocks, shmoozing politicians, purveyors of sausage or of victory odes, bookies, hookers, hooligans, the lot. Armchair anthropology is all very well in its way, but Wilamowitz's dictum is also true: 'sie waren Menschen wie Du und Ich', 'they were human beings like you and I'.

One objection to this might be that I underestimate the degree to which even Christian pilgrimage has a strongly profane side. Exhibit A would of course be the many bawdy elements in Chaucer's *Canterbury Tales*; as Exhibit B I nominate the mock pilgrim badges of the Middle Ages, which show for example penises rather than pilgrims trudging along one after the other. This objection is I think relatively easy to deal with. The basic premiss and the form of the *Canterbury Tales* reflect the special status of Christian pilgrims as they travel and the ideal of pilgrimage as a period of reflection. The fact that pilgrimage has become metaphorical not only for Chaucer but even for a Puritan like Bunyan indicates how firmly established the spiritual ideal of pilgrimage is in international religions. In the Greek world, by contrast, there seems to be no established institution at all, let alone an ideal form of it to humanize, satirize, or employ metaphorically. Most of Chaucer's pilgrims fall well short of the spiritual ideal, but that rather presupposes the ideal than constitutes an argument against its existence. That there were people in the medieval period prepared to produce or buy penis-pilgrim badges is an important fact, but, like (say) Egyptian tomb-robbers or the

---

[32] Xen. *Poroi* 5.4 speaks of 'those keen on things worth seeing or hearing, sacred or secular': οἱ δὲ ἀξιοθεάτων ἢ ἀξιακούστων ἱερῶν ἢ ὁσίων ἐπιθυμοῦντες.

more spectacular sinners among Christian priests, such people are evidence not that powerful cultural models do not exist, but that, despite extravagant claims of cultural determinism, the power of cultural models is limited, particularly perhaps when they run up against some of the rougher or more assertive aspects of our biological inheritance.

I am therefore quite comfortable with the conclusion that in the Greek world so-called 'state pilgrimage' was only intermittently sacred even during the festival itself, and not much like a pilgrimage at all. As a corrective translation of *theōria* of this sort I propose 'festival junketing', and 'Junket' might be a good English name for Aristophanes' Theoria.

The Greek term for pilgrimage undertaken by private individuals can be dealt with much more briefly: there was none. Here again we find in the Greek evidence more or less the opposite of what characterizes pilgrimage in other traditions, where state-pilgrimage is rare and the word 'pilgrim' virtually synonymous with the private, unofficial way-farer. Those who consulted oracles on behalf of a *polis* could be called θεοπρόποι or θεωρός but individuals simply 'consulted the oracle': the Greek verb is μαντεύεσθαι. Those who resorted to healing sanctuaries were called suppliants, ἱκέται. Private persons we are nowadays told were 'making pilgrimages' to oracles, festivals, and healing shrines merely 'went' to them in Greek. Thukydides' report of the peace treaty contemporary with the production of Aristophanes' *Peace* is instructive in this regard; its first clause runs: 'Concerning the common sanctuaries, he who so desires can sacrifice, and go, and consult oracles, and officially attend festivals according to ancestral custom by land and by sea without fear.'[33] What we're encouraged to think of as 'sacred travel' is designated here by the pale verb 'go', and this is surely telling.

Far from using common terminology for private travel to festivals, oracle-consultation, and healing suppliancy, the Greeks linguistically distinguished them one from another, and all the evidence indicates that they were quite distinct practices. In the end, I don't see what is to be gained by lumping them together under the rubric 'pilgrimage'. We have a little evidence from later antiquity for pagan pilgrimage worthy

---

[33] 5.18.2: Σπονδὰς ἐποιήσαντο Ἀθηναῖοι καὶ Λακεδαιμόνιοι καὶ οἱ ξύμμαχοι κατὰ τάδε, καὶ ὤμοσαν κατὰ πόλεις. περὶ μὲν τῶν ἱερῶν τῶν κοινῶν, θύειν καὶ ἰέναι καὶ μαντεύεσθαι καὶ θεωρεῖν κατὰ τὰ πάτρια τὸν βουλόμενον καὶ κατὰ γῆν καὶ κατὰ θάλασσαν ἀδεῶς.

of the name,[34] but the word 'pilgrim' is gaining currency in a weak sense covering practically anybody who—in whatever manner and mood—travels any distance at all to do one thing or another in a sanctuary. 'Pilgrim' in this sense is a term of tremendously wide applicability, but so vague that it ceases to be useful; a term susceptible to what I think of as the W. S. Gilbert objection: 'When everybody's somebody, then no one's anybody.'

We noted that pilgrims in other traditions regard their travel to the sacred site as an essential part of the experience, but their conception of the sacred site itself is also markedly different.[35] In both Jewish and Muslim tradition there is a single pilgrimage destination: Jews return to the Holy Land and the *hajj* leads to Mecca, places of unique, supreme spiritual power, the sacred centres of the Jewish and Muslim worlds. Christian pilgrimage is more diffused, but this is at bottom the result of a historical accident; the Holy Land, previously the principal destination of Christian pilgrimage, became difficult of access when in the tenth century its Muslim rulers grew hostile to Christian pilgrims. The great medieval pilgrimage destinations of Christians were substitutes for the Holy Land, and apart from their particular hagiological associations were all equipped with pieces of the true cross and other relics of the place and persons of Jesus, Mary, and the disciples. Non-Orthodox Christians have mostly reverted to an exclusive focus on the Holy Land, to the extent that they hold with pilgrimage at all. Buddhist pilgrimage sites are all associated with places and events in the life of the Buddha, and are ideally to be visited in the appropriate sequence, as they were by the emperor Ashoka, the model Buddhist pilgrim, in the third century BCE. Hinduism might be described as conceptually or essentially monotheistic but functionally or instrumentally polytheistic, and the many hundreds of pilgrimage sites in India correspond to this paradox: despite the huge variety of gods and avatars to whom they are dedicated, each is also a focus of a divine power that is one and undifferentiated. Moreover, Hindu tradition spiritualizes pilgrimage more intensely than any other: it is a form of renunciation of the world associated with fasting and celibacy and ideally to be undertaken

---

[34] See e.g. Coleman and Elsner (1995), 24–6 with further references.
[35] There are good summary presentations and bibliographies in the appropriate chapters of Coleman and Elsner (1995).

on foot and without creature comforts; many holy men and women spend much of their lives as pilgrims. Neither the unitary focus or centralization nor the intense spiritualization in these pilgrimage traditions has any real counterpart among the Greeks.

This suggests interesting questions about the Greek material, which I can here only raise and address briefly and tentatively. Why did some Greek states and well-to-do individuals travel to panhellenic sanctuaries? Why not rest content with one's local cults? Was there any compelling *religious* motivation for travelling to Olympia or Epidauros or Delphi, or were the primary attractions the wider fame, greater prestige, bigger crowds, and better shows?

In his book on pilgrimage, Matthew Dillon lays great stress on travel to panhellenic sanctuaries. At the festivals there, as Pindar puts it in his Sixth Paian, 'sacrifice is made on behalf of splendid Panhellas', but the distinct treasuries of individual *poleis* at Delphi, Pindar's own epinician odes, with their glorification of local grandees, and indeed the whole course of classical Greek history indicate that the panhellenic is a fleeting and illusive thing. Christiane Sourvinou-Inwood has reminded us that even panhellenic sanctuaries and festivals remain within the control of the local *polis* or amphiktyony, and that so far as we can tell Greeks from other cities or regions could normally only undertake cultic acts at such sanctuaries and festivals through the agency of *proxenoi* or local sponsors.[36] The obstacles to panhellenism were however political rather than religious. Cultic practice was perhaps second only to the Greek language itself as a unifying factor in the Hellenic world, and strictly religious differences were sometimes the ostensible but rarely the real cause of disputes between states. It is therefore unsurprising that the differences between panhellenic and local or ethnic festivals are also more obviously political than ritual or theological in nature. Indeed, it isn't easy to detect in the evidence any consistent distinction between panhellenic and local worship on grounds of ritual practice, divine identity, or religious ideology.

Dillon claims that the power of a god was conceived to be greater at a panhellenic than at a local sanctuary,[37] which if true would not only supply a powerful and specifically religious reason for resorting to

---

[36] Sourvinou-Inwood (1990), 13–15 (in the reprint).
[37] Dillon (1994), 242, summarily at (1997), 76; cf. Krug (1984), 145.

panhellenic sanctuaries, but would imply that when they did so individuals and cities were implicitly acknowledging the secondary status of their local cults of the same gods and their own oracles and healing divinities. Dillon's claim turns out to be based, however, on a single piece of evidence, another *iama* from Epidauros, which will not support the construction he puts on it. Aristagora, troubled by a tape worm, goes to the local Asklepieion at Trozen and dreams that the god's sons remove her head and are unable to reattach it; Asklepios is summoned, returns from Epidauros, and puts things right. The inscription merely speaks of 'the sons of the god—he not being in town (οὐκ ἐπιδαμοῦντος) but being in Epidauros'.[38] Nothing here suggests that Asklepios' being out of town is more than mere happenstance, and the words do imply that he is perfectly at home in Trozen, where the cure is in fact effected. Sons are subordinated to father or apprentices to master rather than the Trozenian Asklepios to the Epidaurian. In the probably original version of the story preserved in a fragment of Hippys of Rhegion (*FGrHist* 554 F 2) god, patient, and temple attendants (rather than sons) are all at Epidauros. The Epidaurian version very probably reflects rivalry with the Asklepieion at nearby Trozen, but Dillon's claim that 'the healing power of the god was felt to be more efficacious at a major sanctuary' is not sustained by this evidence, and so far as I can see there is no better evidence for it.

The relationship between local and panhellenic cults of the same god seems to be rather more complicated; Greeks appear to have acknowledged the pre-eminence of, for example, the Asklepieion at Epidauros without feeling that their local Asklepieion was, in terms of healing as such, a lesser cult. No doubt Delphi was the place to go for an oracle, but given the prominence of Dodona, Claros, Didyma, and other oracles, Delphi's pre-eminence was surely based not on specifically religious grounds but on its antiquity and high repute, its powerfully impressive setting and rich mythology, and above all on the political capital it had amassed.

---

[38] *IG* IV² 1.122.12–14: τοὺς υἱ[οὺς τοῦ θ]εοῦ, οὐκ ἐπιδαμοῦντος αὐτοῦ, ἀλλ' ἐν Ἐπιδαύρωιεόντος,τἀγέ κεφα[λὰν ἀπο]ταμεῖν, οὐ δυναμένους δ' ἐπιθέμενπάλιν πέμψαι τινὰ πο[ὶ] τὸν Ἀσκλ[απιόν, ὅ]πως μόληι.

The normal attitude of classical Greeks in this matter was still going strong in the fourth century CE, when Themistios expressed it in the form of a rhetorical question:

> If we were ill in body and required the help of the god, and he were present here in the temple and the akropolis and were offering himself to the sick, just as even of old he is said to have done, would it be necessary to go to Trikka and sail to Epidauros on account of their ancient fame, or to move two steps and get rid of our illness?[39]

In short, there is little to be said either for the notion that Greeks were great pilgrims, which has a strong whiff of modern religiosity about it, or for the notion that they were limited in their capacity to distinguish secular from sacred, which is more than a little redolent of pop anthropology.

---

[39] Themistios *Orat.* 27.333c.

5

Down-Stream to the Cat-Goddess:

Herodotus on Egyptian Pilgrimage

Ian Rutherford

I. HERODOTUS ON EGYPTIAN FESTIVALS

In his ethnographic survey of Egypt, Herodotus gives an account of Egyptian festivals (2. 58–60), and concomitant pilgrimage-traditions. He says that the Egyptians hold many festivals during the year (there is no dispute about that because we have rich information from Egyptian sacred calendars),[1] and describes six festivals, all from Lower Egypt: the great festivals of Upper Egypt (such as the Opet festival at Karnak, the festival of Good Reunion at Edfu) are omitted by Herodotus, who seems to be preoccupied with northern, and possibly had limited experience of southern Egypt.[2] He also says that festivals were first established in Egypt, along with processions and the offering of sacrificial victims (*prosagōgai*), and subsequently migrated to Greece.

These are the six festivals.

Bastet-Artemis at her principal site at Boubastis, in the eastern Delta, which he says is the best attended, drawing 700,000 pilgrims.

Isis-Demeter at Busiris, a cult centre of Osiris; Herodotus describes this as a festival of lamentation, which means that it is probably identical to

I would like to thank Jane Lightfoot and Elizabeth Frood.

[1] See Casarico (1981). On Egyptian festivals in general: Altermüller, *LÄ* 2. 171–91, s.v. Feste; Bleeker (1967) has bibliography.
[2] Lloyd (1975–88), 2. 268.

the famous festival of Osiris in the month Khoiak (the fourth month of the Egyptian year, in spring in the time of Herodotus), a festival also celebrated elsewhere in Egypt, particularly at the great southern sanctuary of Osiris at Abydos.[3]

Athene-Neith at Sais, a festival involving the burning of lamps, to which Herodotus applies the Greek name *lukhnokaie*.[4] Sais was the main centre of Neith's worship in Egypt, but her cult was much more broadly distributed throughout Egypt.[5] We know from elsewhere that the festival was held on the 13th of the month Epiphi (in late Autumn in the time of Herodotus).[6] Herodotus says that people who did not go to the festival lit lamps at home.

The Sun at Heliopolis; its equivalent in Egyptian sources is uncertain.[7]

Leto-Wadjet at Buto; this is probably the same as the festival of Horus mentioned in the Gmenafharbok stele (see below).[8] Notice that Herodotus represents four of the six festivals he mentions as in honour of goddesses rather than gods; these include the festival for Isis-Demeter at Busiris, even though we have reason to think that it might have been equally a festival in honour of Osiris, and that of Leto-Wadjet at Buto, even though the festival may have been primarily that in honour of Horus (see section v below).

Ares at Papremis. It is equally uncertain where Papremis was and to which Egyptian deity Ares might have corresponded.[9] This festival involved a ritual conflict centred on the image of 'Ares' which one group try to forcibly carry into the temple, while the other group resist.[10]

A consistent feature of all the festivals is sacrifice. In the cases of festivals at Buto and Heliopolis sacrifice is the dominant element (2.63), other festivals have other features as well, such as the ritual conflict at Papremis.

---

[3] Lloyd (1975–88), 2.277. The Egyptian year would have started around mid-December in 450 BCE.
[4] Lamps: Frankfurter (1998a), 83; Dunand (1976).
[5] Hornung (1982), 71.
[6] *P. Hibeh* 27, col. xii, 166; Vandoni (1964), n. 10. Epiphi was the eleventh month.
[7] Lloyd (1975–88), 2.283.
[8] Lloyd (1975–88), 2.284.
[9] Lloyd (1975–88), 2.285.
[10] For the idea of conflict, cf. ll. 6 ff. of the Gmenefharbok-stele cited below.

Herodotus described Egyptian sacrifice earlier on in book 2 (38–41), a full and (as far as we can tell) reasonably accurate account.[11] From this it is clear that the act of sacrifice itself was performed by the priests.

Herodotus' agenda in this section of the *Histories* is partly to highlight the differences between Greek and Egyptian practice but also to suggest that Greek practice could have arisen from the Egyptian. To this end, he chooses some festivals that have no obvious Greek equivalents, such as the festival at Papremis, and some which do, such as the one to Artemis-Bastet, which might perhaps remind the audience of pilgrimage of Artemis to Ephesus.[12] Similarly, some details of the festivals are suggestive of Greek practice, such as sacrifice, and others alien, such as the conflict at Papremis.

The festival and sanctuary which most suggests Greek religion is Buto (2.156), where Herodotus (following Hecataeus) describes the floating island of Khemmis (*3ḫ-bit*), situated in a lake near the sanctuary.[13] There Leto, i.e. the Egyptian goddess Wadjet according to the standard *interpretatio Graeca*, looked after Apollo, i.e. Horus, having received him from his mother Isis, in order to protect him from Typhon, i.e. Seth.[14] Egyptian sources tell us that Horus was born at a place called Khemmis/*3ḫ-bit*, but they do not confirm the other details of the story, and in particular do not mention a floating island; the idea is rather one of a primeval mound located in a marsh-thicket where creation began.[15] Herodotus' account seems to reflect the model of Delos, where Leto gave birth to Apollo, and in some versions Artemis, and which, having originally been a floating island, was rooted down by Zeus in order to provide a safe-place birthplace.[16] The identification between Wadjet and Leto (an identification which is, of course, not perfect in all respects

---

[11] See Lloyd (1975–88), ad loc. I hope to discuss Herodotus' portrayal of sacrifice in Egypt more elsewhere.   [12] Kötting (1950), 56.

[13] Hecataeus: *FGrHist* 1F305, who used the form Khembis; Buto: H. Altenmüller, *LÄ* 1.887–9, s.v.

[14] The name 'Buto' in fact means 'house of Wadjet' (Pr-Uto). For interpretationes Graecae, see Kolta (1968). Herodotus makes the parallel even more explicit in 2.157 by stating that in Egyptian mythology Artemis-Boubastis as well as Apollo-Horus was a child of Dionysus-Osiris and Isis.

[15] See Lloyd (1975–88), ad loc. (esp. 3.145); Gwyn Griffiths (1960), 93–5.

[16] For the cities of Egypt being like the islands of the Aegean when the Nile is in flood, Hdt. 2. 97. For the floating island, see Lloyd (1975–88), 144. A good discussion of the myth and hypotheses put forward to explain it is Gwyn Griffiths (1960), 93 ff. Selden (1998), 389–405 has recently explored aspects of the relation between Apollo and Horus

since it is Isis who gives birth) was probably suggested by the general similarity between these two stories of divine birth, and it may have led the Greeks to project onto the Egyptian myth features from their own mythology, such as the floating island.[17] Elsewhere Herodotus represents Buto as a major oracle, just as sanctuaries of Apollo were oracles.[18] And we should bear in mind that the identification between Delos and Buto is at least as old as Hecataeus and perhaps as early as Ionian settlement in nearby Naukratis.[19] The early Greek settlers are likely to have noticed also that Egyptian pilgrimage to Buto was analogous to Ionian pilgrimage to Delos.

A similar pattern of implications can perhaps be traced in respect of Herodotus' account of Sais, which he described at greater length later on (2.170–1). The circular sacred lake by the temple of Athene-Neith reminds Herodotus of the one at Delos.[20] He also knows that the tomb of Dionysus-Osiris was supposed to be at Sais, and that representations of the sufferings of Osiris (probably part of the Khoiak festival again) were held on the sacred lake. The combination of a sanctuary of Athene with dramatic representations in honour of Dionysus inevitably makes one think of Athens and the dramatic festivals of Dionysus.[21] Later sources, including Diodorus Siculus, explicitly state that Athens was originally an Egyptian colony of Sais, a fiction that perhaps reflects observation of the same parallels.[22]

The similarities between Greek and Egyptian pilgrimage perhaps have three levels. First, Herodotus sees Egyptian religious practices through a filter of Greek ones; second, he may be drawing on

in the Hellenistic period, as represented in Callimachus' Hymns to Delos and to Apollo, touching on the parallel between Chemmis and Delos on p. 404 with n. 553; cf. also Stephens (1998), 180–1.

[17] Gardiner (1944), 54–5. And again the wandering search of Leto in the Greek myth corresponds to the wandering search of Isis in the Egyptian myth. According to Dunand (1975), 157 n. 21, the identification Leto = Wadjet is not found outside of Herodotus.   [18] 2.83, 111, 133, 152.

[19] Gwyn Griffiths (1960), 95; Heidel (1935), 100: 'The situation of Buto in the Delta, not far from Naucratis and Daphnae, leads one to suspect that the temple and its oracle were early known to Greek settlers, who, being for the most part Ionian, would naturally think of their own oracular god Apollo, and his shrine on Delos, which was also supposed to have floated before the birth of the god. Perhaps it was there that the identifications, which later became fixed, of Apollo with Horus, Artemis with Bubastis (Bast) and Leto with Uat, were first made.'

[20] Sais: J. Malek, *LÄ* 5.355–7, s.v.   [21] Lloyd (1975–88), 3.206 ff.
[22] Sources available in Sayed (1982).

generations of Greek visitors and Greek émigrés who had done the same, and perhaps imposed a Greek cultural veneer on Egyptian practice; and third, he consciously moulds his depiction of the Egyptian festivals to suggest aspects of some Greek festivals.

II. PILGRIMAGE IN ANCIENT EGYPT

Of all areas of the Ancient World none had older or richer religious traditions than Egypt, and one might expect that there would be old and entrenched traditions of pilgrimage as well. In fact, the evidence is inconclusive and inconsistent. In the Hellenistic and Roman periods, Egypt offers more evidence for pilgrimage than any other part of the ancient world, mainly in the form of visitor-graffiti left by Greek-speakers at sanctuaries, which record the 'acts of adoration' (*proskunē-mata*) of the pilgrims, but tell us little about the nature of the pilgrimage itself, or the geographical provenance of the pilgrims.[23] Visitor graffiti in Greek and other languages survive from the Memnonion at Abydos from as early as the sixth century BCE, but it is uncertain what the purpose of the visits were.[24]

On the other hand in the main periods of Egyptian history (the Old, Middle, and New Kingdoms), there is very little unequivocal evidence for pilgrimage at all, so little, in fact, that some authorities have stated that none took place.[25] On the usual model, religious activity in Egypt was typically official rather than popular, conducted by priests working inside a closed temple precinct, insulated from the mass of the population outside. Popular religion was typically focused on local temples, and did not involve journeys far afield. Where we find dedications in temples by non-locals, these are usually to be attributed to court officials who were travelling on 'official business', making a 'pilgrimage in passing', to use Yoyotte's felicitous term.[26]

Paradoxically, it was an important part of Egyptian belief about the afterlife that the body of the deceased made a sort of posthumous

---

[23] See Festugiere (1970); Geraci (1971).
[24] See Rutherford (2003).
[25] H. Beinlich, *LÄ* 1.1145–6, s. v. Wallfahrt; Yoyotte (1960); Sadek (1988), 197–8.
[26] See Yoyotte (1960).

pilgrimage to the sacred cities of Abydos in Upper Egypt and to Buto in the Delta. Scenes showing the transportation of the mummified body of the deceased often appear in New Kingdom tombs, but this practice seems to have been imaginary, and not part of real funeral ritual. Similarly, in the Middle Kingdom it was the practice to erect stelai commemorating dead people at Abydos, but few, if any, of these can be attributed to pilgrims to Abydos who had come to attend the great festival of Osiris there; most are to be explained in other ways.[27]

A type of pilgrimage for which we have better evidence is that surrounding the symbolic journey of a deity from one temple to another (the type of journey that Egyptologists refer to as the 'Götterbesuch').[28] The best surviving example is furnished by the instructions for the journey of the goddess Hathor from Dendara to the festival of the Good Reunion (*sḥn nfr*) with Horus at Edfu about 100 miles to the south. This sacred law, written on the Pylon of the temple at Edfu, comes from the late Hellenistic/early Roman period, but there is every reason to think that the basic form of the ritual is much earlier. It gives an account of the festival, divided into three parts. The first part is a list of officials who take part in the festival. The second part is a list of ships that carry them, and third part is a list of the way-stations they call at en route, and seems to mention contributions from other cities south of Thebes, including Elephantine, Hierakonpolis, and Komir (but not Edfu). Towards the end, where the document describes provisions to be supplied, we seem to find reference to popular involvement:

> The chief of Nekhen is to furnish 500 loaves of different kinds, 100 jars of beer and 30 shoulders of small farm animals, for the people of the villages, so they pass their journey seated, to drink and enjoy the festival before the venerable god, to anoint themselves with perfume, to play the tambourine with a great noise, with the people of the town (of Edfu). With music and tambourine they are to sing: 'Eternal joy! eternal joy! It is king NNN, the son of king NNN who has made this foundation for ever, for the voyage to Edfu for millions of years...'[29]

We may well imagine that the journey of the divine statue from Dendara to Edfu was accompanied by large numbers of ordinary people

---

[27] See Beinlich (above, n. 25); Lichtheim (1988).
[28] See U. Rösler-Köller, *LÄ* 2.669–71, s.v. Götterbesuch.
[29] Alliot (1949–54), 2.474–5; Allenmüller (1998), 755.

('people of the villages') who wanted to take part in the festival at Edfu. Though the text is late, the ritual is probably very old, as is the general practice of Götterbesuch.[30] Another example of the same sort of pattern may be a festival of Khnum held at the beginning of the month of Khoiak at Esna, where gods visited Esna from a number of towns in the Third Nome of Upper Egypt, and official delegations will no doubt have arrived from these towns.[31]

The ending of the Edfu text aside, popular pilgrimage is not well attested in Egyptian sources, at least not before the pilgrim graffiti of the Hellenistic period. Its first attestation is Herodotus' account of pilgrimage to the sanctuary of the goddess Bastet at Boubastis. There is no parallel to this in the whole dossier of evidence, with the exception of one demotic text from a few centuries later, the Gmenafharbok stele. Its appearance is so sudden that Egyptologists have generally drawn the conclusion that popular pilgrimage is a late development in Egypt, perhaps even influenced by folk belief and by Graeco-Roman ideas. They may be right, but it is as well to bear in mind that without the testimony of a non-Egyptian source, we would not know about popular Egyptian pilgrimage in the fifth century either.[32] Hence what was new in the fifth century BCE may be not so much new religious phenomena but a new medium to record them.

Prima facie a rare exception to the rule that Egyptian sources never mention popular pilgrimage is a hieroglyphic stele from Buto, probably to be dated to the first century BCE.[33] This stele presents the dead man, Gmenafharbok, as addressing various groups of people who make pilgrimages to Buto. Many details of the Egyptian are difficult to make out, but a rough translation is as follows:

1–3   The one venerated beside Osiris Khentamenti, the prophet who knows
      the mysteries of Buto, Gmenafharbok, child of the lady, good mother
      beside Hathor, princess of the West, W*d*3-šw. He, blessed, says:
      Nobles and servants, embalmers, chiefs of mysteries, people who dispose of
      offerings in performing the function of priests, O all men who pass on roads,

---

[30] Rösler-Köller loc. cit., who points out the practice is well attested in connection with the sed-festival: see, e.g. Gardiner (1910).
[31] Grimm (1994), 57, L27; Sauneron (1962), 47–67. For festivals at Esna, Derchain-Urtel (1998).
[32] Volokhine (1998).
[33] Cairo Museum, 85932; see Drioton (1943)

4–5   whether they come to the necropolis, or pass near this staircase, or go to Imet (Buto) during the day of the full moon to make their oath with the Golden One (Hathor), or to see Wadjet, whose face becomes joyful giving children to pilgrims (?),

5–9   or who come from the country of the god, at the period when the plants are green, to worship during the festival of Horus, and to bring help to Min, when he leaves for his place of rest drawn by horses, decorated with a red band, equipped with a pectoral, when those in front of his resting place tremble seeing him in peril, but when, as he withdraws unharmed, the discouraged man who was inactive rises to his feet, siezes a lance and attacks his enemies, delivering his subjects to the one who is unmovable

9–12 Citizens of Imet and servants, who go and come to kiss the dust in the temple of Silence which has become an antechamber of the tomb, until the king climbs toward the glorious one (Wadjet) at the time of famine when the pilgrims descend toward Min and go in procession to him who presides over the country. And may they recite an appeal us Min that all the grain bhork that the plants spread at the time of their flourishing, and that the destroy of ptt is that of the enemy. they recite an appeal to Min that all the grain blooms, that the plants spread at the time of their flourishing, and that the destiny of Ptt is that of the enemy

Thus, three groups of pilgrims are mentioned: (4–5) those who come to Buto at the full moon to make an oath before Hathor and see Wadjet who grants children; (6 ff.) those who come to make adoration during the festival of Horus and to bring help to Min (the idea of 'bringing help' to the deity suggests the divine conflict at Papremis described by Herodotus); (10 ff.) those who come at time of famine to make appeal to Min.

Three different pilgrimages, then, to the same sanctuary, possibly to different parts of it, since Horus is associated with one part (Chemmis and the locality known as 'Pe') and Wadjet with another part (the locality known as 'Dep').[34] The second of these categories seems most likely to correspond to the festival of Leto/Wadjet at Buto described by Herodotus.[35] The appearance of Min (an ithyphallic god, usually taken as corresponding to Greek Pan) might seem surprising. But we should remember that Min is often identified with Horus in Egyptian religious thinking.[36] The first type of pilgrimage, to Hathor and Wadjet, seems

---

[34] H. Altenmüller, *LÄ* 1.887, s.v. Buto. For Pe: Gutbub (1964), 36 ff.; for Dep: Pyr. 1671 (Faulkner (1969), 248).

[35] See Drioton (1943), who identified it with a festival held in Pauni.

[36] Herodotus: Drioton (1943), 8; Pan and Horus: A. Rusch, *RE* Suppl. 6 (1935), 439–45.

to be a monthly pilgrimage, possibly associated with a fertility cult. The third form seems to be a special pilgrimage envisaged as taking place in time of famine.[37]

In his edition of the inscription Étienne Drioton, noticing that it is unlike any other Egyptian stele, both in so far as it addresses passers-by in this way, and in so far as it gives a typology of pilgrimage, and unlike, in fact, any native Egyptian text in its full description of various types of popular pilgrimage to a sanctuary, suggests that it may have been modelled on a Greek text, possibly a lost Greek epigram.[38] That conclusion may seem desperate, but there are other examples of Greek influence on Egyptian literature in this period.[39] If Drioton's interpretation is right, then the Gmenafharbok-stele is consistent with the hypothesis that references to popular pilgrimage in ancient Egypt are confined to Greek (or Greek inspired) sources. This might be partly a question of a foreign point of view allowing cultural patterns which are taken for granted by natives to be noticed and described, but it is also a question of genre: above all, the development of Greek historiography creates a medium which is well-suited to record patterns of activity in foreign cultures (another example of this would be Lucian's account of pilgrimage to Hierapolis, discussed in Ch. 12 of this volume by Jane Lightfoot). Ancient Egyptian sources tend to be officially sanctioned documents which concentrate on official religion. Many religious-traditions show a contrast between the official organization of the sanctuary and a popular tradition, often supported by a lively pilgrimage tradition, which may focus on different deities.[40] If there were significant movements of popular religion at earlier periods of Egyptian history, they would probably not have been registered in such official Egyptian sources.

---

[37] Cf. link to the gathering of crops in the Canopus decree (*OGIS* 1.56.51), cited below, n. 52.

[38] Drioton (1943).

[39] The dedication in Bernand (1969a), 108 (stele of Moschion). Depauw (1997), 86, 96. Derchain (2000) on child epigrams. And on balance, it seems to me that Drioton is probably right about a Greek source. (While a Greek epigram may have contributed the speech act of an address to passers-by, for the content it seems likelier to me that the source is historiographical, since I do not know any Greek epigram that describes the arrival of pilgrims in this way.)

[40] We see this, for example, at the Mortuary Temple of Hatshepsut at Deir-al-Bahari, where the tradition of healing pilgrimage to Imhotep-Asclepius stands in opposition to the official cult, and at the Memnonion at Abydos in the Roman period where a tradition of pilgrimage to the deity Bes spontaneously develops in opposition to the more official cult of Osiris/Sarapis.

In the case of Buto, there is the additional complexity that the account of pilgrimage to Buto in the stele is so different from Herodotus' account of the festival at Buto. Perhaps we could hypothesize the existence of two simultaneous but contrasting pilgrimage traditions to Buto, one by Greek émigrés or Egyptians with a Greek cultural background, the other by native Egyptians. Here we may be reminded of recent anthropological work on 'competing discourses' in modern Christian pilgrimage.[41] Another possibility is that the Gmenafharbok stele, though Greek-inspired in its form, in fact conveys an attitude of native Egyptian resistance to the Hellenization of Egyptian cults.[42] And in that case the contrast between the two sources will be explained at least partly by a diachronic model: Herodotus' account represents an earlier phase when the dominant form of religious activity at Buto is Greek-inspired, and the stele represents a later phase, when native Egyptian traditions have reasserted themselves again.

III. THE PILGRIMAGE TO BOUBASTIS

Herodotus says that the largest festival was that of Artemis-Bastet at Boubastis/Boubastos in the Eastern Delta.[43] Bastet (Herodotus uses the Greek form Boubastis, which seems to represent a confusion between the name of the goddess with the name of her town)[44] was an important goddess, closely associated with the Pharaoh since the earliest phases of Egyptian history.[45] Bastet was often represented as a lion or a cat, and the mummified corpses of cats were buried in her sanctuary (cf. Herodotus, *Hist.* 2.67).[46] Her main cult site was the eponymously named city of Boubastis (= *Pr-b3stt*, 'the house of Bastet'), capital of the Eighteenth Nome of Lower Egypt, located on the Tanitic branch of the Nile, a city which had been capital of the whole of Egypt in the 22nd

---

[41] Eade and Sallnow (1991).

[42] On native resistance and Egyptian religion, see Frankfurter (1998*a*); Lloyd (1982). On Pilgrimage and resistance more generally, see Elsner 1997*b*.

[43] On the form of the name, see Calderini (1935), s.v. ; there was another place of the same name in the Fayyum.

[44] Harrison (2000), 254–5.

[45] E. Otto, *LÄ* 1.628–30, s.v. Bastet.

[46] See Jentel (1986). With her consort Atum she was mother of another lion god Miysis.

Dynasty. Some of the main structures there date from the period of Osorkon II in the eighth century BCE who built a massive festival hall.[47]

Later on in the History, Herodotus himself claims to have visited the temple of Artemis-Bastet at Boubastis (2.138). The key feature here is that the temple, which is on an island, surrounded by channels that come from the Nile (so too hieroglyphic sources mention an *išrw*, which seems to be a lake or a body of water).[48] It was below the rest of the city, which had been raised up, so that the whole circuit commanded a view down onto it (κατορᾶται πάντοθεν περιόντι). Modern archaeology has confirmed this arrangement.[49] The implication of Herodotus' account is that this practice is unlike that of the Greek world, where the temple is at a higher point than the rest of the city, often on an *akropolis*. This is not the only feature of Boubastis and its festival which is the reverse of Greek practice. It is possible to contrast the pilgrimage of the native Egyptians with the very different visit made by Herodotus himself described later in book 2. Herodotus represents himself as by contrast disengaged from the religious aspects, interested primarily in scientific enquiry. But it is important to remember that both forms of visit—both low level visits to festivals and the higher level contemplation of the intellectual—are covered by the Greek term *theōria*.[50]

Herodotus does not specify when the pilgrimage took place, but from festival calendars preserved in Egyptian temples it is apparent that there was a particularly important festival in the month of Pauni (in Autumn in the time of Herodotus).[51] The decree Canopus mentions both 'Lesser' and 'Greater' Boubastia in the month of Pauni, and seems to correlate this with the gathering of the crops, and the rise of the River Nile.[52] Special note should be taken of a calendar from the temple of

---

[47] L. Habichi, *LÄ* 1.873–4, s.v. Bubastis.

[48] Yoyotte (1962), 101 ff.; Sauneron (1964), 46 ff. Aelian, *Hist. Anim.* 12.29 mentions the fish in the lake at Boubastis.

[49] See Lloyd (1975–88), ad loc., maintaining that Herodotus' account is accurate; Naville (1891), 3.

[50] See Rutherford (2000a). Thucydides uses θεωρέω in this context, but it's not clear that this word was within Herodotus' literary vocabulary. Herodotus does not seem to use any special term for 'pilgrimage' here, except the very general συμφοιτάω.

[51] Lloyd (1975–1988) 2.272; Saite Calendar: Vandoni (1964), n. 10, 145; Casarico (1981) 130–1. Pauni was the 10th month of the year; see n. 6.

[52] *OGIS* 1.56.51; Vandoni (1964), n. 1; Casarico (1981), 139; (238 BCE): ἄγεται δὲ νῦν ἐν τῶι ἐνάτωι ἔτει νουμηνίαι τοῦ Παῦνι μηνός, ἐν ὧι καὶ τὰ μικρὰ

Horus in Edfu in Upper Egypt from the time of Ptolemy X,[53] which specifies that the first of Pauni was a festival in honour of the goddess Hathor of Dendara 'who lives in Boubastis'.

Herodotus' account of the pilgrimage is as follows:[54]

When they travel to Boubastis, this is what they do. They sail thither, men and women together, and a great number of each in each boat. Some of the women have rattles and rattle them, others play the flute through the entire trip, and the remainder of the women and men sing and clap their hands. As they travel on toward Boubastis and come near some other city, they edge the boat near the bank and some of the women do as I have described. But others of them scream obscenities in derision of the women who live in that city, and others of them set to dancing, and others still, standing up, throw their clothes open to show their nakedness. This they do at every city along the riverbank. When they come to Boubastis, they celebrate the festival with great sacrifices, and more wine is drunk at that single festival than in the rest of the year besides. There they throng together, men and women (but no children), up to the number of seven hundred thousand, as the natives say.

Herodotus does not mention where the pilgrims came from. The claim at the end that they numbered 700,000 (far more, clearly, than would attend any Greek festival[55]) indicates that they come from a wide area. Some of them could have started from a long way up the Nile. Women went to Boubastis as well as men, children were excluded. Both women

---

Βουβάστια καὶ τὰ μεγάλα Βουβάστια ἄγεται καὶ ἡ συναγωγὴ τῶν καρπῶν καὶ ἡ τοῦ ποταμοῦ ἀνάβασις γίνεται. Not on the first of Pauni as Casarico says. See Perpillou-Thomas (1993), 74.

[53] A. Grimm (1994), 113, G56; on the nature of the calendar, Grimm (1994), 8. Alliot (1949–54) 1, 232, with a different text.

[54] ἐς μέν νυν Βούβασιν πόλιν ἐπεὰν κομίζωνται, ποιεῦσι τοιάδε. πλέουσί τε γὰρ δὴ ἅμα ἄνδρες γυναιξὶ καὶ πολλόν τι πλῆθος ἑκατέρων ἐν ἑκάστηι βάρι · αἱ μὲν τινὲς τῶν γυναικῶν κρόταλα ἔχουσαι κροταλίζουσι, οἱ δὲ αὐλέουσι κατὰ πάντα τὸν πλόον, αἱ δὲ λοιπαὶ γυναῖκες καὶ ἄνδρες ἀείδουσι καὶ τὰς χεῖρας κροτέουσι. ἐπεὰν δὲ πλέοντες κατά τινα πόλιν ἄλλην γένωνται, ἐγχρίμψ αντες τὴν βᾶριν τῆι γῆι ποιεῦσι τοιάδε. αἱ μὲν τινὲς τῶν γυναικῶν ποιεῦσι τά περ εἴρηκα, αἱ δε τωθάζουσι βοῶσαι τὰς ἐν τῆι πόλι ταύτηι γυναῖκας, αἱ δὲ ὀρχέονται, αἱ δὲ ἀνασύρονται ἀνιστάμεναι. ταῦτα παρὰ πᾶσαν πόλιν παραποταμίην ποιεῦσι. ἐπεὰν δὲ ἀπίκωνται ἐς τὴν Βούβαστιν, ὁρτάζουσι μεγάλας ἀνάγοντες θυσίας, καὶ οἶνος ἀμπέλινος ἀναισιμοῦται πλέων ἐν τῆι ὁρτῆι ταύτηι ἢ ἐν τῶι ἅπαντι ἐνιαυτῶι τῶι ἐπιλοίπωι. συμφοιτῶσι δέ, ὅ τι ἀνὴρ καὶ γυνή ἐστι πλὴν παιδίων, καὶ ἐς ἑβδομήκοντα μυριάδας, ὡς οἱ ἐπιχώριοι λέγουσι.

[55] Compare the audience of 20,000 attested for a festival at Epidauros in Plato, *Ion* 535 b.

and children attended festivals in Greece.[56] The involvement of women is interesting because there is independent evidence of involvement of women in the cult of Bastet.[57] The banning of children perhaps reflects the extreme nature of the festivities there.

The pilgrimage to Boubastis is presented as a continuous celebration. Two details in particular stand out. First, the pilgrims would stop at towns *en route*,[58] shout mockery of the women of the town, and expose themselves. To a Greek reader the self-exposure perhaps suggests Baubo's self-exposure in the Eleusinian myth, but ritual self-exposure is well documented in Egyptian texts and iconography. For example, the figure of Isis pulling up her robe (Isis Anasurmene) is a common theme for Hellenistic and Roman terracottas.[59]

Second, at the sanctuary the pilgrims consume a large amount of wine. We have independent testimony that sacrifice was a characteristic feature of Egyptian festivals, for example in a festival of Hathor preserved in the Dendara calendar.[60] Drunkenness is an authentic detail of Egyptian festivals, though one we would tend to associate with Hathor rather than Bastet, and this is perhaps a sign of the syncretism between Bastet and Hathor mentioned earlier.[61]

In short, the pilgrimage to Boubastis is a model of Victor Turner's *communitas*-pilgrimage, a veritable Bakhtinian carnival of communal

---

[56] Dillon (1997), 183–203.

[57] Women's involvement in pilgrimage to Hathor is documented by Pinch (1993). A total of ten dedications to Boubastis, occasionally accompanied by consorts, survive from Hellenistic and Roman Egypt. Some of them probably come from Boubastis, though the provenance of all of them is not known. Compare Wagner (1983). Some of these dedications are made in the name of children, particularly girls, by their parents, others are made by a man and a woman. Only one is made by a man without a woman. Thus we have a dedication in the name of Galateia daughter of Theudotos (3rd–1st cent. BCE); another in the name of Asteria and Timarion, daughters of Sotion (175–170 BCE); both of these could be either the Boubastis in the Delta or the one in the Fayyum. From the Roman period comes a dedication by Theano mother of Theano (2nd cent. CE; from Alexandria). The role of women is striking, and it is perhaps more likely to be a traditional feature of the cult than a Hellenistic development based on old Greek ideas about Artemis. Compare *CIL* 14.29, from Ostia, by a woman.

[58] Cf. the frequent stops made by Apollonius of Tyana (Philostratus, *VA* 5) as he journeyed up the Nile.

[59] Frankfurter (1998a), 104, has a good discussion with bibliography; Tram Tam Tinh (1990), 780–1, nn. 256–7; Montserrat (1996), 167–70.

[60] Grimm (1994), 105 (G49**).

[61] On drunkenness, Volokhine (1998), 68; H. Brunner, *LÄ* 6.774–7 s.v. Trunkenheit; F. Daumas *LÄ* 2.1034–9 s.v. Hathor-Feste; Daumas (1970), 75–6.

celebration and excess.[62] The festivals that Greek pilgrims attended were times of celebration as well (cf. the account of Theoria/*theōria* in Aristophanes' *Peace*),[63] but not to this degree, and celebration did not spill over into the journey in the same way.

IV. PILGRIMS AND ANIMAL MUMMIES

Herodotus' sketch of pilgrimage to Boubastis looks reasonably reliable, but it should be borne in mind that he does not tell us everything. For example, there could easily be a 'Götterbesuch' dimension to the pilgrimage, as in the festival of Chnum at Esna, with official delegations visiting Boubastis from local towns. Another detail that Herodotus may have omitted is suggested by the fact that one of the most remarkable features of Boubastis are the large deposits of cat mummies, the cat being regarded as a sacred animal specially associated with Bastet. These deposits are so extensive that in the nineteenth century it was considered worth shipping the remains to Europe to manufacture manure.[64] Deposits of animal mummies are features of many Egyptian temples—hawks and ibises were particularly popular.[65] The animals were usually, it seems, raised in the temple.[66] The largest deposits— animal cemeteries as they are called—seem to date from no earlier than the reign of Nectanebo II in the 30th Dynasty (i.e. from about 360 BCE); it may be that they represent an intensification of native religious feeling during this period. But individual burials go back to the reign of Amenophis III.[67]

Greek sources are unanimous in reporting that the Egyptians considered it a capital offence to kill a sacred animal. It is therefore surprising that the mummified animals found in Egyptian sanctuaries show signs of having been deliberately killed, usually by strangulation, and to have been in good health at the time of death.[68] The conclusion

---

[62] Communitas: see p. 5 etc.; Bakhtin: see p. 422.
[63] Cf. Scullion, Ch. 4 in this volume.
[64] Kessler (1989), 150–4.
[65] D. Kessler, *LÄ* 6.579–83, s.v. Tierkult; full list in Kessler (1989), 17 ff.
[66] Ray (1976), 139.
[67] Chatton (1990). Intensification of religious feeling: Lloyd (1975–88), 2.293.
[68] Lloyd (1975–88), 2.300; Chatton (1990); references in Kessler (1989), 151.

seems inescapable that Egyptian priests killed the animals they professed to hold sacred. Once again, different types of evidence from Egypt seem to tell quite different stories.

The motivation and context of deposits of sacred animals must have varied, but it is at least possible that in some cases depositions were made at the behest of pilgrims visiting the sanctuaries; John Ray has suggested exactly this for the ibis cult at Saqqara.[69] As Ray himself says, many questions remain unanswered:

Was each bird allowed to die naturally, or was it put to death in some way? Was this done at the request of one of the many pilgrims who we know were attracted to the site, or did the visitor merely pay for an embalmment which had already taken place?

And there are many other questions as well: for example, did such dedications happen on specific occasions in the ritual calendar or all year round? and what exactly did the pilgrims believe they got out of this procedure?

Could the cat mummies at Boubastis be explained in a similar manner? For the Hellenistic period, the answer has to be yes. However, since the animal cemeteries appear to date from no earlier than the mid-fourth century BCE, over half a century after Herodotus, we cannot be certain that mass deposits of cat mummies were being made this early.

It is interesting that later on in book 2 (65–7) in his account of sacred animals Herodotus describes the interring of animal mummies in sanctuaries:

Cats which have died are delivered to Boubastis, where they are embalmed and buried in sacred receptacles; dogs are buried, also in sacred burial places, in the towns where they belong. Mongooses are buried in the same way as dogs; field-mice and hawks are taken to Buto, ibises to Hermopolis. Bears, which are scarce, and wolves (which in Egypt are not much bigger than foxes) are buried wherever they happen to be found lying dead.

So here we have a sort of system of pilgrimage involving delivery of animal carcasses to three cities: Buto, Bubastis, and Hermopolis (presumably Hermopolis Magna in Upper Egypt, capital of the Fifteenth Nome).[70] There is manifestly a correlation between the animal and the

---

[69] Ray (1976), 143; cf. particularly letter 19 (p.78), verso 8: 'one god in one vessel'.
[70] See Lloyd ad loc.

zoomorphic deity worshipped in these places: the cat corresponds to Bastet, the ibis to Thoth-Hermes, and the hawk and field-mouse to Horus. It all seems like a complex economy of cultic offerings, reminiscent of such systems in classical Greece, except for the funereal nature of the offerings.[71] The idea that the dead animal has to be taken to a sanctuary for burial is reminiscent, perhaps, of the so-called Abydos-fahrt, the journey to the home of Osiris at Abydos that a dead person is sometimes imagined to make after death.[72]

How are we to interpret this? Herodotus' account has some points in common with Ray's hypothesis about Saqqara. In both cases, someone visits a sanctuary and has a mummified animal interred. The difference is that in Herodotus' account the visitor takes a dead animal with him, whereas in Ray's model he acquires a dead animal (or has an animal killed) at the sanctuary. Herodotus also seems to distinguish the delivery of animal corpses from the festival-pilgrimage he describes earlier. There are two principal ways of reconciling this data, both of which yield remarkable conclusions. First, perhaps the practice of killing animals at sanctuaries, whether or not by pilgrims, develops after the period of Herodotus or his sources, and is roughly contemporaneous with the first attestation of the animal cemeteries in the fourth century; this also helps to explain why the Greeks were so convinced that the Egyptians did not kill animals; it had earlier been this way. Thus, in one respect at least the popular pilgrimage in Egypt undergoes a transformation between the fifth century and the Hellenistic period.

On the other hand, it is also possible that a limited number of sacred animals were killed at sanctuaries as early as the fifth century, and that Herodotus may have misunderstood what was going on, perhaps partly because the Egyptian religious officials themselves tended to obscure the truth with their official line about sacred animals. His account of the delivery of animals to the temples could thus be analysed as a bizarre attempt (by him or one of his informants) to reconcile the known fact that sacred animals were buried at sanctuaries with his belief that deliberate killing of sacred animals never took place.

---

[71] The verb ἀπάγω used here is reminiscent of the language of cultic offerings in classical Greece.

[72] See Rutherford (2003) with secondary sources cited there.

V. WHO WAS BASTET? SYNCRETISM AND SACRED GEOGRAPHY

Another respect in which we ought perhaps to question Herodotus' account of pilgrimage to Boubastis is his account of the deity. Comparison of Herodotus' account of Buto with the Gmenafharbok stele suggests that Herodotus simplified the complexity of cult-activity there, ignoring the deity Min who, in Egyptian thinking, is identified with Horus. Could something similar be true of his account of Boubastis?

Generally speaking, Herodotus seems to conceive the Egyptian and Greek panthea as closely corresponding systems, containing an array of equivalent deities.[73] However, a distinguishing feature of Egyptian religion at least as compared with Greek, is that different deities, of whom there are a very large number in the pantheon, are easily and frequently identified with each other in a kaleidoscopic system of creative syncretism.[74] One deity can be represented either as the same as another deity, or as the 'image', 'manifestation', or 'soul' of another deity. Judged against the much more realistic conventions of Greek theology, the results sometimes seem to defy logic or consistency.

In the case of Bastet syncretism seems to operate in at least three dimensions. First, Bastet tends to be identified with other goddesses represented in feline form, such as Tefnut and particularly Sakhmet.[75] A second syncretism that may be in play is with Hathor (Aphrodite in the *interpretatio Graeca*). These two goddesses are closely linked in the religious calendar from the temple of Horus at Edfu, which describes Hathor as 'she who lives in Boubastis', and prescribes sacrifices in 'The Northern Boubastis', in contrast to the southern Boubastis which will be Hathor's primary home at Dendara in Upper Egypt.[76] And the temple of Hathor at Dendara is the source for an inscription in which Hathor is

[73] This point comes out particularly at *Hist.* 2.50; Harrison (2000), 209.
[74] On this, see Hornung (1982), 92–3.
[75] An important text from Philae compares Tefnut to the benign Bastet and the ferocious Sakhmet Philae inscription, ed. Junker (1911); Bergman (1970) believes that Bastet was originally a local variant of Sakhmet.
[76] See Müller (1961); Grimm (1994), 113 (G56); Brugsch (1879–80), s.v. Derchaine (1962) points to an elaborate geographic system represented by the sequence of images on the walls of the Edfu temple where sites in Southern Egypt correspond to sites in North, among them Dendera and Boubastis (pp. 50–1)

described as: 'lady of Bast, mistress of Boubastis in Upper Egypt' (*nb B3sstt hnwt pr.b3 stt š mt*), where 'Boubastis in Upper Egypt' is a kenning for Dendara, implying interchangeability between the two goddesses.[77] Such correspondences between cults in Upper and Lower Egypt are common in sacred texts; for example, a sacred text from Esna in Upper Egypt gives an account of the birth of Neith, of her triumphal journey with the other gods to her home in Sais in Lower Egypt, and of the festival of Neith held there; remarkably, it seems to be implied that the name 'Sais' is understood in the sense of 'Esna'.[78] There, then, the syncretism is between cult-centres, but in the case of Hathor both the cult-centres and the goddesses are identified.

A third important syncretism is that between Bastet and the most important of all Egyptian goddesses Isis.[79] It is telling that in the canonical Hellenistic Isis-aretalogy, composed a few centuries after Herodotus, Isis claims for herself a special association with Boubastis (§11): ἐμοὶ Βούβαστος πόλις ᾠκοδομήθη ('the city of Boubastis was built for me'), a statement which implies a widespread syncretism of Bastet with Isis.[80] Attestations of the divine name Boubastis in Graeco-Roman inscriptions are in many cases probably to be analysed as references to an Isis who has undergone syncretism with Bastet.[81] It might be thought that there would be a tendency especially outside Egypt to identify any Egyptian goddess with Isis, who had come to be regarded as the Egyptian goddess *par excellence* by this period. However, this syncretism was already made in ancient Egypt, as we see in another text from Edfu: *b3 n 3st im m B3stt* ('the soul of Isis is there as Bastet'). Here the name 'Bastet' is creatively and falsely etymologized as the *b3–3st*, that is: *b3* (roughly 'soul') of Isis:[82]

[77] Müller (1961), 37; Brugsch (1879–80), s.v.

[78] Sauneron (1962), 245 ff.

[79] Greatest of gods: Hdt. 2.40; Lloyd (1975–88), 2.179.

[80] Cf. Andrian Hymn to Isis 25; Diodorus Siculus 1.27.4. On the subject, Dunand (1962), 83–6; (1973), 1.118–19.

[81] Cf. Vandebeek (1946); Boubasteia festival in *IG* 9.1.86. For Graeco-Roman references see Vidman (1969). The oddest is a priest of Bubastion (*SIG* 423), which Vidman not unreasonably takes as 'the two goddesses named Boubastis', i.e. the real Boubastis and Isis. In the Oxyrhynchus Aretalogy of Isis (*P.Oxy.* 1380), Isis is said to be worshipped in Boubastis with the name 'τὰ ἄνω', which suggests to J. Bergman (1970), the syncretism between Isis and Sothis, the dog-star. But Totti cites K. F. W. Schmidt, *GGA* 180 (1918), 106–17 and Manteuffel (1920), 2.70–85 for the interpretation Τοανω.

[82] Bergman (1970), 30.

Now the texts cited here are esoteric writings of Egyptian priests, and the extant copies derive from the late Hellenistic and Roman periods. Nevertheless, something like this could be operating at the popular level as well. It follows that it is not necessary that we believe that all the hundreds of thousands of pilgrims who flocked to the festival had a primary interest in Bastet; many of them may have thought of it primarily as a festival of a great Egyptian goddess, most commonly known as Isis and sometimes as Hathor, whose manifestation in this particular locale was as Bastet.[83] And there is a geographical dimension to this correspondence as well: pilgrimage to Boubastis in Upper Egypt is the mirror-image of pilgrimage to Dendara in the South, and so on the symbolic level it represents the activation of a religious network that transcends the political division of Egypt into North and South. In this way, the *communitas* activated through the pilgrimage to Boubastis could have approached the status of a truly pan-Egyptian phenomenon.[84]

[83] Sourdille (1910) points out that a pilgrimage of this magnitude makes more sense if we situate Bastet in the circle of Isis-Osiris. Bergman (1970) suggests that Isis might have been involved in the festival in her role as Sothis, the Dog-Star, a symbol of the new year for Egyptians.

[84] The symbolism of religious geography in Egypt seems to me a neglected subject. As an example of the sort of work that can be done, compare the 'surgical instruments' frieze from Kom Ombo, which contains a sequence of fractions of the Horus eye correlated with different Egyptian cities; as Derchain (1995) and Kurth (1996) suggest, the overall meaning of the frieze is the reintegration of Egypt through the power of Horus and the Emperor.

6

The Philosopher at the Festival:

Plato's Transformation of Traditional *Theōria*

Andrea Wilson Nightingale

In the fourth century BCE, Greek philosophers first articulated the idea that supreme wisdom takes the form of *theōria*. In addition to offering philosophic analyses and discussions of *theōria*, the fourth-century 'theorists' employed powerful rhetoric in the attempt to define this new intellectual practice. None offered a completely neutral or analytic account of theoretical activity; all developed what G. E. R. Lloyd calls 'a discourse, or one might say a rhetoric, of legitimation'.[1] In this chapter I will examine one of the central strategies deployed in the attempt to conceptualize and legitimize philosophical *theōria*, namely, the frequent use of the discourse and structures of traditional pilgrimages of *theōria*. The fourth-century philosophers took over the cultural practice of *theōria* and transformed it for their own purposes. In the venerable and authoritative institution of *theōria*, these philosophers found a model that served to define and defend the new discipline of 'theoretical' philosophy.

The dominant metaphor for philosophic activity in this period was that of *theōria* at panhellenic religious festivals. This comparison of philosophical activity to festival *theōria* was not a casual rhetorical trope: this move had powerful ideological associations. For, by linking philosophical 'theorizing' to an institution that was at once social,

---

[1] G. E. R. Lloyd (1990), 43.

political, and religious, the fourth-century thinkers identified theoretical philosophy as a specific kind of cultural practice. A *theōria* to a panhellenic festival took the form of a journey abroad for the sake of witnessing sacred spectacles or events in a 'space' that transcended the social and ideological practices of any single participant—a space that provided the context for a sacralized mode of viewing and apprehension. The pilgrim—called the *theōros*—could make this journey in a civic or a private capacity. In 'civic' *theōria*, the *theōros* journeyed to a festival as a representative of his city and then returned home with an official report. The journey as a whole, including the final report, was located in a civic context, and had both a political and religious significance. The philosophic appropriation of civic *theōria*—first found in Plato—aimed to ground theoretical philosophy in the world of social and political practice. In the *Republic*, in fact, Plato placed the theoretical philosopher at the very heart of political life, even though the activity of metaphysical contemplation detaches him (for a time) from the practical world.[2] Even when philosophers took 'private' *theōria* as their model—thus removing the philosopher from political affairs—they all claimed that the detached activity of contemplation is (paradoxically) central to the life of a flourishing *polis*.[3]

How, then, did the fourth-century philosophers use the practice of festival *theōria* in their efforts to conceptualize philosophic inquiry and apprehension? Different philosophers offered different accounts of *theōria*: the discipline of theoretical philosophy was a contested enterprise, even among its defenders. In spite of their differences, however, the fourth-century theorists turned to festival *theōria*—in either its civic or its private form—as the model for philosophic practice. Consider, for

---

[2] As I will suggest, the model of 'civic' (as opposed to 'private') *theōria* provides the paradigm for the philosophic theorist in the ideal city. But, as Plato claimed, the philosopher living in a bad city cannot play this role, and therefore must practise *theōria* as a private person who does not participate in politics. The model of 'civic' *theōria*, then, is more of a distant ideal than a true paradigm for ordinary philosophers (who do not live in good cities).

[3] This does not mean that people actually accepted the philosophers' claims (though many influential men did study with these thinkers). Humphreys (1978), ch. 9 offers an excellent analysis of the changing role of the intellectual in archaic and classical Greece. Part of the material on traditional and philosophic *theōria* in this chapter derives from Nightingale (2004), chs. 1–2.

example, a fragment from a dialogue by Heraclides of Pontus (a member of Plato's Academy), which is summarized by Cicero. In this passage, Heraclides draws an explicit parallel between the *theōros* at the Olympic Games and the philosophic theorist, who contemplates 'the nature of things':

> the life of man resembles the festival [at Olympia] celebrated with the most magnificent games before a gathering collected from all of Greece. For at this festival some men trained their bodies and sought to win the glorious distinction of a crown, others came to make a profit by buying or selling. But there was also a certain class, made up of the noblest men, who sought neither applause nor gain, but came for the sake of spectating and closely watched the event and how it was done.[4]

Here, Heraclides depicts three groups of individuals gathered at the Olympian festival: the competitors, who seek glory and honour; the businessmen, who pursue wealth; and the *theōroi*, who go to the festival 'for the sake of spectating'. This latter group provides the model for the theoretical philosophers. For, as Heraclides claims, the philosopher resembles 'the most liberal man at the Olympic festival, who spectates without seeking anything for himself' (*liberalissimum esset spectare nihil sibi acquirentem*). The 'noble' men in this group, Heraclides says, are 'a special few who, counting all else as nothing, studiously contemplate (*intuerentur*) the nature of things'. In this passage, Heraclides claims that the activity of contemplative 'spectating' is disinterested, noble, and liberal: the philosophical theorist engages in the contemplation of metaphysical realities as an end in itself.

Aristotle uses this same 'festival image' in his popularizing dialogue, the *Protrepticus*:

> Wisdom is not useful or advantageous (χρήσιμον ... μηδὲ ὠφέλιμον), for we call it not advantageous but good, and it should be chosen not for the sake of any other thing, but for itself. For just as we go to the Olympian festival for the sake of the spectacle (θέα), even if nothing more should come of it—for the

---

[4] Cicero, *Tusculan Disputations* 5.3 (see also Iamblichus' *Life of Pythagoras* 58); Heraclides puts this idea in the mouth of Pythagoras, thus retrojecting this fourth-century conception of wisdom back onto the ancients and investing it with a venerable pedigree (As Jaeger (1923), appendix, Burkert (1960), and Gottschalk (1980), 29–33 have demonstrated).

theōria (θεωρία) itself is more precious than money; and just as we go to theorize (θεωροῦμεν) the Festival of Dionysus not so that we will gain anything from the actors (indeed we pay to see them)... so too the *theōria* (θεωρία) of the universe must be honored above all things that are considered to be useful (χρησιμόν). For surely we should not go to such trouble to see men imitating women and slaves, or athletes fighting and running, and not think it right to theorize without payment (θεωρεῖν ἄμισθον) the nature and truth of reality. (Düring B44)

Here, Aristotle compares the philosophic 'theorist' to the *theōros* who goes to a festival to see dramatic, musical, or athletic competitions. Aristotle emphasizes that both do this 'for the sake of the spectacle' rather than for profit or gain, though the philosophic theorist is superior to the ordinary *theōros* (who views the inferior spectacles of drama and athletics). The philosophic *theōros*, he claims, contemplates 'the nature of truth and reality', pursuing this as an end in itself rather than for goal-oriented, utilitarian purposes. For this reason, the activity of theorizing is not 'useful or advantageous' and does not offer any 'payment' or wage in the external world—rather, it is a completely free and leisured activity. Like Heraclides, Aristotle claims that the theorist does not seek personal profit but engages in a pure and disinterested act of spectating.

As these passages reveal, Heraclides and Aristotle defined *theōria* in opposition to practical activities: contemplation was starkly contrasted with economic transactions or political affairs. The theoretical philosopher, during the time that he practises contemplation, is disembedded from the social and political systems of exchange in the city and engages in transactions in a completely different sphere. This construction of an opposition between contemplation and action raised the question whether philosophic *theōria* had any role to play in the practical or political realm. How (if at all) did the theorist's contemplation of metaphysical spectacles influence his actions (either practical or political) when he 'returned' to the city? The fourth-century philosophers developed different conceptions of *theōria* and offered different accounts of the theorist's role in civic affairs. In this essay, I will examine the foundational construction of philosophic *theōria*—that articulated by Plato—looking in particular at its appropriation and transformation of the traditional practice of *theōria*.

THEŌRIA AS A CULTURAL PRACTICE

In ancient Greece, *theōria* was a cultural practice characterized by a journey abroad for the sake of witnessing an event or spectacle. In all journeys of *theōria*, the pilgrim or *theōros* travelled away from home to see some sort of spectacle or learn something about the outside world, thus confronting unfamiliar modes of social, civic, and natural life. In classical Greece, the *theōros* could be sent as an official representative of his city, in which case the *theōria* was carried out in a civic and political context. But a *theōros* could also venture forth on his own, performing a 'private' rather than a 'civic' *theōria*. I want to analyse one form of *theōria* quite common in the classical period, namely, the *theōria* to religious festivals. A fuller understanding of this cultural practice will enable us to examine the fourth-century construction of 'theoretical' philosophy from a whole new angle.

Theōria involved a journey abroad. But what counts as travelling 'abroad'? It goes without saying that an individual who travels outside the territory of his own city-state goes abroad (whereas a person who makes a trip to a destination within his city does not). In cases such as Athens, however, which controlled the entire region of Attica, Athenians often travelled to 'extra-urban' sanctuaries or festivals located within the borders of the *polis*-territory but distant from the city proper.[5] Linguistic evidence indicates that such trips did constitute a *theōria*, presumably because they involved a journey of some distance from the city-centre.[6]

---

[5] 'Extra-urban' sanctuaries were located outside of the city proper, often near the borders of the *polis*-territory; these marked the territorial influence of a city and were regional centres for religious activity (Marinatos (1993), 229–30).

[6] Dillon (1997), xviii; Rutherford (2003). See e.g. Euripides *Ion* 1074–80 (on the Athenian *theōros* going to the festival at Eleusis), Herodotus 6.87 (on the Athenian *theōria* to the festival of Poseidon at Sounion), Aristophanes' *Peace* 874 (on the Athenian *theōria* to Brauron). In evaluating the linguistic evidence for the practice of *theōria*, one must distinguish between the technical terms *theōria* and *theōros* from the non-technical verb *theōrein*, which has a very broad semantic range (often signifying 'to observe' anything in one's visual path) and does not by itself serve as a criterion for identifying an actual *theōria*. See, e.g., Koller (1958), 279; Rausch (1982), 15–18; Rutherford (1995), 276, (1998*b*), 132, (2000*a*), 133–8; Ker (2000), 308. Excluding Plato and other thinkers dealing with philosophic *theōria* (who expanded the sense of the term '*theōria*'), there are very few deviations from the technical sense of the nouns *theōria* and *theōros* in the classical period, and these all come from mid to late 4th-cent. texts: Isocrates, *Areopagiticus* 53; Demosthenes, *Contra Macarta* 18.4, *De Corona* 118; Pseudo-Demosthenes, *Eroticus* 16.

For example, an Athenian who travelled from an urban deme in Athens to participate in the rituals at Eleusis (in Attica, 22 kilometres (*c.*14 miles) from Athens) or to the sanctuary of Poseidon at Sounion (on the southern tip of Attica) undertook a *theōria*, whereas the Athenian who went to the City Dionysia in Athens did not. In short, the activity of *theōria* could only take place at a distance from the pilgrim's home-town or city: geographical distance was a precondition for the special kind of viewing and apprehension that characterized the theoric pilgrimage.

Throughout ancient Greece, *theōria* took the form of a pilgrimage in which the *theōros* departed from his city, journeyed to a religious sanctuary, witnessed spectacles and events there (and participated in rituals), and returned home to ordinary civic life. In their anthropological study of Christian pilgrimage, Victor and Edith Turner break this journey into three phases:

> The first phase comprises symbolic behavior signifying the detachment of the individual or group, either from an earlier fixed point in the social structure or from a relatively stable set of cultural conditions; during the intervening liminal phase, the state of the ritual subject (the 'passenger' or 'liminar') becomes ambiguous, he passes through a realm or dimension that has few or none of the attributes of the past or coming state, he is betwixt and between all familiar lines of classification; in the third phase the passage is consummated, and the subject returns to classified secular or mundane social life.[7]

The Turners' discussion places special emphasis on the 'liminal' phase, which includes the journey to and especially the ritual activity at the religious site. During this period, the pilgrim detaches from familiar social structures and enters into foreign and sacred spaces. In this 'liminal' phase, the traveller opens himself to what is new and extra-

---

[7] Turner and Turner (1978), 2 (see also Turner (1974*b*) and (1974*c*)). The Turners focus on the 'liminal' phase of the pilgrimage, i.e. after departure and before re-entry (though they prefer to use the term 'liminoid', since the Christian pilgrimages they study are voluntary rather than 'an obligatory social mechanism', p.35). For criticisms of this thesis, see Morinis (1984), Bowman (1985), Jha (1985) (introduction and essays), Eade and Sallnow (1991) (introduction and essays). Coleman and Elsner (1995), epilogue, offer a more positive assessment of the Turner thesis, though they rightly challenge the claim that pilgrims form a *communitas* that transcends traditional social and political hierarchies. They take '*communitas*' to be an ideal rather than an actual feature of pilgrimages, which are extremely diverse and do not fit the Turners' schematic structure. See also Elsner's discussion of the theory of the 'contestation' of meanings and ideologies at pilgrimage centres (1998 and Ch. 16, this vol.).

mundane. According to the Turners, pilgrimage brings about the partial, if not complete, abrogation of traditional social structures during the period of the journey (rather than reinforcing those structures, as Durkheim suggested).[8]

In 'civic' *theōria* in the classical period, however, the *theōros* made a journey which was structured by political and religious institutions: his activities abroad were, at least in principle, regulated and monitored. This kind of *theōria*, then, does not completely fit the Turners' model. But one should note that the civic *theōros* who journeyed abroad did separate himself, to some extent, from the norms and ideologies of his native city, and he experienced a high degree of freedom during the journey.[9] And this separation from the city was even more pronounced in the case of 'private' *theōria*, since the private *theōros* was in no way answerable to the city and thus enjoyed complete freedom. Whether travelling in a civic or a private capacity, the *theōros* was bound to encounter—and perhaps even embrace—foreign ideas and practices during his journey abroad. There is ample evidence that the Greeks understood that the theoric journey detached the pilgrim from his own community—indeed, this detachment was perceived as a potential threat to the city. We may conclude, then, that *theōria* in the classical period follows the basic pattern of detachment from the city, the 'liminal' phase of the journey itself (culminating in the 'witnessing' of events and spectacles in a religious precinct), and re-entry into the *polis*.[10]

In the classical period, Greek cities made a regular practice of sending *theōroi* as official ambassadors to attend and witness religious festivals. The panhellenic festivals—the Olympian, Pythian, Nemean, and Isthmian—included a variety of religious rituals as well as competitions in athletic and artistic events. And the big Athenian festivals—the City Dionysia and the Panathenaia—featured these same kinds of spectacles (with the addition of dramatic contests at the Dionysia). These festivals drew *theōroi* from all over Greece and provided occasions for different cities to interact with one another. A Greek city sending a *theōria* to the major festivals chose its most illustrious men (generally aristocrats) to

---

[8] Durkheim (1912).
[9] See Nightingale (2004), ch. 1.
[10] Though it did not bring about the *communitas* that the Turners' claim is a defining feature of religious pilgrimage.

represent it in the international arena. The members of this embassy, like those visiting an oracular shrine, returned home with an official account of the *theōria*.[11]

The panhellenic festivals were, first and foremost, religious events that took place in elaborate sanctuaries and featured rituals and sacred spectacles. As Elsner has suggested, *theōria* at a religious festival was characterized by a 'ritual-centred visuality'. The rituals that structured the activities at religious sanctuaries prepared the *theōros* to enter into a specific mode of seeing, since the pilgrim witnessed objects and events that were sacralized by way of ritual structures and ceremonies.

> The viewer enters a sacred space, a special place set apart from ordinary life, in which the god dwells. In this liminal site, the viewer enters the god's world and likewise the deity intrudes directly into the viewer's world in a highly ritualized context.[12]

The viewing of objects and events at a religious sanctuary, then, was a religious activity in itself: the entire precinct, as well as the various rituals and events that took place there, formed part of the spectacle.[13] We must remember, however, that these sanctuaries, with their complex blend of icons, statues, showy dedications, treasuries, architecture, etc., offered a wide array of visual options to the visitor. As Elsner observes, although 'ritual-centred visuality' remained the defining feature of the theoric pilgrimage, the *theōros* could opt for different 'regimes of spectatorship' during his sojourn at a sanctuary—regimes ranging from the aesthetic to the spiritual.[14]

CIVIC VS. PRIVATE *THEŌRIA*

As I have suggested, *theōria* could be conducted privately, as well as in a civic context. In addition to the civic *theōros*, who travelled as a public ambassador, many individuals attended religious festivals in a private

---

[11] In his forthcoming book on *theōria*, Ian Rutherford will discuss Greek inscriptions that dealt with the offical reports of the civic *theōroi* upon returning to the city, and the events and/or rituals that took place when they returned.

[12] Elsner (2000*b*), 61.

[13] Rutherford (1998*b*), 135.

[14] For examples of aesthetic viewing at religious sanctuaries, see Eur. *Andr.* 1086–7, *Ion* 184–218, 233; Aesch. *Theōroi* (*TrGF* fr. 78a), Epicharmus *CGF* fr. 79.

capacity. In the case of 'private' *theōria*, the individual *theōros* would not have been appointed or funded by the state, nor did he offer an official account of the *theōria* on his return home. In principle, he was not accountable to the city for what he saw or learned abroad—his activities as a *theōros* were entirely his own affair.[15]

The civic *theōros* differed from the private *theōros* in that he provided a direct link between the theoric event and his own city and its affairs. This is especially obvious in the case of *theōroi* who returned from an oracular consultation. But it also applied in cases of civic *theōria* to festivals. Consider, for example, Plato's treatment of *theōria* to religious festivals in the *Laws*. In his legislation for the city of Magnesia, Plato positively forbids private *theōria* of any kind (950d), and sets forth many strictures for the practice of civic *theōria*. In particular, he creates a number of strict rules for the return of the *theōros* to the city. As he asserts, the official *theōroi* sent from Magnesia to the Pythian, Olympian, Nemean, and Isthmian festivals must be required, when they return, to spread the report that 'the customs and laws of other countries are inferior to their own' (951a). When the Magnesian *theōros* gets home, he must report 'immediately' to the council of elders who supervise the laws (952b). If he has learned anything on his journey dealing with matters concerning legislation or education or nurture, the *theōros* shall report this to the council (952b). If the council determines that he has brought back valuable information, he may convey this to the young (952a); but if they find that he has been 'corrupted' by his journey, they will forbid him to associate with anyone in the city and compel him to live as a private person (952c). If a *theōros* does not comply, they will try him in the courts and, if he is convicted, execute him on the charge of 'meddling with the culture and the laws' (952c). Here, the re-entry of the *theōros* is treated as a momentous and potentially dangerous political event: the importation of foreign ideas and practices can bring benefits to the city, but it can always bring corruption instead.

---

[15] Goldhill (1999) and Ker (2000) aim to politicize private *theōria*. I agree that 'the *theōros*...is always in some sense the city's representative' (Ker (2000), 310), but we must not overlook the fundamental differences between civic and private *theōria*.

Plato's attempt to control the re-entry of the *theōros* is a reminder that, in civic *theōria*, the ambassador's return home is no less important than the journey abroad. As Rutherford observes,

the return poses a special crisis because it also represents the moment when a piece of information of immense danger and importance is injected into the community. The danger that a corrupt *theōros* will attempt to exploit the situation is ever present (cf. Theognis, 806). And a *theōros* bringing bad news, like a messenger, stands a good chance of being blamed (like Creon in the *Oedipus Tyrannus*).[16]

Though the civic *theōros* and the private *theōros* have much in common, they nonetheless occupy distinct categories. The civic *theōros*, as a public ambassador, performs specific religious and political duties and provides an official link between the theoric event and the city; the private pilgrim or spectator had no such obligations.

THE POLITICS OF *THEŌRIA*

Theōria to religious festivals was a cultural practice that drew people from different Greek cities together in shared religious sanctuaries. This practice had a political as well as a religious dimension. As Sourvinou-Inwood suggests, in ancient Greece 'the *polis* anchored, legitimated, and mediated all religious activity. This is true even in the panhellenic sanctuaries'.[17] In fact, the *theōroi* were always recognized as members of their individual cities:

The *theōroi* of each *polis* conducted ritual acts in the panhellenic sanctuaries in the name of that *polis*. . . . The treasuries erected by individual *poleis* in the great panhellenic sanctuaries are the physical expression of this mediation [of the *polis*], the symbolic representation of the *polis* systems in those sanctuaries.[18]

The *theōroi*, then, were never completely detached from the norms and ideologies of their home cities. The civic *theōros*, in fact, served as a representative of his city, and was perceived as such by the other Greeks assembled at a festival. In spite of his official position, however, the civic *theōros* enjoyed considerable freedom once he left home:

[16] Rutherford (1995), 282.   [17] Sourvinou-Inwood (1990), 297.
[18] Sourvinou-Inwood (1990), 298.

For the individual as citizen of a state, going 'beyond the bounds' was a dangerous move, since community boundaries mark the extent of the security and status conferred by group membership. Yet for the individual, it allowed the freedom to act in whatever way he might deem to be in his own interest.[19]

Even as a civic representative, the *theōros* departed from the social and ideological 'space' of his city and entered a panhellenic 'space' in which Greeks were encouraged to rise above their differences and join together as people sharing a common language, religion, and culture. In this unique 'space', the *theōroi* participated in a religious event which trans- cended—and, to some extent, challenged—the social, political, and ideological structures of any individual city.

In investigating the political valence of the gatherings at theoric events, one must look beyond the local politics of any individual city. Since the major festivals attracted people from all over Greece, they brought disparate (and sometimes hostile) peoples into contact. As Rutherford claims,

an underlying reason for going to a panhellenic sanctuary was to assert the voice of one's own *polis* in the panhellenic community, and hence to gain recognition and prestige throughout the Greek world. The panhellenic significance of the great sanctuaries is so central that we should think of the underlying structure of much Greek pilgrimage as a symbolic movement not so much from 'secular space' to 'sacred space' and back again, but rather between 'local space' and 'panhellenic space'.[20]

Rutherford rightly emphasizes 'panhellenic space' as a defining feature of the theoric event. But it is of course Greek religion and its 'spaces' that provide the institutional and ideological grounding for panhellenic gatherings. It is precisely the confluence of religion and politics that made *theōria* a unique cultural practice, investing it with such great authority and legitimacy.

---

[19] Morgan (1993), 31. As she goes on to explain, the sanctuaries and institutionalized cults within them served (to some extent) to 'limit the actions of individuals to those acceptable to the city'.

[20] Rutherford (1995), 276; Connor (1988), 164 argues that 'in classical Athenian culture the sacred was seen as parallel to and co-ordinate with the other [i.e. "secular"] realm'.

FROM TRADITIONAL TO PHILOSOPHIC *THEŌRIA*

Traditional *theōria* involves 'autopsy' or seeing something for oneself: the *theōros* is an eyewitness whose experience differs radically from those who stay home and receive a mere report of the news. During the period of his journey, the *theōros* encounters what is foreign and different. This encounter with the unfamiliar invites the traveller to look at his own city with different eyes. As Coleman and Elsner observe,

pilgrimage...not only involves movement through space but also an active process of response as the pilgrim encounters both the journey and the goal. It is the experience of travel and the constant possibility of encountering the new which makes pilgrimage distinct from other forms of ritual.[21]

The journey abroad may end up confirming the theorist in his original perpectives and prejudices, but it may also function to unsettle him and even to transform his world-view. *Theōria*, in short, brings an individual into contact with what is foreign and different: it is an encounter with otherness. In the case of festival *theōria*, in fact, the *theōros* not only encounters foreign peoples and places but also interacts with the god who presides over a given festival or shrine (by participating in the sacrifices, prayers, and rituals). Here, the *theōros* approaches the ultimate and most distant 'Other', a divine being.[22]

The following features of festival *theōria* directly influenced the philosophic conceptions of *theōria* developed in the fourth century:

1. Detachment: the *theōros* departs from his native city, leaving behind ordinary practical and political activities; freed from traditional constraints, he is able to achieve a different perspective on the world and his place in it.

2. Spectating: the *theōros* travels to a sacred 'space' where he views spectacles, rituals, and holy objects. Although he might carry this out in the context of an official mission, the act of spectating was,

---

[21] Coleman and Elsner (1995), 206.
[22] Though the *theōros* does not literally 'see' this being, he does look at sacred images and symbols and, by way of ritual, enters into a relationship with a god.

while it lasted, a simple matter of seeing, witnessing, and reflectively responding. This activity is distinct from the journey *per se* and the other activities in the pilgrimage: while spectating, the *theōros* suspended other activities and pursuits and opened himself to the spectacle.[23] In addition, since the *theōros* viewed sacred objects and spectacles, his spectatorial activity had a religious orientation. He thus entered into a ritualized form of seeing in which other (more secular) forms of visualization were filtered out by religious rites and ceremonies.

3. The Return: the *theōros* eventually journeyed home and re-entered domestic and civic life. Like any individual who travels abroad, the *theōros* may have returned from the journey with different perspectives and points of view. The *theōros*' re-entry into the city created apprehension on the part of the citizens, since it was possible that he might bring foreign and 'corrupt' ideas into the *polis*.

As I have suggested, in their appropriation and transformation of traditional *theōria*, the fourth-century philosophers took as their model festival *theōria* (in both its civic and its private forms). The philosophers favoured this paradigm for several reasons. First, they sought to conceptualize a mode of apprehension that took the form of 'seeing' divine essences or truths. *Theōria* at religious festivals—in which the pilgrim viewed icons, sacred images, and ritualized spectacles—offered a good model for this conception of philosophical 'vision'. As we have seen, the rituals which organized the activity of theorizing at religious sanctuaries and festivals made possible a specific mode of seeing—'ritual-centred visuality'. This visual mode 'denies the appropriateness . . . of interpreting images through the rules and desires of everyday life. It constructs a ritual barrier to the identifications and objectifications of the screen of [social] discourse and posits a sacred possibility for vision'.[24] The philosophers of the fourth century conceptualized a mode of 'seeing' that resembled ritualized vision in some key ways. In particular, they conceived of philosophic *theōria* as an activity in which the 'spectating' operated outside of traditional social and

---

[23] See Wallace (1997) for a discussion of 'audience performance' in classical Athens.
[24] Elsner (2000*b*), 62.

ideological spheres. Like the *theōros* at religious festivals, the philosophic theorist detaches himself from ordinary social and political affairs in an effort to contemplate divine and eternal objects. But this theorist goes well beyond the traditional *theōros* in his 'visualization' of divine essences: for the philosopher engaging in contemplation completely detaches himself from his city—and, indeed, from the entire human world—and enters a sphere that is impersonal, disinterested, and objective. Indeed, he practises an entirely new form of spectating that is so far above ordinary human life that the philosophers attributed this contemplative activity to the gods themselves. Unlike the spectatorial activities of the traditional *theōros*, which are not objective or independent of the views of others (there were, after all, huge numbers of *theōroi* at every festival), the philosopher contemplates alone or with a few like-minded associates, seeking to perfect his understanding by turning his back on all traditional views. It is only after contemplation that the philosopher resumes his individual and political identity.

Theōria at religious festivals also offered the philosophers the model of a panhellenic 'space' which (at least in principle) transcended political differences and encouraged a sense of identity which was more universal than that defined by the *polis*. At panhellenic festivals, people from different cities could affirm a single Greek identity based on a shared religion, language, and culture. While the traditional *theōros* at a panhellenic festival did not abandon his political identity, he participated in a religious gathering which operated above and beyond any single political ideology. The fourth-century philosophers took this model to its extreme: philosophic 'spectating' operates in a sphere that completely transcends social and political life. In the activity of contemplation, the theorist rises above all earthly affairs—including his own individual human identity—in order to 'see' eternal and divine beings. Building on the practice of traditional *theōria*, the philosophers developed the notion of the transcendental, impersonal, and impartial 'space' of theoretical activity. This radical separation between theoretical and social/political 'space', of course, inevitably raised the question whether the wisdom acquired in metaphysical contemplation could (or should) play a role in civic affairs. The philosophers thus had to address the question of the theorist's 'return' to the city, which was even more problematic than that of the traditional *theōros*.

THEŌRIA IN PLATO'S *REPUBLIC*

The *Republic* exhibits especially clearly Plato's appropriation and transformation of festival *theōria* in his effort to conceptualize the practice of philosophy. Indeed the traditional practice of *theōria* features quite prominently in this text. At the very opening of this dialogue, Socrates describes his trip to Peiraeus to 'theorize' the festival sacred to the goddess Bendis (327a–b). As he says in the opening lines:

> I went down yesterday with Glaucon the son of Ariston to the Peiraeus, in order to offer my prayers to the goddess [Bendis] and also because I wanted to see (θεάσασθαι) how they would conduct the festival, since this was the first time they celebrated it. I thought that the procession of the citizens was quite fine, but the procession sent by the Thracians was no less fine. After we had offered our prayers and theorized the spectacle (θεωρήσαντες), we began to head back to the city. (327a)

Here, Socrates describes his (private) *theōria* at the festival of Bendis, a Thracian goddess whose worship had just been instituted in Attica.[25] Although we do not know the precise date of this inaugural festival, evidence from inscriptions indicates that it was sometime before 429 BCE.[26] The bustling port of Peiraeus no doubt attracted *theōroi* from many different places; Socrates explicitly mentions a procession 'sent' by the Thracians (no doubt because Bendis was a Thracian goddess), thus reminding us that the festival had international spectators and participants. The fact that this was the first celebration in Athens of a Thracian festival gives it a peculiar status as both Athenian and foreign: for while Athens officially instituted and sponsored the festival, the Thracians played a key role in 'introducing' it and participating in its rituals.[27] The festival, then, is not simply a local Athenian gathering but a true 'theoric event'. Indeed Socrates himself articulates a sentiment that represents

---

[25] The Athenian *polis* had the power to include and exclude forms of worship in this region, and people who wished to introduce new cults or festivals had to seek official sanction (see e.g. Burkert (1985), 176–9; Garland (1992), 14, 19, 137, and *passim*).

[26] Garland (1992), 111–14 suggests that the foundation of the festival was directly connected with inter-state politics, since the Athenians were keen to form an alliance with the Thracian potentate Sitalces at the outbreak of the Peloponnesian War (see also Ostwald (1992), 313).

[27] Garland (1992), 112; Ostwald (1992), 313.

the ideal of panhellenic gatherings when he claims that the Thracian procession was as fine as the Athenian: here, he transcends the Athenocentric point of view and deliberately adopts a panhellenic position.

This instance of *theōria* at the very opening of the *Republic* is carefully woven into the text, and it proleptically anticipates the metaphysical *theōria* set forth in books 5–7. In the scene at the beginning of book 1, some friends who have also come as *theōroi* to the festival apprehend Socrates as he is heading back to Athens, informing him with great excitement that there will be a relay-race on horseback in honour of Bendis that evening, as well as an all-night celebration 'well worth seeing' (ἄξιον θεάσασθαι, 328a). These friends compel Socrates to stay in the Peiraeus so they can see the spectacles together later that night (328a). They then proceed to take him to the festival dinner at Cephalus' house, where Socrates begins the long discussion that occupies the rest of the dialogue. Interestingly, the group never returns to the festival, opting instead to engage in a philosophic search for the nature of justice. This philosophic *theōria* thus interrupts and supplants the *theōria* at the festival. This move from traditional to philosophic *theōria* is clearly emphasized later in the book, when Thrasymachus says that their conversation is itself the feast at the Festival of Bendis (354a–b): here, the literal feast is recast as a 'feast' of words. In the opening scene of the *Republic*, then, Plato introduces several key ideas that will re-emerge later in the dialogue: the activity of spectating at a religious festival; the themes of light and darkness, day and night; and the notion of spectacles 'worth seeing'.

Theōria is also featured at the very end of the *Republic*, for the famous 'myth of Er' is depicted as a journey to a religious festival. In this eschatological tale, a man named Er plays the role of an official *theōros*. According to the story, Er was slain in battle and taken for dead, but when he was brought home and placed on the funeral pyre he woke up and related to his own people the spectacle that he had seen on his visit to the land of the dead. Socrates places great emphasis on Er's journey and its destination: 'Er said that when his soul departed (ἐκβῆναι) he journeyed (πορεύεσθαι) with a great many people, and they came to some sort of divine region' (ἀφικνεῖσθαι σφᾶς εἰς τόπον τινὰ δαιμόνιον, 614b–c). Er, then, has made a pilgrimage with other souls to a foreign and divine place—the region where the souls are judged after death. As Er relates, there he saw the souls coming down from heaven and those coming up from hell after a period of 1,000 years; these souls 'appeared to have come from a long journey (ἐκ πολλῆς πορείας) and happily went to the meadow to camp there as at a festival (ἐν πανηγύρει), and the souls who knew each other embraced; those coming from beneath the earth asked the others about the conditions up above, and those coming from heaven asked how it fared with them' (614d–e). The gathering that Er witnesses, in short, is described as a religious festival (a *panēgyris* is the standard term for a panhellenic festival). The souls at the gathering meet both friends and strangers and, like people on a traditional *theōria*, they give infor- mation to foreigners and receive information from them. The 'space' in which they meet is located outside of ordinary social and political affairs, and transcends the ideology of any given city or peoples. The festival is thus a panhellenic or, perhaps better, 'pan-human' event. At the same time, the souls in attendance maintain the identity of their former life (for which they are rewarded or punished): civic and personal affairs are not completely left behind.

The judges explain to Er that 'he must be the messenger to mankind to tell them of the things here', and they bid him 'to hear and to see everything in this region' (θεάσθαι πάντα τὰ ἐν τῶι τόπωι, 614d). Er, then, takes on the official task of witnessing the 'sights and sounds' in this region.[28] And he must also bring this information back to the human world, thus performing the duties of the civic *theōros*. We know that he does indeed perform this mission for, as Socrates says, when Er was 'brought home' (κομισθεὶς δ᾽ οἴκαδε) and restored to life, 'he related the things that he saw there' (ἔλεγεν ἃ ἐκεῖ ἴδοι).

Plato thus portrays Er as a *theōros* at a peculiar kind of religious festival who interacts with divine beings and brings back a report from this strange and sacred place. In his visit to this 'festival', Er bears witness to competitive and theatrical 'spectacles' (*theamata*, 615d). He watches the newly dead souls being judged for their performance on earth and then rewarded and punished—he sees, in short, the winners and losers in the game of life. He also watches the souls who have returned from heaven and hell choose their next life. This spectacle takes the form of a sort of drama, complete with famous characters like Ajax and

---

[28] This phrase recalls the 'lovers of sights and sounds' in book 5 who, as we will see, are *theōroi* at Dionysian festivals.

Agamemnon and Odysseus, which Er calls a 'pitiful...and ridiculous sight to see' (619e–620a).[29]

Note, finally, that Er says that this spectacle 'was a sight worth seeing' (ταύτην... τὴν θέαν ἀξίαν εἶναι ἰδεῖν), which recalls the scene at the opening of the dialogue where the visitors to the festival of Bendis tell Socrates that the torch-race and nightly events will be 'worth seeing' (328a). This verbal echo reminds us that *theōria* is featured at the very beginning and the very end of the dialogue. Plato's deliberate placement of theoric events at the beginning and end of the dialogue serves to highlight the discussion of '*theōria*' in its central books. Indeed, as we will see, traditional *theōria* plays a prominent role in the very middle of the *Republic*, offering a direct model for the philosopher's journey to the metaphysical region of the Forms and his return 'home' with a report from this region.

In books 5–7 of the *Republic*, Socrates sets forth for the first time in Plato's corpus a detailed account of a new practice that he calls 'philosophy'.[30] In fact, when Socrates brings up the topic of 'philosophy' in book 5, his interlocutors do not understand what he means by this term. It is worth emphasizing that, before the fourth century BCE, the word *philosophein* (and its cognates) meant 'intellectual cultivation' in the broad sense; it did not refer to a specialized discipline or mode of wisdom. It was in fact Plato who first appropriated this term for one particular intellectual discipline. He therefore had to define and describe the 'philosopher' with great care and specificity.[31] Part and parcel of this construction of the specialized discipline of philosophy is the identification of '*theōria*' as the quintessential activity of the true philosopher.

From the very beginning of his definition of the 'philosopher' in the *Republic* bk. 5, Socrates describes him as a new kind of *theōros*. At the opening of this discussion, in fact, Socrates explicitly gestures towards the traditional practice of *theōria*. Socrates begins with the 'love' portion of the 'love of wisdom', inviting his interlocutors to consider individuals who are 'lovers of sights' (φιλοθεάμονες) and 'lovers

---

[29] Pity, of course, conjures up the genre of tragedy, while the ridiculous invokes that of comedy: here, Plato gestures towards the dramatic productions at Dionysian festivals.

[30] On Plato's construction of the specialized discipline of philosophy, see Nightingale (1995).

[31] See Nightingale (1995), ch.1 and *passim*.

of sounds' (φιλήκοοι 475d). Out of all the varieties of 'lover', these ones will provide the model for the lover of wisdom. Who and what are the 'lovers of sights and sounds'? Socrates describes them as people who 'run around to all the Dionysian festivals, never leaving a single one out, either in the towns or in the cities' (475d). The lovers of sights and sounds, then, are clearly identified as *theōroi* who journey abroad to religious festivals to witness the events there.[32] These *theōroi*, in fact, call to mind the men who encounter Socrates at the festival of Bendis at the opening of the dialogue: as we have seen, these men were enthusiastic viewers of the spectacles at that festival. Socrates' friends, then, are living examples of 'lovers of sights and sounds'. In short, all of these *theōroi*— both the friends in book 1 and the (nameless) 'lovers of sights and sounds' in book 5—provide an analogue for this new man called the 'philosopher'. Like the 'lovers of sights', the philosopher loves seeing. But the philosophers love one single kind of spectacle—they are 'lovers of the sight of truth' (τῆς ἀληθείας . . . φιλοθεάμονας).

Plato uses the 'lover of sights' rather than the 'lovers of sounds' as the most direct analogue for the philosopher: having acknowledged that the *theōroi* at religious festivals use both their eyes and their ears, he focuses exclusively on the visual when he makes the move from the traditional to the philosophic *theōros*. Whereas the 'lovers of sights and sounds' delight in the multiplicity of beautiful spectacles performed at Dionysian festivals, the philosopher 'journeys to and looks upon (ἰέναι τε καὶ ὁρᾶν) Beauty itself' (476b–c). The philosopher, then, is a new kind of *theōros*: a man who travels to the metaphysical realm to see the sacred sights in that region.

Plato depicts the journey of the philosophic *theōros* in the Allegory of the Cave (*Republic*, book 7). The story begins in a dark cavern, which houses all human beings in the terrestrial realm; living in chains, these souls are condemned to watch shadowy images of earthly things flickering on the back wall of the cave—a shadow-play that they mistake for substantial reality. Released from bondage, the philosophic soul slowly makes his way up to the mouth of the cave: he makes a sort of journey abroad, experiencing real terror as he leaves the familiar region of the

---

[32] The fact that Socrates mentions that these individuals journey to 'towns and cities' never missing any of the Dionysian festivals (these were held in Greek cities all over the Mediterranean), indicates that the 'lovers of sights and sounds' are men who journey abroad as *theōroi* and do not simply attend local festivals.

cave and turns towards the light. Eventually, the soul comes to the mouth of the cave and enters the metaphysical 'realm' of the Forms, a realm full of light. When he first arrives, the philosopher is temporarily blinded by the light of the sun that shines there. But the eye of his soul slowly adjusts to this radiance, and eventually he can gaze upon the beings in this metaphysical realm—the Forms. Having seen true reality and goodness, the philosopher now recognizes that the shadow-figures in the cave were all copies of the beings in this realm, and that this region is the locus of true 'Being'.

After gazing upon the Forms and thus achieving knowledge, the philosopher returns home, journeying with reluctance back into the cave. Temporarily blinded by the darkness in that realm, his eyes must slowly adjust to the darkness, at which point he can see in that realm better than the prisoners within it (520c). If the philosopher returns to a bad city and communicates his visions to the people there, Socrates says, they will mock and revile him and perhaps even put him to death (517a): the return of the philosophic *theōros* from the foreign realm of the Forms is a potentially dangerous operation. But if the philosopher lives in a good city, his report is (as it were) good news, and it provides the basis for government and politics.

How does the philosopher achieve this vision of truth? As Socrates suggests in book 5, the philosophers must receive a special education designed to lead them to the '*theōria* of all time and of all being' (θεωρία παντὸς μὲν χρόνου, πάσης δὲ οὐσίας; 486a). Trad-itional modes of teaching, Socrates observes, claim to 'put knowledge into a soul that does not yet possess it, as if they were implanting sight in blind eyes' (518b–c); here, he refers to an education that is exclusively aural—the teacher sets forth a *logos* (in poetry or prose) which the student is expected to learn and memorize. On the contrary, Socrates argues, education is an art of 'turning or converting the soul . . . not an art of implanting vision in the soul but rather, assuming that it already possesses vision but is not turned in the right direction or looking where it should, an art of bringing this [turning] about' (518d). The philo-sophic education, as it seems, uses language to forge a path towards the vision of 'true being'. Philosophical discourse—what Plato calls dia-lectic—leads to the contemplation of truth that is the culmination of the philosophic journey. In describing the cultivation of reason and intellection, Plato uses the metaphor of the soul's capacity for 'vision' or 'sight' again and again. Indeed, his philosophic educational system aims, first and foremost, to develop and train the 'eye of the soul' (τὴν τῆς ψυχῆς ὄψιν, 519b). According to Socrates, most humans direct their gaze 'downwards' towards feasting and other physical pleasures, but it can also be directed 'upwards' towards truth and reality (519b). Only an extensive education in philosophy can 'draw the soul away from the world of becoming and towards true being' (521d).

In the *Republic*, then, Plato identifies the philosopher as a new kind of *theōros*, an intellectual ambassador who makes a journey to a divine world to see the spectacle of truth and then brings a report of his vision to the people at home. Note that, in this and other dialogues, Plato identifies the Forms as 'blessed' and 'divine' essences, even though they are not living beings. The philosopher who gazes upon the Forms contemplates divinity, an act replete with wonder and reverence. In the *Republic*, in fact, Plato calls the philosopher's vision of the Forms a 'divine *theōria*' (θείαν ... θεωρίαν, 517d), and he compares the movement of the philosopher from the Cave to the Forms to a journey 'from Hades to the gods' (521c). Like traditional *theōria* at religious precincts and festivals, philosophic *theōria* has a religious orientation. Indeed, this is one of the main reasons why Plato takes as his primary model the *theōria* to religious festivals rather than the *theōria* that takes the form of a search of wisdom (such as that undertaken by Solon).[33] Although the latter is associated with the travels of sages and intellectuals, it is a secular form of *theōria* that focuses on the human and terrestrial world. Since Plato's sage journeys to see 'the most blessed part of reality' (τὸ εὐδαιμονέστατον τοῦ ὄντος, 526e), the model of the religious festival is far more apt.

---

[33] On Solon's *theōria*, see Ker 2000. Note that Herodotus (1.30) says that Solon 'travelled much of the earth philosophizing (φιλοσοφῶν) and pursuing *theōria*', thus linking Solon's *theōria* to the activity of 'philosophizing'. In interpreting this claim, we must remember that, in the 5th cent. BCE, the word *philosophein* and its cognates did not refer to a specialized discipline but rather to 'intellectual cultivation' in the broadest sense (Nightingale (1995), ch. 1). This passage indicates that Solon was cultivating himself as a sage or wise man rather than doing 'philosophy' in our sense of the word. On the travels of sages and (later) philosophers in archaic and classical Greece, see Montiglio (2000) and Hartog (2001). Helms (1988), 8–9 *passim* discusses travel to foreign states for the purpose of acquiring knowledge in premodern societies. On the relation of pilgrimage to tourism, see E. Cohen (1992).

Like civic *theōria*, philosophic *theōria* (in its Platonic form) also has a practical and political dimension. For just as the civic *theōros* must return home to relate the news to his fellow citizens, the philosophic *theōros* depicted in the *Republic* returns back to the city to impart and implement the truths that he has 'witnessed'. As Plato asserts in book 7, the good city will train its philosophers to ascend to the contemplation of reality, but it will also require that they spend part of their lives in political pursuits (519c–520e, 540a). Although they have no desire for political power, the philosophers will nonetheless agree to spend fixed periods of time governing and serving the city (347c–d, 519c–d, 521a–b, 540b). The official requirement that the philosophic *theōros* must return to the city to utilize and disseminate his wisdom clearly gestures towards the practice of civic *theōria*.

We must remember, however, that even in the politically oriented *Republic*, Plato's philosophic theorist does not journey to the Forms simply to apprehend truths that will best serve the city. The activity of philosophic *theōria* serves, first and foremost, to transform the individual soul, conferring upon it a state of wisdom, happiness, and blessedness. For example, Socrates says in the *Republic* that the philosopher who engages in *theōria* will, when contemplating, think he has arrived at the islands of the blessed (518b, 519c; cf. 540b). He also argues that the philosopher who practises dialectic and contemplates the Forms experiences supreme pleasure (book 9). Contemplation, then, is a blessed and pleasurable activity in itself, and it also provides the grounding for virtuous action in the practical world.

In the *Republic*, Plato constructs an ideal city which trains philosophers to journey to the Forms and to 'return' afterwards and play a role in the government of the city. The model of 'civic' *theōria* works well for this philosophic theorist, since his *theōria* is prepared for and carried out in a political context. But what about philosophers living in non-ideal cities? These individuals, Plato states, will stay out of politics altogether (496a–c). The philosopher who lives in a bad city will still make the journey of philosophic *theōria*, but will do this in a private rather than civic capacity. For philosophic *theōria* is the happiest and most blessed for an individual regardless of whether he plays a role in political life.

PRIVATE *THEŌRIA* IN THE
SYMPOSIUM AND *PHAEDRUS*

In developing the notion of 'private' philosophic *theōria*, Plato takes as his model the *theōria* at the Festival of the Greater Mysteries at Eleusis.[34] In his famous speech in the *Symposium*, for example, Socrates (relating the discourse of Diotima) compares the philosopher's vision of the Forms to the mystic revelation at Eleusis.[35] Though brief, the passage nonetheless offers a vivid description of the philosopher's theoric journey away from the physical realm and towards the Form of Beauty (ἰὼν, 210e; ἰέναι, 211c; ἐπανιέναι, 211c).[36] After going through each step of the journey, the philosopher reaches his final destination:

when he views beautiful things, one after another in the correct way, he will suddenly see, at the end, a wondrous (θαυμαστόν) vision, beautiful in nature, which is the final object of all his previous toils. (210e)

According to Socrates, the philosopher who achieves the vision of 'divine Beauty' (τὸ θεῖον καλόν) becomes 'beloved of god and—to the extent possible for any man—immortal' (211e–212a). By contemplating the Forms, the philosopher achieves both wisdom and happiness. And this activity also enables him to 'give birth to virtue'. The vision of Beauty thus renders the philosopher virtuous as well as wise: theoretical contemplation leads to the production and enactment of virtue in the practical sphere. In practising *theōria*, then, the philosopher 'journeys' to the Forms and, having gained wisdom, returns to embody this (in words and in deeds) in the human world.

---

[34] On the Eleusinian Mysteries, see Mylonas (1961); Parke (1977); ch. 3; Burkert (1987); Clinton (1993). Riedweg (1987) offers a useful discussion of Plato's use of the terminology of the Mysteries; see also M. Morgan (1990), ch. 4 and *passim*.

[35] See also *Phaedo* 69c–d and 81a, where Socrates compares philosophers to those who have been 'purified' and 'initiated'. As Rowe (1993), 151, rightly suggests, Socrates refers here to 'initiatory rites in general' (rather than to the Eleusinian Mysteries in particular).

[36] Plato repeatedly uses the language of vision to describe the philosopher's encounter with the Form of Beauty (θεωρῶν, κατίδηι, 210d; θεώμενος κατόψεται, 210e; καθορᾶν, 211b; θεωμένωι, ἴδηις, 211d; κατιδεῖν, 211e; βλέποντος, θεωμένου, ὁρῶντι ὧι ὁρατὸν τὸ καλόν, 212a).

In describing the philosopher's *theōria*, Diotima compares the contemplation of the Forms to the *epoptika* or the moment of revelation at the Eleusinian Mysteries (210a). For example, just before she describes the ascent, she says to Socrates that while he might be initiated (μυηθείης) into the matters discussed thus far, he cannot yet advance to the next stage to see the 'final rites and revelations' (τὰ δὲ τέλεα καὶ ἐποπτικά, 209e–210a). Here, Diotima uses the technical language of the Eleusinian Mysteries, explicitly referring to *theōria* at this famous festival. There were two classes of initiates who came as *theōroi* to this festival: the *mystēs* ('initiate'), who took part in the festival and mystery rites for the first time, and the *epoptēs* ('watcher'), who came to the festival for (at least) a second time to see the *epoptika* or 'highest mysteries'.[37] Diotima identifies Socrates as a *mystēs*, or an initiate who has come to the festival for the first time. He is not, she claims, an *epoptēs* and thus cannot be granted the vision of the highest mysteries. When Diotima goes on to describe these '*epoptika*' in the passage that follows, she is clearly referring to the contemplation of the Forms. As she explains, the philosopher who ascends correctly moves from the 'sight' of one beautiful body to the beauty of all bodies and, from there, to the beauty of the soul; he will then 'behold' the beauty of laws and institutions and, finally, 'theorize' (θεωρεῖν) the Form of the Beautiful (210a–d). In this passage, then, Diotima clearly identifies philosophic *theōria* with the revelation of the highest mysteries at the initiation ceremony at Eleusis.

Although the Festival of the Greater Mysteries at Eleusis was sponsored by Athens, it was attended by *theōroi* from all over Greece. While this festival featured rituals and spectacles similar to those at other religious festivals, it culminated in the unique ritual of initiation (sometimes called the *teletē*). The festival was a public and international event lasting many days, but the initiation ceremony focused on the private individual, offering him or her salvation in the afterlife.[38] After journeying as a *theōros* to the festival of the Mysteries, the person seeking initiation underwent rites of purification (during which he or she was veiled). After participating in various rituals, the individual obtained a

---

[37] Burkert (1985), 287.

[38] Initiation into the Mysteries was open to all Greek speakers, including women and slaves. On the festival and rituals of the Eleusinian Mysteries, see Parke (1977), 55–72; Burkert (1985), 285–90; Dillon (1997), 60–70.

view of the *hiera* or sacred objects, which the hierophant revealed at the climax of the ritual. The precise difference between the experience of the *mystēs* and the *epoptēs* is not clear: both 'saw' the sacred objects, though the *mystēs* may have been veiled during part of the revelation; alternatively, the *epoptēs* may have seen additional sights or perhaps have got a closer look at the sacred objects.[39] Interestingly, the mystic ceremony featured the movement from darkness to light. At the beginning of the ritual, the initiates stood in darkness in a building called the *Telesterion*; when the hierophant opened the door of the *Anaktoron*—a stone chamber at the centre of the *Telesterion*—a stream of light blazed forth from the interior. To receive the revelation, the *mystai* entered the *Anaktoron*, where the *epoptai* were standing with thousands of torches.[40]

The Greeks believed that initiation into the Mysteries guaranteed a good fate in the afterlife: 'blessed among mortals on earth is he who has seen (ὄπωπεν); but the uninitiated never has the same lot once dead in the dreary darkness' (Homeric *Hymn to Demeter* 480–2). We find a similar claim in Sophocles: 'thrice blessed are those mortals who have seen these rites and thus enter Hades: for them alone there is life, but for the others all is misery' (fr. 837 Pearson–Radt).[41] Some Greeks even thought that the mystic revelation had an epistemic as well as a salvific aspect: 'blessed is he who, seeing these thing (ἰδὼν κεῖνα), goes beneath the earth; he knows (οἶδε) the end of life, and he knows (οἶδεν) the god-given beginning' (Pindar, fr. 121 Bowra). According to all the sources, initiation into the Mysteries focused on the afterlife rather than earthly life. The rite of initiation served the individual rather than the community or civic body: it offered personal salvation and blessedness.

It is easy to see why Plato was attracted to this religious festival, since it featured a vision which transformed the initiate and granted him or her salvation in the afterlife. The personal nature of the initiation ceremony offers a model of private *theōria* that has salvific (as well as epistemic) associations. In fact, this kind of *theōria* is so private that the person initiated at Eleusis never offers any account of the mystic

---

[39] Parke (1977), 71; Burkert (1985), 287.

[40] Burkert (1985), 287; Clinton (1993), 118–19; Dillon (1997), 67. Sources from late antiquity provide evidence for certain details of the ceremony.

[41] In the prosaic words of Isocrates, the *mystai* 'have better hopes for the end of life and for all eternity' (4.28).

revelation (though he might have brought news of the other events at the festival). For all the initiates took an oath to keep the central revelation a secret. Just as initiation at Eleusis transformed the individual so that he would achieve salvation in the afterworld, the 'initiation' of the philosophic *theōros*, Plato claims, purifies and transforms the soul and guarantees it a blessed destiny. Plato's philosopher, then, has much in common with the initiate at the Mysteries: in both cases, the *theōros* 'sees' a divine revelation that transforms him at soul. But Plato diverges from his model in his claim that philosophic *theōria* makes the soul wise and happy in this life as well as the next—indeed the philosopher practises *theōria*, first and foremost, to live well in the present.

In the *Phaedrus*, Plato makes an even more prominent use of the model of mystic initiation. We find this in Socrates' second speech, which depicts the experiences of the human soul before incarnation on earth. In this period, he says, souls travelled around the cosmos seeking 'initiation' into wisdom. The human souls followed in the train of the gods, who periodically ascend to the very edge of the universe and engage in the contemplation of the Forms:

Those that are immortal, when they get to the top, pass outside it and take their stand on the outer surface of the heaven; the revolution of the cosmos carries them around as they stand there and they theorize (θεωροῦσι) the things outside the heaven. (247b–c)

Even the gods, as it seems, make a journey of *theōria* to the Forms (247e): travelling to the most distant part of the universe, they 'see the spectacles and have a feast' (as though at a festival) and, after contemplating, return 'back home' (*oikade*). During this *theōria*, the gods gaze upon 'really real Being' (οὐσία ὄντως οὖσα—a term that Plato often uses for the Forms). As Socrates explains, along with the gods, pre-incarnate human souls also attempted to make this upward journey, hoping to gain a vision of reality. Some of these souls, however, failed to reach the edge of heaven and 'went away uninitiated in the vision of reality' (ἀτελεῖς τῆς τοῦ ὄντος θέας ἀπέρχονται); others were more successful, though they achieved at best an unstable and partial view of the Forms, in stark contrast to the gods' full and uninterrupted contemplation (247a–b). Socrates describes the 'initiation' into the knowledge of the Forms as follows:

The mind... of every soul which is destined to receive that which befits it rejoices in seeing being (ἰδοῦσα... τὸ ὄν) for a time and, by theorizing (θεωροῦσα) the truth, it is nourished and made happy until the revolution brings it again to the same place. In the revolution it beholds (καθορᾷ) justice itself, and temperance, and knowledge... and beholding the other true beings in the same way and feeding on them, it sinks back down within the heaven and goes home. (247d–e)

Here, Socrates identifies the 'realities' that the souls behold as the Forms of Justice, Temperance, etc. But he also says that these are 'blessed' and 'holy sights' (μακαρίαι θέαι, 247a; ὧν τότε εἶδον ἱερῶν, 250a), thus emphasizing the divinity of the Forms. The soul that views these beings, he suggests, experiences a sort of religious revelation.

This primordial initiation, Socrates claims, can be re-enacted in one's earthly life. For the 'initiated' soul, when incarnate on earth, can 'recollect' the Forms and theorize them through the practice of philosophy. In particular, the sight of bodily beauty can trigger the recollection of the Form of Beauty (though recollection leads to true knowledge only after long philosophic labour):

When the recent initiate (ἀρτιτελής), who beheld many of those realities there, sees [on earth] a godlike face or the form of a body that offers a good imitation of the Beautiful, he shudders at first and some of the former awe takes hold of him; then, as he looks at it, he reveres (σέβεται) it like a god.... Then, [looking upon the beautiful boy,] his memory is borne back to the true nature of Beauty, and he sees it standing together with Modesty upon a holy pedestal, and when he sees this he is a afraid and falls back in reverence (ἰδοῦσα δὲ ἔδεισέ τε καὶ σεφθεῖσα ἀνέπεσεν ὑπτία). (251a, 254b)

By gazing on the beautiful beloved, the philosophic soul is led to remember the Form of Beauty.[42]

Although the primordial initiation offered the soul a vision of all the Forms, the sight of the Form of Beauty had a particular force. For, unlike the other Forms, Beauty possesses its own special brilliance:

Beauty shone with light at that time when our souls, with a blessed company, saw the blessed sight and vision (μακαρίαν ὄψιν τε καὶ θέαν)... and were initiated into that which is rightly called the most blessed of mysteries (εἶδόν τε καὶ ἐτελοῦντο τῶν τελετῶν ἣν θέμις λέγειν μακαριωτάτην), which

---

[42] Griswold (1986), 111–21 and *passim*.

we celebrated in a state of perfection, when we were without experience of the evils in the later time to come, being initiated and seeing the mysteries in the clear light (μνούμενοί τε καὶ ἐποπτεύοντες ἐν αὐγῆι καθαρᾶι)—sights that were perfect and simple and calm and blessed. (250b–c)

Because the Form of Beauty 'shone with light', it is especially well delineated in earthly beauties; the earthly copies of other Forms, by contrast, 'contained no light' (250b). As Socrates explains, Beauty 'shone in radiance' (ἔλαμπεν) when mortal souls viewed it before birth, 'and now that we have come here we grasp it shining (στίλβον) most clearly through the clearest of our senses' (250d). In recollecting the Form, then, the soul experiences its former, preincarnate 'initiation'. But the person who practises philosophy also undergoes an abiding and continuous initiation in the present: for if he 'employs such recollections rightly', the philosopher 'is always being initiated into perfect mysteries, and he alone becomes truly perfect' (τελέους ἀεὶ τελετὰς τελούμενος, τέλεος ὄντως μόνος γίγνεται, 249c).

Throughout this speech, Plato intermingles the philosophic conception of the recollection and *theōria* of the Forms with the experience of initiation at the Eleusinian Festival (especially the vision of the 'sacred objects' in the initiation ceremony). Both the initiate at the Mysteries and the philosopher theorizing the Forms see a vision that transforms them and brings joy and a blessed destiny. Unlike the ordinary initiate, however, the philosopher looks directly at 'divine' beings (and not just at sacred objects and symbols) and his experience of *theōria* brings him wisdom as well as blessedness. For this vision fulfils the innate desire of the rational part of the soul for truth: 'when it sees Being, the soul attains the knowledge that it longs for and thus encounters true reality' (248b). By comparing philosophic *theōria* to the initiation into the Mysteries, Plato offers a vivid picture of the salvific and epistemic aspects of the practice of theoretical philosophy.

Of course the model of the *theōria* at the Mysteries also conjures up secrecy and exclusion: the initiate is forbidden to talk about the mystic revelation to noninitiates (though he may discuss the other parts of the theoric journey). As Jameson observes,

[at the Eleusinian festival of the Mysteries,] certain sights seen and actions performed distinguished the admitted and the excluded. Here performance was prominent, sometimes spectacular, such as the procession of initiates from

Athens to Eleusis, but the central elements were hidden and the very fact of their obscurity defined the participants. This is an example of what has been called 'advertised secrecy'.[43]

The person initiated at the Festival, then, experiences a sort of *theōria* within a *theōria*: the pilgrimage and rituals take the form of traditional *theōria*, but the initiation offers a vision of a secret and exclusive spectacle. This ritual separates the initiated from the uninitiated.

Like the initiate at the Festival of Eleusis, Plato's theoretical philosopher, of course, sees a spectacle that is inaccessible to ordinary individuals. By practising *theōria*, the philosopher becomes a member of an elite and exclusive group. But this does not mean that he practises secrecy, since he does not endeavour to hide or hoard his wisdom.[44] In the ideal city, in fact, the city requires the *theōros* to introduce his vision and knowledge into the political sphere. The philosophic *theōros* in the *Republic* uses his private (intellectual) wealth for public purposes. Of course, the philosopher can only practise this 'civic' *theōria* in the truly good city. In a bad city, the philosopher will stay out of politics altogether. Nonetheless, Plato makes it quite clear that even the private (nonpolitical) theorist will bring his contemplative wisdom into the practical sphere: virtuous action, performed when the philosopher 'returns' from contemplative activity, is a crucial part of the theoric journey of *theōria* taken as a whole. To the extent that the philosopher embodies his theoretical wisdom in the practical world, he links his theoric 'vision' and learning—his encounter with divine being—to his life as a social and embodied human being. In addition, the philosopher will 'give an account' of his wisdom via dialectic, thus opening it up to scrutiny. He does not, then, live a secretive life focused exclusively on contemplation—on the contrary, he attempts to communicate his vision by way of both action and argumentation.

In this chapter, I have examined Plato's appropriation of traditional forms of *theōria* in his explication of the new discipline of philosophic *theōria*. Plato and his followers turned to traditional *theōria* as a cultural practice that had authority and currency in Greek society in this period. By associating his own philosophic practice with that of traditional *theōria*, Plato claimed legitimacy and status for theoretical philosophy.

[43] Jameson (1999), 334.
[44] Cf. Szlezák (1999), who argues for the esotericist position.

Plato's use of the model of traditional *theōria* does not, of course, tell us very much about the technical aspects of his epistemology. But it does reveal the conceptual and ideological issues involved in the foundational construction of philosophic *theōria*.

PART II

PILGRIMAGE IN
THE ROMAN EMPIRE

7

The Body in Space:

Visual Dynamics in Graeco-Roman Healing Pilgrimage

Alexia Petsalis-Diomidis

In the winter of 149 CE, the orator Aelius Aristides was sent by the god Asklepios on a pilgrimage to Chios for bodily healing. He describes this journey in the *Sacred Tales*, a text which focuses on the author's contact with Asklepios. He makes reference to the difficulty of the journey in adverse weather conditions, to stop-offs at various cities on the way, and also to a divinely-ordered change in the itinerary.[1] Starting out from Pergamon, the pilgrim and his companions get as far as Klazomenai via Smyrna, but from here Aristides is sent to Phokaia and the pilgrimage to Chios is remitted. Finally, the god sends him on to the warm springs at Genais and then back to Smyrna. This emphasis on the pilgrim's location in the landscape of Asia Minor is linked to descriptions of his visions of the god. The following is a description of what he saw in Smyrna:

When we arrived in Smyrna, he appeared to me in some such form. He was at the same time Asklepios, and Apollo, both the Klarian and he who is called

This paper draws on research conducted during the course of my Ph.D. at The Courtauld Institute of Art. I would therefore like to thank my Ph.D. supervisors, Dr Jaś Elsner and Professor Robin Cormack, for their guidance. Thanks are also due to Professor Robin Osborne who read and commented on earlier versions of this research, as well as to Dr Sorcha Carey, Dr Barbara Graziosi, Dr Johannes Haubold, and Harry Boyd-Carpenter. I am also grateful to the University of London Scholarship Fund and the British Academy (Humanities Research Board) for their generous financial support during this period.

[1] *ST* 2.11–23. On this pilgrimage see Rutherford (1999), 144–6.

Kalliteknos in Pergamon and whose is the first of the three temples. Standing before my bed in this form . . . he said that 'this was not a dream, but a waking state', and that I would also know it. And at the same time he commanded that I go down to the river, which flows before the city, and bathe.[2]

Aristides goes on to describe the cold and stormy weather, and his journey to the river, accompanied by a group of friends (including a doctor).

When we reached the river, there was no need for anyone to encourage us. But being still full of warmth from the vision of the god, I cast off my clothes, and not wanting a massage, flung myself where the river was deepest. Then as in a pool of very gentle and tempered water, I passed my time swimming all about and splashing myself all over. When I came out, all my skin had a rosy hue and there was a lightness throughout my body. There was also much shouting from those present and those coming up, shouting that celebrated phrase, 'Great is Asklepios!' . . . My mental state was also nearly the same. For there was neither, as it were, conspicuous pleasure, nor would you say that it was a human joy. But there was a certain inexplicable contentment, which regarded everything as less than the present moment, so that even when I saw other things, I seemed not to see them. Thus I was wholly with the god.[3]

This narrative which culminates in the author's physical and mental healing and ease, and his experience of the intense presence of the god, reveals the importance of space and the visual in this experience of healing pilgrimage. Most fundamentally, there is an emphasis on the role of location in facilitating contact with the divine, communicated through repeated references to the pilgrim's journeys and relocations at the god's commands. On another level, seeing plays an important part in the structure of the pilgrimage narrative: the 'mini-pilgrimage' to the river is signalled by a dream *vision* in which the god *appears* to Aristides, who considers it important to record the appearance of the god, and his similarity to particular cult statues.[4] When the dream *vision* is announced friends and onlookers come to *see* Aristides take his therapeutic

---

[2] *ST* 2.18 (selection). For the text see Keil (1958); all translations of the *ST* and other orations by Aristides are by Behr (1981).

[3] *ST* 2.21–3 (selection).

[4] φαίνεται μοι ἐν τοιῶιδε τινι σχήματι, 'he appeared to me in some such form'; ἐν τούτωι τῶι σχήματι στὰς ἔμπροσθεν τῆς εὐνῆς, 'standing before my bed in this form'; ταῦτα δὲ εἶναι οὐκ ὄναρ, ἀλλ' ὕπαρ, 'this was not a dream but a waking state'; καὶ τὰ μὲν κεφάλαια τῆς ἐπιφανείας ταῦτά ἐστιν, 'this is a summary of the divine manifestation' (2.18).

bath.[5] The effects of the *vision* of the god help Aristides to perform the freezing bath.[6] Furthermore, one of the effects of this divine bath is the transformation of the characters' vision: on the one hand a transformation of the way in which the spectators perceive Aristides (now rosy-coloured) and on the other of the way in which Aristides perceives the world (while seeing, he seems not to see).[7]

This chapter explores both these themes by offering an interpretation of a particular space associated with the worship of Asklepios in the second century CE, the Asklepieion at Pergamon (from where Aristides started this journey). It focuses on visual dynamics within the microcosm of the sanctuary, and through this suggests the centrality of the visual in healing pilgrimage more generally. It is a reading both of the physical layout of the sanctuary—the architectural remains—and of an inscribed set of ritual rules which directed the movement and religious observances of pilgrims. I argue that the architectural context and the system of rules provided the physical and conceptual frameworks in which pilgrims experienced the process of sickness and healing. In the final part of the chapter, I examine a small selection of thank-offerings to the god, including examples of literary, inscriptional, and sculptural dedications, as narratives of individual experiences of pilgrimage within this spatio-ritual context.

This interpretation of the space of the Asklepieion and of the thank-offerings associated with it draws on developments in the discipline of the history of art towards what might be called a history of visuality. These include an emphasis on the scopic regimes of a culture, the role of viewers and the multiplicity of possible viewings, as well as a broadening of the range of objects interpreted with the methodologies of art history to include 'low' art and even inscriptional monuments.[8] Thus an

---

[5] ἐπεὶ δ'ἐξηγγέλθη τὰ τῆς ἐπιφανείας, 'when the divine manifestation was announced'; τῆς ἱστορίας εἵνεκα '[people escorted him] for the purposes of investigation', καὶ πάντ' ἦν κάτοπτα ἀπὸ τῆς γεφύρας, 'and everything was visible from the bridge' (2.20).

[6] ἀλλ' ἔτι τῆς θέρμης τῆς ἐκ τῆς ὄψεως τοῦ θεοῦ μεστὸς ὤν, 'but being still full of warmth from the vision of the god' (2.21).

[7] ὅ τεδὴ χρὼς πᾶς ἤνθει, 'all my skin had a rosy hue' (2.21), ὥστε οὐδ' ὁρῶν τὰ ἄλλα ἐδόκουν ὁρᾶν, 'so that even when I saw other things, I seemed not to see them' (1.23).

[8] Foster (1988); Freedberg (1989); Brennan and Jay (1995); Jones and Galison (1998); Elkins (1999); Nelson (2000).

interpretation of the space of the Asklepieion involves both a broad understanding of visuality in second-century Graeco-Roman culture, and more specifically involves the analysis of the *Lex Sacra*, the publicly displayed inscription of rules which conditioned pilgrims' viewings of the sanctuary. These rules governed both the pilgrims' movements around the Asklepieion and their mental and physical states, for example by requiring fasting and sexual abstinence. An awareness of the infinite multiplicity of possible viewings on the one hand may be said to marginalize the importance of any individual testimony (such as Aristides' *Sacred Tales*) as representative of a generalized pilgrim experience or of silent or lost descriptions of other pilgrims. But, on the other hand it accommodates and indeed celebrates diversity within the whole body of pilgrimage narratives and does not seek to impose a rigid pattern of viewing and experience on all. Finally the range of objects which now fall under the scrutiny of art historians has broadened to include the mass-produced votive body parts, hybrid inscriptional and plastic votives, and inscriptional monuments of the kind found at the Asklepieion.

This kind of art historical approach can be very fruitfully applied to Graeco-Roman pilgrimage principally because of the importance of *place* in this culture's traditions of sacred travel.[9] The immense diversity of cults in the Roman empire and their rich myth-historical traditions resulted in a plethora of attractive pilgrimage centres.[10] Motivations for pilgrimage cross-culturally are notoriously complex and diverse. Nevertheless, within the polytheistic context of Graeco-Roman religion, one factor in deciding on a particular pilgrimage might have been a pilgrim's desire to worship a particular deity and not another. There were, however, numerous shrines dedicated to each deity. The decision to make a pilgrimage to the god at a particular, perhaps more distant, sanctuary must have been partly based on a deeply held sense of the location of the god in *that place*. A candid expression of this feeling can be found at the opening of Aristides' account of his (eventually remitted) pilgrimage to Chios. In this case,

---

[9] On the importance of place in a ritual context generally see Smith (1987).

[10] Generally on religion in the Roman empire see MacMullen (1981); Lane Fox (1986); Turcan (1996); Beard, North, and Price (1998); Edwards, Goodman, and Price (1999).

unusually, the god orders a journey *away* from his sanctuary: 'He sent me to Chios, saying that he sent me for a purgation. We went off on the road to Smyrna, although it was distasteful and we believed that we were without a protector and that we truly sailed alone, once we were outside the temple.'[11]

Gods were 'tied' to particular localities and indeed experienced there by pilgrims through a range of complex processes. I wish to highlight three such visual mechanisms which operated at sanctuaries. The first involves the corroboration of mythical narratives: competing versions of myth, linking a god to a particular locality, were often visually asserted. So for example, the two Asklepieia which claimed to be the birthplace of Asklepios, Epidauros and Thelpoussa (in Arkadia), displayed landmarks to back up this claim: at Epidauros the mountain Myrtion, which is clearly visible from the sanctuary, had been renamed Tithion (Nipple) thus linguistically asserting the story that Asklepios had been suckled by goats there, and at Thelpoussa the tomb of Trygon, the rival human nurse of the divine baby, was pointed out.[12] The association of a sanctuary with a specific aspect of the history of the god, such as his or her birth gave a unique flavour to the experience of the god at that *particular* sanctuary.

Whereas myths suggested an initial association of a god with a particular locality, the display of votive offerings asserted his or her continued presence in the sanctuary. This second visual mechanism, the viewing of thank-offerings (including textual narratives), seems to have been of particular importance in Asklepieia where the efficacy of the god in curing sickness was central to his prestige and worship. Moreover, the establishment of these sanctuaries relatively late (in the fifth and fourth centuries BCE) meant that rich mythical associations were not available to all Asklepieia. Most, in fact, such as those at Athens and Pergamon, were founded by pilgrims who had been cured at Epidauros and who wished to bring the new god back to their cities.[13] In these cases it was through the display of thank-offerings that the

---

[11] *ST* 2.11.

[12] Paus. 2.26.3–7 and 8.25.11.

[13] Paus. 2.26.8. For inscriptional evidence for the foundation of the Athenian Asklepieion see Aleshire (1989), 7 n. 3. See Aelius Aristides *Oration* 38 *The Sons of Asklepios* 11 where a mythical connection between Pergamon and Podalirios and Machaon is made.

presence and charisma of the newly arrived god were asserted. The thank-offerings of past pilgrims then offered evidence of an unbroken line of divine manifestation in that particular place.

The third visual element in the establishment of a god in a particular sanctuary operated on a more profound level. Participation in religious ritual and choreographed processions experientially established the presence of the god in that location for pilgrims. The study of place and visual dynamics in Asklepian pilgrimage, including the three features outlined above, offers the possibility of accessing a part of the religious visionary world that Graeco-Roman pilgrims entered through these sanctuaries.

A major theme which emerges in this chapter is the juxtaposition of order and disorder, both in relation to the sanctuary and in relation to the bodies of pilgrims. It will be argued in the case of the Asklepieion of Pergamon that order and control were imposed on the existing complex of Hellenistic buildings by the second-century CE building programme, and on the sick and disordered bodies of pilgrims by the contemporaneous *Lex Sacra*. These transformations of the landscape and the pilgrims' bodies are traced and linked to the miraculous manifestation of the god both in visions within this sanctuary landscape and in the very bodies of pilgrims.

THE ORDER OF SPACE: ARCHITECTURE AND TRANSFORMATION

By the early second century CE the building history of the Asklepieion stretched back over five centuries. At that point the sanctuary in effect comprised a variety of buildings which had not been conceived as an organic whole, but had been added piecemeal.[14] At this time, and very probably with the involvement of Hadrian who visited Pergamon in 123 and again in 128 CE, an ambitious remodelling of the sanctuary was planned and put into immediate effect.[15] Prominent local aristocrats

---

[14] Ziegenaus and de Luca (1968) and (1975); Ziegenaus (1981); de Luca (1984); Radt (1988), 250–71; Hoffmann (1998), esp. 44–5.

[15] Hoffmann (1998), on Hadrian's involvement esp. 41–7; Le Glay (1976); Birley (1997), 162–9; Fränkel (1895), 258 no. 365.

paid for individual buildings, and no doubt contributed to decision-making.[16] Nevertheless, the new plan was fully co-ordinated and resulted in the transformation of the existing sanctuary into a unified space (Figure 1).

Much effort and expense were required to effect this transformation: several buildings which had been completed in the recent past were demolished and huge earthworks were needed to mould the landscape which is on a natural incline.[17] This raises the question of why the Pergamenes did not choose a new site in which to put into effect their new vision of an Asklepieion, especially in view of the violent history of the existing sanctuary.[18] In general the high value placed on the classical Greek past in the culture of the 'Second Sophistic' militated for the preservation or re-construction of continuities with the past on every level—spatial, artistic, linguistic.[19] More specifically, in the religious context continuity of place was particularly important in order to preserve and honour the presence of a god (as attested in past manifestations) which was not easily transferable. In the Pergamene Asklepieion, in particular, divine charisma had been powerfully manifested in the previous century in a spate of miraculous surgical healings, still remembered and celebrated in the late second century.[20] The building plan

---

[16] On patronage in the Asklepieion see Habicht (1969), 9–11; Hoffmann (1998), 49–50. On A. Claudius Charax (donor of the Propylon entrance) see Andrei (1984); Spawforth and Walker (1986), 93; Halfmann (1979), 161–2, no. 73. On L. Cuspius Pactumeius Rufinus (donor of the temple of Zeus-Asklepios) see Behr (1968), 48 n. 29; Hepding (1933), 93–6 (for inscriptional evidence); Halfmann (1979), 154, no. 66. On Octacilius Pollio (donor of the north portico) see Habicht (1969), 10 and 103–6. On Flavia Melitine (donor of the library) see Habicht (1969), 84–5. On euergetism generally in this period see Veyne (1990), 70–200.

[17] Amongst the buildings demolished during the remodelling of the sanctuary were a temple south-west of the old incubation chambers dated to the Flavian period and an odeion in the area where the Propylon was later built dated to the reign of Trajan. See Radt (1988), 255–7, Hoffmann (1998), 42–7.

[18] In 88 BCE during the rebellion of Mithridates against the Romans Roman citizens were massacred inside the sanctuary where they had sought asylum. In 85 BCE the Roman general C. Flavius Fimbria was murdered in the sanctuary by his own slave. Following these events the right of asylum was taken away from the Asklepieion but was restored in 44 BCE and later confirmed by Tiberius. See Habicht (1969), 4–6.

[19] On the culture of the Second Sophistic see Bowie (1970); Swain (1996); Whitmarsh (2001); Goldhill (2001); Elsner (1998), 169–85.

[20] *ST* 4.64: 'the present priest of Asklepios and this man's grandfather, in whose time, as we have learned, the god performed many great operations'.

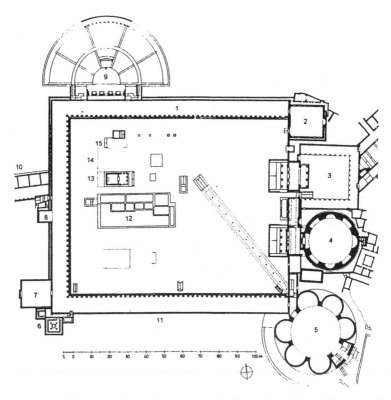

Figure 1. The 'original' second-century CE building plan of the Asklepieion of Pergamon. Scale 1: 2000 (Hoffmann (1998), 60 fig. 2)

Key: 1. North portico, 2. Library, 3. Propylon entrance, 4. Temple of Zeus-Asklepios, 5. Rotunda (treatment centre), 6. Latrines, 7. Room of unknown purpose, 8. Cult niche, 9. Theatre, 10. Hellenistic portico, 11. Southern portico with cryptoporticus for incubation ('the large incubation chamber'), 12. Old incubation chambers, 13. Temple of Asklepios the Saviour, 14–15. Cult buildings and holy spring.

should thus be seen as operating in dialogue with the accumulated legacy of the god's presence, manifested in the existing buildings, statues, and votive offerings of the sanctuary.

A skilful balancing of old and new was required for the success of the remodelling. This was expressed in architectural terms through the sensitive use both of conservative forms (for example, in the new Propylon entrance (Figure 2) and in the old-fashioned plain entablature in the new porticos) and of the latest Roman metropolitan models (for example, in the temple of Zeus-Asklepios which is an exact miniature copy of the Roman Pantheon (Figure 3), and in the *scaenae frons* of the theatre, the first Italian-style three-tiered model to be used in Asia Minor (Figure 4)).[21] Simultaneously a selective 'reading' of the existing sanctuary occurred through alternate 'deleting' and visual 'highlighting' of buildings. For example, a temple south-west of the old incubation chambers and an odeion in the north-east where the Propylon was then built were demolished, while the cluster of temples and incubation chambers in the centre of the sanctuary were given greater prominence by means of their framing by the new peristyle courtyard (Figure 1. 12–15).[22] The decision to give additional prominence to the temple of Asklepios the Saviour and to the old incubation chambers seems to have been predicated on religious rather than aesthetic grounds: these buildings were not in themselves visually impressive, but were, of course, the places in which Asklepios had always manifested himself, both in the form of his cult image and in the form of the incubatory visions he bestowed on his worshippers.

The overriding principle of the new plan was symmetry and order.[23] This is perhaps most clearly evident in the construction of the peristyle courtyard, which created a clearly delineated regular space, within and around which both old and new buildings were organized and

---

[21] On the Propylon see Ziegenaus (1981), 5–29; Radt (1988), 261–2; on the porticos see Hoffmann (1998), 52–9; Radt (1988), 265; on the architecture of the Zeus-Asklepios temple see Ziegenaus (1981), 30–76; Hoffmann (1984); Habicht (1969), 11–14; Ward-Perkins (1994), 277. The internal diameter of the temple of Zeus-Asklepios was just over half the size of the Pantheon (24 m compared to 42 m). On the theatre see Hoffmann (1998), 55–6; Radt (1988), 263–5.

[22] See above n.17. Hoffmann (1998), 42–3.

[23] Hoffmann (1998), 45–8.

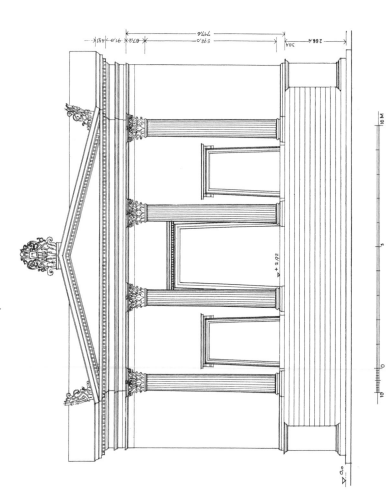

Figure 2. Reconstruction drawing of the west elevation of the Propylon of the Asklepieion of Pergamon (Ziegenaus (1981), Tafel 60)

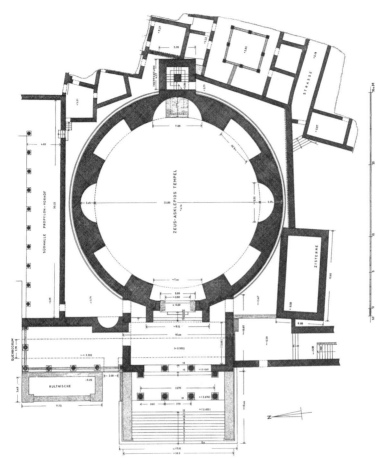

Figure 3. Ground plan of the temple of Zeus-Asklepios in the Asklepieion of Pergamon (Ziegenaus (1981), Tafel 62)

integrated. In addition to framing the old cult buildings, on the east side the courtyard opened on to two new buildings, the Propylon entrance and the temple of Zeus-Asklepios. It seems that these were initially conceived as symmetrical counterparts, as the original plan did not

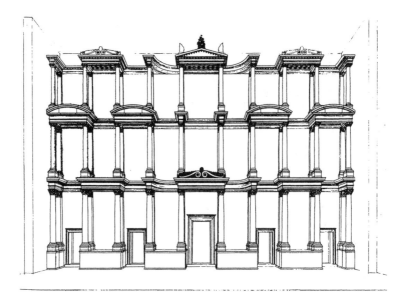

Figure 4. Reconstruction drawing of the *scaenae frons* of the theatre of the Asklepieion of Pergamon (Hoffmann (1998), 61 fig. 4)

include the library and the Rotunda (Figures 5 and 6).[24] This spatial organization impinged not only on the buildings, but also on the pilgrims within the sanctuary. The physical expression of order and structure in the landscape of the sanctuary may have been particularly appropriate for pilgrims whose personal bodily landscapes were 'out of order', in that they were sick and hence out of control.

The remodelled Asklepieion embodied the elite Pergamene vision of the most appropriate space for the meeting of Asklepios with his worshippers. Many scholars have emphasized the elite literary culture of the sanctuary, which is attested on the one hand by the *Sacred Tales* of Aelius Aristides and on the other by the construction of the theatre and library in the sanctuary and by the display of busts of famous fifth- and fourth-century BCE Greek intellectuals, such as

[24] Hoffmann (1998), 48–9. The plan was later modified by the addition of the library in the north-east and the rotunda in the south-east of the sanctuary.

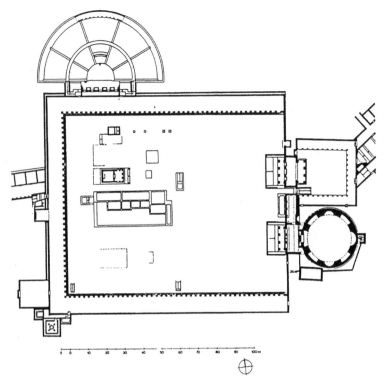

Figure 5. General plan of the Asklepieion in the second century CE. Scale 1: 2000 (Hoffmann (1998), 60 fig. 1)

Sokrates, Euripides, and Xenophon (Figures 7, 8, and 9).[25] Literary and political themes as evoked by image and inscription no doubt informed the experiences of some pilgrims.[26] Simultaneously, though, there is abundant literary and inscriptional evidence for the practice of

---

[25] On the literary culture of the Asklepieion see Behr (1968), 41–60; Habicht (1969), 15–17; Jones (1998); Cortés Copete (1995), 60–77. On the busts, found on the *via tecta*, see de Luca (1984), 102–4.

[26] e.g., the orator Polemo set up a statue of Demosthenes in the Asklepieion (Habicht (1969), no. 33). For inscriptions set up to honour local and imperial public figures see Habicht (1969), nos. 3–62b.

Figure 6. Model of the second-century CE Asklepieion of Pergamon by H. Schleif. View towards east (Radt (1988), 258 Abb. 124)

Figure 7. Bust of Sokrates found on the *via tecta* at the entrance of the Asklepieion of Pergamon (second century CE), Bergama Museum, museum number 772. Height 42 cm. (de Luca (1984), Tafel 43b)

dramatic healing therapies in the sanctuary. For example, Aelius Aristides describes performing a cure at the command of Asklepios which involved smothering his naked body with mud and running three times around the cluster of temples in the centre of the courtyard, during a storm in the night.[27] The remodelled sanctuary provided the physical framework for a broad range of activities, and equally received a range of pilgrims whose bodies covered the spectrum of healthy to sick. In this highly ordered and structured space, pilgrims encountered Asklepios, the god who paradoxically *broke* the laws of

[27] *ST* 2.74–6. For inscriptional evidence of cures in the Asklepieion see e.g. Müller (1987).

Figure 8. Bust of Euripides found on the *via tecta* at the entrance of the Asklepieion of Pergamon (second century CE), Bergama Museum, museum number 773. Height 50 cm. (de Luca (1984), Tafel 42b)

nature in the miraculous cures he offered, but in so doing restored the natural order of health.[28]

THE ORDER OF BODIES: RITUAL AND CHOREOGRAPHY

Within the wider spectrum of worshippers at the Asklepieion was a select group of pilgrims who wished to consult the god during the night in the process of incubation. The *Lex Sacra* quoted and translated

[28] Aeli. Aristid. *Oration* 23 *Concerning Concord* 16: [Asklepios] 'to whom every law of necessity yields'.

Figure 9. Bust of Xenophon found on the *via tecta* at the entrance of the Asklepieion of Pergamon (second century CE), Bergama Museum, museum number 784. Height 49 cm. (de Luca (1984), Tafel 45b)

below is an inscription which set out in detail the rules governing this ritual.[29] The *Lex Sacra* was probably displayed at the entrance of the Asklepieion, perhaps as a guide for pilgrims as they arrived, and a copy may also have been displayed within the courtyard (Figure 10).[30]

---

[29] For the publication of the inscription see Wörrle (1969).

[30] The largest fragment of the *Lex Sacra* (referred to by Wörrle as Fragment A) was found in a ditch by the *via tecta* leading to the Asklepieion. On the basis of its contents Wörrle concluded that the inscription would have been displayed either at the monumental entrance or somewhere inside the sanctuary. Further fragments were found in the courtyard of the Asklepieion. These (referred to by Wörrle as Fragment B and not quoted here) repeat parts of Fragment A suggesting that there may have been two copies, perhaps one at the entrance and one inside the sanctuary. See Wörrle (1969), 167–8.

Figure 10. The *Lex Sacra* from the Asklepieion of Pergamon (second century CE), Inventory number 1965, 20. Dimensions 63 × 40.5 × 13.8 cm. (Habicht (1969), no. 161, Tafel 49)

[-] ϙαὶ τραπεζούσθω σϙ[έ]—   1
[λος δεξιὸν κ]ϙὶ σπλάγχνα κα[ὶ] λαβὼν ἄλλον στέφανον
ἐλάας π[ρο]—
[θυέσθω Διὶ] Ἀποτροπαίωι πόπανον ῥαβδωτὸν ἐννεόμφαλον
καὶ
[Διὶ Μειλιχίω]ι πόπανον ῥαβδωτὸν ἐννεόμφαλον καὶ
Ἀρτέμιδ[ι   4
[...] καὶ Ἀρτέμιδι Προθυραίαι καὶ Γῆι ἑκάστηι πόπανον
[ἐννεόμφ]αλον. ταῦτα δὲ ποήσας θυέτω χοῖρον γαλαθηνὸν
[τῶι Ἀσκλ]ηπιῶι ἐπὶ τοῦ βωμοῦ καὶ τραπεζούσθω σκέλος
δεξ[ι]—
[ὸν καὶ σπ]λάγχνα. ἐμβαλλέτω δὲ εἰ͜ς τὸν θησαυρὸν ὀβολοὺς
τρεῖ[σ].   8
[εἰς δὲ τὴ]ν ἑσπέραν ἐπιβαλλέ[σ]θω πόπανα τρία ἐννεόμφαλα,
[τούτων μὲ]ν δύο ἐπὶ τὴν ἔξω θυμέλην Τύχηι καὶ Μνημοσύνηι,
[τὸ δὲ τρίτ]ον ἐν τῶι ἐγκοιμητηρίωι Θέμιδι. ἁγνευέτω δὲ ὁ
[εἰσπορευ]όμενος εἰς τὸ ἐγκοιμητήριον ἀπό τε τῶν
προειρημέ—   12
[νων πάν]των καὶ ἀφροδισίων καὶ αἰγείου κρέως καὶ τυροῦ
κα[ὶ]
[...]ΙΑΜΙΔΟΣ τριταῖος. τὸν δὲ στέφανον ὁ ἐγκοιμώμενος
[ἀποτιθέμ]ενος καταλειπέτω ἐπὶ τῆς στιβάδος. ἐὰν δέ τις βού—
[ληται ὑπὲρ] τοῦ αὐτοῦ ἐπερωτᾶν πλεονάκις,
προθυέσθω χοῖρο[ν],   16
[ἐὰν δὲ καὶ] ὑπὲρ ἄλλου πράγματος ἐπερωτᾶι, προθυέσθω
χοῖρο[ν]
[ἄλλον κατὰ] τὰ προγεγραμμένα. εἰς δὲ τὸ μικρὸν
ἐγκοιμητήριον
[ὁ εἰσιὼν ἁγ]νείαν ἁγνευέτω τὴν αὐτήν. προθυέσθω δὲ
Διὶ Ἀποτ[ρο]—
[παίωι πόπ]ανον ῥαβδωτὸν ἐννεόμφαλον καὶ Διὶ Μ͜ειλιχίωι
πόπ[α]—   20
[νον ῥαβδω]τὸν ἐννεόμφαλον καὶ Ἀρτέμιδι Προθυραίαι
καὶ Ἀρτέμι—
[δι...]ι καὶ Γηι ἑκάστηι πόπανον ἐννεόμφαλον. ἐμβαλλέ—
[τω δὲ καὶ] εἰς τὸν θησαυρὸν ὀβολοὺς τρεῖς. περιθυέσθωσαν
[δὲ πελανο(?)]ῖς μέλιτι καὶ ἐλαίωι δεδευμένοις καὶ
λιβανωτῶι   24
[πάντες οἱ θ]εραπεύοντες τὸν θεὸν ἑπόμενοι τῶι ἱερεῖ καὶ
ΙΕ[.?]
[...]. εἰς δὲ τὴν ἑσπέραν ἐπιβαλλέσθωσαν οἵ τε ΠΡΟ[.?]

[... ε]ἰς τὸ ἐγκοιμητήριον καὶ οἱ περιθυσάμενοι πάν—
[τες πόπα]να τρία ἐννεόμφαλα Θέμιδι, Τύχηι,
Μνημοσύνηι ἑ—   28
[κάστηι πό]παρνον. καθιστάτωσαν δὲ ἐγγύους τῶν ἰατρείων
  τῶ[ι]
[θεῶι, ἃ ἂν α]ὑτοὺς πράσσηται, ἀποδώσειν ἐντὸς ἐνιαυτοῦ.
[...]ίατρα μὴ νεώτερα ἐνιαυσίων. ἐμβαλέτωσαν δὲ
[εἰς τὸν θησ]αυρὸν τοῦ Ἀσκληπιοῦ τὰ ίατρα, Φωκαΐδα
  τῶι Ἀπό[λ]—   32
[λωνι καὶ Φ]ωκαΐδα τῶι Ἀσκληπιῶι, ὑγιεῖς γενόμενοι
  καὶ ἐάν τι
[ἄλλο αὐτ]οὺς αἰτήσηι ὁ θεός.

                              [... Κ]λώδιος Γλύκων   36
                              [ἱερ]ονομῶν ἀνέθηκεν.

[*vacat*] and he is to set on the table   1
[the right] leg and entrails and once he has taken another
  wreath of olive
he is [to make a preliminary offering to Zeus] Apotropaios of
  a ribbed round cake with nine knobs and
to [Zeus Meilichios] a ribbed round cake with nine buttons
  and to Artemis   4
[...] and to Artemis Prothyraia and to Ge, to each a
  round cake
[with nine]knobs. Then having done this he is to sacrifice a
  suckling pig
[to Askl]epios on the altar and set on the table the right leg
and entrails. Then he is to put three obols into the
  offertory box.   8
[At] evening he is to add three round cakes with nine knobs,
of [these first] two on the outdoors altar for burning (thymele)
  to Tyche and Mnemosyne
[and then the third] to Themis in the incubation chamber.
  He who
[enters] the incubation chamber is to keep himself pure
  from all the things mentioned above   12
and from sex and from goat meat and cheese and
[*c*.14 letters] ... on the third day. The incubant is then to
[lay aside] the wreath and leave it on his straw bed.
    If someone wants
to inquire several times about the same thing, he is to make a

preliminary sacrifice of a pig, 16
[and if he also] makes an inquiry about another matter,
 he is to make a preliminary sacrifice of [another] pig
[according] to the above instructions. He who [enters]
 the small incubation chamber
is to observe the same rules of purity. And he is to make a
 preliminary offering to Zeus Apotropaios
of a ribbed round cake with nine knobs and to Zeus
 Meilichios of a [ribbed] round cake 20
with nine knobs, and to Artemis Prothyraia and Artemis
 [...] and to Ge, to each a round cake with nine knobs.
[And he is also to] put three obols into the offertory box.
All those worshipping the god are to perform a sacrifice in a 24
circle (?) with [cakes] dipped in honey and oil and with
 incense following the priest and [...]
[...] At evening those who [...]
[...] into the incubation chamber and those who have
 sacrificed in a circle (?)
are all to add three round cakes with nine knobs to Themis,
 Tyche, Mnemosyne 28
[to each one] round cake. They are to bring forward guarantors
 [to the god] for any healing fee
which he exacts from them, that they will pay it within a year
[...] healing offering not younger than one year. And then
 they are to put
the payment for the cure [into] the offertory box of Asklepios,
 a Phokaian hekte to Apollo 32
and a Phokaian hekte to Asklepios, once they have become
 healthy, and anything
[else] the god should require. [...]
[... K]lodius Glykon
the sacred official set this up. 36

These rules prescribe in detail the movement of pilgrims around the sanctuary, the nature of offerings to particular gods, and the time and place for these to be made. Specific cult statues and altars are mentioned.[31] Thus the pilgrims' experience of making these offerings—the first stage of the ritual of incubation—was intimately linked to the

---

[31] e.g. line 5, 'Artemis Prothyraia' and line 10, 'the thymele outside'. There are significant problems in the identification of the location of these objects. See Wörrle (1969), 173–4 and 176–7.

topography of the sanctuary so that the rules and the physical layout of the sanctuary operated in tandem to orchestrate the pilgrims' experiences. This choreography governed the way in which pilgrims viewed and experienced the Asklepieion. A literary parallel to this choreography of pilgrimage can be found in Pausanias' description of the sanctuary of Zeus at Olympia which, as the author emphasizes, follows the order of sacrifice at the altars and not Pausanias' actual route.[32]

In effect two alternative journeys through the sanctuary are offered, one leading to 'the incubation chamber' and the other to 'the small incubation chamber'. Although the identification of these buildings is not absolutely certain, it is thought that they refer respectively to the incubation chamber in the cryptoporticus of the southern portico (Figure 1.11) and the old incubation chambers in the middle of the courtyard (Figure 1.12).[33] In addition to the bloodless offerings required from all incubants, those who were to spend the night in the larger incubation chamber were obliged to offer a pig to Asklepios.[34] Socio-economic divisions were thus to some extent maintained in this pilgrimage centre, and were visually and spatially reinforced as pilgrims making the more expensive sacrifice processed to a different incubation chamber.[35]

However, other aspects of the *Lex Sacra* might be said to have fostered what has been described in the anthropology of pilgrimage as *communitas* among pilgrims. The rules of purification for example, which applied to all incubants and involved abstaining from certain foods and from sex, helped create a common pilgrim consciousness.[36] Moreover, all incubants, and possibly also non-incubant worshippers, participated in a communal religious procession before the night of incubation, no doubt a religiously charged experience.[37] The knowledge

---

[32] Paus. 5.14.4 and 10. See Elsner (2000*b*), 53–8; Hutton (Ch. 10 in this volume), 299. For other examples of choreographed processions in religious and civic environments see Lucian's *De Dea Syria* 47 and Rogers (1991), 80–126.

[33] Wörrle (1969), 178; Hoffmann (1998), 55.

[34] *Lex Sacra*, lines 1–2, 6–8, and 18–23.

[35] On social differentiation at pilgrimage centres in other cultures see Pfaffenberger (1979); Morinis (1984); Sallnow (1981) and (1987).

[36] Compare the Turners' interpretation of the effects of fasting among pilgrims in the 1970s at St Patrick's Purgatory at Lough Derg in Ireland (Turner and Turner (1978), 133).

[37] *Lex Sacra*, lines 23–9.

that these purificatory rituals and these very itineraries through the sanctuary had been followed by past pilgrims may have extended *communitas* to an imaginary diachronic community of pilgrims. Within the space of the Asklepieion the *Lex Sacra* in effect set up a radical new taxonomy in which sickness, which in Graeco-Roman culture was considered not only a misfortune but also a sign of divine disfavour, became the necessary prerequisite for prominent participation in religious ritual and for visionary contact with the divine.[38]

The *Lex Sacra* regulated the bodies of pilgrims both by means of nutritional and sexual regimes and by means of obligatory ritual movement. Another fragmentary inscription further suggests that it was not only the internal processes of the body which were regulated by the rules of incubation: the external appearance of pilgrims was also controlled by a specification that pilgrims were to wear a white chiton and were not allowed to wear rings, belts, or shoes.[39] This emphasis on controlling and homogenizing the bodies of pilgrims may have had particular resonance amongst people whose bodies were sick and implicitly out of control.[40]

A parallel can be traced between the way that the building programme imposed a new order on the landscape of the sanctuary, and the way that the *Lex Sacra* imposed control over the bodily landscape of pilgrims (both individual and collective). These two systems of order (architectural and ritual) interlocked and worked in tandem. The interface between these frameworks was the pilgrims: the experience of the pilgrims was constructed on the one hand by the physical space of the sanctuary and on the other by the rules which governed their paths through that space. Simultaneously the presence and religious performances of pilgrims in the sanctuary animated the landscape by confirming the function of buildings and asserting divine presence within them. Both the space of the sanctuary and the space of the pilgrims' bodies

---

[38] On sickness and deformity see Garland (1995).

[39] Fränkel (1895), no. 264 = Edelstein and Edelstein (1945), no. 513. A parallel to these regulations can be found in Lucian's *De Dea Syria* 55, a contemporary account of pilgrimage to the Syrian Goddess: pilgrims are said to shave their heads and eyebrows before setting off; they wear wreaths on their heads, and they are literally marked with tattoos on their wrists or necks. In the *Lex Sacra* the placement and regulation of bodies was applied not only to pilgrims but also to sacrificial animals: it specifies which parts of the animals' bodies are to be laid on the altar (lines 1–2).

[40] See Sontag (1991) on the culturally specific nature of the experience of sickness.

were transformed by the imposition of order and regularity through these architectural and ritual frameworks, and in both cases the ultimate purpose was to receive the god. The space of the sanctuary and the very bodies of pilgrims were portals for access to the divine.

PILGRIM TESTIMONIES: MIRACLES IN THE ASKLEPIEION

Within the regulated space of the sanctuary and the regulated bodies of pilgrims there was scope for an infinite variety of experiences of contact with the divine, especially in visions during the night. Thank-offerings describe aspects of those experiences through image and text. After the departure of a pilgrim the thank-offering remained in the sanctuary and thus 'extended' the pilgrimage. The display of collections of offerings stretching back over generations visually constructed a diachronic community of healed pilgrims. The dedications offered subsequent pilgrims glimpses into that realm for two main reasons. First, there are many references to the god specifying the kind of offering he wanted: in other words viewers were aware that the offerings were 'designed' by the god.[41] Second, they often explicitly narrate the moment of contact between the pilgrim and the god.[42] Inscriptional and sculptural

[41] *Lex Sacra*, lines 31–2. The following phrases used in thank-offerings imply obedience to a command given by the god in a moment of human/divine contact, usually in a dream vision: κατὰ ἐπιταγήν ('in accordance with a command') (Habicht (1969), nos. 72, 139); κατὰ συνταγήν ('in accordance with a command') (Habicht (1969), nos. 69, 120, 123); κατὰ κέλευσιν τοῦ θεοῦ ('in accordance with the order of the god') (Müller (1987), 194, Line 6); κατ' ὄνειρον ('in accordance with a dream') (Habicht (1969), nos. 75, 76, 77, 91, 116); κατ' ὄναρ ('in accordance with a dream') (Habicht (1969), nos. 117, 127); κατὰ ἐνυπνίου ὄψιν ('in accordance with the vision of a dream') (Habicht (1969), no. 132). Aelius Aristides writes that his literary thank-offering was composed at the command of the god (*ST* 2.1–4). Compare also stories of the god ordering specific thank-offerings in the 4th-cent. BCE Epidaurian 'miracle inscriptions' e.g. Ambrosia was ordered to offer a silver pig to the god as a memorial of her ignorance because she had scoffed at the stories of miraculous cures narrated by thank-offerings on view (LiDonnici (1995), 88–9 (A4)).

[42] For example, the 4th-cent. BCE Epidaurian 'miracle inscriptions' describe occurrences during incubation, including the application of drugs and the performance of operations by the god (e.g. LiDonnici (1995), 88–9 (A4), 92–3 (A9), 96–7 (A17), 98–9 (A18 and A19), 100–1 (B1), 102–3 (B3), 104–5 (B5), 106–7 (B7, B8, and B9), 108–9 (B10, B11, and B12), 112–13 (B18), 114–15 (B20, B21)), and conversations between

thank-offerings on display in the sanctuary could thus function as gateways into the experience of past pilgrims and into a realm of visionary contact with Asklepios.

This interpretation of the effect of the display of thank-offerings in Asklepieia rests on an understanding of visuality in Graeco-Roman culture and in particular in the context of religious spaces. Descriptions of art and sculpture in second-century texts suggest that viewers expected to 'read out' themes and narratives from images. For example several passages of Achilles Tatius' *Leukippe and Kleitophon* offer detailed imaginative readings of images.[43] In the context of pilgrimage, ritual viewing of the cult image and votive dedications, *theōria*, was of great significance.[44] The display of exegetical inscriptions next to thank-offerings in sanctuaries invited viewers to read narratives into images with the guidance of the texts.[45] Priests and guides may also have helped pilgrims to interpret thank-offerings.[46] In addition to evidence for this in-depth, religious viewing of thank-offerings there are also references to

Asklepios and the incubant (e.g. LiDonnici (1995), 86–7 (A2 and A3), 88–9 (A4), 90–1 (A7), 92–3 (A8), 110–11 (B14)). Similarly, marble votive reliefs often depict the pilgrim approaching Asklepios (e.g. Athens Archaeological Museum, nos. 1330, 1339, 1377), or Asklepios curing the pilgrim (e.g. Athens Archaeological Museum, nos. 1841, 2373).

[43] Achilles Tatius, *Leukippe and Kleitophon* 1.2 (in the temple of Astarte), 3.6–8 (temple of Zeus of Mount Cassius at Pelusium—paintings of Andromeda and Prometheus), 5.3–4 (painting of Prokne and Philomela; theory of interpreting a picture as a prophetic sign). See Bartsch (1989), esp. 30–1, 40–79. On visuality in Graeco-Roman culture see Elsner (1996) and (2000*b*); Goldhill (2001), 154–94.

[44] Rutherford (2000*a*) and (2001*a*), esp. 42–5. Cf. Pausanias' descriptions of votive dedications at other sanctuaries, for example at the sanctuary of Zeus at Olympia, *Description of Greece* 5 and 6. See also Lucian's *De Dea Syria* 10 where ἀρχαῖα ἀναθήματα καὶ πολλὰ θαύματα are amongst the noteworthy features of the sanctuary mentioned by the narrator. See also Chariton *Kallirhoe* 3.5.3 where Chaireas comes to the shrine of Aphrodite and looks at the votive offerings and recognizes the ἀνάθημα which Dionysios has set up—a golden statue of Kallirhoe.

[45] It has been argued that the Epidaurian miracle inscriptions were a compilation of exegetical inscriptions which originally glossed wooden plaques depicting scenes of miraculous healing (LiDonnici (1995), 40–75). See Herodas *mimiamboi* 4, lines 14–17 and 21–25 (Edelstein and Edelstein (1945), no. 482) for the concurrent reading of image and text in a Hellenistic poetic narrative of pilgrimage to the Asklepieion at Kos. Pausanias and Arrian demonstrate the 2nd-cent. CE practice of concurrent readings of images and accompanying inscriptions: on Pausanias see Arafat (1992), 397 and Habicht (1998), 64–94; see Arrian, *Peripl. M. Eux.* 1 (he comments both on the statue of Hadrian—its likeness to him—and on its accompanying inscription).

[46] See Plut. *De Pyth. Or.* 394e where guides conduct the visitor around the ἀναθήματα at Apollo's oracle at Delphi.

their status as testaments to the power and presence of the god, as proof of the stories they constructed.[47]

Beyond the multiplicity of possible viewings and readings at any time, a twenty-first-century European reading of a thank-offering from the Asklepieion is without doubt temporally and culturally removed from a second-century Graeco-Roman pilgrim's reading. However, the following analysis of a selection of thank-offerings is sensitized to the frameworks in which these were viewed by pilgrims in the second century—the broad cultural context of the Greek east in the Roman empire, with particular reference to discourses of visuality and religion, and the specific spatial and ritual context of the Pergamene Asklepieion. The interpretation of the sanctuary and the *Lex Sacra* in the first part of this paper emphasized the construction of *communitas* through spatial and ritual regulation of the pilgrim body as a whole. The thank-offerings, however, focus exclusively on the experience of the individual pilgrim-dedicant, even though this was constructed within and by the communal space and ritual. The *Lex Sacra* organized pilgrims into one visible communal procession and united them through common purificatory rituals, while the communal incubation chambers physically gathered pilgrims together. By contrast the thank-offerings asserted the pilgrims' individuality by means of choices both of presentation in text and image, and of display, as there were a variety of spaces in which to make the dedications.[48] Both the *Lex Sacra* and the thank-offerings focused on the bodies of pilgrims: but whereas the former attempted to homogenize them, the latter differentiated them through narratives of individual bodily healing and engaged in a discourse of therapeutic competition.

There was a wide range of genres of thank-offerings and the first one to be examined is literary and also perhaps the most eloquent thank-offering associated with the Asklepieion, Aelius Aristides' *Sacred Tales*.[49]

---

[47] See e.g. Plut. *De Pyth. Or.* 408f–409a (votives are adduced as proof of the truth of the Pythia's pronouncements); Kallimachos' *Epigrammata* 55 (Edelstein and Edelstein (1945), no. 522) (if Asklepios forgets that the pilgrim has paid for the cure the tablet will bear witness); Epidaurian miracle inscriptions (LiDonnici (1995), 86–9 (A3 and A4)).

[48] Thank-offerings have been found all over the Asklepieion, in particular in the northern area of the sanctuary.

[49] On the *ST*: on the literary context see Boulanger (1923); Cortés Copete (1995). On the religious dimensions see Festugière (1954), 85–104; Dodds (1965), 41–5; Bompaire (1989). On pilgrimage see Rutherford (1999). On conversion see Weiss

Important differences of effect certainly arise from the choice of genre of thank-offerings. For example, literary thank-offerings could be heard or read outside the Asklepieion whereas marble statues and inscriptions narrating similar stories of healing could only be read and viewed within the context of the sanctuary.[50] Aristides himself, however, on one level treats oral and physical narratives in thanks for healing as comparable.[51] Simultaneously he does specify that his choice of genre—λόγοι—in which to give thanks was particularly appropriate to him and his story of contact with the god as he was an orator and his oratorical skills had been advanced by contact with Asklepios.[52] Thus in this instance the

(1998). On the social and public context see Brown (1978), 27–53. On autobiography see Misch (1973), 495–510; Quet (1993). On the literary role of documentation see Pearcy (1988). On dream narratives see Michenaud and Dierkens (1972); Cox Miller (1994), 184–204. On pain and the body see Perkins (1992) and (1995), 173–99; King (1999). On references to the space of the Pergamene Asklepieion see Jones (1998). Hostile interpretations of the *ST* and its author in the light of the notion of hypochondria include Phillips (1952); Behr (1968), 44–46; Bowersock (1969), 72; Reardon (1971), 258, 261, 262; Misch (1973), 495–510 (esp. 502, 506–8); Brown (1978), 41; MacMullen (1981), 9, 15; M. Gourevitch and D. Gourevitch (1968); D. Gourevitch (1984), 17–71; Lane Fox (1986), 160; Hoffmann (1998), 54.

[50] Several passages from Aristides' writings strongly suggest that the *ST* was known beyond the confines of the Pergamene Asklepieion: *ST* 2.2, *Oration* 42 *An Address Regarding Asklepios* 4 and 10. See also *ST* 4.30 which suggests the therapeutic public reading of the third book of the *ST* in the Asklepieion, presumably for a select audience. Philostratos' reference to the *ST* presupposes its publication, *Vitae Sophistarum* 581: 'For the nature of his disease, and the fact that he suffered from muscle spasms he himself writes in the Sacred books; and these books served him in some sort as diaries, and the diaries are good teachers of the art of speaking well on every subject.' Lucian's *De Dea Syria*, which makes the temple public for a wider (Greek-speaking) audience, could be regarded as literary thank-offering.

[51] Ael. Aristid. *Oration* 42 *An Address Regarding Asklepios* 7: 'But some, I mean both men and women, even attribute to the providence of the god the existence of the limbs of their body, when their natural limbs had been destroyed; others list other things, some in oral accounts, some in the declarations of their votive offerings' (οἱ μὲν ἀπὸ στόματος οὕτωσὶ φράζοντες, οἱ δὲ ἐν τοῖς ἀναθήμασιν ἐξηγούμενοι).

[52] Ibid. 2–3: 'Of course I am concerned to express my gratitude and show my respect by means of sacrifice and incense, whether this takes place in keeping with Hesiod's advice or even with greater enthusiasm than my means allow. But the expression of gratitude through oratory appears particularly proper to me. For if in general the study of oratory (λόγοι) means for man the point and, as it were, the sum of life, and of speeches those concerning the gods are the most necessary and just, and our career in oratory clearly is a gift from the god himself, there is no fairer means of showing gratitude to the god, I think, than through oratory, nor would we have a better use to which to put oratory.' On the simple literary style of the *ST* as a deliberate technique which functions primarily to convey Aristides' image of simplicity, piety, and ἀφέλεια see Weiss (1998),

choice of genre expresses the pilgrim's individuality and the nature of his personal contact with Asklepios.

The *Sacred Tales* focuses exclusively on Aristides, in particular on his body and his oratory. Scholars have been disappointed by his apparent lack of interest in the building activity which must have been going on in the Asklepieion during his two-year stay, his 'kathedra', in 145–7.[53] There are no references to the communal activities set out in the *Lex Sacra*, and very few references to other pilgrims at all—and these are highly selective as they refer almost exclusively to men of the social, political, and intellectual elite of Asia Minor.[54] These choices construct a narrative which reflects the experience, or perhaps more accurately, the ideal of pilgrimage to the Asklepieion of one intellectual aristocrat; it is one pilgrim's voice amongst many, most of which were not recorded in either text or image or, if recorded, were subsequently lost.

An important feature of Aristides' 'voice' is its highly competitive tone.[55] He presents himself as the pilgrim whose sickness is the most severe, whose suffering is the most painful, whose powers of endurance are the most extraordinary, and whose recovery is the most miraculous.[56] He also claims to have had the most frequent and intense visionary contact with Asklepios and to have received more favours

---

47–73, and esp. 52–72. See Rutherford (1998*a*), 101 for Aristides' later reputation as a writer in the ἀφελές style.

[53] e.g. Jones (1998), esp. 74. For Aristides' references to his 'kathedra' see *ST* 2.70 and 3.44.

[54] For example, in the narrative of Aristides' 'kathedra' in the Asklepieion he is said to have contact with: L. Sedatius Theophilus, citizen of Nikaia on the Kayster and Laodikaia ad Lycum, of praetorian rank; L. Cuspius Pactumeius Rufinus consul in 142 CE and donor of the temple of Zeus-Asklepios; L. Salvius Julianus consul 170/1 CE; and Q. Fabius Julianus Optatianus consul 128 CE and proconsul of Asia 145/6 CE. Philosophers and orators are also mentioned at IV.19, 23 and 27. However, there is evidence external to the text for the presence of different types of worshippers—women and non-elite. See Habicht (1969) for inscriptional evidence for female worshippers at the Asklepieion. In addition to thank-offerings by women, Flavia Melitine built the library and dedicated the statue of Hadrian in this building. Material evidence for poor pilgrims is inevitably lacking because of the perishable nature of cheap offerings. However, according to the *Lex Sacra* (lines 8, 22–3) the fee for incubation in this period was not very high (3 obols), suggesting that poorer pilgrims were not excluded.

[55] This has been interpreted in light of the competitive and public 'face to face' culture of the second century. On Aristides see Brown (1978), 27–53; Cox Miller (1994), 184–204; and generally on competitive 'reading' of appearance in second century culture (physiognomics) see Gleason (1995), 55–81; Barton (1994), 95–131.

[56] e.g. *ST* 2.47.

from him than any Greek at any time.[57] His therapeutic contact with Asklepios is exclusive: if others try the cures that Asklepios has prescribed to Aristides, they fall ill, and if Aristides follows the advice of human doctors—even if it is identical with that of Asklepios!—he does not recover.[58] Aristides' dependence on Asklepios is mirrored by the god's dependence on his new-found servant, διάκονος.[59]

Aristides' discourse of personal divine favour is initially played out on the stage of his suffering body and involves a series of violent illnesses and gruelling treatments. In the first three books of the *Sacred Tales* Aristides' sickness is presented as a serious impediment to his career as a public orator (ironically in a highly sophisticated literary medium).[60] Gradually though, and especially in books four and five, a symbiotic relationship is depicted between Aristides' sickness and his oratory because of the contact with Asklepios that the former condition entails.[61] Asklepios the god of healing, becomes the ideal teacher of oratory: he orders Aristides to resume writing and public speaking, he directs his course of study, introduces him to the great intellectuals of the past such as Plato and Sophokles, and sometimes even writes his speeches for him![62] An apologetic passage indicates that Aristides was

---

[57] *ST* 2.55 (frequent visions), *Oration 42 Address Regarding Asklepios* 1 (most favoured of all the Greeks).

[58] *ST* 2.76, 2.73; examples where doctors are proved wrong 1.62–8 and 3.8–9.

[59] e.g. *ST* 1.71–7: Aristides saves his foster father Zosimos from sickness (1.74: τῶι τε θεῶι χάριν ἔχων τῆς προνοίας καὶ τῆς διακονίας ἐμοί 'being both thankful to the god for his providence and to me for my service'); 3.38–40 Aristides puts a stop to a spate of earthquakes (3.40: προνοίαι μὲν καὶ δυνάμει τῶν θεῶν, διακονίαι δ' ἡμῶν ἀναγκαίαι, 'on the one hand on account of the providence and power of the gods, on the other hand on account of my necessary service'); 4.33–7 Aristides saves his travelling companions from a storm (4.36: εὐεργέτην, σωτῆρα ὀνομάζοντες, συγχαίροντες τῆς παρὰ τῶν θεῶν προνοίας 'calling me "benefactor" and "saviour", and rejoicing with me at the providence of the gods').

[60] *ST* 2.5–7 and 60–70 (he contracted his illness on a journey to Rome to perform as an orator), and 5.56 (illness has prevented him from touring and performing).

[61] *ST* 4.25 (his contact with the healing god was the most valuable part of his oratorical training), 4.27 (he became ill by divine good fortune in order that his oratory be improved), 4.29 (he realizes that the god intended his healing therapies not only to save him but to help him in his oratory). See Perkins (1992) and (1995), 173–99, and King (1999) on the narrative function of pain and suffering in the *ST*.

[62] *ST* 4.14 (Asklepios orders him to resume oratory), 4.24 (reading list and introductions to the great past masters), 4.25–26 (Aristides' compositions aided in dream visions), 4.59–62 (visions of all the great literary figures of the past). Compare the role of the hero Protesilaos in Philostratos *Heroikos* 26–42 in revealing the (dead) Trojan heroes to the vinegrower (and through him to the Phoenician merchant and the reader).

aware of the unusual nature of Asklepios' contact with him.[63] The presence of Asklepios in Aristides' body and words is repeatedly asserted in narratives of competitive therapeutic and oratorical performances. Aristides' very existence is attributed to the god repeatedly saving him and this theme is expressed in a story in which Asklepios bestows the name Theodoros ('gift of the god') on Aristides.[64] The text offers glimpses into Aristides' intense, personal, charismatic relationship with the god; this is only reinforced by occasional tantalizing suggestions that some encounters with the divine cannot be revealed to the reader.[65]

Aristides' literary thank-offering is of some length and enables the author to describe a series of illnesses and recoveries, and to present the development of his relationship with Asklepios. Inscriptional thank-offerings found in the Asklepieion are much shorter: complex narratives are telescoped into short graphic summaries. But the focus on the individual is an important feature in a similar manner to Aristides' narrative. The pilgrim's identity and story of divine contact are conveyed in a number of ways. Cultural affiliation is stated through choice of language—Greek or Latin.[66] The pilgrim's name is a vital feature of identity and is included in almost every thank-offering.[67] Occupation and social or military rank are further autobiographical features present in many inscriptions.[68] Place of origin further identifies the individual and simultaneously evokes a narrative of the pilgrim's journey from home to the Asklepieion.[69] The pilgrim's visionary contact with Askle-

---

[63] *ST* 5.36.

[64] *ST* 4.53 and 70.

[65] *ST* 1.71; 3.46, 3.48; 4.50–1. Pausanias too withholds religious information from his readers, e.g. 1.38.7 (about Eleusis) and 4.33.4–5 (about the Karnasian grove outside Messene). For a discussion see Habicht (1998), 156; Elsner (1992), esp. 20–5. See also Apuleius, *Apology* 61 and *Metamorphoses* 11.22 for tantalizing references to the knowledge of initiates (on the latter see Beard, North, and Price (1998), 287–8). On the theme of documentation and testimony in the *ST* see Pearcy (1988).

[66] Most of the inscriptions are in Greek. Latin examples include Habicht (1969), nos. 67, 68, 107.

[67] Contrast Lucian's *De Dea Syria* 1 and 60 where there is a play on (the witholding of) the name of the author/pilgrim. See Elsner (2001*b*), 126–7, 152–3.

[68] e.g. Habicht (1969), nos. 67 (lictor to the proconsul of Asia), 77 (soldier of the first legion), 106 (corn supplier to the sixth legion), 125 (treasurer of lower Mysia); for references to rank see nos. 79, 106, 120.

[69] e.g. Habicht (1969), nos. 74 (Troas), 75 and 76 (Nikaia), 78 (Antiocheia), 88 (Kos), 102 (Mylasa), 127 (Rhodes).

pios is often referred to in formulae such as κατ' ὄναρ.[70] Such brief statements do not compare in intensity and detail to Aristides' literary descriptions of his visionary contact with Asklepios at Pergamon and beyond. For example:

> But it was made as clear as possible, just as countless other things also clearly contained the presence of the god. For there was a seeming, as it were, to touch him and to perceive that he himself had come, and to be between sleep and waking, and to wish to look up and to be in anguish that he might depart too soon and to strain the ears and to hear some things as in a dream, some as in a waking state. Hair stood straight, and there were tears with joy, and the pride of one's heart was inoffensive. And what man could describe these things in words? If any man has been initiated, he knows and understands.[71]

The plain κατ' ὄναρ of inscriptions could have been read as a sign pointing to this kind of experience, encouraging pilgrims to imagine it most effectively for themselves.

The inscription set up by Julius Meidias focuses on the pilgrim's body, and in particular on the painful treatment he underwent at the command of Asklepios (Figure 11): Ἰούλιος Μειδί[ας] φλεβοτομηθεὶς ὑπὸ τοῦ μυὸς κατὰ ἐπιταγὴν ἀνέθηκ[ε]. ('Julius Meidi[as] set this up in accordance with a command having been bled underneath his muscle').[72] Meidias' inscription creates a narrative of his body's sufferings and endurance on account not of sickness (though this is implicit), but of the therapy imposed by the god. Within the confines of the Asklepieion at least, this pilgrim chose to identify himself with a narrative of therapeutic bodily suffering in accordance with the will of the god. The god's takeover of Meidias' body through the treatment was paralleled by his claiming part of the space of the god with this dedication: it was found in the courtyard of the Asklepieion between the temple of Asklepios the Saviour and the old incubation chambers. The 'inscribing' of the pilgrim's body through cutting (bloodletting) is paralleled by the permanent 'inscribing' of the god's landscape by the

---

[70] See above n. 41.
[71] *ST* 2.31–3. Compare the description of the vinegrower's contact with the hero Protesilaos in Philostratos, *Heroikos* 10–11.
[72] Habicht (1969), no. 139.

Figure 11. Votive inscription from the Asklepieion of Pergamon, dedicated by Julius Meidias. Inventory number 1933, 40. Dimensions 17 × 18 × 3.0 cm. (Habicht (1969), no. 139, Tafel 41)

setting up of the votive inscription in the very area where he manifested himself in his cult statue and in dream visions.

Text and image are used together in thank-offerings very effectively to focus on the particular part of the pilgrim's body which had been sick and was subsequently healed by the god. For example, the pilgrim Tapari dedicated a bronze image of her eyes attached to a plaque which identified both her and the god by name (Figure 12).[73] On the basis that this thank-offering was found in the courtyard of the sanctuary it is presumed that it had been displayed in this area. Consequently, after her departure a representation of the part of Tapari's body which had been miraculously healed remained close to the god. In this case the gaze of the pilgrim which had beheld the god in his cult

[73] Habicht (1969), no. 111b: Ταπαρι ʾΑσ- | κληπιῶ εὐχή<ν> ('Tapari to Asklepios a votive'). For a purely inscriptional account of the healing of eyes see Habicht (1969), no. 86.

Figure 12. Bronze plaque with eyes from the Asklepieion of Pergamon, dedicated by Tapari. Bergama museum, inventory number 1959, M 3. Dimensions of plaque 5.9 × 2.1 × 0.2 cm. (Habicht (1969), no. 111b, Tafel 30)

image or perhaps in a dream vision, was frozen in a permanent state of healed transformation in the sanctuary and looked out not only on the sacred space of the god but also on subsequent pilgrims.[74] In the context of the sanctuary this image and short text told an eloquent story of divine healing. Within the taxonomy of the Asklepieion the very part of the body which had been perceived as the locus of illness and pain was transformed into the miraculous part.

The thank-offering of Fabia Secunda also uses a combination of text and image (Figure 13).[75] It is unclear whether the ear depicted

---

[74] On the gaze in Late Antique and Medieval Christianity see Frank (2000*b*) and Hahn (2000).

[75] Habicht (1969), no. 91: Ἀσκληπιῷ Σω-|τῆρι Φαβία Σεκοῦν-| δα κατ' ὄνειρον ('To Asklepios the Saviour Fabia Secunda in accordance with a dream').

Figure 13. Bronze plaque with gilded ear from the Asklepieion of Pergamon, dedicated by Fabia Secunda. Inventory number M 1959; Dimensions 9 × 4.3 (top) and 7.3 (bottom) × approximately 0.5 cm. (Habicht (1969), no.91, Tafel 30)

represents the ear of the pilgrim (whether sick or healed) or the ear of the god, listening to the pilgrim's request.[76] The dedication is made of relatively expensive materials (bronze and silver) and is visually impressive. By means of their thank-offerings pilgrims such as Meidias, Tapari, and Fabia Secunda competed to catch and hold the attention not only of

---

[76] The depiction of ears on votive dedications is a motif found in sanctuaries of many gods. The idea of Asklepios listening to pilgrims is expressed in the epithet ἐπήκοος ('listening'), for example Habicht (1969), nos. 99, 100, and 101. Compare also accounts of conversations between Asklepios and the incubant in the 4th-cent. BCE Epidaurian miracle inscriptions (see above n. 42). See also literary testimonies Oribasius, *Collectiones Medicae* 45. 30. 10–14 (Edelstein and Edelstein (1945), no. 425); Philostratos, *Vitae Sophistarum* 568 (the sophist Antiochos converses with Asklepios at the sanctuary of Asklepios at Aigai). For examples of Aristides conversing with Asklepios in dream visions narrated in the *ST* see 1.71 and 4.50.

the god but also of other pilgrims. These dedications were dispersed throughout the sanctuary, but together constructed a community of past pilgrims in bronze and marble. Competition and *communitas* can thus be identified as features of the process of making a thank-offering as well as of the performance of incubation, as analysed above, and of the general cultural construction of the sanctity of Pergamene Asklepios.

Several common themes emerge from the analysis of this small selection of thank-offerings. The text of Aristides, the inscription of Meidias and the body parts of Tapari and Fabia Secunda express diverse personal experiences of healing in individualized ways. All focus on the bodies of the pilgrims and on their contact with Asklepios. They present narratives of the miraculous presence of the god in sick bodies, of personal salvation and transformation through divine favour, of the restoration of order to fragmented bodies. These highly personal and intimate stories were, however, experienced in the public domain of the Asklepieion and expressed in the public discourses of texts and images. In this way highly individualized pilgrim responses, which were themselves moulded and to some extent controlled by the range of meanings available within the context of the sanctuary, became part of that 'objective' reality of the Asklepieion.

CONCLUSIONS

This interpretation of pilgrimage to the Pergamene Asklepieion in the second century has emphasized the importance of the visual and of place, where place is understood as architectural space in conjunction with the rules that governed the pilgrims' collective movement and mental state within it. This emphasis on the common space and rituals engendering a sense of *communitas* was the starting point, the framework in which therapeutic competition and individual experiences of contact with the divine were then located and interpreted. It has been argued that the order and regulation offered by the architecture of the sanctuary and rules of the *Lex Sacra* were important aspects of the experience of healing pilgrimage. This communal element was both reinforced and paradoxically undermined by the intensity of individual contact with the god and his presence in individual bodies. Both the landscape of the sanctuary and bodies of the pilgrims were transformed by the imposition of spatial and ritual order. But it was the miraculous, often violent transformation through the presence of Asklepios that both these systems were designed to achieve. A perilous struggle of order and chaos lay at the core of healing pilgrimage to this sanctuary: between order expressed in the architecture and in the regulated bodies of pilgrims, and the chaos of illness and miracle.

8

Mucianus and a Touch of the Miraculous:

Pilgrimage and Tourism in Roman Asia Minor

George Williamson

> Moreover the Mucianus who was three times consul has stated recently that, when governor of Lycia, he had read a certain letter of Sarpedon written on paper at Troy.[1]

The scene is familiar from countless imperial settings: locals eager to impress upon a newly-arrived governor both the antiquity of their land and its impeccable Homeric credentials, and unlike many such encounters it was relics not speeches which formed their proof. A letter from Sarpedon, prince of the Lycians in Homer's *Iliad*, a hero worth showing off to an incomer and recipient of cult in his *heroon* on the acropolis at Xanthos, was something worth dangling before the Roman's nose, something wonderful (*mirabile*).[2] Is this an anecdote about tourism? The effects of imperial power? Does it tell us about belief in relics, or belief in heroes? Is it secular, or religious? Why did this Mucianus choose to write about it? Why did Pliny the Elder choose to quote it

---

[1] Pliny, *NH* 13.88 = Peter fr. 22. Pliny goes on to cast doubt on this letter, stating that 'this seems to me even more remarkable since when Homer was writing, Egypt [the source of papyrus] did not yet exist'. The fragments of Mucianus are collected (with several omissions) in vol. 2 of Peter (1870), 101–7. His ordering will be used throughout this chapter, and an appendix at the end presents translations.

[2] For the cult of Sarpedon on the acropolis at Xanthos see Appian *BC* 4.10.71–8. Worship is attested as early as the Hellenistic period, see for example *TAM* 2.265 for a dedication by the general Aichmon to the 'heroes Sarpedon and Glaukos'.

in his all-encompassing *Natural History*? And why should it have any relevance in a discussion of ancient pilgrimage?

DEFINING ANCIENT PILGRIMAGE

What counts as ancient pilgrimage? Notoriously neither Latin nor Greek provides exact equivalents.[3] Certain modern definitions might distinguish between travel undertaken either for sacred or secular purposes—in speaking of pilgrimage we might think of Chaucer's pilgrims loquaciously wending their way to Canterbury, or the annual participants in the Muslim Hajj. Whatever they might see or take in en route, their primary motivation is religious: to visit a site of special religious or numinous significance.[4] By contrast, tourism is seen as either mere recreational activity, or at best as visiting beautiful buildings, landscapes, or works of art to evoke an aesthetic response of wonder. Such distinctions have been challenged as overschematic and unhelpful, and it might be argued that only the most consumerist definition of tourism need exclude the ideal of 'sacral fulfilment' which Elsner and Rubiés see at work in all modern constructions of travel, including anthropology and tourism.[5] The object of this paper is to show how difficult it is to fit the travels of one man, described in his fragmentary memoirs, into either category.[6]

Alternatively, such issues can fall under the rubric of 'Wonder': we might argue that whilst a sense of wonder is at the heart of both pilgrimage and tourism, in either case its origins are very different. In

---

[3] Dillon (1997) argues that there is no such vocabulary in Greek at all, whereas Rutherford (2000*a*) more plausibly demonstrates that there is a range of terms covering aspects of a modern definition of pilgrimage, including the term *theōria* denoting a state-pilgrimage.

[4] See Morinis (1992*b*) and Cohen (1992) for works which attempt to make such clear-cut distinctions.

[5] See the introduction to Elsner and Rubiés (1999).

[6] On the difficulties of making the distinction between tourism and pilgrimage see Rutherford (2001*a*), 41–4. In their introduction Elsner and Rubiés (1999) avoid simple dichotomies, and argue that the history of travel since the Renaissance has been 'a dialectic of dominant paradigms between two poles, which we might define as the transcendental vision of pilgrimage and the open-ended process which typically characterizes modernity' (5). In other words, much of the most avowedly secular writing has had at its heart an engagement with varieties of spiritual fulfilment.

the case of religion, that wonder is grounded in the operation of divine power or presence in either objects (for instance, saints' bones, pieces of the True Cross) or a sacred site, leads to accounts of pilgrimage not merely evoking this wonder but linking it explicitly to statements of divine power or involvement.[7] On the other hand, tourism, and the wonders evoked by a visit to, say, the Uffizi Museum or the Taj Mahal, connects to the availability of an aesthetic response, an operation grounded either in admiration of the power of Man or Nature.[8] Yet if the separation of religious and secular spheres was never simple or clear-cut even in the post-Enlightenment period—for Romantics like Wordsworth or Blake it was precisely *through* Nature that God was revealed—such distinctions cannot be applied straightforwardly to the world of the Roman empire. The writings of Gaius Licinius Mucianus reveal a continual awareness of the importance of both witness (autopsy) and physicality (the sense of touch). It is these, as much as ritual activity such as sacrifice or ablutions, which take us to the heart of ancient religious contemplation.

This chapter aims to investigate the very different conditions of travel and belief found in the early Roman empire, looked at through the eyes of Mucianus, a man well known for his political career, but much less well known for his travels.[9] It will ask whether in a polytheistic 'World full of Gods' such clear-cut distinctions between travel for religious and travel for aesthetic purposes can be made.[10] I will suggest that the travels of a Roman governor—for which Mucianus is perhaps our best witness—although including much that is non-religious in any strict sense, should not be placed in a category of secular travel; that the approach of an ancient who adhered to a polytheistic structure of beliefs should be

---

[7] Brown (1981) argues throughout for the importance of the special dead in late antique Christianity, and in particular at 88–94 discusses the function of relics as instances of divine mercy. The gradual development of a particular Christian topography of the Holy Land and its need to excavate the physical remains of the Gospels is the theme of a seminal essay by Maurice Halbwachs. See Halbwachs (1992).

[8] On the aesthetics of wonder see Fisher (1998). Daston and Park (1998) is a contribution to the history of science, examining how monsters, miracles, and the wonders of nature were described in the Renaissance and then filtered into early modern scientific enquiry, becoming crucial in the construction of institutions such as museums.

[9] Hunt (1984) provides an excellent analysis of the opportunities for travel opened up by the *pax Romana*. He also emphasizes the need to distinguish religious travel in the Roman empire from the very specific form of Christian pilgrimage.

[10] The phrase comes from the title of Hopkins (1999).

seen as motivated by a range of impulses, and that religious motivation cannot be considered 'off the agenda'. What was Mucianus' motivation in visiting sanctuaries and then writing about this? Analogies have been drawn between the collections of modern museums and those of ancient sanctuaries with their votives, but I want to suggest that the relationship and motivation of the visitor to both is radically different.[11]

Attempts by scholars to distinguish pilgrimage and tourism often result in their privileging those forms of travel and experience that centre on a deeply felt set of inner convictions. Erik Cohen's effort to inject theoretical rigour into the topic in the end produces a caricature of pilgrimage as essentially a serious, internalized process, opposed to an image of tourism as merely frivolous.[12] Morinis produces a similarly high-minded argument that a journey cannot be a pilgrimage if 'the intent of the journey does not involve a quest for an ideal'.[13] There is just enough ancient evidence which fits this model to have made it govern the assumptions underlying much recent work in this area—for example, Aelius Aristides and his *Sacred Tales*, or the elaborate ritual described by Lucian in his account of the cult of the Syrian Goddess at Hierapolis/Membij in *On the Syrian Goddess* both present intellectualized first person narratives dwelling on religious experience and practices to the exclusion of everything else.[14] Such works refer to the exceptional experiences of religious over-achievers rather than presenting a normative picture of ancient religion.[15] Without wishing to detract from the power that ancient religious experience might engender, experiences such as the powerful vision of the goddess Isis described in the ending of Apuleius' *Golden Ass* are the exception.[16] Is the focus on

---

[11] Pearce (1995), 88–92 looks at the growth of collecting within the sanctuaries of the Graeco-Roman world, drawing particularly on the evidence of Pausanias.

[12] Cohen (1992).

[13] Morinis (1992*b*), 7.

[14] Throughout his *Sacred Tales* Aristides refers to journeys he had been ordered to make by the god Asclepius, for instance 5.1, 'While I was in Smyrna during this time, the god indicated a journey to me. And I had to leave immediately. And we went out on the road to Pergamon.' Cf. Rutherford (2001*a*), 51–2. See also Rutherford (1999).

[15] Elsner (2001*b*) argues for the sophistication of the authorial self-presentation in Lucian's *On the Syrian Goddess* as well as considering its importance as a work about pilgrimage. Rutherford (2001*b*) 51–2 treats the *ST* as a pilgrimage text, stressing that Aristides' travels were 'always motivated by divine instruction'. See also Swain (1996), 254–97.

[16] Apul. *Met.* 11. 3–6.

emotional conversion, or intensity, which has been seen by scholars such as Nock as the crucial quality of religious experience in many ancient cults, not just Christianity, really the best way to approach ancient religious experience?[17] Should the study of pilgrimage in the ancient world concern itself with the ideas of spiritual quest or inner pilgrimage identified by those working on the topic in the modern period? Into what paradigm can we best fit the incessant temple visiting we can recover from the fragments of Mucianus' work? Tourism, pilgrimage, neither, or both?

INTRODUCING MUCIANUS

The fame of Gaius Licinius Mucianus is generally derived from his public career, not his writings, partly because of the salacious reputation he acquired in biographical sources for homosexual practices, but more important, for his role in the events of 69 CE, the 'Year of the Four Emperors'.[18] For Tacitus he served as a literary foil to Vespasian through his portrait of a man who might have been emperor, but preferred to support another.[19] His origins are unknown, although Syme has speculated that they might lie either in Spain or Apennine Italy, and we know nothing of his early career, except that he served as a legionary legate under Domitius Corbulo in Armenia,[20] and that at some point he fell into severe disfavour with Claudius, and seems to have pre-empted exile by taking himself off to Asia Minor.[21] He returned to favour under

---

[17] Nock (1933). This whole focus on intense devotion has been questioned, in particular by the work of Ramsay MacMullen. See MacMullen (1984).

[18] Suet. *Vesp.* 13.

[19] On Mucianus' role in 69 CE see Syme (1958) s.v. 'Mucianus', and Syme (1977). Also Levick (1999), and Wellesley (1975) On Mucianus as a foil to Vespasian see Tac. *Hist.* 1.10.10, 'He found it more congenial to hand over power (*imperium*) than to win it for himself.'

[20] Fr 7. See *PIR*² 5.1.50.

[21] Tac. *Hist.* 1.10.5, 'Removed to a remote part of Asia he came as close to being an exile as later he did to becoming emperor.' On this period in Mucianus' life see Syme (1958), 790–1. Some have thought the location of his exile to have been Rhodes on the basis of his description of a temple there (fr. 25), for instance the editors of *PIR*², but given the close connections between Lycia and Rhodes it is equally plausible that this visit took place during his time as imperial legate to Lycia under Nero. For the location of his exile on Rhodes see Bowersock (1965) 77, 'Rhodes had been the home of many other

Nero (perhaps the vagaries of his personal life so denigrated by Tacitus endeared him to the new emperor), and was sent on a series of provincial postings, first as imperial legate to the province of 'Lycia et Pamphylia', probably some time after 57 CE.[22]

His career is important both as an example of how a Roman governor might make use of his time in the provinces, and also because of the close connections between his postings and the texture of his writings. In 64 he went on to become suffect consul, and to achieve this position twice more (in 70, and two years later in 72) as a reward for throwing the support of his four legions in Syria behind the candidacy of Vespasian in 69.[23] He had been governor there since 66.[24] Consular honours were accompanied by triumphal honours granted in the immediate aftermath of the Flavian victory by a somewhat mistrustful Senate.[25] Such honours and his prominence in the early Flavian period has led Syme to go so far as to describe him as Vespasian's 'chief minister', though he probably presented as many problems to Vespasian as earlier Grand Viziers such as Burrus, Sejanus, and Tigellinus had to Tiberius.[26] Here was a man who knew where the bodies were buried.

Also, like Cicero, Caesar, and Sallust before him, he combined a public career with literary interests. In part these were antiquarian—he edited various volumes of *Acts* and *Letters*, including the great figures of Roman Republican history such as Pompey and Crassus—as a passage in Tacitus' *Dialogus* attests, though the evidence is too slim to place a political construction upon such historiography.[27] Certainly praise of Republican heroes such as Brutus and Cassius as a veiled attack upon the emperor could, as Cremutius Cordus discovered to his cost, lead to condemnation.[28] And Pompey too might stand in as an opposition

---

political refugees from Rome in earlier days'. It was the place Tiberius left Rome for. See Jones (1978*b*), 26–35 on the condition of Rhodes in the 1st cent. CE.

[22] See *PIR*² 5.1.50–1.

[23] See Nicols (1978), 71–3, 113–18 on the understanding between the two men.

[24] Syme (1958), 264.

[25] Tac. *Hist.* 4.4.

[26] Syme (1958), 212.

[27] Tacitus, *Dialogus* 37.

[28] For Cremutius Cordus see Tac. *Hist.* 3.4.5. On the use of literature as a form of opposition see the comments of Raaflaub (1986) at 17, 'indirekter Kritik durch historische und literarischen Auspielungen'. See also MacMullen (1975) for the ways in which Republican heroes might act as symbols for contemporary opposition under the Caesars.

figure during the early principate.[29] But without any remains of these works it is impossible to determine whether Mucianus praised or condemned Pompey and Crassus.

REDEEMING THE FRAGMENTS:
THE NATURE OF MUCIANUS' TEXT

All that has come down to us under Mucianus' name are a number of citations in the *Natural History* of the Elder Pliny. Translations of these are presented at the end of this chapter in an Appendix. In the form that Pliny presents them many appear from a work on *mirabilia*. Some are natural prodigies, creatures or natural phenomena that exceed what Remus has termed the 'canon of the ordinary'.[30] For instance, he reports a *mullus* fish captured in the Red Sea that weighed 80 pounds, or a plane tree growing in Lycia that was so large that Licinius was able to host a dinner party for 22 inside it.[31] As for natural phenomena another citation describes a 'flesh-eating' rock which is found both at Assos in the Troad, and also in Lycia: within 40 days any body placed there is consumed apart from its teeth, and personal items such as mirrors or clothes become stone. The few modern scholars who have studied these fragmentary citations have assumed that they come originally from a collection of *mirabilia* and belong to a genre known as 'paradoxography'.[32] For instance the latest edition of the *Oxford Classical Dictionary* states that 'he wrote a book of geographical mirabilia ("wonders") much used by Pliny the Elder'.[33] Syme came to a similar conclusion, and so does Baldwin.[34] In a recent article on paradoxography, Schepen and

---

[29] Consider Pompey's portrayal in Lucan's *Pharsalia*. Leigh (1997) argues that the figure of Pompey is presented in places as an epic hero, but problematizes this picture by suggesting that he cannot be seen as a fully sympathetic Republican hero. Nevertheless, 'a Republican voice is there to be found' (157). Masters (1992), 87 argues a similar case for the complexity of Lucan's supposed pro-Pompeian stance.

[30] Remus (1983).

[31] Frs. 16 (= Pliny *NH* 9.68) and 21 (= Pliny *NH* 12.9).

[32] On Mucianus' literary work there is little: Traiana (1987), and a short recent article Baldwin (1995) which accepts the orthodox view of Mucianus.

[33] *OCD*[3] s.v. Licinius Mucianus.

[34] On this aspect of Mucianus see Syme (1969), 203–4, 'Mucianus was eager for *curiosa* and *mirabilia* about men and animals, buildings and works of art.' Baldwin (1995), 292, 'he also wrote a book or books in which there was much about the natural and unnatural curiosities he had himself seen.'

Delcroix place Mucianus unproblematically within the genre.[35] Likewise, Bardon thinks Mucianus to have been interested in miracles,
although he briefly raises an alternative possibility—close to that
which will be argued in this chapter—before dropping it, that Mucianus
was writing a 'Journal des voyages'.[36]

Natural marvels and bizarre phenomena were a staple of Greek
writers at least as early as Herodotus, but the development of a formal
genre of paradoxography, concentrating on pseudo-scientific collections
of marvels to the exclusion of other material, was a Hellenistic phenomenon.[37] The pseudo-Aristotelian 'On Marvellous Things Heard', provides a good introduction to the genre. It is arranged as a series of
discrete anecdotes arranged thematically. For instance, the statement
'Men say that among the Chalybians, in an islet situated beyond them,
gold is collected by mice in large numbers' is followed by the observation that 'On the island of Gyaros it is said that mice eat iron'.[38] In
contrast to Greek ethnographic or geographical writing there is no claim
here to autopsy. The oldest genuine work appears to be that of Calli-
machos whom the Suda attests as an author of a 'Collection of marvels
which relate to every land'.[39] The use of the term 'collection (*synagōgē*)'
to describe this work makes it clear that it is a derivative collection
of material, not a first person investigation.[40] Writers include Agath-
archides of Cnidos, Antigonus of Carystus, Myrsilus of Methymna,[41]
and from the Roman period, Isigonus of Nicaea and Phlegon of

---

[35] Schepen and Delcroix (1996), 430, 'The fragments we have deal with *paradoxa* of
geographical and zoological character, on human activities etc., and seem to have belonged
to a real paradoxographical collection, rather than to a *Chorographia* or a *Periegesis*'.

[36] Bardon (1952), 179–81.

[37] On paradoxographers the 1839 collection of Westermann et al. (1963) is still
useful. There is a more recent collection edited by Giannini (1966), and work is currently
underway to fulfil Jacoby's plans for a fascicle of *FGrH* (4E) which will include
paradoxographical work. There is almost nothing in standard histories of Greek literature on paradoxography, for instance, just passing comments in Lesky et al. (1966), and
no standard monograph in English. Schepen and Delcroix (1996), however, provide a
recent and very useful introduction with an extensive bibliography, and rightly state that
'this is a branch of literature that has hardly been able to attract the attention of more
than a few scholars over the past century' (375). Articles and editions, however, exist for
several of the most important authors.

[38] [Aristotle] *On Marvellous Things Heard* 24–5.

[39] Westermann et al. (1963), x.

[40] Schepen and Delcroix (1996), 389.

[41] See Jackson (1995).

Tralles.[42] Of course, paradoxographical 'digressions' are also to be found in other genres, as Helen Morales has shown for the Greek novel.[43]

As a genre it focuses on strange, or indeed miraculous, natural happenings: odd creatures, weird behaviour, bizarre natural phenomena. Examples are taken from all over the known world, and tend to be in the form of short anecdotes that confound the reader's expectations. In his article on the oldest preserved of these treatises, that of Antigonus of Carystus, Jacob insists that the educative value and aesthetic pleasure of reading such treatises go hand in hand.[44] He stresses that these are serious works of compilation which borrow anecdotes from a range of earlier writers, in the case of Antigonus from sixteen named writers. An educative function is perhaps true for an early writer like Antigonus, in whose text Jacob traces a close relationship to Aristotle's *Historia Animalium*, but this is less likely for later writers like Phlegon who developed the sensational aspects of the genre. Indeed it is this aspect, the shading of paradoxical stories into pure fictions that lies at the heart of Lucian's satirical attack in his *True History*.

The orthodox interpretation of Mucianus as a paradoxographer can be challenged in two ways. First, it fails to take satisfactory account of all the relevant citations. At least a third are hard to class as examples of *mirabilia*. These include several references to distances (fr. 4, circumference of Syros; fr. 5 circumference of the Black Sea), as well as fr. 3, the observation that Delos has twice suffered earthquakes, and fr. 7, on the source of the Euphrates. Then there are descriptions of the 3,000 statues to be found on the island of Rhodes (fr. 30), the materials that were used in the construction of the temple of Artemis at Ephesos (fr. 24), the strength of the local wine in Thrace (fr. 23), the qualities of oysters from various localities (fr. 29), the workmanship of Amasis' corselet dedicated in the temple of Athena at Lindos (fr. 25), and details about the propagation of saffron (fr. 26). Many of the anecdotes really relate to religious contexts, and it appears that Mucianus had a great interest in the religious topography of Old Greece. His comments on the epiphany of Dionysos at the god's temple on the island of Andros (frs. 1 and 27),

---

[42] Hansen (1996) for commentary and English translation.
[43] Morales (1995) emphasizing the use of animals as exotica in Achilles Tatius' *Leukippe and Klitophon*.
[44] Jacob (1983).

used by Pliny to illustrate a miracle, might equally be regarded as part of an extended description of the rites and architecture of the sanctuaries he visited. Certainly in the case of the Temple of Artemis at Ephesos he is particularly interested in the wooden cult statue of the goddess (fr. 24).

Second, the geographical spread of his work differs from many paradoxographers. Whereas Carey has recently suggested that '*mirabilia* are particularly associated with places on the edge of empire',[45] Mucianus describes the heart of the old Greek world, the cities of the Roman province of Asia, the neighbouring islands, Lycia, and Egypt. Moreover, they are generally not perversions of nature, but exaggerated reports of fairly ordinary phenomena (an over-sized mullet-fish (fr.16), a vast plane-tree (fr. 12), and the sarcophagus stone (fr. 21)). In addition, his *mirabilia* are set *within* the society to which Mucianus belongs rather than *outside* it. This is contrary to the usual pattern, found in Philostratos' *Life of Apollonios of Tyana*, or Ktesias' *Indika*, or indeed Lucian's parodic *True History*, where places like India, Ethiopia, China, and Scythia become the setting for marvels because they stand outside the settled rule of Rome and the civilizing effects of its *humanitas*. It is therefore difficult to see Mucianus as part of the long tradition of geographical and ethnographic works in both Greek and Latin.[46]

Our problems in understanding the nature of Mucianus' text result from failing to take sufficient account of the ways in which Pliny has subtly refashioned information and anecdotes taken from Mucianus in order to suit his own rhetorical purposes.[47] This is common in paradoxographical works where sensational details are stripped from their original contexts and denuded of any rational explanations.[48] Pliny can be classed amongst the paradoxographers, so long as we remember that this is to excerpt a single feature from his much larger project in a work which attempts to produce an inventory of the known Roman world,

---

[45] Carey (2000), 5.

[46] There is a growing bibliography on such works, most recently see Romm (1992) on ethnographic writings and Clarke (1999) on geographical material. The topic of travel within the Roman empire is now a popular one, for instance the recent collection of essays in Adams and Laurence (2001).

[47] Baldwin (1995) makes no mention of it, despite his interest in Pliny's relationship to Mucianus.

[48] Schepen and Delcroix (1996), 394 on 'rewriting' of original sources by paradoxographers.

collecting its natural and man-made elements in a single text.[49] Nevertheless, a striking part of this was an interest in the natural world and it is here that the strongest links are with works dealing with the marvellous, since Pliny seems to have been fascinated with tales of natural prodigies, even if he is sometimes sceptical.[50] Discussion of several fragments will indicate the problems involved.

The anecdote with which this chapter opened, the letter of Sarpedon, is used by Pliny as an attack upon a bogus *mirabile*, arguing that paper was not yet available to the heroes of the *Iliad* and that they had to make do with wooden writing tablets.[51] Mucianus, by contrast, seems originally to have reported this incident without such scepticism. We are therefore approaching Mucianus through a very particular kind of filter, in which the narrative unity of the original work is broken up, and excerpts are chosen simply for their peculiarity. Can we uncover any of the original organizational principles of his work? Fragments hint at a connection between his official career and his writings. For instance, his comments on the source of the Euphrates in Armenia (fr. 7) surely relate to his serving there early in his career as a legionary legate under Domitius Corbulo. Likewise, the information regarding his dinner party in the enormous plane tree is explicitly linked to his governorship in Lycia (fr. 21).

Mucianus' work appears to have had frequent reference to geographical information, distances and the like.[52] This is hardly a typical paradoxographical feature, but is entirely consistent with another genre, that of the memoir or *commentaries*. Take, for instance, the best known of this genre, Julius Caesar's *Gallic Wars*, which often introduces such geographical data into its narrative.[53] It is also a feature shared with geographical writers such as Strabo, but unlike them this appears to be a first-person narrative.

[49] Schepen and Delcroix (1996), 410 on Pliny as paradoxographer.
[50] e.g. his continual scepticism about the phoenix, see *NH* 7.153, 10.3–5, although at 11.121 he seems to accept its existence.
[51] Pliny *NH* 13.88.
[52] e.g. fr. 4 (circumference of Syros), fr. 5 (circumference of the Black Sea), fr. 6 (circumference of Lake Moeris), and fr. 9 (distance between Rhodes and Alexandria).
[53] e.g. at *BG* 1.2 (description of the territory of the Helvetii, 'which was 240 miles long, and 180 miles wide').

Table 1. The Geography of Mucianus' Fragments found in Pliny

Region	Fragment nos. (Peter)
Achaea	10
Armenia	7
Asia Provincia	5, 10, 15, 17, 18, 20, 24, 25, 28, 29, 30, 31
Cycladic Islands	1, 3, 4, 27
Egypt	6, 16 (if Red Sea)
Hispania	29
Italy	2, 12
Lycia	19, 21, 22, 26, 32
Lydia	11
Rhodes	9[54]
Syria	8
Thrace	23
Unknown	13, 14

Table 1 immediately makes clear that his work did not comprise a geographical description of the whole known world, which rules out the possibility that it is a geographical treatise. Nothing here can be definitely placed west of Italy, except perhaps for the comparison involving Spanish oysters; to the praise of those from Cyzicus he states that they are fuller than those of Ilici in Spain (fr. 29). If we can take this as evidence that Mucianus had actually visited Spain—indeed Syme felt it possible that he might in fact have been of Spanish origin, in which case Ilici will be a reasonable candidate for his birthplace—this is his only reference in these fragments to the western half of the empire.[55] Aside from two further fragments which refer to the wonders of Italy, the first discussing the urbanization of the Pomptine Marsh (fr. 2), the second treating the arrival of several elephants at Puteoli (fr. 12), the rest relate in the main to the Greek East, especially Asia Minor, and a few perhaps to neighbouring regions such as Phoenicia and Egypt. Given that we have already seen that these fragments represent parts of a first-person

---

[54] Rhodes had been annexed by Rome in 44 CE, but recovered its liberty in 53 after an eloquent speech before Claudius by the young Nero, see Tac. *Ann.* 12.58. Cf. *IGRR* 4. 1123, a Rhodian decree honouring the ambassadors who had helped to obtain this grant.

[55] See Syme (1958), 598.

autopsy, their geography will therefore bear some resemblance to Mucianus' own travels.

Most of the fragments come from three neighbouring regions: the first (and largest) group relates to the cities and islands within the Roman province of Asia (that is, not just within Asia Minor, but in that part constituting the province created out of the bequest of the Attalid kings). These fragments presuppose a wide range of travels within the province, from the Propontis and Troad (as far as Byzantium) through the major cities of the province, Ephesos, Smyrna, Iasos, Cyzicus, and to some of the offshore islands such as Samos and Knidos. In none of them is any official position stated (unlike his sojourn in Lycia where Pliny describes him as, 'legatus provinciae' (fr. 21), 'cum praesideret' (fr. 22)), and we have no evidence that Licinius ever held an official position in Asia. It is unlikely that Mucianus would have had time when governor of Lycia and Pamphylia to visit the sights of Asia, and so we must find another period when Mucianus could have had sufficient time in Asia to make such extensive journeys. Fortunately, a neat solution is to link this with Tacitus' statement that Mucianus went into virtual exile ('in secretum Asiae sepositus') during the reign of Claudius.[56] Syme thinks this section of the work formed a digression, although it is not clear how he envisaged the structure of the whole.[57]

The geographical range of Mucianus' travels enables us to suggest that it was indeed the province of Asia, rather than the island of Rhodes, that formed the landscape of his exile. In many ways this anticipated the cosmopolitan awareness of the historical landmarks of the Greek East by which many writers of the Second Sophistic paraded their Greek identity.[58] It also gives us a glimpse of how a young Roman aristocrat might have spent his time whilst in exile in the eastern part of the empire holding no official position. For the most part he seems to have followed an established tourist trail, so for example his visit to one of the Seven Wonders of the Ancient World, the temple of Artemis at Ephesos, where his interest seems partly in the materials used to construct the roof and the cult statue.[59] The anecdote only survives because of Pliny's

---

[56] Tac. *Hist.* 1.10.5.

[57] Syme (1969), 204 thinks that 'these features impel to a digression'.

[58] Elsner (1992) treats the issue of self-definition, in this case as a Hellene, through the work of Pausanias.

[59] Fr. 24.

interest in types of timber, and its original shape is distorted because of Pliny's 'framing' narrative. Originally it may have comprised not only a description of the construction of the temple but also its treasures and the cult practised there. Pliny's heading, 'It is believed that ebony lasts an extremely long time, and also cypress and cedar' introduces his topic (the longevity of certain types of timber), and this therefore accounts for the shape into which Mucianus' anecdote is fitted.

In any case, aside from the famous temple of Artemis, Mucianus paid attention to various other sanctuaries, included the equally famous temple of Aphrodite at Knidos, best known for its nude cult statue created by Praxiteles.[60] These were two of the most important tourist attractions during the imperial period. Other sites he saw in Asia are not quite in the first rank, and reflect either quirky interests, or Pliny's bias in the way he has excerpted the text. These include a boy who had previously been a girl at Smyrna;[61] dolphins off the coast near Iasos;[62] a spring with magical properties near Cyzicus;[63] the quality of the oysters also at Cyzicus;[64] and a sarcophagus stone found at Assos in the Troad.[65]

The second largest geographical distribution of fragments comes from Lycia (five examples); in this case we are told explicitly that these relate to Mucianus' tenure of the province as governor, perhaps in 57 CE. His anecdote about the *anthias* fish, common off the coast of Lycia, is less a tourist tale than a legal case relating to a dispute between two partners in a fishery business, which had presumably come to Mucianus' attention in his official capacity as governor.[66] The use of the phrase 'when he was in charge' (*cum praesideret*) and the appearance of anecdotes relating to his official career might suggest some sort of memoir. Mucianus' original text is likely not merely to have recounted the anecdote, but also to have explained his role in it or his status as observer. Likewise, his story of the unfeasibly large plane tree is connected with the discharge of his official duties, since we are told that Mucianus used this spot to 'hold a banquet with eighteen members of his retinue inside the tree'.[67] Interest in the religious topography of the Greek East may also have been part of his gubernatorial duties. He visited a sanctuary where Sarpedon's letter was displayed,[68] as well as the temples of Artemis at Ephesos, Aphrodite at Cnidos, Dionysus on the

[60] Fr. 17.   [61] Fr. 10.   [62] Fr. 15.   [63] Fr. 28.   [64] Fr. 29.
[65] Fr. 31.   [66] Fr. 19.   [67] Fr. 21.   [68] Fr. 22.

island of Andros,[69] and the famous temple of Athena at Lindos on Rhodes.[70]

The third most important area of interest seems to be the Cyclades: Mucianus made visits to Andros, Delos, and mentions Syros. When and why did he visit these? Pliny does not describe the visit to Delos: he merely uses Mucianus as an authority that Delos had in fact suffered earthquakes, *contra* the view of Varro. Even so, given that the fragment relating to Andros appears close in Pliny's text, and the fact that Pliny describes this island as 'celebrated for its temple of Apollo', and also the clear interest Mucianus had in temple-visiting, it is not far-fetched to see the trip as also motivated in part by a desire to visit a famous sanctuary. When, however, did Mucianus visit these islands? Once more, like Asia Provincia, there is no evidence that he ever held any official position there. However, the positioning of fragments in Pliny's work may give some clues. Although the texts have been excerpted from Mucianus' original text, and therefore should not necessarily be expected to remain in their original order, there is a strong possibility that Pliny's methods were not as random as this: fragments from geographically proximate regions tend to be bunched suspiciously together, so that he uses Mucianus as a source for the Cyclades twice in succession (frs. 3, 4), and indeed all his fragments relating to the Cyclades appear early (frs. 1, 3, 4); likewise the Lycian material, although distributed in a section of the *Natural History* that is ostensibly thematic rather than organized on a geographical principle, nevertheless is also surprisingly bunched together (frs. 19, 21, 22).

If there is anything in these observations, it suggests that much of the Asia material occurs *between* these two points and may be arranged on some kind of chronological scheme. Mucianus' exile will have come first, with perhaps the Cyclades as a stop-off point en route to Asia. Next Asia, and later the material relating to his term in Lycia. A memoir of some kind where Mucianus describes his career in imperial service does seem a plausible place for him to make reference to his service under Domitius Corbulo as legionary legate in Armenia (fr. 7).[71] It similarly accounts for his brief reference to Arados, an island city which lay within the province of Syria of which Mucianus was governor after 66/7 CE. He describes only that at Arados fresh water is brought up from a source under the sea, a phenomenon which also attracted the attention of Strabo.[72] This falls outside the chronological scheme just outlined because Pliny quotes Domitius Corbulo first, and only later Mucianus.

Mucianus' interest in Arados may, however, have been more than its water supply. Referred to as an important maritime and commercial city in the Old Testament, Arados by the Roman imperial period had declined from its wealthy heyday when it controlled a *peraia*, or mainland territory, encompassing a number of cities on the coastline opposite,[73] and was, until the provincial reforms of Septimius Severus, a part of the province of Syria.[74] Mucianus may have visited it during his tenure as governor, especially since its greatest attraction fits in with what we know of his interests more generally, an ancient sanctuary of Aphrodite, mentioned in Chariton's novel, *Chaereas and Callirhoe*:

Arados is an island three or four miles from the mainland. It contains an old shrine of Aphrodite; the women lived there as in a house, feeling completely secure.[75]

Even for a Christian like Clement of Alexandria, Arados might serve as a suitable tourist attraction. In one of his *Homilies* he describes how some of his party stopped off at the island in order to see two enormous wooden pillars, and also various works by the fifth-century BCE Greek artist Pheidias.[76] Mucianus seems once again to have taken advantage of his position as governor in order to visit a celebrated city within his province; one that Rey-Coquais has described as a 'ville-musée', though

---

[72] Strabo 16.2.13 gives a detailed description of the mechanism by which water was collected from the underwater spring. He describes how the Aradians let down a leather tube to which a lead funnel had been attached at one end. The fresh water was pumped up through this funnel, into the pipe, and then collected in various containers and brought back to the city.

[73] Rey-Coquais (1974), esp. 164–9 on its vicissitudes under the Roman Empire. Strabo 16.2.12, 14 mentions the *peraia*, much of which was given in gratitude for help given by the Aradians to Seleukos Kallinikos. See also Millar (1993), 270–2 on the evidence for local cults at Arados, and suggestions of Phoenician survivals.

[74] On these reforms see Millar (1993), 121–2, emphasizing the changes in the 190s CE and the creation out of the original province of Syria of two separate provinces of Syria Coele and Syria Phoenicie. Also, 127–41 on the frontier under Severus. Its earlier status as part of the province of Syria is best attested in the find of a statue base honouring the governor of that province in 102–4 CE, Julius Quadratus (*IGLS* 7.4010).

[75] 7.5.

[76] 12.12.1.

Pliny has typically chosen to focus on Mucianus only as a source for its water supply.[77]

Two fragments, dealing with Egypt, do not immediately fit this model of a memoir. One (fr. 9) reports the distance between Rhodes and Alexandria, yet we have no indication of his holding any official position in Egypt—as a senator he cannot have held the equestrian governorship of the province—and under the regulations governing it since Augustus he would have had to seek special imperial dispensation to pay a visit.[78] Of course, it does not rule out the possibility of a visit with imperial permission—perhaps during his time as governor of neighbouring Syria, but the fact that Pliny does not quote any *mirabilia* from this section might indicate that he did not indulge in his usual tourist habits of visiting local sanctuaries and other curios, or that Pliny for some reason has chosen not to use this part of his work as a source. Another explanation might therefore be more plausible. If part of the purpose of this work was to recount Mucianus' career, then surely (as we have seen) an important part of this will have focused on the events of 69 CE. From ancient sources we can reconstruct the route that Mucianus took back to Rome in 69 when fighting in support of Vespasian. He set out through Asia Minor, via Byzantium, Thrace and into Moesia.[79] It is possible that Mucianus presented a parallel narrative giving some indication of what Vespasian (whom he supported as his candidate for the throne) was up to. At this time, he was holed up in Alexandria for the winter of 69–70 CE where he stayed until August 70.[80] Shipping during the winter months was almost impossible during antiquity.[81] After this he seems to have returned to Rome via the island of Rhodes, as Josephus reports:

Now at the time when Titus Caesar was assiduously besieging Jerusalem, Vespasian, embarking on a merchant vessel, crossed from Alexandria to Rhodes.[82]

---

[77] Rey-Coquais (1974) 259.

[78] On Augustus' dispensations regarding Egypt see Lewis (1983), 16. On the need for senators to seek imperial permission to visit Egypt see Tac. *Ann.* 2.59. Also, note the discussion of various types of official pass required for visiting Egypt in Sidebotham (1986), 79–81.

[79] See Syme (1977).

[80] See Halfmann (1986), 178–80, esp. 178. On Vespasian's sojourn in Alexandria see Henrichs (1968).

[81] See Pryor (1988), ch. 3; Horden and Purcell (2000).

[82] Josephus 7.2.1, Dio 66.12.

A plausible context for the reference to the distance between Alexandria and Rhodes is therefore to the voyage made by Vespasian in 70. A second passage relating to Egypt makes mention of Lake Moeris and might come in the context of Mucianus' describing the wonders of Egypt, a land he had never himself seen; it had certainly formed a centrepiece in Herodotus' description of the marvels of Egypt. Moreover, the Fayūm, containing what remained of Lake Moeris, continued as a tourist destination during the imperial period.[83] His description draws heavily on a written source such as Herodotus.

Other fragments fit neatly into place within the scheme of a memoir. Pliny quotes Mucianus' observations about Thracian wine, and whilst a journey through Thrace during his exile in Asia is possible, we have definite evidence of his travelling through the region in 69 with his Syrian legions en route to Italy after passing through Asia Minor.[84] His reference to the long-lived Tempsis at Mt. Tmolus (fr. 11) presumably refers to a visit to Lydia, a region neighbouring the province of Asia and thus most likely undertaken during his sojourn there. Finally, even his story about the clever alphabetic elephants he encountered at Puteoli (fr. 12) can be explained within this structure. It makes an appearance as the port Titus sailed to in 71 on his route back from Alexandria, being a terminus on a regular route between Italy and Egypt.[85] During the early imperial period it served as one of the main ports for commerce between Rome and the eastern Mediterranean, facilitated by the existence of the *Via Appia*. In particular, it had close trading connections with the island of Delos and with Alexandria, for it was to Puteoli that the Egyptian grain fleet sailed.[86] Such North African connections are perhaps hinted at in Mucianus' comment about seeing elephants unloaded there. It would, however, be to build hypothesis upon hypothesis to suppose that

[83] See Foertmeyer (1989) 17 for the 'paltry remains' of tourist graffiti; later she refers to the rather more extensive literary and papyrological evidence for visiting the Fayūm, for instance at 19 she discusses Germanicus' visit in 19 CE during his extensive tour of Egypt.

[84] Tac. *Hist.* 2.83. See Syme (1977).

[85] See Suet. *Tit.* 5.3. See Frederiksen and Purcell (1984) 180. On the Puteoli–Alexandria route compare Pliny *NH* 19.3 for a record-breaking journey of 9 days.

[86] See Frederiksen (1959), 2046. D'Arms (1974) argues against older views of an economic decline at Puteoli after the development of Ostia under Trajan. *CIL* 10.1613.1797 records a dedication made in the temple of Augustus by the 'mercatores qui in Alexandr. Asiai Syriai negotiantur', demonstrating the ethnically mixed character of the port.

Mucianus was recording an encounter between himself and Titus at Puteoli. Purcell's view that it was a 'packet port', serving embassies and officials making the journey between Italy and the East, makes better sense of Mucianus' presence there.[87] The anecdote might then belong to any of several official journeys that he made East during his career.

Overall the work shows strong signs of having been a memoir dealing with an official life, written during Mucianus' retirement in the early 70s CE.[88] This contrasts with the standard view of it as a work of paradoxography, since its geographical scope belongs within the known world, not outside. It only mentions places with which Mucianus is known to have had official dealings, and in several cases alludes to events which happened during his tenure as governor. Scholars have overstated its taste for the bizarre, and in fact it is visits to sanctuaries that make up the largest grouping of fragments. Pliny's role in its miscategorization cannot be underestimated, for to a Flavian propagandist like him a figure like Mucianus to whom the Flavians owed so much, and could offer so little, was a real difficulty.[89]

---

[87] See Nicholas Purcell's chapter on Campania in Frederiksen and Purcell (1984), 319–49.

[88] Given that Mucianus had used his tenure as imperial governor in order to gather information for this work, the total absence of any material referring to his tenure in Syria after 66/7 CE might be taken as a sure indication that the work had already been completed by that point. This would give a date before 66, but the continual use by Pliny of the phrase to describe Mucianus of 'who had recently been governor of Lycia', somewhat inappropriate if this is Pliny writing in the 70s CE, some fifteen to twenty years after the events had taken place, may in fact be taken over from the original language of Mucianus. In which case, a date in the years 58–60 might very well be appropriate. However, the appearance of material from the Propontis and the movement through Thrace (see Levick (1999), 48–9) undoubtedly dates to the events of 69, and strongly points to a final date of composition after 69. See Levick (1999), 48–9.

[89] If Pliny has deliberately excluded certain elements of the original work, why? Was he was only interested in strange natural phenomena, or is the absence of a framing narrative for these anecdotes proof of a bias against Mucianus? Why, for example, does he *not* tell us what Mucianus was doing in Thrace, when he seems perfectly happy to explain what he was doing in Lycia? For this we need to understand the historical context within which Pliny was writing—consideration of the preface to the *Natural History* (1.1) should leave us in little doubt of its ostensible purpose as a work of Flavian propaganda, intended to highlight the achievements of the dynasty. It was all very well for Tacitus, writing from a retrospective vantage, to suggest that Mucianus was close to seizing *imperium* for himself, and to make clear the enormous debt that Vespasian owed to Mucianus in the winning of the empire, but this is a debt that the Flavians could only repay in indirect gestures such as the repeated consulships Mucianus held, and could not be revealed directly in the coin of military glory. Pliny's exclusion of Mucianus' military

TOURIST OR PILGRIM?

By now it ought to be clear that the landscape of the Greek world was, as far as Mucianus was concerned, above all a religious topography. For it is sanctuaries—at Andros, Ephesos, Lindos, Knidos, and probably in Lycia and at Arados—which form the subject of the single largest group of citations in his name. What were the attitudes and expectations he brought to his travels? Was he a naive Roman visitor? Modern tourism obscures the sacred geography of these sanctuaries by opening them up to tourist traffic and ignoring the original sacred ways linking city and sanctuary. Such options were not open to Mucianus. His visit, for example, to the sanctuary of Aphrodite at Knidos (fr. 17), or Athena on Lindos (frs. 1 and 27) would have been along the usual sacred way linking city to sanctuary. His visit may not have been during one of the major festivals of the year when the whole city processed out to the sanctuary, although his comments on the miracle of transubstantiation seen at the sanctuary of Dionysus on the island of Andros every January 5th might refer to his having been a participant in some festival like the Athenian Lenaea. Nevertheless the route taken by him was precisely that taken by the regular procession. Mucianus was both making and re-making the same pilgrimage. Even 'tourism', then, might cover the same geography as proper pilgrimage. One might object that the difference lies in the attitude of mind towards the sanctuary, its history, ritual, and the miracles claimed by it. Was merely an aesthetic or historical appreciation embodied in Mucianus' behaviour? What sort of attitude did he display towards these sanctuaries?

Mucianus was respectful and credulous, showing an interest in the objects (dedications) on display in sanctuaries, which acted both as a repository of physical objects, but also became a focus of stories and memories that encapsulated the identity of the community. He apparently sought out the priests and asked for their interpretation of what was on show, without any show of disbelief. Moreover the anecdotes reported of the temple of Dionysus on Andros (frs. 1 and 27, the

exploits is therefore a move, calculated not to detract from the military glory of the ruling house—the critical role played by Mucianus in 69 might be acknowledged privately, but was at least problematic for the propagandists of the regime.

miraculous transformation of water into wine) are used by Pliny to create an encyclopaedia of bizarre natural phenomena. Reinserted into their original socio-religious setting they must surely belong to the cultic calendar and sacred myths attached to the sanctuary itself. They are comparable to the miracles associated with Dionysus' epiphany elsewhere in literature, most obviously in Euripides' *Bacchae*. The date of the marvel—early January—almost precisely matches that of the Athenian Lenaea and of the winter solstice, and suggests a nexus of connections made between the rebirth of the year and the rebirth of the god. Turning water into wine represents the literal epiphany of the god.[90] Pliny's statement that 'Mucianus believes' (*credit*), if we accept that he accurately represents the sense of Mucianus' original text, is crucial for our understanding of the nature of Graeco-Roman pilgrimage and views of *mirabilia*, suggesting as it does that Christianizing distinctions between pilgrims (those visiting with a religious purpose in mind) and other forms of tourism may be misplaced. Mucianus' visit to the temple presumably led to his being told the miracle of water turned into wine, which he approached without incredulity. Whatever his original motives for visiting the temple, unlike Pliny his is not the voice of scepticism.

We also know Mucianus to have visited the sanctuary of Aphrodite at Knidos, best known to us as the home of Praxiteles' famous cult statue of the goddess, though in this case also important for an earlier incident.[91] Mucianus recounts a story given by the priests there as an aetiology for a series of murex shells which had been dedicated. These fish, he says, had by their actions prevented a group of noble youths from being castrated by the tyrant Periander of Corinth.[92] Another version of this incident is told in Herodotus; that the Samians had rescued these youths after they had sought sanctuary there by a subterfuge which involved bringing them ritual cakes to eat. Presumably Mucianus' story is a later tradition, perhaps invented or at least transmitted by the priests in order to account for a particularly unusual

---

[90] Kerényi and Manheim (1976), 299. Otto (1965), 98 gives parallels such as the Thyia festival at Elis where empty basins were locked away and miraculously filled with wine, and wine pouring from a spring on Naxos.

[91] On the Aphrodite of Praxiteles as a destination for sightseers see Ps(?)-Lucian's *Amores* 11.

[92] Pliny *NH* 9.79 = Peter, fr. 17.

dedication. The story emphasizes his interest not only in the votives on display, but also the sacred narratives which explained the function and origin of such objects. Mucianus seems to have accepted that many of these were evidence of divine epiphany; and *mirabilia* may be discussed not—as in paradoxography—to express a sense of the weird, but rather to accept the efficacy of the divine.

HERODOTUS' EYES

The work as a whole appears to have had a degree of literary sophistication. There is an emphasis on autopsy, a Herodotean trope, but one also found in a whole series of other travel literature, later also to be the mode employed by Pausanias.[93] In their current form the anecdotes attributed to him cannot be taken as accurate evidence for his original phrasing; at the very least they have been placed in indirect speech, and we may suspect that Pliny has changed the language altogether. Even so Pliny often makes it clear that Mucianus based his authority upon autopsy, generally stating that something had been 'seen by him' (*visum a se* or *visam sibi*). For example, under the heading 'it is no tall story that women turn into men', Pliny quotes Mucianus as saying that 'Arescontes *had been seen by him* at Argos, whose name used to be Arescusa'.[94] The ethnographic trope of first person autopsy is elsewhere used to give authority to his statement that he had seen (*visam sibi*) a certain type of goat.

In this Mucianus differs from later writers like Phlegon of Tralles or the *mirabilia* found in Aelian's *Varia Historia*, for his statements are given the imprimatur of personal autopsy—they are not collections of other people's accounts, the second-hand versions employed in Pliny's text, where he is not so much the collector of the world as its cataloguer. Mucianus' travels are perhaps better seen as an early precursor of the sorts of travel undertaken or described by later writers of the Second Sophistic such as Pausanias, Lucian, or Aelius Aristides, for like them he was no naive tourist.[95] His travels are informed with

---

[93] On the importance of autopsy as a mode in Herodotus see Marincola (1997).
[94] Fr. 10.
[95] Rutherford (2001*a*), 49–50 argues that 'In the Second Sophistic, pilgrimage assumed a high profile'. His evidence is both literary and epigraphic.

knowledge of the Greek past, both literary and actual, and his eyes were often those of Herodotus himself, as three instances demonstrate.[96] His description of Lake Moeris is set in the past tense, 'There was once a lake', and he makes no claim of autopsy. Whilst the context may well be Vespasian's visit to Egypt, the observation surely draws on Herodotus' self-proclaimed—and often disbelieved—autopsy in book 2 of his *Histories* of the artificial complex including the so-called Labyrinth of which Lake Moeris was only a part.[97] Mucianus seems to have followed Herodotus reasonably closely here—his figure for the circumference of Lake Moeris, 420 miles, is close to Herodotus' 450 miles, and either figure may have suffered the vagaries of the manuscript tradition.

Moreover, two stories to which Mucianus alludes—that of the mistreatment of several noble youths at the hands of Periander (fr. 17), and the breastplate dedicated by the Egyptian king Amasis (fr. 25) are told in different versions in Herodotus. Indeed both narratives follow each other in Herodotus, and it is surely more than coincidence that both also appear in Mucianus. Finally, two fragments (14 and 15), which give no indication of their geographical provenance, have a strong Herodotean flavour, though nothing exactly parallels them in his text. They allude to the cleverness of animals: first, goats who devise a stratagem for crossing a narrow bridge: second, monkeys capable of distinguishing false nuts from real ones, as well as possessing a precocious religious sense.[98] The latter anecdote might suggest a more exotic location than

---

[96] For the influence of Herodotus on Second Sophistic literature see Elsner (2001*b*), 127–8, and n. 24 giving bibliography for specific influence on his work 'On the Syrian Goddess'. Herodotus was a source both of inspiration to writers of the period and the subject of intellectual attack for his supposed lack of credibility.

[97] Armayor (1985) who argues at 3 that 'Lake Moeris is out of the question in the real Egypt of history', and prefers to substitute a symbolic reading of it as a Pythagorean lake of the dead.

[98] Peter's collection of fragments quotes Mucianus as a source for the intelligence of monkeys. In fact the early part of this fragment derives originally from one of the fragmentary Alexander historians, Cleitarchus. A very similar description of monkeys escaping traps using bird lime is referred to both in Diodoros 17 (without naming the source), and also in Aelian *VH* 17.25 where a passage with comparable wording is attributed to Cleitarchos. Pliny names no source other than Mucianus, but this is only for the latter part of the information, and we should not assume (as Peter did) that Mucianus mentioned the earlier details.

those we have so far examined, but monkeys were in fact to be found in more familiar places. Not only were they important in Egypt as animals sacred to the god Thoth, they were also used as performers and kept as pets.[99] They were well known as mimics.[100] Moreover religiously curious monkeys can be compared to Aelian's superstitious suppliant elephants that gesture to the new moon.[101] Overall we might suggest that the taste for marvels displayed in Mucianus' work is as likely to be influenced by the Herodotean precedent as it is by the whole genre of paradoxography.

Considered together this suggests a strong Herodotean influence, in the tone of the work, its use of specific narrative devices such as claims to autopsy, its interest in *thaumata* and also in allusions to particular passages. Taken out of its paradoxographical frame and reconstituted as evidence of Mucianus' travels another anecdote draws out some of the associations sanctuaries had both to their local constituency and to visitors. Just as the letter of Sarpedon was displayed amongst the treasures of the sanctuary, so too during another visit, this time to the Temple of Athena at Lindos on the island of Rhodes, Mucianus became interested in another object with an (ancient) history. Sarpedon's letter had provided the sanctuary with a tangible link back to the heroic age; Lindos could if asked do just as well, but Mucianus' attention was drawn to a linen corselet which had belonged to the Egyptian pharaoh Amasis and had been dedicated by him to the goddess at some point during the sixth century BCE:

This may surprise people who do not know that in a breastplate that belonged to a former king of Egypt named Amasis, preserved in the temple of Minerva at Lindos on the island of Rhodes, each thread consisted of 365 separated threads, a fact which Mucianus who held the consulship three times quite lately, stated that he had proved true by investigation, adding that only small remnants of the breastplate now survive owing to the damage done by persons examining its quality.

---

[99] McDermott (1938), 3–14 on their presence in Egypt. Cleopatra is said to have kept one as a pet (Lucian, *Apol.* 5), and Cicero refers to the one kept in Rome by Publius Vedius (*Att.* 6.1.25).

[100] Ael. *NA* 5.26 states that the monkey is 'the most imitative (*mimelotaton*) creature'. At 6.10 he speaks of how the Egyptians taught baboons their alphabet, how to dance, and how to play various musical instruments.

[101] Ael. *NA* 4.10.

This is an object with both an oral and a written tradition. The corselet had already been mentioned in Herodotus' narrative, and so there was a version of its history which stood outside the priestly tradition. Mucianus' claim to authority is both a device to encourage confidence in his work, and also the reference to the constant wear and tear of those examining the celebrated thread-work provides valuable witness to the interests of those visiting such sanctuaries. Mucianus was only the latest—and most literary-minded—of a considerable body of visitors, pilgrims if you like, who had made an examination of the temple treasures at least one of the objectives of their trip. Why did such objects become so important a focus of attention? An elaborate temple inventory from this very sanctuary, discovered in 1904 by its Danish excavators, gives us clues. In its present form it is a Hellenistic text, dating probably from the second century BCE, and opens as follows:

Since the temple of Lindian Athena is the oldest and most glorious and has been adorned with many beautiful votives from the earliest times on account of the *epiphaneia* of the goddess, it happens that most of the votives along with the inscriptions have been destroyed by time.[102]

This preface details the decision taken by the authorities at Lindos to write up an inventory on stone pillars of the votives which had been dedicated at the temple, using as sources 'letters, public records (*chrēmatismoi*), and other testimonies'.[103] The dedicators map exactly onto the mythical history of the city, beginning with its eponymous hero Lindos who dedicated a *phialē* of 'unknown material' on which was written 'Lindos [dedicates this] to Athena Polias and Zeus Polieus'. There then follow a series of dedications from mythical figures, for example the Telchines, Kadmos, Minos, and Herakles, and also historical figures such as Phalaris tyrant of Akragas, the Persian general Artaphernes, Alexander the Great, Ptolemy I, Pyrrhos of Epiros, and the latest entry is for King Philip III of Macedon.[104] Partly to demonstrate that the sanctuary can compete in magnificence with the major

---

[102] Blinkenberg (1915) Text A, 3–5.
[103] Blinkenberg (1915) Text A, 6–7.
[104] All references are to Blinkenberg (1915): Telchines (Text B, 2), Kadmos, (Text B, 3), Minos (Text B, 4), Herakles (Text B, 5), Phalaris (Text C, 27), Artaphernes (Text C, 32), Alexander (Text C, 38), Ptolemy (Text C, 39), Pyrrhos (Text C, 40), and Philip III (Text C, 42).

mainland sanctuaries of Delphi and Olympia, it also stresses the function that sanctuaries had, not as museums, but as repositories of the memories of the local community. This is hardly surprising given that many Greek states made clear in the publication clauses of civic decrees that a copy was to be displayed in the local sanctuary—religious space could be regarded both as public space and as a sort of archive. Amasis' dedication is therefore part of a sequence of dedications, which mirror the city's changing political relationships from the moment of its (legendary) foundation by the hero Lindos down to the Hellenistic period.

If objects on display were in some sense traces of divine epiphany, as the preamble to the Lindos Temple Chronicle suggests, then for an individual like Mucianus, enmeshed in a polytheistic system for which belief is an inappropriate criterion of participation, there are crucial differences between his experience of visiting, inquiring about, even touching these votives, and modern visitors to the glass-cases of a museum. Mucianus' visits—even if we wish to class them as tourism—were very much about an autoptic experience of wonder, a wonder prepared by Herodotus and Homer and actually experienced in Mucianus' contact with relics.

Mucianus' response helps us to understand how the difference between the Christian and Graeco-Roman discourse regarding miracles arose, for although Mucianus recognized the transformation of water into wine on Andros as evidence for the power of Dionysus, there is no evidence he conceptualized this as distinct from natural phenomena whose wondrous aspects were not directly related to the divine. Miracles had long been a part of both Graeco-Roman and Jewish religion, and had indeed often been taken as a sign of divine power, but the Graeco-Roman tradition did not distinguish between divine and natural marvels.[105] As Christianity developed intellectually it developed means of identifying *mirabilia* as either true miracles and therefore the workings of divine authority in the world, or as false miracles and thereby to be attributed to demonic power.[106] Indeed in part Christianity played up the importance of its 'true miracles' by virtue of

---

[105] Kolenkow (1980).

[106] Kee (1986), 69–94 on the earlier Hellenistic and Jewish background to pagan miracles. Theissen and Riches (1983), 252–9 argues that within Christian tradition miracle stories arose originally in a lower-class milieu and served an important missionary function. With the growing influence of developed theology such miracles had to be resituated within a coherent model of God's creation.

contrast with and polemic against false miracles.[107] Pagan miracles could also be denigrated as 'magic'.[108] Such distinctions are inappropriate for the Greco-Roman world. Mucianus' text should prompt us to reconsider the separation by Christian writers of *mirabilia* and *miracula* into different categories. Augustine ascribed the power of miracles even to lower beings such as demons, but argued that true miracles belonged to God.[109] In the subtlest exposition of such doctrines Aquinas redefined miracles as actions that take place 'outside the order of nature', and therefore the provenance of God alone.[110] Marvels seen in the natural world might be *mirabilia*, but unless one could find divine reference for them they could not be considered *miracula*.[111] Theologians therefore drew strict boundaries around phenomena which were ascribed to legitimate divine intervention in the natural world (approved and under the control of the Church) and marvels (*mirabilia*), which were not evidence of divine power. The strict separation was useful to the early Christians as it enabled them to develop a theology in which marvels claimed by pagans could be denigrated as the work of demons.[112] The usage familiar to Mucianus did not draw these sharp boundaries between divine signs and those of the natural world—the word *miraculum* had not yet taken on its later theological overtones, as is suggested by the definition offered by the commentator that 'a miracle (*miraculum*) is that which is wonderful (*mirum*)'.[113]

CONCLUSION

Mucianus' work is important for a number of reasons. Given he was writing in Latin in the mid-first century CE his interests in the religious

[107] Note the role played by Simon Magus in *Acts of the Apostles* and the denial of the pagan Apollonius of Tyana's miracles by Eusebius in his *Against Hierocles*. On the latter see Swain (1999), 192–3.

[108] Remus (1983) 55 discusses Justin's 'demon theory' of pagan religion.

[109] Augustine, *The Trinity*, 3.2 discussing the issue of miracles wrought by demonic power.

[110] Aquinas, *Summa Theologica*, First Part, Question 110.

[111] Aquinas, *Summa Contra Gentilos*, 3/2, 103. 'Accordingly, although such effects cannot be called *miracles* absolutely, since they result from natural causes, yet are they *wonderful* to us.'

[112] Remus (1983).

[113] Servius on *Aeneid* 3.366, quoted in Remus (1983), 52.

history and topography of the Greek East, which he had visited in the course of his official career, make clear that the enormous increase in interest in travel literature often taken as characteristic of the cultural phenomenon known as the 'Second Sophistic' has its roots in journeys undertaken by educated Romans as well as Greeks. His travels were made possible by the deep structural changes effected by Roman power. His early date and the fact that he is from the Latin-speaking half of the Roman empire make him a more important literary figure than has been supposed.[114] His continual temple-visiting and following a tourist trail that encompassed the great monuments of Roman Asia Minor suggests that writers such as Pausanias were simply fitting into a pre-existing cultural pattern. As a little-studied writer he in fact provides valuable evidence both of the attraction of sanctuaries to an educated Roman visitor and also of their importance to local communities. Just as Pausanias would later take the opportunity to describe the objects on display at Greece's sanctuaries, for instance, the Chest of Kypselos at Olympia (5.17.5), Mucianus shows an interest in these.[115] Moreover, the *range* of Mucianus' travels puts him in a category with Pausanias.[116]

The gap between tourism and pilgrimage closes from two directions: first, because visitors such as Mucianus might visit with pious intent or at least with their credulity intact; second, because sanctuaries served a range of purposes—they were not merely a goal of sacred focus and intent, but also the appropriate locus for the display of votives and epiphanies, which might form the raw material for accounts of *mirabilia*. The usual analogy is that sanctuaries acted like proto-museums, but quick comparison with even the earliest of the late medieval/early Renaissance *Wunderkammern* or early collections such as that of Tradescant which formed the basis of Oxford's Ashmolean Museum, suggest that the eclectic range of collections characteristic of the modern museum was not shared with ancient sanctuaries which were focused on the history and memory simply of the god(dess) and the local community.[117]

---

[114] Swain (1996) dates the Second Sophistic as early as 50 CE, although none of the writers he discusses belong earlier than the late 1st cent. CE.

[115] On the Chest see Snodgrass (2001).

[116] Rutherford (2001*a*), 41 comments on the range of detours in Pausanias's journey.

[117] On these early collections there is now a considerable body of work. A good starting point is Impey and MacGregor (1985). Kaufmann (1995) details the development of the museum from its origins in the late medieval *Wunderkammern* associated with various noble and princely patrons.

Above all, Mucianus' credulous attitude towards the many sanctuaries he visited suggests that much material often considered under the heading of 'tourism' may have to be taken seriously by students of pilgrimage.

Appendix of Translated Texts

[Fragment numbers correspond to those of *Historicorum Romanorum Reliquiae*]

1. It is accredited by the Mucianus who was three times consul that the water flowing from a spring in the temple of Father Liber on the island of Andros always has the flavour of wine on 5 January: the day is called Theodosia (God's gift day). (= Pliny *NH* 2.231)

2. Another marvel not far from Circello is the Pomptine Marsh, a place which Mucianus who was three times consul has reported to be the site of twenty-four cities. (= Pliny *NH* 3.59)

3. By far the most famous of the Cyclades and lying in the middle of them is Delos, celebrated for its temple of Apollo and its commerce. According to the story, Delos for a long time floated adrift; and it was the only island that down to the time of Marcus Varro had never felt an earthquake shock. Mucianus, however, states that it has twice suffered from earthquake. (= Pliny *NH* 4.66)

4. Next to Delos is Rhene... Syros, stated by old writers to measure 20 miles in circuit, but by Mucianus 100 miles. (= Pliny *NH* 4.67)

5. The whole circumference of the Black Sea according to Varro and the old authorities generally is 2,150, but Cornelius Nepos adds 300 miles, while Artemidorus makes it 2,119 miles, Agrippa 2,540, and Mucianus 2,425. (= Pliny *NH* 4.77)

6. Between the Arsinoite and Memphite nomes there was once a lake measuring 250, or according to Mucianus' account, 450 miles round, and 250 feet deep, an artificial sheet of water called the Lake of Moeris after the king who made it. (= Pliny *NH* 5.50)

7. A description of the Euphrates also will be most suitable in this place. It rises in Caranitis, a prefecture of Greater Armenia, as has been stated by two of the persons who have seen it nearest to its source—Domitius Corbulo putting its source in Mount Aga, and Licinius Mucianus at the roots of a mountain the name of which he gives as Capotes, 12 miles above Zimera. (= Pliny *NH* 5.83)

8. Then in the Phoenician sea off Joppa lies Paria, the whole of which is a town—it is said to have been the place where Andromeda was exposed to the monster—and Arados, mentioned already; between which and the mainland, according to Mucianus, fresh water is brought up from a spring at the bottom of the sea, which is 75 feet deep, by means of a leather pipe. (= Pliny *NH* 5.128)

9. But the most beautiful is the free island of Rhodes, which measures 121, or if we prefer to believe Isidore, 103 miles round, and which contains the cities of Lindos, Camiros, and Ialysos, and now that of Rhodes. Its distance from Alexandria in Egypt is 583 miles according to Isidore, 468 according to Eratosthenes, 500 according to Mucianus, and it is 176 miles from Cyprus. (= Pliny *NH* 5.132)

10. Transformation of females into males is not an idle story...Licinius Mucianus has recorded that he personally saw at Argos a man named Arescon who had been given the name of Arescusa and had actually married a husband, and then had grown a beard and developed masculine attributes and taken a wife; and that he had also seen a boy with the same record at Smyrna. (= Pliny *NH* 7.36)

11. Mucianus is the authority for one Tempsis having lived 150 years at the place called Mount Tmolus Heights. (= Pliny *NH* 7.159)

12. Mucianus who was three times consul states that one elephant actually learnt the shapes of the Greek letters, and used to write out words in the language: 'I myself wrote this and dedicated spoils won from the Celts.' And also that he had personally seen elephants that, on having been brought by sea to Puteoli, were made to walk off the ship, were frightened by the length of the gangway stretching a long way out from the deck, and turned around and went backwards so as to cheat themselves in their estimation of the distance. (= Pliny *NH* 8.6)

13. Mucianus has described a case of this animal's cleverness seen by himself —two goats coming in opposite directions met on a very narrow bridge, and as the narrow space did not allow backing blindly on the passageway with a rushing torrent flowing threateningly below, one of them lay down

and so the other one passed over, treading on top of it. (= Pliny *NH* 8.201)

14. The kinds of apes which also are closest to the human shape are distinguished from each other by the tails. They are marvellously cunning: people say that they use bird-lime as ointment, and that they put on the nooses set out to snare them as if they were shoes, in imitation of the hunters; according to Mucianus the tailed species have even been known to play at draughts, are able to distinguish at a glance false nuts made of wax, are depressed by the moon waxing and worship the new moon with delight. (= Pliny *NH* 8.215)

15. Mucianus' account of the same kind of fishing in the Iasian gulf differs in this—the dolphins stand by their own accord and without being summoned by a shout, and receive their snare from the fisherman's hands, and each boat has one of the dolphins as its ally although it is in the night and by torchlight. (= Pliny *NH* 9.33)

16. Licinius Mucianus has recorded the capture from the Red Sea of a mullet weighing 80 lbs. (= Pliny *NH* 9.68)

17. Mucianus states that the murex is broader than the purple and has a mouth that is not rough nor round, and a back that does not stick out into corners, but is stuck together like a bivalve shell, and that owing to murexes clinging to the sides a ship was brought to a standstill when in full sail before the wind, carrying dispatches from Periander ordering some noble youths to be castrated, and that the shell-fish that rendered this service are worshipped in the shrine of Venus at Knidos. (= Pliny *NH* 9.79)

18. Mucianus has stated that he has also seen in the Dardanelles another creature resembling a ship under sail: it is a shell with a head like a boat, and a curved stern and beaked bow. In this (he says) the *nauplius*, a creature like the cuttle-fish, secretes itself, merely by way of sharing the game. The manner in which this takes place is twofold: in calm weather the carrier shell strikes the water by dipping its flappers like oars, but if the breezes invite, the same flappers are stretched out to serve as a rudder and the curves of the shell are spread out to the breeze. (= Pliny *NH* 9.94)

19. Nor is it proper to omit the stories about the *anthias* fish that I notice to have won general acceptance. We have mentioned the Chelidonian Isles situated off a promontory of Mt. Taurus in the rocky sea off Asia; this fish is frequent there, and is quickly caught, in one variety. . . . There is a story that a disaffected partner in a fishery lay in wait for the leader fish, which

was very well known, and caught it with malicious intent; Mucianus adds that it was recognized in the market by partner who was being victimized, and that proceedings for damages were instituted and a verdict given for the prosecution with damages. (= Pliny *NH* 9.180)

20. Mucianus has stated that he saw a Samothracian named Zocles who grew a new set of teeth when 140 years old. (= Pliny *NH* 11.167)

21. At the present day there is a celebrated plane tree in Lycia, allied with the amenity of a cool spring; it stands by the roadside like a dwelling-house, with a hollow cavity inside it 81 feet across, facing with its summit a shady grove, and shielding itself with vast branches as big as trees and covering the fields with its long shadows, and so as to complete its resemblance to a grotto, embracing inside it mossy pumice-stones in a circular rim of a rock—a tree so worthy to be deemed a marvel that Licinius Mucianus who was three times consul and recently governor of the province, thought it worthy handing down to posterity that he held a banquet with eighteen members of his retinue inside the tree, which itself provided couches of leafage on a bounteous scale, and that he had then gone to bed in the same tree, shielded from any breath of wind, and receiving more delight from the agreeable sound of the rain dropping through the foliage than gleaming marble, painted decorations, or gilded panelling could have afforded. (= Pliny *NH* 12.9)

22. Moreover the Mucianus who was three times consul has stated recently that, when governor of Lycia, he had read a certain letter of Sarpedon written on paper at Troy—which seems to me even more remarkable if even when Homer was writing, Egypt did not yet exist. (= Pliny *NH* 13.88)

23. This class of wine (wine of Maronea) in the same district (Thrace) still retains its strength and its insuperable vigour, since Mucianus, who was three times consul, ascertained when actually visiting that region that it is the custom to mix with one pint of this wine eight pints of water, and that it is black in colour, has a strong bouquet, and improves in substance with age. (= Pliny *NH* 14.54)

24. It is believed that ebony lasts an extremely long time, and also cypress and cedar, a clear verdict about all timbers being given in the temple of Diana at Ephesus, in as much as though the whole of Asia was building it the temple took 120 years to complete. It is agreed that its roof is made of beams of cedar, but as to the actual statue of the goddess there is some dispute, with all the older writers saying that it is made of ebony, but

one of the people who have most recently seen it and wrote about it, Mucianus, who was three times consul, states that it is made of the wood of the vine, and has never been altered although the temple has been restored several times, and that this material was chosen by Endoeus—Mucianus actually specifies the name of the artist which for my part I think surprising since he assigns to the statue an antiquity that makes it older than not only Father Liber but Minerva also. He adds that nard is poured into it through a number of apertures that the chemical properties of the liquid may nourish the wood and keep the joins together. (= Pliny *NH* 16.213)

25. This may surprise people who do not know that in a breastplate that belonged to a former king of Egypt named Amasis, preserved in the temple of Minerva at Lindos on the island of Rhodes, each thread consisted of 365 separate threads, a fact which Mucianus who held the consulship three times quite lately, stated that he had proved to be true by investigation, adding that only small remnants of the breastplate now survive owing to the damage by persons examining its quality. (= Pliny *NH* 19.12)

26. [Saffron]. Mucianus is an authority that in Lycia after six or seven years it is transplanted to a well-dug bed; in this way it recovers from its degeneration. (= Pliny *NH* 21.33)

27. Mucianus states that on Andros, from the spring of Father Liber, on fixed seven-day festivals of the god, flows wine, but if the liquid is carried out of sight of the temple the taste turns to that of water. (= Pliny *NH* 31.16)

28. A spring at Cyzicus is called Cupid's Spring: those who drink of it, Mucianus believes, lose their amorous desires. (= Pliny *NH* 31.19)

29. So much for the bodies of oysters. I will now speak of the countries that breed oysters, lest the shores be deprived of their proper fame; so I shall do so in the words of another, one who was the greater connoisseur of such matters in our time. These are the words of Mucianus, which I will quote: 'Oysters of Cyzicus are larger that those of Lake Lucrinus, fresher than those of the British, sweeter than those of Medulla, sharper than the Ephesian, fuller than those of Ilici (in Spain), less slimy than those of Coryphan, softer than those of Histria, whiter than those of Circeii.' (= Pliny *NH* 32.62)

30. Yet it is stated by Mucianus who was three times consul that there are still 3000 statues at Rhodes, and no smaller number are believed to exist at Athens, Olympia, and Rhodes. (= Pliny *NH* 34.36)

31. At Assos in the Troad we find the Sarcophagus stone, which splits along a line of cleavage. It is well known that corpses buried in it are consumed within a period of forty days, except for the teeth. Mucianus vouches for the fact that mirrors, scrapers, clothes and shoes placed upon the dead body are turned to stone as well. There are similar stones both in Lycia and in the East; and these, attached even to living persons, eat away their bodies. (= Pliny *NH* 36.131)

32. Theophrastus, again, and Mucianus express the opinion that there are certain stones which give birth to other stones. (= Pliny *NH* 36.134).

9

Pilgrimage as Elite *Habitus*:

Educated Pilgrims in Sacred Landscape During the Second Sophistic

Marco Galli

A Rita Zanotto Galli,
con profonda amicizia e stima

PATTERNS OF RELIGIOUS MEMORY AND PAIDEIA DURING THE SECOND SOPHISTIC

Is it possible to reconstruct, at least in part, the suggestive and intricate frame that connected the monuments and images, the ritual actions, and the pilgrim who actively and subjectively participated as collector and observer of sacred experience? What indices permit us to trace the emotional reactions of pilgrims in contact with the sacred landscape? What mental processes and emotional reactions made the tangible objects (the monuments, the images, and the rites) into mental objects, and how did these become fixed in the memory of the pilgrim? With these questions as guidelines, I shall argue that we can apply a contemporary approach to the investigation of the social functions of ancient pilgrimage. For the exploration of the relationship between the religious experiences of the pilgrim and social instances of collective memory for the reconstruction and reactivation of a sacred traditional landscape, we may turn to a moment in history that provides an unusually dense

representation of the internal states of sacred experience.[1] This is the
period dubbed 'The Second Sophistic'. It was a period virtually obsessed
with the problem of memory, when even religious tradition, because it
formed one of the most significant communicative functions of collective life, was subjected to fundamental revision within the process of
social memory.[2]

Plutarch's writings cast light on the role of memory and its interaction
with religious tradition. In his dialogues 'On the Pythian Oracles'
Plutarch expresses a clear awareness of how a religious geography
would be possible by means of a fuller, more active, contribution of
memory:[3]

Men in those days had to have a memory for many things. For many things
were communicated to them, such as signs for recognizing places, the times for
activities, the shrines of gods across the sea, secret burial-places of heroes, hard
to find for men setting forth on a distant voyage from Greece!

(Plut. *De Pyth. Or.* 27.407 f)

In this passage memory emerges as a fundamental support for pilgrimage. Whereas for the ancients preceding Plutarch the dimensions of the
pilgrimage trip and the search for focal points in the sacred landscape
might be understood as collective memory,[4] for Plutarch's Second
Sophistic contemporaries these were better definable in terms of *paideia*.
Intellectual competence and educated *habitus*[5] are not simply a leit-

---

[1] For an example of a topographically constructed memory, see Cancik (1985/6). On
the configuration of the sacred sphere see in general the recent contribution of Graf
(1996); on the concept of 'The Sacred' see Burkert (1977), 420: 'Für die Griechen
ist zweifellos hieros seit mykenischer Zeit der entscheidende Begriff, um die Sphäre des
Religiösen abzugrenzen'. For the semantics of the sacred sphere see Morani (1983).

[2] Bowersock (1969) formed innovative and fundamental criteria for the contemporary discussion of this period. See also Schmitz (1997); Swain (1996); Gleason (1995);
Anderson (1993). On self-representation in this cultural climate: Smith (1998); Zanker
(1995), ch. 5. Regarding the question of social memory in this period see Alcock (2001):
I owe my thanks to S. E. Alcock for her generous permission to view the paper before the
date of publication.

[3] Many new approaches to the religious *habitus* of Plutarch in Gallo (1996),
esp. Burkert (1996) and Sfameni-Gasparro (1996).

[4] On memory and religion see Assmann (2000).

[5] For the key concept *habitus* I use notions drawn from Pierre Bourdieu's social
theory: for a schematic account see the editor's introd. in Bourdieu (1991): 'The habitus
is a set of dispositions which incline agents to act and react in certain ways. The

motif in the literary panorama of the Second Sophistic nor a mere matter of erudition in restricted circles.[6] It is crucial, for a greater understanding of the *mentalité* of the Second Sophistic, to grasp the particular function of *paideia* as an active support for reactivating mental images and making them collectively accessible.[7] Of particular significance is the role of *paideia* as a catalyst for public behaviour. Plutarch in the Delphic dialogues offers examples of how cultural patrimony—that baggage of notions, traditions, and habits—became a dynamic channel of communication.

Using local guides (more or less learned),[8] distinguished members of the local and international elite 'visit' the most famous oracular sanctuary of ancient times.[9] A group of friends is climbing the Sacred Way in Delphi, starting at the beginning and arriving at the Temple of Apollo. Engrossed in lively discussion, they make various stops:

BASILOCLES. You people have kept it up till well into the evening, Philinus, escorting the foreign visitor around among the statues and votive offerings. For my part, I had almost given up waiting for you.

PHILINUS. The fact is, Basilocles, that we went slowly, sowing words, and reaping them straightway with strife, like the men sprung from the Dragon's teeth, words with meanings behind them of the contentious sort, which sprang up and flourished along our way.

BASILOCLES. Will it be necessary to call in someone else of those who were with you; or are willing, as a favour, to relate in full what your conversation was and who took part in it?

PHILINUS. It looks, Basilocles, as if I shall have that to do. In fact. it would not be easy for you to find anyone of the others in the town, for I saw most of them once more on their way up to the Corycian cave and Lycoreia with the foreign visitor.

---

dispositions generate practices, perceptions and attitudes which are "regular" without being consciously co-ordinated or governed by any "rule". (...) The habitus also provides individuals with a sense of how to act and respond in the course of their daily lives', ibid. pp. 12–13.

[6] On the notion of the 'intellectual' and its legitimated application in antiquity see the approach to this question by Mazza (1982) and the recently published contribution of Anderson (1998). In regard to the social implications of the religious activity for the Roman imperial elites see Bowersock (1973).

[7] Concerning the social implications of the cult of *paideia* see Flinterman (1995), 31–55; Anderson (1989), 104 ff esp. n. 149.

[8] On guides see Jones (2001).

[9] For a general description of the Delphic Sanctuary see Maass (1993).

BASILOCLES. Our visitor is certainly eager to see the sights, and an unusually eager listener.

PHILINUS. But even more is he a scholar and a student. However, it is not this that most deserves our admiration, but a winning gentleness, and his willingness to argue and to raise questions, which comes from his intelligence, and shows no dissatisfaction nor contrariety with the answers.

(Plut. *De Pyth. Or.* 1.394 e)

The text shows how these individuals travelled towards the sacred site, arrived there, and how they visited it. That such visits became new opportunities for a close interaction between place, object, and observer, is clearly evident in Plutarch's picture of the relations between a visitor-observer and a bronze statue in the sanctuary.[10] Through the subtle filter of a cultivated approach, the notable group of Lysander erected near the beginning of the Delphic sanctuary became an object for immediate personal reaction (Figure 1).

PHILINUS. The guides were going through their prearranged programme, paying no heed to us who begged that they would cut short their harangues and their expounding of most of the inscriptions. The appearance and technique of the statues had only a moderate attraction for the foreign visitor, who, apparently, was a connoisseur in works of art. He did, however, admire the patina of the bronze, for it bore no resemblance to verdigris or rust, but the bronze was smooth and shining with a deep blue tinge, so that it gave an added touch to the sea-captains (...) as they stood there with the true complexion of the sea and its deepest depths.

(Plut. *De Pyth. Or.* 1.395 b)

This commentary on the Lysander group at Delphi shows the impossibility of applying modern touristic or 'museum' type perceptions.[11] The responses dramatized by Plutarch are not about a deep study of the objects nor the acquiring of new knowledge nor even the correction of information. This is implied by the lack of interest in the oral accounts of the local guides who were following a set programme. The example

---

[10] Cf. Coleman and Elsner (1995), 202–6.

[11] Swain (1996), 76 Delphi as 'museum of the Greek past'; for another point of view—Delphi as place of cultural memory—see Jacquemin (1991); for a new approach in considering the Roman Greece simply as 'Museum' see Alcock (1993), 201: 'The notion that Greece was simply "a country learning to be a museum" has been rejected as the central fact about Roman Greece, but the conscious cultivation of the glorious past was patently in operation.'

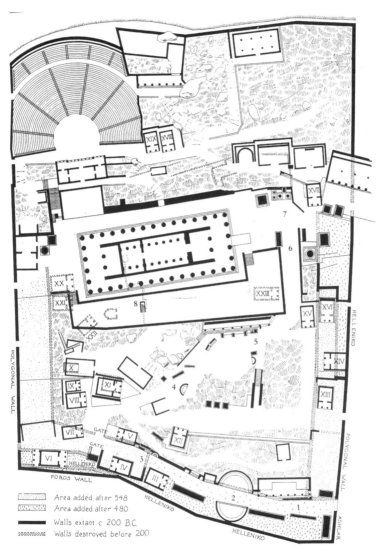

Figure 1. Delphi, Sanctuary of Apollo, Plan (from BCH 36, 1912, pl. 8)

demonstrates the force of the tight connection between sacred place and object, whose sanctity could always be reactivated by a cultivated observer of the imperial period. The group of Lysander is not a simple 'attribute' of the place nor even an object of erudite discussion, but rather constitutes one of the strong stimuli which the cultivated observer faced. The interaction of mental images, already present in the observer, and their activation via emotional tensions generated by contact with a sacred place, constitute the catalyzing experience of the pilgrimage here.

A passage in another of Plutarch's works is indicative of those processes of emotional involvement during a religious event and of the amplification of such public behaviour. Even if the majority of men were afraid of the divine, Plutarch argues, the feeling of hope outweighs their fear. The notion that a spirit, full of hope, might become serene provides proof that religious rituals and ceremonies comforted men.

> This is proved by the strongest kind of evidence: no visit delights us more than a visit to a temple; no occasion more than a holy day; no act or spectacle more than what we see and what we do ourselves in matters that involve the gods, whether we celebrate a ritual or take part in a choral dance or attend a sacrifice or ceremony of initiation. For on these occasions our mind is not plunged into anxiety (. . .). No, wherever it believes and conceives most firmly that the god is present, there more than anywhere else it puts away all feelings of pain, of fear and of worry, and gives itself up so far to pleasure that it indulges in a playful and merry inebriation
>
> (Plut. *Non posse suaviter vivi secundum Epicurum*, 1101 e)

These considerations comment on how an individual's emotional involvement may spread to become a collective experience. The community's external expressions (above all the visual and gestural movements—ὧν ὁρῶμεν ἢ δρῶμεν αὐτοὶ περὶ τοὺς θεούς) seem to correspond directly to the internal expressions of the individual participants. Plutarch seems to foreground here one of the most important components of visiting Greek sanctuaries: the direct participation in rituals that defined the key moments of pilgrimage. In their visits, educated pilgrims not only comment on the monuments, but also actively participate in the rituals. Both for many *pepaideumenoi* (educated and antiquarian travellers), contemporaries of Plutarch, and for Plutarch himself—a philosopher in the tradition of Plato and at the same time a priest of Apollo at Delphi—the religious dimension was perceived in its emotional function. Plutarch's experience here anticipates that of somewhat later contemporaries like Pausanias and Aelius Aristides. To understand better the mental dynamics of pilgrimage during the Second Sophistic, it may be useful to compare two different experiences that allow us to regard the Athenian Acropolis as a mental concept.

FREUD'S AND PAUSANIAS' DISTURBANCES OF MEMORY ON THE ACROPOLIS

Athens, August–September 1904: The founder of psychoanalysis climbs the Acropolis at Athens for the first time. This experience and the heavy emotional involvement that followed his visit to the sacred centre of antiquity was analyzed by Sigmund Freud many years later in a famous passage:[12]

When, finally, on the afternoon after our arrival, I stood on the Acropolis and cast my eyes around upon the landscape, a surprising thought suddenly entered my mind: 'So all this really does exist, just as we learnt at school!' To describe the situation more accurately, the person who gave expression to the remark was divided, far more sharply than was usually noticeable, from another person who took cognizance of the remark; and both were astonished, though not by the same thing. The first behaved as though he were obliged, under the impact of an unequivocal observation, to believe in something, the reality of which had hitherto seemed doubtful... The second person, on the other hand, was justifiably astonished, because he had been unaware that the real existence of Athens, the Acropolis, and the landscape around it, had ever been objects of doubt. What he had been expecting was rather some expression of delight or admiration.

Now it would be easy to argue that this strange thought that occurred to me on the Acropolis only serves to emphasise the fact that seeing something with one's own eyes is after all quite a different thing from hearing or reading about it.

The experience of estrangement on the Athenian Acropolis testifies to the strong emotional participation that arises from the contrast between the real perception of a place and its mental counterpart as activated in

---

[12] Freud (1964), 240–1. On this document see also some notable considerations by Smith (1987), 24 ff.

the memory of a specific individual. The disturbance of memory acutely analysed by Freud provides exemplary documentation of how the experience of an emblematic landscape of the past may spark a series of mental chain reactions. The experience of seeing a real place forcefully evokes the mental image of the same place and interacts with it. For Freud the mental image had already been created before he actually saw the place. The passage provides decisive evidence for the priority given to a mental construct. The context of an urban Athenian sanctuary visited by Freud in 1904 could not possibly have corresponded to the Acropolis that he had studied as a student in the years around 1870.[13] The intense excavations begun in 1885 had radically changed the medieval and Turkish citadel into a 'classical landscape' of ancient ruins. For the young Sigmund Freud, in a Viennese gymnasium, the Acropolis of Athens was an emblem of Greek civilization conforming to the models of his education, that is to say, to the bourgeois *paideia* of the *Mitteleuropa*. This curious interference of memory on the Acropolis in Athens in the case of an educated pilgrim does not correspond to an antiquarian or nostalgic attitude. Freud's visit to the Acropolis and its mental reactivation is full of significant anxieties and unconscious desires. It is, therefore, not about a simple discrepancy between that which is read and thought and that which one experiences in person, but rather about a deeper disturbance, a situation characterized by strong emotional participation on the part of the individual which, as Freud reveals, 'umfaßt meine Person, die Akropolis und meine Wahrnehmung derselben'.

For a *pepaideumenos* like Pausanias, just as for Freud and even for Plutarch, the experience of the sacred landscape of antiquity was the result of a significant interplay between perception of the actual place and reactivation of the mental memory connected to the place.[14] For Pausanias (as for Freud), the Acropolis before the viewer was certainly not that of the complete Periclean splendour of the fifth century BCE; it was rather the product of successive reinterpretations that persisted at least until the Antonine period. Yet, this chronological aspect did not seem particularly to interest the author of the *Periegesis*. Fidelity to a

---

[13] For further discussion of this point see Smith (1987).

[14] Alcock (1996) offers a thorough approach to the landscape of memory in Pausanias' work; see Assmann (1999) too, with other references.

historic continuity was not a necessity taken into consideration in its structure. The awareness of symbolic overload, in the pilgrimage made by Pausanias to the sacred centre of Hellenic civilization, causes him to declare 'that religious fervor is more intense among the Athenians than it is among other peoples'.[15] The beginning of his visit to the Acropolis is exhausting on account of the complicated series of 'chain reactions' that include the visual perception of the sacred landscape, a complex of emotional reactions in the observer, the mental recreation of the 'real place', the presence in the observer of an already existing memory, the contextual image of the same place filtered by the complex of cultural values, and, finally, a frame of disturbances and integrations of memory.

> There is but one entry to the Acropolis. It affords no other, being precipitous throughout and having a strong wall. The gateway has a roof of white marble, and down to the present day it is unrivalled for its beauty and the size of its stones.

> (Paus. 1.22.4)

The periegete's eyes move upwards: notwithstanding its brevity, the glance directly follows the position of the monumental entrance. What remains of the strong impact with this imposing rite of access? Behind the framework of topical rhetoric (*kosmōi kai megethei*, arrangement and size), the brightness of the stone (*lithou leukou*) stands out in Pausanias' text. It is a note that seems generic and indefinite but is in reality a telling statement about the interaction between the visitor and the monumental background. It is a considerably more efficient way of communicating the visual impact than a precise architectural description. It is precisely this quality, the blinding whiteness of the marble, that seems to constitute for Pausanias some form of continuity between his experience as an educated pilgrim in Greece during the Antonine period and that of his predecessors (μέχρι γε καὶ ἐμοῦ προεῖχε).

This past-in-present dimension,[16] which Pausanias seems to affirm, remains purely a fragment of collective memory.[17] In fact, immediately

---

[15] Paus. 1.17.1 and 1.24.3; in general on bk. 1, see Beschi and Musti (1982).

[16] Anderson (1989), 140–5, esp. p. 139: 'the past is simply being used to communicate the present in the most familiar way'.

[17] For the 'past-in-present' dimension in Pausanias' work see Bowie (1996).

after the strong visual first impression, interferences of memory begin
to arise.

> Now as to the statues of the horsemen, I cannot tell for certain whether they are
> the sons of Xenophon or whether they were made merely to beautify the place.
> On the right of the gateway is a temple of Wingless Victory. From this point the
> sea is visible, and here it was that, according to legend, Aegeus threw himself
> down to his death.
>
> (Paus. 1.22.4)

The quoted version of the myth of Theseus completes the mental report
of the sacred place. In this connection the mythical memory is reactivated
as a sort of 'interface' between the real sight and the mental reconstruction of the religious experience. We should consider these first short
narrative remarks as exemplary of the way the periegete proceeds on his
peregrinatio. They represent not just the way he carries out his specific
'visit' to the Acropolis but also how he registers the visual and emotional
effects of pilgrimage in various different sacred landscapes. It is the myth
that generated the places which become the object of memorialization.

Certainly it is true that Pausanias takes particular care to affirm that
he is writing from autopsy. But far from being a Blue Guide or a
Baedecker for the ancients, the *Periegesis* takes the form, above all in
its way of understanding sacred landscapes, of a sort of visual and
emotional breviary of ancient sacredness. Thus, Elsner's thesis that the
Periegesis represents a sort of interior emigration needs to be supple-
mented by an examination of the internal images that Pausanias de-
ploys.[18] In this sense, the experience of Freud and that of Pausanias
represent two extremes (but not opposites) of the *anamnesis* of place as
institutionalized and codified by *paideia* and by cultural tradition, and
marked by the mental projections of their respective historic eras. The
two 'visits' to the Acropolis constitute paradoxically two extreme ways of
reacting to mental images of a place that is overloaded with symbolic
connotations. Both these experiences go beyond being a recording of a
moment lived in the present and take on the value of an experience of
memory.

In Freud the state of uneasiness and the contrast that it creates
between internal and external reality is overcome in a process of accurate

---

[18] Elsner (1992), 9–10.

analysis. Recollecting the various levels of memory he traces the extremely personal dynamics that lead to the formation of such mental places. Pausanias, in contrast, focuses on recovering and reproducing in language, in a 'book of memory', an entire complex framework of multiple interactions between sacred places, objects, and emotions of the observer–pilgrim. Even though they are chronologically disparate, the dynamics of the two experiences of the same sacred place lead us to reconsider the relationship between locus and memory. This concept of memory differs from how the relationship was conceived in antiquity, as summarized by Cicero in his famous passage on the *vis admonitionis* of certain places.[19] The place should not be considered a passive recipient but an active product of an intellectual and psychological process that is activated by the intellect of the observer.

THE PERFORMATIVE ACTS OF PILGRIMAGE: FORMS OF RELIGIOUS AND SOCIAL COMMUNICATION

The points made up to now provide some premises on which certain characteristics of the full network of interferences and exchanges that occur between an individual and a system of social norms can be reconstructed. One of the factors behind the strong interest and direct involvement (personal and collective) of the well-to-do classes in pilgrimage is the role of pilgrim experience as a force of social cohesion. A tight connection between collective memory and an effort to strengthen the identity of the group underlies the revival of pilgrimage in the Antonine period. Thorough examination of the communicative structure of the ritual and symbolic sequences of pilgrimage seems necessary here, not just to register the social dynamics of the phenomenon but also to reconstruct the chain of emotional reactions that rises between the individual and the collective group. In the cultural climate of the Second Sophistic the ruling classes of the Roman empire appear to have adopted comparable patterns of communication about politics, culture, and religion. Some of the connotations of this pilgrim behaviour

[19] Cic. *De Fin.* 5.1. On this passage see Assmann (1999), 298.

and the hierarchical structuring of the pilgrim-group are stressed by different literary sources.

In the Delphic dialogues of Plutarch some situations demonstrate the interrelationship of intellectual occupations, practical religious functions, and sacred space. I note briefly the dramatic structure of the *De defectu oraculorum*.[20]

Yet a short time before the Pythian games, which were held when Callistratus was in office in our own day, it happened that two revered men coming from opposite ends of the inhabited earth met together at Delphi, Demetrius the grammarian journeying homeward from Britain to Tarsus, and Cleombrotus of Sparta, who had made many excursions in Egypt and about the land of the Cave-dwellers, and had sailed beyond the Persian Gulf; his journeyings were not for business, but he was fond of seeing things and of acquiring knowledge; he had wealth enough, and felt that it was not of any great moment to have more than enough, and so he employed his leisure for such purposes; he was getting together a history to serve as a basis for a philosophy that had as its end aim theology, as he himself named it. (. . .)

Proceeding onward from the temple, we had by this time reached the doors of the Cnidian Clubhouse. Accordingly we passed inside, and there we saw sitting and waiting for us the friends to whom we were going. There was quiet among the other people there because of the hour, as they were engaged in taking a rub-down or else watching the athletes.

(Plut. *De Def. Or.* 2.6–7, 410, 412d)

This passage opens a dialogue between different *pepaideumenoi* or individuals who aspire to be such. The dialogue occurred, or was imagined to have occurred, inside the sanctuary at Delphi. The brief information about the two main characters proves itself not to be secondary but rather exemplary for the social composition and cultural motivations that characterize the different components of the pilgrim group. Whereas they come from diverse geographic backgrounds— we speak of the international elite of the second century CE[21]—the pilgrims belong to the same privileged social class. A fact of central importance emerges: the desire to obtain cultural enrichment which motivated the *pepaideumenos*-pilgrim to fulfil the rituals of pilgrimage

---

[20] On this dialogue see the recently published contribution of Santaniello (1996).

[21] Emblematic for the 'international' scope of the Roman elites is the (re)institution of the Hadrianic panhellenion in the Greek East, in general see Spawforth and Walker (1985).

was strictly connected to an emotional tension of equal intensity: ἀνὴρ φιλοθεάμων ὢν καὶ φιλομαθής.

There is also another singular element in the plot of the same dialogue. This is the explicit reference to the famous *leschē* of the Cnidians as a meeting point inside the Delphic sanctuary where animated discussions between sages and their students were held. This information about the active function of a much older building that was still used in its ancient role shows that at the time of Plutarch such a monument clearly maintained the legibility of its original functions. That the clubhouse of the Cnidians continued to maintain a historic-artistic value of great importance is demonstrated by Pausanias who, during his visit to the Delphic sanctuary, dwells at length on this monument.[22] Certainly both for Plutarch and for Pausanias the connotations that the clubhouse of the Cnidians evoked were still strong in the high imperial period. In addition to this connection between a sacred space and a form of social communication, Plutarch provides further information:

On many occasions when the subject had been brought up in the school I had quietly turned aside from it and passed it over, but recently I was unexpectedly discovered by my sons in an animated discussion with some strangers, whom, since they proposed to leave Delphi immediately, it was not seemly to try to divert from the subject, nor was it seemly for me to ask to be excused from discussion, for they were altogether eager to hear something about it. I found them seats, therefore, near the temple, and I began to seek some answers myself and to put questions to them; influenced as I was by the place and the conversation itself, I remembered what, when Nero was here some years ago, I had heard Ammonius and others discussing, when the same question obtruded itself in a similar way.

(Plut. *De E apud Delphos*, 385b)

This dialogue features a discussion of the mysterious meaning of the sacred symbol, the E. A group of interested youths and the circle of learned 'friends' of Plutarch participate in the discussion. In contrast to the precise location of the *De Defectu Oraculorum* inside a building, the

---

[22] Paus. 10.25.1–31, 12; LSJ 1040 s.v. λέσχη. Assembling many literary and archaeological sources: Nafissi (1991), 318–27; 331–41; Galli (2001), for the existence of such architectural spaces as meeting-places of *thiasoi* in famous Greek sanctuaries, as Epidauros and Eleusis.

dialogue about the E of Delphi takes place on the steps of a temple in a less formal setting. This location is no less relevant for the relationship or role—much discussed in this text—of memory in the interaction of sacred place (mental and actual) and emotional involvement. As parallels to the situations described by Plutarch, one might consider a short note concerning a similar occasion of collective pilgrimage at Delphi under the guidance of an influential intellectual, recorded by Aulus Gellius.[23]

> When the philosopher Taurus was on his way to Delphi, to see the Pythian games and the throng that gathered there from almost all Greece, I was his companion. And when, in the course of the journey, we had come to Lebadia, which is an ancient town in the land of Boeotia, word was brought to Taurus there that a friend of his, an eminent philosopher of the Stoic sect, had been seized with illness and had taken to his bed.
>
> (Aulus Gellius 12.5.1)

The trip was taken by the author himself under the guidance of the philosopher Calvenus Taurus, one of the most prominent Middle-Platonists of the reign of Antoninus Pius and the teacher of Gellius and Herodes Atticus. One may conjecture from Gellius' portrait that the 'visit' to the supreme Platonic site, seat of Apollo, was an obligatory stop on the spiritual route. Dörrie pointed out that philosophical *paideia*, in the form of Pythagorean wisdom, was acquired under harsh conditions of asceticism.[24] Such widsom was not a matter of antiquarianism but of the formation of an elite caste of initiates. This characteristic remains a topos for the philosophical elite of later periods. Directly comparable with the cases raised by Plutarch and Gellius, is the activity of another holy man, Apollonius of Tyana.[25] To summarize the intense interest and social impact of Apollonius, at least as he is constructed by Philostratus, consider:

---

[23] According to the author himself, who is considering the entire experience of the 'Attic Nights' as a *subsidium memoriae* (*Praef.* 2), the work of Aulus Gellius has to be interpreted as a mental journey in the memory of Greek culture. On the philosopher Taurus see the study of Dörrie (1976).

[24] Ibid.

[25] On Philostratus' account see Anderson (1986), and esp. on holy men, Anderson (1994).

And when he visited these temples and corrected the rites, the priests went in his company, and the votaries followed in his steps, and goblets were set up flowing with rational discourse and the thirsty quaffed their wine.

(Phil. *VA* 4.24)

The conversations which Apollonious held in Olympia turned upon the most profitable topics, such as wisdom and courage and temperance, and in a word upon all the virtues. He discussed these from the platform of the temple, and he astonished everyone not only by insight he showed but by his forms of expression.

(Phil. *VA* 4.31)

A strong relationship between the pietas of the *pepaideumenos* and an ideal or effective restoration of a religious memory is clearly affirmed by Philostratus.

And I have gathered my information partly from the many cities where he was loved, and partly from the temples whose long-neglected and decayed rites he restored, and partly from the accounts left of him by others and partly from his own letters.

(Phil. *VA* 1.2)

These examples bear witness to how particular forms of educated pilgrimage were constructed in the literary record as important occasions for *pepaideumenoi* and their followers to display elite status and make 'cultural capital'.[26]

'ALL SACRED THINGS MUST HAVE THEIR PLACE'

The richest source for the multiple aspects of sacred experience in the Antonine period are the recollections contained in the *Sacred Tales* of Aelius Aristides.[27] They attest to a complete spiritual cycle in the sacred

---

[26] Regarding the definition of 'cultural capital' of the French sociologist P. Bordieu see the considerations of Gleason (1995), xxi. About the euergetistic involvement of famous Antonine *pepaideumenoi* in the Greek sanctuaries see Galli, (2001); concerning the tight connection between euergetistic *habitus* and reconfiguration of religious memory in general: Bendlin (1997), 55.

[27] On emotional involvement see Sfameni Gasparro (1998); see also Rutherford (1999), Petsalis-Diomidis, Ch. 7 in this vol.

context of the sanctuary of Asclepius at Pergamon. These actions could not have possibly been imagined as separate from a particular and specific scenic background (Figure 2).[28] They do not constitute normal behaviour—'ordinary' acts in which attitude and behaviour are expressed directly—but rather ritualized acts. It must be stressed that Aristides' rituals are emphasized for their public resonance before an audience. They show in what way the embellished performance of pilgrimage guaranteed social communication. They also permit the analysis of how various moments of the ritual action were articulated in precise dramatic sequence.

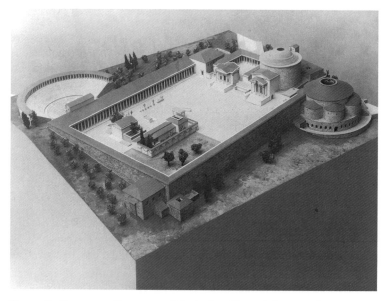

Figure 2. Pergamon, Sanctuary of Asclepius, Plan of the second century CE (DAI Istanbul, Neg. Nr. Pergamon Repro 83/3–2)

[28] Lévi-Strauss (1962) quoted by Smith (1987), 24 ff. who is pointing out the strong relationship between the sacred place and the location of ritual context. About the sanctuary of Pergamon see the most recent contribution of Alexia Petsalidis and Galli (2001).

The Arrival and Entrance of the Pilgrim
to the Sanctuary

Arrival at the sanctuary and the access to it had strong sacred connotations.[29] How this performative sequence is emphasized in a wider
context of ritual patterns can be seen in the following passage.

On the second, I dreamed that I was in the Temple of Asclepius at dawn, having
come straight from some journey, and was glad because it had been opened
early. I dreamed also that the boys sang the old song, which begins.

> 'I celebrate Zeus, the highest of all'

and were singing the following part of the song:

> 'By far, by far the essence of life for me.
> Is to sing of the gods and in joy
> To soothe my heart under such a teacher.'

> (Behr 1.30)

The revelation of the sacred space, as the pilgrim enters it, is here
imaginatively underscored by the collective ceremony of the choral
song that accompanies the pilgrim's entrance.[30] In addition, the action
occurs at the suggestive moment of dawn. In another dream, a similar
situation of approach and entrance to a sacred point is described more
fully. Aristides is at Smyrna and does not pass up the occasion to 'visit'
the temple of his divine protector there.

On the twenty-second, I dreamed that, as it were, in Smyrna, I went at
evening to the Temple of Asclepius, which is in the Gymnasium. And I went
with Zeno. And the Temple was larger and covered as much of the portico
as was paved. At the same time, I also pondered about this, as it were, about
a vestibule. And while I prayed and called upon the God, Zeno said, 'Nothing
is more gentle.'

> (Behr 1.17)

The dreamlike structure of the story permits a deliberate visual deform-
ation that emphasizes the orator's personal involvement in approaching
the divinity's house. Aristides writes: 'At the same time, I also pondered

---

[29] Other examples collected Lane-Fox (1986).
[30] On the choral prose of Aelius Aristides see Russell (1990).

about this, as it were, about a vestibule.' Given its strong emotional content, this dream-like experience is related to the type of perception that Pausanias demonstrated in front of the Athenian Propylaion. The brief report of the pilgrimage to the Asklepieion of Smyrna is yet more significant for how it communicates the mental reconstruction of a single ritual gesture. The perception notably marked by the pronaos functions to evoke another thought:

And he himself addressed the God and named him a refuge and such things. I noticed, as if in the vestibule, a statue of me. At one time I saw it, as if it were of me, and again it seemed to be a great and fair statue of Asclepius. And I recounted to Zeno himself these things which appeared to me in my dream. The part about the statue seemed to be very honorable.

(Behr 1.17)

This new situation corresponds apparently to the strong desire to insert and fix in the imagined context a precise visual sign, in this case a statue representing the orator, from his own individual experience; naturally the whole situation is elaborated publicly, becoming an object of communal discussion. The episode of the Asklepieion at Smyrna offers evidence that clarifies the ties between the mental reconstruction of an individual experience and the collective framework of communication which shaped the religious experience of the pilgrims' performance.

An explicit reference to the rites that occurred inside the monumental entry to the sanctuary creates a correspondence between literary tradition and archaeological evidence. This 'rite of passage' connected with the arrival and the stepping over the threshold of the sacred place by the pilgrim is well described in an often neglected passage of the *Sacred Tales* relating to Pergamon.

I dreamed that I stood at the propylaea of the Temple. And many others were also gathered together, as whenever there is a purificatory ceremony, and they wore white garments, and the rest was of an appropriate form. Here I cried out other things to the God and called him 'the arbiter of the fate', since he assigned men their fates. And my words began with my own circumstances. And after this there was wormwood, made clear in some way. It was made clear as possible, just as countless other things clearly contained the presence of the God.

(Behr 2.31)

In this case the monument described—belonging to the architectural project financed by the Pergamene *pepaideumenos* Claudius Charax—is significant (Figure 3).[31] From Aristides' account the strong symbolic value of the euergetism of Claudius Charax emerges. The pilgrims dressed in white and intent on participating in the sacred ceremony of purification designate the site as not only a simple place of entrance but a sort of pre-sanctuary area. This architectural project of the Propylaia was a product of a complete reordering of the sanctuary of Pergamon in the Antonine period. The structure with its rectangular plan featuring a series of colonnaded porticoes that surround a central open-air court-yard functions in accordance with the dynamics of the described rites.

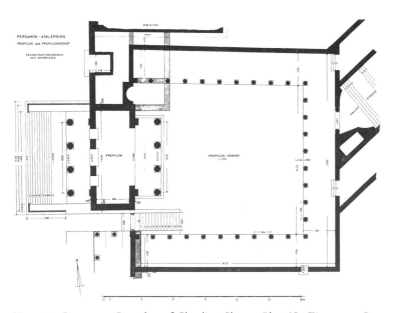

Figure 3. Pergamon, Propylon of Claudius Charax, Plan (O. Ziegenaus, *Das Asklepieion, 3. Die Kultbauten aus römischer Zeit an der Ostseite des heiligen Bezirks*. Altertumer von Pergamon 11, 3 (1981) pl. 5)

---

[31] Andrei (1984); for the Asclepieion of Pergamon as a 'centre of the spiritual life' during the Antonine age in general see Habicht (1969), 16 ff. On the Asclepieia and the structure of their ritual and monumental space see Graf (1992).

Regulating the path of the pilgrims from the *via sacra* to the true monumental entrance, this area takes on the function of preparing the pilgrims for the ensuing holiness of the place.

Some Acts of Individual and Collective Ritual Praxis

Other passages allow us to consider the gestures and the liturgies that marked the rituals undertaken by a cultivated pilgrim once he had reached the sacred space. Once again due to the dreamlike dimension of the account, certain images recorded by Aristides have significant documentary value.

Therefore I marvelled that the song appeared spontaneously. Again since my birthday was approaching, I sent servants to the Temple conveying certain offerings, and I also wrote down inscriptions on that which they conveyed. And I used artifice for a good token, so that my speaking might succeed in all that was necessary.

On the third, the lamps appeared to be brought into the temple by the porters in accordance with a prayer on my behalf, and it was necessary to vomit. I vomited.

(Behr 1.31 and 32)

Here Aristides dramatizes some of the symbolic acts in the Asklepieion; the desire to leave or install visible and durable proof of one's presence, that would testify that one had been there and carried out the ritual.[32] A significant body of documentation consists of poetic dedications associated with votive objects. The whole mechanism of votive rituals is described in an even more detailed manner. Take the following episode:

And I also gave public choral performances, ten in all, some of boys and some of men, and the following took place, when I was going to bring on the first chorus. (. . .)

---

[32] Pointing out the tight connection between strategy of power and epigraphic *habitus* of the Roman elites Beard (1991), esp. p. 57 argus that 'Writing, or the capacity of writing to preserve the redundant, could allow obscurantism to flourish—and, with it, the sense of an exclusive elite group privy to the arcane secrets of religion. Writing is necessarily connected with power. At the same time as it opens up new intellectual possibilities, new ways of representing human (in our case religious) experience, it raises the problem of closure and control: who has the right to determine or interpret those written representations'.

Again after the completion of the tenth performance, in which I happened to have omitted some song, because it was written entirely impromptu, with little thought, and, as they say, 'almost only for itself', a dream came, which demanded this too, and we also offered it. When these things were accomplished, it seemed fitting to dedicate a silver tripod, as a thank-offering to the god, and at the same time as a memorial of the choral performances which we gave. And I prepared the following elegiac couplet:

> The poet, judge, and backer all in one,
> Has dedicated to you, O King, this monument of his choral
>   performance.

Then after this were two other verses, one of which contained my name, and the other that these things occured under the patronage of the god. But the god's version prevailed. For on the day, I believe, on which it was necessary to make the dedication, or a little before it, around dawn, or even still sooner, a divinely inspired inscription came to me, which ran as follows:

> Not unknown to the Greeks, Aristides dedicated this,
> The glorious charioteer of everlasting words.

And I dreamed that I had this inscribed and that I was going to make the dedication, as it were, to Zeus.(...)

After this, when we took counsel in common about the dedication, it seemed best to us, the priest and the temple wardens, to dedicate it in the Temple of Zeus Asclepius, for there was no fairer place than this. And so the prophecy of the dream turned out. And the tripod is under the right hand of the god, and it has three golden statues, one on each foot, of Asclepius, of Hygieia, and of Telesphorus. And the inscription is inscribed, and it has been added that it is from dream. I also dedicated to Olympian Zeus the inscription and another dedication, so that the oracle was in every way fulfilled.

(Behr 4.43–6)

This full narrative section describes a detailed ritual session. A chain of different dramatic actions appears clearly:

1. ritual act (institution and organization of choral performances)
2. dedication of a votive silver tripod
3. composition and placement of a poetic text
4. the public resonance of and collective participation in the ritual action
5. the choice of a public location in which to display the votive.

What is important here is not so much the object or the ritual action in itself, but the individual and collective involvement and simultaneously the desire of the dedicator to leave a sign of his presence. The performance of the choruses and the sumptuous dedication of the silver tripod inside the Asklepieion at Pergamon exemplify the numerous links between the personal experience of an individual and his public behaviour. This complex framework of ritual actions which show the individual participation of Aristides as pilgrim–observer–archivist is always marked by a high level of emotional involvement.

I immediately held fast to the inscriptions, as I rejoice in my sleep and while I was still waking. And I practiced it and studied, that it might not slip my mind. And so I mastered it.

(Behr 4.45)

(...) When the inscription was made, I became much more eager, and it seemed in every way to be fitting to hold rhetoric, as our name would live even among future man since the God had called my speeches 'everlasting'. And so it happened in the matter of the Choral performances.

(Behr 4.47–8)

Aelius Aristides himself expresses an awareness of an emotional participation little short of exultation that fixes the religious experience in his personal memory. Mental processes, emotional reactions, and memory are intensely linked here.

As in the comparison of Freud and Pausanias at the Athenian Acropolis, a more detailed analysis of the pilgrimages made by Aristides to sacred sites demonstrates how sacred travel was interiorized as journey to a mental site. One may note that it is memory itself which is consciously presented by the author as a determining factor in his entire experience. The link between the memory process and a series of emotional reactions becomes the play of consciousness in the *pepaideumenos* pilgrim:

Come let us also recall earlier events, if we are able. From the first it did not occur to me to write anything about these, because I did not believe that I would survive. Next my body was also in such a state that it did not give me leisure for these things. And again as time passed, it seemed to be an impossibility to remember each thing and to tell it precisely. Therefore I thought that it was better to keep completely silent than to spoil such great deeds.

(Behr 2.1)

Where should one begin, when there are so many different things and at the same time, when all are not remembered, only the gratitude because of them?

(Behr 2.11)

These examples from the *Sacred Tales* illustrate a process of *anamnesis* of the numerous pilgrimages undertaken—a kind of mental recapitulation that might serve as a repetition of actual pilgrimage in the mind. Yet again, such an experience is only seemingly isolated and individual. In reality the need to produce written documentation of interior experience springs from a need to present the pilgrimage process publicly as a collective reflection.

And for these reasons I made many excuses both to the god and to my friends, who were ever asking me to speak and write about these things. Now so many years afterwards, dream visions compel us to bring these things to light. Still I can say this much that straight from the beginning the god ordered me to write down my dreams. And this was the first of his commands. I made a copy of my dreams, dictating them, whenever I was unable to write myself. However I did not add in what circumstances each took place nor what resulted after them.

(Behr 2.1–2)

The individual experience of the pilgrim–observer–archivist and the relationship with a common social *habitus* belonging to the cultured class of the Second Sophistic, is not exclusive to the *Sacred Tales*. Other certainly less elaborate but equally significant documents show comparable patterns. I will compare two examples of extreme psychological reactions by educated pilgrims.

HOMO VIATOR: THE PILGRIMAGES OF AELIUS ARISTIDES AND MARCUS APELLAS

The concept of *homo viator*, the traveller on his journey, is fundamental to early Christian and medieval thought.[33] It conjures up an image of a man on a journey through terrestrial life as an exile, estranged from the world, headed towards the final destination of a heavenly home. The oscillation between the two dimensions, the human and the divine, is

---

[33] Ladner (1967).

particular to the post-classical conception of the pilgrim: 'man is a wayfarer. He is a wanderer between two worlds, but in more than one sense. He may have around himself an aura of divine being like the long-suffering godlike Ulysses or Plato's Eleatic Stranger or Prospero, Shakespeare's exiled island prince.'[34] The social dynamics that determine the medieval conception of the *homo viator* are foreign to classical antiquity, as we have seen it so far in this article. Two important aspects are absent in antiquity. First, the idea of alienation from life on earth as an ascetic response to the human condition; and second, the pervasive down-playing of the value of human existence by contrast with a future heaven.

Nonetheless, there are some similarities—which may well imply the generation of a post-classical pilgrimage ideal in pre-Christian pagan practices during the Second Sophistic.[35] The individual condition of mystic alienation on pilgrimage, an aspect particular to the medieval definition of *homo viator*, is already present as a catalysing factor in the pilgrimage experience of the second century CE. This justifies the application of the *viator* concept to the interpretation of certain aspects of pagan pilgrimage in the high imperial period. Two different reports of the spiritual fervour of pre-Christian pilgrimage experience bear witness to how the wayfaring *habitus* of the educated took on the form of a strong emotional involvement.

Aelius Aristides' experience at the sanctuary of Asclepius at the springs of the Aesepus (in the beginning of the fourth *Sacred Tale*) significantly documents how the pilgrimage trip becomes a process of mystical purification (Figure 4). The motivation for the trip is consciously expressed as the need to return to the roots of the author's interior and physical sickness. The awareness of having to close an eternal cycle, that is, to end a sickness where it had been conceived, transforms the real journey into spiritual and mental one, as well as recapitulating the memory of the disease. We could almost say that the journey to the springs of the Aesepus turns into an *itinerarium mentis in Deum* of the pagan religious experience of the Antonine period.

At the beginning of the tenth year of my illness, a vision came and said the following: 'Sick with the same disease, at the start of the tenth year, by the will

---

[34] Ladner (1967), 233.
[35] See Introd. to Elsner and Rubies (1999).

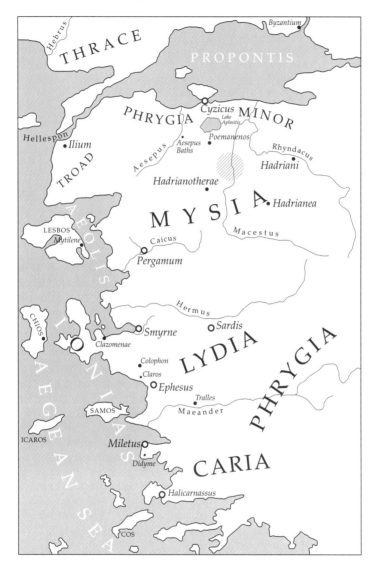

Figure 4. Mysia, Pilgrimage of Aelius Aristides from his Laneion estate (the shaded circle) to the rural sanctuary of Asclepius and to the springs of the Aesepus (by courtesy of D. Dinelli)

of Asclepius, I went to the places where the disease began, and was rid of it.'
Such was what was said, and it seemed to have been written. Then too we were
staying at the temple of the Olympian Zeus. It was winter, a little after the
solstice, but the air was gentle. When these oracles were given, I was, as is likely,
joyful and wonderfully eager to depart. The Aesepus and the warm springs near
it are a two days journey from the region of the Temple. (. . .)

Then we set out, in high spirits, as on a pilgrimage. The weather was
marvelous, and the road inviting. (3) Poemanenos is a place in Mysia, and in
it is a sacred and famous temple of Asclepius. Here we completed about one
hundred and sixty stades, and nearly sixty of these at night, as we started when
the day was advanced, and about this place we also met with some mud from
earlier rains, which was not easy to cross. The journey was made by torch light.
(4) Here I was completely consecrated, as it were, and possessed. And I
composed many lyrics to the Savoir himself, while I was sitting in the carriage,
and many to the Aesepus, the Nymphs, and Artemis Thermaea, who keeps the
warm springs, to free me from all my troubles and to return me to my original
state.

(5) When I reached Poemanenos, the god gave me oracles and kept me there
for some days, and he purged my upper intestinal tract and that nearly once and
for all. And a farmer, who did not know me, except my reputation, had a
dream. He dreamed that someone said to him that Aristides had vomited up the
head of a viper. Having seen this vision, he told one of my people and he told
me. So much for this.

(6) When the god sent me to the Aesepus, he ordered me to abstain from the
baths there, but he prescribed my other regimen every day. And here there were
purifications at the river by libation, and purgations at home through vomiting.
And when three or four days had passed, there was a voice in a dream saying
that it was over and it was necessary to return. It was all not only like an
initiation into a mystery, since the rituals were so divine and strange, but there
was also coincidentally something marvelous and unaccustomed. For at the
same time there was gladness, and joy, and a contentment of spirit and body,
and again, as it were, an incredulity if it will ever be possible to see the day when
one will see himself free from such great trouble, and in addition, a fear that
some one of the usual things will again befall and harm one's hopes about the
whole. Thus was my state of mind, and my return took place with such
happiness and at the same time anguish.

(Behr 4.1–7)

The usual oscillation in the *Sacred Tales* between the different layers in
the account—the dream-like aspect, memory, and direct narrative—
creates a characteristic tension. The *peregrinatio* that Aristides is about to

undertake is explicitly defined as *theōria*, the semantic value of which (to see and be seen) refers in principle to a collective ritual, but is here used by Aristides to designate a personal mystical purification. The mysterious elements and initiations of the *peregrinatio* are consciously emphasized. The decisive divine consecration occurs during a nocturnal journey lit by torches. Writing that he composes religious poetry in honour of the god 'while I was sitting in the carriage', Aristides evokes the 'in-between' initiate space of a rite-of-passage *in itinere* to the realm of the deity. Such liturgical activity that we can define as *in itinere* becomes a symbol of this sought-after alienation and entrance into the realm of the deity itself. In this case, what is presented is not, as is often said, an exaggerated spirituality on the part of the author, but rather a textual attempt to recreate a complete physical and spiritual involvement in the sacred sphere.

This description of a traveller on a mystical journey, his complete fixation on the divinity, the account of the complex and detailed series of curative prescriptions, the ritual acts, and the final healing that marks the conclusion of the mystical purification do not represent an isolated or unique instance of a tormented hypochondriac in the Second Sophistic. There are parallels and it is worth examining less well-known but similar evidence. For example, an important epigraphic document of the second century CE reports the stages of a pilgrimage to Epidauros:

I, Marcus Iulius Apellas, from Idrias (a suburb of Mylasa), was summoned by the god, for I was often falling into illnesses and suffering from indigestion. During my journey by boat he told me, in Aegina, not to be so irritable all the time.

When I entered the sanctuary he told me to keep my head covered for two days; it was raining during this time. (He also told me) to eat bread and cheese and celery with lettuce, to bathe without any assistance, to run for exercise, to take lemon rind and soak it in water, to rub myself against the wall near the 'Place Where Supernatural Voices Are Heard', to go for a walk on the 'Upper Portico', to swing on a swing [or, to engage in passive exercise?], to smear myself with mud, to walk barefoot, to pour wine all over myself before climbing into the hot pool in the bathing establishment, to bathe all alone, to give an Attic drachma to the attendant, to offer a joint sacrifice to Asclepius, Epione, and the goddesses of Eleusis, and to drink milk with honey.

One day when I drank only milk, the god said: 'Put honey in your milk, so it can strike through' [or, have the right effect, i.e., act as a laxative]. When I urged the god to heal me more quickly, I had a vision: I was walking out of the sanctuary toward the 'Place Where Supernatural Voices Are Heard', rubbed with salt and mustard all over, and a little boy was leading me, and the priest said to me: 'You are cured; now you pay the fee.'

I did what I had seen [i.e., acted out my vision]. When they rubbed me with salt and liquid mustard, it hurt, but after I had taken a bath, it hurt no longer. All this happened within nine days after my arrival. The god touched my left hand and my breast. On the following day, as I was offering a sacrifice, the flame leapt up and burned my hand so that blisters appeared. After a while my hand healed. I stayed on, and the god told me to use anise with olive oil for my headache. Actually, I had no headache.

But after I had done some studying it happened that I suffered from congestion of brain. Taking olive oil, I got rid of my headache. [I was also told] to gargle with cold water for my swollen uvula—for I had asked the god for help with this problem, too—and the same for the tonsils. The god also told me to write all this down. I left, feeling grateful and restored to health.

$$(IG\ 4.955\ (=SIG^3\ 1170))$$

Georg Luck has emphasized the importance of this document of the second century CE, which was found in the sanctuary of Asclepius at Epidauros: 'the Apellas inscription is remarkable because it shows that this particular patient was almost constantly in touch with the god Asclepius.'[36] A comparison with Aelius Aristides is enlightening. Present in the text from Epidauros, as in Aristides, are the various stages of pilgrimage that lead Apellas from his home-city to the centre of Asclepian sanctity where he will remain, as he himself affirms, for nine days. The process of the whole ritual sequence is articulated in distinct phases.

1. The affirmation of the sickness and the summons by the divinity; thus, a relationship is immediately formed with the god.

2. A series of significant intermediate steps: the stop-over at Aegina may indicate particpation in the mysteries celebrated on the island into the Roman period.

3. Arrival at the sanctuary.

4. Minute details of the performative acts (better testimony in fact than in the *Sacred Tales*). These include requirements, rules, and taboos concerning diet (both solid and liquid foods) for pilgrims to Epi-

---

[36] Luck (1985), 146.

dauros, and the usual obligation to participate in collective ritual (sacrifice).

The concern with bodily gestures and expression particularly stands out. Apellas notes clothing accessories (the covered head) and frequent washing in water, which may be connected to rites of sacrifice and purification. Finally he lists ritual actions of movement—running, walking (even barefoot), swaying, and rubbing against a wall—as well as non-verbal bodily expressions and the use of foreign substances, for example, covering oneself in dust and mud, pouring wine on oneself, and spreading salt and mustard over the body. Whereas these formulas could be explained as purely curative, this would reductively exclude their visual and olfactory significance as showing the purification process in action. Even if it lacks the literary quality of Aristides' writings—the sophist himself notes the difficulty of his literary undertaking more than once—the account of the pilgrim Apellas articulates a complex framework of Asclepian pilgrimage that incorporates vision, a dreamlike aspect, and immediate or direct reporting. The element that dominates the story, just as in Aristides' tale of the springs of Aesepus, is the concentration on the divinity.

Apellas, like Aelius Aristides, is an example of an educated *homo viator*, and his experience a further instance of pilgrimage *habitus* as a form of mystical alienation. The relative brevity of the epigraphic form used bears witness, in the most durable form possible, to the phases of purification (both spiritual and corporeal) that Apellas underwent. As for Aristides, so for Apellas, sickness becomes only an exterior sign of a much more complex emotional involvement on the part of the individual. The full text of the Apellas inscription is carried on a marble stele crowned with a small tympanum. Particular care is given to the layout of the text (Figure 5) and the object is likely to have been exhibited in a visible location inside the sanctuary.

EDUCATED PILGRIMS IN THE
SACRED RURAL LANDSCAPE

My account of the sacred wayfaring *habitus* of the educated elite of the high imperial period results from an attempt to understand and connect the internal states of a sacred experience, as well as the individual and

Figure 5. Epidauros, Stele (IG IV 955) of Marcus Iulius Apellas in the sanctuary of Asclepius (Th. Papadakis, *Epidauros. Das Heiliglum des Asklepios*, Athens, 1971, fig. 23)

collective reactions to the sacred environment, as a series of complex and intriguing interactions with social dynamics. I have for the most part neglected individual parts of the sacred space that framed the actual reactions of viewers to real landscapes, often ignoring their topographical and archeological details. I have discussed above all the configuration of the landscape in its generic values, that are more or less marked by the presence of monuments. One of the most original aspects of the pilgrimage phenomenon of the Second Sophistic is the reconstruction and reactivation of the sacred rural landscape. In addition to the large panhellenic sanctuary complexes, cultivated *euergetai* also chose small rural centres, outside the major pilgrimage itineraries.

In understanding the particular forms of pilgrimage discussed here, the direct participation of imperial authority may be said to sanction their symbolic value. The ascent of *montes divini* may help in throwing light on this issue.[37] In the *Historia Augusta*, the emperor Hadrian, who is an exceptional protagonist of *peregrinationes ad loca sancta,* is reported to have climbed Etna, probably around 125 CE:

Afterwards he sailed to Sicily, and there he climbed Mount Etna to see the sunrise, which is many hued, they say, like the rainbow.

(SHA *Hadr.* 13.3)

Mount Etna is particularly interesting both because it is a volcano and because it was studied in regard to natural phenomena connected to the sun. Hadrian's famous *curiositas* (Tert. *Apol.* 5, 7: *omnium curiositatum explorator*) was not probably limited to Mount Etna as a source of *thaumasia* and *paradoxa* by means of natural phenomena. Mountains were worshipped as divinities and could host different cults, not only in Asia Minor but also in ancient Italy. In the specific case of Etna, as Ferguson has pointed out, Hadrian's climb goes beyond scientific curiosity to a religious dimension (perhaps connected with the cult of Zeus).[38] The literary context in which the Etna episode occurs reinforces its religious point, immediately after the report of the emperor's panhellenic initiation at Eleusis and after the mention of

[37] The *peregrinatio* of Hadrian to Mount Casius was recently analysed with different perspectives by Biffi (1995); on *montes divini* it is still useful to see Lenormant (1887), more recently Bernandi (1985).

[38] Ferguson (1970), 50. See further Petsalis-Diomidis, Ch. 7 in this vol.

Hadrian's participation in sacrifice dressed in the clothing of an ordinary private citizen.[39]

During Hadrian's long journey between 129 and 130 in the eastern provinces, he stopped at Antioch on the Orontes, where we are informed of his second ascent of a divine mountain:

As he was sacrificing on Mount Kasios, which he had ascended in order to see the sunrise, a storm arose, and a flash of lightning descended and struck both the victim and the attendant.

(SHA *Hadr.* 14.1–3)

The religious activity performed by the famous pilgrim is tightly connected, according to the account, with a vision of a natural phenomenon (*cum videndi solis ortus... sacrificanti*) after he had reached the top of the mountain. The custom of imperial pilgrimage to *montes divini* is not to a restricted monumental space nor does it partake of a liturgical apparatus with a complex ritual sequence for the accomplishment of the pilgrimage. It rather involves natural phenomena. Second, the participation and religious experience of this kind of imperial pilgrimage to natural divinity was highly exclusive. We may imagine that what made this type of religious experience extraordinary was the participation of few officiants and the following of a faithful circle of friends.[40]

On what one might call an imperial model, cultivated pilgrims, like Aelius Aristides and Herodes Atticus were led back to the traditional sacred landscape. In the *Sacred Tales*, Aelius Aristides often emphasizes that his private sphere is characterized by a close connection to the surrounding area of sacred rural spaces. His Laneion estate, the property of his father, is his preferred place of leisure and is similarly a place of familiar traditions. It is often spoken of as the πατρῴια ἑστία or πατρῴια οἰκία.[41] It was topographically close to neighbouring cult areas (Figure 4). A temenos and temple of Asklepius lay directly in

---

[39] SHA 13.2: 'After this he sailed along the coast of Asia and past the islands to Achai, and undertook the Eleusinian rites, following the example of Hercules and Philip; he conferred many benefits on the Athenians and took his seats as president of the games. During this stay in Achaia, care was taken, they say, that when Hadrian was present none should come to a sacrifice armed, whereas generally many used to carry knives. Afterwards he sailed to Sicily.'

[40] On the cult of Zeus Kasios see Koch (1993).

[41] Behr 1.43; 3.13, 16, 20; 4.28, 49; 5.10.

front of his paternal house,[42] as did a rural sanctuary of Olympian Zeus.[43] The outlying territory, thus, constituted a background against which he developed his personal religious tendencies. The sacred areas in the vicinity formed a framework that allowed Aelius Aristides to express his religious interests.

For on about the sixth or seventh day before the earthquakes began, he ordered me to send to the old hearth, which is at the Temple of Oympian Zeus, and make a sacrifice, and to establish altars on the crest of the hill of Atys. And these things were just finished, when the earthquake came and so ravaged all the other land in between that not an inn was left standing, except some small ruin. But it did not proceed up the Atys, nor to our Laneion Estate at the south of the Atys, except only to perceive it, and ravaged nothing beyond.[44]

(Behr 3.41–2)

L. Robert profitably compared topographic and epigraphic research in northern Mysia with the evidence from the literary picture given by Aelius Aristides.[45] North of Hadrianoutherai and 80 km south of Kyzikos is the country estate Laneion (see Figure 4); north of this is the hill of Atys and not far off is the sanctuary of Zeus. Robert was able to document evidence of the *pietas* of Aelius still in situ on the hill in the area of 'Asar Kale'. The inscription corresponds to a similar text on an altar which Robert found in the neighbouring village Omer Köy Fand.[46] Both inscriptions read:

Δίκηι	(κ)αὶ Σαράπι–
καὶ Νεμέσει	δι
Ἀριστείδης	Ἀριστείδης

The literary wording is in keeping with the unpretentious style of some orators and sophists of this period.[47] The first example shows a great attention to the accurate execution of the lettering.[48] The manifestations of rural religion do not appear to be confined simply to familiar environs. In addition to these and other scattered traces[49]

---

[42] 4.49.   [43] 4.48, 1–2, 21, 71, 105; 3.41.   [44] 3.41–2.

[45] Robert (1937).   [46] Robert (1937), 216–20.

[47] Jones (1978), 232; on the literary production of the Second Sophistic see Bowie (1989), esp. p. 235 regarding the 'clean simplicity' of Herodes Atticus.

[48] Robert (1937), pl. 13, nos. 2 and 4.

[49] Robert (1937), p. 211 dedication of a statue of Hera, p. 212 an altar for Zeus, p. 214 a fragment of another dedication.

from his estate, there is the further evidence of other inscriptions of similar content and formulated in Sophistic style which the sophist left behind at sites he had visited as evidence that he had been there.[50] The different stops of his learned pilgrimages were sanctioned with respective dedications commemorating religious acts.[51] As a pilgrim in Attica, Aelius Aristides erected another altar. This time the typically laconic text is dedicated to the triad of Asklepius, Hygieia, and Telesphoros (Figure 6).[52]

$$[Ἀσκληπιῶι καὶ]$$
$$[Ὑγ(ι)είαι] κα[ὶ]$$
$$[Τελε]σφόρ[ωι]$$
$$[Ἀρι]στείδης$$
$$εὐ[ξ]άμενος$$

(Altar *IG* 2.2. 4531)

The find spot of the altar in the chapel of Profitis Ilias on Mount Pentelikon, not far from the well-known Penteli monastery, is remarkable (Figure 7).[53] Since the neighbouring area was rich in watersprings, the inscription of Aelius Aristides suggests that the cult statue on the Mount Pentelicon mentioned by Pausanias was located in this area.[54] The search for remote cult places for both dedications and ritual acts, as demonstrated by the dedication on the hill of Atys, implies that the choice of what might be called 'romantic' sacred areas in Attica played a special role for the *pepaideumenos*. Not only the choice of divinities to honour but also the particular selection of the natural spaces in which to honour them emphasize the exclusive character of these religious interests.

The religious experience of an educated pilgrim in the Second Sophistic so self-consciously demonstrated by Hadrian and Aelius Aristides can be compared to some offerings of Herodes Atticus in the

[50] See Jones (1978), 232 together with no. 64: dedication of an altar in honour of Asclepios in Mythiline.

[51] Elsner (1992) with literature, see esp. the right statement in regard to the typical behaviour of the donor-sophists: 'A religious tourist visiting sacred sites is *not* simply a tourist, he or she is also a pilgrim (...) Pausanian travel was as much about making contact with the sanctity embodied in a place as it was about tourism' (pp. 7–8).

[52] Jones (1978), 213 f.

[53] Find spot: Mersch (1996), 173 f. Travlos (1988), 329 f.

[54] Paus. 1.32.2.

Figure 6. Attica, Altar of Aelius Aristides with the dedication (*IG* II² 4531) to Asclepius, Hygieia, and Telesphoros (DAI Athens, Neg. Nr. Att. 142)

Figure 7. Attica, Penteli Monastery on Mount Pentelicus, Map (E. Curtius and J. A. Kaupert, *Karten von Attika*, Berlin, 1881–1903)

Attic landscape.[55] A unique example shows us the type of interaction that could exist between acts of eugertism completed by a sophist and pilgrimages to cult locales in the countryside. In the area of the ancient deme of Myrrhinous (Merenda)[56] in south-east Attica was located the following dedication of Herodes Atticus:[57] 'Herodes Attikos of Marathon rebuilt the temple and dedicated the statue to Athena.' In the dedication's concise formula are the two key points of the offering: the restorative act, that is to renew the substance and visual aspect of the cult (ἐπισκευάζειν),[58] and the religious act, that is the giving of the cult statue.[59] This piece of euergetism on the part of Atticus has many parallels in the rich documentation of this sophist's activity.[60]

SOME EXPERIMENTAL CONCLUSIONS: DYNAMICS AND CONFLICTS BETWEEN MENTAL IMAGES AND EMOTIONAL PERCEPTIONS

I have isolated cases where pilgrimage experience was subjected to two factors: mental models, preserved and kept in the memory, and the emotion of actual experience. The awareness that pilgrimage (sacred

[55] On sophistic activity in Attic territory see Tobin (1997), and Galli (2002).

[56] One should note the choice of the place. The rich archaeological documentation of this settlement runs from the geometric to the classical period; there is no evidence, in contrast, for activity in the Roman period (See the literature in Mersch (1996), 23, 153 ff). It is still possible that the cult site at Merenda, to which Alcock ascribes rural cults, had continuous meaning in the Roman period even though the settlement no longer existed (Alcock (1993), 200 ff.). Pausanias shows that there was cult activity practised there in the second century CE when he recounts in his excursus on Attic Demoi about the ancient Xoanon of Artemis Kolainis (Paus. 1.31.4–5: Beschi and Musti (1982) 385 f.).

[57] *IG* 22. 3191, base of a statue h. 0.834 m; b. 0.78 m; Eng. tr.: Tobin (1997), 280. First published by A. Milchhöfer, *AM* 12 (1897), 277; found in the chapel of the church of Panagia: precisely located by Mersch (1996), 153. Merenda is situated appr. 4 km east of Markopoulo: Mersch (1996), 23 esp. no. 139, about the excavations and archaeological finds pp. 153 ff; Travlos (1988), 365 fig. 465. About the local cults see *RE* (1935) 1146 s.v. Myrrhinus (Wrede).

[58] For the meaning as 'to restore' see LSJ 656 s.v.

[59] Anderson (1989), 140 ff. esp. p. 142: 'in such a climate building and restoration could be invested with new meaning (. . .) To practise restoration itself was to build oneself into the past'.

[60] On the donations of Herodes Atticus see Tobin (1997); Galli (2002).

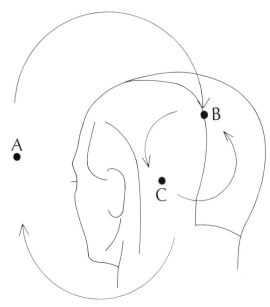

Figure 8. Dynamics between mental images and emotional perceptions (A = experience, B = emotions, C = memory) (courtesy of Martina Schwarz)

wayfaring) tradition was already codified and fixed in a long sequence of collective memory is clearly illustrated by the passage in Plutarch about the memory of the ancients (*De Pyth. or.* 27407f). In many ways the mental image of a sacred place becomes active only on account of its emotional connotations (see Figure 8). Examples are: Pausanias' experiences with the Propylaea and the group of the sons of Xenophon on the Acropolis of Athens; Plutarch's discussion of the statuary group of Lysander in the Delphic sanctuary; the 'Dedication of the silver Tripod' by Aelius Aristides, and his *peregrinatio* to the springs of the Aesepus, as well as the ascent of divine mountains and the devotional practices performed there by various educated pilgrims.

10

The Construction of
Religious Space in Pausanias

William Hutton

One barrier to the study of pilgrimage in ancient Greece has been the scarcity of first-hand accounts of pilgrimage in the preserved literature.[1] Recognition of this scarcity in recent years has brought fresh attention to the second-century CE author Pausanias. Pausanias is known today for a single surviving work, a ten-volume topographical account of the Greek mainland entitled *Periegesis Hellados* (*Description of Greece* or *Guide to Greece*). The *Periegesis* is a unique work, one that consists partly of topographically arranged descriptions of sites, buildings, monuments, and artworks, partly of historical and mythological accounts related to the places and objects he describes. For much of the twentieth century it was customary to view the *Periegesis* as a repository of useful information rather than a work worth studying for its own value. In the last few decades, however, that has begun to change.[2] The period in which Pausanias lived, the time of Hadrian and the Second Sophistic, is

---

[1] Cf. Dillon (1997), xvii.

[2] The recent re-evaluation of Pausanias begins with Habicht (1985) and Veyne (1988) 95–102; within the last decade the most important works include monographs: Bearzot (1992); Arafat (1996); Pritchett (1998 and 1999); collections of essays: Bingen (1996); Pirenne-Delforge (1998a); Alcock, Cherry, and Elsner (2001); Knoepfler and Piérart (2001); substantial sections of monographs: Elsner (1995), 125–55; Hartog (1996), 144–61; Swain (1996), 330–56; and a large number of separate articles. Among older scholarship, fundamental is Gurlitt (1890), upon whom the more accessible Frazer (1898) frequently depends. Regenbogen (1956) offers an excellent synopsis of many important issues, and also to be commended for her thoroughness is Heer (1979).

gaining recognition as one of the more dynamic eras in Greek history.[3] In spite of the fact that the Greek city-states had been subject to the Roman empire for several centuries and had been on a path of economic and demographic decline for at least as long, Greek culture was revered among the educated elite of the day from one end of the Mediterranean to the other.[4] This unusual combination of cultural predominance, physical decay, and political subjugation makes this period a complex and conflicted one for the Greeks. Pausanias presents a valuable perspective on Greek culture and Greek identity in this environment as well as on the contemporary material state of Greece's cities and shrines.

PAUSANIAS AS PILGRIM?

While Pausanias' testimony regarding Greece in the second century explains much of his modern appeal, his particular relevance to this volume and to the study of pilgrimage remains to be explained. For this one must recognize two characteristics of his work. First, the *Periegesis* is based substantially on the author's own travels.[5] Pausanias' descriptions of Greek landscapes are eyewitness descriptions (something that cannot be taken for granted in the case of ancient geographical and topographical authors), and he writes about the country as a visitor or immigrant rather than as a native. Though in terms of language and what we would call ethnicity he appears to be thoroughly Greek, his home lay not within the mainland territories he wrote about but in Asia Minor, probably Magnesia on Sipylos.[6] The second important charac-

---

[3] A far-from-exhaustive sample of recent work from the last decade or so, encompassing literary, historical, cultural, and archaeological studies: Spawforth and Walker (1985 and 1986); Cartledge and Spawforth (1989); Walker and Cameron (1989); Engels (1990); Willers (1990); Bowie (1991); Alcock (1993); Anderson (1993 and 1994); Brunt (1994); Woolf (1994); Gleason (1995); Jones (1996); Swain (1996); Schmitz (1997); Boatwright (2000); Goldhill (2001); Whitmarsh (2001).

[4] Alcock (1993), 24–32 argues convincingly that the extent of this decline is exaggerated for moralistic and literary purposes in our sources. Even an exaggerated decline is a decline, however; cf. the same author's later thoughts: Alcock (1997*b*).

[5] The unsupportable notion that Pausanias copied significant portions of his account from previous eyewitness reports can now safely be said to have been laid to rest. Cf. Habicht (1985), 165–75.

[6] Gurlitt (1890), 1.56–7; Frazer (1898), 1.xix–xx; Habicht (1985), 13–15; cf. Paus. 5.13.7 and 1.24.8 (e.g.). Elsner (1995), 129, 131, 154, cites as a critical distinction

teristic to note is that Pausanias' travels seem to be motivated in part by genuine religious sensibilities. He is far more likely to include religious structures and artworks in his descriptions than items that are completely secular, and several times in the course of his account he records his own participation in religious cults and his observance of religious taboos.[7] To a certain extent his religiosity must be seen as part of a deliberate *mimesis* of credulous ancient models, chiefly Herodotus, but in the self-conscious and hyper-referential literature of the period, highly mannered and ironic expressions on the subject of religion are not necessarily incompatible with genuine piety,[8] and in some respects Pausanias' religious devotion seems to go beyond what is required for the presentation of a classicizing persona. Perhaps most tellingly, Pausanias forgoes a number of opportunities to describe interesting religious sites and practices when commanded not to do so by dreams.[9]

Elsner was the first to suggest that the conjunction of Pausanias' travels and his religious interests renders it profitable to consider him as a sort of pilgrim.[10] Given the aforementioned scarcity of pilgrimage accounts from ancient Greece, the identification of Pausanias as a pilgrim would open a new window on an element of Greek religion and culture that is poorly understood. Some scholars, however, have objected to this identification,[11] and it is true that any comparison of Pausanias' text to pilgrimage literature should begin with a number of caveats. For instance, while the *Periegesis* is based on the author's travels, it is not the record of a single, continuous journey. Though he makes some effort to obscure the fact, Pausanias' text is almost certainly

---

between Pausanias and other pilgrims the fact that Pausanias was travelling within his own homeland. This is an important observation, but one that is true only in a broad sense, since the places covered in his *Periegesis* were geographically, politically, and to some extent culturally distinct from the place he called home.

[7] Participation in cult: 2.30.4; 9.39.5–14, etc. Observation of prohibition: 1.37.4; 2.3.4; 2.17.4; 2.35.8; 2.37.6; 5.15.11; 8.37.9; 8.42.11; 9.25.5; For an analysis of Pausanias' religious attitudes, see Frazer (1898), 1.xxv–xxvii, li–lx; Heer (1979), 127–314. More recently, Lacroix (1992); Elsner (1995); Pritchett (1998), 61–363, and (1999), 223–320; Ekroth (1999); Hughes (1999); and several articles in Pirenne-Delforge (1998*a*).

[8] Cf. Elsner (2001*b*); Lightfoot (2003), 184–208.

[9] Most notoriously at the sanctuary of Demeter at Eleusis (1.38.7), but see also 1.14.3; 4.33.5. Cf. Elsner (1995), 145–52.

[10] Elsner (1992), 8 (= (1995), 130). Cf. Elsner (1994).

[11] Most notably Arafat (1996), 10; Swain (1996), 334.

a composite based on a number of different journeys made over the course of several years, if not decades.[12] If one speaks of Pausanias' travels as pilgrimage, therefore, one is speaking not of a unitary undertaking, but of several separate pilgrimages which Pausanias has amalgamated in the composition of his account.

In addition, if one looks to the *Periegesis* for a vivid reflection of a pilgrim's subjective experience, one is bound to be disappointed. In dealing with any aspect of Pausanias' mentality and inner life, one must confront the author's notorious reticence about himself. He tells us nothing about his family or his background, his profession or previous life (aside from some references to previous travels), little about the conditions of travel or the people he meets on his journeys.[13] While he sometimes offers his opinion on matters moral or historical, in general he hides the exertions and pains of his fieldwork behind an objectivizing persona of effortless authority.[14] To say almost anything about the effect that his travels and his religious experiences had on him we must resort to reading what he says about his activities and engaging our capacity for empathetic imagination to divine what his experiences would have meant to him. This procedure is naturally speculative.

Even more fundamentally, whether one views Pausanias as a pilgrim also depends on which of the many available definitions of 'pilgrim' and 'pilgrimage' one is using. If one adopts the strict Turnerian definition favoured by Scott Scullion (Ch. 4 in this volume), whereby the journey itself functions as a rite of passage and is at least as important to the traveller's spiritual experience as is his or her encounter with the shrine or monument at the journey's end, then it is difficult to see the *Periegesis* as a pilgrimage account. Given his nearly complete silence about any experiences he may have had that were enlightening or life-changing, it

---

[12] On the chronology of the various books, see Gurlitt (1890), 1.58–62; Frazer (1898), 1.xv–xvii; Regenbogen (1956), 1010; Habicht (1985), 9–12, with some important innovations over his predecessors, and Bowie (2001). Book 1 was composed before *c.* 160 CE (7.20.6), and perhaps considerably earlier (cf. Beschi and Musti (1982), xii–xviii). Book 5 and subsequent books were composed in or after 173 CE (5.1.2), with 180 (the end of the reign of Marcus Aurelius, the latest emperor mentioned by Pausanias) being a plausible *terminus ante quem* for the entire project.

[13] For what Pausanias tells us, and what we can otherwise surmise, about his biography, cf. Frazer (1898), 1.xiii–xcvi (esp. xv–xxii); Gurlitt (1890), 1–55; Regenbogen (1956), 1012–14; Habicht (1985), 1–27; Arafat (1996), 8–12; Bowie (2001), 20–5.

[14] Cf. Alcock (1996), esp. 260–1.

is hazardous to assume that his travels functioned for him as a sort of 'kinetic ritual' to produce a transformative liminal experience.[15] Elsner and others have suggested that Pausanias experienced such a life-changing epiphany in the 'conversion' that he claims to have undergone by the time he began his account of Arkadia, the eighth book of the *Periegesis*.[16] In 8.8.3 Pausanias states that up to that point he regarded much of the divine mythology of the Greeks as nonsense, but that upon reaching Arkadia he realized that the ancient tales presented profound truths in allegorical fashion. This is an interesting statement in a number of respects, but it hardly reflects a road-to-Damascus revelation, since on previous occasions Pausanias shows himself open to an allegorical interpretation of myths and divinities (e.g. 1.17.1; 7.23.7). While this passage may show some spiritual development on Pausanias' part, normal life-experience and sedentary study may have had a hand in bringing about his change in attitude. The fact that Pausanias was writing about Arkadia some fifteen years or more after his first visits to the Greek mainland makes it difficult to ascribe his spiritual enlightenment (such as it is) solely to the experience of travelling.[17]

All of these considerations can be raised as obstacles to seeing Pausanias' text as an account of pilgrimage in any narrow sense. Nevertheless, even if we hesitate to grant Pausanias the title of 'pilgrim' plain and simple, there are still a number of benefits to comparing Pausanias' work to more familiar examples of pilgrimage literature. Although no word in Greek corresponds precisely to the uses of the English word 'pilgrimage', Ian Rutherford has recently argued that a number of the activities that Pausanias engages in, activities that might seem to betray his identity as a 'tourist' rather than a 'pilgrim', are common features of religiously motivated travel in the ancient Greek world; these include 'sightseeing', antiquarian study of objects and artifacts, and making various gods and various shrines the object of one's travel rather than a single pilgrimage centre.[18] Even without Rutherford's insights, Pausanias and his text can be comfortably accommodated under a more synthesizing and inclusive definition of pilgrimage such as that offered by Morinis: 'a journey

---

[15] Cf. Turner and Turner (1978; new edn. 1996), 1–39. The phrase 'kinetic ritual' comes from Edith Turner's preface to the 1996 edn., p. xiii.
[16] Elsner (1995), 144; cf. Veyne (1988), 98–100.
[17] See n. 12 above concerning the chronology of the work.
[18] Rutherford (2001*a*).

undertaken... in quest of a place or a state that [the pilgrim] believes to embody a valued ideal'.[19] Such a definition is particularly useful in the case of Pausanias, in that it avoids any specific emphasis on 'religion'. One of the prominent characteristics of Greek religion was that it was traditionally a civic religion, a fact that makes dividing the sacred from the profane problematic. Consideration of this interconnectedness of religious and civic identity in Pausanias' world should allay the concerns of Arafat, who objects to the characterization of Pausanias as a pilgrim on the grounds that 'pilgrimage implies a journey by a devotee in pursuance of a primarily religious goal', and that Pausanias shows a 'complementary interest in non-religious matters'.[20] Pilgrimage need not be defined so narrowly, and in the case of Pausanias and many of his contemporaries, both the religious and the non-religious cooperate in an indissoluble fashion to embody a 'valued ideal', namely the ideal of Hellenism.

At this point we come to another prominent characteristic of Pausanias' outlook: his distinct preference for the history, monuments, and artworks of Greece's pre-Roman past over those of his own time. The great majority of buildings, statues, anecdotes, and historical events that Pausanias refers to in his account date no later than the middle of the second-century BCE, the period in which Rome put the final touches on its subjugation of mainland Greece.[21] As was mentioned before, such reverence for classical Hellenic culture was typical among the educated classes in Pausanias' day. In the period of the Second Sophistic, upper-class youths throughout the empire, non-Greek as well as Greek, were raised on the literature and oratory of classical Greece. As a result, both their historical imaginations and their sense of identity as cultured individuals were rooted in that distant period. The Hellenizing sensibilities of the entire educated elite, including those of its members who were Greek themselves, focused not on the culture of contemporary Greek communities but on the fabled Greece of Plato, Themistocles, and Demosthenes.[22]

---

[19] Morinis (1992*b*), 4.

[20] Arafat (1996), 10.

[21] Cf. Frazer (1898), 1.xxxiii–xxxv; Habicht (1985), 23. Bowie (1970 and 1996); Alcock (1996); Arafat (1996), 43–79, who wisely cautions against overestimating this bias.

[22] Cf. Bowie (1970 and 1991); Anderson (1993), 101–32; Swain (1996), 65–100; Schmitz (1997), 18–26; Whitmarsh (2001), 90–130.

In many respects the *Periegesis* can be seen as a portrait of Greece that filters out almost everything in the landscape that would not appeal to an antiquarian sense of Greek identity, and Pausanias' reverence for deities and sacred localities is—in part—one means by which he manifests this reverence for the past.[23] He devotes the bulk of his attention to the cults of the traditional Greek gods and heroes, and spends little time on the cults of latter-day immigrant gods like Isis and Serapis.[24] Moreover, as we shall see, he shows a marked lack of interest and respect for the most widespread new religion in the Greece of his day, the 'imperial cult' devoted to deified Roman emperors and their families. The religions Pausanias privileges, therefore, are themselves reminders of the former Greece that he and his contemporaries so admired. Insofar as he pursues the historical *and* religious ideal of Hellenism in his travels, there is every reason to regard Pausanias as a pilgrim of sorts, and whether one regards him a pilgrim or not there is still every reason to consider his texts in comparison to those of other pilgrims, since similarities will emerge in their treatment of privileged localities.

THE CONSTRUCTION OF RELIGIOUS TOPOGRAPHIES

When pilgrims write accounts of their journeys they tend to select and organize the remembrances of their experiences in a manner that reflects their subjective perspectives on the places they visit. In doing so they are not unique: the accounts of all writers who describe journeys or places reflect the authors' cognitive mapping;[25] that is, their contours arise

---

[23] Cf. Pirenne-Delforge (1998*b*).

[24] Pausanias does not ignore Isis and Serapis completely: see especially 1.18.4 and 10.32.13–18. In most other cases, however, he does little more than record the presence of a temple or statue without further elaboration (e.g. 1.41.3, 2.4.6, 2.34.10, 3.22.13, 4.32.6). As is suggested by these citations, Pausanias refers to Isis and Serapis far more frequently in the first four books of his works (the only examples from the latter six being 7.21.13, 7.25.9, 7.26.7, 9.24.2 and the aforementioned 10.32.13–18). Perhaps Pausanias' interest in these new gods even decreased over the course of his travels.

[25] For the phrase 'cognitive mapping' see Tolman (1948). For studies examining the formation and communication of spatial perceptions as discursive processes, see e.g. Culler (1981); Cosgrove (1984); Pratt (1992); Rose (1993). For the application of similar perspectives to classical literature, see Hartog (1988 and 2001); Nicolet (1990); Romm (1992); Elsner (1997*a*); Clarke (1999).

from the intersection of the physical landscape and the cognitive landscape of personal and cultural preconceptions that resides in the observer's mind. The formation of a cognitive topography can begin even before the traveller first encounters a landscape, if, as is the case with Pausanias and with the majority of pilgrims, the places he or she visits are ones that he or she is already familiar with from oral or written accounts. On site, the predisposition of the visitor's mind manifests itself both in the differential attention he or she pays to various elements of the landscape and in the staying power that those elements have in his or her memory. The actual writing of a text like the *Periegesis* represents only the crystallization of an ongoing interaction between observation and cognitive predilection.

While such things can be said about all travel writing and, for that matter, all writing that describes landscapes, pilgrimage accounts are particularly interesting since the authors' fidelity to their motivating ideology tends to make the mental topography of their preconceptions more tangible and rigid. For pilgrims, as for Pausanias, the places they are visiting are not random or unfamiliar sites but ones that form the physical backdrop for the narratives that play a large role in creating their sense of religious and cultural identity. Thus pilgrims tend to approach their destinations with deeply held expectations, and their accounts are suffused with the tension between these expectations and their on-site experiences.[26] Although there is no room in this essay to analyse other pilgrimage accounts in detail, this dialogue between the two competing sources of conceptions about landscapes, the cognitive and the perceptual, has been noted in the two Christian pilgrimage accounts that are closest to Pausanias in time, the spare and utilitarian itinerary of the so-called Bordeaux Pilgrim and the epistolary pilgrimage account of Egeria.[27]

Pausanias' text clearly reflects this 'pilgrim outlook' in the case of a number of monuments and sites. Not surprisingly, the most

[26] Some recent work on the growing field of pilgrimage studies, with particular reference to late antique and early Christian pilgrimage: Turner and Turner (1978); Hunt (1982 and 1984); Campbell (1988 and 1991); MacCormack (1990); Holum (1990); the articles in Eade and Sallnow eds. (1991); Morinis, (1992*a*); Clark (1996); Elsner (1997*a* and 2001*b*); Frank (2000*a*). See further references in the next note.

[27] On the Bordeaux pilgrim see Leyerle (1996). For Egeria: Sivan (1988*a* and 1988*b*); Campbell (1988), 20–33; Elsner (1995), 134–5, 144–5; Westra (1995); Leyerle (1996); Wilkinson (1981), 1–48.

obvious examples occur at religious shrines. To take one well-known example, in Pausanias' description of Olympia, he first separates the rich array of monuments in the sacred precinct into various categories, and then treats each category separately. In enumerating the altars, which constitute one such category, he does not handle them in topographical sequence but in the order in which sacrifices were performed at them during Elean festivals (5.14.4). In this way, Pausanias' account not only describes the religious objects, but also reflects in ritual order the devotee's experience.[28] The way he handles Olympia thus provides us with one of the more marked examples of how his religious interests, combined probably with a desire to add some variation to his methods, can shape his construction of a topographical account.

While one might expect Pausanias' piety to exert a noticeable influence on the texture of his descriptions when it comes to sites that are primarily religious in nature, the same is also true for sites that are ostensibly secular. I would suggest, in fact, that the extent to which a pilgrim's selective perception of the landscape surfaces in Pausanias' treatment of cities and other places that include a mixture of sacred and non-sacred shows how intertwined the religious and secular aspects of Hellenism were for him. The remainder of this essay will discuss how, in the manner of a pilgrimage account, Pausanias' religious sensibilities inspire and shape his literary construction of a particular civic landscape in Greece, the city of Corinth.

PAUSANIAS' CORINTH[29]

Corinth was one of the mother cities of the pre-Roman civilization that Pausanias and his contemporaries so admired, and even in Pausanias' day Corinth had few rivals among Greek cities in terms of size,

---

[28] Though as befits his self-distancing ethnographic stance, he does not present this as his own religious experience, but specifically that of the Elean locals. For an illuminating discussion of Pausanias' construction of Olympian topography, see Elsner (2001*a*).

[29] Work on this chapter was substantially complete when two new articles on the subject of Pausanias in Corinth became available to me: Torelli (2001) and Osanna (2001). I'm happy to see that the conclusions of these scholars, while different, are not, in general, incompatible with my own.

prosperity, importance, and renown.[30] But the city that Pausanias visited and the one that flourished in classical times were not identical. In 146 BCE, during one of the last conflicts between Rome and independent Greece, Corinth was destroyed by the Roman general Mummius. Afterwards the city and its land remained desolate and only sporadically inhabited for a period of more than a hundred years. In 44 BCE, either Julius Caesar or his successors in the triumvirate established a colony on the site of the old Greek city. New people moved in, most of them probably freedmen and veterans from Italy; the land was resurveyed and redistributed; roads, buildings, temples were re-designed and rebuilt.[31] It was this resurrected city that Pausanias saw some two hundred years later, a city which, through the vicissitudes of Roman rule, had been given a new identity distinct from its ancient origins. As a result of this unusual situation, the description of Corinth is a task that confronts Pausanias with unprecedented problems, and puts his normal methods of constructing a description to a severe test.

The inability of contemporary Corinth to live up to Pausanias' archaizing expectations causes him a certain amount of discomfort, as is discernible from the very start of his description of the city (2.2.6):

λόγου δὲ ἄξια ἐν τῆι πόλει τὰ μὲν λειπόμενα ἔτι τῶν ἀρχαίων ἐστίν, τὰ δὲ πολλὰ αὐτῶν ἐπὶ τῆς ἀκμῆς ἐποιήθη τῆς ὕστερον. ἔστιν οὖν ἐπὶ τῆς ἀγορᾶς —ἐνταῦθα γὰρ πλεῖστά ἐστι τῶν ἱερῶν—Ἄρτεμίς τε ἐπίκλησιν Ἐφεσία καὶ Διονύσου ξόανα ἐπίχρυσα πλὴν τῶν προσώπων...

Worth mention in the city are the remaining antiquities, but most things are products of the latter period of prosperity. There is then on the agora—for that is where most of the shrines [*hiera*] are—an Artemis surnamed Ephesia, and ancient images [*xoana*] of Dionysos, which are gilt except for the faces...

The reinvention of Corinth in the Roman era is not limited to its new buildings and monuments, however; it also extends to the people and their cultural and religious practices. Though by Pausanias' time Corinth had become a predominantly Greek-speaking city once again,[32] the new inhabitants had no necessary connection to the old

---

[30] Engels (1990); Alcock (1993), 156–64.

[31] Wiseman (1979); Romano (1993); Walbank (1997); Torelli (2001) 135–40.

[32] The gradual 'Hellenization' of the colonists is attested to in inscriptions. See Kent (1966).

inhabitants or their customs.[33] One of Pausanias' responses to the absence of tradition in contemporary Corinth is to make his description relatively spare and brief. Little that Pausanias sees in the city inspires him toward the expansive mythological or historical reflections he tends to engage in elsewhere, and he devotes less text to his topography of Corinth than he does to any other major city and even less than he does to many of the smaller cities, such as Corinth's neighbour to the west, Sikyon. In the midst of what to him must have seemed a terrain of desolate prospects, however, Pausanias still discerns some things that respond to his religious and cultural expectations. Through a series of compositional techniques he manages to highlight these elements and present a picture of Corinth which, if not comprehensive, is nevertheless coherent in its cultural and cognitive structure.

The most obvious strategy that Pausanias follows in his reconstruction of Corinth is the one we have mentioned already as one of his general tendencies, namely selectivity or exclusion. Although Roman Corinth was a vibrant place full of busy markets and offices, with costly and imposing buildings accentuating the visible scenery (Figure 1), Pausanias avoids mentioning nearly all of the structures of the city that have a primarily secular function (with a few important exceptions that we will encounter below). Most of the landmarks that exist within Pausanias' frame of reference, the only ones that register on the cognitive landscape of his classicizing mind, are religious landmarks. This selectivity is evident from the very first sentence of his description (quoted above): he begins in the agora 'for that is where most of the shrines are'. With this explanatory phrase, Pausanias announces more explicitly than he does anywhere else that the framework of his topography is structured on religious sites. In a manner that embodies the close connection in his mind between religion and antiquity, his attention quickly focuses on a pair of cult images that must have been among the (purportedly) oldest artefacts that Pausanias laid eyes on in Corinth, the ancient wooden statues (*xoana*) of Dionysos.[34]

After the *xoana* of Dionysos, however, the religious monuments that Pausanias will go on to describe are no older than the non-religious

---

[33] Cf. Pausanias' comments in (2.3.7) on the failure of the new Corinthians to maintain the traditional cult practices in honour of Medea's children.

[34] Osanna (2001), 187–8.

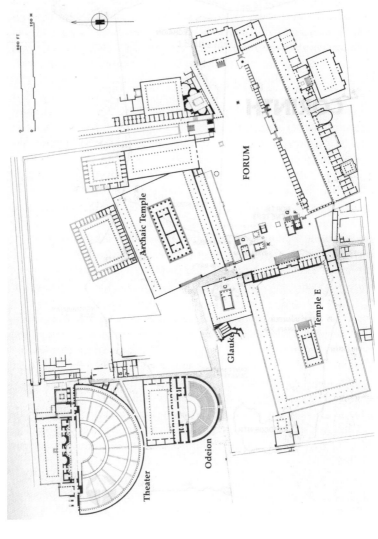

Figure 1. Central Corinth in Pausanias' day (from Williams and Zervos (1990), 332)

structures he ignores, so he must employ other strategies to reclaim them for traditional Hellenism. The first of these techniques we will consider might be called transformation: Pausanias often reinterprets or highlights certain aspects of a monument so as to emphasize its connection to ancient traditions. A particularly good example of this comes immediately after the introductory statement that was quoted above (2.2.8):

ἔστι δὲ καὶ Τύχης ναός· ἄγαλμα ὀρθὸν Παρίου λίθου· παρὰ δὲ αὐτὸν θεοῖς πᾶσίν ἐστιν ἱερόν. πλησίον δὲ ᾠκοδόμηται κρήνη, καὶ Ποσειδῶν ἐπ’ αὐτῆι χαλκοῦς καὶ δελφὶς ὑπὸ τοῖς ποσίν ἐστι τοῦ Ποσειδῶνος ἀφιὲς ὕδωρ. καὶ Ἀπόλλων ἐπίκλησιν Κλάριος χαλκοῦς ἐστι καὶ ἄγαλμα Ἀφροδίτης Ἑρμογένους Κυθηρίου ποιήσαντος. Ἑρμοῦ τέ ἐστιν ἀγάλματα χαλκοῦ μὲν καὶ ὀρθὰ ἀμφότερα. τῶι δὲ ἑτέρωι καὶ ναὸς πεποίηται. τὰ δὲ τοῦ Διὸς, καὶ ταῦτα ὄντα ἐν ὑπαίθρωι. τὸ μὲν ἐπίκλησιν οὐκ εἶχε. τὸν δὲ αὐτῶν Χθόνιον καὶ τὸν τρίτον καλοῦσιν ῞Υψιστον.

There is also a temple of Tyche; upright statue of Parian marble. Beside it is a shrine for all the gods. Nearby a fountain has been built, and a bronze Poseidon is on it and a dolphin under the feet of Poseidon emitting water. Also there is a bronze Apollo surnamed Klarios and a statue of Aphrodite, the work of Hermogenes of Kythera. There are statues of Hermes in bronze and both of them are upright, but for one of them a temple also has been built. As for the statues of Zeus (and these also are in the open), one of them had no surname, but one of them they call Chthonios and the third they call Hypsistos.

This passage lists a series of temples, shrines, and statues that scholars for decades have associated with the western side of the Corinthian forum (Figure 2):[35] at this end, the limit of the forum is defined by a terrace surmounted by a number of small structures. One fixed point that helps us orient Pausanias’ description is the structure that stands in the centre of the terrace, which can, through the nature of the archaeological remains, be identified with some certainty as the fountain of

[35] Scranton (1951), 3–73, with important corrections by Williams in Williams and Fisher (1975), 25–9 (cf. Williams (1987 and 1989); Williams and Zervos (1990), 351–6). See also Roux (1958), 107–112; Wiseman (1979), 521–30; and Torelli (2001), 141–55 for further discussion of the identification of the temples. Many questions remain as to the specific identity of these structures, but the general association of them with this section of Pausanias’ text and the identification of the temple of Aphrodite and the Fountain of Poseidon seem universally accepted.

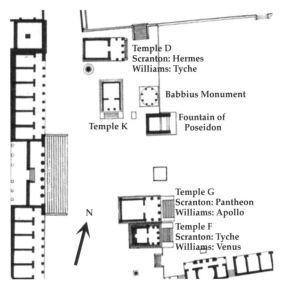

Figure 2. The west end of the Corinthian forum (adapted from Williams and Zervos (1990), 332)

Poseidon mentioned by Pausanias.[36] Since Pausanias specifies that many of the structures mentioned in this list stand in proximity to one another, it is also likely that the other landmarks he refers to are to be found in the vicinity of this fountain on the western terrace. But at this point a problem arises: in Pausanias' day there were at least five structures on the terrace apart from the fountain, at least three of them buildings in the form of a temple,[37] yet in his description of the terrace Pausanias mentions only two temples explicitly, the second one only as an afterthought to the statue of Hermes that it housed. Aside from these

---

[36] Scranton (1951), 32–6; Williams (1989). The remains in question include the bases of rectangular waterproofed basins and a number of sculpted and inscribed elements found in the vicinity that Williams (op. cit.) convincingly reconstructs into an arched fountain structure.

[37] Four, counting 'Temple K', which, however, is so badly preserved that even its identity as a temple is in question. Cf. Scranton (1951), 51–2; Williams and Zervos (1990), 353. Torelli (2001), 145–52, reviving and expanding on his suggestions in Musti and Torelli (1986), identifies it as the 'Pantheon' (i.e. 'Shrine for All the Gods').

two temples and the shrine (*hieron*) of all the gods, Pausanias mentions only a number of statues. While some of these statues were probably standing in the open air (as Pausanias specifies in the case of the three Zeus statues and one of the Hermes statues) it has long been suspected that the remaining two statues, those of Apollo and Aphrodite, were housed in two of the temples of the West Terrace. This is particularly likely to be the case for the statue of Aphrodite, since a tympanum block from the southernmost of the temples, conventionally labelled 'Temple F', has an inscription that identifies its inhabitant as Venus (i.e., in Greek terms, Aphrodite).[38]

Thus it seems likely that at least in the case of the Aphrodite, and perhaps also in the case of the Apollo, Pausanias has chosen to mention a religious work of art and to ignore completely the temple it is housed in. This is a curious omission, since temples are one type of structure that our pious topographer can usually be counted on to make note of. A possible explanation for this lies in the architectural form of these temples. Though little of them exists today aside from their foundations, most can plausibly be restored as prostyle podium temples, an architectural style that is (from our perspective, at least) distinctly Roman.[39] It is an open question whether such structures would have been perceived as 'Roman' by Pausanias' contemporaries, since the architectural *koinē* of the empire had by this time come to encompass an amalgamation of 'Greek' and 'Roman' forms and techniques.[40] Nevertheless, the differences between these temples and the more traditional sort of Greek temple would probably not have been lost on a careful observer like Pausanias.[41]

One could therefore argue that when Pausanias comes to this point in his description, he simply passes over the Roman-style architecture and acknowledges only the Greek (or Greek-style) works of art found within. In effect, Pausanias has read the Roman elements out of the landscape

---

[38] Scranton (1951), 58, with the essential correction by Williams in Williams and Fisher (1975), 25–9.

[39] Williams (1987), 26–7.

[40] On the problematic nature of 'Romanization', cf. Yegül (1991), 345–55; Freeman (1993), 438–45; Woolf (1994 and 1997); Alcock (1997*b*), 1–7; and the articles in Webster and Cooper (1996), Hoff and Rottroff (1997), Mattingly (1997), and Laurence and Berry (1998).

[41] See Arafat (1996), 45–58, on Pausanias' sensitivity to visual cues as indicators of age.

and foregrounded those elements of it that are Hellenic. It is not that Pausanias is deliberately misrepresenting the state of things. In the unlikely event that he intended to deceive the reader he could have easily mentioned the temples without discussing their style, leaving it for the reader to assume that they were like the typical Greek-style structures that he describes elsewhere. This selective vision is more likely an unconscious tendency arising from the way Pausanias' cognitive disposition encourages him to make note of certain things more readily than others.

A similar phenomenon occurs in the case of the building known as Temple E. Temple E was the largest and most remarkable religious structure in the central part of Corinth (Figure 1). It was situated on high ground to the west of the forum and would have been an impressive landmark to anyone visiting the city. The only mention Pausanias seems to make of this major temple is a brief remark that comes soon after his description of the west terrace (2.3.1):[42]

ὑπὲρ δὲ τὴν ἀγοράν ἐστιν Ὀκταβίας ναὸς ἀδελφῆς Αὐγούστου βασιλεύσαντος Ῥωμαίων μετὰ Καίσαρα τὸν οἰκιστὴν Κορίνθου τῆς νῦν.

Beyond the agora [forum] is a temple of Octavia, the sister of Augustus, who ruled the Romans after Caesar, the founder of present-day Corinth.

The terseness of Pausanias' acknowledgement of such an impressive religious structure is not the only thing that is remarkable here. In

---

[42] Both Torelli (2001), 164–7, and Osanna (2001), 193–4, resurrect the suggestion of Sarah Freeman in the original publication of the temple (Stillwell, Scranton, and Freeman (1941), 232–6), that Pausanias makes reference to Temple E later on when he mentions a shrine (ἱερόν) of 'Zeus Kapetolios' (sc. Jupiter Capitolinus) which he locates 'beyond' (ὑπέρ) the theatre (2.4.5). If correct, this would not have much effect on the point I am making here, since the discrepancy between the grandeur of Temple E and the brevity of Pausanias' reference to it would be the same. However, having spent much time at the site of Corinth examining the topography of Pausanias' account, I find myself in complete agreement with Walbank (1989), 367, who argues that this point in Pausanias' itinerary through Corinth would be an exceedingly strange place in which to mention Temple E. This is by no means a conclusive argument. As Osanna correctly points out (194), Pausanias was not writing a simple travel guide in which one can expect directional information to be full and unambiguous; yet there is, in general, what Torelli himself calls an 'aspetto odeporico' (164) to Pausanias' account—a topographical logic that adheres with reasonable fidelity to the physical contours of the landscape and to a commonsensical experience of that landscape—and one should not assume radical departures from that logic without firmer evidence. As Walbank realizes, one can argue for the identification of Temple E as the Capitolium without supposing that Pausanias is referring to Temple E in his later reference to 'Zeus Kapetolios'.

identifying this temple as the temple of Octavia, it is probable that Pausanias is making one of the most serious misidentifications in the entire *Periegesis*. Although the purpose to which Temple E was dedicated is a subject of controversy,[43] one thing that is relatively certain is that it was not a temple for Octavia. Pausanias has an impressive record of having the last word over scholars who accuse him of error,[44] but at present there is no evidence that Octavia was given permanent divine honours anywhere in the Greek East, and no reason to think that the Corinthians in particular would enshrine her cult in their most impressive temple.[45] Mary Walbank has made an attractive suggestion as to the origin of this apparent error: she hypothesizes that the colonnade surrounding the temple precinct was dedicated to a woman named Octavia (whether Augustus' sister or another), and that when he was told this Pausanias leapt to the conclusion that the entire precinct, including the temple itself, was sacred to Octavia.[46] While there will probably never be enough evidence to confirm this speculation, one thing we can safely say is that Pausanias exercises an uncharacteristic degree of negligence in not pursuing the issue of the actual dedicatee of this major religious structure.

As with the smaller temples in the forum, we are left with the question of why Temple E seems to register so feebly in Pausanias' perception of the Corinthian landscape. Again, architectural taste may have something to do with it: in Pausanias' time, Temple E was a larger and grander version of the sort of podium temple that he ignored on the

[43] The most widely accepted suggestion, based partly on Pausanias' reference and partly on numismatic evidence (Imhoof-Blumer and Gardner (1887; repr. 1964), 22, Plate E; Amandry (1988), 59–66) is that Temple E served as a temple for the imperial cult (on which, see below): Williams (1989); Williams and Zervos (1990). More recently Mary Walbank has suggested that Temple E was built as the Capitolium for the Roman colony: Walbank (1989) (cf. Walbank (1996), 204–6; (1997), 122). Though he vehemently disagrees with some aspects of Walbank's interpretation, Torelli (2001), 157–67, strongly endorses the identification of Temple E as the Capitolium. However, reviving and expanding on suggestions he made in Musti and Torelli (1986), he does not believe that Pausanias' reference to the temple of Octavia pertains to Temple E, but to a temple of the *Gens Iulia* located somewhere in unexcavated territory to the east of the forum.

[44] Cf. Pritchett (1999), 1–167, for an extensive catalogue of examples.

[45] See Walbank (1989), 370–2. Octavia was offered divine honours in Athens alongside her husband Mark Antony during the triumvirate, but there is no evidence of this becoming a permanent cult. See Raubitschek (1946), 146–50.

[46] Walbank (1989), 365–70.

west terrace. A more fundamental explanation, however, may lie in the purpose for which Pausanias thought the building was used. From his reference to the worship of Octavia it is clear that he believed the temple was used for some form of the imperial cult. It matters little for our purposes whether Pausanias was right about this, what is important is that this is what he somehow came to believe. Although the imperial cult was an everyday part of life in most communities of the Greek East, and included some of the leading Greek intellectuals and politicians in its priesthood, it is an institution for which Pausanias seems to have nothing but disdain, as one can see most clearly in the following passage from the introduction to his volume on Arcadia (8.2.5):[47]

ἐπ᾽ ἐμοῦ δὲ—κακία γὰρ δὴ ἐπὶ πλεῖστον ηὔξετο καὶ γῆν τε ἐπενέμετο πᾶσαν καὶ πόλεις πάσας—οὔτε θεὸς ἐγίνετο οὐδεὶς ἔτι ἐξ ἀνθρώπου. πλὴν ὅσον λόγωι καὶ κολακείαι πρὸς τὸ ὑπερέχον.

In my day, however, since evil has grown to such an extent and has spread over the entire land and into every city, no one from the race of humans ever becomes a god any more, except in name only, and in flattery addressed to the powerful.

Here, in fact, is one distinction that Pausanias is never given enough credit for: this passage is the strongest and most unequivocal condemnation of the practice of ruler worship by any Greek author of the Roman period. Other writers, Plutarch for instance, go so far as to say it is virtue that makes someone divine, not a civic decree (*Romulus* 28), but Pausanias is the only one who rules out apotheosis entirely, leaving no room for even a virtuous emperor to join the ranks of the gods.[48] While he does not mention the emperors explicitly, his emphatic assertion that he is talking about what happens in his own day (ἐπ᾽ ἐμοῦ) leaves little doubt that he has in mind the emperors and their familiars,[49] and not Hellenistic kings or other objects of deification

---

[47] Torelli (2001), 179–85, also calls attention to this passage, and to Pausanias' general distaste for the imperial cult.

[48] On the response to the imperial cult by Greek intellectuals (not including Pausanias), see Bowersock (1973).

[49] A few pages later (8.9.7) Pausanias deals with what must have seemed to him to be a particularly egregious example of deification, the cult established in honour of the emperor Hadrian's favourite, Antinoos, in the Arcadian city of Mantineia. It may be that this explains why Pausanias makes so strong a denunciation of deification at this point in the *Periegesis*. Swain (1996), 349, is of the opinion that Pausanias, induced by his

ensconced safely in the distant past.[50] In his brief and careless treatment of Temple E we possibly see the attitude Pausanias has toward the imperial cult impressing itself upon his construction of the topography of Corinth. Once again, as in the case of the temples of the western terrace, it is a matter of the removal or diminution of the Roman imprint on the Greek landscape.

So far, I have discussed strategies that remove or obscure parts of the landscape; but what do Pausanias' cognitive predispositions add to the landscape? One of the most important qualities Pausanias lends to the plethora of sites, monuments, and territories he deals with is a sense of order. From the time of Herodotus and even before, we know that a mind moulded by classical Greek tradition tends to conceive of geographical space as well ordered and symmetrical.[51] In cities, Pausanias' descriptions often convey a sense of symmetry and proportion that is absent from the landscape when we look at it with modern eyes. As an example, Figure 3 is a plan of the Athenian Agora as it has emerged from modern excavations, with the zigzagging course that Pausanias' text seems to trace between the monuments indicated. Contrast that with Figure 4, a hypothetical map of the same agora which Carl Robert published in 1909, basing his design solely on Pausanias' text. Admittedly this rectilinear version of the agora tells us as much about Robert's cognitive predispositions as it does about Pausanias': Robert clearly expects that any expression of the Greek spirit, even in the realm of urban landscapes, will exhibit the qualities of symmetry and proportion. But the point is that Pausanias does nothing to disabuse him of that expectation. Even in a case where Pausanias himself lists the monuments in a seemingly haphazard sequence, the mental image his text conveys is a world of straight lines and right angles.

---

admiration for Hadrian, forgets his previous objection to deification and accepts Antinoos' godhood without complaint (cf. Arafat (1996), 187). But Pausanias' reference to Antinoos' cult is actually quite sarcastic: he claims that he never saw Antinoos while he was 'among humans' (μετ' ἀνθρώπων), echoing his previous assertion that nobody becomes a god 'from among humans' (ἐξ ἀνθρώπων).

[50] As suggested by Swain (1996), 346. Although Swain recognizes that the remark refers to the present he finds its contemporary relevance blunted by the fact that 'the context is not connected to Rome'. Hellenistic kings, however, are even further removed from the context, and, as the previous note suggests, Roman practices may well have been fresh on Pausanias' mind.

[51] Cf. Dilke (1985), 21–7; Romm (1992), 9–44.

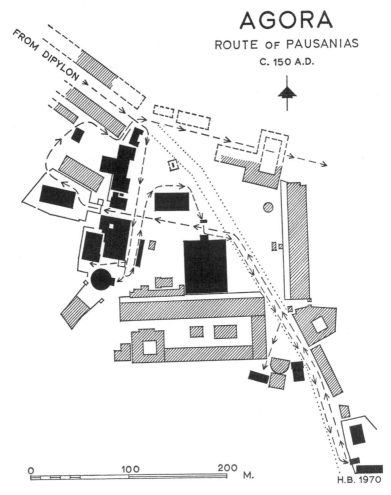

Figure 3. The Athenian agora with the route traced by Pausanias (from Thompson and Wycherley (1972), 206)

Pausanias' normal (and normative) procedure is to impose this sort of order on landscapes that, from our point of view, partake of a certain degree of natural disorder. Occasionally his efforts to do so become plainly visible, as at Olympia, where the problems presented

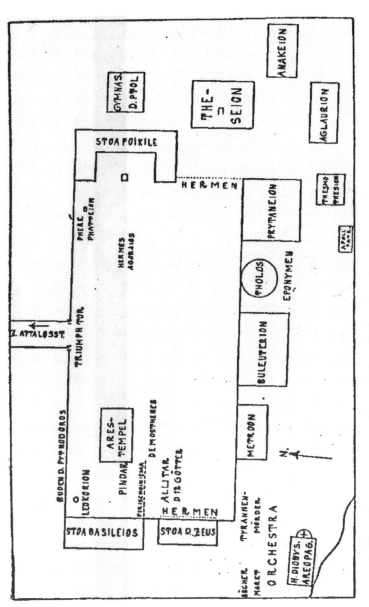

Figure 4. The Athenian agora according to Robert (Robert (1909), 330)

by the bewildering jumble of monuments occupying the Altis cause him to make the unusual organizational methods he adopts for this site particularly explicit with a number of signposting statements (5.14.4, 14.10, 21.1, 25.1).[52] In most cases, however, the extent to which Pausanias constructs rather than reflects a well-ordered landscape only becomes clear from inspection on-site. This is particularly clear in Corinth when we compare Pausanias' description with the excavated finds. When he has finished describing the site of the forum and Temple E, Pausanias traces a series of three routes that branch out from the forum in different directions. The objects he mentions on these three routes are listed in Table 1.

The first thing one might notice is that Table 1 confirms what we said before about Pausanias' almost exclusive focus on religious items in Corinth.[53] This is a complete list of things Pausanias mentions along

Table 1. Objects listed by Pausanias on three routes from the Corinthian forum

Lechaion Road (2.3.2–2.3.5)	Sikyon Road (2.3.6–2.4.5)	Acrocorinth Road (2.4.6–2.4.7)
	Temple of Apollo	
Propylaia	Fountain of Glauke	Two Shrines of Isis
Bronze Herakles	Odeion	Two Shrines of Serapis
Spring of Peirene	Tomb of Medea's Children	Altars of Helios
Peribolos of Apollo	Temple of Athena Chalinitis	Shrine of Necessity and Force
Bronze Hermes	Theatre	Temple and Throne of the Mother of the God
Poseidon group	Herakles by Daedalus	Temple of Moirai
Baths of Eurykles	Shrine of Zeus 'Kapetolios'	Temple of Demeter and Kore
Poseidon Statue	Gymnasium	Shrine of Hera Bounaia
Artemis Statue	Spring of Lerna	
Bellerophon Fountain	Temple of Zeus	
	Temple of Asclepius	

[52] Cf. Elsner (2001*a*), esp. 8–16.
[53] For more detailed remarks concerning Pausanias' selection of monuments on these routes, see Osanna (2001).

these three routes, and the number of items that have no immediate connection to religion number less than ten. Even some of these 'secular' items, such as the propylaia and the baths of Eurykles, were adorned with statues of divinities that serve as the actual focus of Pausanias' attention. For present purposes, however, what is important about the lists in Table 1 is their relative length. Pausanias offers no more information than what is given here about how far or in what direction his routes between the sights on these roads proceed. Since he describes roughly the same number of points of interest along each of the three routes,[54] one might be tempted to suppose that all three routes are comparable in length, but that supposition would be far from the truth: as Figure 5 shows, the first route, following the Lechaion Road, proceeds only a couple of hundred yards beyond the forum.[55] The second, the road towards Sikyon, follows a winding course all the way to the city wall,[56] while the third (Acrocorinth) route, is in fact the longest, proceeding all the way up the slope of the citadel as far as the Demeter sanctuary.[57] If all one had to go on was Pausanias' text there would be no way of sensing the disparity between these three routes. By choosing judiciously which monuments to include and which to exclude on each of the routes, Pausanias transforms an asymmetrical landscape into a balanced narrative. By locating the religious monuments of Corinth within this classicizing framework of proportion and symmetry, he further recovers them for the classically minded tradition of contemporary Hellenism. His treatment of Corinth here replicates in small scale the strategies he employs in his treatment of the entire territory of Greece: each of his ten volumes (with the exception of books 5 and 6, both dedicated to Elis and Olympia) treats one of the major geographical subdivisions of the Greek mainland. Some of these subdivisions, such as the territories of Messenia (book 4) and Achaea (book 7) have far

---

[54] The three lists would be even closer to equal in length if I had given separate listings to multiple items that Pausanias refers to as a group, such as the two shrines of Isis.

[55] For location of sites along this route see Fowler et al. (1932), 159–92, 135–41, 135–58; Stillwell in Stillwell, Scranton, and Freeman (1941), 1–53; Hill (1964), 1–115. The end point, Pausanias' Baths of Eurykles, would seem to be located immediately north of the 'Peribolos of Apollo'; cf. Williams (1969), 62–4 and Williams, MacIntosh, and Fisher (1974), 25–33. The prominent Lechaion Road bath is probably a different structure; cf. Biers (1985), 25–6 and 63–4.

[56] For the course of this route, see Williams in Williams and Zervos (1984).

[57] For the location of items Pausanias mentions on this route see Bookidis and Stroud (1997), 3–8.

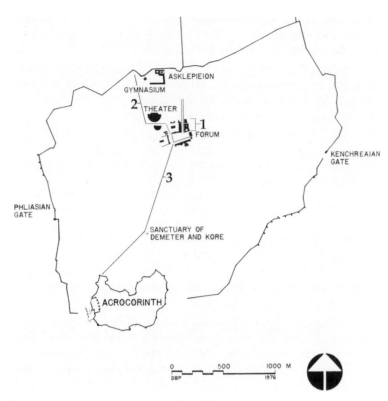

Figure 5. Routes Pausanias traces from the Corinthian forum (after Bookidis and Stroud (1997), pl. 12)

fewer interesting sites and monuments than the other territories, but rather than let the account of these territories be overwhelmed by the descriptions of their monument-rich neighbours, Pausanias compensates by adding more information of different sorts, chiefly historical and mythological, so that each territory can be the subject of a comparably-sized book.

There are other ways in which Pausanias places the monuments in a context that expresses his ideology of Hellenism. Part of his re-creation of the Hellenic identity of Greek institutions consists of portraying them as vital elements within living communities. This impulse to situate the religious monuments he describes within a functioning civic context may explain what he does in the following passage from his description of sights on the Lechaion road (2.3.5):

λουτρὰ δὲ ἔστι μὲν πολλαχοῦ Κορινθίοις καὶ ἄλλα. τα μὲν ἀπὸ τοῦ κοινοῦ, τὸ δὲ βασιλέως Ἀδριανοῦ κατασκευάσαντος . . . κρῆναι δὲ πολλαὶ μὲν ἀνὰ τὴν πόλιν πεποίηνται πᾶσαν ἅτε ἀφθόνου ῥέοντος σφισιν ὕδατος καὶ ὃ δὴ βασιλεὺς Ἀδριανὸς ἐσήγαγεν ἐκ Στυμφάλου.

The Corinthians have baths in many places, some of them built at public expense, one built by the emperor Hadrian . . . Many fountains have been built throughout the whole city, since they have plenty of flowing water in addition to what the Emperor Hadrian brought in from Stymphalus.

The peculiar thing about this passage is the way Pausanias seems to abandon the tendencies we noted elsewhere. Where previously he had overlooked Roman architecture, here he mentions baths (a quintessentially Roman sort of structure), and an aqueduct built by the emperor Hadrian. At first glance, this would seem to be an inconsistency in Pausanias' standards of inclusion, but on closer inspection that seeming inconsistency turns out to be merely part of a more complex coherence. We can tell at various points in his work that Pausanias' sense of what makes a viable community is based to some extent on the community's physical infrastructure. In an oft-cited passage (10.4.1) Pausanias wonders whether the Phocian community of the Panopeans deserve the name *polis* (city-state) since it lacks certain physical markers of development and sophistication: public offices, gymnasia, a theatre, marketplace, and water works. These things are not the *only* signifiers of communal vitality and *polis*-identity for Pausanias—in the end he does allow that the Panopeans constitute a valid *polis*—but where such things exist they appeal to Pausanias' desire to see the old Greek cities as entities that still function as living communities.

As with the facilities Pausanias mentions in his discussion of Panopeus, baths and aqueducts can be part of the community infrastructure that marks any city as a going concern rather than a forlorn relic. Though Pausanias finds Corinth far from the most stimulating city he visits from the point of view of his antiquarian interests, he still makes an effort to grant it a minimum level of civic functionality, and the 'Roman' items he mentions suit his requirements in this context. The argument I am advancing here is in some ways the mirror image of one made by Karim Arafat, who suggests that Pausanias' focus on religion comes mainly from his desire to convey a sense of the communal vitality of the cities he visits.[58] That religious monuments and institutions can fulfil that function is beyond doubt, but in Corinth, we see almost the reverse going on. Since the main thing linking contemporary Corinth to the privileged past was the fact that the modern Corinthians had shrines and statues of many of the traditional gods, in Pausanias' construction the landscape of Corinth becomes nearly as exclusively religious as that of Olympia or Delphi. The secular items mentioned play the role of making this religious landscape a living one rather than a desolate open-air museum. Here we can see one of the benefits to examining Pausanias' pilgrim-like outlook: taken out of context, such references to modern structures like baths and aqueducts can be used as evidence that Pausanias did not despise or avoid the contemporary world and its Roman realities as much as has typically been thought.[59] Looked at in context, however, with a critical eye on the strategies Pausanias' follows to make the physical landscape conform as much as possible to his cognitive expectations, we can see that such 'Roman' elements may paradoxically play a role in creating a coherent landscape embodying traditional Hellenism.

It may seem strange to suggest that Pausanias would avoid mentioning Roman-style temples in one part of his account and go out of his way to mention Roman-style structures in another. Part of the answer, no doubt, is that the religious associations of the temples made their incongruous form more problematic for Pausanias. In the end, however, there is no denying at least a superficial inconsistency. This brings us, by way of conclusion, to an important point of terminology: I have referred to the processes by which Pausanias shapes his account as 'strategies', but I do not mean to imply by this term that Pausanias was pursuing *deliberate* tactics in service of some subversive end. Instead, I use the term as shorthand for the way Pausanias' cultural predilections filter his sensory experiences and condition the ways he composes his text. I imagine that this was largely an unconscious business for him. If it were conscious, it would probably be more consistent on the superficial level—Roman baths and aqueducts built by Hadrian would be symbols of Greece's subjugation rather than symbols of civic viability. Instead,

---

[58] Arafat (1996), 10–11.   [59] As does Arafat (1996), 111.

what we are dealing with, I suggest, is an ingenuous and largely spontaneous way of seeing Corinth that develops from the thought patterns that Pausanias' upbringing and his piety give rise to. If this way of seeing seems self-contradictory in some respects, that is only to be expected. As we have seen, the period in which Pausanias wrote was a paradoxical period in Greek history that produced complex and conflicting attitudes towards questions of cultural identity in most Greeks whose writings are preserved.

In his sending of mixed signals about what was noteworthy to a Greek-speaking Roman subject visiting Greece, Pausanias is no oddity. But the overall trend of his approach remains clear: through the strategies we have examined here Pausanias resurrects a functioning, if not thriving, religious landscape from a physical reality that must in many respects have been dissonant with his cognitive expectations. Examining Pausanias' account as one that embodies a pilgrim's selective and highly preconditioned viewpoint can both reclaim his text as unique testimony to the experience of pilgrimage in ancient Greece and also lead to a better understanding of the *Periegesis* and its author.

11

A Journey to the End of the World

Andrew Fear

Traditionally founded in *c.*1100 BCE and attested archaeologically from the ninth century BCE, the city of Cadiz has a strong claim to the title of western Europe's earliest town. The settlement was founded by Phoenicians from Tyre and it is their name, Gaddir, or fortified place, which has produced, via Latin and Arabic, the modern name of Cadiz. The town grew into one of the most prosperous cities of the western Roman empire.[1] Changes in the coastline now mean that the town is a peninsula, but throughout antiquity, Cadiz was a true offshore island.

Ancient Cadiz's most striking feature was its temple of Hercules. This was erected away from the urban centre, most probably at the other end of the then island, in the environs of what is now the island of Sancti Petri.[2] Unfortunately the changes which have joined Cadiz to the mainland have submerged the site of the temple itself which is now lost to modern investigation. The Hercules of the temple is in fact the product of *interpretatio romana;* the god being in fact the Phoenician God Melqart, or Lord of the City. The town and surrounding district never shed its Punic roots. Cadiz appears to have had a Punic

---

[1] Strabo 3.5.3.

[2] Our clearest statement comes in Pomponius Mela, 3.46: *in altero cornu eiusdem nominis urbem opulentam in altero templum Aegyptii Herculis.* ('at one end of the island is the wealthy city which bears the same name, at the other is the temple of Egyptian Hercules') 'Egyptian' is the standard name given to the syncretized version of Melqart. See also Strabo 3.5.5. The area has produced bronze figurines of Phoenician-type male deities, A Blanco Freijeiro (1985). The most detailed survey of the temple is García y Bellido (1963*a*) and (1963*b*).

constitution until the time of Caesar,[3] its coinage, normally sporting an image of classical Hercules, had bilingual inscriptions in Latin and neo-Punic, the latter being in praise of Melqart until minting ceased in the reign of Tiberius. Punicizing names such as Saturninus, and indeed Herculaneus, are commonly attested in the epigraphy from the town.[4] Nor did Cadiz stand out from the surrounding region in this respect: Agrippa, when compiling his map of the world, remarked that the population of the entire region was Punic in origin.[5]

Like the town, the temple of Hercules reflected the area's strong Punic heritage. Strabo's reference to the inner shrine (ναός) inside the Heracleum ('Ηράκλειον),[6] implies that the temple was, like many Near Eastern shrines, found within a large surrounding precinct. The temple itself still had a noticeably semitic form in the imperial period,[7] possessing a flat roof, if its depiction on coins can be trusted, and allegedly still retaining some of its original woodwork.[8] Although the precinct contained many statues, including famously one of Alexander the Great which provoked an anguished outcry from Caesar,[9] in accordance with Near Eastern custom there was no cult statue of the god himself.[10] The temple's door was flanked by two nine-foot tall pillars. Such pillars were again a typical semitic feature found most famously in Solomon's temple at Jerusalem.[11]

The semitic nature of the temple was mirrored by the rituals practised there which also remained firmly Punic throughout the Roman period. Both Arrian[12] and Appian[13] describe these as 'Phoenician' making it clear that they are referring to their own time. The temple had a celibate priesthood[14] who shaved their hair, went barefoot, and sacrificed doves

---

[3] Cic. *Pro Balbo* 14.32.

[4] Saturninus: *CIL* 2.1751, 2.1898, 2.1908; Herculaneus: *AE* 1995 791, 810, 817.

[5] Pliny, *NH* 3.1.8.

[6] Strabo 3.5.9.

[7] Arrian, *Alex* 2.16.4, 'The Temple has been built according to Phoenician custom and the sacrifices are offered in that fashion there.'

[8] Diod. Sic. 5.20; Sil. Ital. 3.17–20.

[9] Suet. *DJ* 7; Dio 37.52.

[10] Sil. Ital. 3.30–1.

[11] Posidonius *apud* Strabo 3.5.6; for Jerusalem see I Kings 7:15–22.

[12] See n. 7.

[13] Appian, *Ib.* 2.

[14] Sil. Ital. 3.32–44.

daily to the deity:[15] all semitic traits. The gates of the temple are
described in detail by Silius Italicus.[16] The striking feature here is the
fact that while Silius' ecphrasis purports to be of the Labours of
Hercules, only ten labours rather than the customary twelve are
described. Albright and Tsirkin have argued persuasively that the scenes
in fact are an oriental myth cycle which refers to Melqart and are
unconnected with classical Hercules.[17] There is unfortunately little
evidence that this outpost of Middle Eastern culture retained links
with her mother city. However Quintus Curtius' comments that a
delegation from Carthage, another Tyrian colony, happened to be
present at Tyre 'to honour Hercules' during Alexander's siege of Tyre
in 332 BCE may suggest that some religious contact between the mother-
cult and those established in Tyre's colonies did persist.[18]

The temple appears to have had a longer life than the town of Cadiz
itself. Avienus writing in the fifth century CE, notes that 'now [Cadiz] is
poor, small, deserted, nothing but a pile of ruins',[19] adding that, 'apart
from the rites of Hercules we saw nothing to wonder at in these parts'.[20]
The shrine's final demise is uncertain, Avienus' comments show that it
managed to weather the initial storm of Theodosius the Great's anti-
pagan legislation and we can see from the longevity of the temple of the
Sun at Baalbek that some semitic cults were extremely tenacious. In the
long-run however the rising tide of Christianity must have been too
much: the temple had certainly vanished by the time of St Fructuosus'
visit to the ruined town in the seventh century.

Given that the temple was plundered by Mago, the last Carthaginian
governor of Spain, before he fled from the town to Ibiza in 206 BCE, we
can assume that it enjoyed a large number of visitors who made
dedications there in the Punic period.[21] A substantial number of these

---

[15] Porph. *De Abstin* 1.25.

[16] Sil. Ital. 3.32 ff.

[17] Tsirkin (1981) developing Albright (1968). For doubts about the theory see
Bonnet (1988).

[18] Quintus Curtius 4.2.10–11. According to Bonnet (1992), 'À Carthage Melqart
demeure populaire et sert de pivot aux relations entre colonie et métropole'. On
pilgrimage to Tyre, see Introduction, p. 27.

[19] *OM* 271–2.

[20] *OM* 273–4.

[21] Livy 28.36.2. Aubet (1993), 234–6 attributes this wealth to the temple's role in
local commerce but provides no firm evidence of this.

visitors would have been sailors as Gades lay at the end of a major Phoenician trade route. For the Phoenicians Melqart was the patron god of sailors (the coins of Tyre depict the god riding on a hippocampus) and it became customary to dedicate to him after a safe passage round the Straits of Gibraltar.[22] Can we call such visitors to the Heracleum pilgrims? Here we need to define our terms, no easy feat. When looking at pilgrimage two considerations seem to be important. One is uncontroversial—namely that pilgrimage involves a special journey to a specific spot. The other is more problematic. This is the question of whether to qualify as a pilgrimage the journey to a place in itself rather than merely arriving at the designated place is an important part of the traveller's overall experience and purpose.[23] Certainly, given that the temple lay over ten miles from the town of Cadiz and its harbours, it required some effort to make a dedication at the Heracleum. On the other hand, that journey had no intrinsic significance other than taking the dedicants to the shrine. For many moderns who would insist on the journey itself as having significance, this would seem to discount such journeys as pilgrimage. Such a view however would be a mistake as there is little sign of such a notion in antiquity even to journeys which it would be hard to deny were pilgrimages. This is best seen in early Christian accounts of visits to the Holy Land where there is little trace of the sense that the journey to the Middle East had any intrinsic value. The nun Egeria when travelling to the Holy Land in the fourth century CE, for example, has nothing to say about her journey as a spiritual experience: it is merely a means to an end, not an end in itself. Consequently, it seems anachronistic to impose this modern criterion on the ancient world and there is no reason why we should not see the sailors' journey to the Heracleum as acts of pilgrimage.

The temple was not, however, merely a site for seadogs to dedicate to their god. The earliest attested famous visitor to the Heracleum was Hannibal who came here from Cartagena in order to fulfil vows that he had made to Melqart and make further promises of dedications in the event of a favourable outcome of his projects. Hannibal made his visit as he was mustering his troops to march on Rome after the capture of

---

[22] Strabo 3.5.5.

[23] This view has its most famous exemplar in Bunyan's *Pilgrim's Progress*. On the definition of pilgrimage, see further Introduction, Section 1.

Saguntum in 219 BCE.[24] After the region's absorption into the Roman empire, the temple's attraction to those in power continued. The governor of *Hispania Ulterior*, Q. Fabius Maximus Aemilianus, came to the town to sacrifice at the Heracleum prior to launching a campaign against Viriathus in 145/4 BCE.[25] It has been asserted that Pompey visited the shrine during the Sertorian wars and dedicated a statue of Alexander the Great there, but there is no firm proof of this.[26] More well known is Julius Caesar's visit to the temple while holding a *conventus* court in Cadiz in 68 BCE during his stay as quaestor in *Hispania Ulterior*. It was during this visit that Caesar saw fit to lament his own inadequacy when he saw this statue of Alexander the Great in the temple precinct.[27]

If we are to believe Diodorus Siculus, many other Roman 'great men' also made and completed their vows to Hercules Gaditanus.[28] Diodorus does not tell us whether all these great men were connected with the province of *Hispania Ulterior*, but his choice of words suggests that this was not the case. We can therefore assume that during the Republican period a section of the Roman great and good made the trip to Gades and the Heracleum. The fact that the temple was plundered twice in the Roman civil wars, first by Varro in 49 and then by Caesar in 45 BCE, suggests that Diodorus is right about the popularity of the temple and about it having a high-class clientele.[29]

Despite the violence done to it, the temple seems to have recovered rapidly from the civil war period; Porphyry refers to it as 'extremely wealthy', πλουσιώτατος in 38 BCE, although he could be speaking about his own day.[30] Certainly interest in the Heracleum did not wane in the imperial period. Its fame can be seen from the fact that even trivial poetry such as the *Priapea* saw fit to mention Gades among a list of sites which 'belonged to famous deities'.[31] The Heracleum was a temple

---

[24] Livy 21.21.9.

[25] Appian, *Ib.* 65.

[26] Gagé (1940) 425–38.

[27] Suet. *Caes.* 7; Dio 37.52.2.

[28] Diod. Sic. 5.20: πολλοὶ δὲ καὶ τῶν Ῥωμαίων ἐπιφανεῖς ἄνδρες καὶ μεγάλαςπρά ξειςκατειργασμένοι.

[29] Varro: Caesar, *BC* 2.18.2 The treasure was restored by Caesar as a propaganda gesture, *BC* 2.21.4; Caesar: Dio 43.39.4.

[30] Porph. *De Abstin.* 1.25.

[31] *Priapea* 75.

which was legally permitted to inherit property, a feature shared only with eight other shrines throughout the empire.[32]

Both Trajan and Hadrian struck coins which featured Hercules Gaditanus.[33] It has been suggested that this was to emphasize their own Spanish backgrounds, but this seems unlikely and it seems more probable that the shrine's fame was the reason for its appearance on these coins. The Gallic emperor Postumus also struck coins bearing the legend *Hercules Gaditanus.*[34] Postumus identified himself with several local versions of Hercules throughout his break-away empire and his choice of Hercules Gaditanus shows the power of the cult in this part of his realm. As has been noted, Avienus tells us that the temple was still in operation at the beginning of the fifth century CE.

What then was the attraction of Cadiz? For the local population of the *conventus* of Cadiz and the Punic regions of Spain beyond, the temple would have held an appeal as the largest local centre of their particular religious beliefs. Dedications to Hercules are found throughout the *conventus,* and while it is reasonable to urge a note of caution in identifying all dedications to Hercules in the Iberian peninsula with *Hercules Gaditanus*, it would seem unwise to deny that many, especially in the near locality, may well have had this version of the god in mind.[35] The attraction of visiting the largest shrine of their most important god would exercise a powerful pull on such individuals. Nor must we forget the strong degree to which Punic religion had influenced native Iberian religious beliefs. For this group too the Heracleum might have seemed a natural place to make a dedication.

Such visitors could be styled 'local pilgrims'. There may well have been pilgrims inspired to visit the temple from further afield for the same reasons. The North African coast was a stronghold of Punic

---

[32] Ulpian, 22.6. The other shrines were Jupiter Capitolinus (Rome), Apollo Didymus (Miletus), Mars ('Gaul'), Minerva Iliense (Troy), Diana (Ephesus), Mater Deorum (Sipylus), Nemesis (Smyrna), and Caelestis Saliniense (Carthage).

[33] Trajan: *BMCRE* 3 nos. 81–3, pl. 10, 14–16 with Strack (1931). 1.95 ff; Hadrian: *BMCRE* 3 nos. 98–9 pl. 48, 17–18 with Strack (1931), 2.85 ff. These coins which show statues of Hercules are often taken as implying that a cult image was present in the temple by the beginning of the 2nd cent. CE, it may not follow however that the image depicted was necessarily the focus of the temple.

[34] *RIC* 5.2 p. 365, no. 346.

[35] See Thouvenot (1940), 287 and Toutain (1917), 1.402. For a more cautious approach see Mangas (1996). An explicit dedication to Hercules Gaditanus has been found at Cartagena, *CIL* 2.3409.

culture and contact between the two areas common.[36] King Juba II of Mauretania held an honorary duovirate at Cadiz and Columella speaks of African rams being sold in the market there.[37] In this sense the temple of Hercules can be seen as a religious centre which was also in some ways a geographical centre lying at the heart of an area with shared religious beliefs.

Hannibal and Fabius Maximus, on the other hand, travelled much further out of their way to go to Cadiz, doubtless in the belief that propitiating the god would bring them success. In both cases the journey to Cadiz happened before a major military undertaking, and the shrine lay well away from the obvious route of that undertaking. One of Melqart's titles was 'the bringer of Victory' and it is this aspect of the god's powers which must have attracted the two generals.[38] The action is readily understandable on the part of Hannibal who would naturally have turned to Melqart, but the case of Maximus shows the pull of the god the more clearly. Maximus must have identified the god of the Heracleum, despite the semitic nature of the cult, with *Hercules Victor* or *Hercules Triumphalis*. This cult grew in popularity in the mid-second century BCE as can be seen from Mummius' vow to *Hercules Victor* on his capture of Corinth, made a year before Maximus' visit to the Heracleum at Cadiz.[39] *Hercules Victor* was to become not merely a favourite deity of Roman generals, but also a legitimating force for the Roman empire itself.[40] Given the general identification of Melqart with Hercules, his role as bringer of victory could easily be assimilated to this Roman version of the cult of Hercules and the large number of wars in the peninsula throughout the Republican period means that it is likely that Maximus was not the only commander who sought the god's aid. This form of patronage would also help to account for the shrine's

---

[36] The most famous literary evidence is Hor. *Odes* 2.2 which is amply supported by archaeology, see Fantar (1990) and Pensabene (1990).

[37] Juba, see Avienus *OM* 280–4; Columella 7.2.4.

[38] This was a common attribute of gods at the head of a semitic pantheon, see the Brëô stele = *KAI* 201.

[39] *ILS* 20. The vow was completed by a dedication in 142 BCE after Mummius' triumph.

[40] Fears (1981), 773 ff. and López Castro (1995), 104–6, 263–71. The presence of such a legitimating force at the very end of the earth must have been heartening for the Roman mind.

wealth, as the custom of the *decuma Herculis*, or the dedication of one-tenth of the spoils of war to the god, grew.[41]

Caesar may also have fallen into this category of pilgrim, but unfortunately our sources are silent as to whether he visited the shrine as governor of the province in 60 BCE when he campaigned against the Lusitanians and sought a triumph for his campaign. On his attested visit to Cadiz as quaestor in 68 he was what one might call an opportunistic visitor, as he was already in the town on other business. His motive for visiting the temple is unclear and might have been simply sight-seeing, albeit he would still have had to make a special ten mile journey to reach the Heracleum.

On the other hand, the account of his visit implies that Caesar did have a specific reason for his trip along the island, although one different to that of looking for help in battle. We are told that on the night following his visit Caesar had a strange dream in which he had sex with his mother and that this was later explained as a sign of future greatness by local 'soothsayers' who were presumably connected to the temple.[42] This suggests that Caesar may have gone to the temple in the hope of learning something about his future.[43] Melqart was a god connected with prophecy: a Greek inscription from Tyre refers to him as 'Lord Hercules the Prophet', (κύριος ‘Ηρακλῆς προμαντεύς) and dreams are specifically linked to the god's mantic powers. Arrian has Tyrian Hercules appear to Alexander the Great in a dream near the city of Tyre[44] and Justin records that popular opinion had it that Cadiz itself was founded in response to a divine command given in a dream at Tyre.[45] Nor was Caesar's dream the only such story connected with the Heracleum. Porphyry's *De Abstinentia* has a tale which tells how the high priest of the temple received instructions in a dream about how to remedy the lack of sacrificial victims caused by the siege of Cadiz by the Mauretanian king, Bogud, in 38 BCE—the dream is said to have

---

[41] See Plut. *Sulla* 35, and *Crassus* 2.

[42] Dio 37.52.

[43] The story has a pleasing parallel with Alexander's visit to the oracle of Zeus Ammon at Siwah in the sense that both oracles are located in far-away places; Caesar, the future conqueror of the West's lamentations before the statue of Alexander, the conqueror of the East, make a convenient link in the reader's mind between the two.

[44] Arrian, *Alex.* 2.18.

[45] Justin 44.5.2.

been fulfilled the following day.[46] Silius Italicus has Hannibal visit Cadiz and, after a description of the Heracleum and the odd phenomena found in the ocean nearby, significantly describes how it is here that Jupiter sent Hannibal a false dream which incited him to march on Italy.[47] Finally Dio makes an explicit reference to an oracle at the shrine stating that Caracalla put Caecilius Amilianus, a former governor of Baetica, to death in 215 CE on the grounds that he had 'made use of the Heracleion at Cadiz'.[48] This must be a reference to the governor consulting the oracle at the temple, presumably to discover either his own political future or that of the emperor. It is clear therefore that the Heracleum possessed an oracle and there is a substantial weight of circumstantial evidence to suggest that this oracle was associated with oneiromancy. The lack of any mention of special incubation areas is no objection to such a view, as oneiromancy in the Phoenician heartland also lacked such features.[49]

The Heracleum's mantic powers would have been sufficient reason in themselves to draw visitors to it. The temple also had other attractions in terms of the exotic dedications made there and the lure of such material in antiquity is easily seen from Pausanias. According to Philostratus the Heracleum's treasures included Teucer's baldric and a golden olive tree with emerald fruit given to the shrine by Pygmalion.[50] Adjacent to town lay another island, Erytheia, which had become the traditional site for one of the Labours of Hercules, the theft of Geryon's cattle, and by extension one of the traditional burial places of Hercules' adversary, Geryon.[51] This was certainly Pausanias' belief when he refuted the view that the body of Geryon was to be found in Lydia.[52] According to others 'Tyrian' Hercules (i.e. Melqart) himself was buried in Cadiz.[53] Such stories about Hercules had a powerful pull on the

---

[46] Porph. *De Abstin* 1.25.

[47] Sil. Ital. 3.163–213. Silius is here echoing the false dream of *Iliad*, and goes on to echo the catalogue of ships. Prior to the dream we have a passage which parallels Hector's encounter with Andromache in *Iliad* 6.390 ff.

[48] Dio 77.78.

[49] See Hajjar (1990) 2294.

[50] Philostratus 5.5.

[51] See Pliny, *NH* 4.22.120, Philost. *Vit. Apol.* 5.5 where the grave is marked by strange trees, and Arrian's protests about the tradition *Alex* 2.16. For a general discussion of Hercules' myths in this area see Schulten (1984).

[52] Paus. 1.35.6

[53] Arnob. *Adv. Gentes* 1.36, Pomponius Mela 3.46.

ancient popular imagination. The Elder Pliny exercises his superiority over the masses by grandly denouncing them as mere fables when discussing the region.[54]

Other religious sites may also have brought visitors. Avienus speaks of an island to the west of Gades with a cave and oracle of *Venus Maritima*. The island is probably to be identified with the islet of San Sebastian and the goddess concerned is likely to be the major female deity of the Punic pantheon Tanit/Astarte who was again seen as a protector of sailors.

Cadiz offered other attractions from the natural world too in the form of tidal surges and springs of fresh water to which could be added a variety of confusing stories about the nature of the Atlantic itself. These phenomena again may well have been taken for divine wonders by many, but they also had an irresistible appeal for the natural scientists of antiquity who were drawn to the site to study them. The philosopher Posidonius spent several days in the shrine contemplating these phenomena, and it is probable that these phenomena were also what attracted Artemidorus and Polybius to the town.[55]

But apart from such material the Heracleum also possessed another even stronger exotic attraction: namely its position beyond the Pillars of Hercules and hence at the very end of the known world. This would not only have been of mere geographic interest; it cannot be divorced from the religious appeal of the town as places at the edge of the world were renowned in classical antiquity as sites where wise men and manifestations of the divine were to be found. Ironically therefore we have a 'centre' of pilgrimage which owes its position as a centre precisely to being on the periphery of the world; perhaps equally curious is the fact that although this was the western end of the world what was to be found there was firmly eastern.

That these different categories of attraction ought not to be treated as exclusive to one another is shown by Philostratus' *Life of Apollonius of Tyana*. It appears to have been a combination of the remote and divine which attracted Apollonius to Cadiz. At one level, it is important for the work that the sage goes to both ends of the earth, so his trip to Cadiz is

---

[54] Pliny, *NH* 3.1.8.
[55] See the discussion in Strabo 3.5.7–9, the length of Posidonius' stay is found in Strabo 3.5.9.

significant to Philostratus in terms of its location. In India Apollonius encounters wonders of nature combined with wise men. We find exactly the same combination at Cadiz. Philostratus is happy to dwell on the natural wonders of the site. We are told that one reason Apollonius wished to go to Cadiz was to see the Ocean and various descriptions of its currents etc. then follow in his account. Apollonius' motive here seems to have been in part one of scientific enquiry. However, there is a second reason given for his visit. Philostratus tells us that Apollonius had also heard of the φιλοσοφία of the people of Cadiz (later described by Philostratus as 'exceptionally devout'[56]) which consisted in 'their great advances in religious matters' and that this too drew him to the town and inevitably to the Heracleum.

The above discussion has centred on pilgrimage by the great and the good to Cadiz. Sadly the loss of the site of the Heracleum to the sea means that this is inevitable as the votives of the more lowly pilgrims have been lost to the waves.[57] Our most likely reference to a humble visitor to the town is found in an aside in Pausanias. This is a reference to a visit to Cadiz by the otherwise unknown Cleon of Magnesia on the Hermus. Cleon is often assumed to have been a sailor, but Magnesia is an inland town and the probable date of his visit was outside the sailing season so this assumption seems unlikely.[58] His origins on the opposite side of the Mediterranean to Cadiz show the pull exercised by the temple. In Pausanias Cleon is used as an example of an anti-rationalist who is quoted as saying that men believe too little in wonders and goes on to talk about a sea monster he himself had seen in order to defend the authenticity of the tomb of Tityus in Phocis despite its enormous size (its mound was 75 yards (*c.* 70 m) in circumference). Cleon saw this monster while returning to Cadiz after being excluded from it 'by command of the God'.[59] He was not alone in this, as he tells us that he returned with the 'multitude' or ὄχλος that had been so excluded. Ὄχλος here should be taken in the sense of 'non-citizen body'. This

---

[56] Philost. *Vit. Apol.* 5.4: περιττοὶ δέ εἰσι τὰ θεῖα.

[57] Two statuettes recovered from the sea near Sancti Petri are likely to have been ex votos. Only one is now extant, this is of bronze and carries the inscription H(ercules) G(aditano). See Oria Segura (1996), 210–11 and Lam. 16.

[58] It is made, for example, by Peter Levi in his Penguin edition of Pausanias (vol.1, p. 412, n. 21) despite him previously noting that Magnesia was an inland town (vol. 1 p. 1).

[59] Paus. 10.4.4.

obscure passage is likely to refer to a form of religious exclusion from the
city. The most likely candidate for such a ritual seems to be a version of
the ceremony performed at Tyre in the month of Peritios (February/
March) known as the *egersis* or 'Awakening of Heracles' which involved
the ritual cremation and rebirth of the god.[60] Such ceremonies were
common in semitic religion, the most well known being the rites of
Cybele and Attis, which were also held in March and would normally
last for several days. It is unlikely that the ritual exclusion was for the
whole of the festival and that the ceremonies connected as they were
with Melqart and the Heracleum would have drawn a substantial
number of visitors.

These visitors would not have had a difficult journey for despite its
emblematic remoteness in literature, Cadiz was highly accessible to the
wider Roman world. The voyage from Cadiz to Rome took some 6–9
days of sail.[61] The outward journey (Rome to Cadiz) would have been a
little more difficult than the return, given the nature of currents in the
Straits of Gibraltar, and some travellers elected to make the last leg of the
journey on foot, putting in at Malaga. In addition to this, Cadiz lay on
the busy olive oil trade route from Baetica (the sea-captain from Spain is
already a topos in Horace's poems),[62] so the journey would not only be
swift, but ships frequent. The trip could also be made entirely on foot.
Cadiz lay at the end of the arterial *via Herculea* (renamed the *via Augusta*
in the imperial period) which ran along the length of the Mediterranean
coast of Spain.[63] The town itself which had grown to rival any in the
western empire would present no hardships either. In this respect
perhaps ancient Cadiz can be seen in the same light as modern-day
Lourdes. It had all the attractions of the exotic and mysterious, but in
fact was easy to get to and comfortable enough to stay in.

Even after the temple's collapse, the attraction of the site remained. In
the seventh century St Fructuosus of Braga ended his peregrinations

---

[60] Josephus, *AJ* 8.146. It is possible that there is an allusion to the ceremony in Elijah's
taunting of the priests of Baal on Mt Carmel, *I Kings* 18.27. For a summary of the *egersis*
see *RE* XX sv Phoiniker, cols 362 and 375.

[61] Pliny, *NH* 19.1 and Plut. *Galba* 7.

[62] *Odes* 3.6.

[63] The trip was made in the opposite direction as is attested by four silver jars made in
the form of mileposts and listing the itinerary from Cadiz to Rome. These were found in
the healing springs at Vicarello, *CIL* 11.3281–4. The journey listed is 840 Roman miles
long.

through Spain by going to 'Island of Cadiz' and founded a monastery there and two others nine miles away.[64] The hagiographer goes out of his way to say that the monastery on the island of Cadiz was on its Western side. The point here is to make the religious foundation as near to the edge of the world as is humanly possible. Sadly no trace of any of these foundations survive. Fructuosus specialized in visiting the sites of famous martyrs, most notably the shrine of Sta Eulalia at Merida. We have a record of the martyrdom of Sts Servandus and Germanus at Cadiz, but they were later buried elsewhere.[65] Fructuosus' anonymous hagiographer makes no mention of any buildings at Cadiz himself, not even the 'tower' which was later to attract the excitement of arabic geographers, and all that we have elsewhere is a garbled account of a female hermit living here.[66] It is likely that the appeal of Cadiz to Fructuosus was the same which had attracted visitors in the past, namely its position at the end of the world. For Fructuosus, and no doubt his biographer, the journey to Cadiz which the saint claimed was divinely ordained would have been seen as one to conquer the ends of the earth for Christ.[67] At the beginning of the hagiography Fructuosus is compared to the Egyptian desert fathers and so just as in the pagan quasi-hagiography of Philostratus the eastern and western ends of the world are linked. In the *Life* the desolate nature of Cadiz emphasizes its peripheral position not just in the geographical, but also the civilized and spiritual worlds and this again allows a comparison with the far East—like the fathers of Egypt Fructuosus by constructing his monasteries made the desert a city. Fructuosus' trip however was very different to that of his classical forebears. They travelled *en masse* and in relative comfort to a wealthy city and there is no sign that the journey or personal privation formed any part of the value of a trip to Cadiz. Fructuosus' journey on the other hand was not to a holy place but to make a place holy. It was solitary, dangerous, difficult, and to an area which was uninhabited. For his hagiographer, the difficulties encountered by Fructuosus during his journey do seem to have possessed spiritual value. As we look at how the notions of pilgrimage have changed over time, perhaps it would be best to see Fructuosus not as the last ancient, but as the first modern pilgrim to Cadiz.

[64] [Valerius of Bierzo] *Life of Fructuosus of Braga*, chs.11–12.
[65] Usuard, Matyrology, *PL* 124 609–10.
[66] Castro (1858).
[67] [Valerius of Bierzo] *Life of Saint Fructuosus*, ch.14.

12

Pilgrims and Ethnographers:
In Search of the Syrian Goddess

J. L. Lightfoot

What might we mean when we talk about pilgrimage in Roman Syria? As scholarship on pilgrimage gathers pace, so the grip of Christian and/or Muslim paradigms relaxes, and scholars become more enthusiastic about the possibilities that open up when one embraces broad and non-restrictive definitions of pilgrimage: journeying to a sacred place (we now acknowledge) may be for spiritual or pragmatic ends, or both; it may be connected with festivals, vow-making, life-events or initiations, healing-cures, oracles, or none of the above; it may have no definite end in sight at all. But what is the evidence for Roman Syria? With what sites is it associated, what types of behaviour, and what groups might be involved? The answers could have an important bearing on several areas. For example, what light might it shed on (perceptions of) ethnicity in the area? It is well established that different pilgrimage centres may have different catchment areas and be frequented by different groups; what might patterns of attendance tell us about demarcations of, and relations between, communities in the area—that whole subject so tantalizingly evoked by Iamblichus' distinction between 'the Greeks who inhabit Syria' and 'the autochthonous people'?[1] Or again: pilgrimage becomes enormously important when

---

[1] Photius, *Bibliotheke*, cod. 94; scholium on 75b.

Syria is Christianized;[2] what is the connection between the new pilgrimage sites and centres of the old religion?

As so often, our evidence lets us down badly. Even where Syria's
grandest and most glamorous religious monuments are concerned, is
there evidence for anything that can usefully be called pilgrimage?
Take Palmyra: can we detect any patterns of religious visitation even
to this spectacular and well-documented urban centre in the middle
of the Syrian desert? (Answer: not unless as-yet unpublished Safaitic
inscriptions turn out to document patterns of visitation by desert
nomads to certain of the city's temples; even then, it would remain to
determine when and for what purpose those visits were made.[3]) Of
course, we do have fragmentary, tantalizing evidence from scattered
sites. One well-known example is the temple of Zeus at Baetocaece,
located in a dip in the mountains inland from Arados in northern
Phoenicia. An inscription from approximately the middle of the third
century CE, but preserving material that may go back as far as the third
century BCE (*IGLS* 7.4028), documents the occurrence of sacrifices
($\theta \upsilon \sigma \acute{\iota} \alpha s$, B.24) every month, and fairs ($\pi \alpha \nu \eta \gamma \acute{\upsilon} \rho \epsilon \iota s$, B.26) twice a
month; those who attend these gatherings are called 'worshippers'
('pilgrims'?), $\pi \rho o \sigma \kappa \upsilon \nu \eta \tau \alpha \acute{\iota}$ (D.35). The latest treatment of this inscription brings out the contrast between apparent remoteness, difficulty of
access, the role of distance in creating a sense of the divine, and yet the
presence of fairs and commerce that were clearly at the heart of these, as
of so many other, sacred gatherings.[4] Another example: the temple of
Baalshamin (the supreme god of the sky) at Siʿ in the Hauran, which
seems to be mentioned in Safaitic graffiti as the object of sacred
visitation, a possibility that is certainly supported by the temple's size
and commanding location at the juncture of a network of roads. The
interesting suggestion has been made that this was another node of

---

[2] See most recently Peña (2000). Note also the cult of the Christian martyr, St Sergius,
whose first church was established in the earlier 5th cent. by Bishop Alexander of
Hierapolis at Rusafa near the Euphrates in 'the barbarian plain' (*c*.120 km south-east
of Hierapolis), but whose influence had an extraordinary reach throughout peoples of
Syria and Mesopotamia: Key Fowden (1999) (thanks to Jaś Elsner for this reference).
[3] Visitation by desert nomads of cult-places belonging to sedentary populations is a
phenomenon observed elsewhere in the Arab world: see Henninger (1981), 38 and n. 16.
But for a very different assessment of Palmyra as a 'ville de pèlerinage', see Bounni, (2000).
[4] Steinsapir (1999), with earlier bibliography. For the frequent association of pilgrimage and commerce, see Preston (1992), 43; Eade and Sallnow (1991), 25–6.

communication between nomadic and sedentary peoples, and that economic exchange took place here too.[5]

Neither Baetocaece nor Siʿ is mentioned in Greek literary sources, and it is worth pausing to reflect on the disparity, or rather the only very partial coincidence, between epigraphical and archaeological data (on the one hand), and the religious map of Syria delineated by classical literary sources (on the other).[6] For the places that fall within the sight-lines of classical literary culture are not, in the main, the inland, let alone rural, centres. They are the great and ancient mercantile centres of coastal Phoenicia—Sidon, Tyre, Byblos—which had long been accommodated within classical frameworks, kitted out with mythologies (Cadmus, Europa, Agenor, Adonis), and literary traditions (Homer referred to Sidon, Herodotus actually claimed to have visited Tyre in the course of his researches in a capacity straddling that of pilgrim, tourist, and ethnographer). Heliopolis/Baalbek in the Beqaʾ valley also finds its way into imperial literature; it had (as far as we can tell) neither antiquity nor a classical mythological tradition to recommend it, but it was in the territory of Berytus, an almost unique 'island of Romanness and the Latin Language in the Near East', and the centre of a highly visible cult that spread throughout the Roman empire.[7] But does the fact that classical sources take notice of such sites have any implications for the scope of their appeal? Is there any sense of disjunction between religious centres that have become visible, or amenable, to classical observation, and 'native' cult centres in the culture of Roman Syria—or is that a false dichotomy?

These are not the only questions posed by the text that is the subject of this chapter, the treatise 'On the Syrian Goddess'

[5] Most recently: Healey (2001) 65, 124; see esp. Dentzer (1986) 405–7. For the Safaitic material, see Littmann (1943) 90–1, no. 350.

[6] The disjunction is noted by Millar (1993) 246; Polański (1998*a*), 99 (= 1998*b*: 181). For the literary map of Roman Syria, see Lucian, *DDS* §§3–9 (Tyre, Sidon, Heliopolis/Baalbek, Byblos and its satellite Afqa, as a prelude to Hierapolis); Macrobius, *Sat.* 1.17–23 (Hierapolis, Heliopolis/Baalbek, Byblos and Afqa). It is often supposed that Macrobius' source here is Porphyrius, the third-century neo-Platonist philosopher who was himself a native of Tyre; but note the more hesitant approach of Liebeschuetz (1999), 197–200.

[7] Millar (1993), 124, 281–5. The standard works on this site are Hajjar (1977) and (1985). For 'pilgrimage' there, see Hajjar (1977), 1.179, 2.521, and (1985), 274.

($\Pi\epsilon\rho\grave{\iota}$ $\tau\hat{\eta}_S$ $\Sigma\upsilon\rho\acute{\iota}\eta_S$ $\Theta\epsilon o\hat{\upsilon}$).[8] The text deals with Hierapolis (Aramaic Manbog, modern Membij), near the west bank of the Euphrates in the north of Syria, a city which—unlike the maritime cities of Phoenicia— had not fallen within Greek sight-lines from the archaic period onwards, and although it had attracted piecemeal treatments since the Hellenistic period, it had no Homer or Herodotus to ground its appeal to classical observers. And yet, in the imperial period, it attracted the attention of an author who was (I believe) none other than the satirist Lucian of Samosata (fl. second century CE), who treated it to a full-scale Herodo-teanizing ethnography, or rather, *periēgēsis* of its temple in the style of Ionic ethnographical narrative. Hierapolis was the Holy City of Atarga-tis, known to classical observers and devotees as the Syrian Goddess (Figure 1). She seems to have been a particular, local configuration of that classic divine figure, an all-powerful benefactress, patronness of human life and promoter of fertility, queenly and merciful, and especially associated with life-giving water whose visible symbols were her sacred fish. The earliest evidence for the cult is a series of coins from Hierapolis (at that time called by its pre-Greek name Manbog) at the dawn of the Hellenistic period;[9] from that point onwards, though with gaps, we can watch her encounters with classical civilization, and glimpse something of the way she is reconstituted in the process—in particular, her ever-intensified contact with the classicized Phrygian 'Mother' goddess, Cybele.

Without 'On the Syrian Goddess' (henceforth *DDS*, from its Latin title *De Dea Syria*), we would have had little idea that Hierapolis was a centre of pilgrimage. The city has never been excavated, and now probably never will be. There is hardly anything left; the last remnants of the temple disappeared at the end of the nineteenth century; even the city's most famous topographical feature, its sacred lake, is now grassed over and turned into a football pitch. Nor do other literary sources touch on any tradition of religious visitation to the city. Only one, Procopius, writing at the beginning of the sixth century, speaks of a holy city, which he does not name, in the east, whose 'holy rituals' attracted international crowds, from India, Persia, Phoenicia, Scythia, Greece, and 'all Ionia'.[10] This city is often identified as Hierapolis, though it

---

[8] See Lightfoot (2003). What follows, on the character of the goddess and on the author and character of *DDS*, is a much-condensed resumé of the first two sections of this book.   [9] Seyrig (1971).   [10] *PG* 87.3, 2817.

Figure 1. Cult relief of Atargatis, the Syrian Goddess, and her consort, from the temple of Atargatis, Dura Europos

does not seem to me that the matter is settled: the context of the report is that the Byzantine emperor relieved its water-shortage with an aqueduct, which does not seem to fit Hierapolis itself, a city which owed its original, Semitic name to its springs and copious water supplies.[11] Even if we could be sure that Procopius meant Hierapolis, however, the Byzantine emperor's generosity would be best explained on the hypothesis that the city had by then been Christianized (we know that it came to appropriate the bones of St Matthew). That could open up interesting possibilities about continuity between pagan and Christian pilgrimage centres in Syria;[12] still, my focus here is only on the former, and

[11] Drijvers (1980), 94, and in *RAC* s.v. Hierapolis, 27.

[12] The description of holy men in Hierapolis who ascend pillars in front of Atargatis' temple for a limited period twice yearly (*DDS* §§28–9) cannot but recall those magnets of Christian pilgrimage, the stylites who inhabited their pillars in almost the same area of northern Syria three centuries later, but the relationship (if any) between the two is highly controversial; most recently, Frankfurter (1990).

although there is no other direct evidence for pilgrimage there, there is clear testimony to the pagan city's prestige in well-defined areas remote from Hierapolis itself. First, an inscription from the village of Kafr Haouar in the Antilibanon, in which a certain Lucius of Acraba set up an altar to a goddess he identified as both Atargatis and the 'Syrian Goddess of the Hierapolitans' (the title reappears on Hierapolis' Roman coins).[13] Secondly, the use of, 'Mambogaios' as a personal name throughout Commagene, Coele Syria, especially the Antilibanon, Hermon, and the Hauran.[14] What deserves emphasis, and has not so far received it, is that this is a practically unique example of the use of a city-ethnikon as a personal name in Greek inscriptions of Roman Syria, and that it determinedly clings to the non-Greek name which all literary sources relegate to the past in favour of 'Hierapolis'. Some have seen it as evidence that the holder received the name after he, or his parents, went on pilgrimage there;[15] I doubt that it can be pressed that far, but the use of these names and their relatively thick attestation in clearly-defined areas marries up well with other, physical, evidence, to suggest Atargatis' special prestige in those areas. Particular, local forms of the, or a, Syrian Goddess occur throughout Syria, but it is hard not to wonder whether, in these areas, Hierapolis/Manbog held the status of a high-level shrine or locus of especial sanctity, whether or not there was any aspiration on the parts of their inhabitants to travel there. Moreover, the pointed use of the non-Greek form of the name raises interesting questions: was this a deliberate rejection of Greekness or simply an aesthetic preference—or was there no necessary discontinuity between Greek and non-Greek perceptions of the Syrian goddess at all?

DDS itself is riddled with notions of pilgrimage to Atargatis' Holy City. It describes it; it enacts it; it even offers its readers a vicarious experience of it. And yet before going any further we have to face the formidable difficulties that this source raises. The problem of unique-

---

[13] Fossey (1897), 59–61 no. 68.

[14] See Lightfoot (2001).

[15] Cf. *IGLS* 6.2981, where Μανβογêος is rendered 'pèlerin de Mabbûg'; on *IGLS* 4.1780, the editors (L. Jalabert, R. Mouterde, and C. Mondésert) commented: 'Le nom...pourrait rappeler un pèlerinage à ce grand sanctuaire syrien, ou une naissance attribué à la Déesse syrienne qui y était particulièrement honorée. Comparer l'emploi moderne des titres de Ḥaǧǧ et de Moqaddasi pour ceux qui ont visité la Mecque ou Jérusalem.'

ness is only the beginning. For if (the argument has been) the ascription to Lucian is correct, then we have every right to regard *DDS* as a work of satire, as unsympathetic and deconstructive in its attitude to religion as the satirist's other works.[16] Doubts find confirmation in the treatise's literary texture, which imitates and exaggerates the mannerisms of Herodotean ethnography to sometimes (though not consistently) humorous levels. I contend, on the basis of parallels with the rest of the Lucianic corpus, that the treatise is indeed genuine, but believe that 'satire' is the wrong set of problematics (for what gives us the right to confine the brilliant Lucian to writing always in a single mode and with the same agenda?). Rather, the difficulties begin with those inherent in all ethnography. It is not simply that Greek descriptions of ritual are generally content to describe rather than explain. Rather, accounts of foreign peoples and practices suffer from two simultaneous tendencies: they implicitly, by default, position their object as an exotic 'other' to be objectified and served up as marvels for the delectation of a Greek audience, and yet they view it, overtly or implicitly, through Greek eyes and a Greek explanatory framework, a problem of which it is merely the most obvious manifestation in *DDS* that Hierapolis' deities all bear Greek names. These problems are raised to a higher degree insofar as *DDS* exaggerates the idiosyncrasies and stylistic twitches of its Herodotean model (rather than systematically parodies them, in which case it would be easier to regard *DDS* as a spoof of the kind one encounters, for example, in Lucian's own *True Stories*). Another problem is the extent to which what is registered is predetermined by the literary model: how far is the quality of *DDS*'s observation compromised by the existence of 'slots' or *topoi* which Herodotean ethnography had created? And finally, the situation is complicated to a far greater degree by the author/narrator's own self-positioning as an Assyrios, and by the sting in the treatise's tail, when he reveals that he, too, took part in Hierapolis' rituals in his youth. It becomes evident that he is both outsider (like the Herodotean ethnographer and tourist) and insider—an 'Assyrian' counterpart to Pausanias, the periegete but also 'initiate viewer' vis-à-vis the holy places of old Greece.[17] Is he, as his self-confession might insinuate,

---

[16] For the two most recent challenges to its authenticity, see Dirven (1997) and Polański (1998*a* and *b*).

[17] Elsner (1992) (on Pausanias) and (2001*b*) (on Lucian, and all the themes of the above paragraph). Elsner observes to me that the closeness of both authors' focus might

really offering privileged access into a barbarian holy place? Or, just when we might seem to catch a glimpse of Atargatis in all the intimacy of her holiest temple, does the window cloud over again with a mist of generic convention and Herodotean role-play?

And yet *DDS* is packed with rich and seductive detail. Detail after intimate, circumstantial observation cries out for commentary, context, exegesis. The chapters on pilgrimage to the Holy City are among this text's unique insights, potentially a glimpse of something very important indeed, if only we could contextualize them. How should we approach it? Historically, perhaps, seeking contexts for its data, looking for corroboration as far as the evidence will permit. Yet this would be unduly positivist if it ignored the literary context, the intimate relationship with Herodotus and other periegesis literature. One could also focus on its cultural implications and interpretative contexts, what *DDS* says for the author itself and for the culture(s) in which it originated and was received. And because of the complex nature of the text, a truly satisfying reading would have to marry (at least) all three approaches.

First and foremost, the text represents Hierapolis as a religious centre: not the city, nor even the goddess herself, is at the heart of this text, but the temple. The text is a *periēgēsis*, of a very restricted locale; and before we look further into what the text says, it is worth considering what it does *not* say. The central section of *DDS*, in particular, is a very precise guide to the layout of the temple, leading from the outside into the *naos* and the Holy of Holies where Atargatis is enthroned with her consort, around the other divine statues in the temple, then back outside once more to the courtyard and sacred animal enclosure (§§28–41). Yet landscape—as opposed to topography—barely figures. The temple in Hierapolis is located on a hill in the centre of the city, near to the sacred lake (§§28, 45), and processions take place 'to the sea' (§§13, 33, 48); but there is little sense that the numinous is embedded in the landscape, and practically none of either Hierapolis' urban setting (save the private houses in §51), or of its wider geographical context ('not far from the river Euphrates', §1). The temple is simply itself, needing minimal context, a spiritual magnet which draws peoples from all over the

be considered another similarity between them: Lucian concentrates on a single place, while Pausanias essentially offers a sequence of restricted locales, the largest in literary scope being the Altis in Olympia which occupies most of books 5 and 6.

Near East. It might have been otherwise, as with pilgrimage texts that describe or prescribe routes to a holy centre and indicate the intensification in holiness through the increasing concentration of monuments and markers as one approaches the focus of pilgrimage.[18] *DDS*, in contrast, knows only a centre.

Nor is there any indication that the temple at Hierapolis might have subsumed, or been complementary to, other rival shrines. The temple is offset—to its advantage—against Syria's other 'great and ancient' temples, but there is no sense that they, or any other religious centre, might have come into competition with it. The author pays considerable attention to the city's curious oracle (§§35–7), a self-moving statue which delivers responses by propelling its bearers forwards or backwards, and since Macrobius gives an almost identical account of an oracle in Heliopolis/Baalbek, it is tempting to speculate that the acquisition of an oracle here, as elsewhere, might 'in reality' have belonged in a competition for pre-eminence among originally local cults.[19] But such considerations are far from the outlook of the author himself, who sees the Holy City and that alone.

What made it so potent? 'No temple is holier, no land more sacred', the text tells us; 'the gods are extremely manifest to them' (§10). This self-promotional theme also chimes in with the 'presence' or 'visibility' that is so frequent an attribute of Hellenistic godhead. Large numbers of inscriptions from Asia Minor, and to a lesser extent Syria, contemporary with this text, refer to 'manifestations', 'manifest gods'.[20] Was there a sense, in Hierapolitan pilgrimage, of travelling to a place where the sense of the numinous was particularly strong or concentrated? And if so, was perception of age and antiquity an issue? For Lucian insists on the past throughout his account. Hierapolis surpasses Syria's other 'ancient temples' (§10); it is crammed with ancient offerings (§11); and the foundation traditions of the present temple (which, since it has a podium, is apparently Roman) are retrojected to the Seleucid period which is already enveloped in a hazy Assyrian antiquity (§§17–27). May

---

[18] Like the *Itinerarium Burdigalense*: Elsner (2000*a*), 190–4.

[19] Macrob. *Sat.* 1.23.13. For the importance of oracles in the 'competitive creativity' of Egyptian local religion by the 2nd cent. CE, see Frankfurter (1998*b*), 23–4, 32; Hajjar (1985), 274 cites the Heliopolitan oracle precisely *à propos* of 'processions et pèlerinages'.

[20] The language of ἐπιφάνειαι, ἐναργεῖς θεοί: see Lane Fox (1986), 102–67; for Syria, see e.g. *IGLS* 7.4002 (Arados).

we infer that engagement with the past was an important element of Syrian religious life in the Roman period?[21] Or is this merely a literary posture, struck on the analogy of the Greek awe for Egypt's magisterial antiquity which underpins Lucian's literary model, Herodotus' second book? That is possible, but Herodotus tends not to remark explicitly on the age of Egyptian temples and monuments (perhaps because they are usually already tied in with the reign of a particular pharaoh), much less does he present it as a wonder to be registered in its own right, and it figures in none of his set-piece descriptions of foreign shrines.[22] Is this distinctive feature of *DDS*, then, the author's perspective rather than, or as well as, that of the Syrians of whom he speaks? In either case, it may reflect antiquarian leanings. Yet at the same time, Hierapolis was precisely that religious centre of Roman Syria whose pre-Roman, even pre-Hellenistic, existence we can document from the remarkable series of coins struck under its priest-kings.[23] Whatever transformations, whatever reconfigurations the cult underwent, it would be of some importance to know whether conscious appeal to the past was a major theme of its self-presentation. (Could it even be awareness of that past to which the continued use of 'Mambogaios' as a personal name alludes?)

Sacred visitation to Hierapolis is made central right at the inception of *DDS*. 'I shall declare', announces the narrator in his programmatic statement, 'what customs (νόμους) they practise with regard to the sacred rites (ἱρά), the festivals (πανηγύριας) they celebrate and the sacrifices (θυσίας) they perform' (§1); he adds that he knows some of them by autopsy. Later, after a splendidly resonant list of the eastern peoples who have contributed to the temple's riches, he explains that 'for no other people are so many festivals (ἑορταί) and sacred gatherings (πανηγύριες) appointed' (§10). Of the festivals which dramatize Hierapolis' holiness and which, by implication, generate its wealth, two are labelled 'greatest' (πανηγύριες ... μέγισται). In one, the cult statues are paraded to the waterside in order to be washed (a ritual with parallels in Roman, Greek, Anatolian, indeed Hittite and Meso-

---

[21] For the rise of antiquarian attitudes to Egypt's past in the New Kingdom, and then among the Greeks, see Volokhine (1998), 76–7, 83.

[22] A temple's age is noted in Hdt. 1.105.3; 1.171.6; 2.52.2; cf. 2.44.4.

[23] Seyrig (1971).

potamian traditions[24]), in the other a procession 'to the sea' takes place, where water is fetched and poured down a cleft inside the temple supposedly to commemorate a flood myth (§§47, 48, cf. also §§13, 33). The orbit of this second festival is described as 'all Syria and Arabia, and many people from beyond the Euphrates' (§13). A third festival, labelled by the narrator 'the greatest of all festivals which I know' (ὀρτέων τε πασέων τῶν οἶδα μεγίστην, §§49–50), takes place in the spring, when 'many people arrive from Syria and all the surrounding countries' to attend a great bonfire and holocaust in the forecourt of the temple. It is at this festival that new devotees, swept away by the ecstasy of the moment, castrate themselves in honour of the goddess to the accompaniment of *auloi* and pulsing drums (§§51–2).

I reserve remark on these festivals for my commentary; what interests me here is their insistent labelling as πανηγύριες and their attendants as πανηγυρισταί (the account of whom immediately follows that of the three main festivals of Hierapolis' sacred calendar). First, before the fourth century CE, the word πανηγυριστής is quite rare. It is cited as the title of a couple of Hellenistic comedies; Strabo also uses it, to distinguish festival-goers and revellers in the sanctuary of Sarapis at Canobus from those in search of cures and oracles.[25] After him, it only occurs five times in Lucian (here and on four other occasions); and then the word is not attested until the Christian theologians. All Lucian's other uses of the noun are of Olympia (once of a gathering compared to Olympia), and the same pattern can be discerned in his use of πανήγυρις.[26] A πανήγυρις, in the other writings of Lucian, generally refers to the great panhellenic centres, especially Olympia; on one single occasion it is extended to gatherings outside Greece that are, in their own way, representative of, or the culmination of, a cultural tradition (*Icar.* 24, including also πανηγύρεις of Artemis in Ephesos, Asclepius in Pergamon, Bendis in Thrace, Anubis in Egypt). Perhaps, then, the festivals of Hierapolis are implicitly being raised to parity with the greatest of the Greek panhellenic gatherings (whether or not there 'really' was a constituency of Syrians who conceived of their land as a

---

[24] See my commentary; one of the best-known parallels is with the *lavatio* in the Roman rites of Cybele, for which see Ov. *Fast.* 4.337–40; Arr. *Tact.* 33.4; Arnob. *Adv. Nat.* 7.32; Dio 48.43.5; *CIL* 1.2.260, cf. *CIL* 6.2305.

[25] *Suda* δ1152, π 1708; Strab. 17.1.17.

[26] *Peregr.* 19, *Pseudol.* 2, *Herod.* 2, 8.

country or cultural unity in the same way as a Greek could think of Greece). However, it is just as important to register that Lucian's use of the noun πανήγυρις throughout *DDS* corresponds better to Herodotus' than to his own elsewhere. He uses it four times, both of specific events in Hierapolis' sacred calendar, and of the general density of such events in the Holy City. Herodotus himself uses πανήγυρις twice of Greek events (the festival of Hera at Argos and the Panathenaia),[27] but by far its greatest density occurs in his discussion of Egyptian festivals (2.59–63) in the ethnography which is Lucian's main literary model. Here he repeatedly uses πανήγυρις and the derivative verb πανηγυρίζω ('celebrate a festival'), claiming that the Egyptians invented religious festivals (cf. *DDS* §2), and going into great detail about the very various ways in which the Egyptians celebrate them. Lucian recalls and trumps this, by claiming that no other people have as many festivals and sacred gatherings (ἑορταὶ ... καὶ πανηγύριες) as the Hierapolitans.[28]

On one level, then, the fact that the pilgrimage-theme is foregrounded in *DDS* may be due to the fact that Herodotean ethnography had already created a niche for it, had formed the expectation that it would be there. It may also have predisposed the choice of word, πανήγυρις, and facilitated that of the agent noun, πανηγυριστής. It inclines us, in turn, to view 'pilgrimage' to Hierapolis primarily in terms of the category that anthropologists have labelled 'normative': it is part of a ritual cycle, specifically, it forms part of the city's festival year.[29] But the text also suggests other reasons for sacred visitation to the Holy City. The author/narrator himself mentions that he visited the temple in his youth to take part in one of its hair-cutting rituals: young men (νεηνίαι) offer up the first shavings of their beard, while another category of the youth (νέοι) dedicate sacred locks which are grown since birth, then shaven on arrival in the temple and deposited in inscribed containers. This too can be accommodated in modern taxonomies: it is 'initiatory', a sacred journey connected with life-events or *rites-de-passage*;[30] and it is interesting that hair-cutting has precisely this function at certain Hindu pilgrimage shrines too (as well as carrying other meanings in other

---

[27] 1.31.3, 6.111.2.

[28] On this section, see Rutherford, Ch. 5 in this volume.

[29] Morinis (1992*b*), 11–12.

[30] Morinis (1992*b*), 13–14; for hair offerings in Greek and Roman pilgrimage, Rutherford (2005)

contexts).[31] Lucian places it last, immediately after a reference to the fact that 'all bear marks' (as later pilgrims to Jerusalem would wear tattooes[32]): the temple leaves its mark on its devotees, while they leave behind a physical part of themselves, and their name, within it. Needless to say, this is far more intimate and personal a gesture than anything that takes place in Herodotus' Egypt (where temples are in fact closed to the public).

And it affects an enormous range of people. The Spring festival, we are told, was attended by 'many people from Syria and all the surrounding countries' (§49), and the procession to fetch water from the 'sea' by 'all Syria and Arabia and many people from the other side of the Euphrates' (§13). The temple itself is full of exotic dedications which come 'from Arabia and the Phoenicians and Babylonians and more from Cappadocia, some brought by the Cilicians, more by the Assyrians' (§10), while the goddess herself is adorned with precious stones, among them the sardonyx, hyacinths, and emeralds 'which come from Egyptians, Indians, Ethiopians, Medes, Armenians, and Babylonians' (§32). These are resonant and evocative names, they complement the exoticism of the temple's offerings and the cult statue's gems. Yet 'all Syria and Arabia' also purports to describe the extent of the temple's appeal, and the implications—even granted the usual imprecision of ancient geographical terms—are astonishing. How much weight can they bear? 'Arabia', for example, need not literally mean the peninsula, but might mean further south in Syro-Palestine, areas inhabited by Nabataeans or Ituraeans, or (as often) refer to an area inhabited by those who lived a certain way of life, desert-dwellers, nomads, peoples outside the cultivated areas that were under Roman control ('Syria'?). Could this centre, then, in the middle of Roman Syria— indeed, in the middle of an area that had been under Macedonian and Roman control since the dawn of the Hellenistic era—have conserved enough of its indigenous character to retain an appeal (even granted that it had ever had one) to nomads of the steppe? And could it simultaneously be visited by those who might well have spoken different

---

[31] For Hindu *muṇḍana* ('an important initiatory rite marking the passage from infancy to childhood'), see Bhardwaj (1973), 150, 154, and table on 155–7. For hair-cutting at a pilgrimage centre (tīrtha), which is conceived as a liberation from sin, cf. Salomon (1985), 274–309.

[32] Jones (1987), 141, 144–5.

languages or dialects—let alone Greek-speakers? More fundamentally still, could it be visited by 'all' the inhabitants of such broadly defined areas? Collecting and analysing all the data from other cities of Syro-Phoenicia is way beyond the scope of this chapter, and each site has its individual characteristics and problems; but, where evidence is available, it tends to suggest that cities were visited by the peoples of their own hinterland on the one hand, and by their overseas colonies (where they had them), on the other: a much narrower focus.[33] The effect, in *DDS*, is to represent Hierapolis once more as a sort of Syrian answer to Greece's pan-Hellenic centres: 'all' go there to attend festivals and to receive tattoos, in an ethnographic flourish that applies this well-known Herodotean badge of national identity (Thracians and other Balkan tribes wear them[34]) to visitation of a specific, central, temple.

The other point to note is the text's silence about Greeks—despite the fact that the text itself is a most accomplished product of Greek literary culture. This foreignness is emphasized by the account of pilgrimage practice in §§55–6 (and possibly in the succeeding chapters):

I shall also describe what each festival-goer does. When a man first (?)sets out for (lit. 'arrives in') the Holy City, he shaves his head and eyebrows, and afterwards, having sacrificed a sheep, he cooks and eats all the rest of it, but laying the fleece on the ground he kneels on it, and takes the feet and head of the animal upon his own head. At the same time he prays for the present sacrifice to be well received, and promises a larger one next time. This done, he garlands his own head and those of the others who are travelling the same road; and setting out from his own country he proceeds on his journey, using cold water for washing and drinking and always sleeping on the earth. It is not holy for him to climb into bed before he has completed his journey and returned

---

[33] Tyre, for example, was visited by Carthaginian envoys, who rendered first-fruits there, as to their mother-city (Polyb. 31.12.11–12; Quint. Curt. 4.2.10; Arr. *An.* 2.24.5–6); Alexander instituted four-yearly games in honour of Heracles/Milqart, which survived into late antiquity (Arr. *An.* 2.24.6); Achilles Tatius mentions delegations from Byzantium to take part in the thusia for Heracles, but the novel sets up family connections between these two cities (Achill. Tat. 2.14–18; cf. 7.14.2, τὴν τῶν Ἡρακλείων ἑορτήν); other, more casual, thank-offerings: Achill. Tat. 8.18.1; Charit. 8.5.2 (the Great King offers ἐπινίκια to Heracles). Herodotus visits Tyre in 2.44, and Lucian in *DDS* §3.

[34] Hdt. 5.6.2, cf. Cic. *Off.* 2.25 and Dyck ad loc. (Thracians), and Jones (1987), 145–6; Strab. 7.5.4 (Thracians, Illyrians, and an Alpine tribe); Plin. *NH* 22.2 (Dacians and Sauromatians); Herodian 3.14.7 (Britons); Xen. *Anab.* 5.4.32, Diod. Sic. 14.30.7 (a Pontic tribe).

home again. In the Holy City a host whom he does not know receives him: there are appointed hosts there for each city, and this office is handed down in their families. They are called 'teachers' by the Assyrians, because they instruct them in everything.

Although this is structured according to the stages important to any pilgrim, ancient or modern—setting out, the journey, arrival at the sacred centre itself, its ritual specialists and hospitallers, and the return home—I know of no comparable procedural description of Greek pilgrimage. Partly it is a matter of singling out details unusual or unattested in Greek tradition. Head-shaving I have already mentioned; it is interesting that it also marks the *termination* of certain pilgrimages of pre-Islamic Arabia and of the modern Hajj.[35] The ascetic practices *en route* are reminiscent of the sort of penitential behaviour and bodily mortification associated with Christian pilgrimage, although it is impossible to tell whether that is a more relevant, or less misleading, context than that of the Arabian *ihram*, Hebrew nazirite, and other traditions in which self-imposed privations are willingly undergone until a sacred duty is completed (a state of affairs that may be terminated by head-shaving).[36] Partly, it is a matter of singling out details that specifically contrast with Greek practice (sacrificing a sheep oneself and donning the skin: as opposed to the Greek—as well as Hebrew and Punic—practice of giving the hide of the sacrificed animal to the priest).[37] And partly, it is a case of the deliberate defamiliarization of practices that would not necessarily look odd to Greek eyes at all. For example, the combination of guide, exegete, and hospitaller is not necessarily something so untoward that it could not have been found at a Greek sanctuary too, but here it is glossed and treated as if in need of interpretation into a more familiar idiom. More remarkably: the preparatory sacrifice is a *sine qua non* of Greek practice too, but Lucian has

[35] Henninger (1981), 287–8, with references; cf. also Healey (2001), 134 (cult of Manāt). Allegedly an *Egyptian* custom, observed μέχρι τῶν νεωτέρων χρόνων, for those on journeys to grow their hair until their return home, according to Diod. Sic. 1.18.3.

[36] Wellhausen (1897), 122–4 (comparing Hierapolis); for the Nazirite, see Num. 6:1–21; Acts 21:23–4; Henninger (1981), 290–1. For physical hardships (fasting, sleeping on the ground, walking barefoot, celibacy) endured in order to increase merit in Hindu pilgrimage, see Salomon (1985), 219–73.

[37] Puttkammer (1912), 7; Burkert (1983), 7; Brown (1995), 213–14; West (1997), 42.

chosen to designate it with the verb κρεουργεῖν, which equates with the English 'butcher' in its more loaded sense. It is at home in contexts of (human) slaughter, of human beings slaughtered like animals (as on the tragic stage), and could hardly have read as the standard, unloaded vocabulary of animal sacrifice.

Was Hierapolis 'really' as strange, foreign, and exotic as this? We might be able to diagnose the strategy of defamiliarization, even if we cannot see beyond it. There are (at least) two sets of problems. The first is with the literary genre, which implicitly, tacitly, positions its subject as an 'other' to a Greek reader or spectator. Yet the narrative hardly reads like a formulaically constructed antitype to Greek pilgrimage either, certainly not the kind of self-definition-by-opposites that proponents of binary models have discerned elsewhere.[38] And indeed, in other respects the practices of the Hierapolitans may be presented in a way that could be recognizable to Greeks, perhaps deliberately polyinterpretable: I owe to Ian Rutherford the interesting suggestion that the ritual processions 'to the sea' (ἐς τὴν θάλασσαν) could have resonated with an audience familiar with the processions 'seawards' (ἅλαδε) in the Eleusinian mysteries (a tradition whose preparatory fasting, incidentally, may provide one of the best Greek analogues for the sense of hardship undergone in preparation for attaining the sacred centre).[39]

The second set of problems concerns the historical Hierapolis' culture in the second century CE and the extent of Hellenism's penetration there. If it really was the case that 'all Arabia and Syria' continued to visit this temple-town in the heart of Roman Syria, in a landscape dominated by Macedonian city-foundations (Antioch, Beroea, Apamea, Laodicea, Cyrrhus) and practise some or all of the rituals that Lucian said they did, did they do so with a deliberate sense of difference from, or even resistance (or potential resistance) to, classical civilization? Or, without articulating any such feelings, were they maintaining loyalty to a sacred centre whose status and prestige had long preceded

---

[38] Such as Herodotus' Scythians in the mirror of Hartog (1988); for a pointed critique of the binary approach, see Dewald (1990).
[39] *IG* 2.2.847.20 (Eleusis, 215/14) τῆς ἅλαδε ἐλάσεως, cf. *IG* 1.84.35 (Attica, 418/17) εἰ ἅλαδε ἐ[χ]σελαύνοσι οἱ μύσται; Ephorus, *FGrH* 70 F 80; Polyaen. *Strat.* 3.11.2; Hesych. a 2727. For preliminary fasting, see Ov. *Fast.* 4.535–6; Clem. Al. *Protr.* 2.21.2; a sense of spiritual preparation for the Eleusinian mysteries in S III 4ᵃ Ar. *Pl.* 845 f. καὶ ἔστι τὰ μικρὰ ὥσπερ προκάθαρσις καὶ προάγνευσις τῶν μεγάλων.

the arrival of the Macedonians? (In this respect, the Mexican pilgrimage centres studied by Victor Turner might provide illuminating parallels: Turner showed how pilgrims to the shrine of Our Lady of Ocotlán, near Tlaxcala City, preferred to go 'almost pointedly to the ancient heartland', although the main modern episcopal centre lay elsewhere.)[40] But at the same time (and not necessarily in contradiction to the foregoing): to what extent had, or might have, Hellenism in fact altered matters, either by consolidating the cult's local power-base (by giving it a new and powerful vocabulary in which to express itself) or by extending its appeal and broadening its catchment area?[41] Was Hellenism in fact *supportive* of the 'foreign' cult in its midst? To a large extent we can only shadow-box with this central question, because the surviving remains from Hierapolis are so pitiful. Nonetheless, if only from the city's coins, we can see how the goddess evolved between the fourth century BCE (when she is labelled *Ateh* or *(A)tarateh* and has some seeming archaic or archaistic traits) and the imperial period, by which time she had appropriated much of Cybele's repertoire including her paired lions or lion-mount, mural crown, and tympanum, and dropped her native, Aramaic name in favour of the international 'Syrian Goddess of the Hierapolitans'.[42] It is easy to see how all of this might have helped a Graeco-Roman viewer to understand Atargatis, even if it was only to construe her as exotic, in terms of an already familiar encyclopaedia or frame of reference. But of course there is no evidence (in Hierapolis at least) for whether or how they did so. Except, that is, for *DDS* itself, where Atargatis lends herself to comparison with a remarkable number of goddesses: Hera and Rhea (§15), with further visual similarities to Athena, Aphrodite, Selene, Rhea, Artemis, Nemesis, and the Fates (§32).[43] None of this shows conclusively how a 'real' devotee genuinely might think, but does at least suggest ways in which an originally local

---

[40] Turner (1974), 211–15.

[41] For this series of questions see Frankfurter (1998*b*), 23, 32–3.

[42] For the early coins, see Seyrig (1971): on the fifth coin in his series, the goddess' hairstyle closely recalls that of a goddess on an ivory pyxis from Ugarit (cf. p. 14). For Hierapolis' imperial coins, see *BMC Syria*, 138–46 (from Trajan (98–117) to Philip the Arab (244–9)). The full iconographic dossier in *LIMC* s.v. Dea Syria (H. J. W. Drijvers).

[43] Contrast, however, Elsner (1997*b*), 194, for whom '[w]hat all this succeeds in affirming (despite, even perhaps because of, the attempt to assimilate the gods of Hire to those of Greece) is the radical difference, the cultural otherness, of Lucian's Syrian religion'.

goddess, the divine patronness of Manbog, could have found means of self-expression that helped her to transcend parochialism.

All of which brings us, finally, to the author himself. His account of his pilgrims, and their festivals, is in the main highly formal, normative, and prescriptive—that of an outsider looking on, whether that outsider is cast as a Herodotean ethnographer or a specimen of the more recent breed of Graeco-Roman tourist-pilgrim. While the latter is especially associated with Egypt, there are examples from Syro-Phoenicia, as when, at the beginning of Achilles Tatius, the narrator who finds himself in Sidon after a storm first pays a thank-offering to its goddess Astarte and then goes on a tour of the city to inspect its other dedications.[44] And yet, as we have seen, at the very end of the treatise the perspective narrows down so that in a final sentence fraught with implication the narrator reveals himself to be precisely one such pilgrim: in his youth, he tells us, he dedicated a lock of hair and left it behind in the temple in a sealed container bearing his name (§60). Herodotus' journey to Tyre surely lies in the background of Lucian's Phoenician peregrinations,[45] just as Graeco-Roman tourism-cum-pilgrimage can help to give it a contemporary context. Yet neither engaged Herodotean intellectual inquiry, nor even the quest for the exotic of the Graeco-Roman tourist-pilgrim, can account for this naked confession of 'what I did in my youth'. In a way, it invites a reappraisal of the text itself and of certain aspects of its author/narrator's personality. Take his repeated use of first-person verbs of sense-perception, $εἶδον$, $ἐθεασάμην$, $ὄπωπα$, and so on (all renderings of 'I saw'). On the most obvious level, they have the same function as Herodotus' first-person verbs of sense-perception: they assure the reader that he was there and saw and can be trusted. 'I saw—and you will believe me because I say so.' But there is another level at which the insistent verbs of seeing are an essential component of the narrative of a sacred traveller to a holy place, like the women in the temple of Asclepius in Herodas' fourth mime, or—especially—the chorus in the Delphi of Euripides' *Ion*, who thrill to the sight of Apollo's

---

[44] 1.1.2 $περιιὼν οὖν καὶ τὴν ἄλλην πόλιν καὶ περισκοπῶν τὰ ἀναθήματα...$ For Egypt, see Foertmeyer (1989); and for a study of modern pilgrimage *versus* tourism, Cohen (1992).

[45] 2.44; compare Herodotus' $ἔπλευσα... πυνθανόμενος$ with *DDS* §9 $ἀνέβην πυθόμενος$.

temple.[46] 'I saw... I saw' says Lucian, of the temple's sculptures, just like Creusa's women before the magnificent sculptures on the temple's pediment. Lucian is a spectator, both as ethnographer and as pilgrim, and we have no choice but to look through his eyes. The product of this autopsy, the written travelogue itself, might even be seen as offering readers a vicarious pilgrimage in an ethnography which, in this respect, has interesting resonances of the sophistic ecphrasis[47]—not only a periegete's dry or objectifying catalogue, but also an attempt to bring it vividly and evocatively alive as spectacle before our eyes.

Despite the neglect it has received in this respect, *DDS* could serve as a focus for some of pilgrimage studies' classic debates. The basic difficulty is evidential: is Lucian giving the 'official' programme of what pilgrims do, or a personal interpretation, and how can we tell when so little survives to serve as a corrective? As things stand, these problems are insurmountable—yet cannot inhibit further questions. For example, we might want to ask about Hierapolis' 'actual' constituency (if it was more than a local centre, as surely it was, then what region or regions did it command), about the languages in use among its constituents, and about the extents to which they retained their local identities and perspectives when they visited the sacred centre (in this respect, Lucian's datum that separate communities were lodged apart is highly interesting). Ultimately, these questions perhaps reduce themselves to much bigger, underlying ones about the identities of those who travelled there and what they found there, whether a centre or a periphery. For in one sense, Hierapolitan pilgrimage is centripetal, about bringing people together, as the Syrians and Arabians come together to receive a badge of their ethnicity in the form of a tattoo, and/or to leave their hair in the temple. Furthermore, they are travelling to an urban centre in the middle of a Roman province, not to some out-of-the-way place, a mountainside or site in the desert: difficulty of access is not, as far as we can tell, an issue. But from another angle, travelling to Hierapolis might be seen as centrifugal, 'antistructural', leading its

---

[46] Rutherford (2000*a*), 138–42; Eur. *Ion* 184–218, cf. 232–4; Herod. *Mim.* 4.20–78.

[47] See the excellent remarks of Polanski (1998*a*), 100–2 = (1998*b*), 182–4, on the description of the cult-statue in §32. Note also the affect-laden §46 δοκέοις ἄν, 'you might think'—a feature of sophistic ecphrasis, of which there is another example in Itin. Burdig. 591: cf. Elsner (2000*a*), 195.

pilgrims *away* from the centre, as it might lead a cultured Greek away
from the cultural or political centres of the empire to celebrate a holy
place on its periphery—and in turn accord it a centrality that it lacked in
the Greek mainstream.[48] Yet Lucian, of course, is not simply Hellenic,
but a Hellenized Syrian, a native of Samosata (some 130 km. north east
of Hierapolis). He never lost sight of his origins, referring in numerous
other works to his race and to a childhood in which (if he is to be
believed) he barely spoke Greek and wore a caftan.[49] Which Lucian is
the author of this text? If he is, after all, a cultured Greek travelling to
and celebrating a peripheral, barbarian holy place, it is worth registering
the complete absence of one of the frequent features of Greek treatments
of peripheral or exotic peoples: there is no attempt to present the
Hierapolitans as purveyors of ancient wisdom or esoteric 'Chaldaean'
lore. Or is he in some sense travelling back to a sacred base or centre—
and in so doing exploiting to brilliant effect a master-text, Herodotean
ethnography, whose author was the 'lover of barbarians', φιλοβάρβαρος,
par excellence?[50] And lastly, what does it say for the relations between
Hellenism and non-Greek paganism that he has been able to do so with
such subtle ambiguity about where he stands?

[48] Elsner (1997*b*), 193, 195.
[49] *Bis Accusatus* 27; see also *Hist. Conscr.* 24; *Scyth.* 9, *Adv. Indoct.* 19, *Hal.* 19, *Bis Acc.*
14, 25–34 (Σύρος); *Bis. Acc.* 34, *Scyth.* 9, *Hal.* 19 (βάρβαρος). See further Millar (1993),
245–6, 454–6; Swain (1996), 299.
[50] Plut. *Mor.* 857a.

13

Divine and Human Feet:

Records of Pilgrims Honouring Isis

Sarolta A. Takács

An individual who travelled to a sacred place[1] in order to worship, seek guidance, or ask for help might feel compelled to leave behind a token that commemorated the journey, the visit, the personal request, or gratitude. In the study of Graeco-Roman cult sites, it is the surviving testimonia of pilgrims that offer us invaluable information not only about the site but also about the relationship the ancients had to their gods. Graeco-Roman religion was a votive religion and driven by a reciprocal relationship dynamic. A person seeking and receiving a cure at a shrine would have to acknowledge the positive outcome in form of a thanksgiving, which could be a prayer, a dedication, or a votive offering. Even if giving thanks was not a compulsory action, the cured ones 'were clearly expected by the religious personnel and didactic warnings made clear the risks involved in not giving an offering'.[2] At some ancient sites, these votive offerings were representations of anatomical parts.[3]

Many heartfelt thanks to Ian Rutherford and Jaś Elsner for their critical reading of this paper and the countless other things that made its fruition possible.

[1] Bhardwaj (1997), 2: 'The minimum elements of pilgrimages include the religiously motivated individual, the intended sacred goal or place, and the act of making the spatial effort to bring about their conjunction. Whatever the religion, or the terminology employed for religious journeys, one fact is common to all types of pilgrimage—the physical traversing of some distance from home to the holy place and back.'

[2] Dillon (1997), 169.

[3] For general and concise discussion see ibid. 169–72.

The purpose of this chapter is to provide an analysis of inscriptions with depictions of feet in honour of Isis. A representation of a foot or feet, bare or shod, could be a votive or a commemoration of a visit to a shrine and imply even a wish for a successful return home. A depicted foot or feet could also belong to a god.[4] Inscriptions with feet, in connection with Isis, have been found in Abydos, Philae, Delos, Chaeroneia, Thessaloniki, Maroneia, Catania, Rome, Lanuvium, Industria (Monteù da Po), and Augusta Vindelicorum (Augsburg). The dedicators were predominantly Greeks. Most inscriptions are from the first century CE and later. As a group, however, they constitute only a small portion of inscriptions dedicated to Isis all across the Mediterranean,[5] though it is still widely assumed that the Egyptian goddess Isis worked her healing throughout the Mediterranean world. Her healing shrine in the Nile delta at Menouthis serves as a good example of her role as a healer, although the evidence is based on literary sources. In the Canopus Isis healed a broad spectrum of diseases, most often with the help of plants and honey as well as through incubation and visions.[6] Mother Isis, who almost lost her son, Horus, to a snake bite, could feel compassion for the ill and deliver, if not everlasting health, at least a cure. And a cure-seeker might have called out: 'O Isis, you great healing goddess, heal me, let all bad and evil things, which belong to Seth, let all demonic illness flow from me, just as you healed your son Horus!'[7]

One of the most powerful stories of Isis comes from an Egyptian hieratic text, which describes Isis as an old hag who knows formulae and incantations that make her the most prominent healer in Egypt.[8] It is a universal commonplace that old women can be, or become, extremely knowledgeable and ultimately powerful. In a way, their a-sexual-ness, the fact that they can no longer produce children, makes them acceptable retainers of useful and powerful knowledge. They move from female to male space; they are self-sufficient and, maybe even, subject to no one. In this tale, Isis is remarkably cunning. Ra, the sun god and

---

[4] Kötting (1983), 197–201 and Dunbabin (1990). Castiglione (1970) studied 'ancient footprints and foot representations of religious character' as a result of his 'study tours in Egypt' (p. 95).

[5] Collected by Vidman (1969).

[6] Takács (1994); and Montserrat (1998).

[7] Ebers Papyrus, lines 12–16 (Ebers (1987), 23).

[8] For a translation of this myth of Ra, see J. A. Wilson in Pritchard (1955), 12–14.

most powerful of all gods, is old and spit falls from his mouth. Isis fashions a snake out of Ra's spit and clay. This snake then bites Ra, who calls Isis to him by calling out all his own names, except his secret name. Isis hears this and comes. 'Divine Father,' she says, 'tell me your name, since the one who speaks his own name will be healed.' But, the great name of Ra is hidden in his heart. Finally, in pain and close to death, Ra has his secret name move from his body into Isis' body. Ra allows that his name is taken from his body. Isis becomes the owner of his secret name and, consequently, the mistress of the universe and supreme healing deity. She knows now the unknown and unspeakable,[9] the secret name of Ra, and thus has acquired power.

Prayers and magic formulae, consisting of a chain of nonsensical letters, were (are) believed to give humans the means to come in direct contact with the divine. The one praying would be enabled to entreat a deity without mediation. His words would have the power to bring the deity to perform or bring about the desired end. In his *Metamorphoses*, Apuleius has Lucius the ass, who cannot bear any longer to be a mistreated animal, utter a very traditional prayer in request for help. Gazing at the moon, Lucius prays:

you appear as Ceres, bountiful and primeval bearer of crops, or celestial Venus, or the sister of Phoebus, or ... the horrid Proserpina ... but by whatever name or rite of image it is right to invoke you ... let this be enough toils and enough dangers. (11.2)

Isis appears, reveals herself, and instructs Lucius how to regain his human form (11.5–6). In exchange for her help, Lucius will have to devote his life to Isis. It was dabbling in magic that transformed Lucius into an ass. Experiencing the harshness of an animal existence with a human mind; i.e., having to exist outside human society, brings Lucius to the realization that he wants to be human. It is at this crucial emotional point that Isis intervenes directly.

[9] Isis, in effect, killed Ra and committed an unspeakable crime. Clay (1982) shows how the seer Teiresias, in Sophocles' play, reluctant to utter the unspeakable and forbidden (murder and incest) tries to convey the truth to Oedipus without saying what is unspeakable. In some ways, Teiresias has greater power over Oedipus than Oedipus over the seer. Socio-political standing is suspended. Teiresias' words bring about violent reactions in Oedipus and, ultimately, make him realize the (ugly) truth.

Isis, however, also had a political aspect. Her hieroglyph was a throne and each pharaoh was the embodiment of her son, Horus. Together with her Ptolemaic consort, Sarapis, she was linked to the imperial house (*domus Augusta*) at Rome from the time of the emperor Vespasian. Literary texts alone (and very sparsely) record that Isis or Sarapis related prophecies. The most well-known prophecy is the one given by Isis' partner, Sarapis, to two men, one lame and one blind, at the time of Vespasian's ascent to power.[10] Vespasian's troops had proclaimed him emperor in Alexandria, which made him *de facto* pharaoh of Egypt. Consequently, the new emperor was the embodiment of Horus and, by virtue of his position, was able to heal the two men just as Sarapis had suggested to them in a dream. It does not really matter whether there is any historical truth to this story, for it is the message to the ancient reader that counts. Vespasian had extraordinary powers and was worthy of the political position given to him. If this seems a bit far-fetched, one need only read through the inscription from Rome, which describes all the powers Vespasian held.[11] The only item missing in this list is the healing power attributed to him in the story above. Even outside Egypt, the Flavians remained devoted to Sarapis and Isis; their *pietas* demanded it. The legions had proclaimed Vespasian emperor in Alexandria. Alexandria's guardian deities since the Ptolemaic period were Sarapis and Isis, and, as a result, the two deities became linked to the *domus Augusta* and the Roman state.

Seeking out Isis for medical help, future guidance, even for political or annual ritualistic reasons, follows established patterns of ancient pilgrimage. Interestingly enough, as will be seen below, most of our epigraphic evidence comes from Egypt; and very little data comes from other regions of the Roman empire. While literary texts record healings and prophecies, very few inscriptions record a healing. Most dedicatory inscriptions to Isis with the iconographic component of an incised foot or feet are in Greek and from the Hellenistic period. In her article, *Le impronte del quo vadis*, Guarducci stated that in the classical period monuments that depicted feet showed human rather than divine feet. The latter was very much the case in pre-classical period.[12] However,

---

[10] Tac. *Hist.* 4.81; Suet. *Vesp.* 7; Cass. Dio 66.8.
[11] *CIL* 6.930.
[12] Guarducci (1942–3). There is no definition for 'classical period' in Guarducci's article. I am assuming that the term stands in contrast to 'pre-historic', a time without

even in classical times, one could argue, some feet, and here I am thinking of the *foot of Sarapis*, can designate, if not the presence, the perceived existence or an acknowledgement of a god.[13]

Herodotus, in the fourth book of his *Histories*, writes that Scythia, besides its rivers and the vast extent of its plains, had one other interesting thing: a footprint left by Heracles. The natives, Herodotus remarks further, show this to visitors on a rock by the river Tyras. It is like a man's footprint, but it is two cubits long.[14] Lucian more humorously notes that there existed a footprint of Heracles with one of Dionysus next to it but that Heracles' foot happened to be much bigger than that of Dionysus.[15] Cicero in his philosophical treatise *De Natura Deorum* (3.5.11) has Gaius Aurelius Cotta ask Quintus Lucilius Balbus:

do you believe that the horseshoe-like impression on a flint rock, which is still visible today at lake Regillus, was brought about by Castor's horse? Would you not rather believe, what seems much more likely, that the souls of extraordinary human beings... are divine and eternal, rather than those, who had been once and for all cremated, were able to ride on horseback and fight in battle?[16]

historiography and intellectual reflection. If this assumption is correct, the classical period begins with Herodotus.

[13] Study on this curious representational type provided by Dow and Upson (1944). All known 'Sarapis feet' are right feet. Dow and Upson concluded that most of the feet belong in the Antonine period with one exception belonging into the Flavian period. One cannot but help thinking that the Flavians' *pietas* toward the Alexandrian god and later Hadrian's interest in Egypt might have inspired the production of these feet. There is also an inscription from Alexandria (Breccia (1911), no. 104a), which has a foot imprint and reads: 'Ἴσιδος πόδας'. In the same collection there is also a dedication to Hermanubis with a right, bare foot (no. 120, fig. 75). The toes point towards the reader of the inscription.

[14] The actual passage (4.82) reads: 'θωμάσια δὲ ἡ χώρη αὕτη οὐκ ἔχει, χωρὶς ἢ ὅτι ποταμούς τε πολλῶι μεγίστους καὶ ἀριθμὸν πλείστους. τὸ δὲ ἀποθωμάσαι ἄξιον καὶ πάρεξ τῶν ποταμῶν καὶ τοῦ μεγάθεος, τοῦ πεδίου παρέχεται. εἰρήσεται ἴχνος Ἡρακλέος φαίνουσι ἐν πέτρηι ἐνεόν. τὸ οἷκε μὲν βήματι ἀνδρός. ἔστι δὲ τὸ μέγαθος δίπηχυ. παρὰ τὸν Τύρην ποταμόν.

[15] The travelers having set out for the western ocean from the Pillars of Hercules arrived at a wooded island on the eightieth day. *Ver. Hist.* 1.7: προελθόντος δὲ ὅσον σταδίους τρεῖς ἀπὸ τῆς θαλάσσης δι' ὕλης ὁρῶμεν τινα στήλην χαλκοῦ πεποιημένην Ἑλληνικοῖς γράμμασιν καταγεγραμμένην. ἀμυδροῖς δὲ καὶ ἐκτετριμμένοις. λέγουσαν Ἄρχι τούτων Ἡρακλῆς καὶ Διόνυσος ἀφίκοντο. ἦν δὲ καὶ ἴχνη δύο πλησίον ἐπὶ πέτρας. τὸ μὲν πλεθριαῖον. τὸ δὲ ἔλαττον—ἐμοὶ δοκεῖν. τὸ μὲν τοῦ Διονυσίου. τὸ μικρότερον. θάτερον δὲ Ἡρακλέος.

[16] 'illud in silice quod hodie apparet apud Regillum tamquam vestigium ungulae Castoris equi credis esse? nonne mavis illud credere, quod probari potest, animos

Cotta, the proponent of the Academy, wants philosophical proof from Balbus, the Stoic, which the latter seems unable to provide. Whether he ever brought forth reasoned explanations rather than old wives' tales (*fabellas aniles*), we never learn.

Divine beings, these three ancient authors imply, were believed to walk (or ride upon) the earth and leave behind imprints; that is, tangible evidence of their appearance and, by extension, existence.[17] A divine footprint could be a tourist or pilgrim attraction like Heracles' footprint in a faraway, utterly un-Greek place like Scythia or a wooded, nameless island. This very footprint, it would seem, gave Greeks a foothold in the unknown. Where a Greek hero left a footprint, Greek civilization had touched and could ultimately prosper. On the other hand, a divine footprint could be turned into a reflective, literary pun as Lucian showed. Dionysus, the younger god, had smaller feet than the demi-god, but older, Heracles. Divine beings had human bodies and could show age. Xenophanes already suggested something similar in one of his poems (DK 15), when he declares that divine beings look like their creators. Cicero's philosophical dialogue *De Natura Deorum* goes beyond Herodotus' description and Lucian's witty adaptation. Physical evidence, based on an old wife's tale or on interpretation/speculation, does not prove the actual appearance of a divine being. Without any physical evidence of a divine epiphany, there could not be a perceived, concrete, reality of a god's appearance. This, of course, is a circular

---

praeclarorum hominum ... divinos esse et aeternos, quam eos qui semel cremati essent equitare et in acie pugnare potuisse'.

[17] Kötting (1983), 198, points to Augustine's *De Doctrina Cristiana* 2.1.1 (*CCL* 32.32), who stated: 'For a sign is a thing which, beyond the impression it makes on the senses, makes something else come to mind as a consequence of itself: just as when we see a footprint, we conclude that an animal whose trace it is has passed by' (signum est enim res, praeter speciem quam ingerit sensibus, aliud aliquid ex se faciens in cogitationem venire: sicut vestigio viso, transisse animal cuius vestigium est, cogitamus). The fact that gods have a non-physical existence might be the reason, according to Kötting, that there are very few clear examples of such traces in Graeco-Roman religion. In addition, since Greeks and Romans started to depict their gods early on, there was no need for visible imprints of any kind vouching for their existence (p. 198).
    When there are divine imprints of any kind, however, they are worth a mention and a visit, maybe even a pilgrimage. Pausanias (1.26.5) describes an outline of Poseidon's trident on the rock of the salt-water cistern on the Athenian acropolis; part of the evidence for Poseidon's claim on the land. As long as there was a visual marker of any kind, the abstract belief (that Poseidon had a claim on Athens) had concrete proof and, consequently, was legitimate and, at the same time, legitimized.

argument, and also one that Cotta wanted Balbus to avoid when he asked for philosophical proof. However, human beings worship gods and find artistic ways of representing them. If we agree that human reality is a constructed reality, that there is a dialectical relationship between the creators of culture and their creation, then we can also find footprints, or representations of divine feet that are objects, which can become subjects of analysis.

Physical monumentalization stands opposite narration. The construct of belief, and ultimately of pre-text-based history, is simply more tangible with physical evidence. The location where the divine being left his footprint became a marked place.[18] This sacred location is where the divine and the human spheres intersected. Consequently, the places *where the footprint appears* held extraordinary powers, for with the physical evidence at hand the god's presence and the place's magic were guaranteed.[19] Even when religious systems changed, these places retained their importance. People kept visiting such sites. Imprints of pilgrims' feet would tell others that they had been physically there. Feet marked a location. They imprinted and created a memory. Dedications of representations of feet not only announced that a person was physically present at a specific site, a pilgrimage site, but also gave the dedicator a chance to have an existence beyond that of his physical life. The pilgrim, by leaving behind an inscription or graffito with feet imprints, had created a monument, a physical memory immediately accessible to anyone visiting the site. Through the inscription or graffito, the pilgrim inhabited (in a sense, timelessly) the sacred space s/he had visited to pay homage to a god who was thought to inhabit the space.

The incised feet of the temple of *'Ain Dara* dated to the mid-eighth century BCE, provide an intriguing parallel to our data analysed here. Although a universal rather than the specific precursor, the almost one metre in length foot imprints might memorialize the visitation of a

---

[18] In the Mediterranean world of antiquity, male pagan gods (Herakles, Dionysos, Asklepios/Sarapis, and Mithras), Christ and the prophet Mohammed left behind footprints (Kötting (1983) and Castiglione (1970) *passim*). Goddesses, on the other hand, do not seem to have left behind such markers.

[19] Eusebius in his *Vita Constantini* 3.42 recounts the empress Helen's visit to Galgatha where she admired and honoured the saviour's footprints. See Kötting, (1983), 200, for discussion. Jesus' footprints (barefeet), supposedly dating back to the time when he appeared to Peter, can still be seen in Rome (Guarducci (1942–3), 305–7 and fig. 1).

divine being, or indicate to a visitor how to walk into the innermost part of the sanctuary (*cella*): both feet together, left, and then right. It is the right foot then that touches the *cella* first. By stepping into the oversized footprint, the pilgrim could also feel an immediate connection with the divinity.[20] In contrast to the *'Ain Dara* footprints stand the graffiti drawings of private citizens on the terrace of the Memnonion in Abydos. The editors of the graffiti interpreted the imprints as 'a kind of cartouche, which signified the pilgrimage; a kind of pictogram having the same meaning as the written graffiti formulae τὸ προσκύνημα τοῦ δεῖνα. ὁ δεῖνα ἧκε (the act of worship of so-and-so, so-and-so came).'[21] The votive feet inscriptions found in the temple of Isis of Philae are in part more elaborate than those of Abydos that have only names or partial names. The Philae προσκύνημα inscriptions come from one family whose members were officials of the cult of Isis.[22]

---

[20] Abu Assaf (1990), 11 and pl. 11.

Vidman (1979), 145–7, discusses the *planta pedis* of the Mithraeum in Ostia (see also Dunbabin (1990) 93–4). Since this Mithraeum was situated on the same street as the Serapeum, some scholars postulated an Egyptian influence. The depiction of a sole of a foot, Vidman states, is 'atypical in Egyptian religion'. Divine and human footprints can be found all across the ancient Mediterranean and beyond, they are not solely an Egyptian phenomenon. However, as Dunbabin noted (p. 88), 'it is in Egypt that the practice seems to be most at home'; i.e., most of the surviving data comes from there. The Sarapis sanctuary in Panóias (Portugal) has to be mentioned in this context. There, eroded granite rocks served a Celtic and then Romanized population as a place of blood sacrifice. 'On one of the...rocks beside a small sacrificial hole...and beside the canal leading out of it to the edge of the rock, three sunk-in footprints were found. ... Here, too, the footprints served to perpetuate the persons offering the sacrifice (Castiglione (1970) 101).' The fact that there are three footprints seems odd and defies an easy explanation. While one can step into one footprint and thus symbolically come in contact with the deity, three is one too many unless one thinks of the tripartite arrangement of Isis, Sarapis, and Horus. Alföldy (1995), provides a thorough analysis of the Panóias sanctuary. The cult in honour of the *Dii Severi*, of which *Hypsistos Serapis* was the most prominent, was introduced by the senator Gaius Calpurnius Rufinus at the end of the 2nd or beginning of the 3rd cent. CE. In the Panóias sanctuary, *mystes* were initiated into a cult of gods of the netherworld; an initiation that seems to have involved a fair amount of blood from sacrificial animals.

[21] Perdrizet and Lefebvre (1919), 117: 'L'empreinte du pied forme comme une sorte de cartouche, qui signifiait le pèlerinage; c'est une sorte de pictographe ayant le même sens que les formulas τὸ προσκύνημα τοῦ δεῖνα. ὁ δεῖνα ἧκε des graffites écrits.' Perdrizet and Lefebvre recorded sixteen feet graffiti (nos. 642–658); only one inside the temple structure in the Hall of the King's table (no. 325). This graffito includes, besides the pictogram of a foot, a palm branch and a vessel. The palm branch and the vessel served the pilgrim, according to the editors, in his lustration (p. 63).

[22] Bernand (1969*b*), 2. 217–21 (nos. 188–9), 234–7 (no. 196), 247–8 (no. 198); nos. 188 and 196 pl. 57 and 58.

The four inscriptions (nos. 188, 189, 196, and 198) are from the early fifth century CE. Nos. 188 and 196 show a right and a left foot next to each other to indicate that the dedicator stood on the upper terrace of the temple of Isis ahead of which lay the *cella*. There were, as the feet of *'Ain Dara* tell us, still steps to go until the actual sanctuary of the goddess was reached.

Philae, no. 188

πόδας Σμητχῆμ ἐκ πατρὸς | Παχουμίου προφήτης ᾽Ισιδος | Φιλῶν
Smetchem's feet, son of Pachoumios, prophet of Isis of Philae

Philae, no. 189

This inscription, now in the museum of Alexandria (Inv. 11850), was found in the 'parement' of a Coptic church, which is located north of the Great Temple.

Παχομίου |ρ[κ]η'
(Feet) of Pachomios (year) 127

Philae, no. 196

Σμητχ[ῆμ] ὁ πρωτοστολιστὴς| υἱὸς Π[αχουμ]ίου προφήτου'| Χοιὰκ δι|ρξε'
Διοκλ(ητιανοῦ)
Smetchem, prōtostolistēs, son of Pachoumios, prophet. 15th Choiak, year 168 of the Diocletian period.

Philae, no. 198

This inscription comes from the same Coptic church as no. 189. It is now in the Museum of Alexandria (Inv. 11849).

Σμηταχάτης|Σμητο', μητρο's|Τσαουῆλ, ροα'
Smetachates, (son of) Smeto (and of) Tsaouel, his mother, (year) 171.[23]

Maspero thought Smetchem and his family were priests at Philae. Wilcken, following Krall, put forth what seems a more convincing hypothesis, especially in light of the incised feet. These priests of Isis, Wilcken thought, were Blemmydes who made their way north to

---

[23] Bernand offers a detailed discussion of the family and the relationship of the members mentioned in these inscriptions, ibid. 237–46.

Philae.[24] This group had received special permission from Diocletian to come to Philae and worship Isis,[25] a right they exercised until Justinian I put an end to the worship in 537 CE. The two inscriptions that offer cultic titles (nos. 188 and 196) point to the highest ranks of cult magistracy: the prophet and the *prōtostolistēs*. A cult association had perhaps five priests. If we believe Apuleius' description of the Isis procession, the *navigium Isidis* celebrated in March officially to open the sailing season (*Met.* 11.10), then each of these five priests carried different cult insignia. Greeks in Egypt called the highest-ranking priest prophet whose equivalent outside Egypt seems to have been the *pastophoros* (the one carrying the statue of the goddess). The *stolistēs* (statue dresser) held the second-highest honour in the Egyptian cult system; with the *prōtostolistēs* mentioned in no. 196 we have a statue dresser of first rank, which would mean that this cult association had at least two ranks of dressers.

The island of Delos was of great importance in the propagation of the cult of Isis. Italian traders returned to Italy after Mithridates VI's sack of the island in 86 BCE. While these merchants did not per se introduce the cult, they intensified the cult 'pockets' already existent in Italy. A now, unfortunately, lost inscription from the Capitoline region of Rome dated around 90 BCE links Delos and Rome through a family engaged in slave trade.[26]

The two inscriptions from Delos not only have footprints but they also state that τὸ βῆμα/τὰ βήματα (foot/feet) were placed as dedications. *CE* 60 speaks of an *aretalogos* who followed the command of Sarapis (κατὰ πρόσταγμα Σαράπιδος). (Σαράπιδος is a supplement.) Purgias, the *aretalogos*, dedicated his inscription to Isis and Anubis. The only other occurrence of the title *aretalogos* comes from Beroia in

---

[24] Bernand offers a detailed discussion of the family and the relationship of the members mentioned in these inscriptions, ibid. 242–3.

[25] The years mentioned in the inscriptions count the years from Diocletian's rule forward.

[26] *CIL* 12.1263 = 6.2247 = *SIRIS* 377: 'A. Caecili(us) A. l(ibertus) Olipor | Cn. Caecili A. [l(iberti)] Silonis | Caeci[li]a A. et Cn. l(iberta) Asia | A. Caecili A. Cn. l(iberti) Alexsandri|[5] Polla Caecilia Spuri [f(ilia)] | A. Cae[c]ili A. f(ilii) Pal(atina) Rufi | T. Sulpici T. f(illi) {Caecili} sac(erdotis) Isid(is) Capitoli(nae) | Porcia T. l(iberta) Rufa {sac(erdos)} Sulpici {Capitoli(nae)} | T. Porcius T. f(ilius) Col(lina) Maxsimus|[10] T. Sulpicius T. l(ibertus) Primus | C. Valerius C. l(ibertus) [P]hilar[g]urus | Q. Lolius Q. [f(ilius)] H]or(atia) Rufus | D. Aurelius D. l(ibertus) Stella (?) | H(oc) m(onumentum) <h>e(redes) non seq(uetur).' On this inscription and the introduction of the cult of Isis in Rome, see Takács (1995).

Macedonia (*SIRIS* 119). *Hymnodos* (singer), which as a professional cult title does not appear outside Egypt, seems a close equivalent to *aretalogos*.

CE 60 (I Delos 1263 =*IG*11⁴ 1263)

A white marble slab, the location of its original position is unknown, text inscribed round the edge of the slab from right to left.

Πυργίας ἀρεταλόγος|κατὰ π[ρ]όσταγ
[μα Σαράπιδ]
|ος· τὸ βῆμα--μυρίς
Μαιανδρία σησάμη|ʼΙσι Ανούβι

Purgias, the *aretalogos*, following the command of Sarapis, a foot--a box of unguents, Maeandrian sesame, to Isis and Anubis

CE 122 dated after 114/13 BCE was dedicated by a Milesian citizen to Isis Δικαιοσύνη (Iustitia).

CE 122 (I Delos 2103)

A white, square marble base, which was found in the Serapeion C. On the upper part, two feet are depicted.

ʼΑπατούριος Διοδώρου|Μιλήσιος τὰ βήματα|ἀνέθηκεν ʼΤσιδι|Δικαιοσύνηι|
κατὰ πρόσταγμα|ἐπὶ ἱερέως ʼΑριστίωνος τοῦ|Εὐδόξου Μελιτέως

Apatourios, the Milesian, son of Diodoros, placed the feet to Isis Dikaiosune following the command in the presence of the priest Aristionos, son of Eudoxos of Miletus.

In all inscriptions dedicated to Isis, this epithet δικαιοσύνη occurs only thrice, once more on Delos (*CE* 117) and on a marble stele found in Athens dated to the first century BCE. There is no occurrence of it in the Latin-speaking part of the empire.[27]

SIRIS 61 = IG 4.3414[28]

A white marble basis from Chaeronea (Boeotia) with two sandalled feet planted next to each other on the top of the basis dated to the imperial period.

Φῦρος Σωτέου|ἐπιταγῆι Εἴσιδος
Phuros, son of Soteos, following the (oracular) command of Isis

---

[27] Plutarch, however, does mention the epithet in his treatise *De Iside*.
[28] Manganaro (1961), 187, fig. 9–9a.

SIRIS 111a:[29]

A white square marble slab from the temple of Sarapis in Thessalonike dated to the first century BCE. Underneath the inscription two feet planted next to each other are depicted in relief. The name of the dedicator, Caecilia Polla, seems to point to the Roman inscription of 90 BCE (*SIRIS* 377), n. 18.

Καικιλίαι Πώλλαι Σαράπιδι|Εἴσιδι κατ᾽ ἐπιταγήν
For Kaikilia Polla, to Sarapis and Isis, following a(n oracular) command

SIRIS 111b:[30]

A white marble slab from the same location as *SIRIS* 111a and with the same design, the feet, however, are imprinted rather than in relief. The date of the inscription might be a bit more recent than *SIRIS* 111a.

Βενετύα Πρεῖμα|κατ᾽ ἐπιταγήν
Venetia Prima, following a(n oracular) command

SIRIS 111c:[31]

A white marble slab with a right foot imprint. The inscription comes from the same location as *SIRIS* 111a and b and its date is thought to be the same as *SIRIS* 111b. The slab breaks off at the third line. The sigmas are reversed.

Ἰερητεύοντος Νεικίου τοῦ Ἀντ|έρ]ντος ἀρχινακοροῦντος Ἀμ[ε]ιμήτ]ου?τοῦ Δημακράτους
Of the priest Neikios, son of Anteron, of the chief temple warden Ameimetos, son of Demokratos

SIRIS 111d:[32]

A white broken marble slab found in the same location as *SIRIS* 111a, b, and c. There are two incised feet planted next to each other. The slab is broken from the left and the feet imprints remain only partially. The date of the inscription is probably the first century CE. The dedicator was a freedman of Greek origin.

Ἴσισι Νύμφηι Αἰμίλιος Εὔτυ|χος
To Isis the Nymph, Aimilios Eutuchos

[29] Manganaro (1964), 292, pl. 69.1.
[30] Ibid., pl. 69.2.
[31] Ibid., pl. 69.3.
[32] Ibid. 292–3, pl. 70.1

Tacheva-Hitova no. 52:[33]

A marble base from Maroneia, a coastal city in Thrace. It features two oversized pairs of bare feet on top of the base. The feet point towards the reader of the inscription. The *ex voto* dedication is to Serapis (a newer rendering of the name than Sarapis), Isis, Anubis, and Harpokrates. The 'p' and 'k' of the name are aspirated. The inscription has been dated to the late second or the beginning of the third century CE. The feet are somewhat oversized (33 cm right foot and 35 cm of left foot of the left pair and 40 cm of the right pair).

'Αγωνοθέτης 'Απολλώνιος 'Απολλωνίου Σεράπιδι|'Ίσιδι'Ανούβιδι 'Αρφοχρά- τηικατὰ πρόσταγμα

The judge Apollonios, son of Apollonios, to Serapis, Isis, Anubis, Harpokrates in accordance with a command

SIRIS 379 = *CIL* 6.351 = *ILS* 4354:[34]

A marble disc from the Church of Santa Maria in Aracoeli in Rome. The inscription is from the imperial period. A foot is depicted in the middle of the disc. The dedication is to Isis *frugifera*, an epithet that occurs rarely on inscriptions.[35]

Isidi | frugiferae | ---| --ene | --donum | posuit
To Isis the fruitbringer ---has put this gift

SIRIS 416 = *CIL* 6.31107:[36]

A marble slab from the via Nomentana in Rome. Underneath the inscription there are two incised pairs of feet. The toes of the left pair point downwards, the right pair upwards. The dedicator was a freedwoman of Greek origin.

Licinia Philete | pro salute sua et suor(um) | d(e) s(uo) p(osuit)
Licinia Philete has put this up from her own funds for her and the well-being of her family

SIRIS 449 = *CIL* 6. 15782

A small marble slab whose upper part is broken. Between a sistrum to the right and the left there are two soles depicted. The origin of the inscription is not known; it is now in Rome.

---

[33] Tacheva-Hitova (1983), 31; Grandjean (1975), 119–120, pl. 5; Dunbabin (1990), 86, fig. 2.

[34] Guarducci (1942–3), 315.

[35] The two other examples are *SIRIS* 724 (Latin) and 317 (Greek).

[36] Manganaro (1961), 188.

L. Claudius Stacus | Herennia G(aia) l(iberta) | Laudica
Lucius Claudius Stacus Herennia Gaia Laudica, freedwoman

SIRIS 515:[37]

A slab of Lunensian marble broken in many parts from Catania (Sicily). The date of the inscription is probably first to second century CE. Two bare feet in relief in a frame facing towards the reader of the inscription, which is below the frame.

M(arcus) Antonius Cal[l]istus

SIRIS 523 = ILS 4355:[38]

A marble slab from Lanuvium with two sets of feet imprints between three lines of inscription. The first line above the feet mentions the addressee: Isis Regina, and the two lines below the feet, the dedicator. One set (sandalled feet) move away from the viewer of the inscriptions, while the other set (bare feet) move towards him/her. The inscription comes from the first to second century CE and has one orthographic transposition, 'Crhyseros' for 'Chryseros' and a peculiarity: 'solbuit' for 'solvit'. The dedicator was a freedman of Greek origin.

Isidi reginae | C(aius) Sempronius Crhyse | ros votum solbuit
To Isis the queen, Gaius Sempronius Chryseros fulfilled his vow

SIRIS 645 = CIL 5. 7488:[39]

A marble slab from Industria (Monteù da Po in Liguria) with two feet in relief. In the middle of the feet are two hederae which sandwich a sistrum. Left from the left foot is a 'v' for 'votum' and right of the right foot an 's' for 'solvit'.

Avilia Ambilis | v(otum) s(olvit)
Avilia Ambilis fulfilled her vow

---

[37] Ibid. 184 n. 2, 190, fig. 7. From Catania also comes an inscription (1st to 2nd cent. CE) with incised, bare feet on the surface of a marble slab. The feet point towards the viewer and below them are written three lines. Based solely on the photograph, it would seem to me that the third line is by a different hand: D(is) M(anibus) | Vibia Arete vix[it annis] | XXX (To the Gods of the Netherworld, Vibia Arete who lived 30 years). Then written on the front side of the slab: Vibius Aptitian(us) Pi---. Manganoro interpreted the feet as representing the husband's visit to his wife's grave. I would argue differently; namely, that Vibia had visited a sacred place and was returning to those visiting her 'memorial'.

[38] Manganaro (1961), 189 n. 2, fig. 11.

[39] Ibid. 189 n. 1, fig. 10.

The most interesting and telling of all these inscriptions is, in my opinion, one found at Augsburg in the Romanized outskirts of the empire. Following Tacitus' description, we should imagine the provincial capital of Raetia as a relatively sophisticated town. Its ethnic make-up was mixed; among the indigenous Celtic population there were imperial administrative employees, Italian merchants, and immigrants from various areas of the empire. The inscription was discovered close to the cathedral, where two buildings, one with murals and a mosaic, were also uncovered. East of this area a *hypocausteum* was unearthed and further, in the same direction, a bath and a cistern turned up.[40] The text of the inscription was written downwards in three columns with the concluding line written across the bottom of the three columns. Between the first and second and the second and third column, the dedicator, Flavius Eudiapractus, had a pair of bare feet depicted in relief. Incised on the left foot is a wavy line interpreted to be a snake.[41] The depiction of a snake occurs quite often on these inscriptions with footprints. A possibility, positivistic as it might be, could be that snakes posed a threat to people travelling on foot. The poison of the snake was also a perfect *pharmakon*; able to heal as well as to kill. Another possibility is that the snake simply symbolizes Isis. The *uraeus* could represent Isis as the asp was sacred to the pharaoh.

SIRIS 646:

first column	Fl(auius)| Eu|dia|prac|tus
second column	Isi|di| Reg(inae)
third column	ex| uo|to
below first column	s(oluit)
below second column	l(ibens)
below third column	m(erito) p(osuit) [42]

Flavius Eudiapractus gladly and deservedly fulfilled his vow to Isis the Queen, and put this up

The dedicator's *cognomen* suggests Greek origin. The palaeography and the lack of a *praenomen* suggest the third century as a possible date range

---

[40] Ohlenroth (1954), 76–85. The inscription was found in Fronhof 6, previously Kremerhaus D 115, which corresponds on Ohlenroth's map with no. 42.

[41] Vidman called it a *uraeus*.

[42] *SIRIS* 646 and new reading *AE* 1982, 726. See Takács (1995) for discussion.

for the inscription. Eudiapractus' dedication might have followed the healing of a foot ailment.[43] Despite the lack of further archaeological detail of the area where the inscription has been found, the proximity of a *hypocausteum*, a bath, and a cistern implies that Eudiapractus found a cure through water treatment.

Water played a significant part in the cult of Isis and Sarapis. It had an important place in the Egyptian as well as Celtic world of ideas.[44] The life-giving Nile came into existence by Isis crying for her murdered husband/brother, Osiris. All sanctuaries of Isis in Noricum, a heavily Celtic area, are located on ancient 'holy mountains' and all of them have rich water sources.[45] Assigned to the celestial, as well as to the terrestrial sphere, water was thought to be magical. Its magic ranged from bringing forth the essential crops to healing various bodily ailments.

A look at the small town of Aquae Helvetiorum, Baden in Switzerland, should help in understanding the inscription from Augsburg in a larger context. Aquae, as its name suggests, possessed thermal springs. Excavations have brought forth a Roman bath complex.[46] Its size suggests that the Aquensians were quite affluent. The discovery of a building complex, approximately 300 m west of the baths, yielded, in addition to a large number of mural painting remains, a large number of medical instruments.[47] An inscription suggests that there was also a temple of Isis in this area.

SIRIS 714 = CIL 13.5233

Deae Isidi templum a solo | L. Annusius Magianus | de suo posuit vik(anis) Aquensib(us) | ad cuius templi ornamenta |⁵ Alpinia Alpinula coniunx | et Peregrina fil(ia) (denarios) C dede | runt l(ocus) d(atus) d(ecreto) vicanorum

L. Annusius Magianus has built on his own and with his own money this temple for the goddess Isis among the Aquensian villagers on a location given by the decree of the villagers while his wife Alpinia Alpinula and his daughter Peregrina gave a hundred denarii for the embellishment of this temple

---

[43] See *AE* 1982, 726.
[44] I understand this concept as a socially constructed reality.
[45] For the importance of water in the cult of Isis and Sarapis see Wild (1981).
[46] Drack and Fellmann (1988), 352.
[47] Ibid. 349.

The initial reason for Annusius Magianus' interest in Isis remains unknown and any attempt to pinpoint one would be pure speculation. Certain conditions, however, facilitated the construction of an Isis sanctuary. The river Limmat recreated, although admittedly much less exotically, a Nilotic environment, the very basic topographical condition that would allow the integration of the cult of Isis and Sarapis. While the economic position of the dedicator, Annusius Magianus, in the Aquensian community must have been a decisive factor in the public allocation of village owned property, the council of the Aquensians had to be well disposed towards Isis as well. The construction of a temple on publicly owned land could only take place when the deity for whom the temple was built was not perceived as impeding the *pax deorum* (peace among gods) and, subsequently, the *pax hominum* (peace among human beings). This inscription, assigned to the second or third century CE, falls into a period in which the cult of Isis and Sarapis was well established as a public religious rite (*sacrum publicum*).[48]

There are too few surviving inscriptions with feet imprints in honour of Isis to draw broad conclusions; although, some might still believe that here is enough proof that the goddess' cult swept through the Roman empire and bound most of its inhabitants to it. But the reality is that this goddess was certainly not a rival to the healing and miracle-working Jesus and his religion. Isis had her pilgrims, though. Most of them came to celebrate Isis at one of the annual festivals, fulfilling a vow or following a divine command, others came to seek a cure. Besides a written record (a name or a more detailed inscription), some of these pilgrims had also (their) feet depicted. Some of them came in sandals, some of them barefoot. Those who came with shod feet might have taken off their shoes at the threshold of the sanctuary. They stood in front of the sanctuary (two planted feet), they walked towards and into it (single feet away from the viewer of the inscription), and on occasion, they stepped into pre-made footprints, and then they returned (single feet towards the viewer of the inscription). They completed their journey (two planted feet towards the viewer of the inscription). Here, in the sacred space inhabited by the goddess Isis, the pilgrims left their mark. They marked their space and thus imprinted their memory. Spaces we can still view and memories that can be recalled even today.

---

[48] The introduction of the cult as a *sacrum publicum* occurred around 40 CE.

PART III

JEWISH AND CHRISTIAN PILGRIMAGE

14

Rabbi Aqiba Comes to Rome:

A Jewish Pilgrimage in Reverse?

David Noy

People from Palestine travelled to Rome throughout the second, third, and fourth centuries CE, for a variety of reasons.[1] Some journeys made by Jewish sages are mentioned in rabbinic literature. They are usually described as travelling individually or in pairs (although some of them were wealthy men who probably took their entourages with them).[2] The journey that is discussed most often in the Talmud was made by a group of four rabbis: Aqiba, Gamaliel, Joshua b. Hananiah, and Eleazar b. Azariah.[3] There are many anecdotes about their journey and some of their experiences while they were at Rome. This visit is usually dated to 95 CE (on less than compelling grounds; see below), and must at any rate have taken place at the end of the first or beginning of the second century CE.

Various theological problems seem to have arisen during the voyage. They were at sea during the Feast of Tabernacles, and found that only Gamaliel had a lulab (palm-branch); they decided that if each of them 'fulfilled his obligation with it' and then gave it as a gift to the next one,

---

[1] For full discussion, see Noy (2000), 85–127, 255–67.

[2] e.g. b. Horayot 10a, Midrash Gen.R. 13.9 p.118; Midrash Deut.R. 2.24; y. Sanhedrin 7.19 52d. See Finkelstein (1962), 332 n.2.

[3] References include: b. Abodah Zara 54b; Midrash Gen.R. 13. 9, 20.4; Midrash Ex.R. 30.9; Midrash Deut.R. 2.24; Midrash Eccl.R. 10.7. Some or all of these men probably made more than one visit, as noted by Solin (1983), 660, so the various references do not necessarily all refer to the same one.

they would all satisfactorily fulfil their obligations.[4] As was common for travellers from the East at this date, they appear to have landed at Puteoli, from where they could allegedly hear the noise of the crowds in Rome.[5] Bacher suggested reading 'Palatine' rather than 'Puteoli', on the incontestable grounds that it would not be possible to hear the noise of Rome from Puteoli,[6] but it seems more likely that, unless their hearing was supposed to be supernaturally acute, the passage is deliberately exaggerating to make its point. According to one rabbinic source which echoes the same view about the city:[7]

Our Rabbis taught: Were it not for the revolution of the sun, the sound of the tumult of Rome would be heard: and were it not for the sound of the tumult of Rome, the sound of the revolution of the sun would be heard.

After spending some time at Rome, they sailed home from Brindisi.[8] The following story, of which one interpretation suggests that they had had enough of each other's company by the end, is probably set during the return journey:[9]

They [R. Gamaliel and R. Joshua] once travelled on board a ship. R. Gamaliel had with him some bread only, while R. Joshua had with him bread and flour. When R. Gamaliel's bread was consumed he depended on R. Joshua's flour. 'Did you know', the former asked him, 'that we should be so much delayed that you brought flour with you?' The latter answered him, 'A certain star [i.e. comet] rises once in seventy years and leads the sailors astray, and I suspected it might rise and lead us astray.' 'You possess so much knowledge', the former said to him, 'and yet must travel on board a ship!'

Most scholars until recently accepted that the journey of Aqiba and his colleagues actually happened. Finkelstein gives a dramatic and somewhat imaginative account.[10] He claims that it was motivated by governmental threats to the Jews of Rome in response to the conversion of Flavius Clemens and other prominent figures; this idea, apparently first proposed by Vogelstein, is the origin of the dating to 95 CE, but was

---

[4] b. Sukkah 41b. All translations of talmudic passages are from the Soncino edn.
[5] Noy (2000), 143; b. Makkoth 24a–b = Midrash Lam.R. 5.18.
[6] Bacher (1896), 195–6.
[7] b. Yoma 20b.
[8] m. Erubim 4.1.
[9] b. Horayoth 10a.
[10] Finkelstein (1962), 136.

flatly rejected by Leon.[11] The reliability of the whole story is question-able, however, and Catherine Hezser is sceptical about it:[12]

Although visits to Rome are repeatedly mentioned, their historicity, just as the historicity of stories about meetings of rabbis and government officials, is doubtful. The authors of all of these stories may have tried to enhance the image of the particular sage by depicting him in close contact with power-holders and on journeys to the center of authority.

The factual nature of any event recorded in a rabbinic text is always open to question. However, Hezser's reasons for scepticism in this case do not seem entirely well founded. The rabbis are not represented as having any dealings with authority figures at Rome, and their activities in the city do not enhance their image in any obvious way. Their theological credentials as interpreters of Torah and upholders of Jewish tradition are stressed, but they are not shown as successful on a political level. Furthermore, the collegial nature of their trip does not fit the idea of trying to enhance the image of a particular sage. There is a story about a witty exchange between the emperor's daughter and Gamaliel (in which she gets the better of him and her father), but it is not said to take place at Rome.[13] Trips to Rome did not necessarily enhance prestige: a separate visit by R. Meir ended in an embarrassing incident with non-kosher food or a prostitute, as a result of which he ran away to Babylon.[14] There was apparently some discussion about whether a ruling given by R. Eleazar b. Jose at Rome was valid elsewhere, which implies that doing something at Rome did not necessarily give it any particular authority within the rabbinic world.[15] One exception con-cerns some dealings between R. Joshua and the emperor, which are probably set at Rome, and may be part of the group visit, although the other rabbis are not mentioned and Westenholz thinks that the emperor is Hadrian.[16] However, the miracles which occur in this story (all the pregnant women miscarry; the walls of Rome fall down; the emperor's

---

[11] Leon (1960), 36.
[12] Hezser (1997), 170.
[13] b. Sanhedrin 39a; the exchange concerns God removing Adam's rib to create Eve.
[14] b. Abodah Zara 18b.
[15] b. Nidah 58a.
[16] Westenholz (1995), 90.

daughter contracts leprosy) seem to put it in a rather different genre from the mundane details of the other rabbinic activities at Rome.[17]

I shall work on the assumption that, even if the trip of the four rabbis did not happen exactly in the way described in the sources, similar trips certainly did happen, and the stories throw some light on what it was like for influential people from Palestine to travel to Rome. They do not, however, throw much light at all on why such people made the journey. None of the accounts offers a specific reason; Finkelstein's ideas of a political motive are not directly based on anything in the sources. The best documented Jewish embassy to Rome, the one from Alexandria to Caligula in which Philo participated, was an attempt to get the emperor to intervene in a local dispute. There is one talmudic discussion of why an embassy (probably not R. Aqiba's) was sent to Rome.[18] 'For the Government had once issued a decree that [Jews] might not keep the Sabbath, circumcise their children, and that they should have intercourse with menstruant women.' R. Reuben b. Istroboli had it removed temporarily, but when it was reimposed, '[The Jews] then conferred as to who should go [to Rome] to work for the annulment of the decrees.' The embassy attributed elsewhere to R. Simon b. Yohai and R. Eleazar b. Yose is probably the one referred to here, most likely in the reign of Antoninus Pius on the assumption that the anti-Jewish legislation belongs to Hadrian.[19] On another occasion, R. Nahum of Gimzo was robbed at an inn of the gift he was bringing for the emperor,[20] but he was not necessarily on a political mission; other people are recorded as paying their respects to the emperor in the hope of advancing their careers,[21] and it may have been common for people to leave some sort of gift (probably without seeing the emperor in person) in the hope that they would be under his protection while at Rome. When a new emperor came to power, communities all over the empire sent delegations to Rome in his honour, and delegations were also sent to Rome for many local reasons;[22] some rabbinic visits may

---

[17] b. Hullin 59b. b. Nedarim 50b reports a non-miraculous exchange between R. Joshua b. Hananiah and the emperor's daughter, in which he gets the better of her.
[18] b. Me'ilah 17a.
[19] *Jewish Encyclopaedia* (*JE*) 6.599–600; Westenholz (1995), 90.
[20] *JE* 12.796; Ginzberg (1925–38), 4.203.
[21] Noy (2000), 146.
[22] Noy (2000), 100–6.

have fallen into this category, since it is unlikely that such theologically irrelevant information would be mentioned in the Talmud.

Aqiba and his colleagues *may* have had dealings with the authorities, but there is no particular reason to suppose that they did, and the journey could be made by people from Palestine with no political purposes at all. An anecdote which is probably set during the group's visit may even suggest their general reluctance to become involved with the Roman elite: R. Joshua went to the house of an influential noble-woman, but was very worried about how his 'disciples' would interpret his actions while he was there (removing his *tefillin* and shutting the door) and when he came out (taking a ritual bath).[23]

It is very likely that Aqiba and his colleagues would have had dealings with the local community leaders at Rome, since by the mid-second century some of them were well thought-of by the Palestinian rabbis. R. Matthiah b. Heresh established an academy at Rome.[24] On his first voyage there from Palestine, he is said to have reached Puteoli and then turned back because of longing for the land of Israel.[25] Matthiah is recorded as questioning R. Simeon b. Yohai, during his visit to Rome, about the Ark of the Covenant and the blood of reptiles.[26] One anecdote with a questionable chronological basis connects Matthiah with a member of Aqiba's group:[27] 'R. Matthiah b. Heresh asked R. Eleazar b. Azariah in Rome: have you heard about the four kinds of sins, concerning which R. Ishmael has lectured?' This perhaps implies an interest among the Jews of Rome in being kept up to date with the latest theological thinking.

Todos or Theudas (perhaps versions of the name Theodosius) of Rome, who was active at a similar time, was presumably also a Hebrew scholar in view of his high prestige among the sages of Palestine, on account of which actions by him were approved which would have been condemned if they had been done by anyone else.[28] It is not stated that he was an immigrant to Rome, but his prestige seems more plausible in someone born in Palestine than in a native of Rome. He was also a figure

---

[23] b. Shabbath 127b. Other anecdotes about the visit do not mention 'disciples', so perhaps this is a misunderstanding of the role of the other rabbis.

[24] b. Sanhedrin 32b.

[25] *JE* 11.1132, quoting Sifre Deut. 80; this could well be an addition for the purposes of anti-emigration propaganda.

[26] b. Yoma 53b, b. Me'ilah 17a.

[27] b. Yoma 86a.

[28] b. Bezah 23a; t. Yom Tov 2.15; y. Moed Qatan 3.1.

of influence among the Jews of Rome, to whom he introduced the practice of eating a 'helmeted kid' (or possibly a lamb) roasted whole on Passover night (implying that there were large gatherings to celebrate the occasion).[29] There is also a story about how R. Joshua rescued a Jewish child who had been captured during the Revolt; the child gave a theologically approved answer about the reason for the Jews' defeat, saying that God punished them for their disobedience, and became a sage himself, R. Ishmael b. Elisha.[30] This could not have happened on a visit in the 90s CE, which would of course be much too late for any prisoners to be describable as 'children', but even if it is imaginary it shows that there was a later belief that rabbinic sages could be found at Rome. There seems to be an underlying assumption of regular contact between Palestine and Rome, and visits like that of Aqiba's group must have been an important way of maintaining it, even if that was not the only reason why they went.

There are some more anecdotes about the rabbis at Rome. R. Aqiba sent out 'a member of his household' to buy some food in the market, which may indicate that they had travelled with their servants, as would be expected for people of their status.[31] Another text describes a debate at Rome between the rabbis and some pagan 'philosophers', probably on this occasion.[32] Rabbinic texts are a useful source for how people reacted when they first came to Rome, an experience which is rarely described in any other sort of literature. The sheer scale of Rome, as well as the noise, undoubtedly struck visitors, as in this grossly inaccurate saying attributed to R. Judah the Prince:[33]

There are three hundred and sixty five thoroughfares in the great city of Rome, and in each there were three hundred and sixty five palaces; and in each palace there were three hundred and sixty five storeys, and each storey contained sufficient to provide the whole world with food.

Such impressions presumably explain why there are some other hyperbolic descriptions of the city, not necessarily derived from eye-witnesses. The school of R. Shila said that Rome had as much 'fine gold' as the rest of the world put together.[34] A third/fourth-century CE rabbi expressed a

---

[29] y. Pesahim 7.34a; Bokser (1990); Rutgers (1995), 204.   [30] b. Gittin 58a.
[31] Midrash Ruth 6.1.   [32] b. Abodah Zara 54b.   [33] b. Pesahim 118b.
[34] b. Gittin 58a.

very unrealistic view of how the corn-dole system worked, and of how big the city was:[35]

Ulla said: 'Greek Italy' is the great city of Rome, which covers an area of three hundred *parasangs* by three hundred. It has three hundred markets corresponding to the number of days of the solar year. The smallest of them is that of the poultry sellers, which is sixteen *mil* by sixteen.[36] The king dines every day in one of them. Everyone who resides in the city, even if he was not born there, receives a regular portion of food from the king's household, and so does everyone who was born there, even if he does not reside there. There are three thousand baths in it, and five hundred windows the smoke from which goes outside the wall. One side of it is bounded by the sea, one side by hills and mountains, one side by a barrier of iron, and one side by pebbly ground and swamp.

It would not be surprising if someone who had previously regarded Tiberias or Sepphoris as a big city was overwhelmed by Rome, and Aqiba's group probably reacted in a similar way. Rabbis also noticed the social conditions, and the contrast between rich and poor:[37]

When R. Joshua b. Levi visited Rome, he saw there pillars covered with tapestry so that in winter they should not contract and in summer they should not split, but in the market he saw a poor man wrapped in a single mat—others say, in half an ass's pack saddle.

These texts illustrate what the rabbis did at Rome and how they felt about what they found there, but they still fail to answer the question of why they went there in the first place. I wish to argue that Rome, as the centre of the empire, had some specific attractions for Jewish visitors. Naturally, the Talmud has no interest in what they thought of the Colosseum or the Pantheon,[38] but non-Jews certainly travelled to Rome in order to enjoy the entertainment there and to see the sights of the city. Ovid says that 'a great world was in the city' for Augustus' Naumachia.[39] Martial lists the people from the eastern fringes of the

---

[35] b. Megillah 6b.

[36] A *mil* corresponds to 7.5 stades and a *parasang* to 30 stades; roughly 1.5 km and 6 km.

[37] Midrash Gen.R. 33.1.

[38] However, in the 12th cent., the Jewish traveller Benjamin of Tudela described the Colosseum and imperial palaces.

[39] *AA* 1.174.

Roman empire who came for the opening of the Colosseum.[40] The
partly preserved work by Florus, *Vergilius Orator an Poeta* (1.1), set in
the early second century CE, begins with some men from Baetica who
have been to Rome for the games being blown off course on the journey
home. Enough people came from Cadiz in the third/fourth centuries to
have their own designated seats at the Colosseum.[41] In 403, the monk
Telemachus came from the East to try to stop the gladiatorial games at
Rome, and was lynched as a result.[42] Touristic sightseeing at Rome was
certainly a possibility for those with available time and money, like
Antonius Theodorus, a Phoenician who became an important official in
Egypt, and who 'a citizen in sovereign Rome, spent much time there and
saw the wonders in that place and the things there'.[43]

There is, however, one sort of sightseeing at Rome which was specific to
the Jews, and which might be thought to cross the boundary between
sightseeing and pilgrimage: going to see the objects of Jewish cult which
were captured at Jerusalem in 70 CE. The Arch of Titus depicts the ones
which were presumably the most eye-catching when displayed in the
triumph: the menorah, shewbread table, trumpets and vessels for the
Temple cult (Fig. 1). There were clearly others too with less visual
impact for general spectators (see below). The public display of objects
representing Roman military success was already well-established: the
most prominent one was probably the obelisk installed in the centre of
the Circus Maximus bearing an inscription stating that 'Egypt having
been brought into the power of the Roman people, (Augustus) gave it as
a gift to the Sun'.[44] Displaying the cult objects of the Jewish God may
even (accidentally or deliberately) have recalled the archaic practice of
evocatio, where a deity associated with the enemy was encouraged to
come over to Rome. Vespasian built the Temple of Peace as part of the
new Forum of Peace, and that was where most of the objects were placed
after the triumph over the Jews:[45]

---

[40] *Spect.* 3.
[41] CIL 6.32098. l, m. They may, of course, have been in Rome for other reasons.
[42] Theodoret, *HE* 5.26 (PG 82.1256).
[43] *IGR* 1.1211 = SB 1002.
[44] *CIL* 6.702.
[45] Josephus, *BJ* 7.162.

Figure 1. The spoils of Jerusalem carried in the triumph of Vespasian and Titus. Photograph: DAI ROME INST. NEBG. 57.893.

There [i.e. the Temple of Peace] too he laid up the golden vessels from the Temple of the Jews, for he prided himself on them; but their Law and the crimson curtains of the Inner Sanctuary he ordered to be deposited in the Palace[46] for safekeeping.

The 'Law' mentioned by Josephus must have consisted of scrolls saved from the Temple. There is also a very late reference to a scroll being preserved somewhere other than in the Palace. *Midrash Genesis Rabbati*, probably attributable to the eleventh-century Moses ha-Darshan of Narbonne, mentions variant readings taken from a scroll which had been brought from Jerusalem to Rome and was stored in the '*kenishta* of Severus';[47] this has usually been taken as a synagogue and often linked to the emperor Alexander Severus,[48] but Siegel argues that it could be any sort of public building connected to someone called Severus. He

---

[46] The Palace would at this date be the Domus Tiberiana. I am grateful to Tony Brothers for information about the buildings in Rome.
[47] Genesis Rabbati ed. Albeck p. 209; Siegel (1975), 15; *JE* 14.1200.
[48] Frey (1975), LXXXI; Leon (1960), 162–3 takes a sceptical view.

also notes that such a document, if it existed, would be more likely to survive in private than public hands.[49]

There are various references in rabbinic texts to some of the objects from Jerusalem being seen, but always with reference to one visitor, R. Eleazar b. Jose. There is no obvious reason why he is the only one mentioned. He was a pupil of R. Aqiba, and presumably visited Rome some time in the early or mid-second century CE. He is said to have seen three items, only one of which is mentioned in the non-rabbinic sources: the remains of Solomon's throne,[50] the High Priest's headband (*ziz*),[51] and the curtain from the Holy of Holies (*parokhet*).[52] He reported that 'Holy unto the Lord' was written in one line on the headband, and that there were bloodstains from sacrificial offerings on the curtain. The objects in the Temple of Peace were no doubt on public display, since the Flavians lost no opportunity to make propaganda out of their Jewish victory. Where Eleazar would actually have seen the curtain is unclear. It seems highly unlikely that a Jewish sightseer would have been allowed into the Palace, where Josephus says the curtain was, and more probably it was eventually placed in the temple with the other objects.

Eleazar was successful in his attempt to see the spoils of Jerusalem, and the interest which he took in recording specific details about them suggests that they were the reason why he was in Rome. The other rabbis who visited Rome must surely have seen them as well; it is hard to imagine that they would not have gone to the Temple of Peace, even if their visits are unrecorded. Pilgrimage was a traditional duty for Jews until 70 CE. When pilgrimage to the Jerusalem Temple was no longer possible, the idea of a sort of substitute pilgrimage to see its relics at Rome must have been appealing; even if Jews travelled to Rome for other reasons, it would be natural for them to act like Eleazar and go to the temple of Peace. The tradition of displaying war trophies as reminders of national success and failure was revived in the nineteenth and twentieth centuries: in the early nineteenth century the Louvre displayed objects looted by victorious French armies, and in white-ruled Rhodesia the National Museum gave pride of place to nine chiefs' ceremonial staves or emblems captured by the British South African

---

[49] Siegel (1975), 53, 59.   [50] Midrash Esth.R. 1.12.
[51] b. Shabbath 63b; b. Sukkah 5a.   [52] b. Yoma 57a.

Army in 1899.[53] Such objects kept in western museums receive visits from people who may still regard them as things to venerate in their own right, or see them as reminders of the consequences of imperialism.[54] Jewish visitors to the Temple of Peace may have experienced the same feelings.

However, their visits may only have been possible for a limited period, and there is probably a good reason why there are no references to anyone after Eleazar visiting the relics. The temple of Peace was largely destroyed by fire in 192 CE:[55]

And a fire that began at night in some dwelling leaped to the Temple of Peace and spread to the storehouses of Egyptian and Arabian wares, whence the flames, borne aloft, entered the Palace [or Palatine] and consumed very extensive portions of it, so that nearly all the state records were destroyed.

The fire was very destructive, and some of the rich who had deposited their valuables in the temple for safety are said to have been left destitute.[56] There are no direct references to what happened to the Jewish trophies, but they are not likely to have escaped undamaged, especially those like the curtain which did not have any obvious monetary value. The Temple of Peace was restored by Septimius Severus, but without the works of art which had characterized the original building. The lack of any later references to the relics of Jerusalem in rabbinic literature may therefore simply be due to the fact that they were no longer on public display.

It seems that the objects were not all destroyed in the fire, however, since there are some much later references to them; they may have been kept in the Palace after 192, although this is not stated. Procopius provides two apparently contradictory accounts. He says that Germans besieging Carcasiana in Gaul in 507 were trying to capture the booty which Alaric had taken from Rome in 410, including 'the treasures of Solomon, the king of the Hebrews, a most noteworthy sight; for the most of them were adorned with emeralds'.[57] But he also says that, at

---

[53] Duncan (1999), 309; Munjeri (1991), 448.

[54] cf. Clifford (1999), 451.

[55] Cassius Dio 73(72).24.1–2.

[56] Herodian 1.14.2–3. Galen (13.362, 14.66, 19.19) refers to the fire as destroying the Palatine libraries.

[57] Procopius, *Wars* 5.12.42. Two capitals from the synagogue at Ostia depict a menorah whose branches are apparently encrusted with precious stones.

the triumph of Belisarius at Byzantium in 534, there were displayed the objects which Gizeric the Vandal had plundered from Rome in 455 and taken to Carthage, including 'the treasures of the Jews, which Titus the son of Vespasian, together with certain others, had brought to Rome after the capture of Jerusalem'. As a result of a warning from a Jewish spectator, who said that Gizeric had specifically targeted them and others might do so again in the future, they were sent to the Christian churches of Jerusalem rather than being kept in Justinian's palace.[58] If these objects really were the original spoils, they must have been items of obvious value like the menorah; it seems very unlikely that scrolls or curtains would have survived the original fire, let alone subsequent plundering. However, since the symbols of the defeat of Judaism would have been very useful in Christian propaganda, it is perhaps also possible that the objects which were plundered in the fifth and sixth centuries were not the originals at all, but fourth-century replacements. The fact that both Alaric and Gizeric could be credited with taking them (assuming that it is not simply an error by Procopius) might suggest that there was so much to plunder because valuable objects of various provenances came to be identified as 'the treasures of the Jews'. This could also be the origin of two bronze columns which Benjamin of Tudela saw in the Church of St John Lateran in the twelfth century and believed to have come from the Temple, 'the handiwork of King Solomon'.[59]

It thus seems likely that the opportunity for Jews to make a 'pilgrimage' to Rome may have existed for only about a century: from the triumph of Titus and Vespasian until the destruction of the original Temple of Peace. Therefore it would have been only of antiquarian interest to the compilers of the Talmud, which would explain why it is not discussed there specifically. It can never have been of great theological importance, in view of the relative scarcity of even indirect references to it. However, the psychological leap between pilgrimage being of paramount importance to Jews before 70 CE and impossible for them afterwards must have been very considerable. To ameliorate it by making a pilgrimage-style journey to see the objects which they would

---

[58] Procopius, *Wars* 4.9.5–9. 3.5.1–5 mentions Gizeric's plundering of the Palace and the Temple of Jupiter Capitolinus without referring to the spoils of Jerusalem.

[59] Benjamin of Tudela (ed. Adler), p. 10.

have venerated at Jerusalem would be a natural course of action for anyone who was in a position to do so. I would therefore suggest that, even if it was not their only reason for travelling to Rome, Aqiba and his companions treated their journey as a pilgrimage in reverse.

15

'Intermingled Until the End of Time':

Ambiguity as a Central Condition of Early Christian Pilgrimage

Wendy Pullan

THE AMBIGUITY OF PILGRIMAGE

Pilgrimage, along with its accompanying states of alienation and sojourning, is one of the visible threads that meanders through the many permutations of early Christian thought and practice. The persistence of the theme is confirmed by the frequency with which it appears in the New Testament and both eastern and western patristic literature.[1] For Tertullian, even truth itself is on pilgrimage in this world,[2] and Augustine began *City of God* with the basic characterization of the Christian entity as 'a stranger among the ungodly'.[3] Yet, despite its pervasiveness, pilgrimage is distinguished by ambiguity and impre-

---

[1] John 17:14,16; Gal. 4:26; 2 Cor. 5:6–8; Eph. 2:19; Phil. 3:20; 1 Pet. 1:4, 1:9, 1:17, 2:11–18; Heb. 11:13–16, 13:13–14; 1 Clement, salutation; 2 Clement, 5.5; *Diognetus*, 5; Tert. *Apol.* 1.2; 42; Iren. *Adv. Haer.* 4.21.3; Clem. Alex. *Strom.* 4.26; Orig. *Cont. Cel.* 8.75; Euseb. *Mart. Pal.* 11:8–13; Jerome, *Ep.* 22.1; *Hom. 63 on Ps. 83(84)*; *Hom. 66 on Ps 88(89)*; Leo the Great, *Serm.* 74.5; John Chrysostom, *Hom. 12 on Matt. 4*; *Hom. 15 on 2 Cor. 5*; *Hom. 16 on 2 Cor. 6*; *Hom. 23 on Eph.*; *Hom. 79 on John 3*; Gregory the Great, *Moralia*, 8.54. Augustine refers to pilgrimage in much of his work; he reinforces it in his sermons (e.g. 14.4, 80.7, 177.2, 178.9; see also: Brown (1990), 313 ff.), and repeats it throughout *City of God*; van Oort (1991), 131–8, quotes a number of the references.

[2] Tert. *Apol.*, 1.2; Leo the Great, *Serm.* 74.5 states that those who 'have entered on the way of Truth are sojourning in the vale of this world'.

[3] Augustine, *Civ. Dei* 1. pref.

cision. It is not a sacrament, has no doctrine, and unlike the Hebrew Bible and the Qur'an, the New Testament does not make it obligatory. Little written theology of the period is devoted exclusively to a discussion of pilgrimage;[4] it does not have the primacy of trinitarian and christological issues in the development of early Christian theology, although it is basic to soteriology and eschatology, and to the understanding of Christian ethics. In pilgrimage there is a rejection of worldly eminence in favour of a higher and more distant order; but with ideas and manifestations ranging from life as a state of continuous estrangement, to the undertaking of a distinct physical journey with a clear destination, it has a multifarious nature that is rooted in a complex and sometimes incongruous combination of the ephemeral and the concrete. Certainly the absence of a firm doctrine and official status makes pilgrimage difficult to grasp. On the other hand, the phenomenon has an inherent ambiguity, and it is perhaps more fruitful to seek an understanding of it that is situated within its own paradoxes. The observations in this chapter attempt to do so.

Rendered by the tension between this world and the next, early Christian pilgrimage can first of all be described as an alien citizenship, where the terrestrial sojourn was understood to be in a state of perpetual estrangement, regarded as a journey beyond earthly concerns, on the way to, but not yet arrived at, the heavenly kingdom. The situation is well characterized in the second-century *Letter to Diognetus*:

The difference between Christians and the rest of mankind is not a matter of nationality, or language, or customs. Christians do not live apart in separate cities of their own, speak any special dialect, nor practise any eccentric way of life. The doctrine they profess is not the invention of busy human minds and brains, nor are they, like some, adherents of this or that school of human thought. They pass their lives in whatever township—Greek or foreign— each man's lot has determined; and conform to ordinary local usage in their clothing, diet, and other habits. Nevertheless, the organisation of their community does exhibit some features that are remarkable, and even surprising. For instance, though they are residents at home in their own countries, their behaviour there is more like that of transients; they take their full part as citizens,

---

[4] True, even in Augustine, although Markus (1966), 433 notes that while the concept of estrangement is of secondary importance in his work, it is 'part of a cluster of ideas which stand at the centre of his thought'. See also: Claussen (1991).

but they also submit to anything and everything as if they were aliens. For them, any foreign country is a motherland, and every motherland is a foreign country. Like other men, they marry and beget children, though they do not expose their infants. Any Christian is free to share his neighbour's table, but never his marriage bed. Though destiny has placed them here in the flesh, they do not live after the flesh; their days are passed on the earth, but their citizenship is above in the heavens.[5]

The passage depicts a dialectic of heaven and earth with ordinary Christians partaking in limited ways of both; their lives may be seen as a form of pilgrimage which mediates between the two domains in a state of 'here but not here'. These spatial ambiguities are augmented by, and indeed inseparable from, the temporal 'now and not yet',[6] for the pilgrim's final haven remains beyond the world in the celestial city, and all destinations on earth are only prefigurations of the ultimate one to come with the Last Judgement. Compounded together are both the ongoing apocalyptic, or vertical eschatology, activated by partial salvation achieved in Christian baptism, and the hope for full redemption at the end of time.[7] In its spatial and temporal ambiguousness, pilgrimage is the vehicle through which the world is seen and experienced; and yet, as a fundamental condition of Christian life on earth, it also becomes the world.[8]

In the early centuries, many of the textual references to earthly estrangement and pilgrimage, like *Diognetus* 5, focus on orienting a life of Christian praxis to the transcendent promise of the Heavenly Jerusalem. One is struck by the effort made to define Christian existence in terms of living life properly and avoiding entanglement 'in treacherous snares',[9] and especially for accommodating mundane life within the transient state of pilgrimage, so that one may grow in faith and spirit.[10] John Chrysostom explains the conflict succinctly: 'For our citizenship is

---

[5] *Diog.* 5.

[6] Rowland (1985), 292 ff.

[7] On the importance of both vertical and horizontal eschatology in early Christianity, see: Rowland (1982), esp. 356–7.

[8] Käsemann (1984) maintains that for bearers of revelation, pilgrimage is an existential necessity; see also: Ladner (1967), 233, 237.

[9] Leo the Great, *Serm.* 74.5.

[10] As well as *Diog.* 5, see: 1 Pet. 1:13–17, 2:11–18; Clement of Alexandria, *Paed.* 2.1.1; Tert. *Apol.* 42; Iren. *Adv. Haer.* 4.21.3. John Chrysostom encourages parishioners to put up with difficulties precisely because they are sojourning in a foreign land, but reminds them that 'the dreadful thing would be to suffer so in our own country' (*Hom. 79 on John*, 3).

in heaven. And our life is here.'[11] It is a demanding obligation with contradictions that, not unexpectedly, were never properly reconciled; the uneven and often unsuccessful attempts to put a life of extended pilgrimage into practice reflect the many inconsistencies in Christianity of the first centuries.[12] On an everyday basis, the combination of alienation and assimilation was confusing and elusive. An apt example is Eusebius' account of the impasse created at the trial of the Christian Pamphilus when the defendant adamantly declared himself a citizen of (Heavenly) Jerusalem, a city unknown to the Roman judge, who immediately suspected the Christians of establishing an undisclosed town hostile to the empire.[13] Greer's term for such tension is 'marvellous paradox', where Christians 'bear the same relation to the world as the soul does to the body', and discover that the Roman cities which imprison and reject them also unify and remind them of their heavenly destiny.[14] It is within the ontological nature of the paradox that early Christian pilgrimage should be seen, situated neither in earth nor in heaven but in the fluid and reciprocal relationship between the two. Notwithstanding the difficulties of implementation, the ideal of pilgrimage was extensive and ongoing; Greer emphasizes that the vision of alien citizenship was always a dominant one for early Christians for two powerful reasons: its contradictions fostered dialogues that made the Church stronger, and, more significantly, it enabled an understanding of Christ's victory that promised a new order.[15]

Greer concedes practical failures primarily at a social level, but ultimately the relevance of pilgrimage is soteriological and eschatological.[16] Although implicit in the earlier textual sources already mentioned, a full theological exposition of *peregrinatio* as a metaphor for Christian life appears only with Augustine in *City of God*.[17] Contributing to this was his development of the idea of the journey of the soul as an inner pilgrimage for individuals while still in the body, yet which

---

[11] John Chrysostom, *Hom. 15 on 2 Cor. 5.*
[12] Demonstrated well by Greer (1986), ch. 6, in his discussion of Tertullian, Clement of Alexandria, the Christian commonwealth as understood by Eusebius and Lactantius, and the transformation of the paradox by John Chrysostom and Augustine.
[13] Euseb. *Mart. Pal.*, 11.8–13.
[14] Greer (1986), 141.
[15] Ibid. 160–1; see also Rowland (1985), 293.
[16] Greer (1986), 159; cf. Markus (1989), 167, *passim.*
[17] Claussen (1991), 33.

recognized the spiritual superiority of the soul as extending beyond the mortal domain, so that 'virtue enables it [the soul] to raise itself up even in this life...that virtue's and piety's reward is God himself, that is Truth itself.'[18] With this understanding, the condition of homelessness, where Christian life is maintained in a state of pilgrimage that in itself may offer certain ethical dimensions, becomes an embodiment of the soul's journey with the final destination in heaven. Resolving the tension between soteriology and eschatology requires that the focus on salvation for the individual must ultimately be reconciled with the corporate factors inherent in redemption for all of the righteous at the end of time.[19] During the first Christian centuries, changing eschatological beliefs were reflected in the nature and value of lifelong pilgrimage, for as expectation of an imminent *parousia* diminished, history was understood no longer as an overlapping of old age and new, but as a time of extended waiting and journey.[20] What had been, in hope, a short present, became a more lengthy existence; in the belief that God alone ordained the postponement of the end of the world, Christian sojourners even prayed for Rome, the emperor and empire.[21] Here, pilgrimage is not simply a means to bring one closer to God, but, in extending its own mediational capacity through time, also a matter of delaying or distancing humanity from the divine. Saint Jerome expresses this by comparing the departure from his own land of the biblical patriarch Abraham to the soul's need to 'go out from its own land and its kindred'.[22] Clearly both pilgrimages, of the soul and of Abraham,

---

[18] Aug. *Quant. Anim.* 36.81. For a description of the *itinerarium animae* see Aug. *Conf.* 7.17, and esp. *Quant. Anim.* 33.70–6. The seven stages or levels are: *animatio, sensus, ars, virtus, tranquillitas, ingressio, contemplatio* (vitalization, sensation, art, virtue, tranquillity, initiation, contemplation). Gilson (1991), ch. 9 points out that a full resolution of the Christian understanding of body and soul comes only later with St Thomas Aquinas.

[19] Aug. *Quant. Anim.* 36.80; *Immort. Anim.* 15.24; this is a large and complex theme with extensive bibliography; see for example: Markus (1989), ch. 7 *passim*.

[20] Rowland (1985) 285–94.

[21] Tert. *Apol.* 30.4–5,32.1, 39.2; see also Lact. *Div. Inst.* 7.25, who believed that the preservation of Rome restrained the end of the world; but, cf. John Chrysostom, *Hom. 16 on 2 Cor.*, 6, who emphasises providence: 'it is the lot of sojourners to be ejected when they think not, expect not', and brevity: 'the sojourning is but for a short and little time' (*Hom. 79 on John*, 3). The short sojourn may be seen in contrast to the eternity of the final home.

[22] Jerome, *Ep.* 22.1; cf. 2 Cor. 5:6–8.

require delay and distance. As well, in Jerome's hands, the two are analogous, the material form of the latter illustrates and embodies the more exclusively spiritual nature of the former. In maintaining distance, pilgrimage 'fleshes out' Christian life on earth and more fully mediates human participation in the divine while still in the mortal realm. Within such a context, we cannot be surprised to find pilgrimage appear in a highly concrete guise, as a physical journey to a sacred place or person,[23] or even as life in a monastery or in the Holy Land.

If then, in a broad and enduring sense, pilgrimage may be regarded as the participatory condition of Christian life, it is probably fair to say, that for the majority of people, this entailed living ethically in the community of the Church with full engagement in the sacraments; but for some, such an imperative demanded a journey. Sometimes the relationship between the more general state of estrangement and a voyage to an earthly destination was close, almost indistinguishable, as John Rufus' account of the fifth-century priest and pilgrim, Peter the Iberian, reveals: when he 'grew in age and spiritual love, he experienced a compelling urge to retire from the world and its emptiness and undertake a pilgrimage, that most virtuous of enterprises'.[24] It began as a pilgrimage to Jerusalem and extended through the rest of his life as he progressed in holiness; but only in death could he 'reach that goal which is the crown of God's heavenly call'.[25] In another example, Paulinus of Nola links the pilgrimage to Jerusalem of the Roman Melania with a departure from her own body to a higher state of the soul that in itself becomes a pilgrimage.[26] The physical and spiritual aspects of pilgrimage overlap most obviously and completely when the journey to a holy place becomes a lifetime pursuit, but some form of spiritual content must be present in all modes of pilgrimage. Both body

---

[23] This essay focuses on the role of place in pilgrimage; for a study of early Christian pilgrimage to monks and ascetics see: Frank (2000*a*).

[24] Lang (1956), 63 on a synopsis/translation of John Rufus, *Life of Peter the Iberian*.

[25] Ibid. 78. This pattern is familiar in accounts of many of the extended pilgrimages to the Holy Land: Jerome, Paula, the two Melanias, Palladius, Rufinus, Sabas, etc. Most people who remained in Palestine in the fourth to seventh centuries did so within some sort of monastic framework. For the history of many of these pilgrim-settlers see: Hunt (1984).

[26] Paulinus of Nola, *Ep.* 29.10: 'Abandoning worldly life and her own country, she chose to bestow her spiritual gift at Jerusalem, and to dwell there in pilgrimage from her body. She became an exile from her fellow citizens, but a citizen amongst the saints.'

and soul share the final destination and linking the two asserts the Christian opposition to dualism. Movement is crucial. Dupront's image of 'une prière marchée',[27] unites two significant factors of pilgrimage, movement and human participation in the divine; but this laconic description omits a destination, ultimately achieved through time, for all pilgrimage is a prefiguration of the eschaton, with the pilgrim 'experiencing proleptically the joys of worship amid the cultus of heaven'.[28]

These comments are intended not to fix a definition of early Christian pilgrimage but to establish conditions from which to generate an understanding of its content. So far, it is possible to say that as a phenomenon, pilgrimage is multi-dimensional in its practice and meaning, having to do with the way that one participates in the divine. Estrangement is the broad context for Christian life, providing distance so that the soul may grow. In taking on the form of a physical journey, pilgrimage may act, in a rather specialized way, to embody demands beyond the material world. Ambiguities and paradoxes are inherent to pilgrimage because of its own nature in the temporal world and, thus, offer us important insights, but true resolution is possible only eschatologically, that is, with the end of pilgrimage.

STRANGERS AND SOJOURNERS

As a primary horizon of understanding, language offers insights into many of the fundamental ambiguities of pilgrimage. Although various tongues were used by early Christian pilgrims, Hebrew, Greek, and Latin represent major traditions from which the religion developed and their terms help to illuminate the discussion at hand.[29] It is clear that no one word exists in ancient Hebrew or Greek for 'pilgrim', and

---

[27] Dupront (1973).

[28] Johnsson (1978), 247; also Markus (1994), 151–2.

[29] A complete linguistic survey of the terms for pilgrimage is not the intent here. For more extensive philological treatment, see Friedrich (1967), esp. ξένοι, 5.1–36; παροικία, 5.841–53; for a survey of early Christian sources see: Solignac, 12/1, col. 890; for Hebrew and Greek meanings see: Estes (1988), 25–32, 134–8; on *paroikoi*, with an emphasis on social interpretation, see: Elliot (1981), 24–8, 38; for Hebrew traditions see Guttmann (1926). For the background of Augustine's use of the word see: Claussen (1991), 35–42.

the Hebrew Bible, Septuagint, and Greek New Testament use a variety
of terms which express the ideas of 'stranger', 'alien', 'exile', 'wanderer',
and 'sojourner'. In many ancient cultures the unknown foreigner was
considered threatening—an enemy—as well as one needing hospitality
and protection—a friend; within this tension the political and social
status of the foreigner became defined.[30] In Hebrew, the term *gēr*
referred to a resident alien,[31] falling in between *nokhri*, a foreigner
temporarily in the land, and *ezrah*, a citizen with full rights and
obligations. In the Hebrew Bible, the term *gēr* is often used with *toshav*
meaning 'sojourner'.[32] While these may be seen as socio-political terms,
their meanings cannot be separated from the theological sense inherent
in the relationship of the Israelites to the land as promised to them by
God. In Hebrew thought, while the world as a whole is estranged from
God, the Israelites are granted the privilege of living in Canaan, God's
own country, as *gērim* under his protection.[33] This usage constitutes
basic tension of the human status which, although without the Christian eschatological context, establishes a mode of existence recognizable
in the later Christian paradox of alien citizenship.

   While the Hebrew understanding of estrangement, which sees God as
foreign to the world, is essentially theological, the Greek view is primarily anthropological, based on the separation of the soul from the
world.[34] The theological ideas in early Christian alienation can be seen
as a development of the Hebrew view,[35] with the difference that in
Christ human beings become alien to the world, as is God. In the
Septuagint, Philo, and other Greek intertestamental literature, *toshav*

---

[30] Friedrich (1967), 5.2–8.
[31] Guttmann (1926), 1–2, 14.
[32] Ibid. 5.842–46; the connection between stranger and sojourner is seen in the Septuagint where sometimes κατοικεῖν (to dwell) is used when one would expect παροικεῖν
(p. 843); see also: Estes (1988), 25–32.
[33] Friedrich (1967), 5.26–7.
[34] Friedrich (1967), 5.26. The fundamental fissure in Hebrew tradition is in the
Genesis account of the fall of man where the human world becomes estranged from God;
see also: Phan (1988), 11. The Greeks regarded the human being more as an incarnate
soul, with separation between soul and body at death (Plato, *Phaedo* 64c; echoed by
Plotinus, *Ennead*, 1.6; see also: Vernant (1991*b*), 192; Gilson (1991), 172 ff.).
[35] This is not to diminish the considerable contact between Greek and Hebrew points
of view in early Christianity; see: Friedrich (1967), 5.26 ff. See also: Markus (1966),
431–50, who thinks that Augustine's image of the pilgrim on his way to the heavenly
patria may build upon Philo's dichotomy of sojourning (παροικεῖ) and dwelling
(κατοικεῖ) and represent a fusion of Stoic and scriptural themes (435–7).

(and sometimes *gēr*) is translated as *paroikos*.[36] *Paroikos* was a legal status, below *polites*—citizens, and above *xenos*—strangers. When taken over into Christianity, these terms were a kind of 'constitutional terminology',[37] applied to heaven, earth, and the city of God. *Paroikia*, meaning 'the stay or sojourn of one who is not a citizen in a strange place', became 'parish...a community of strangers',[38] the permanent earthly status of Christians and the basic unit of the Christian Church. In most books of the New Testament, *xenoi* and *paroikoi* are used to describe full-fledged Christians as strangers, sojourners, and exiles on earth (1 Pet. 1:17, 2:11; Heb. 11:13).[39] But Ephesians 2:19 distinguishes between those before conversion who were 'strangers and sojourners' (ξένοι καὶ πάροικοι) to Christianity, and those after conversion who are 'fellow citizens with the saints' (συμπολῖται τῶν ἁγίων). The prevailing socio-political understanding of the stranger and sojourner inhabiting a state of static discontinuity has now been substituted by a non-residential citizenship with clear destinations that are first of all soteriological and then, eventually, eschatological.

As in Greek, the Classical Latin *peregrinus* is a legal term, meaning stranger or foreigner, which denotes the status of a non-citizen and offers a certain level of protection. But it also introduces more forcefully the notion of wandering, although initially with no particular destination. From this we have the modern English 'peregrination'. In Christianity, the use of *peregrinatio* to combine physical movement and destination is first found in Tertullian when he describes Mary coming to visit Christ (Luke 8:20),[40] however, in the patristic period, a variety of other terms are used: *itinerarium* as well as *peregrinatio* was employed in the general sense of physical travel to a holy place or person and Augustine uses the words *via* and *viator* almost as frequently as *peregrinatio* and *peregrinus*.[41] *Peregrinatio* also refers to spiritual exile and sojourn of the Christian community on earth: *ecclesia peregrina*, and the pilgrimage of the soul: *peregrinatio animae*. The fourth-century pilgrim

---

[36] Elliot (1981), 25; also: Estes (1988), 137–8.
[37] Friedrich (1967), 5.29.
[38] Bauer (1979), 629.
[39] Παρεπίδημος is also used. For pilgrimage vocabulary in Hebrews see: Johnsson (1978), 241.
[40] *Carne Christi*, 7.7, in Solignac (1983), col. 890.
[41] Ladner (1967), 236 n. 14.

Egeria applies *peregrinus* to a candidate for baptism,[42] implying a spiritual journey facilitated by sacrament. By the outset of widespread pilgrimage to the Holy Land in the fourth century,[43] there was still little consistent use of any particular term, Greek or Latin, in pilgrims' literature: authors spoke of 'going to pray' at a place,[44] or simply of 'departing for' or 'going to see' a particular place.[45] However, from the fourth to the sixth centuries we can find some stabilization in the use of the words, such as the account of the Piacenza Pilgrim (*c.*570) where *peregrinus* and *peregrinatio* are used frequently.[46]

It is difficult to know to what extent such words as 'exile', 'stranger', 'sojourner', 'alien', 'wanderer', etc., were understood as metaphors for 'pilgrim' in the early Christian period and an attempt to designate exact equivalents risks the creation of a closed referential system.[47] The terms correlate in an open and fluid manner that reflects the changing and developing phenomenon of early Christian pilgrimage; moreover, this brief survey of language shows the terms of pilgrimage to be inclusive and ambiguous over a long period of time. The foreigner exists in a socio-political limbo with a paradox in the resident-alien status: he is both a stranger *and* a sojourner. The connotation is both positive and negative, a dialectical situation where the foreigner inhabits a mediated zone. When seen in Christian theological terms, the same words are used for both spiritual and physical pilgrimage, because the distance travelled is ultimately the one between earth and heaven; it is the

---

[42] Egeria, *Itinerarium*, 45.4.

[43] Although there are textual references for earlier pilgrims, it is unclear, and heavily debated, whether pilgrimage of this sort can be said to have existed before the legalization of Christianity in 313. It is a topic beyond the scope of this essay, but, I think, reasonable to point out that it is unlikely pilgrimage suddenly sprang into being as a mature phenomenon in the early fourth century, as this investigation of language indicates. The literature of early Christian pilgrimage is chronologically documented in Leclerq (1907–), col. 65–176 and Wilkinson (1977), 209–16. Walker (1990), 10–13 and Hunt (1984), 3–4 summarize what is known of the situation before 313. On the possibility of a syncretic period of Jewish and Christian popular pilgrimage see: Wilkinson (1990); Simon (1973), 99, 103–4. Holum (1990), 67 ff. reviews a number of the arguments for and against pilgrimage before 313, but comes out against it; Hunt (1999) argues for it.

[44] Wilkinson (1977), 33.

[45] Gregory of Nyssa's *Ep. 2*, is known today as 'On Pilgrimage', but in the introduction he uses the more general expression simply 'departing for Jerusalem' (ἀπελθεῖν εἰς Ἱεροσόλυμα).

[46] Piacenza Pilgrim, *Itinerarium*, 159; 175; 177; 180.

[47] On the advisability of open references and contextuality, see: Soskice (1989), 150–1.

distance of time represented by space, the distance from birth to death and finally eschatological rebirth. Saint Jerome describes the pilgrimage of his friend Paula in *Letter* 108 as many different things: the bearing of witness (108.2), faith (108.7,13), disinheritance and inheritance (108.6), affliction (108.18), martyrdom (108.32), citizenship (108.32). All of this is pilgrimage; the language is wide-ranging and comprehensive, the language of a whole life.[48]

Christian pilgrimage is perpetually hopeful for attainment of the final destination, yet invariably conscious of the place left behind. The alien citizen becomes pilgrim because he or she resides in an intermediate area where the old life is left behind because of faith, and the new life exists in hope, also because of faith.[49] In a letter encouraging the Spaniard Lucinius to make pilgrimage to Bethlehem, Jerome again uses Abraham as the prototype for the stranger and sojourner of the Christian pilgrim.[50] At God's calling Abraham journeyed from Mesopotamia to the Holy Land, and Jerome describes how the uncertainties of the venture are pitted against his newly found faith, for he 'seeks what he knows not, not to lose Him who he has found' (71.2). The means to do so is temporal, 'forgetting these things which are behind, he reaches forth to that which is before'. The negative notion of strangeness is not just countered by the positive one of faith, but subsumed by it, for a requirement of faith is estrangement from non-faith; here exile and faith together become citizenship.[51] But even this is transient, for until the final home in heaven is reached, the journey is in a foreign land: 'what [Christian pilgrims] are no longer, they still are in a different form, namely in relation to the earth, on which they still wander.'[52] The paradox intensifies when the indeterminacy of estrangement is bolstered by the security of membership in the community of the Church: the *ekklēsia* as *paroikia* is itself in a state of exile as well.[53]

[48] Sister Catherine of Siena Mahoney has argued that Augustine's use of *peregrinatio* in *City of God* means simply 'this life'; see Mahoney (1935), 144, 150, as noted in Claussen (1991), 33 n. 33.

[49] Aug. *Civ. Dei* 19.17.

[50] Jerome, *Ep.* 71.

[51] In Christian terms, absence of faith also means estrangement, but from God rather than the world. On these two meanings see: Ladner (1967), 234–8.

[52] Friedrich (1967), 5.851.

[53] *Diog.* 5, is an apt description; also: Aug. *Civ. Dei*, 19.17. For Augustine, the fate of individual and city are inextricably linked (*Civ. Dei* 19.17 *passim*, *En. Ps.* 147.20).

Ambiguity and inclusiveness may often imply vagueness, but this is not the case here. When Augustine talks of 'home', 'journey', 'citizens', and 'pilgrims' it is quite clear that he refers, ultimately, to the pilgrimage of Christians to heaven. But within its temporal parameters, these words also refer to the earthly situation of alienation. The language is ambiguous and inclusive because it finds its place within the mediative phenomenon of pilgrimage which, between the absolutes of heaven and earth, negotiates a way through the potential variety and richness of the world.

THE PARTICULARITY OF PLACE

The imposition of the human will upon particular places in Christendom may be regarded as an attempt to order mimetically the world in which pilgrims found themselves alienated. In his study of medieval alienation and order, Ladner states:

The type of alienation which meant detachment from this world somehow belonged together with man's attempts to re-establish the disturbed terrestrial order of creation in such a way that it would reflect, however imperfectly the celestial order.[54]

Pilgrimage appears to have been a major driving force for ecclesiastical building in the Christian Holy Land,[55] which had begun under the emperor Constantine's directive in 325; this, as a reflection of celestial order in the terrestrial empire, materializes as the architecture of political supremacy.[56] Eusebius writes that in Jerusalem the Constantinian

---

[54] Ladner (1967), 238. Ladner notes that in late antiquity some gnostics also had the idea of double alienation, from world and from God, but only the Christians linked it with human efforts to reestablish earthly order.

[55] Hunt (1984), 18–27, 103; Holum (1990), 75–7; Maraval (1985), 60; Wilkinson (1976), 82. This is also evident in the architecture of the churches—the Nativity in Bethlehem, the Holy Sepulchre at Golgotha, and especially the Eleona on the Mount of Olives—where caves and crypts appear to have been designed for the visibility and/or accessibility of pilgrims; see: Pullan (2000), 310–12. But I would like to stress that a variety of factors contributed to these early churches; certainly in accounts of pilgrims like Egeria, it is difficult to distinguish between pilgrimage and purely liturgical churches.

[56] Even in the terse *Itinerarium Burdigalense*, the pilgrim author tags each mention of a basilica with 'built by command of Constantine'. Sulpicius Severus, *Historia Sacra* 2.33, reports that Helena 'cast down the idols and temples' which she found in Jerusalem,

basilicas were large and splendid.[57] The reaction of Egeria was probably typical; of the complex at Golgotha she wrote:

the decorations are too marvellous for words . . . They are beyond description, and so is the magnificent building itself. It was built by Constantine, and under the supervision of his mother it was decorated with gold, mosaic, and precious marble, as much as his empire could provide, and this not only at the Great Church, but at the Anastasis and the Cross, and the other Jerusalem holy sites as well.[58]

Yet rather than an affirmation of power on earth, pilgrimage offers exile and the hope of a heavenly citizenship; its emphasis is on the way, which ends only in the distant perfection of heaven. Although impressed by the richness of the Constantinian basilicas, Egeria shifts away from worldly matters and ends her brief description above: 'But I must get back to the point.'[59] Jerome writes admiringly of the modesty of pilgrims, yet reminds us that the churches of Shiloh and Bethel and other places 'are set up like standards to commemorate the Lord's victories'.[60] He stresses the simplicity of the grotto at Bethlehem, 'this poor crevice of the earth [where] the Creator of the heavens was born', and even asks, 'Where are the spacious porticoes? Where are the gilded ceilings?'[61] The truth of the matter is that although not particularly large, the Church of the Nativity was probably more sumptuous than Jerome was willing to admit.[62]

The problem of how the spiritual way should be fabricated on earth was often overshadowed by the ongoing argument of whether such

and 'through the exercise of her royal powers' erected churches. There has been considerable examination of this subject; see e.g. Telfer (1957), 696–700; Krautheimer (1982), 66–7. On the image of Jerusalem in the Byzantine Empire see: Holum (1990), 75–6.

[57] Constantine's letter to Macarius, Bishop of Jerusalem, in Euseb. *V. Const.* 3.30–2; also quoted by Socrates, *Hist. Eccles.* 1.9. Soz. *Hist. Eccles.* 2.2, states that the church on Golgotha 'was executed in the most magnificent and costly manner possible'.

[58] Egeria, *Itin.* 25.8–10.

[59] Ibid. 25.10.

[60] Jerome, *Ep.* 46.13.

[61] Ibid. 46.11.

[62] Jerome complained that the clay manger was replaced by one of gold and silver; see: *Hom. 88 on the Nativity.* Euseb. *V. Const.* 3.43, states that Empress Helena 'honoured with rare memorials the scene of her travail who bore this heavenly child, and beautified the sacred cave with all possible splendour. The emperor [made] princely offerings, and added to his mother's magnificence by costly presents of silver and gold, and embroidered hangings.' See also Egeria, *Itin.* 26.8. On the symbolic representation of the divine by splendid decoration, especially with the use of gold, see Janes (1998).

embodiment should exist at all: the fundamental dilemma, which finds its source in the Second Commandment, was whether one could search for God in a particular place, a problem articulated by Paul: 'God who made the world and everything in it, being the Lord of heaven and earth, does not dwell in shrines made by man' (Acts 17:24). Three hundred years later even Bishop Cyril of Jerusalem, who was a devotee of the city and an advocate of the power of the holy sites, stated clearly that God could not be contained in a particular place:

This Father of our Lord Jesus Christ is not circumscribed in any place nor is He less than the heavens; but the heavens are the works of His fingers, and the whole earth is held in His palm. He is in all things and about all.[63]

While there is little doubt that in the fourth century Christian attitudes towards holy places did shift towards particularity,[64] the Constantinian building programme and increased pilgrimage did not alleviate the tension between the universality of the divine and the concreteness of place.[65] In fact, when pilgrimage increased substantially after 313 CE, the issue was no longer hypothetical: the contradictions inherent in a God who is uncontained yet connected to a specific place were presenting themselves daily in the churches of Jerusalem.

PILGRIMAGE'S WORTH

Patristic texts illustrate conflicting and ambivalent feelings for pilgrimage to the holy sites, pondering and sometimes doubting the value of physical manifestation of the spiritual. In the third century Origen

[63] Cyril, *Catecheses* 4.5.
[64] Markus, (1994), 264–5; cf. White (1992), whose archaeological investigations of pre-Constantinian architecture indicates that the Constantinian revolution was more evolutionary than previously thought. On Eusebius' and Cyril's attitudes to the holy places, see: Walker (1990). For a more extensive study of the relationship of place and religious understanding, see Smith (1987), esp. ch. 4.
[65] Earlier Jewish tradition attempted to resolve this tension by equating place with the divine; in Hebrew the word *maqōm*, which means place, is one of the words for God; see Montgomery, (1905), 17–26. In the 1st cent., Philo gave place three levels of meaning from material to spiritual: 'firstly that of a space filled by a material form, secondly that of the Divine Word, which God Himself has completely filled throughout with incorporeal potencies . . . [and] a third signification, in keeping with which God Himself is called a place, by reason of His containing things, and being contained by nothing whatever' (*De Somnis* 1.62).

wrote that 'the whole earth itself was cursed by the works of Adam';
this included Jerusalem and Judaea, although he does concede that
they may be 'a symbolic shadow of the pure land which is good and
large and lies in a pure heaven'.[66] Generally the fourth century was
more positive: Eusebius of Caesarea, Cyril of Jerusalem, and Paulinus
of Nola exalted the testimonial role of the sacred sites.[67] Still, Athanasius told a group of pilgrims that their tears at departing from
Jerusalem were unnecessary because Jerusalem, and therefore Christ,
lives not in the place but within the person who leads a saintly life.[68]
Sustained expressions of ambivalence about pilgrimage may be found
in a number of letters by Jerome and Gregory of Nyssa.[69] Jerome was
resident in Bethlehem from 386 CE onwards, and as the men wrote
both as theologians and pilgrims, their insights are particularly revealing to us.

Gregory of Nyssa travelled to the Holy Land in *c*.383 for church
business and pilgrimage; two letters document this visit. *Letter 2* was
advisory, according to 'the Gospel rule of life' (2.15), on the matter of
monks and nuns travelling to Palestine. Gregory contends that 'when
the Lord invites the blessed to their inheritance in the kingdom of
heaven, He does not include a pilgrimage to Jerusalem amongst their
good deeds' (2.29–33), and on the contrary, the mixing of members of
the opposite sex during pilgrimage make it 'so far from being worth an
honest pursuit, that it actually requires the greatest caution to prevent
him who has devoted himself to God from being penetrated by any of
its hurtful influences' (2.44–8). He mounts other objections: moral—
pilgrimage does not help the wicked (2.158–64); theological—the
Holy Spirit facilitates the dispersion of Christianity far beyond Jerusalem (2.168–87); logical—'if the Divine grace was more abundant
about Jerusalem than elsewhere, sin would not be so much in fashion
amongst those who live there' (2.95–8); and spiritual—'wherever thou
may be, God will come to thee, if the chambers of thy soul be found of

---

[66] Orig. *C. Cels.* 7.29.
[67] Euseb. *V. Const.* 3.28, 3.42; Cyril, *Cat.* 10.19, 13.9, 14.22–3; Paulinus, *Ep.* 49.14.
[68] Athan. *Letter to the Virgins*, in Elm (1989), 220.
[69] Jerome, *Ep.* 46; 58; 108; Gregory, *Ep.* 2; 17. From the Reformation until today
these letters have been used as a basis for debate on the value of pilgrimage and the holy
places. See e.g. Maraval (1986), 131–46; Williams (1998), 94–131.

such a sort that he can dwell in thee and walk in thee' (2.155–8). For Gregory, place is ultimately the human soul.

In *Letter 17: To Eustathia, Ambrosia, and Basilissa*, also written *c*.383, Gregory begins enthusiastically, thanking these friends in Palestine for their contribution to his very stirring journey. Here he acknowledges a link between the saving tokens of the human soul and those of holy places:

> The meeting with the good and the beloved, and the memorials of the immense love of the Lord for us men, which are shown in your localities, have been the source to me of the most intense joy and gladness. Doubly indeed have these shone upon divinely festal days; both in beholding the saving tokens of the God who gave us life, and in meeting with souls in whom the tokens of the Lord's graces are to be discerned spiritually in such clearness, that one can believe that Bethlehem, and Golgotha, and Olivet, and the scene of the Resurrection are really in the God-containing heart (17.1–14).

But this sort of experience is only for the sufficiently righteous, whose 'flesh with cloud-like lightness accompanies the ascending soul—such a one, in my opinion, is to be counted in the number of famous ones in whom the memorials of the Lord's love for us men are to be seen' (17.26–31). In *Letter 2*, Christians partake of God's gift 'according to the proportion of their faith, not in consequence of their pilgrimage to Jerusalem' (2.184–7); but in *Letter 17* the holy places contain 'the saving tokens of the God who gave us life' (17.7–8). The two documents, about the same subject and from the same time, appear inconsistent; however, Gregory's opinions may be more a matter of degree than of absolute contradiction.[70] He regards physical pilgrimage positively if undertaken when the soul has also made the proper journey beyond its bodily restrictions, hence it is often difficult to know if he refers to physical localities or to symbolic places of God and/or the human soul (17.1–14, 31–4). He implies that there is a reciprocity between the soul and the holy places: the soul can be nurtured by the saving symbolism instilled in the holy places (17.2–5, 7–8) but the spiritual value of the holy places depends upon the capacity of the human soul to understand and appreciate them (17.8–14, 28–31). Gregory is emphatic that pil-

---

[70] Wilken (1992), 118, calls Gregory 'as much a theologian of the Incarnation as he was of transcendence'; see pp.117–22, for Wilken's discussion of Jerome's and Gregory's views on the holy places.

grimage does not aid the wicked (2.158–64), and that a simple monk must ascend from the body not via the sacred sites (2.165–8); however, for a person well-advanced in holiness the sight of holy places and people brings pure joy (17.35–6). Gregory points out the fact that even 'the spot itself that has received the footprints of the very Life is not clear of wicked thorns' (17.47–9), and he knows that it is 'an impossible thing for a human being to enjoy unmixed with evil any blessing'(17.37–9). Even at the best of times pilgrimage is not an entirely good thing, and at no time is it automatically beneficial; one has to be properly pious to receive its virtues.

Jerome is generally more positive towards pilgrimage and the holy sites than Gregory, but taken in total his letters are equivocal as well.[71] His first reactions after settling in Bethlehem in 386 are of unbridled enthusiasm. *Letter 46* written in that year in the name of his travel companions, Paula and Eustochium, tries to convince a third friend, Marcella, to leave Rome for the Holy Land. Jerome finds Palestine sublimely pious:

> Wherever one turns the labourer at his plough sings alleluia, the toiling mower cheers himself with psalms, and the vine-dresser while he prunes his vine sings one of the lays of David. These are the songs of the country: these in popular phrase, its love ditties. (46.12)

It is the love-song of a newly smitten sojourner in the Holy Land. Barbed criticism about Jerusalem of the sort made by Gregory is refuted in an eloquent apologia for the city,[72] and in doing so, Jerome tackles the problem of the disparity between the Jerusalem which was the site of the crucifixion and the Jerusalem which is the holy city in the Book of Revelation. He realizes that 'it is no answer to say that the Jerusalem which is called holy is the heavenly one which is to be, while that which is called Sodom is the earthly one tottering to its downfall' (46.6); mystical rather than literal understanding is necessary to understand the present world as well as the future Jerusalem of Revelation (46.7). At

---

[71] Jerome, *Ep.* 5.1, 77.8; as well as 46; 108.

[72] Jerome, *Ep.* 46.7–10. There is no evidence that Jerome knew of or read Gregory's letter according to Maraval (1988), 353. However, negative opinions of Jerusalem and the holy places were still common enough near the end of the fourth century, hence the need to convince Marcella of the city's virtues. On these attitudes see: Cardman (1982), 18–25.

the same time, we must not mistake for the celestial city the Jerusalem where the 'rocks rent, and the graves were opened, and many bodies of the saints which slept arose and came out of the graves after his resurrection' (Matt. 27:51, 53); it is indeed the holy city, but on earth, for in heaven 'the apparition there of the bodies of the saints could be no sign to men of the Lord's rising' (46.7). Not entirely terrestrial or celestial, Jerusalem is interpreted by Jerome in terms of pilgrimage: it is the city where 'the psalmist (Ps. 132:7) commands us to worship the Lord "at his footstool" ' (46.7).

By c.395 Jerome's romantic view of Palestine seems to have been overcome by the realization of its short-comings: he refers no more to psalm-reciting labourers, instead lamenting that Jerusalem is populated with 'prostitutes, playactors, and buffoons'.[73] It is clear that he is concerned with the moral fabric of the city[74] and its pilgrims: 'what is praiseworthy is not to have been at Jerusalem but to have lived a good life while there' (58.2). His disapproval is translated once again into the problem of place as mediation between God and human beings:

It is not, I believe, for nothing that I, like Abraham, have left my home and my people. But I do not presume to limit God's omnipotence or to restrict to a narrow strip of earth Him whom the heaven cannot contain.   (58.3)

Like Gregory, Jerome feels that the holy places profit only those people who show themselves worthy (58.3), but ultimately the value of place is surpassed because, 'access to the courts of heaven is as easy from Britain as it is from Jerusalem; for "the kingdom of God is within you" ' (58.3). However, near the end of the letter, Jerome regains a little of his earlier optimism, conceiving of a golden age to be gleaned in part from the power and goodness of the holy places; he addresses Paulinus:

Oh that it were mine to conduct a genius like you, not (as the poets sing) through the Aonian mountains and the peaks of Helicon but through Zion and Tabor and the high places of Sinai. If I might teach you what I have

---

[73] Jerome, *Ep.* 58.4, written to Paulinus of Nola to dissuade him from making pilgrimage to Jerusalem.

[74] Maraval (1988), 353. At this time Jerome was also embroiled in the Origen conflict which probably played a role in his disillusionment with Jerusalem; on Jerome's personal and political situation see: Kelly (1975), 194 ff.

learned myself and might pass on to you the mystic rolls of the prophets, then might we give birth to something such as Greece with all her learning could not show.   (58.8)

Whether Jerome wished to actually escort Paulinus to the high places, or just to guide him through their theological meanings, is not entirely clear. What is significant is that Jerome's vision of a repository for Christian culture is rooted in and symbolized by particular places. The tapping of these mountain sources is dependent upon Paulinus' genius, Jerome's erudition, and the mysticism of the prophets, a combination of knowledge and faith which is greater than learning alone, even that of Greece.

Jerome's *Letter 108* to Eustochium on the death of her mother Paula in 404 CE somewhat reconciles his ambivalence about pilgrimage; this is not by directly addressing the question of whether God can be contained in a place, but by balancing the extremes of earth and heaven with the more immediate spectrum of mediation created by exile and faith. Paula was Jerome's dear friend and colleague in Bethlehem and by eulogizing her he is able to relive in considerable detail the passion of their first pilgrimage to the holy places (108.7–14), and at the same time put into a mature perspective a whole lifetime of pilgrimage. Paula aspired to a spiritual existence, achieved in death when 'after a long martyrdom she won her crown' (108.32); but her spirituality in life, described by Jerome, is earthy and direct. At the holy sites 'she threw herself down in adoration', and 'licked with her mouth the very spot in which the Lord's body had lain' (108.9); in her Bethlehem convent she slept 'on the hard ground covered only with a mat of goat's hair', disfigured her face and mortified her body, having pleased her husband in 'the world in the past, desir[ing] now to please Christ' (108.15). The corporeal/spiritual dialectic is the basis for Paula's scriptural understanding:

The holy scriptures she knew by heart, and said of the history contained in them that it was the foundation of the truth; but, though she loved even this, she still preferred to seek for the underlying spiritual meaning and made this the keystone of the spiritual building raised within her soul.   (108.27)

Exile is a dominant theme, both as Paula's way to God by 'disinheriting herself upon earth that she might find an inheritance in heaven' (108.6), and as estrangement from God, 'for as long as she was in the body she was absent from the Lord and would constantly complain... my soul hath been this long time a pilgrim' (108.1). Faith is what drove her forward, on to all the holy places (108.13), and throughout her life, so that 'she has finished her course, she has kept the faith, and now she enjoys the crown of righteousness' (108.22).

In arguing for and against pilgrimage to the holy places, Jerome and Gregory of Nyssa grapple with the relationship between immanent and transcendent domains. They demonstrate that spiritual pilgrimage is often expressed in a mundane, naive, and corporeal way, and that it is concomitant with physical pilgrimage which itself exists to concretize the intangible, and to create a link with the elusive and mysterious. The physical cannot be separated from the spiritual; it represents and pre-figures it, with arrival at the earthly haven offering a glimpse of a pilgrim's destiny at the end of time. However, the great desire for transcendence sometimes made it difficult to value the particularity of the places of pilgrimage. Jerome sums up the problem in his observation that the hermit Hilarion went only once to Jerusalem, 'in order not to seem, on the one hand, to despise the holy places... nor, on the other, to seem to enclose the Lord in one place'.[75] Gregory stresses more emphatically the distance between the physical and spiritual, suggesting that it is better 'to be absent from the body to go to our Lord, rather than to be absent from Cappadocia to go to Palestine'.[76] We recognize in this the common, almost innate, tendency to favour the contempla-tive as a higher state and goal, which is nonetheless coupled with the nagging realization that we are bound by the physicality of our situation in the world. Pilgrimage has the ability to mediate between the two; while it is never a solely physical act, it was also seen to fall short of a purely contemplative state.[77] In the end, the reality of the pilgrim's situation is a constant negotiation, as Jerome acknowledges:

[75] Jerome, *Ep.* 58.2.
[76] Gregory, *Ep.* 2, 166–8.
[77] The reciprocity of the contemplative and the physical is rooted in Plato's divided line. The predilection for philosophical contemplation over *theōria* as pilgrimage may be found in classical texts as well as Christian; for example, see Arr. *Epict. Diss.* 1.6.20–4; Iamb. *Protr.* 9. I am grateful to Ian Rutherford for these references. The late Middle Ages saw a linking of pilgrimage and contemplation, but it is only with early modernity that contemplative pilgrimage became fathomable and complete in itself; see e.g. Smith (1987), 117 on Ignatius of Loyola's pilgrimage of the mind.

[Paula] sowed carnal things that she might reap spiritual things; she gave earthly things that she might receive heavenly things; she forewent things temporal that she might in their stead obtain things eternal.[78]

On the one hand, to seek heaven was an obvious and natural aspiration for the Christians of these early centuries. Yet the constant reiteration of distance from the divine was the primary means of acknowledging one's mortality and orienting humanity's place in the cosmos; the holy places, especially because of their physical immediacy and appeal to all the human senses,[79] provided a significant way of establishing distance. The constant tension of proximity and remoteness may be seen to constitute ontological movement; this was disclosed within the reciprocity of heaven and earth, and brought to a level of visibility through pilgrimage.

THE INTERMINGLED CITY

The ambivalent feelings towards pilgrimage and the veneration of place in the fourth and fifth centuries were part of the wider reorientation of Roman and Near Eastern culture to Christianity. Jerome's varying responses to pilgrimage and Jerusalem are less a case of his fickle temperament than a genuine struggle to understand the situation of an individual place as it embodies the universality of the divine. His concern is directly represented in his perceptions of the city; the Heavenly Jerusalem may be the final destination but its earthly counterpart contains the particularities of the sites of the incarnation, as well as the universality of Christ's significance, in order to reflect and prefigure the celestial *telos*. The necessary ontological distance is available only in the terrestrial city; this is why the spiritual journey required external and concrete anchoring.

The holy places of Palestine were particularly effective in broadening and deepening the mediative spectrum beyond the internal and the ephemeral, providing an embodied setting for the pilgrims' mimetic participation in the incarnation. Peripatetic veneration on well-worn

---

[78] Jerome, *Ep.* 108.20.
[79] On the importance of sight and touch see Frank (2000a), 118–33, *passim*.

routes took them from the grotto of the nativity in Bethlehem, to the hill of the crucifixion and sepulchre of the resurrection at Golgotha, and finally to Olivet and its cave of the teaching of the mysteries and rock of the ascension. Jerusalem was believed to be the place of Final Judgement, and lying just east of the city, the Mount of Olives was often prophesied as the place of the *parousia*.[80] The churches and shrines at the various sites marked not only the paradigmatic past of the religion's founding events, but in the promise of the Second Coming, they also represented the eschatological future. By making their way through the ritual topography of Jerusalem, the pilgrims re-enacted scriptural narrative, and in doing so, proleptically traced history to its end on earth. As a spiritual path that was embodied by the physical journey, pilgrimage was further grounded in the holy sites of Jerusalem; moreover, with its own eschatological quest in tow, pilgrimage securely dovetailed with the city's ritual topography.[81]

Clearly, the understanding of eschatological pilgrimage was particularly explicit in the sites and topography of Jerusalem. At the same time, early Christian pilgrimage quickly became widespread and journeys to other shrines, persons and relics could not symbolize the detailed narrative of the incarnation in the same way. Many of the new churches referred to prior events, commemorating the heroic deeds and exemplary life of a martyr or saint; however, history, in this sense, is not primarily a view of the past but an opening to transcendence.[82] All destinations would have been venerated for their spiritual capacity; as such, commemorative sites, and even living people, would have stood both as witness to and prophecy of the truth.[83] More specifically, because the notion of Christian alienation was, by its very nature, an expression of the temporal past *and future* manifested in the spatial, pilgrimage to all destinations symbolized eschatological hope as well as

---

[80] Euseb. *Dem. Evang.*, 6.18.287c, 288d–289; Cyril, *Cat.* 14.30.

[81] I have written about the ritual topography of early Christian Jerusalem in some detail elsewhere; see Pullan (1993), (1997–8), (2000). Full bibliographic details are included.

[82] Rahner (1990), 22 writes: 'History only becomes history in contrast to nature through what one calls transcendence. . . . Transcendence is not the business of human beings *alongside* history, but is lived and realized in concrete history and in freedom.'

[83] Gadamer (1975), 275, states that 'a religious proclamation is not there to be understood as a merely historical document, but to be taken in a way in which it exercises its saving effect.'

paradigmatic memory. Thus, pilgrimage in all of its permutations can be understood as a primary means of mediating between the earthly and Heavenly cities, and it takes on all of the contradictions and ambiguities inherent in them.

Jerome rejects facile solutions which oppose the two cities, and struggles with the inherent contradictions.[84] But it is Augustine who formulates the state of temporal ambiguity as a mingling of the two cities until the end of time:

> this mortal condition of the two cities, the earthly and the Heavenly, which are mingled together from the beginning to the end of their history. One of them, the earthly city, has created for herself such false gods as she wanted. . . . The other city, the Heavenly City on pilgrimage in this world, does not create false gods. . . . Nevertheless, both sites alike enjoy the good things, or are afflicted with the adversities of this temporal world state, but with a different faith, a different expectation, a different love, until they are separated by the final judgement, and each receives her own end, of which there is no end.[85]

This intermingled city exists 'horizontally' through history until the eschatological end, and 'vertically' in its stratified meanings which embody the soul's ascent within the salvation of the world. Its paradoxes lie in this simultaneity and, with direct reference to pilgrimage, its ability to accommodate the ever-shifting configuration of distance and proximity. It is this city which the pilgrim negotiates, for just as pilgrimage must not be removed from devotion it cannot be separated from history. The intermingled city was, thus, a constant reminder not just of God, but of one's own finitude, allowing true human experience. For the homeless pilgrims of the early Christian centuries, the intermingled city provided a true and proper home on earth.

---

[84] The problem is addressed at some length by Jerome in *Ep.* 46.6–7; he states: 'The apocalypse was written by John long after the Lord's passion, yet in it he speaks of Jerusalem as the holy city. But if so, how can he spiritually call it Sodom and Egypt? It is no answer to say that the Jerusalem which is called holy is the heavenly one which is to be, while that which is called Sodom is the earthly one tottering to its downfall' (46.6).

[85] Aug. *Civ. Dei.* 18.54

16

Piety and Passion:

Contest and Consensus in the Audiences for Early Christian Pilgrimage

Jaś Elsner

She . . . started to go round visiting all the places with such burning enthusiasm that there was no taking her away from one unless she was hurrying on to another. She fell down and worshipped before the Cross as if she could see the Lord hanging on it. On entering the Tomb of the Resurrection she kissed the stone which the angel had removed from the sepulchre door; then, like a thirsty man who has waited long, and at last comes to water, she faithfully kissed the very shelf on which the Lord's body had lain. Her tears and lamentations there were known to all Jerusalem—or rather to the Lord himself to whom she was praying.

(Jerome, *Ep.* 108 (*ad Eustochium*) 9.2–3)

An early version of this chapter first saw light in Liz James's 'Son et Lumière' day conference on audiences and response at Sussex. Ian Rutherford persuaded me to give a version at the 'Seeing the Gods' conference in Reading, and it subsequently had outings in Elizabeth Jeffrey's Byzantine Seminar in Oxford (where I particularly treasure the memory of Henry Chadwick's humorous intervention) and in the 'Art and the Sacred' conference on pilgrimage and the visual jointly organized by myself and Linda Seidel at the University of Chicago. I am particularly grateful to Sebastian Brock, Simon Coleman, and James George for their comments, and to Ian Rutherford for his editorial discussions.

Thus wrote St Jerome in 404 CE about a pilgrimage he had made with
the Roman noblewoman Paula nineteen years earlier.[1] This letter, addressed to Paula's daughter Eustochium, served as Jerome's obituary of
Paula, with whom he had set up a monastery in Bethlehem. The passage
quoted, and the letter as a whole, are vibrant testimony to the piety and
passion of early Christian pilgrimage, as well as to the almost visionary
idealism of our ancient sources on the subject. Other writers besides St
Jerome emphasize the vividness with which the holy sites of Palestine
inspired the pilgrim imagination, they too emphasize the 'burning
enthusiasm' of pilgrims, even Jerome's presentation of weak female
pilgrims as if they had acquired the physical strength of men. What I
would like to stress, before we embark on some of the problems of early
Christian pilgrimage, is that even in its contemporary historiography,
what was crucial was the *response* of pilgrims to the Holy Land.[2]

I want to begin, as I think we are told *never* to begin, by presenting a
few deliberately undigested bits of primary evidence. Here, without the
benefit of historians' careful explications and classifications of the material, is some of the primary stuff out of which a history of early
Christian pilgrimage must be created.

Figure 1. A lead-alloy ampulla from the Holy Land dating from the later
sixth century CE. The majority of such objects, mass-produced from
moulds relatively cheaply in pewter, survive in the Treasuries of the
Cathedrals at Bobbio and Monza in Italy to which they were probably
donated as collections of prize relics from Palestine by the seventh-
century Lombard queen, Theodolinda.[3]

Figures 2 and 3. The ruins of one out of a great many fifth- and sixth-
century churches from Christian Syria and Palestine—Qal'at Siman,

---

[1] On these kinds of hyper-real responses to the sights of the Holy Land, see now
Frank (2000*a*), 104–111, 118–20.

[2] For the visual structuring of shrines to heighten the 'sight of the holy' and hence to
support faith, see Hahn (1997), 1084–92 on the East. For the importance of visual
response in asceticism generally, see Cox Miller (1994), 138–9, and in pilgrimage in
particular, see Frank (2000*a*), 102–33 and Frank (2000*b*).

[3] See Grabar (1958), 15–16, 32–3. See also Engemann (1973) 7 (and nn. 16 and 17)
on the material (Grabar mistakenly believed they were silver and so more valuable than in
fact they were, 11). For the latest article on this class of objects see Engemann (2002)
with bibliography.

the monastery and pilgrimage centre of St Simeon the Stylite (who died in 459).

Figure 4. A casket which may have contained relics: the late fourth-century ivory so-called 'lipsanotheca' now in Brescia—a beautiful and outstanding piece of workmanship which may in fact have been a container for eucharistic bread.[4]

Figures 5, 6, and 7. Three early icons from the collection gathered at the monastery of St Catherine at Mt Sinai. Even a cursory glance shows the Virgin and Child with Angels and Saints (from the sixth century and usually attributed to Constantinople) is of very different style from the other two images. The different styles may point to different provenances.[5]

Table 1. Some comparative lists of the stations at which liturgy was celebrated in Jerusalem on the octave of feast days during Epiphany, according to (*a*) the late fourth-century pilgrimage account of a Spanish lady called Egeria (col. 2); and (*b*) according to the two surviving manuscripts of an Armenian Lectionary produced in Jerusalem from the early to mid-fifth century (cols. 3 and 4).[6]

I should say that this is not really a representative selection of primary materials, since most scholars working on early Christian pilgrimage have hardly referred to the art and archaeology, basing their work much

Table 1. Liturgical stations at Jerusalem during Epiphany

Feast	Egeria	AL-J	AL-P
5 Jan.	Bethlehem	10th hour Shepherds	Shepherds
Epiphany 6 Jan.	1st hour Martyrium	Martyrium	Martyrium
2nd Day	Martyrium	Mart. of St Stephen	Mart. of St Stephen
3rd Day	Martyrium	(Sun.) Martyrium	Martyrium
4th Day	Eleona	Sion	Sion
5th Day	Lazarium	Eleona	Eleona
6th Day	Sion	Lazarium	Lazarium
7th Day	Anastasis	Ad Crucem	Ad Crucem
8th Day	Ad Crucem	Anastasis	Anastasis

Source: Baldovin (1987), appendix 2.

[4] See Tkacz (2002).
[5] See Weitzmann (1976) nos. B3, B33 and B40: respectively pp. 18–21, 58–9, and 67.
[6] This list comes from Baldovin (1987), 282–3.

Figure 1. Pewter ampulla from Palestine now in Monza, sixth century CE. The obverse (shown here) depicts the adoration of the Magi and shepherds. The texts Greek read: 'Magi' (to the left of the wise men), 'Emmanuel, God is with us' (in the horizontal band below the main image) and 'the oil of the wood of life from the holy places of Christ' (in the circular inscription on the circumference).

Figure 2. View from the north-east of the great cruciform complex of Qal'at Siman in Syria, *c*.470 CE. The complex consisted of four basilicas, each with a nave and two aisles radiating from a central octagon built around the pillar on which St Symeon the Stylite had stood. Photograph: Courtesy of the Conway Library, Courtauld Institute of Art.

more on textual evidence such as Egeria's travelogue, Jerome's letter to Eustochium, or the early saints' lives.[7] However, from this exercise, one thing should be clearly apparent: first, the primary sources and objects are fragmentary, scattered, bitty. Unlike later periods in history or the history of art, early Christian scholars must construct their story out of a paucity of eclectic materials which demand much interpretative work in order to be integrated into a coherent analysis. Thus, although the lists from Egeria and the Armenian Lectionary are primary sources, the original texts out of which these entries come have undergone considerable textual and interpretative criticism before they could be compared in this manner. Second, one is struck by the great distance

[7] See e.g. Maraval (1985). His 'remarques sur les sources de cette étude' are symptomatic: he devotes nearly 7 pages to literary sources (13–19), and less than half a page to 'les sources non littéraires' (19–20). For a theologian's programmatic plea that patristic historians shift 'some of our interest, attention and hermeneutical energy' from written documents to 'popular Christianity' in the form of images, see Miles (1985).

Figure 3. View within the central octagon of Qal'at Siman. In the foreground is all that remains of St Symeon's pillar. Photograph: Courtesy of the Conway Library, Courtauld Institute of Art.

between the primary sources in their somewhat messy diversity and the kinds of secondary accounts—fluent, digested, smoothly argued—which generations of scholars have given to explain them. Critical history is always a highly creative construct.

How then are we to interpret all this primary stuff? Histories of early Christian pilgrimage have synthesized the material into coherent narratives with rather different ends. In the hands of the great English school of narrative history—especially Edward Gibbon and his successors, such as Bury, Jones, and Runciman—early Christian pilgrimage to Palestine represents the worst excesses of what has been called 'heady credulity'.[8] Gibbon himself strikes the note with his magnificent ironies:[9] the piety of the earliest Christian pilgrims 'was authorized by

[8] The phrase is from Hunt (1982), 247. His book is in effect a detailed (though in some aspects sympathetic), attack on this view.

[9] Gibbon (1929; first pub. 1776), 2.480–5. See also Jones (1964), 2.957–64 ('the growth of superstition') and Runciman (1951), 1.38–50 which has some ironic comments about pilgrims feeling 'mystical contact' (38).

Figure 4. Ivory Casket now in Brescia, probably third quarter of the fourth century, from Italy. On the lid are busts of Christ and two saints on either side of him. On the three tiers of the main body of the casket are Jonah being eaten by and vomited by the Whale (on either side of the lock); Christ with Mary Magdalene, Christ teaching, and Christ at the door of the sheepfold (in the larger-scale central band) and scenes showing Susanna and the Elders, Susannah before Daniel, and Daniel in the Lion's Den in the lower tier. Photograph: Courtesy of the Conway Library, Courtauld Institute of Art.

the example of the empress Helena, who appears to have united the credulity of the age with the warm feelings of a recent conversion' (p. 480). He writes of the 'pious art of the clergy of Jerusalem and the active credulity of the Christian world' (p. 485), but does not hesitate to suggest that avarice as well as zeal was a significant cause of the clergy's support of pilgrimage (pp. 480–1). In a wonderfully rhetorical crescendo, the true horror underlying all the piety (to which all the credulous were hopelessly blind) is exposed: 'every species of vice, adultery, theft, idolatry, poisoning, murder, was familiar to the inhabitants of the holy city' (pp. 481–2).

Figure 5. The Virgin and Child enthroned between St Theodore and St George, with angels and the Hand of God above. A spectacular and large-scale portable icon (some 69 cm. in height and 50 cm. wide) in wax encaustic, this panel is usually dated to the sixth-century, possibly associated with the imperial refoundation of the monastery at Sinai by Justinian, and often thought to have been made in Constantinople. Photograph: Courtesy of the Michigan-Princeton-Alexandria Expedition to Mount Sinai.

Figure 6. Pair of triptych wings of which the central panel has not survived. From Sinai. The saints depicted are Paul and Nicholas (left) and Peter and John Chrysostom (right)—all inscribed. Associated with Coptic or Palestinian art, and usually dated to the seventh or eighth century. Photograph: Courtesy of the Michigan-Princeton-Alexandria Expedition to Mount Sinai.

Figure 7. Bust-length icon of the Virgin and Child of the Hodegetria type, probably the central panel of a triptych whose wings are now missing. From Sinai. Again associated with Coptic or Palestinian style, and usually dated to the eighth or ninth century. Photograph: Courtesy of the Michigan-Princeton-Alexandria Expedition to Mount Sinai.

This school, deeply indebted to a combination of Enlightenment and Protestant scepticism about all charismatic religious phenomena, systematically implicated the development of Christianity (particularly— but by no means exclusively—in its more popular forms) with a decline and fall from the grandeur and sobriety of Rome. This approach has the merit of synthesizing the diverse materials into a coherent narrative. It takes seriously the piety and passion of late antique pilgrims as genuine—only to dismiss the sentiment as a kind of populist hysteria, possibly manufactured and certainly manipulated by a cynical hierarchy. Such deep condemnation of the attitudes of the peoples one studies is not exactly politically correct by modern standards nor anthropologically valid, but it served well historians like Gibbon—since their concern was to use the phenomena of Christianity as a pawn in a very different and rather more contemporary argument about decline and the Enlightenment.

By contrast, historians of the rise of early Christendom (and particularly those writing from within the Church) have presented a very different story.[10] Far from being a significant low-point in European culture's long slide into the Dark Ages, early Christian pilgrimage to the Holy Land represents an ideal of communal spirit among the faithful in a still unified Church. This sort of account sees 'the power of the holy places in keeping their devotees to a sober, historical truth'.[11] Despite all kinds of theological and political vicissitudes, it finds 'the holy places, and the solid piety which surrounded them, very evidently answering to the newly confident Christianity of the later Roman empire'.[12] Particularly in studies of the Jerusalem liturgy—that crucial theatre in which pilgrims encountered the holy places in their most charged and miracle-working form on the most special of holy days—the fourth and fifth centuries are seen as an ideal period of uniform and orthodox development.[13] Despite the complex diversity of sources from which the liturgy is reconstructed—the Latin text of Egeria from the 380's,[14] the two

---

[10] The basic general accounts are Kötting (1950), 89–111 (on Palestine between 330 and 500 CE) and Maraval (1985).

[11] Chitty (1966), 114.

[12] Hunt (1982), 248.

[13] The key studies are Baldovin (1987), and Baldovin (1989).

[14] Text in Maraval (1982) and translated with extensive English commentaries in Wilkinson (1971).

manuscripts of an Armenian Lectionary said to be based on a lost Greek original from anywhere between 417 and 495,[15] and a Georgian Lectionary also assumed to follow a Greek source from after the 450s[16]—liturgical scholarship traces a monolithic evolutionary progression of ritual practice in Jerusalem.[17] It is as if the myth of one universal and apostolic Church can find its vindication in the religious practices of the international pilgrim environment of Christianity's most holy places.

This approach is highly 'internalist' in its motivations—taking its enthusiasm about early Christian pilgrims from a medieval tradition going right back to Jerome's eulogy of Paula, which turned the pilgrimage account into a hagiography.[18] It has interesting parallels with the anthropological study of pilgrimage pioneered in the 1970s by the Roman Catholic anthropologists Victor and Edith Turner.[19] The Turners argued that pilgrimage fostered and still fosters 'communitas' for its participants—by which they meant 'a state of unmediated and egalitarian association between individuals who are temporarily freed from the hierarchical roles and statuses which they bear in everyday life'.[20] The Turners' highly idealist model, which has similarities with Mikhail Bakhtin's idealizing theory of carnival as an egalitarian rupture from the constraints of social hierarchies,[21] finds its historical partner in studies of early Christian pilgrimage liturgy. Here, the single, systematic ritual system of a unitary faith is portrayed as evolving organically in

[15] On which see Renoux (1961), 361–85 and Renoux (1969 and 1971). For the range of dates, see Renoux (1963), 168.

[16] For a brief discussion and literature, see Baldovin (1987), 72–80.

[17] The fullest synthetic view is Baldovin (1987), 55–104. See also Wilkinson (1971) 253–77, Maraval (1987), and Bradshaw (1999). Baldovin's assumption in Baldovin (1989), 5–6 that fourth to seventh century Jerusalem liturgy can in fact be seen in synchronic and uniform terms is perhaps the most extreme expression of the monolithic view.

[18] See e.g. the eulogy on Egeria written by the seventh century monk Valerius in Wilkinson (1971), 174–8 with Coleman and Elsner (1995), 92–3.

[19] Turner and Turner (1978). The Turners have an interesting passage on Holy Land pilgrimage (163–6), seeing it as 'prototypical' (163). Rather like Valerius on Egeria, they idealize 'the earliest known pilgrims' as 'for the most part devout souls, most of them clergy or in religious orders' (164).

[20] This is the characterization of *communitas* in Eade and Sallnow (1991), 4. For the Turners' own (long) definition (speaking of 'full, unmediated communication, even communion, between definite and determinate identitites' etc.), see Turner and Turner (1978), 250–1, 252–5.

[21] See Williams (1998), 273–4.

response to new church buildings, new discoveries of sacred relics (such as those of St Stephen the proto-martyr in 415), and imperial patronage.[22] The pilgrim in this view is an implicitly positive *exemplum* of piety and passion—not to be dismissed as a religious fetishist but to be upheld as a paradigm of Christian perfection.

Art-historical scholarship on pilgrimage arts has had relatively little to contribute to the themes of viewing and audience until recently. Traditionally the surviving arts of the holy places and in particular the imagery of ampullae has been seen as evidence for lost monumental works.[23] In the 1980s interest developed in the phenomenology of surviving objects as reliquaries, 'blessings' (*eulogiae*), and talismans with healing and devotional properties.[24] Art history has largely accepted the general approach of those historians sympathetic to the Church and has seen the products of Holy Land pilgrimage as the material evidence of a uniform tradition in which the real Jerusalem attempted, and even succeeded, in matching the ideal Jerusalem—the celestial city evoked in a famous fourth-century mosaic in the apse of the church of Sta Pudenziana in Rome.[25] In effect, art historians have followed an argument constructed by historians of religion and liturgy. The need for a steady evolution in the Jerusalem liturgy is tied to a scholarly project in which Jerusalem is represented as emerging in the fourth century as the paradigmatic Christian holy place and the liturgy of its Church as the crucial model for that of other Churches.[26] The internationalism of Jerusalem pilgrimage, the range of arts it produced (whether deliberate imitations of lost buildings or simply sacred mementos), the diffusion of the image of the Holy City—all this is implicitly presented as a comfortable paradigm of Christian unity.

In the end, despite their radical disagreement on the value of Christianity itself, the two approaches outlined here have much in common. We are offered a unifying use of the evidence, an acceptance of the piety

[22] See Baldovin (1987), 45–104 for his discussion of the Jerusalem stational liturgy. The assumption of a unitary development is shared by Renoux (1969), 29 and Renoux (1977), 267.
[23] See Grabar (1958), 44–50 and Weitzmann (1974).
[24] See e.g. Vikan (1982), (1984), 81–4, (1990) and Hahn (1990). A number of Vikan's papers on these issues are now collected in Vikan (2003).
[25] On Sta Pudenziana, see e.g. Hellemo (1989), 41–64; Schlatter (1992); Mathews (1993), 92–114.
[26] For this theory and a critique of it, see Markus (1994), 265–8.

and passion reported by our primary sources, a systematic narrative of development. Instead of the condemnation implied by Gibbon and his followers, the historians of the Church offer praise. The enthusiasm of our sources about pilgrims is accepted at their word, but it is idealized rather than despised. Both approaches take the development of history as evolutionary (whether they read the process as progression or decline). Both approaches take the early pilgrims—the central but always somewhat shadowy figures in the drama—as sharing a consensus of pious responses to the Holy Land, much on the anthropological model of *communitas* advanced by Victor and Edith Turner.

As I said earlier, lying deep in all this historical reconstruction are some assumptions about audience-response. Early Christian pilgrims are taken as a group out of which one can generalize: all the diverse bits of evidence, from art, inscriptions found on archaeological field-surveys, descriptions in hagiographic texts, and first-person narrative accounts are utilized to forge a single model of pilgrimage which presupposes a single model of pilgrim-response. Might this not be a little too cosy and comfortable? It certainly makes for an easy straw-man to beat up or for a pleasant ideal to applaud. But might there be other ways of taking the primary evidence and of interpreting it?

Contemporary anthropology of Christian pilgrimage has roundly attacked the Turnerian ideals of consensus and *communitas* as the goal and the reality of pilgrim experience on the grounds that these are unrealistically idealizing, and moreover have not been corroborated by observations in the field. In their elegant deconstruction of contemporary Christian pilgrimage, John Eade and Michael Sallnow argue that pilgrimage centres are religious voids into which multiplicities of different pilgrim-groups read their own (often conflicting and contested) interpretations.[27] Writing about modern Jerusalem in their edited book, Glenn Bowman makes the point that modern Orthodox, Roman Catholic, and Protestant pilgrims not only visit different sites within the Holy Places but also interpret them in very different ways depending on the differential structure of the 'ontology of their particular sectarian allegiances'.[28] Elsewhere, analysing the heady mix of na-

---

[27] Eade and Sallnow (1991), 15.
[28] See Bowman (1991), 107. Cf. also Bowman (1995). Bowman's position has arguably been reinforced by C. Lock's historical reflections on the differing distances of the gaze in Protestant and Orthodox relations to Holy Land pilgrimage, see Lock (2002).

tionalism with religion in the occupied territories of modern Israel, Bowman makes the case for a wide variety of differing responses to sites in Palestine like the Shrine of Elijah.[29] In one case, 'the semantic multivocality of one holy place...is seen to reflect the diversity of interests of the various communities which revere it';[30] in another, Muslim and Christian Palestinians of all denominations may worship together at the same places and times as a demonstration of an over-arching Palestinian identity in opposition to the Israeli state.[31]

I don't wish simply to replace one anthropological model for another in interpreting early Christian pilgrimage. Indeed the contestation model is open to certain substantive criticisms. First, Bowman's articulate presentation of numerous contemporary Christianities in competition at Jerusalem nonetheless reifies each Christian denomination he discusses (Orthodox, Catholic, and Protestant) as if these were single entities as opposed to fissile and fractured groups of multiple views and from numerous backgrounds. In fact, given the diversity within any one sect or denomination, we have to entertain the possibility of individuals or small groups constructing their own patterns of pilgrimage or ritual within a site either to complement any 'official' or authoritative structure approved by their denomination, or in opposition, or both.[32] Second, on a more theoretical level, it is not clear that multiplicity need necessarily imply contestation.[33] We might in principle extend the range of characterizations of multiplicity to include—in addition to contestation—such options as juxtaposition, diversity, conflict, and negotiation as well as 'communitas'. One way forward is to argue that in setting out on a sacred journey and converging on a pilgrimage centre, pilgrims generate the desire for some kind of sacred experience which may well correspond to something like the Turners' 'communitas' (on the level of desire), though it may have other—much more personal—investments and aims as well (or instead). In actuality, both from the subjective viewpoints of participants and in the external

---

[29] Bowman (1993).

[30] Ibid. 431 (quote), 433–9.

[31] Ibid. 439–51.

[32] At least, this is an upshot of observations in the field at contemporary Walsingham, which like Jerusalem is a site of Christian pilgrimage by diverse denominations. See Coleman and Elsner (1998).

[33] For this point in relation to ancient religions, see Goodman (1994), 1, 17–18.

reflections of observers, there will always be a multiplicity of experiences which may not only conform to any point on the imaginary scale between 'communitas' and 'contestation' but may also change along that scale in relation to the ritual process that takes place and the memories of it thereafter.

Nonetheless, it is worth looking back at the historical record of early Christian Palestine to see if something of this problematic of multiplicities of experience and potentially of contestation may be relevant to Holy Land pilgrimage of the fourth and fifth centuries. The historical record, it is worth stressing, is already a complex set of documents (quite apart from its fragmentation as a set of diverse and eccentrically surviving material sources) in that it conflates actuality with memory, experience with a variety of succeeding idealizations. Quite apart from a continuing pagan polytheism certainly until the fifth century (which tends to be underrated),[34] we have evidence, in the Palestine of the first few centuries after the Peace of the Church, of multilingual communities both of temporary pilgrims and of settlers (permanent pilgrims, one might say, like St Jerome). Many of the latter were monks but others were aristocrats associated with the court, such as the empress Eudocia and the noblewomen Paula, Eustochium, and the two Melanias.[35] Egeria describes the Jerusalem liturgy being performed in Greek with translations into Latin and Syriac (she may mean Aramaic).[36]

In the midst of this strongly international community, comprising pilgrims of many social classes, one factor affecting the Church of Jerusalem no less than the other ecclesiatical provinces in this period was the unrelenting series of internal divisions over heresy and what constituted orthodox doctrine.[37] In the time covered by Baldovin's lists of liturgical stations (from say 380 to 460), Palestine experienced three

---

[34] See e.g. Geiger (1998); Rubin (1998); Belayche (2001), 296–309.

[35] For some of these aristocratic female pilgrims, see Hunt (1982), 155–79, 221–48 (Eudocia) and Holum (1982), 183–6 (Melania the Younger), 217–28 (Eudocia).

[36] On linguistic diversity, see Hunt (1982), 152–4 and Renoux (1984). On the different provenances of visitors to Palestine, see Maraval (1985), 105–113 and Binns (1994), 85–95. For Arab pilgrimages, see Shahîd (1998), 374–7. For a 'bird's eye view' of Palestinian monasticism in the period, with bibliography, see Perrone (1995).

[37] See esp. Perrone (1980). On the local politics between the sees of Caesarea and Jerusalem, see e.g. Rubin (1999).

major disputes over heresy: in the 390s when the Church divided over Origenism, in the teens of the fifth century when the Jerusalem hierarchy split over the Pelagian controversy, and above all after 451 and the Council of Chalcedon.[38] The details of each of these disputes are perhaps less important than the fact that they involved a division of the establishment with significant figures in the ecclesiatical, monastic, and political spheres supporting rival theological parties. Pilgrims were inevitably drawn into these polarized factions, as much by where they happened to receive hospitality as by theological inclination.[39]

In the 390s Bishop Epiphanius of Salamis in Cyprus (a native of Palestine) sided with Jerome and Paula against the monks who favoured Origen's speculative theology, while Bishop John of Jerusalem along with Rufinus and the Elder Melania in their monastery on the Mount of Olives supported the Origenists.[40] Reverberations of this argument lasted well into the sixth century in Palestinian monasticism.[41] In 418, the British-born monk Pelagius was finally condemned for heresy, after residing in the Holy Land from around 412 and being solemnly pronounced orthodox by a local Council of Palestinian bishops at Diospolis in 415 led by John of Jerusalem.[42] Again the controversy caught up a number of locals (with Jerome leading the batting against Pelagius and Bishop John the defence).[43] But by far the deepest crisis (and one whose effects are still in evidence in Coptic and Armenian Christianity) was over the Council of Chalcedon in 451. After Bishop Juvenal of Jerusalem had deserted the party of the Patriarch Dioscorus of Alexandria to side with the winners in a council which anathematized most of the Egyptian and Syrian Churches as Monophysite heretics, he was opposed almost unanimously by the monks of Palestine.[44] They deposed Juvenal from his episcopal throne and installed an anti-Chalcedonian bishop, Theodosius, to replace him. Theodosius then put

[38] Generally on events before Chalcedon, see Perrone (1977), 212–49.

[39] See Hunt (1982), 180–4.

[40] On Origenism and Palestine, see Perrone (1980), 204–12; Hunt (1982), 180–202; Kelly (1975), 195–209; Rubenson (1995).

[41] See Binns (1994), 201–17.

[42] On Pelagius, see Evans (1968); Brown (1972), 183–226; and Kelly (1975), 309–25.

[43] For Pelagianism and Palestine, see Hunt (1982), 203–220.

[44] For these events and a portrait of Juvenal in the light of ecclesiastical politics, see Honigman (1950). On Chalcedon and the rise of Monophysitism, see Frend (1972), 1–49.

Monophysites into all the bishoprics in his jurisdiction. Only in 453 was Juvenal—still considered an apostate and a Judas by the majority of his flock—able to return, with the help of imperial troops. During the half-century after Chalcedon, the successive Patriarchs of Jerusalem followed the vagaries of imperial policy on whether the council had been Orthodox, and it was only after 490 that Palestine (as opposed to Egypt, Syria, and parts of the Levant less than 100 miles from Jerusalem) emerged on the Chalcedonian side.[45]

Clearly the literary texts, from which so much of our narrative of this fierce series of conflicts is reconstructed, could hardly fail to be the bearers of the polemics involved.[46] Take the *Life of Melania the Younger*, the Roman aristocrat who settled in Palestine before 420 and founded monasteries, martyria, and churches on the Mount of Olives.[47] This was probably composed by the monk Gerontius, who took over the direction of Melania's monasteries after her death in 439 and himself died in the last quarter of the fifth century. Gerontius was an ardent Monophysite—one of those who aided in the deposition of Juvenal from the Patriarchal see of Jerusalem in 451 and who assisted in the elevation of the anti-Chalcedonian Theodosius (at whose behest the text may have been written).[48] The Monophysite allegiance of this text is striking—nowhere is Juvenal mentioned, although he was bishop from 422 to 458 (with the twenty-month interval of Theodosius' tenure in 451–3) and despite the fact that Melania is constantly represented as honouring and being honoured by bishops.[49] On the Chalcedonian side, the same events were depicted with no less partiality. In the *Life of Euthymius*, the first of the *Lives of the Monks of Palestine* written by Cyril of Sythopolis in the mid-sixth century, the saint is approached in 451 by two emissaries from Theodosius ('in appearance a monk, but in reality a precursor of Antichrist') shortly after the ousting of Juvenal. One of these is Gerontius, author of the *Life of Melania*. Euthymius refuses to

---

[45] On Chalcedon and its after-effects in Palestine, see Perrone (1980), 89–113, and Binns (1994), 183–99. For the Monophysite episcopate, see Honigman (1951).

[46] Briefly on such 'militant' hagiography in Palestine, see Perrone, (1998), 87–90.

[47] See Clark (1984), 83–119 on life and activities.

[48] Clark (1984), 17–22.

[49] Clark (1984), 19. What Clark calls the text's 'tendentious, indeed propagandistic, qualities' extend to the exclusion of others tainted with what Gerontius saw as heresy, notably the elder Melania (his heroine's grandmother and predecessor in a long Palestinian sojourn)—see Clark (1984), 148–52 (quote from 152), and 170.

change his position on Chalcedon, withdraws into retreat in the desert and upholds Orthodoxy as he waits for the enemy to fall (41.4–45.4). Clearly, any more than the historical narratives we derive from them, texts like this do not deliver us actual pilgrims and their beliefs or the competitive confessional adherences of places of pilgrimage. But given that the monasteries provided the principal tour guides, hostels, and in some cases even the central attractions (in the form of living saints or the relics of departed ones) for the practice of Palestinian pilgrimage,[50] it would be surprising to find these intensely-felt doctrinal divisions to have had no impact on the pilgrim experience.

This background of conflict and dispute, in which the Palestinian monasteries were the principal players,[51] can hardly be separated from the practices of pilgrimage. It is worth adding at this point that contestation is certainly a historically valid model also for the internal relations of the hierarchy of the Church in Rome (the Christian world's other paradigmatic pilgrimage centre) during the third and fourth centuries.[52] At this point the Roman Church was split by a series of doctrinal and political schisms about rival centres of authority; rival sites of cult—above all for Rome's premier saints, Peter and Paul—persisted within the structures of Roman pilgrimage and urban liturgy at least till the end of the fourth century.[53] In the context of Palestine, we know that different religions shared major pilgrimage venues, such as the sanctuary of Mamre which continued to attract Jews and polytheists well beyond the Constantinian Christianization of the site.[54] The rival

---

[50] On monks and theology, see Binns (1994), 183–217; on monks and pilgrimage see Binns (1994), 83–5 and esp. Frank (2000*a*), which focuses on monks as both pilgrims and objects of pilgrimage. The model of holy man as pilgrim goes back to pre-Christian antiquity in the form of Apollonius of Tyana, with Elsner (1997*a*).

[51] The best discussion of the complex nature and interrelations of Palestinian monasticism (though not focused on pilgrimage) is Perrone (1998).

[52] On this dynamic, see Brent (1995) 381–4 on the 4th cent. and 389–540 on the 3rd cent.; also Curran (2000), 129–42 on the 4th cent. For the effects of this on visual production, see Elsner (2003).

[53] There is a vast literature on the problem of the three sites involved—what have become the traditional tombs of Peter and Paul at the Vatican and on the Via Ostiense outside the walls of Rome respectively, and the famous joint site on the Via Appia (from which there is a great deal of archaeological evidence), known as 'ad catacumbas' (from which the term 'catacomb' is derived) which later became known as San Sebastiano. See for instance O'Connor (1969), 116–206 and Snyder (1985), 98–114, 141–7.

[54] See Perrone (1998), 71; Kofsky (1998), 24–8 with earlier bibliography; Belayche (2001), 96–104.

Christian factions occasionally established shared sanctuaries—as was
the case at Amida in Syria and at the Shrine of St Menas as well as that of
Sts Cyrus and John at Menouthis, both near Alexandria, in all of which
Monophysites worshipped alongside Chalcedonians.[55] Equally, competing Christianities established alternative places of worship—as when
the Chalcedonians began devotion to the Mother of God on Mount
Zion, after the Tomb of Mary at Gethsemane had fallen into Monophysite hands,[56] or when the Arab Monophysite bishop Ahudemmeh
set up a rival Shrine of St Sergius to that dominated by the Chalcedonians at Rusafa in Qasr Sarij near Balad in Syria (in about 565).[57] The
evidence of late antique Egypt offers pilgrimage sites shared by Christians not only with 'heretics' but even with pagans.[58] It raises the theme
of contested space not only within various 'paganisms',[59] but also within
the Church hierarchy,[60] and among the monastic establishment,[61] as
well as between multiple forms of Christianity (Coptic and Orthodox).[62] It shows clear evidence of Christian usurpation of pagan sites.[63]

These hints certainly echo the patterns of pilgrimage as an affirmation
of contested and segmentary religious positions proposed by Bowman
for modern Jerusalem; they also look back to earlier Christian appropriation of Pagan, Jewish, and Samaritan holy sites.[64] Moreover, the
divergent provenances of pilgrims to Jerusalem before it fell to Islam in
638 argue for more than merely linguistic and national differences.
While Western and Constantinopolitan visitors may have been largely

---

[55] On Amida, see Key Fowden (1999), 156–7. On St Menas, see Kötting (1950),
190–2; Maraval (1985), 83; Binns (1994), 198. On Menouthis, see Key Fowden (1999),
157. Note that the sharing of space did not entail the sharing of liturgy or liturgical
implements.

[56] See Maraval (1985), 75; Binns (1994), 198.

[57] See Key Fowden (1999), 122–5. In Rusafa itself, as possibly in Zenobia to the
south-east on the Euphrates, it may be that there were (at least) two churches serving the
different rites: see Key Fowden (1999), 91–2.

[58] See Frankfurter (1998c), 29–39.

[59] See Rutherford (1998c), 230–1 and 250–3.

[60] See Behlmer (1998), 351–4.

[61] See Goehring (1997).

[62] On the specificity of Coptic pilgrimage—its spaces and rituals—see MacCoull,
(1998); Timbie (1998); Krawiec (1998); McNally (1998).

[63] See Montserrat (1998), 257–60.

[64] See Wilkinson (1990) and Taylor (1993), 318–32. On the development of the
Christian idea of holy places and a holy land, see Walker (1990); Wilken (1992); and
Markus (1994).

Chalcedonian, Persian Christians (who came in reasonable numbers)[65] were probably Nestorian—which is to say out of communion with both Chalcedonians and Monophysites since the Council of Ephesus in 431, while Armenians, Georgians, Copts, and Syrians were principally Monophysite.[66] Some Monophysite texts argue that the holy sites had lost their sanctity on falling into Chalcedonian hands, and others such as the Acts of the Armenian Council of Dvin in 536 banned pilgrimage to Palestine.[67] Meanwhile, despite these attempts on the part of the Monophysite clergy to prevent their flocks from straying to the Holy Land, there is much evidence nevertheless of Armenian sacred travel. For instance, several sixth- and seventh-century texts refer to Armenian pilgrims in Palestine or Sinai,[68] and archaeological surveys have yielded large numbers of Armenian inscriptions on pilgrim routes to Sinai different from those mentioned by our mainly western pilgrim accounts.[69] It remains possible, of course, that these particular Armenians, for whom the evidence survives, were Orthodox, or that the doctrinal differences on which so much weight has been traditionally put meant rather less among people on the ground than to polemical theologians and hagiographers writing in their libraries.

In effect, it is clear that the Holy Land was host to a constant mixture of nationalities, races, and Christianities which participated in the holy places in their own ways, more or less officially. The extent of 'heretic' participation in Orthodox services was not, to be sure, a subject either side was keen to publicize (all sides of course considered themselves Orthodox and the others heretical), and therefore the problem is all but ignored in the literature.[70] Likewise, the possibility— let alone the extent—of alternative rites from those run by the dominant Chalcedonians at different places or at the same places at different hours has hardly been raised. Yet, if we take together the evidence of

---

[65] See Maraval (1985), 110–12, 135.

[66] See Maraval (1985), 112–13, 134 f., 160 f. For a general discussion of Nestorian and Monophysite pilgrimage to Jerusalem, see Fiey (1969).

[67] See Maraval (1985), 135 (for the desanctification argument), 75 (for the Dvin edict).

[68] On Jerusalem and Armenia, see the overview by Thomson (1985), 77–91, and on Sinai, Chitty (1966), 174–5.

[69] Mayerson (1982), 44–57.

[70] Save for Maraval's brief comments: Maraval (1985), 134–5, 160–1.

vehement religious division, of different racial and sectarian groups apparently treading different paths to the Holy Sites and of multiple languages, we may find that the existing testimony of the primary sources reads a little differently from the neat unfolding of a consensual and unified tradition which modern accounts have conspired to describe.

Take Baldovin's (1987) list of stations in the Jerusalem liturgy (Table 1).[71] For him the differences between Egeria's presentation of stations in, say, the Octave of Epiphany (which is to say, the eve of the sixth of January and the eight days following it) and those listed by the Armenian Lectionary in its two early manuscripts (J and P) 'clearly show an evolution from the practice of Egeria's time to that of the early fifth century' (p. 94). He reads the differences as 'signs of an evolving pattern' (p. 95), and thus creates a unifying narrative of 'major developments' (p. 96) to bridge the temporal and evidential gaps.[72] We need add no further primary information, however, to reverse his interpretation and assert that the differences could equally be due to competitive liturgies organized by contesting racial or national groups which may already have been denying communion to each other in the late fourth, let alone the early to mid-fifth centuries. The literature on the Jerusalem liturgy uniformly claims that the Armenian calendar (preserved in a language and by a Church out of communion with the Chalcedonians since 451) is really a translation of a Greek liturgy like that reported by Egeria but more advanced.[73] On the face of it, this seems rather like special pleading—a deliberate fixing of the evidence even before its consider-

---

[71] Baldovin (1987) appendix 2, 282–4; Baldovin (1989), 35–7. His discussion of development in the hagiopolite liturgy is (1987), 94–102.

[72] Clearly new evidence is susceptible to being imported into the grand narrative. For instance, a fragmentary Christian Palestinian Aramaic manuscript of the Gospels with lectionary rubrics, reused as a palimpsest by the Georgian scribe Zosimus in the 10th cent., adds to Luke 2:8 the rubric: 'Fifth lection: of the Martyrion of the Shepherds, before the vigil of the Theophania.' As Sebastian Brock points out, this accords with the Armenian Lectionary in placing the eve of the Nativity (celebrated on 6 January), at the 'place of the Shepherds at the 10th hour'. However, the use of 'Martyrium' is unique of the Church of the Shepherds and not all of this manuscript's lectionary indications correspond with the Armenian Lectionary, so it is by no means clear whether this kind of additional evidence supports or undermines the evolutionary interpretation. See Brock (1999), 765–6.

[73] Renoux (1969), 21, 29; Baldovin (1987), 65.

ation in order for it to yield the desired results.[74] As I remarked earlier this whole argument is part of a larger project which sees the Jerusalem liturgy as the model for liturgy throughout Christendom,[75] and which sees Jerusalem itself as the paradigmatic holy place.[76]

Clearly, liturgy does evolve gradually on something like the pattern Baldovin has proposed. But whether its evolution in Palestine was as consensual, or as bishop- and hierarchy-centred, as Baldovin would like is what is at issue.[77] Although we are apparently dealing with historical problems of the development of pilgrimage practices over time, in fact the bottom line of the possible theoretical frames underlying the writing of this history is embedded in our assumptions about the responses of pilgrims. Do we want those pilgrims to be a unified body, in full communion with an undivided and Orthodox episcopate—an ideal community of worshippers, in other words—as do Baldovin and historians of his persuasion? Or are we willing to conceive of a more chaotic climate of disparate, diffracted, and sectarian groups, possibly in conflict with each other, with those who run the site and with their forebears? Both versions and the histories derived from them are driven by a more or less implicit theory of audience-response. Either model will help us to construct a coherent historical account to explain the evidence.

Again, a surprising number of the grander pilgrims known to us from late antiquity were women.[78] No published study to date has addressed the problematics of gender in the pilgrim community or the question of possible differentiation in gendered responses to the holy places. Indeed

---

[74] Likewise Baldovin's comprehensive definition of stational liturgy (1987, 35–7) as presided over by the local bishop begs a series of questions—not least whether a text like the Armenian Lectionary (which mentions dates, places, and gospel readings), really represents a stational liturgy as Baldovin assumes. Moreover, what happens in the case of rival bishops appointed by rival communions?

[75] See e.g. Baldovin (1989), 5 and 44.

[76] See Markus (1994), 265–8.

[77] For attempts to resolve divergences in our liturgical sources (instead of exploiting their potential conflict) see e.g. Johnson (1988), and Baldovin (1989), 11–13. For the traditional attempt to derive the Syriac lectionary from the Greek (and hence implicitly to even-out conflicts by chronologizing difference as evolution), see Metzger (1969). On the ways Syriac lectionaries may in fact borrow their *structure* from the Greek lectionary but use different and potentially conflicting Syriac materials, see Brock (1970).

[78] On female pilgrims to Palestine in late antiquity, see Brubaker (1997); Holloway (1998), 31–9; Davis (1998), 323–33; Smith (1999). ·

the scholarship has conspired to present pilgrims as a united front—their credulity being all the more plausible in women according to the cynics, and their ideal piety all the more archetypal in the women (the true visionaries of medieval culture) for the believers. No less than doctrinal division, gender difference has been elided—suppressed—in the standard accounts.

Personally, I think it is hard to resist entirely the theory of contestation suggested equally by modern anthropological observation, by the evidence of early Christian doctrinal divisions and by even a very brief survey of the national, racial, and gender differences so marked among the late antique pilgrims. Nonetheless, contestation is an interpretative assumption applied to the evidence—and it is certainly not in the flavour of the saints' lives and first-hand pilgrim accounts (like Egeria or Jerome on Paula) which form the bulk of our written evidence. Of course, one would expect such accounts to be idealizing, and the ideals they express clearly reflect the desire, if not necessarily the actual experience, of many early Christian pilgrims. In the end, we write history as plausibly and coherently as possible in accordance with a series of our own—often unconscious—presuppositions about how the world is. I don't want to be taken as arguing for some kind of transhistorical postmodernism as a more appropriate means of approaching the early Christian world than earlier theoretical approaches. However, some of the insights of the current deconstructive drive towards pluralism, competing views, and contestation have a value in throwing light on one aspect of early Christian pilgrimage—an important aspect—which earlier more communalistic and perhaps less cynical scholarship failed to notice. More careful work on the range of possible audience-responses clearly offers an important way into making conscious and self-aware choices about the models we decide to apply.

17

Urban Shrine and Rural Saint in Fifth-Century Alexandria

David Frankfurter

I. RELICS AND POLITICS

By the middle of the fifth century CE, Egypt's Christianity—or those parts of Egypt that had come to embrace Christianity—included a broad network of pilgrimage shrines, some of international fame like Apa Mena west of Alexandria, some of local or regional importance, like the oracle-granting cult of St Philoxenus in Oxyrhynchus, or the healing cult of St Colluthus in Antinoë, or the numerous cults of living saints in and around monasteries or in the desert. It was a Christianity acculturated to the Egyptian landscape and its religious idioms.[1]

This relic-centred Egyptian Christianity also lay in some theological and cultural tension with the episcopal and imperial Christian world that had been developing in Alexandria and beyond. Already in the fourth century CE Athanasius of Alexandria decried the rush for martyrs' bones, the invention of holy places, and the ecstatic devotions he saw going on at the Egyptian shrines.[2] Athanasius sought to rein in the

Originally delivered at the International Medieval Conference, Leeds, July 1999. I am grateful to David Brakke, Jaś Elsner, Georgia Frank, David Johnson, Vassiliki Limberis, and Terry Wilfong for criticisms of earlier drafts, and to the editors of this volume for inviting its contribution.

[1] See Lefort (1954); Baumeister (1972), esp. ch. 2; and now Papaconstantinou (2001). On indigenous aspects of the Egyptian martyr cult see Frankfurter (1994) and Clarysse (1995).

[2] Brakke (1997), (1998).

charismatic monks and hermits, to subsume them in an ecclesiastical world where scripture held sway and bishops governed flocks and interpreted that scripture.[3] Saints' shrines and relics, of course, were never the exclusive preserve of some popular or 'semi-' Christianity, since most classes and cultures of the empire came to subscribe to their blessings.[4] And yet the kind of distaste that Athanasius showed in his time for the intimate rituals developing around martyria began to characterize a certain class of urban bishop throughout the Christian empire—including Ambrose in the west and Jacob of Sarug in Syria. In their late fourth-century CE criticisms of the martyr cult, Peter Brown has observed, 'we are dealing with the claims of an austere, transcendent monotheism put forward by the clergy in the name of their own monopoly of access to the divine.'[5] Holiness, they sought to instruct Christendom, should be found in scripture, in the Mysteries, in the ecclesiarchy, rather than in relics. Nevertheless, by the early fifth century, cults of saints were becoming a precious and ineradicable aspect of Christianity, its landscape and urban self-definition; and archbishops and emperors alike gained protection and prestige for their newly Christian cities through importing and enshrining new relics.

But whose relics? A subtle tension seems to have developed in this process—at least in the eastern Mediterranean world—between the saints that the urban bishops held dear and authoritative and those that marked the Christianized landscape of particular cultures like Egypt. The urban authorities, we find, sought relics of predominantly *biblical* saints—patriarchs, prophets, apostles—who signified the defining authority of scripture in the Christian church and whose body parts could bridge the tension between the urban centres of Christendom and a Holy Land revered as mythical centre.[6] And while scriptural saints like Elijah and John the Baptist had certainly provided the principal models of Christian ascetic and charismatic self-definition throughout Egypt,

---

[3] Brakke (1994) and (1995), ch.2.

[4] See esp. Brown (1981), 11–22.

[5] Brown (1998), 661.

[6] See in general Baynes (1949); Brown (1981), ch. 5; Hunt (1981); Limberis (1994), 52–53; Orselli (1999); plus Theodoret, *History of the Monks of Syria* 21.20. On the use of relics to forge ideological links with the Holy Land see Elsner (1997c). Gibb (1999) discusses similar conceptions of Muslim saints in the contemporary Ethiopian city of Harar, offering protection, history, and social identity to city-dwellers.

Egyptian Christians beyond the cities were also constructing a Christian landscape made up predominantly of relics of *Egyptian* martyrs or holy men, who functioned as mediators between the local culture and a broader Christian ideology.[7]

One cannot, of course, polarize the urban ecclesiastical and rural monastic worlds in any absolute way, since debates over the nature of saints, the use of relics, and the function of shrines stretched across city, *chōra*, monastery, village, and church.[8] Furthermore, western church officials, far from the Holy Land, took the reverse approach to authenticate their basilicas and shrines, 'inventing' local saints right and left, like Gregory's cult of St Martin and the two obscure martyrs that Ambrose exhumed for the benefit of his new basilica in Milan.[9] Yet by the fifth century CE we can detect, in Egypt particularly, two *roughly* distinct Christian cultures—in theological tendency, language, attitude towards scripture and Christian lore, and—particularly for my purposes—concepts of the saint's shrine: biblical and Egyptian.

In this chapter I will not so much try to push this cultural dichotomy as to examine incidents of its *convergence*: when a rural holy man himself contributed to the authentication or indigenization of a shrine to a biblical saint.

II. JOHN THE LITTLE AND THE SHRINE OF THE THREE HEBREWS

In the early fifth century CE, Archbishop Theophilus instituted a building programme designed to Christianize the very infrastructure of

---

[7] See Lefort (1954); Brakke (1998), 463–72; Frankfurter (1998c), 28–39; Papaconstantinou (2001), 230–3 and *passim*; and general observations on the mediating capacity of relics, Boesch Gajano (1999).

[8] See Reymond and Barns (1973), 5 and Wipszycka (1992), esp. 126–28. Debates over the meaning of relics and holy space could arise in quite extra-urban milieux: the 5th-cent. upper-Egyptian abbot Shenoute decries relic veneration in one sermon (Lefort 1954), while his biographer Besa and people in his region came to view him in his life and thereafter as himself a saint of great intercessory and thaumaturgical power: see Bell (1983), Timbie (1998), and Frankfurter (1996), 191–3.

[9] On Ambrose: McLynn (1994), 209–17 and Humphries (1999), 54–6. On Gregory, St Martin, and the Gallic predilection for local saints: Van Dam (1985), 167–70, 199–201, 214–16, 230–55.

Alexandria and its surroundings. In this endeavour Theophilus reflected the growing sense in late antique Mediterranean culture that what distinguished a Christian city and what gave a city prestige was its saints—its protectors and axes to heaven.[10] His most important urban shrine, to John the Baptist and Elisha, I will turn to shortly; but one particular shrine was dedicated to the three Hebrew youths who survived the furnace in the Book of Daniel (3:1–30). No archaeological evidence exists for this church, but a medieval Coptic homily places it in the ruins of a native temple just outside the city.[11] This same homily goes on to describe a series of inaugural miracles wrought by the Three Hebrews, even their appearance during the martyrion's construction. Indeed, a good number of Coptic texts promoting the Three Hebrews or the shrine show a real propaganda effort to establish the saints in the evolving Christian landscape of Alexandria and the Egyptian delta.

But why the Three Hebrews, instead of some Egyptian martyr like Apa Mena or John and Cyrus, both active and renowned cults outside Alexandria by the fifth century CE?[12] Constructed against a religious topography full of miracle-working hermits and active cults to little-known Egyptian martyrs, Theophilus' intentions would have had a discernibly political cast. Installing this shrine would demonstrate his protective patronage of Alexandria's fortune by bringing in new 'city-guardians'—a distant recollection of Ptolemy I's retrieval of the body of Alexander from Babylon to legitimize the nascent Alexandria.[13] More-over, Theophilus' act would stake out Alexandrian ground for the heroes of scripture rather than for the obscure martyrs of Egyptian tradition, thus acknowledging (and importing) the pre-eminence of the Holy

[10] On Theophilus' building programme, see Haas (1997), 206–14. On new notions of the city and its saints in late antiquity, see Caseau (1999), 36–8; Gauthier (1999), 207–9; and sources in n. 6 above.

[11] Cyril of Alexandria (attrib.), *Miracles of the Three Children*, ed. De Vis (1990), 2.164–6. It should be noted that another tradition, inscribed in Sophronius' *Miracles of Ss John and Cyrus* (7th cent.), attributes the building of this shrine to the 6th-cent. archbishop Apollinaris. Here the 'biblical' cult is indigenized through its inclusion of relics of the local healing saints John and Cyrus. See Gascou (1984), 334–5 and, on the John and Cyrus cult, Montserrat (1998).

[12] On the Apa Mena cult, see Grossmann (1998). The Apa Mena cult had international renown: see Delahaye (1997).

[13] On Ptolemy I and the relics of Alexander see Strabo 17.1.8 (794), and Green (1990), 13.

Land during this period as the paradigmatic religious landscape.[14] In this way, shrines of more *local* or *regional* authority would, at least in Alexandria, be pre-empted for the sake of the authority of scripture and the international prestige of having well-known saints in residence. To be sure, it was a nod to the Egyptian martyrological tradition to bring in the Three Hebrews—proto-martyrs, who had suffered under Nebuchadnezzar, and archetypal holy men whose secret names were often invoked in amulets.[15] But it was an ideological statement nonetheless, constructing Alexandria's sacred landscape according to the Bible rather than the popular legends of Egyptian martyrs.

Theophilus seems to have been faced with a more glaring problem, however, than tension with Coptic local cults. As two Coptic hagiographies note, the *relics* of the Three Hebrews remained in Ctesiphon, in Babylonia. There they had been 'discovered' around 420 CE (the same time as Theophilus' building programme).[16] Thus the shrine of the Three Hebrews in Alexandria would have presented a rather questionable degree of power, of saintly 'presence', especially in a landscape already rich in real bones. If the heroes resided distant in Babylonia, what efficacy could they have in the shrine in Alexandria? Why would people come to an empty martyrion?[17]

---

[14] See Elsner (1997c).

[15] Three Hebrews in Coptic spells: Van der Vliet (1991), 236–9. On the broader Coptic veneration of the Three Hebrews, see *Martyrdom of Shenoufe* 120 Rii-Vi, tr. Reymond and Barns (1973), 204; Gascou (1984); Van Esbroeck (1991); and Papaconstantinou (2001), 198–200. See early iconographic evidence in Walters (1974), 129, 133; Van Loon (1999), 167–76.

[16] *Life of John the Little*, ed. Amélineau (1894), 316–413, tr. Mikhail and Vivian (1997); Theophilus (attrib.), 'Sermon on the Three Hebrews,' ed. De Vis (1990), 2:121–57. According to an Armenian account of their invention, the cult of the Three Hebrews in Ctesiphon seems to have started under the reign of Vahram V, perhaps with the relics' transfer from the Jewish community: see Garitte (1959), esp. 69–75 on history of Ctesiphon cult, and (1961). The *Life of Daniel the Stylite* (ch. 92) attests to the relics' translation to Constantinople under emperor Leo I (457–74) and placement over Daniel's tomb at his burial in 493 (Dawes and Baynes 1977: 64–5).

[17] So also Gascou (1984), 334. It is conceivable that this rivalry with Babylon over important relics recalled Ptolemy I's claim of Alexander's body to sanction Alexandria. See above, n. 13. But rivalry among shrines to the same divinity over the divinity's 'presence' is well-known elsewhere in the Mediterranean world: propagandists for the dominant shrine of Asclepius at Epidauros asserted the god's *absence* at his shrine at Troizen; and if one insisted on visiting Troizen, Asclepius would have to make a special trip *over from* Epidauros: Epidauros B3, C5, on which see LiDonnici (1995), 71–73. On empty shrines compare also Heyberger (1998), 126.

It is the resolution of this problem that occupies one chapter of the Coptic *Life of John the Little*, holy man of the monastery of Scetis in the late fourth and early fifth centuries CE.[18] John, according to the *Life* (ch. 75), was asked by Archbishop Theophilus to intercede with the Three Hebrews themselves off in Babylon. Acceding to his wishes, the holy man took off immediately to the distant city—by remarkable means:

he began to pray, and immediately at that hour a cloud carried him and placed him in Babylon where lay the bodies of the holy and excellent athletes of Christ God. Our holy father saw the perfect gift of the tomb of the saints by means of the light of the Holy Spirit who guided him. He worshiped upon the earth three times before he reached them. When our father approached them he threw himself down on his face and embraced their holy relics with a display of many sweet tears.[19]

In his capacity as supernatural mediator, John speaks directly with the Three Hebrews and implores them to allow their relics' translation to Alexandria. The heroes, however, explain that they have to remain in Babylon: 'Tell the archbishop that it is not at all possible for our bodies to be translated to another place and remain there forever; they must remain where they are now, according to the commandment of God the Creator.'[20] The heroes make this promise instead:

Let them decorate the shrine [in Alexandria] and hang all the lamps without oil or wicks, and gather there with all the people and clergy. At night we will come and place in it the power and blessing of the Lord and in this way sanctify the house of God, . . . And by the power of the God of Israel, while the archbishop lives we will spiritually dwell in it through signs and wonders [ⲧⲉⲛⲛⲁϣⲱⲡⲓ

[18] On John the Little see Evelyn White (1932), 2.106–11, and Vivian in Mikhail and Vivian (1997), 3–16.

[19] ⲁϥϯ ⲛⲟⲩⲉⲩⲭⲏ ⲥⲁⲧⲟⲧϥ ⲇⲉ ϧⲉⲛ ϯⲟⲩⲛⲟⲩ ⲁ ⲟⲩϭⲏⲡⲓ ϥⲁⲓ ⲙⲙⲟϥ ⲟⲩⲟϩ ⲁⲥⲭⲁϥ ⲉϩⲣⲏⲓ ϧⲉⲛ ⲑⲃⲁⲃⲩⲗⲱⲛ ⲉϥⲙⲁ ⲉⲧⲉⲣⲉ ⲡⲥⲱⲙⲁ ⲛⲧⲉ ⲛⲓⲁⲅⲓⲟⲥ ⲛⲅⲉⲛⲛⲁⲓⲟⲥ ⲛⲁⲑⲗⲏⲧⲏⲥ ⲛⲧⲉ ⲡⲭ̅ⲥ̅ ⲟ̅ⲧ̅ ⲭⲏ ⲙⲙⲁⲩ ⲉⲧⲁϥⲛⲁⲩ ⲇⲉ ⲛϫⲉ ⲛⲉⲛⲓⲱⲧ ⲉⲑⲟⲩⲁⲃ ⲉⲧⲇⲱⲣⲉⲁ ⲉⲧⲭⲏⲕ ⲉⲃⲟⲗ ⲛⲧⲉ ⲡⲥⲕⲏⲛⲱⲙⲁ ⲛⲛⲓⲁⲅⲓⲟⲥ ϩⲓⲧⲉⲛ ⲫⲟⲩⲱⲛⲓ ⲙⲡⲓⲡⲛ̅ⲁ̅ ⲉⲑⲟⲩⲁⲃ ⲉⲧϭⲓ ⲙⲱⲓⲧ ϩⲁⲭⲱϥ ⲁϥⲟⲩⲱϣⲧ ϩⲓϫⲉⲛ ⲡⲓⲕⲁϩⲓ ⲛⲅ ⲛⲥⲟⲡ ⲙⲡⲁⲧⲉϥⲫⲟϩ ⲉⲣⲱⲟⲩ· ⲉⲧⲁϥϧⲱⲛⲧ ⲇⲉ ⲉⲣⲱⲟⲩ ⲛϫⲉ ⲡⲉⲛⲓⲱⲧ ⲁϥϩⲓⲧϥ ⲉϩⲣⲏⲓ ⲉϫⲉⲛ ⲡⲉϥϩⲟ ⲉϥⲉⲣ ⲁⲙⲁⲗⲏⲝ ⲉϫⲉⲛ ⲛⲟⲩⲗⲉⲓⲯⲁⲛⲟⲛ ⲉⲑⲟⲩⲁⲃ ϧⲉⲛ ⲧⲁⲓⲥⲑⲏⲥⲓⲥ ⲛϩⲁⲛ ⲉⲣⲙⲱⲟⲩⲓ ⲉⲩϩⲟⲗϫ, ed. Amélineau (1894), 384, tr. Mikhail and Vivian (1997), 48.

[20] ⲛⲉⲛⲥⲱⲙⲁ ⲙⲉⲛ ⲙⲙⲟⲛ ϣϫⲟⲙ ⲉⲡⲧⲏⲣϥ ⲉⲑⲣⲟⲩⲟⲩⲟⲑⲃⲟⲩ ⲉⲕⲉⲙⲱⲓⲧ ⲉⲑⲣⲟⲩϣⲱⲡⲓ ⲛϩⲏⲧϥ ϣⲁ ⲉⲃⲟⲗ ⲥⲁ ⲃⲟⲗ ⲙⲡⲁⲓⲙⲁ ⲉⲧⲟⲩⲭⲏ ⲛϩⲏⲧϥ ϯⲛⲟⲩ ⲕⲁⲧⲁ ⲫⲟⲩⲁϩⲥⲁϩⲛⲓ ⲙⲡⲓⲣⲉϥⲥⲱⲛⲧ ⲫϯ. ed. Amélineau (1894), 385, tr. Mikhail and Vivian (1997), 49.

ⲚϨⲎⲦϤ ⲠⲚⲀⲦⲓⲔⲰⲥ ϨⲓⲦⲉⲚ ϨⲀⲚ ⲘⲎⲓⲚⲓ ⲚⲉⲘ ϨⲀⲚ ⲱⲫⲎⲣⲓ], glorifying the blessed one forever for the healing [ⲟⲩⲭⲀⲓ] of souls.[21]

John then asks for the Youths' blessing and returns by cloud to Alexandria, where

> the Archbishop immediately gathered all the clergy and the other holy bishops and the whole city near the martyrion of the saints for their holy consecration. In the middle of the night a great light suddenly appeared in the holy place and clouds of pure sweet fragrance were in the air, especially above the city of Alexandria and the dwelling-place of the saints, and all the torches were immediately lit, burning so brightly that one could almost say the whole place was on fire. All these things were a sign of the presence of the saints in the city.[22]

Thus by virtue of his preternatural ability to travel miraculously to distant cities and converse with their heavenly guardians, John the Little was able to guarantee the efficacy of a shrine lacking relics.

In its broadest outlines this legend of an *imported* shrine's authentication by a *local* figure resembles many situations of religious conversion that revolve around the acculturation and localization of alien gods. In the Graeco-Roman period, inscriptions and local legends celebrate local patrons who import Sarapis cults to their towns following dreams of the god's appearance.[23] And so more vividly in colonial Latin America: the Virgin of Guadalupe is established on a hill outside Mexico City following her apparition to a local peasant; Jesus is received in Qolluriti, Peru, after he frolics with a shepherd boy beneath a sacred peak in the Andes.[24] These latter legends, of course, depend on the lowly status of the authenticator compared to the elite Spanish promoters of the new gods Mary and Jesus. In contrast, John the Little, by the time this story was supposed to have taken place, was the leader of a major monastery in Scetis, a charismatic figure who, according to the monastic tradition, had 'all Scetis hanging from his little finger'.[25] Thus the hagiography

---

[21] *Life of John the Little*, ch. 75, ed. Amélineau (1894), 586, tr. Mikhail and Vivian (1997), 49.

[22] *Life of John the Little*, ch. 75, tr. Mikhail and Vivian, 49–50.

[23] See Sokolowski (1974), 442–3.

[24] On Guadelupe, see Turner and Turner (1978), 80–90. On Qolluriti, see Sallnow (1987), 207–42. Both Turner and Turner and Sallnow analyse the legends of native authenticators.

[25] *Apophth. Patr.*: John the Little 36.

describes an Archbishop's appeal to an *established native holy man* in order to authenticate a new shrine.

Furthermore, John does not simply give his blessing to the shrine: he goes to *meet with* the Three Hebrews by virtue of his own supernatural powers.[26] This feat was clearly beyond the capabilities of an Archbishop (as this role was construed in the fifth century CE). Yet such quasi-shamanic powers as mediation with otherworldly figures to secure this-worldly benefits fairly typified the limitless supernatural services of Egyptian ascetics, who were renowned not only for powers of healing, cursing, and prophecy, but also apocalyptic visions and journeys.[27] John's intercessory cloud-journey may recall the biblical prophet Eze-kiel's (chs. 8–9); but it was clearly more than biblical typology by John's time. The great fifth-century CE abbot Shenoute visited the emperor Theodosius by cloud, an achievement detailed in his *Vita* and still described in a hymn centuries later.[28] The sixth-century CE Apa Pisen-tius beheld the patriarchs and apostles while 'caught up in ecstasy' before his death.[29] Otherworldly travel had become a pre-eminent virtue in the hagiographical tradition, ascribed to the greatest of prophets by disciples and devotees.

---

[26] A Coptic sermon on the Three Hebrews falsely attributed to Theophilus himself proposes that John's journey to Ctesiphon was overland, not by cloud, and took seven months, whereupon John met with the Three Hebrews and received various spiritual instructions (ed. De Vis 1990: 2.135–51). However, the extravagant travelogue suggests that this account has less historical reliability than the hagiography's claim that John procured the saints' presence through his own intercession *in situ*. The Arabic *Synaxar-ium* (for 17 Oct.), apparently on the basis of the *Life of John the Little*, also describes his cloud-journey (*PO* 1.3.353–54).

[27] Brown (1975), chs. 3–4; (1982); (1995), ch. 3. See also Dunand (1991); and on visionary powers of holy men, Frankfurter (1996), 174–85. The formal parallels to central Asian shamanism, revolving around the performance of otherworldly mediation by a socially ordained expert, aid us in moving beyond purely literary details or biblical typology to speculate on the public drama that suggested such a cloud journey. In general on shamanic performance and 'flight' see Siikala (1987), Desjarlais (1996), and on applications of the category 'shaman' to ancient Mediterranean phenomena, Brown (1981).

[28] Besa, *V. Shenoute*, 53–67 (tr. Bell 1983: 57–61); Hymn 'on the prophet Apa Shenoute': 'Now our father Apa Shenoute, when the emperor sent for him, was seized by a cloud and taken to the palace ed./tr.Kuhn/Tait (1996), 144–5.

[29] *V. Pisentius*, ed. Amélineau (1887), 155–6; cf. Budge (1913), 317–18.

The appeal to and intercession by John the Little to establish the saints' presence in the new Alexandrian shrine thus exposes the complexity of defining Christian holy space in a city whose topography was hotly contested. On the one hand, having demolished the Serapeum and other sanctuaries, Theophilus and his successors were systematically purging the city of heathen presence—inaugurating a Christian city. On the other hand, the countryside had itself long been engaged in assimilating Christian notions of power into the landscape and the rhythms of culture, chiefly through an extensive network of living saints and martyrs who stood between the ecclesiastical and popular worlds.[30] A shrine like that of the Three Hebrews represented the ultimate authority of scriptural heroes over local saints and martyrs; but to establish such a shrine in Alexandria—and in competition with the relics away in Babylon—required deference to the local wielders of authority. That at least was the intention of John the Little's eighth-century hagiographer.

III. MACARIUS OF TKOW AND THE SHRINE OF JOHN AND ELISHA

The subsequent fortunes of the Alexandrian shrine are lost from both archaeological and hagiographical records. But another project of Theophilus' building programme, a martyrion to John the Baptist and Elisha the prophet, seems to have become one of the centres of Alexandrian Christianity over the fifth century, cited as an urban landmark in papyri of the 490s, its Byzantine remains still visible in excavations this century.[31]

The legends of this martyrion's construction revolve around two themes: the *rescue* of John the Baptist's relics from the depredations of the emperor Julian (an adventure curiously featuring Athanasius)[32] and

---

[30] See Frankfurter (1994), Clarysse (1995).

[31] Papyri: *P. Oxy* 63, 4394, 4395; archaeology: Rowe (1957), 502–5 and Papaconstantinou (2001), 112–15, 283; cf. Martin (1984), 222, 223 n. 72, proposing two different churches to John the Baptist.

[32] *Chronicle of John of Nikiu* 78.42–7; Paris copte 129 (14), f.110, ed. Orlandi (1969), 23–6; *History of the Patriarchs of Alexandria*: Theophilus (ed./tr. B. Evetts, *PO* 1.4.426); compare Arabic *Synaxarium*: October 16 (ed. Basset, *PO* 1.3.346–7), which

the *function* of the martyrion to neutralize and reconsecrate the grounds of the newly defunct Serapeum, symbol of traditional religious vitality until 391 CE.[33] Neither theme, however, depends on an intrinsic link between John the Baptist and Alexandria. It was a case of the relics' 'translation' *into* the city; and as in the case of the Three Hebrews, the importation of the relics carried ideological overtones: the authority of the scriptural martyr and the pre-eminence of the Holy Land whence the relics came.

But there was a more subtle function to bringing in relics of John the Baptist and—soon afterwards—the prophet Elisha. For, along with the great Elijah himself, these two figures served as the chief heroes for the monks and hermits at that point dominating Egyptian Christian culture.[34] So the establishment of this particular shrine atop the fractured symbol of heathenism may have served in some way as an acknowledgement of the monks' prestige.

Yet the martyrion of John and Elisha must have struck some as alien to the monastic landscape, whether for its restriction to scriptural saints, its Alexandrian location, or its focus on departed 'Elijahs' rather than the living 'Elijahs' known to appear regularly to, or through, desert hermits. Such tensions emerge in a sixth-century CE hagiography, the *Panegyric on Macarius of Tkow*, who was an early fifth-century holy man and bishop in upper Egypt.[35] Macarius is the epitome of the rural saint: Greek-illiterate, so wild-looking as to be unpresentable in the imperial court, famous for healing and for opposing native temples with heav-

describes the shrine as built over hills, with no mention of the Serapeum. On the cult of John the Baptist in general, see *DCL* 1.883, s.v. 'John the Baptist, Saint'.

[33] Rufinus, *HE* 11.27–28, with Thelamon (1981), 264–6.

[34] Frankfurter (1993), 65–77. There are several Coptic homilies on John the Baptist that testify to his importance in Egyptian Christianity. An anonymous Panegyric preserved in Sahidic and Bohairic mss. exalts him as model ascetic and martyr and promotes the healing powers of his and Elisha's shrine: ed. De Vis (1990), 1.48, 50. Another, attributed to Archbishop Theodosius, ed. Kuhn (1966, plus additional fragments ed. Kuhn 1975) provides no indication as to place, cult, or context. Another, attributed to John Chrysostom includes such Egyptianizing details as John the Baptist's otherworldly role as ferryman over a river of fire to the third heaven, meant as propaganda for an historical shrine, which might suggest an endeavour to indigenize John the Baptist for an Egyptian audience (much as Enoch was presented as a Thoth-like figure), ed. Budge (1977), 128–45, 335–51. See also Perez (1991).

[35] Dioscorus (Attrib.), *Panegyric on Macarius of Tkow*, ed./tr. Johnson (1980); see also id. (1991).

enly fire, militantly opposed to the council of Chalcedon, and remembered as the very avatar of the prophet Elijah.[36]

The *Panegyric* consists of the alleged reminiscences of one Dioscorus of Alexandria, a monk who met Macarius on a ship to Constantinople and learned from others of his exploits in upper Egypt. Dioscorus himself receives a vision of John the Baptist and Elisha, who reveal that 'the Saviour sent us to ... summon this elder, the man of Tkow, that his body should rest beside our own.'[37] Time passes as Macarius and Dioscorus both alienate themselves thoroughly from the Chalcedonian church leadership; and finally Dioscorus hears that Macarius has died in Alexandria after an assault by Chalcedonian thugs (13.6–7; 15.8). In accordance with Dioscorus' vision, Macarius' disciples bring his body to the martyrion of John and Elisha for burial. But when they arrive, the Alexandrian bishop objects: 'What are you doing with this unclean Egyptian, burying him in the sanctuary of the holy men?'[38] The bishop is immediately struck dead by lightning, and a mute child standing nearby suddenly announces that John the Baptist and Elisha themselves have arrived to welcome Macarius into the martyrion. Thus the crowd cheers the addition of the Egyptian saint (16.2–4).

Even a sympathetic reader might find it somewhat presumptuous of Macarius' devotees to claim a place for him in this grandest of Alexandrian churches, alongside two ancient biblical saints—as if some rural populist leader from Mississippi were to be added to the Lincoln Memorial in Washington DC. Before I address the larger issues around Macarius' burial in this shrine, let me briefly discuss how the hagiography itself justifies it. Beyond the basic claim that it was God's own will, the text asserts that Macarius' own 'city was unworthy of your holy body because they worship idols in your region'.[39] Macarius, that is, deserves a better cult-place than that semi-Christianized backwater Tkow. This is an unusual point of view among the countless hagiographical justifications that hermits' corpses should remain where they drop, in caves or on mountain tops or at least near the villages that

---

[36] On Elianic references see *Panegyric on Macarius* 13.4; 15.8.

[37] ⲚⲦⲚⲔⲀⲀⲓ ⲘⲠⲈⲓⲌⲀⲗⲟ ⲚⲢⲈⲘⲦⲔⲱⲟⲗ ⲬⲈⲈⲢⲈⲠⲈϥⲤⲱⲘⲀ ⲚⲀⲞⲨⲱⲌ ⲌⲀⲌⲦⲈⲘⲠⲱⲚ (*Panegyric on Macarius* 6.1, ed. Johnson (1980), 1.41, tr. 2.31; see also 12.2).

[38] ⲈⲦⲈⲦⲚⲢⲞⲨ ⲘⲠⲈⲓⲈⲔⲨⲠⲦⲒⲞⲤ ⲚⲀⲔⲀⲐⲀⲢⲦⲞⲤ ⲈⲦⲈⲦⲚⲦⲱⲘⲤ ⲘⲘⲞϥ ⲌⲘⲠⲘⲀⲢⲦⲨⲢⲓⲟⲚ ⲚⲚⲈⲦⲞⲨⲀⲀⲃ (*Panegyric on Macarius* 16.1, ed. Johnson (1980), 1.124, tr. 2.96).

[39] *Panegyric on Macarius* 16.5, tr. Johnson (1980), 2.98.

revered them. Often hagiographies reflect strong local sentiment to keep bones, if discovered, accessible to the community.

Another argument for Macarius' inclusion that extends throughout the text is that Macarius, by his powers and behaviour, is himself an avatar of the prophet Elijah; and as such he completes the 'Elianic set' of Elisha and John the Baptist: 'Where there were formerly two,' the text says, 'they have now become three, as the type of the Holy Trinity.'[40] As a true Elijah, Macarius certainly belongs in a shrine built to Elianic figures.

Finally, in the very presumptuousness of claiming an Alexandrian martyrion, the *Panegyric on Macarius* exhibits a certain desire to appropriate the city, its sacred landscape, and ecclesiastical power—at the very least to rescue it from the evil Chalcedonians. The bishop who tries to exclude 'this unclean Egyptian' represents not a Greek Christianity in opposition to an Egyptian one but rather a sacred city that has been taken over by heretics as blind to true saintly charisma as they are to true doctrine. Macarius belongs in that shrine, the text argues, as surely as Monophysite Christianity belongs in the Church of Alexandria. It was an issue of contested space: the shrine of John the Baptist as symbol of Christian Alexandria.

IV. CONCLUSION: HERMITS AND THE LEGITIMATION OF SCRIPTURAL SAINTS

But there are broader implications to Macarius' burial in the Alexandrian church: above all, what is being contested around the shrine of John and Elisha. Every instance of a shrine's establishment, especially under the aegis of a larger religion, involves a contestation of space, for every shrine mediates the particularity of a saint or the immediacy of a local cult with the broader ideological claims of the religious institution.[41] A shrine of John the Baptist *needed* the corpse of a local Elijah in order to be acceptable—meaningful in the wider Egyptian Christian landscape. In this respect, the monks' attempt to intrude Macarius into

---

[40] ϫⲉⲉⲩⲟ ⲛⲥⲛⲁⲩ ⲛ̄ϣⲟⲣⲡ̄ ⲧⲉⲛⲟⲩ ⲇⲉ ⲁⲩⲉⲣϣⲟⲙⲛⲧ̄ ⲙ̄ⲡⲧⲩⲡⲟⲥ ⲉⲧⲉⲧⲣⲓⲁⲥ ⲉⲧⲟⲩⲁⲁⲃ (*Panegyric on Macarius* 16.5, ed. Johnson (1980), 1.127, tr. 2.99).

[41] See Eade and Sallnow (1991), and Frankfurter (1998c), 18–28.

the John the Baptist shrine is not unlike an episode at another shrine of John the Baptist, this one in early fifth-century CE Cyrrhus, in Syria. One James of Cyrrhestica, a saint of radical privations and great supernatural power, takes sick at one point; and in a story famous in the annals of desert hermits, armed devotees from the city of Cyrrhus steal his comatose body before he could die and his relics be claimed for the local village.[42] And where does this mob take James? To the shrine of John the Baptist. When he recovers, of course, he demands to be returned to his hilltop. But later James reaffirms his connection to this same shrine: he informs the hagiographer—who was also the bishop responsible for importing the relics and building the martyrion—that he, James, had actually harboured doubts as to the relics' authenticity. But then, James says, he met John the Baptist in a vision and received assurance they were real.[43] Thus, like John the Little and the martyrion of the Three Hebrews, James establishes himself as authenticator of relics by virtue of his supernatural clairvoyance.

All three stories illustrate the function of a rural, *living* saint in authenticating a shrine to a *scriptural* saint: as 'arbiter of authenticity'. He renders alien *sacra* or vacant shrines meaningful and powerful within the immediate landscape. He appropriates or redefines the value of those *sacra*—or is himself appropriated to mark the shrine's cultural authenticity.[44] It is, indeed, a negotiation between distinct systems of sacred presence and meaning: a regionally based monastic system emphasizing charismatic leadership and active visionary intercession, and an imperial ecclesiastical system that elevated 'safely scriptural' saints as sources of authority and prestige.[45]

---

[42] Theodoret, *History of the Monks of Syria*, 21.9–10. See Nau (1906), 200–1, and Baynes (1949), 170–1 on the hijacking of the corpse of the Constantinopolitan monk Isaac from an imperial convoy in order to be interred in a shrine of St Stephen.

[43] Theodoret, *History of the Monks of Syria*, 21.19–21.

[44] In the story of Daniel the Stylite, relics of the Three Hebrews are added to his martyrion rather than vice versa (ch. 95), allegedly to prevent worship of Daniel's relics and encourage worship of the scriptural relics (Dawes and Baynes (1977), 66–7). There are cases of local hermits in 16th-cent. Spain also promoting official images or relics as especially beneficial to the immediate region: see Christian (1981), 111.

[45] The *Vitae Prophetorum*, compiled in the 4th or 5th cents., seems to reflect a similar ideology, promoting biblical prophets remembered through Bible and landscape in such a way as to 'replace' living holy men. See Satran (1995), 2–6, 97–117.

We must admit, finally, another dimension to these stories: that of the hagiographies themselves. Assembled well after the lives of their protagonists, after the traumatic schisms over the council of Chalcedon, and—many—under Arab rule, they retroject a world in which holy men truly held sway over the shrines of Alexandria. In these texts, the emperor Julian and advocates of Chalcedon are damned, Athanasius becomes a trafficker in relics, archbishops defer to monks, and monks authenticate the sanctity of known shrines. It is indeed an idealized world that these documents retroject, although it was clearly situated in a recognizable landscape with real figures.[46] Thus we might well wonder whether Macarius of Tkow was only interred with John the Baptist in the fantasy of the hagiographer and his audience,[47] and what sort of performance the historical John the Little could have put on, beyond mere assurance, in order to guarantee the Three Hebrews' presence. These questions, of course, do not gainsay the larger historical picture I have drawn of holy men and saint's shrines, nor the problems these stories divulge about the relationship of local holy men and scriptural saints. But they do press us to consider the culture and era when this larger picture became vital religious history. Perhaps these hagiographies could be linked to a Coptic literary 'invention of tradition' carried out under Muslim rule. Like the many Coptic annals and chronicles deriving from this period (e.g., the Cambyses legend, the *Chronicle of John of Nikiu*, and the *History of the Alexandrian Patriarchs*), these legends of holy men in Alexandria may have been part of a continual monastic endeavour at creating a preferred sacred history in text when the politics of the real landscape were less than ideal.[48] Indeed, by the time of these hagiographies, the memories and often the very relics of the monastic holy men glorified in their pages would most likely have been preserved in monasteries rather than in cities under Muslim rule.[49] Thus, in the end, rather than their serving Archbishop Theophilus and his programme of sanctifying the great

---

[46] See Patlagean (1983), esp. 109–10 on hagiographies' use of space.

[47] Relics of Macarius of Tkow were later claimed to reside at the monastery of Macarius the Great, where there were also reliquaries of John the Baptist and Elisha. See Johnson (1991), 1493.

[48] On the political context of medieval Coptic hagiography, see Wilfong (1998), 188–90.

[49] See Papaconstantinou (2001), 308.

city of Alexandria with alien relics, it was the monks of the Egyptian countryside who ended up the heroes, the emperor and his city mere literary foils to their powers.[50]

---

[50] The appeal of local monks as principal saints and intercessors persists in Coptic Egypt: see Mayeur-Jaouen (1998), 182–3.

Bibliography

ABU ASSAF, A. (1990), *Der Tempel von 'Ain Dara* (Mainz).

ADAMS, C., and R. LAURENCE, (2001), *Travel and Geography in the Roman Empire* (London).

ALBRIGHT, W. F. (1968), *Yahweh and the Gods of Canaan* (London).

ALCOCK, S. E. (1993), *Graecia Capta: The Landscapes of the Roman Greece* (Cambridge).

—— (1996), 'Landscapes of Memory and the Authority of Pausanias', in J. Bingen (ed.), *Pausanias Historien*. Fondation Hardt pour l'étude de l'antiquité classique. Entretiens 41: 241–67.

—— (1997*a*), 'Minding the Gap in Hellenistic and Roman Greece', in S. Alcock and R. Osborne (eds.), *Placing the Gods: Sanctuaries and Sacred Space in Ancient Greece* (Oxford), 247–61.

—— (1997*b*), 'Greece: a Landscape of Resistance?' in Mattingly (1997), 103–15.

—— (2001), 'The Reconfiguration of Memory in the Eastern Roman Empire', in S. E. Alcock, T. D. Altroy, K. Morrison, and C. Sinopoli (eds.), *Empires: Perspectives from Archaeology and History* (Cambridge), 323–50.

—— J. F. CHERRY, and J. ELSNER, (eds.) (2001), *Pausanias: Travel and Memory in Roman Greece* (Oxford).

ALESHIRE, S. (1989), *The Athenian Asclepieion: The People, their Dedications, and the Inventories* (Amsterdam).

ALFÖLDY, G. (1995), 'El santuario rupestre de Panóias', *Madrider Mitteilungen des Deutschen Archäologischen Instituts* 36, 252–8 and pls. 22–4.

ALTERMÜLLER, H. (1998), 'Die Fahrt der Hathor nach Edfu und die "Heilige Hochzeit" ', in W. Clarysse, A. Schoors, and H. Willems (eds.), *Egyptian Religion. The Last Thousand Years. Studies Dedicated to the Memory of Jan Quaegebeur* (Leuven), 2. 753–66.

ALLIOT, M. (1949–54), *Le culte d'Horus à Edfou au temps des Ptolémies*, Bibliothèque d'Étude 20 (Cairo).

AMANDRY, M. (1988), *Le monnayage des duovirs corinthiens*. BCH Suppl. 15 (Paris).

AMANDRY, P. (1939), 'Convention Religieuse conclue entre Delphes et Skiathos', *BCH* 63, 183 ff.

—— (1950), *La mantique Apollinienne à Delphes* (Paris).

AMÉLINEAU, E. (1887), *Étude sur le christianisme en Égypte au septième siècle.* (Paris).

—— (1894), *Histoire des monastères de la Base Égypte.* Annales du Musée Guimet (Paris).

ANDERSON, G. (1986), *Philostratus. Biography and Belles Lettres in the Third Century A.D.* (London).

—— (1989), 'The *Pepaideumenos* in Action: Sophists and their Outlook in the Early Roman Empire', *ANRW* 2.33.1, 79–208.

—— (1993), *The Second Sophistic. A Cultural Phenomenon in the Roman Empire* (London).

—— (1994), *Sage, Saint and Sophist: Holy Men and their Associates in the Early Roman Empire* (London).

—— (1998), 'L'intellettuale e il primo impero romano', in S. Settis (ed.), *I Greci* 2: 3. 1123 ff.

ANDREI, O. (1984), *A. Claudius Charax di Pergamo. Interessi antiquari e antichità cittadine nell'età degli Antonini* (Bologna).

ARAFAT, K. W. (1992), 'Pausanias' attitude to antiquities', *The Annual of the British School at Athens* 87, 387–409.

—— (1996), *Pausanias' Greece: Ancient Artists and Roman Rulers,* (Cambridge).

ARAVANTINOS, V. L., L. GODART, and A. SACCONI, (2001), *Thèbes. Fouilles de la Cadmée I. Les tablettes en linéaire B de la Odos Pelopidou. Édition et commentaire* (Rome).

ARMAYOR, O. K. (1985), *Herodotus' Autopsy of the Fayoum: Lake Moeris and the Labyrinth of Egypt* (Amsterdam).

ARNUSH, M. (2000), 'Argead and Aetolian Relations with the Delphic Polis in the Late Fourth Century BCE', in R. Brock and S. Hodkinson (eds.), *Alternatives to Athens: Varieties of Political Organization and Community in Ancient Greece* (Oxford), 293–307.

—— (2002), 'Sanctuary of Apollon at Delphoi', *Ancient World: Coins, Cults, History and Inscriptions,* 32(2), 153–63.

ARRIAN (1998), *Discourses of Epictetus,* ed. R. Hard (London and Rutland, Vermont: 1995); tr. R. F. Dobbin (Oxford).

ASSMANN, A. (1999), *Erinnerungsräume. Formen und Wandlungen des kulturellen Gedächtnisses* (Munich).

ASSMANN, J. (2000), *Religion und kulturelles Gedächtnis* (Munich).

ATTRIDGE, H. W., and R. A. ODEN, (1976), *The Syrian Goddess* (Missoula, Mont.).

AUBET, M. E. (1993), *The Phoenicians and the West* (Cambridge).

BACHER, W. (1896), 'Rome dans le Talmud et le Midrasch', *REJ* 33, 187–96.

BADIAN, E. (1981), 'The Deification of Alexander the Great', in *Ancient Macedonian Studies in Honour of Charles F. Edson* (Thessalonika), 27–71.

BALDOVIN, J. (1987), *The Urban Character of Christian Worship: The Origins, Development, and Meaning of Stational Liturgy* (Rome).

—— (1989), *Liturgy in Ancient Jerusalem* (Bramcote).

BALDWIN, B. (1995), 'Pliny the Elder and Mucianus', *Emerita* 63, 291–301.

BARDON, H. (1952), *La littérature latine inconnue* (Paris).

BARRETT, W. S. (1954), 'Bacchylides, Asine, and Apollo Pythaieus', *Hermes* 82, 421–44.

BARTON, T. S. (1994), *Power and Knowledge: Astrology, Physiognomics and Medicine under the Roman Empire* (Ann Arbor).

BARTSCH, S. (1989), *Decoding the Ancient Novel: The Reader and the Role of Description in Heliodorus and Achilles Tatius* (Princeton).

BASANOFF, V. (1947), *Evocatio* (Paris).

BATAILLE, A. (1951), *Les inscriptions grecques du temple de Hatshepsout à Deir el Bahari* (Cairo).

BAUER, W. (1979), *A Greek–English Lexicon of the New Testament and Other Early Christian Literature* (Chicago and London).

BAUMEISTER, T. (1972), *Martyr Invictus: Der Martyrer als Sinnbild der Erlösung in der Legende und im Kult der frühen koptischen Kirche*. Forschungen zur Volkskunde 46. (Münster).

BAYNES, N. H. (1949), 'The Supernatural Defenders of Constantinople', *Analecta Bollandiana* 67, 165–77.

BEARD, M. (1991), 'Writing and Religion: Ancient Literacy and the Function of the Written Word in Roman Religion', in J. H. Humphrey (ed.), *Literacy in the Roman World*, *JRA* Suppl. 3, 35–58.

BEARD, M., J. NORTH, and S. PRICE (1998), *Religions of Rome*, 2 vols. (Cambridge).

BEARZOT, C. (1992), *Storia e storiografia ellenistica in Pausania il Periegeta* (Venice).

BEHLMER, H. (1998), 'Visitors to Shenoute's Monastery', in Frankfurter (1998*b*), 341–58.

BEHR, C. A. (1968), *Aelius Aristides and the Sacred Tales* (Amsterdam).

—— (1981), *The Complete works of P. Aelim Aristides* Vol. II *Oratious XVII–LIII* (Amsterdam).

BEINLICH, H. (1977), 'Gauprozession', *Lexikon der Ägyptologie* (Wiesbaden) 2. 417–20.

BELAYCHE, N. (1987), 'Les pèlerinages dans le monde romain antique', in Chelini and Branthomme 1987, 136 ff.

—— (2001), *Iudaea-Palaestina: The Pagan Cults in Roman Palestine* (Tübingen).

BELL, C. (1992), *Ritual Theory, Ritual Practice* (New York).

—— (1997), *Ritual: Perspectives and Dimensions* (New York).

BELL, D. N. (1983), *Besa: The Life of Shenoute*, CSS 73 (Kalamazoo, Mich.).

BELTING, H. (1994), *Likeness and Presence: A History of the Image Before the Era of Art* (Chicago).

BENDLIN, B. (1997), 'Peripheral Centers–Central Peripheries: Religious Communication in the Roman Empire', in Cancik and Rüpke (1997), 35–68.

BENVENISTE, E. (1969), *Le vocabulaire des institutions indo-européennes* (Paris).

BERGMAN, J. (1968), *Ich bin Isis : Studien zum memphitischen Hintergrund der griechischen Isisaretalogien* (Uppsala).

—— (1970), *Isis-Seele und Osiris-Ei: zwei ägyptologische Studien zu Diodorus Siculus I 27,4–5* (Uppsala).

—— (1980), 'Isis', *LÄ* 3, 186–203.

BERNAND, É. (1969*a*), *Inscriptions métriques de l' égypte gréco-romaine. Recherches sur la poésie épigrammatique des grecs et égypte* (Paris).

—— (1969*b*), *Les inscriptions grecques et latines de Philae*, 2 vols. (Paris).

—— (1988), 'Pèlerins', in M.-M. Mactoux and E. Geny (eds.) *Mélanges Pierre Leveque*. Annales littéraires de l'Université de Besançon; 367, Centre de recherches d'histoire ancienne v. 79 (Paris), 1.49–63.

BERNARDI, A. (1985), 'Il divino e il sacro nella montagna dell'Italia antica', in F. Broilo (ed.), *Xenia. Scritti in onore di Piero Treves* (Rome), 1–8.

BESCHI, L., and D. MUSTI, (eds.), (1982), *Pausania, Guida della Grecia. Libro I L'Attica* (Milan).

BHARDWAJ, S. M. (1973), *Hindu Places of Pilgrimage in India (A Study in Cultural Geography)* (Berkeley).

—— (1997), 'Geography and Pilgrimage: A Review', in R. H. Stoddard and A. Morinis (eds.), *Sacred Places, Sacred Spaces: The Geography of Pilgrimages* [= *Geoscience and Man* 34] (Baton Rouge), 2.1–24.

—— and G. RINSCHEDE (eds.), (1988), *Pilgrimage in World Religions* (Berlin).

—— —— and A. SIEVERS (eds.), (1994), *Pilgrimage in the Old and New Worlds* (Berlin).

BIERS, J. C. (1985), *The Great Bath on the Lechaion Road*. Corinth, v.17 (Princeton).

BIFFI, N. (1995), 'Adriano sul monte Casio Curiosità e pratica devozionale', *Invigilata Lucernis* 17, 17–38.

BILLOT, M.-F. (1992), 'Apollon Pythéen et l'Argolide archaïque. Histoire et Mythes', *Archaiognosia* 6, 35–98.

BINGEN, J. (ed.) (1996), *Pausanias Historien*. Fondation Hardt Entretiens sur l'antiquité classique. 41 (Geneva).

BINNS, J. (1994), *Ascetics and Ambassadors of Christ: The Monasteries of Palestine 314–631* (Oxford).

BIRLEY, A. R. (1997), *Hadrian: the Restless Emperor* (London).

BLANCO FREIJEIRO, A. (1985), 'Los nuevos bronces de Sancti-Petri', *Boletín de la Real Academia de la Historia* 182(2), 207–16.

BLECH, M. (1982), *Studien zum Kranz bei den Griechen* (Berlin).

BLEEKER, C. J. (1967), *Egyptian festivals: Enactments of Religious Renewal* (Leiden).

BLINKENBERG, C. (1915), *Die lindische Tempelchronik* (Bonn).

BLÜMEL, W. (1987), *Die Inschriften von Mylasa. Teil 1: Inschriften von der Stadt* [= *IGSK* 34] (Bonn).

BOATWRIGHT, M. T. (1994), 'Hadrian, Athens and the Panhellenion', *JRA* 7, 426–31.

—— (2000), *Hadrian and the Cities of the Roman Empire* (Princeton).

BOESCH, P. (1908), *Theōros: Untersuchung zur Epangelie griechischer Feste* (Berlin).

BOESCH GAJANO, S. (1999), 'Reliques et pouvoirs', in E. Bozoky and A.-M. Helvètius, (eds.), *Les reliques: Objets, cultes, symboles*. Hagiologia 1 (Turnhout), 255–69.

BOËTHIUS, A. (1918), *Die Pythaïs: Studien zur Geschichte der Verbindungen zwischen Athen und Delphi* (Diss. Uppsala).

BOKSER, B. M. (1990), 'Todos and rabbinic authority in Rome', in J. Neusner et al. (eds.), *New Perspectives on Ancient Judaism I: Religion, Literature and Society in Ancient Israel, Formative Christianity and Judaism*, Brown Judaic Studies 206 (Atlanta), 117–30.

BOMPAIRE, J. (1989), 'Le Sacré dans les discours d'Aelius Aristides (XLVII–LII Keil)', *REG* 102, 28–39.

BONNECHERE, P. (2003), *Trophonios de Lébédée : cultes et mythes d'une cité béotienne au miroir de la mentalité antique* (Leiden).

BONNET, C. (1988), *Melqart* (Leuven).

—— (1992), *Dictionnaire de la Civilisation Phénicienne et Punique*.

BOOKIDIS, N., and R. S. STROUD (1997), *The Sanctuary of Demeter and Kore: Topgraphy and Architecture. (Corinth XVIII.iii)* (Princeton).

BOSANQUET, R. C. (1908–9), 'Excavations at Palaikastro. IV. 8 The temple of Dictaean Zeus', *BSA* 11, 298–9.

—— (1939–40), 'Dicte and the temples of Dictaean Zeus', *BSA* 40, 60–77.

BOTTRO, J. (1987), 'Processions et pèlerinages en Mesopotamie ancienne', in Chelini and Branthomme 1987, 45–54.

BOULANGER, A. (1923), *Aelius Aristide et la sophistique dans la province d'Asie au IIe siècle de notre ère*, (Paris).

BOUNNI, A. (2000), 'Palmyre, ville de pèlerinage', *Bulletin d'Etudes Orientales* 52, 195–7.

BOURDIEU, P. (1991), *Language and Symbolic Power* (Cambridge).

BOWERSOCK, G. W. (1965), *Augustus and the Greek World* (Oxford).

Bowersock, G. W. (1969), *Greek Sophists in the Roman Empire* (Oxford).

—— (1973), 'Greek Intellectuals and the Imperial Cult in the Second Century A.D', in den Boer 1973, 179–206.

Bowie, E. L. (1970), 'The Greeks and their Past in the Second Sophistic', *Past and Present* 46, 3–41.

—— (1989), 'Greek Sophists and Greek Poetry in the Second Sophistic', *ANRW* 2.33.1, 209–58.

—— (1991), 'Hellenes and Hellenism in Writers of the Early Second Sophistic' in Said (1991), 183–204.

—— (1996), 'Past and Present in Pausanias', in Bingen (1996), 207–30.

—— (2001), 'Inspiration and Aspiration: Date, Genre, and Readership' in Alcock, Cherry, and Elsner 2001, 21–32.

Bowman, G. (1985), 'Anthropology of Pilgrimage', in M. Jha (ed.), *Dimensions of Pilgrimage: An Anthropological Appraisal* (New Delhi), 1–9.

—— (1991), 'Christian Ideology and the Image of a Holy Land: The Place of Jerusalem Pilgrimage in the various Christianities', in Eade and Sallnow 1991, 98–121.

—— (1993), 'Nationalizing the Sacred: Shrines and Shifting Identities in the Israeli-occupied Territories', *Man* 28, 431–60.

—— (1995), 'Contemporary Christian Pilgrimage to the Holy Land', in O'Mahoney 1995, 288–310.

—— (1999), ' "Mapping History's Redemption": Eschatology and Topography in the Itinerarium Burdigalense', in Levine 1999, 163–87.

Brading, D. (2001), *Mexican Phoenix. Our Lady of Guadelupe: Image and Tradition across Five Centuries* (Cambridge).

Bradshaw, P. F. (1999), 'The Influence of Jerusalem on Christian Liturgy', in Levine 1999, 251–9.

Brakke, D. (1994), 'Canon Formation and Social Conflict in Fourth-Century Egypt: Athanasius of Alexandria's Thirty-Ninth *Festal Letter*', *HThR* 87(4), 395–419.

—— (1995), *Athanasius and the Politics of Asceticism* (Oxford).

—— (1997), 'Athanasius of Alexandria and the Cult of the Holy Dead', *Studia Patristica* 32, 12–18.

—— (1998), ' "Outside the Places, Within the Truth": Athanasius of Alexandria and the Localization of the Holy', in Frankfurter 1998*b*, 445–81.

Breccia, E. (1911), *Catalogue général des Antiquités Égyptiennes du Musée d'Alexandrie no. 1–568: Iscrizioni greche e latine* (Cairo).

Brelich, A. (1966), *Introduzione alla storia delle religioni* (Rome).

—— (1979), *Storia delle religioni, perché* (Naples).

BREMER, J. M., and W. D. FURLEY. (eds.) (2001), *Greek Hymns: Selected Cult Songs from the Archaic to the Hellenistic Period.* 2 vols., Studien und Texte zu Antike und Christentum 9, 10 (Tübingen).

BREMMER, J. N. (1998), ' "Religion", "Ritual" and the Opposition "Sacred vs. Profane": Notes Towards a Terminological "Genealogy" ', in F. Graf (ed.), *Ansichten griechischer Rituale. Geburtstags-Symposium für Walter Burkert* (Stuttgart and Leipzig, 1998), 9–32.

BRENNAN, T., and M. JAY, (eds.) (1995), *Vision in Context: Historical and Contemporary Perspectives on Sight* (London).

BRENT, A. (1995), *Hippolytus and the Roman Church in the Third Century* (Leiden).

BRESCIAN, E. (1993), 'Éléments de rituel et d' offrande dans le texte démotique de l' "Oeil du Soleil" ', in J. Quaegebeur (ed.), *Ritual and Sacrifice in the Near East* (Leuven).

BROCK, S. (1970), *Journal of Semitic Studies* 15, 268–70.

—— (1999), *Journal of Theological Studies* 50, 760–7.

BROGIOLO, G. P., and B. WARK-PERKINS, (eds.) (1999), *The Idea and Ideal of the Town Between Late Antiquity and the Early Middle Ages. The Transformation of the Roman World*, 4 (Leiden).

BROWN, J. P. (1981), 'The Mediterranean Seer and Shamanism', *Zeitschrift für Alttestamentliche Wissenschaft* 93, 374–400.

—— (1995), *Israel and Hellas*, 1 (Berlin and New York).

BROWN, P. (1971), 'The Rise and Function of the Holy Man in Late Antiquity' *JRS* 61, 80–101.

—— (1972), *Religion and Society in the Age of St Augustine* (London).

—— (1975), *The Meaning of Late Antiquity* (Cambridge, Mass.).

—— (1978), *The Making of Late Antiquity* (Cambridge, Mass.).

—— (1981), *The Cult of the Saints: Its Rise and Function in Latin Christianity* (London).

—— (1982), 'The Rise and Function of the Holy Man in Late Antiquity', in id., *Society and the Holy in Late Antiquity* (London): 103–52.

—— (1990), *Augustine of Hippo: a Biography* (London and Boston).

—— (1995), *Authority and the Sacred: Aspects of the Christianisation of the Roman World* (Cambridge).

—— (1998), 'Christianization and Religious Conflict', in A. Cameron and P. Garnsey (eds.), *The Cambridge Ancient History*, 13: *The Late Empire, A. D. 337–425* (Cambridge), 632–64.

BRUBAKER, L. (1997), 'Memories of Helena: Patterns of Imperial Female Matronage in the Fourth and Fifth Centuries' in L. James (ed.), *Women, Men and Eunuchs* (London, 1997), 52–75.

BRUGSCH, H. K. (1879–80), *Dictionnaire géographique de l'ancienne Égypte* (Leipzig).

BRUIT ZAIDMAN, L., and P. SCHMITT PANTEL, (1992), *Religion in the Ancient Greek City* (Cambridge).

BRUNEAU, P. (1970), *Recherches sur les cultes de Delos à l'époque impériale* (Paris).

BRUNT, P. A. (1994), 'The Bubble of the Second Sophistic', *PCPhS* 40, 25–52.

BUDGE, E. A., WALLIS (1913), *Coptic Apocrypha in the Dialect of Upper Egypt* (London) [repr. New York, 1977].

BURKERT, W. (1960), 'Plato oder Pythagoras? Zum Ursprung des Wortes "Philosophie" ', *Hermes* 88, 159–77.

—— (1977), *Griechische Religion der archaischen und klassischen Epoche* (Berlin).

—— (1983), *Homo Necans: The Anthropology of Ancient Greek Sacrificial Ritual and Myth*, tr. P. Bing (Berkeley).

—— (1985), *Greek Religion* (Oxford and Cambridge, Mass.).

—— (1987), *Ancient Mystery Cults* (Cambridge, Mass.).

—— (1993), 'Concordia Discors: the literary and the archaeological evidence on the sanctuary of Samothrace', in N. Marinatos and R. Hägg (eds.), *Greek Sanctuaries: New Approaches* (London), 178–91.

—— (1996), 'Plutarco: Religiosità personale e teologia filosofica', in Gallo (1996), 11–28.

—— (2002), ' "Initiziazione": Un concetto moderno e una terminologia antica', in B. Gentili and F. Perusino (eds.), *Le Orse di Brauron* (Pisa).

BUSOLT, G., and H. SWOBODA, (1926), *Griechische Staatskunde*, 3rd edn. (Munich).

BUXTON, R. (1992), 'Imaginary Greek Mountains', *JHS* 112, 1–15.

—— (ed.) (2000), *Oxford Readings in Greek Religion* (Oxford).

CANCIK, H. (1985/6), 'Rome as sacred Landscape', *Visible Religion* 4/5, 250–65.

CANCIK, H., and J. RÜPKE, (eds.), (1997), *Römische Reichsreligion und Provinzialreligion* (Tübingen).

CALDERINI, A. (1935), *Dizionario dei nomi geografici e topografici dell' egitto greco-romano* I.1 (Cairo).

CAMPBELL, M. B. (1988), *The Witness and the Other World: Exotic European Travel Writing, 400–1600* (Ithaca, NY).

—— (1991), ' "The Object of One's Gaze": Landscape, Writing, and Early Medieval Pilgrimage', in Westrem (1991), 3–15.

CARDMAN, F. (1982), 'The Rhetoric of the Holy Places: Palestine in the Fourth Century', *Studia Patristica* 17, 18–25.

CAREY, S. (2000), 'The Problem of Totality: Collecting Greek Art, Wonders and Luxury in Pliny the Elder's *Natural History*', *Journal of the History of Collections* 12, 1–14.

CARLIER, P. (1992), *La royauté en Grèce avant Alexandre*. Etudes et travaux: Association pour l'étude de la civilisation romaine 6 (Strasbourg).

CARTLEDGE, P., and A. SPAWFORTH, (1989), *Hellenistic and Roman Sparta: A Tale of Two Cities* (London).

CASARICO, L. (1981), 'Note su alcune feste nell' Egitto tolemaico e romano', *Aegyptus* 61, 121–42.

CASEAU, B. (1999), 'Sacred Landscapes', in G. W. Bowersock, P. Brown, and O. Grabar (eds.), *Late Antiquity: A Guide to the Postclassical World* (Cambridge, Mass.), 21–59.

CASPARI, O. B. (1915), 'The Ionian Confederacy', *JHS* 35, 173–88.

CASTIGLIONE, L. (1970), 'Vestigia', *Acta Archaeologica* 22, 95–132.

CASTRO, A. (1858), *Historia de Cádiz* (Cadiz).

CAUVILLE, S. (1997), *Le temple de Dendara. Les chapelles osiriennes*, 3 vols. (Cairo).

CHAMBERS, H. E. (1980), 'Ancient Amphictionies. Sic et Non', in C. D. Evans, W. W. Hallo, and J. B. White (eds.), *Scripture in Context II. More Essays on Comparative Method* (Pittsburg).

CHANIOTIS, A. (1988), 'Habgierige Götter, habgierige Städte. Heiligtumsbesitz und Gebietsanspruch in den kretischen Staatsverträgen', *Ktema* 13, 21–39.

—— (1996*a*), *Die Verträge zwischen kretischen Poleis in der hellenistischen Zeit*. Heidelberger althistorische Beiträge und epigraphische Studien 24 (Stuttgart).

—— (1996*b*), 'Conflicting Authorities: Asylia between Secular and Divine Law in the Classical and Hellenistic *Poleis*,' *Kernos* 9, 65–86.

—— (1996*c*), 'Asylon', in *DNP* 2: 143–4.

CHANTRAINE, P. (1968–83), *Dictionnaire étymologique de la langue grecque* (Paris).

CHATTON, A. (1990), 'Massacres d' animaux à la Basse Époque', Revue d'Égyptologie 41, 209–13.

CHELINI, J., and H. BRANTHOMME, (1987), *Histoire des pèlerinages non chrétiens. Entre magique et sacré: le chemin des dieux* (Paris).

CHITTY, D. J. (1966), *The Desert a City: An Introduction to the Study of Egyptian and Palestinian Monasticism under the Christian Empire* (London).

CHRISTIAN Jr., W. A. (1981), *Local Religion in Sixteenth-Century Spain*. (Princeton).

CHRISTIDIS, A.-F., S. DAKARIS, and I. VOKOTOPOULOU (forthcoming), χρηστήρια ἐλάσματα ἀπό το μαντείο της Δωδώνης (Athens).

CLARK, E. A. (1984), *The Life of Melania the Younger* (Lewison).

CLARK, G. (1996), 'Cosmic Sympathies: Nature as the Expression of Divine Purpose', in Shipley and Salmon 1996, 310–29.

—— (2001), 'Translating Relics: Vitricius of Rouen and the Fourth Century Debate', *Early Medieval Europe* 10, 161–76.

CLARKE, K. J. (1999), *Between Geography and History: Hellenistic Constructions of the Roman World* (Oxford).

CLARYSSE, W. (1995), 'The Coptic Martyr Cult', in M. Lamberigts and P. van Deun (eds.), *Martyrium in Multidisciplinary Perspective: Memorial Louis Reekmans*. Bibliotheca Ephemeridum Theologicarum Lovaniensium 117 (Leuven), 382–93.

CLAUSSEN, M. A. (1991), ' "Peregrinatio" and "Peregrini" in Augustine's *City of God*', *Traditio* 46, 33–75.

CLAY, D. (1982), 'Unspeakable Words in Greek Tragedy', *AJP* 103, 277–98.

CLAYMAN, D. L. (1980), *Callimachus' Iambi*. Mnemosyne Supplement 59 (Leiden).

CLIFFORD, J. (1999), 'Museums as contact zones', in D. Boswell and J. Evans (eds.), *Representing the Nation: A Reader* (London), 435–57.

CLINTON, K. (1989), 'The Eleusinian Mysteries: Roman Initiates and bene-factors, Second Century B.C. to A.D. 267', *ANRW* 2.18.2 (1989), 1498–539.

—— (1993), 'The Sanctuary of Demeter and Kore at Eleusis', in Marinatos and Hägg 1993, 110–24.

—— (2001), 'Initiates in the Samothracian Mysteries, September 4, 100 B.C.' *Chiron* 31, 27–36.

—— (2003), 'Stages of Initiation in the Eleusinian and Samothracian Myster-ies', in Cosmopoulos 2003, 50–78.

—— and C. KARADIMA-MATSA, (2002), 'Korrane, a Sacred Woman in Samo-thrace', *ZPE* 138, 87–92.

COHEN, E. (1992), 'Pilgrimage and Tourism: Convergence and Divergence', in Morinis 1992, 47–61.

COHEN, G. M. (1996), 'A Dedication to the Samothracian Gods', *Studia Troica* 6, 201–7.

COLE, S. G. (1984), *Theoi Megaloi: The Cult of the Great Gods at Samothrace*. EPRO 96 (Leiden).

—— (1989), 'The Mysteries of Samothrace during the Roman period', in *ANRW* 2.18.2 (1989), 1565–98.

COLEMAN, S., and J. ELSNER. (1991), 'Contesting Pilgrimage: Current Views and Future Directions', *Cambridge Anthropology* 15, 63–73.

—— —— (1995), *Pilgrimage: Past and Present in the World Religions* (London).

—— —— (1998), 'Performing Pilgrimage: Walsingham and the Ritual Construction of Irony', in F. Hughes-Freeland (ed.), *Ritual, Performance, Media* (London), 46–65.

—— —— (eds.) (2002), *Pilgrim Voices: Narrative and Authorship in Christian Pilgrimage* (Oxford).

CONNOR, W. R. (1988), ' "Sacred" and "Secular" ', *Ancient Society* 19, 161–88.

COOK, J. M. (1962), *The Greeks in Ionia and the East* (New York).

CORTÉS COPETE, J. M. (1995), *Elio Aristides: un sofista griego en el Imperio Romano* (Madrid).

COSGROVE, D. (1984), 'Prospect, Perspective and the Evolution of the Landscape Idea', *Transactions of the Institute of British Geographers*, NS 10, 45–62.

COSMOPOULOS, M. B. (ed.) (2003), *Greek Mysteries: The Archaeology and Ritual of Greek Secret Cults* (London).

COX MILLER, P. (1994), *Dreams in Late Antiquity. Studies in the Imagination of a Culture* (Princeton).

—— (1994), 'Desert Asceticism and the "Body from Nowhere" ', *Journal of Early Christian Studies* 2, 137–53.

CRUMRINE, N. R., and A. MORINIS (eds.) (1991), *Pilgrimage in Latin America* (New York).

CULLER, J. (1981), 'The Semiotics of Tourism', *American Journal of Semiotics* 1, 127–40.

CURRAN, J. (2000), *Pagan City and Christian Capital: Rome in the Fourth Century* (Oxford).

DARENBERG, C., and E. SAGLIO (1877–1919), *Dictionnaire des antiquités grecques et romaines: d'après les textes et les monuments* (Paris).

D'ARMS, J. H. (1974), 'Puteoli in the Second Century of the Roman Empire: A Social and Economic Study', *JRS* 64, 104–24.

DASSMANN, A. (1975), 'Ambrosius und die Martyrer', *JbAC* 8, 49–68.

DASTON, L., and K. PARK (1998), *Wonders and the Order of Nature, 1150–1750* (Cambridge, Mass.).

DAUMAS, F. (1970), 'Les objets sacrés d'Hathor à Dendara', Revue d' Égyptologie 2, 75–6.

DAUMAS, M. (1998), *Cabiriaca: recherches sur l'iconographie du culte des Cabires* (Paris).

DAUX, G. (1943), *Chronologie delphique. Fouilles de Delphes, v. III: Épigraphie.* Extr. Fasc. (Paris).

DAVIES, J. K. (1993), *Democracy and Classical Greece* (London).

—— (1994), 'First Sacred War', in S. Hornblower (ed.), *Greek Historiography* (Oxford), 193–212.

DAVIES, J. K. (2001), 'Rebuilding a Temple: The Economic Effects of Piety', in D. J. Mattingly and J. Salmon (eds.), *Economics Beyond Agriculture in the Classical World* (London), 209–29.

DAVIS, S. J. (1998), 'Pilgrimage and the Cult of St Thecla in Late Antique Egypt', in Frankfurter (1998), 303–39.

—— (2001), *The Cult of St Thecla* (Oxford).

DAWES, E., and N. H. BAYNES (1977), *Three Byzantine Saints.* (Crestwood, NY).

DAWSON, C. M. (1950), 'The Iambi of Callimachus', *YCS* 11, 1–168.

DELEHAYE, G.-R. (1997), 'La diffusion des ampoules de Saint-Ménas en Gaule', *Le monde copte* 27/8, 155–65.

DELEHAYE, H. (1912), *Les origines du culte des martyrs* (Brussels).

—— (1927), *Sanctus: Essai sur le culte des saints dans l'antiquité* (Brussels).

—— (1930), 'Loca Sanctorum', *Analecta Bollandiana* 48, 5–64.

DEN BOER, W. (1973), *Le culte des sourverains dans l'empire Romain.* Entretiens sur l'antiquité classique 19 (Vandœuvres, 1973).

DENTZER, J.-M. (1986), 'Conclusion: Développement et culture de la Syrie du Sud dans la période préprovinciale', in id. (ed.), *Hauran I: Recherches archéologiques sur la Syrie du Sud à l'époque hellénistique et romaine*, 2. (Paris), 387–420.

DEPAUW, M. (1997), *A Companion to Demotic Studies.* Papyrologica Bruxellensia 28, (Brussels).

DE POLIGNAC, F. (1994), 'Mediation, Competition and Sovereignty: The Evolution of Rural Sanctuaries in Geometric Greece', in S. Alcock and R. Osborne (eds.), *Placing the Gods: Sanctuaries and Sacred Space in Ancient Greece* (Oxford), 3–18.

DERCHAIN, P. (1962), 'Un manuel de géographie liturgique á Edfou', *CdE* 37, 31–63.

—— (1995), 'Miettes (suite)', *RdE* 46, 89–92.

—— (2000), *Les impondérables de l'hellénisation: littérature d'hiérogrammates* (Brepols).

DERCHAIN-URTEL, M.-T. (1998), 'Die Festbesucher in Esna', in R. Gundlach and M. Rochholz (eds.), *Ägyptologische Tempelagung. Feste im Tempel* (Wiesbaden), 3–15.

DES BOUVRIE, S. (forthcoming), 'The Pilgrimage to Olympia. Settings and Sentiments', in M. Wedde (ed.), *Celebrations: Sanctuaries and the Vestiges of Cult Practice.* Papers from the Norwegian Institute at Athens 6 (Bergen).

DESJARLAIS, R. R. (1996), 'Presence', in C. Laderman and M. Roseman (eds.), *The Performance of Healing* (New York), 143–64.

DE VIS, H. (1990; repr. of 1922–9), *Homélies coptes de la Vaticane*, 2 vols. (Copenhagen).

DEWALD, C. (1990), Review of Hartog 1988, *CPh* 85, 217–24.

DIBELIUS, M. (1933), *Die Formgeschichte des Evangeliums*, 2nd edn. (Tübingen).

DILLON, M. P. J. (1990), ' "The House of the Thebans" (FD, iii.1 357–358) and Accommodation for Greek Pilgrims', *ZPE* 83: 64–88.

—— (1994), 'The Didactic Nature of the Epidaurian *Iamata*', *ZPE* 101, 239–60.

—— (1997), *Pilgrims and Pilgrimage in Ancient Greece* (London).

DILKE, O. A. W. (1985), *Greek and Roman Maps* (London).

DIRVEN, L. (1997), 'The Author of *De Dea Syria* and his Cultural Heritage', *Numen* 44, 153–79.

DITTENBERGER, W. (1903). *Orientis Graeci Inscriptiones Selectae. SIG* Suppl. (Leipzig).

DODD, D., and C. FARAONE (eds.) (2003), *Initiation in Ancient Greek Rituals and Narratives* (London).

DODDS, E. R. (1965), *Pagan and Christian in an Age of Anxiety* (Cambridge), 41–5.

DÖRRIE, H. (1973), 'L. CALVENUS TAUROS. Das Persönglichkeitsbild eines platonischen Philosophen um die Mitte des 2. Jahrh. n. Chr.' *Kairos* 15, 24–35 (=Dörrie 1976).

—— (1976), *Platonica minora. Studia et testimonia antiqua* 8. 310–23.

DOUGLAS, M. (1973), *Natural Symbols* (New York).

DOUGLASS, L. (1996), 'A New Look at the *Itinerarium Burdigalense*', *Journal of Early Christian Studies* 4, 313–33.

DOW, S., and F. S. UPSON, (1944), 'The Foot of Sarapis', *Hesperia* 13, 58–77.

DRACK, W. and R. FELLMANN (1988), *Die Römer in der Schweiz* (Stuttgart and Jona SG).

DRIJVERS, H. J. W. (1980), *Cults and Beliefs at Edessa* (Leiden).

DRIJVERS, J. W. (1992), *Helena Augusta. The Mother of Constantine the Great and the Legend of Her Finding of the True Cross* (Leiden).

DRIOTON, E. (1943), 'Les fêtes de Bouto', *Bulletin de l'Institut d'Égypte* 25, 1–19.

DUBISCH, J. (1995), *In A Different Place: Pilgrimage, Gender and Politics at a Greek Island Shrine* (Princeton).

DUNAND, F. (1962), 'Une "interpretatio romana" d'Isis: Isis, déesse des naissances', *REL* 40, 83–6.

—— (1973), *Le culte d'Isis dans le bassin oriental de la Méditerranée*, 3 vols. (Leiden).

—— (1975), 'Les syncrétismes dans le religion de l'Égypte Romaine', in F. Dunand and P. Levêcque, *Les syncrétismes dans les religions de l'antiquité* (Leiden), 154–85.

—— (1976), 'Lanternes gréco-romaines d'Égypt', *Dialogues d'histoire ancienne* 2, 71–95.

DUNAND, F. (1991), 'Miracles et guérisons en Égypte tardive', in N. Fick and J.-Cl. Carrière (eds.), *Mélanges Étienne Bernand*, (Paris), 235–50.

—— (1997), 'La consultation oraculaire en Egypte tardive: l'oracle de Bes à Abydos', in J. G. Heintz, (ed.), *Oracles et propheties dans l'antiquité. Actes du colloque de Strasbourg 15–17 juin 1995* (Paris), 65–84.

DUNBABIN, K. M. D. (1990), '*Ipsa deae vestigia*... Footprints divine and human on Graeco-Roman monuments', *JRA* 3, 85–109.

DUNCAN, C. (1999), 'From the princely gallery to the public art museum', in D. Boswell and J. Evans (eds.), *Representing the Nation: A Reader* (London): 304–31.

DUNCAN-FLOWERS, M. (1990), 'A Pilgrim's Ampulla from the Shrine of St. John the Evangelist at Ephesus', in Ousterhout 1990, 125–39.

DUPRONT, A. (1973), 'Pèlerinage et lieux sacrés', in *Méthodologies de l'histoire et des sciences humaines: Mélanges en l'honneur de Fernand Braudel*, 2 (Toulouse), 189–206.

DÜRING, I. (1961) *Aristotle's Protrepticus* (Göteborg).

DURKHEIM, E. (1912), *The Elementary Forms of Religious Life*, New York 1995, Eng. tr. by K. E. Fields of *Les formes élémentaires de la vie religieuse* (Paris, 1912).

EADE, J., and M. J. SALLNOW (eds.) (1991), *Contesting the Sacred: The Anthropology of Christian Pilgrimage* (London).

EBERS, G. (ed.) (1987), *Papyros Ebers* (Osnabrück).

EBERT, J. and P. SIEGERT. (1999), 'Eine archaische Beamtenurkunde aus Olympia mit Vorschriften für Ringkämpfer und Kampfrichter', in A. Mallwitz (ed.), *XI Bericht über die Ausgrabungen in Olympia* (Berlin), 391–412.

EDELSTEIN, L. and E. EDELSTEIN (1945), *Asclepius. Collection and Interpretation of Testimonies* (Baltimore).

EDWARDS, M., M. GOODMAN, and S. PRICE, (eds.) with C. ROWLAND (1999), *Apologetics in the Roman Empire: Pagans, Jews and Christians* (Oxford).

EKROTH, G. (1999), 'Pausanias and the Sacrificial Rituals of Greek Hero-cults', in Hägg (1999), 146–58.

EL-SAWI, A. (1979), Excavations at Tell Basta: report of seasons 1967–71 and catalogue of finds (Prague).

ELKINS, J. (1999), *The Domain of Images* (Ithaca, NY).

ELLIOTT, J. H. (1981), *A Home for the Homeless* (Philadelphia).

ELM, S. (1989), 'Perceptions of Jerusalem Pilgrimage as Reflected in Two Early Sources on Female Pilgrimage (3rd and 4th centuries A.D.)', *Studia Patristica* 20, 219–23.

ELSNER, J. (1992), 'Pausanias: A Greek Pilgrim in the Roman World', *Past and Present* 135, 3–29.

—— (1994), 'From the Pyramids to Pausanias and Piglet: Monuments, Travel and Writing', in S. Goldhill and R. Osborne (eds.), *Art and Text in Ancient Greek Culture* (Cambridge), 224–54.

—— (1995), *Art and the Roman Viewer: The Transformation of Art from the Pagan World to Christianity* (Cambridge).

—— (1996), 'Image and Ritual: Reflections on the Religious Appreciation of Classical Art', *Classical Quarterly* 46, 515–31.

—— (1997*a*), 'Hagiographic Geography: Travel and Allegory in the *Life of Apollonius of Tyana*' *JHS* 117, 22–37.

—— (1997*b*), 'The Origins of the Icon: Pilgrimage, Religion and Visual Culture in the Roman East as "Resistance" to the Centre', in S. E. Alcock (ed.), *The Early Roman Empire in the East* (Oxford), 178–99.

—— (1997*c*), 'Replicating Palestine and Reversing the Reformation', *Journal of the History of Collections* 9(1), 117–30.

—— (1998), *Imperial Rome and Christian Triumph* (Oxford).

—— (2000*a*), 'The *Itinerarium Burdigalense*: Politics and Salvation in the Geography of Constantine's Empire', *JRS* 90, 181–95.

—— (2000*b*), 'Between Mimesis and Divine Power: Visuality in the Graeco-Roman World', in R. S. Nelson (ed.), *Visuality Before and Beyond the Renaissance: Seeing As Others Saw* (Cambridge), 45–69.

—— (2001*a*), 'Structuring "Greece": Pausanias's *Periegesis* as a Literary Construct', in Alcock, Cherry, and Elsner (2001), 3–20.

—— (2001*b*), 'Describing Self in the Language of the Other: Pseudo (?) Lucian at the Temple of Hierapolis', in Goldhill (2001), 123–53.

—— (2003), 'Inventing Christian Rome: The Role of Early Christian Art', in C. Edwards and G. Woolf (eds.), *Rome the Cosmopolis* (Cambridge), 71–99.

—— and J.-P. RUBIÉS (1999), *Voyages & Visions: Towards a Cultural History of Travel* (London).

EMLYN-JONES, C. J. (1980), *The Ionians and Hellenism: A Study of the Cultural Achievement of the Early Greek Inhabitants of Asia Minor* (London).

ENGELS, D. (1990), *Roman Corinth* (Chicago).

ENGEMANN, J. (1973), 'Palästinische Pilgerampullen im F. J. Dölger Institut in Bonn', *JbAC* 16, 5–27.

—— (2002), 'Palästinische frühchristliche Pilgerampullen', *JbAC* 45, 153–69.

ESTES, D. J. (1988), 'From Patriarch to Pilgrim: The Development of the Biblical Figure of Abraham and its Contribution to the Christian Metaphor of Spiritual Pilgrimage' (unpublished Ph.D. Diss., University of Cambridge).

EVANS, R. F. (1968), *Pelagius: Enquiries and Reappraisals* (London).

EVANS-PRITCHARD, E. E. (1965), *Theories of Primitive Religion* (Oxford).

EVELYN WHITE, H. G. (1932), *Monasteries of the Wadi 'n Natrun*, 2 vols. (New York).

FANTAR, M. (1990), 'Survivances de la civilisation punique en Afrique du Nord', in A. Mastino (ed.), *L'Africa romana: atti del VII convegno di studio, Sassari* (Sassari, 1990), 53–70.

FANTASIA, U. (1986), 'Samo e Anaia', in *Serta historica antiqua*, 2 vols. Pubblicazioni dell'Istituto di storia antica e scienze ausiliarie dell'Università di Genova 15 (Rome), 113–43.

FAULKNER, R. O. (1969), *The Ancient Egyptian Pyramid Texts, Translated into English* (Oxford).

FEARS, J. R. (1981), 'The Theology of Victory at Rome: Approaches and Problems', *ANRW* 17.2, 736–826.

FERGUSON, J. (1970), *The Religions of the Roman Empire* (London).

FERRARA, A. J. (1973), *Nanna-Suen's Journey to Nippur* (Rome).

FESTUGIÈRE, A. J. (1954), *Personal Religion among the Greeks* (Berkeley).

—— (1970), 'Les proscynèmes de Philae', *REG* 83, 175–97.

FIEY, J. M. (1969), 'Le pèlerinage des Nestoriens et Jacobites a Jerusalem', *Cahiers des civilization médiévale* 12, 113–26.

FINKELSTEIN, L. (1962), *Akiba. Scholar, saint and martyr* (Cleveland and New York; first published 1936).

FISHER, P. (1998), *Wonder, the Rainbow, and the Aesthetics of Rare Experiences* (Cambridge, Mass.).

FLACELIÈRE, R. (1937), *Les Aitoliens à Delphes* (Paris).

—— (1965), *Greek Oracles* (London).

FLINTERMAN, J.-J. (1995), *Power, Paideia, and Pythagoreanism: Greek Identity, Conceptions of the Relationship between Philosophers and Monarchs and Political Ideas in Philostratus' Life of Apollonius* (Amsterdam).

FOERTMEYER, V. A. (1989), *Tourism in Graeco-Roman Egypt* (Diss. Princeton).

FONTENROSE, J. (1978), *The Delphic Oracle: Its Responses and Operations with a Catalogue of Responses* (Berkeley and Los Angeles).

—— (1988), *Didyma: Apollo's Oracle, Cult and Companions* (Berkeley and Los Angeles).

FOSSEY, C. (1897), 'Inscriptions de Syrie', *BCH* 21, 39–65.

FOSTER, H. (ed.) (1988), *Vision and Visuality* (Seattle, Wash.).

FOUCAULT, M. (1970), *The Order of Things* (London).

—— (1974), *The Archaeology of Knowledge* (London).

FOWLER, H. N., R. STILLWELL, C. W. BLEGEN, B. POWELL, and C. A. ROBINSON, (1932), *Introduction: Topography, Architecture. (Corinth I.i)* (Cambridge, Mass.).

FRANK, G. (2000a), *The Memory of Eyes: Pilgrims to Living Saints in Christian Late Antiquity* (Berkeley).

FRANK, G. (2000*b*), 'The Pilgrim's Gaze in the Age before Icons', in R. Nelson (ed.), *Visuality Before and Beyond the Renaissance* (Cambridge), 98–115.

FRÄNKEL, M. (ed.) (1895), *Altertümer von Pergamon* VIII, 2 *Die Inschriften von Pergamon. 2 Teil: Römische Zeit* (Berlin).

FRANKFURTER, D. T. M. (1990), 'Stylites and *Phallobates*: Pillar Religion in Late Antique Syria', *VChr* 44, 168–98.

—— (1993), *Elijah in Upper Egypt: The Coptic Apocalypse of Elijah and Early Egyptian Christianity*. Studies in Antiquity and Christianity 7 (Minneapolis).

—— (1994), 'The Cult of the Martyrs in Egypt Before Constantine: The Evidence of the Coptic *Apocalypse of Elijah*', *V Chr* 48, 25–47.

—— (1996), 'The Legacy of the Jewish Apocalypse in Early Christian Communities,' in J. C. VanderKam and W. Adler (eds.), *The Jewish Apocalyptic Heritage in Early Christianity*. Corpus Rerum Iudaicarum ad Novum Testamentum III.4 (Assen/Maastricht and Minneapolis), 129–200.

—— (1998*a*), *Religion in Roman Egypt: Assimilation and Resistance* (Princeton).

—— (ed.) (1998*b*), *Pilgrimage and Holy Space in Late Antique Egypt* (Leiden).

—— (1998*c*), 'Introduction. Approaches to Coptic Pilgrimage,' in Frankfurter 1998*b*, 3–48.

FRASER, P. M. (1960), *Samothrace*, 2.1. *The Inscriptions* (London) (= Lehmann and Lehmann (1959–1998), vol. 2.1).

—— (1972), *Ptolemaic Alexandria* (Oxford).

FRAYN, J. M. (1993), *Markets and Fairs in Roman Italy* (Oxford).

FRAZER, J. (1898), *Pausanias's Description of Greece*, 5 vols. (London).

FREDERIKSEN, M., and N. PURCELL, (1984), *Campania* (London).

FREDERIKSEN, M. W. (1959), 'Puteoli', *RE* 23.2, 2036–60.

FREEDBERG, D. (1989), *The Power of Images. Studies in the History and Theory of Response* (Chicago).

FREEMAN, P. W. M. (1993), 'Romanisation and Roman Material Culture,' *JRA* 6, 438–45.

FREND, W. H. C. (1972), *The Rise of the Monophysite Movement: Chapters in the History of the Church in the Fifth and Sixth Centuries* (Cambridge).

FREUD, S. (1964), *Standard Edition of the Complete Psychological Works*, ed. James Strachey, 22 (London).

FREY, J.-B. (1975), *Corpus Inscriptionum Judaicarum*, 1 (New York; first published 1936).

FREY, N. (1988), *Pilgrim Stories: On and off the Road to Santiago* (Berkeley).

FRIEDRICH, G. (ed.) (1967), *Theological Dictionary of the New Testament* (Grand Rapids, Mich.).

FRISK, H. (1955–72), *Griechisches etymologisches Wörterbuch* (Heidelberg).

GADAMER, H.-G. (1975), *Truth and Method* (London).

GAGÉ, J. (1940), 'Hercule-Melqart, Alexandre, et les Romains à Gades', *REA* 42, 425–38.

—— (1955), *Apollon Romain. Essai sur le culte d'Apollon et le développement du <ritus Graecus> à Rome des origines à Auguste* (Paris).

GALLI, M. (2001), 'Pepaideumenoi am "Ort des Heiligen": Euergetische Initiativen und Kommunikationsformen in griechischen Heiligtümern zur Zeit der Zweiten Sophistik', in Chr. Reusser (ed.), *Griechenland in der mittleren und späteren Kaiserzeit. Neue Forschungen zur Skulptur, Architektur und Topographie. Festschrift zum 60. Geburtstag von Dieter Willers, HASB* Suppl. 3, 43–70.

—— (2002), *Die Lebenswelt eines Sophisten. Untersuchungen zu den Bauten und Stiftungen des Herodes Atticus* (Mainz).

GALLO, M. (ed.) (1996), *Plutarco e la religione, Atti del VI convegno plutarcheo. Ravello 29–31 maggio 1995* (Naples).

GARCÍA Y BELLIDO, (1963*a*), 'Hercules Gaditanus', *Archivo Español de Arqueologia* 36, 70–153.

—— (1963*b*), 'Subsidios para la historia del Herakleion gaditano', *Boletín de la Real Academia de la Historia* 153, 145–51.

GARDINER, A. H. (1944), 'Horus the Behdehite', *JEA* 30, 23–60.

GARITTE, G. (1959), 'L'Invention Géorgienne des trois enfants de Babylone', *Le Muséon* 72, 69–100.

—— (1961), 'Le texte arménien de l'invention des trois enfants de Babylone,' *Le Muséon* 74, 91–108.

GARLAND, R. (1992), *Introducing New Gods: The Politics of Athenian Religion* (Ithaca, NY).

—— (1995), *The Eye of the Beholder: Deformity and Disability in the Graeco-Roman World* (London).

GASCOU, J. (1984), 'Notes de papyrologie byzantine II, 1: Les sanctuaries dédiés aux Trois Saints Jeunes Gens Égypte byzantine', *Chronique d'Égypte* 59, 333–7.

GAUTHIER, H. (1931), *Fêtes du dieu Min* (Cairo).

GAUTHIER, N. (1999), 'La topographie chrétienne entre idéologie et pragmatisme', in Brogiolo and Ward-Perkins (1999), 195–209.

GEERTZ, C. (1973), *The Interpretation of Cultures* (New York).

GEIGER, J. (1998), 'Aspects of Palestinian Paganism in Late Antiquity' in Kofsky and Stroumsa (1998), 3–17.

GERACI, G. (1971), 'Ricerche sul Proskynema', *Aegyptus* 51, 3–211.

GIANNINI, A. (1966), *Paradoxographorum Graecorum reliquiae* (Milano).

GIBB, C. C. T. (1999), '*Baraka* without Borders: Integrating Communities in the City of the Saints', *Journal of Religion in Africa* 29(1), 88–108.

GIBBON, E. (1929), *The History of the Decline and Fall of the Roman Empire*, ed. J. B. Bury (London).

GIFFORDS, G. F. (1991), *The Art of Private Devotion: Retablo Painting of Mexico* (Fort Worth).

GILSON, E. (1991), *The Spirit of Medieval Philosophy*, tr. A. H. C. Downes (Notre Dame and London; first pub. 1936).

GINOUVÈS, R. (1962), *Balaneutiké, Recherches sur le bain dans l'antiquité grecque* (Paris).

GINZBERG, L. (1925–38), *The Legends of the Jews* (Philadelphia).

GIORDANO, M. (1999), *La supplica. Rituale, istituzione sociale e tema epico in Omero* (Diss. Naples).

GLEASON, M. (1995), *Making Men: Sophists and Self-presentation in Ancient Rome* (Princeton).

GÖDDE, S. (1998), 'Hikesie', in *DNP* 3. 554–5.

GOEHRING, J. E. (1997), 'Monastic Diversity and Ideological Boundaries in Fourth-century Christian Egypt', *Journal of Early Christian Studies* 5, 61–83.

GOLDHILL, S. (1999), 'Programme Notes', in Goldhill and Osborne (1999), 1–29.

—— (ed.) (2001), *Being Greek under Rome: Cultural Identity, the Second Sophistic and the Development of Empire* (Cambridge).

—— and R. OSBORNE, (eds.) (1999), *Performance Culture and Athenian Democracy* (Cambridge).

GOLLEDGE, R. G., and R. J. STIMSON (1997), *Spatial Behavior: A Geographic Perspective* (New York).

GOODMAN, M. (1994), *Mission and Conversion: Proselytizing in the Religious History of the Roman Empire* (Oxford).

—— (1999), 'The Pilgrimage Economy of Jerusalem in the Second Temple Period', in Levine (1999), 69–76.

GOODY, J. (1961), 'Religion and Ritual: The Definitional Problem', *British Journal of Sociology* 12, 142–64.

—— (1997), *Representations and Contradictions* (Oxford and Malden, Mass.).

GOTTSCHALK (1980), *Heraclides of Pontus, the Younger* (Oxford).

GOULD, J. (1973), 'Hiketeia', *JHS* 93, 74–103.

GOUREVITCH, D. (1984), *Le Triangle Hippocratique dans le monde Gréco-Romain* (Rome).

GOUREVITCH, M., and D. GOUREVITCH (1968), 'Aelius Aristide ou mémoires d'un hystérique au IIe siècle', *Information psychiatrique* 44(10), 897–902.

GRABAR, A. (1958), *Ampoules de Terre Sainte* (Paris).

GRAF, F. (1992), 'Heiligtum und Ritual. Das Beispiel der griechisch-römischen Asklepieia', in A. Schachter (ed.), *Le sanctuaire grec*, Entretiens Fondation Hardt 37, 159–99.

—— (1996), 'Gli dei greci e i loro santuari', in *I Greci. Storia, cultura, arte, società, 2. Una storia greca*, 1, 343–80.

470   *Bibliography*

GRAF, F. (1999*a*), 'Kabiren', in *DNP* 6, 123–7.

—— (1999*b*), 'Pompai in Greece. Some Considerations About Space and Ritual in the Greek Polis', in R. Hägg (ed.), *The Role of Religion in the Early Greek Polis* (Stockholm), 55–65.

—— (2002*a*), Review of *Pilgrims and Pilgrimage in Ancient Greece* by M. Dillon, *History of Religions* 42, 193–6.

—— (2002*b*), 'What is New about Greek Sacrifice?' in H. F. G Hortmanschaft et al. (eds.), *Kykeon: Studies in Honour of H. S. Versnel* (Leiden, 2002), 113–25.

—— (2003), 'Initiation: A Concept with a Troubled History', in Dodd and Faraone (2003), 3–24.

GRANDJEAN, Y. (1975), *Une nouvelle arétologie d'Isis à Maronée. EPRO* 49 (Leiden).

GREEN, P. (1980), *Alexander to Actium* (Berkeley).

GREEN, T. M. (1992), *The City of the Moon God: Religious Traditions of Harran* (Leiden).

GREER, R. A. (1986), *Broken Lights and Mended Lives. Theology and Common Life in the Early Church* (University Park and London).

GRIMM, A. (1994), *Die altägyptischen Festkalender in den Tempeln der griechisch-römischen Epoche* (Wiesbaden).

GRISWOLD, Jr., C. L. (1986), *Self-Knowledge in Plato's Phaedrus* (New Haven; repr. Philadelphia, 1996).

GROSSMANN, P. (1998), 'The Pilgrimage Center of Abu Mina', in Frankfurter (1998*b*), 281–302.

GRUEN, E. S. (1990), *Studies in Greek Culture and Roman Policy* (Leiden).

—— (1992), *Culture and National Identity in Republican Rome.* Cornell Studies in Classical Philology. Townsend lectures 52 (Ithaca, NY).

GUARDUCCI, M. (1929), *Poeti vaganti-e conferenzieri dell'età ellenistica; ricerche di epigrafia greca nel campo della letteratura e del costume.* Memorie della R. Accademia nazionale dei lincei. Classe di scienze morali, storiche e filologiche . . . ser. 5; vol. II, fasc. IX (Rome, 1929).

—— (1934), 'I "miracoli" di Asclepio a Lebena', *Historia* 8, 410–28.

—— (ed.) (1935–50). Inscriptiones Creticae. 4 vols. (Rome).

—— (1942–3), 'Le impronte del Quo Vadis e monumenti affini, figurati ed epigrafici', *Rendiconti della Pontificia Accademia di Archaeologia* 19, 305–44.

—— (ed.) (1935–50). *Inscriptiones Creticae,* 4 vols. (Rome).

—— (1974). 'Ancora sull' inno cretese a Zeus Dicteo', in *Antichità cretesi: studi in onore di Doro Levi,* 2 (Catania), 36–8.

GURLITT, W. (1890), *Über Pausanias* (Graz).

GUTBUB, A. (1964), 'Remarques sur les dieux du nome Tanitique à la Basse Époque (suite)', *Kemi* 17, 35–60.

GUTTMANN, M. (1926), 'The Term "Foreigner" נכרי Historically Considered', *Hebrew Union College Annual* 3, 1–20.

GWYN GRIFFITHS, J. (1960), *The Conflict of Horus and Seth*, (Liverpool).

HAAS, C. (1997), *Alexandria in Late Antiquity: Topography and Social Conflict.* (Baltimore and London).

HAAS, V. (1982), *Hethitische Berggötter und hurritische Steinddämonen: Riten, Kulte und Mythen: eine Einführung in die altkleinasiatischen religiösen Vorstellungen* (Mainz am Rhein).

HABACHI, L. (1957), *Tell Basta* (Cairo).

HABERMAS, J. (1981), *Theorie des kommunikativen Handelns* 1–2 (Frankfurt), Eng. tr. by T. McCarthy, *The Theory of Communicative Action*, 1 (Cambridge, 1984), 2 (Cambridge, 1987).

HABICHT, C. (1969), *Altertümer von Pergamon* VIII.3. *Die Inschriften des Asklepieions* (Berlin).

—— (1970), *Gottmenschentum und griechische Städte.* Zetemata, Heft 14; 2nd edn. (Munich).

—— (1985), *Pausanias' Guide to Ancient Greece* (Berkeley; repr. 1998).

—— (1994), 'Iasos and Samothrake in der Mitte des 3. Jh. v. Chr.', *Chiron* 24, 69–74.

HÄGG, R. (1999), *Ancient Greek Hero Cult: Proceedings of the Fifth International Seminar on Ancient Greek Cult, organized by the Department of Classical Archaeology and Ancient History, Göteborg University, 21–23 April 1995* (Stockholm).

HÄGG, T. and P. ROUSSEAU (eds.) (2000), *Greek Biography and Panegyric in Late Antiquity* (Berkeley).

HAHN, C. (1990), 'Loca Sancta Souvenirs: Sealing the Pilgrim's Experience', in Ousterhout (1990), 85–96.

—— (1997), 'Seeing and Believing: The Construction of Sanctity in Early-Medieval Saints' Shrines', *Speculum* 72, 1079–106.

—— (2000), '*Visio Dei*: Changes in Medieval Visuality' in Nelson 2000, 169–96.

HAJJAR, Y. (1977), *La Triade d' Héliopolis-Baalbek: son culte et sa diffusion à travers les textes littéraires et les documents iconographiques et épigraphiques*, 2 vols. (Leiden).

—— (1985), *La Triade d'Héliopolis-Baalbek: iconographie, théologie, culte et sanctuaires* (Montreal).

—— (1990), 'Divinités oraculaires et rites divinatoires en Syrie et en Phénicie a l'époque gréco-romaine', *ANRW* II.18.4, 2236–320.

HALBWACHS, M. (1992), 'The Legendary Topography of the Gospels in the Holy Land', in L. Coser (ed.), *On Collective Memory, Maurice Halbwachs*, (Chicago).

472 *Bibliography*

HALFMANN, H. (1979), *Die Senatoren aus dem östlichen Teil des Imperium Romanum bis zum Ende des 2. Jahrhunderts n.Chr.* (Göttingen).

—— (1986), *Itinera Principum. Geschichte und Typologie der Kaiserreisen im Römischen Reich* (Wiesbaden).

HALL, J. M. (1997), *Ethnic Identity in Greek Antiquity* (Cambridge).

—— (2002), *Hellenicity: Between Ethnicity and Culture* (Chicago).

HANSEN, W. (1996), *Phlegon of Tralles' Book of Marvels* (Exeter).

HARRIS, W. V. (1989), *Ancient Literacy* (Cambridge, Mass.).

HARRIS, R. (1999), *Lourdes: Body and Spirit in the Secular Age* (London).

HARRISON, J. E. (1908–9), 'The Kouretes and Zeus Kouros: a study in prehistoric sociology', *BSA* 15, 308–38.

—— (1912), *Themis: A Study of the Social Origins of Greek Religion* (Cambridge).

HARRISON, T. R. (2000), *Divinity and History: The Religion of Herodotus* (Oxford).

HARTOG, F. (1988), *The Mirror of Herodotus: The Representation of the Other in the Writing of History* (Berkeley).

—— (1996), *Mémoire d'Ulysse: Récits sur la frontière en Grèce ancienne* (Paris).

—— (2001), *Memories of Odysseus: Frontier tales from Ancient Greece* (Chicago).

HEALEY, J. F. (2001), *The Religion of the Nabataeans: A conspectus* (Leiden).

HEER, J. (1979), *La personnalité de Pausanias.* (Paris).

HEIDEL, W. A. (1935), *Hecataeus and the Egyptian Priests in Herodotus, Book II.* American Academy of Arts and Sciences, Memoirs, xviii, 2 (Boston).

HELLEMO, G. (1989), *Adventus Domini* (Leiden).

HELMS, M. W. (1988), *Ulysses' Sail: An Ethnographic Odyssey of Power, Knowledge and Geographical Distance* (Princeton).

HEMBERG, B. (1950), *Die Kabiren.* (Upsala).

HENNINGER, J. (1981), *Arabica Sacra: Aufsätze zur Religionsgeschichte Arabiens und seiner Randgebiete* (Freiburg and Göttingen).

HENRICHS, A. (1968), 'Vespasian's Visit to Alexandria', *ZPE* 3, 51–80.

HEPDING, H. (1933), 'ROUFINION ALSOS', *Philologus* 88, 90–103.

HERMAN, G. (1987), *Ritualised Friendship and the Greek City* (Cambridge).

HERZOG, R. (1931), *Die Wunderheilungen von Epidauros. Ein Beitrag zur Geschichte der Medizin und der Religion* (Leipzig).

HEZSER, C. (1997), *The Social Structure of the Rabbinic Movement in Roman Palestine, TSAJ* 66 (Tübingen).

HEYBERGER, B. (1998), 'Sainteté et chemins de la perfection chez les chrétiens du Proche-Orient (xviie–xviiie siècles)', *RHR* 215, 117–137.

HILL, B. H. (1964), *Corinth I.vi: The Springs: Peirene, Sacred Spring, Glauke* (Princeton).

HOFF, M. C., and SUSAN I. ROTROFF (eds.) (1997), *The Romanization of Athens* (Oxford).

HOFFMANN, A. (1984), 'Zum Bauplan des Zeus-Asklepios-Tempels im Asklepieion von Pergamon', in *Bauplanung und Bautheorie der Antike: Diskussionen zur Archäologischen Bauforschung* 4 (Berlin), 95–103.

—— (1998), 'The Roman Remodeling of the Asklepieion' in Koester 1998, 41–61.

HOHLWEIN, N. (1940), 'Déplacements et tourisme dans l' Égypte Romaine', *Chronique d' Égypte* 15, 253–78.

HOLLOWAY, J. B. (1998), *Jerusalem: Essays in Pilgrimage and Literature* (New York).

HOLUM, K. (1982), *Theodosian Empresses: Women and Imperial Dominion in Late Antiquity* (Berkeley).

—— (1990), 'Hadrian and Saint Helena: Imperial Travel and the Origins of Christian Pilgrimage', in R. Ousterhout (ed.), *The Blessings of Pilgrimage* (Urbana, Ill. and Chicago, 1990), 66–81.

HOMMEL, P., G. KLEINER, and W. MÜLLER-WIENER (1967), *Panionion und Melie* (Berlin).

HONIGMAN, E. (1950), 'Juvenal of Jerusalem', *DOP* 5, 211–79.

—— (1951), *Évêques et évêchés monophysites d'Asie antérieure au VIe siècle* (Louvain).

HOPKINS, K. (1999), *A World Full of Gods: Pagans, Jews and Christians in the Roman Empire* (London).

HORDEN, P., and N. PURCELL, (2000), *The Corrupting Sea: A Study of Mediterranean History* (Oxford).

HORNBLOWER, S. (1982), 'Thucydides, the Panionian Festival, and the Ephesia (iii. 104)', *Historia* 31, 241 ff.

—— (1991), *A Commentary on Thucydides. 1. Books I–III* (Oxford).

—— (1992), 'The Religious Dimensions of the Peloponnesian War', *HSCP* 94, 169–97.

HORNUNG, E. (1982), *Conceptions of God in Ancient Egypt: The One and the Many* (Cornell).

HORSFALL, N. (1987), 'The Aeneas-legend from Homer to Virgil', in J. N. Bremmer and N. M. Horsfall (eds.), *Roman Myth and Mythography. BICS* Suppl. 52 (London), 12–24.

HUGHES, D. (1999), 'Hero Cult, Heroic Honors, Heroic Dead: Some Developments in the Hellenistic and Roman Periods', in Hägg 1999, 168–75.

HUMPHREYS, S. C. (1978), *Anthropology and the Greeks* (London).

HUMPHRIES, M. (1999), *Communities of the Blessed: Social Environment and Religious Change in Northern Italy, AD 200–400* (Oxford).

HUNT, E. D. (1981), 'The Traffic in Relics: Some Late Roman Evidence', in Sergei Hackel (ed.), *The Byzantine Saint: University of Birmingham 14th Spring Symposium of Byzantine Studies* (London): 171–80.

—— (1982) *Holy Land Pilgrimage in the Later Roman Empire. AD 312–460*, (Oxford).

—— (1984), 'Travel, Tourism and Piety in the Roman Empire: A Context for the Beginnings of the Christian Empire', *Echos du monde classique*, 3, 391–417.

—— (1999), 'Were there Christian Pilgrims before Constantine?' in J. Stopford (ed.), *Pilgrimage Explored*, (Woodbridge), 25–40.

HUNTER, R. L. (1979), 'The Comic Chorus in the Fourth Century', *ZPE* 36, 34–5.

HUXLEY, G. L. (1972), *The Early Ionians* (Shannon).

IMHOOF-BLUMER, F., and GARDNER P. (1887). *A Numismatic Commentary on Pausanias* (London).

IMPEY, O. and A. MACGREGOR, (1985), *The Origins of Museums: The Cabinet of Curiosities in Sixteenth-and Seventeenth-Century Europe* (Oxford).

JACKSON, S. (1995), *Myrsilus of Methymna, Hellenistic Paradoxographer* (Amsterdam).

JACOB, C. (1983), 'De l'art de compiler à la fabrication du merveilleux. Sur la paradoxographie grecque', *Lalies* 2, 121–40.

JACOBSEN, T. (1987), *The Harps that Once: Sumerian poetry in translation* (New Haven).

JACQUEMIN, A. (1991), 'Delphes au IIe. siècle après J.-C. Un lieu de la mémoire grecque', in Said (1991), 217–31.

JAEGER, W. (1923), *Aristoteles, Grundlegung einer Geschichte seiner Entwicklung* (Berlin), trs. R. Robinson as *Aristotle: Fundamentals of the History of his Development*, 2nd edn., (Oxford, 1948).

JAMESON, M. H. (1999), 'The Spectacular and the Obscure in Greek Religion', in Goldhill and Osborne 1999, 321–40.

JANES, D. (1998), *God and Gold in Late Antiquity* (Cambridge).

JESSEN, H. (1913), 'Hikesios, Hikesia', *RE* 8.2, 1592–3.

JENTEL, M.-J. (1986), 'Bubastis', *LIMC* 2. 81–3.

JHA, M. (ed.) (1985), *Dimensions of Pilgrimage: An Anthropological Appraisal* (New Delhi).

JOHNSON, D. W. (1980), *A Panegyric on Macarius, Bishop of Tkōw, Attributed to Dioscorus of Alexandria* 1–2. CSCO 415–16, S. Coptici 41–42 (Louvain).

—— (1991), 'Macarius of Tkow, Saint', *Coptic Encyclopaedia* 5, 1492–4.

JOHNSON, M. (1988), 'Reconciling Cyril and Egeria in the Catechetical Process in Fourth-century Jerusalem', in P. Bradshaw (ed.), *Essays in Early Eastern Initiation* (Bramcote), 18–30.

JOHNSSON, W. G. (1978), 'The Pilgrimage Motif in the Book of Hebrews', *Journal of Biblical Literature*, 97/2, 239–51.

JONES, A. H. M. (1964), *The Late Roman Empire 282–602* (Oxford).

JONES, C. A., and P. GALISON, (1998), *Picturing Science Producing Art* (London).

JONES, C. P. (1978*a*), 'Three Foreigners in Attica', *Phoenix* 33, 222–34.

—— (1978*b*), *The Roman world of Dio Chrysostom* (Cambridge, Mass.).

—— (1996), 'The Panhellenion', *Chiron* 26, 29–56.

—— (1987), '*Stigma*: Tattooing and Branding in Graeco-Roman Antiquity', *JRS* 77, 139–55.

—— (1998), 'Aelius Aristides and the Asklepieion', in Koester 1998, 63–76.

—— (2001), 'Pausanias and his Guides', in Alcock, Cherry, and Elsner 2001, 33–9.

JORDAN, B. (1975), *The Athenian Navy in the Classical Period: A Study of Athenian Naval Administration and Military Organization in the Fifth and Fourth Centuries B.C.*, UCPCA 13 (Berkeley).

JUNKER, H. (1911), *Der Auszug der Hathor-Tefnut aus Nubien* (Berlin).

KÄSEMANN, E. (1984), *The Wandering People of God*, tr. R. Harrisville and I. Sandberg (Minneapolis: Augsberg).

KAUFMANN, T. D. (1995), *Court, Cloister, and City: The Art and Culture of Central Europe, 1450–1800* (Chicago).

KEE, H. C. (1986), *Medicine, Miracle and Magic in New Testament Times* (Cambridge).

KEIL, B. (1958), *Aelii Aristidis Smyrnaei quae supersunt omnia. 2: Orationes XVII–LIII Continens* (Berlin).

KELLY, J. N. D. (1975), *Jerome: His Life, Writings and Controversies* (London).

KENT, J. H. (1966), *Corinth VIII.iii: The Inscriptions 1926–1950* (Princeton).

KER, J. (2000), 'Solon's *Theôria* and the End of the City', *Classical Antiquity* 19, 304–29.

KERÉNYI, K., and R. MANHEIM, (1976), *Dionysos: Archetypal Image of the Indestructible Life* (London).

KERKESLAGER, A. (1998), 'Jewish Pilgrimage and Jewish Identity in Hellenistic and Early Roman Egypt', in Frankfurter 1998*b*, 99–228.

KERKHECKER, A. (1999), *Callimachus' Book of Iambi* (Oxford).

KERN, O. (1919), 'Kabeiros, Kabeiroi', *RE* 10, 1428–9.

KESSLER, D. (1989), *Die heiligen Tiere und der König* (Wiesbaden).

KEY FOWDEN, E. (1999), *The Barbarian Plain: Saint Sergius Between Rome and Iran* (Berkeley/London).

KILLEN, J. T. (1994), 'Theban Sealings, Knossos tablets, and Mycenean state Banquets', *BICS* 39(1), 67–88.

KING, H. (1999), 'Chronic Pain and the Creation of Narrative', in J. I. PORTER (ed.), *Constructions of the Classical Body*, Ann Arbor, 269–86.

KITZINGER, E. (1954), 'The Cult of Images Before Iconoclasm', *DOP* 8, 85–150.

KLEINER, G., P. HOMMEL, and W. MÜLLER-WINER (1967), *Panionion und Melie* (Berlin).

KLEES, H. (1975), *Herren und Sklaven*. Forschungen zur antiken Sklaverei 6 (Wiesbaden).

KNOEPFLER, D. (2001), 'La Fête des Daidala de Platées chez Pausanias: Une Clef pour l' Histoire e la Béotie Hellénistique', in Knoepfler et Piérart 2001, 343–74.

KNOEPFLER, D., and MARCEL PIÉRART (eds.) (2001), *Éditer, traduire, commenter Pausanias en l'an 2000*. (Neuchâte).

KOCH, K. (1993), 'Hazzi-Sapan-Kasion. Die Geschichte eines Berges und seiner Gottheiten', in B. Janowski, K. Koch, and G. Wilhelm (eds.), *Religionsgeschichtliche Beziehungen zwischen Kleinasien, Nordsyrien und dem Alten Testament. Internationales Symposion Hamburg 17–21. März 1990*. Orbis Biblicus et Orientalis 129 (Freiburg and Göttingen), 171–223.

KOESTER, H. (ed.) (1998), *Pergamon Citadel of the Gods*, Harvard Theological Studies 46 (Pennsylvania).

KOFSKY, A. (1998), 'Mamre: A Case of A Regional Cult?' in Kofsky and Stroumsa (1998), 19–30.

—— and G. STROUMSA (eds.) (1998), *Sharing the Sacred: Religious Contacts and Conflicts in the Holy Land* (Jerusalem).

KOLENKOW, A. B. (1980), 'Relationships between Miracle and Prophecy in the Greco-Roman World and Early Christianity', *ANRW* 23.2 (1980), 1470–506.

KOLLER, H. (1958), 'Theoros und Theoria', *Glotta* 36, 273–86.

KOLTA, K. S. (1968), *Die Gleichsetzung ägyptischer und griechischer Götter bei Herodot* (diss. Tübingen).

KOPPERSCHMIDT, J. (1967), *Die Hikesie als dramatische Form. Zur motivischen Interpretation des griechischen Dramas* (diss. Tübingen).

KÖTTING, B. (1950), *Peregrinatio Religiosa: Walllfahrten in der Antike und das Pilgerwesen in der alten Kirche* (Regensburg).

—— (1983), 'Fußspuren als Zeichen göttlicher Anwesenheit', *Boreas* 6, 197–201.

—— (1988), *Ecclesia Peregrinans*, 2 vols. (Munster).

KOWALZIG, B. (2004), 'Changing Choral Worlds: Song-Dance and Society in Athens and Beyond', in Murray and Wilson 2004, 39–65.

—— (forthcoming) *Singing for the Gods* (Oxford).

KRAUTHEIMER, R. (1982), *Three Christian Capitals: Topography and Politics* (Berkeley, Los Angeles).

KRAWIEC, R. (1998), 'Space, Distance and Gender: Authority and Separation of Communities in the White Monastery', *The Bulletin of the American Society of Papyrologists* 35, 45–64.

KRUG, A. (1984), *Heilkunst und Heilkult. Medizin in der Antike* (Munich).

KUELZER, A. (2002), 'Byzantine and Early Post-Byzantine Pilgrimage to the Holy Land and Sinai', in R. Macrides (ed.), *Travel in the Byzantine World* (Aldershot, 2002), 149–61.

KUHLMANN, K. P. (1988), *Das Ammoneion: Archäologie, Geschichte und Kulturpraxis des Orakels von Siwa* (Cairo).

KUHN, K. H. (1966), *A Panegyric on John the Baptist attributed to Theodosius Archbishop of Alexandria* 1–2. CSCO 268–9, S. Coptici 33–4 (Louvain).

—— (1975), 'Three Further Fragments of a Panegyric on John the Baptist Attributed to Theodosius, Archbishop of Alexandria', *Le Muséon* 88, 103–12.

—— and W. J. TAIT, (1996), *Thirteen Coptic Acrostic Hymns from Manuscript M574 of the Pierpont Morgan Library* (Oxford).

KUPER, A. (1999), *Culture: The Anthropologists' Account* (Cambridge, Mass.).

KURTH, D. (1996), 'Die Ritualszene mit den medizinischen Instrumenten im Tempel von Kom Ombo (Nr.950)', in (ed.), M. Schade-Busch, *Wege öffnen. Festschrift für Rolf Gundlach*, AAT 35 (Wiesbaden), 149–64.

LACROIX, L. (1992), 'À propos des offrandes à l'Apollon de Delphes et du témoinage de Pausanias: du réel à l'imaginaire', *BCH* 116, 157–76.

LADNER, G. (1967), 'Homo Viator: Medieval Ideas on Alienation and Order', *Speculum* 42, 233–59.

LAJTAR, A. (1991), 'Proskynema Inscriptions of a Corporation of Iron-Workers from Hermonthis in the Temple of Hatszepsut in Deir El-Bahari: New Evidence for Pagan cults in Egypt in the 4th Cent. A.D.', *Journal of Juristic Papyrology* 21, 52–70.

LAMBROUDINAKIS, B. (1990), 'Un retugié argien à Épidaure au ve siècle' *CRAI*: 174–85.

LANE FOX, R. (1986), *Pagans and Christians in the Mediterranean World from the Second Century A.D. to the Conversion of Constantine* (London).

LANG, D. M. (1956), *Lives and Legends of the Georgian Saints* (London).

LARSON, J. (2001), *Greek Nymphs: Myth, Cult and Lore* (Oxford).

LAURENCE R., and J. BERRY (eds.) (1998), *Cultural Identity in the Roman Empire* (London).

LAWALL, M. L. (2003), '"In the Sanctuary of the Samothracian Gods:" Myth, Politics, and Mystery Cult at Ilion', in Cosmopoulos 2003, 79–111.

LE GLAY, M. (1976), 'Hadrien et l'Asklépieion de Pergamon', *BCH* 100, 347–72.

Lebrun, R. (1987), 'Pèlerinages royaux chez les Hittites', in Chelini and Branthomme 1987, 83 ff.

Leclercq, H. (1907–), 'Pèlerinages aux Lieux Saints', in F. Cabrol and H. Leclercq (eds.), *Dictionnaire d'archéologie chrétienne et de liturgie* (Paris), 14, cols. 65–176.

Lefèvre, F. (1998), *L'amphictionie pyléo-delphique: histoire et institutions*. Bibl. des Écol. Fr. d'Ath. et de Rome 298 (Paris).

Lefort, L.-Th. (1954), 'La chasse aux reliques des martyrs en Égypte au IVᵉ siècle', *La nouvelle Clio* 6, 225–30.

Lehmann, K. (1998), *Samothrace, A Guide to the Excavations and the Museum*, 6th rev. edn. (Thessalonike).

—— and P. W. Lehmann (eds.) (1959–98), *Samothrace. Excavations Conducted by the Institute of Fine Arts of New York University* (vols. 1–4 London 1959–69; vols. 5–11 Princeton 1982–98).

Lehmann, P. W., and Denys Spittle (1982). *Samothrace, 5. The Temenos* (Princeton) (= Lehmann and Lehmann (1959–98), vol. 5).

Leigh, M. (1997), *Lucan: spectacle and engagement* (Oxford).

Lenormant, F. (1887), *Montes divini*, Daremberg–Saglio III.2.

Lenschau, T. (1944), 'Die Gründung Ioniens und der Bund am Panionion', *Klio* 36, 201–37.

Leon, H. J. (1960), *The Jews of Ancient Rome* (Philadelphia).

Lesky, A., J. Willis, and C. Heer (1966), *A History of Greek Literature* (London).

Lévi-Strauss, C. (1962), *La pensée sauvage* (Paris).

Levick, B. (1999), *Vespasian* (London).

Levine L. I. (ed.) (1999), *Jerusalem: Its Sanctity and Centrality to Judaism, Christianity and Islam* (New York).

Lewis, N. (1959), *Samothrace, 1. Literary Sources* (London) (= Lehmann and Lehmann (1959–98), vol. 1).

—— (1983), *Life in Egypt under Roman Rule* (Oxford).

Leyerle, B. (1996), 'Landscape as Cartography in Early Christian Pilgrimage Narratives', *Journal of the American Academy of Religion* 64, 119–43.

Lichtheim, M. (1988), *Ancient Egyptian Autobiographies, Chiefly of the Middle Kingdom. A Study and an Anthology*. OBO 84 (Göttingen).

LiDonnici, L. R. (1995), *The Epidaurian Miracle Inscriptions: Text, Translation, and Commentary* (Atlanta).

Liebeschuetz, W. (1999), 'The Significance of the Speech of Praetextatus', in P. Athanassiadi and M. Frede (eds.), *Pagan Monotheism in Late Antiquity* (Oxford), 185–205.

Lightfoot, J. L. (2001), 'Μαμβογαῖος, *Epigraphica Anatolica* 33, 113–18.

LIGHTFOOT, J. L. (2003), *Lucian, On the Syrian Goddess: Edited with Introduction, Translation, and Commentary* (Oxford).

LIMBERIS, V. (1994), *Divine Heiress: The Virgin Mary and the Creation of Christian Constantinople* (London and New York).

LINDERS, T. (1987), 'Gods, Gifts and Society', in T. Linders and G. Nordquist (eds.), *Gifts to the Gods: Proceedings of the Uppsala Symposium 1985* (Uppsala, 1987).

LITTMANN, E. (1943), *Syria: Publications of the Princeton University Archaeological Expeditions to Syria in 1904–5 and 1909: IV,C: Safaitic Inscriptions* (Leiden).

LLOYD, A. B. (1975–1988), *Herodotus Book II*, 3 vols. (Leiden).

—— (1982), 'Nationalist Propaganda in Ptolemaic Egypt', *Historia* 31, 33–55.

LLOYD, D. W. (1998), *Battlefield Tourism: Pilgrimage and the Commemoration of the Great War in Britain, Australia and Canada, 1919–1939*. The Legacy of the Great War Series (Oxford).

LLOYD, G. E. R. (1990), *Demystifying Mentalities* (Cambridge).

LLOYD-JONES, H. (1976), 'The Delphic Oracle', *G&R* 23, 60–73.

LOCK, C. (2002), 'Bowing Down to Wood and Stone: One Way to Be a Pilgrim', *Journeys* 3, 110–32.

LÓPEZ CASTRO, J. L. (1995), *Hispania Poena* (Barcelona).

DE LUCA, G. (1984), *Das Asklepieion. 4. Teil: Via Tecta und Hallenstrasse, die Funde. Altertümer von Pergamon* XI, 4 (Berlin).

LUCK, G. (1985), *Arcana Mundi. Magic and the Occult in the Greek and Roman World* (Baltimore).

MA, J. (2000), *Antiochus III and the Cities of Western Asia Minor* (Oxford).

MAASS, M. (1993), *Das antike Delphi. Orakel, Schätze, und Monumente* (Darmstadt).

MACCORMACK, S. (1990), 'Loca sancta: The Organisation of Sacred Topography in Late Antiquity', in Ousterhout 1990, 9–20.

MACCOULL, L. S. B. (1998), 'Chant in Coptic Pilgrimage', in Frankfurter 1998*b*, 403–14.

MCCREDIE, J. R. (1968), 'Samothrace: Preliminary Report on the Campaigns of 1965–7', *Hesperia* 37, 216–34.

—— (1979), 'Samothrace: Supplementary Investigations, 1968–1977', *Hesperia* 48, 1–44.

MCDERMOTT, W. C. (1938), *The Ape in Antiquity* (Baltimore).

MACGILLIVRAY, J. A., J. M. DRIESSEN, and L. H. SACKETT, (2000), *The Palaikastro Kouros: A Minoan Chryselephantine Statuette and its Aegean Bronze Age Context*. BSA Studies 6 (London).

MCLYNN, N. B. (1994), *Ambrose of Milan: Church and Court in a Christian Capital* (Berkeley).

MacMullen, R. (1975), *Enemies of the Roman Order: Treason, Unrest, and Alienation in the Empire* (Cambridge, Mass).

—— (1981), *Paganism in the Roman Empire* (New Haven).

MacMullen, R. (1984), *Christianizing the Roman Empire, AD 100–400* (New Haven).

McNally, S. (1998), 'Transformations of Ecclesiastical Space: Churches in the Area of Akhmim', *The Bulletin of the American Society of Papyrologists* 35, 79–95.

Macready, S., and F. H. Thompson (eds.) (1987), *Roman Architecture in the Greek World* (London).

Magnetto, A. (ed.) (1997), *Gli arbitrati interstatali Greci. Introduzione, testo critico, traduzione, commento e indici* (Pisa).

Mahoney, Sr. Catherine of Siena (1935), *The Rare and Late Latin Nouns and Adverbs in S. Augustine's De Civitate Dei: A Morphological and Semasiological Study*, Patristic studies 44 (Washington, DC).

Malaise, M. (1987), 'Pèlerinages et pèlerins dans l' Égypte ancienne', in Chelini and Branthomme 1987, 55 ff.

Manganaro, G. (1961), 'Ricerche di Epigrafia Siceliota', *Siculorum Gymnasium*, 175–98.

—— (1964), 'Peregrinazioni Epigrafiche', *Archeologia Classica* 16, 291–5.

Mangas, J. (1996), 'El culto de Hercules en la Bética', in J. M. Blázquez and J. Alvar (eds.), *La Romanización en Occidente* (Madrid).

Mango, C. (1990a), 'Constantine's Mausoleum and the Translation of Relics', *BZ* 83, 51–62.

—— (1990b), 'Constantine's Mausoleum: An Addendum', *BZ* 83, 434.

Manteuffel, G. (1920), *De opusculis graecis Aegypti e papyris ostracis lapidipidusque collectis* (Warsaw).

Maraval, P. (1982), *Egérie: Journal de voyage* (Paris).

—— (1985), *Lieux saints et pèlerinages d'Orient: Histoire et géographie des origines à la conquête arabe* (Paris).

—— (1986), 'Une Querelle sur les pèlerinages autour d'un texte patristique (Grégoire de Nysse, *Lettre 2*)', *Revue d'Historique et de Philosophie Religieuses*, 66, 131–46.

—— (1987), 'Liturgie et pèlerinage durant les premiers siècles du christianisme', *Le Maison Dieu* 170, 7–28.

—— (1988), 'Saint Jérôme et le pèlerinage aux lieux saints de Palestine', in Y.-M. Duval (ed.), *Jérôme entre l'Occident et l'Orient* (Paris), 345–53.

—— (2002), 'The Earliest Phase of Christian Pilgrimage to the Near East (before the Seventh Century AD)', *DOP* 56, 63–74.

Marcovich, M. (1991), 'Philodamus' Delphic Paean', *ZPE* 18 (1975) 167–8 = *Studies in Greek Poetry*, *ICS* Suppl. 1 (Atlanta), 143–4.

MARINATOS, N. (1993), 'What were Greek Sanctuaries? A Synthesis', in Marinatos and Hägg 1993, 228–33.

—— and R. HÄGG (eds.) (1993), *Greek Sanctuaries: New Approaches* (London, 1993).

MARINCOLA, J. (1997), *Authority and Tradition in Ancient Historiography* (Cambridge).

MARKUS, R. A. (1966), '*Alienatio*. Philosophy and Eschatology in the Development of an Augustinian Idea', *Studia Patristica* 9(3), 431–50.

—— (1989), *Saeculum: History and Society in the Theology of Saint Augustine* (Cambridge; first pub. 1970).

MARKUS, R. A. (1994), 'How on Earth Could Places Become Holy? Origins of the Christian Idea of Holy Places', *Journal of Early Christian Studies* 2, 257–71.

MARTIN, A. (1984), 'Les premiers siècles du christianisme à Alexandrie: Essai de topographie religieuse', *Revue des Études Augustiniennes* 30, 211–25.

MASSON, O. (1982), 'Pèlerins chypriotes en Phénicie (Sarepta et Sidon)', *Semitica* 32, 45–9.

MASTERS, J. (1992), *Poetry and Civil War in Lucan's Bellum Civile* (Cambridge).

MATHEWS, T. (1993), *The Clash of Gods: A Reinterpretation of Early Christian Art* (Princeton).

MATTINGLY, D. J. (ed.) (1997), *Dialogues in Roman Imperialism: Power, Discourse, and Discrepant Experience in the Roman Empire*. Journal of Roman Archaeology Supplementary Series, no. 23 (Portsmouth, RI).

MAYEUR-JAOUEN, C. (1998), 'Saints coptes et saints musulmans de l'Égypte du XXe siècle', *RHR* 215, 139–86.

MAYERSON, P. (1982), 'The Pilgrim Routes to Mount Sinai and the Armenians', *Israel Exploration Journal* 32, 44–57.

MAZZA, M. (1982), 'L' intellettuale come ideologo: Flavio Filostrato ed uno "speculum principis" del III secolo d. C.', in P. Brown, L. Cracco Ruggini, and M. Mazza (eds.), *Governanti e intellettuali, Popolo di Roma e popolo di Dio (I–VI secolo)* (Turin), 93 ff.

MEIGGS, R. (1972), *The Athenian Empire* (Oxford).

MERSCH, A. (1996), *Studien zur Siedlungsgeschichte Attikas von 950 bis 400 v. Chr.* (Frankfurt).

METZGER, B. (1969), 'A Comparison of the Palestinian Syriac Lectionary and the Greek Gospel Lectionary', in E. Ellis and M. Wilcox (eds.), *Neotestamentica et Semitica* (Edinburgh), 209–26.

MICHENAUD, G. and J. DIERKENS, (1972), *Les Rêves dans les 'Discours Sacrés' d'Aelius Aristide IIe siècle ap. J.-C. Essai d'analyse psychologique* (Brussels).

MIKHAIL, M. S., and T. VIVIAN (1997), 'Life of Saint John the Little: An Encomium by Zacharias of Sakha', *Coptic Church Review* 18 (1–2), 17–64.

MILES, M. R. (1985), ' "The Evidence of Our Eyes": Patristic Studies and Popular Christianity in the Fourth Century', *Studia Patristica* 18, 59–63.

MILLAR, F. (1993), *The Roman Near East, 31 BC–AD 337* (Cambridge, Mass.).

MIRHADY, D. (1996), 'Torture and Rhetoric in Athens', *JHS* 106, 119–32.

MISCH, G. (1973), *A History of Autobiography in Antiquity*, 2 (Westport, Conn.).

MITCHELL, S. (1998), *Pisidian Antioch: The Site and its Monuments* (London).

MOGGI, M. (1996), 'L'excursus di Pausania sulla Ionia', in J. Bingen, ed., *Pausanias historien*. Entr. Hardt 41 (Vandœuvres), 79–105.

—— and M. OSANNA (comm.) (2000), *Pausania. Guida della Grecia. Libro VII: L'Acaia* (Milano).

MOMIGLIANO, A. (1934), 'Il re degli Ioni nella provincia romana di Asia', in *Atti del III Congresso Nazionale di Studi Romani*, Roma, 1934: 429–43 =*Quinto Contributo* 1. (Rome, 1975) 205–10.

MONTGOMERY, J. A. (1905), ' "The Place" as an Appellation of Deity', *Journal of Biblical Literature* 24, 17–26.

MONTIGLIO, S. (2000), 'Wandering Philosophers in Classical Greece', *JHS* 120, 86–105.

MONTSERRAT, D. (1996), *Sex and Society in Graeco-Roman Egypt* (London).

—— (1998), 'Pilgrimage to the Shrine of SS Cyrus and John at Menouthis in Late Antiquity', in Frankfurter (1998*b*), 57–79.

MORALES, H. (1995), 'The Taming of the View: Natural Curiosities in *Leukippe and Kleitophon*', in H. Hofmann, (ed.), *Groningen Colloquia on the Novel*, 6 (Groningen), 39–50.

MORANI, M. (1983), 'Sull' espressione linguistica dell' idea di "santuario" nelle civiltà classiche', in M. Sordi (ed.), *Santuari e politica nel mondo antico. Contributi dell' Istituto di Storia Antica* 4, 3–33.

MORGAN, C. A. (1989), 'Divination and Society at Delphi and Didyma', *Hermathena* 147, 17–42.

—— (1990), *Athletes and Oracles: The Transformation of Olympia and Delphi in the Eighth Century BC* (Cambridge).

—— (1993), 'The Origins of Pan-Hellenism', in Marinatos and Hägg 1993, 18–44.

MORGAN, M. (1990), *Platonic Piety: Philosophy and Ritual in Fourth-Century Athens* (New Haven).

MORINIS, E. A. (1984), *Pilgrimage in the Hindu Tradition: A Case Study of West Bengal* (Delhi).

—— (ed.) (1992*a*), *Sacred Journeys: The Anthropology of Pilgrimage* (Westport, Conn.).

—— (1992*b*) 'Introduction: The Territory of the Anthropology of Pilgrimage', in Morinis (1992*a*), 1–28.

MÜLLER, D. (1961), *Ägypten und die griechischen Isis-Aretalogien* (Berlin).

MÜLLER, H. (1987), 'Ein Heilungsbericht aus dem Asklepieion', *Chiron* 17, 193–233.

MUNJERI, D. (1991), 'Refocusing or Reorientation? The Exhibit or the Populace: Zimbabwe on the Threshold', in I. Karp and S. D. Lavine (eds.), *Exhibiting Cultures* (Washington, DC), 444–56.

MURRAY, G. (1908–9), 'The Hymn of the Kouretes', *BSA* 15, 364–65.

MURRAY, O. (1988), 'The Ionian Revolt', in *CAH* 4.2 (Cambridge), 461–90.

MURRAY, P., and P. WILSON (2004), *Music and the Muses: The Culture of 'Mousike' in the Classical Athenian City* (Oxford).

MUSTI, D., and M. TORELLI (1982), *Pausania, Guida della Grecia Libro I: L'Attica* (Milan).

—— —— (1986), *Pausania, Guida della Grecia Libra II: La Corinzia e L'Argolide* (Milan).

MYLONAS, G. (1961), *Eleusis and the Eleusinian Mysteries* (Princeton).

NAFISSI, M. (1991), *La nascita del kosmos. Studi sulla storia e la società di Sparta* (Naples).

NAIDEN, F. (2004), 'Supplication and the Law', in E. Harris and L. Rubenstein (eds.), *The Law and the Courts in Ancient Greece* (Duckworth).

NAQUIN, S., and C. Yü (1992), *Pilgrims and Sacred Sites in China* (Berkeley).

NAU, F. (1906), 'Notes sur les mots πολιτικός et πολιτευόμενος et sur plusiers textes grecs relatifs à saint Étienne', *Revue de l'orient chretienne* 11, 198–216.

NAVILLE, E. (1891), *Bubastis* (London).

NEHRBASS, R. (1935), *Sprache und Stil der Iamata von Epidauros: eine sprachwissenschaftliche Untersuchung. Philologus* Suppl. 27.4 (Leipzig).

NELSON, R. S. (2000), *Visuality before and beyond the Renaissance: Seeing as Others Saw* (Cambridge).

NICOLET, C. (1990), *Space, Geography and Politics in the Early Roman Empire* (Ann Arbor).

NICOLS, J. (1978), *Vespasian and the Partes Flavianae* (Wiesbaden).

NIGHTINGALE, A. W. (1995), *Genres in Dialogue: Plato and the Construct of Philosophy* (Cambridge).

—— (2004), *Spectacles of Truth in Classical Greek Philosophy: Theoria in its Cultural Context* (Cambridge).

NILSSON, M. P. (1916), 'Die Prozessionstypen im griechischen Kult', *Arch. Jahrb.* 31, 309–39. (Repr. in *Opuscula Selecta*, 1 (Lund, 1951), 166–214).

—— (1967–74), *Geschichte der griechischen Religion* (Munich).

NOCK, A. D. (1933), *Conversion: The Old and the New in Religion from Alexander the Great to Augustine of Hippo* (Oxford).

—— (1934), 'A Vision of Mandaulis Aion', *HTR* 27, 53–104 = *Essays on Religion and the Ancient World* (Oxford, 1972), 1. 357–400.

NOCK, A. D. (1941), 'A Cabiric rite', *AJA* 45, 577–81.

NOHLEN, K., and W. RADT (1978), *Kapikaya: ein Felsheiligtum bei Pergamon.* Altertertümer von Pergamon, XII (Berlin).

NOTH, M. (1930), *Das System der zwölf Stämme Israels* (Stuttgart).

NOY, D. (2000), *Foreigners at Rome: Citizens and Strangers* (London).

O'CONNOR, D. (1969), *Peter in Rome* (London).

OHLENROTH, L. (1954), 'Augusta Vindelicum', *Germania* 32, 76–85.

OLSON, S. D. (ed.) (1998), *Aristophanes* Peace. *Ed. with introd. and comm.* (Oxford)

O'MAHONEY, A. (ed.) (1995), *The Christian Heritage in the Holy Land* (London).

ONIANS, J. (1951), *The Origins of European Thought about the Body, the Mind, the Soul, the World, Time, and Fate: New Interpretations of Greek, Roman and Kindred Evidence also of some Basic Jewish and Christian Beliefs* (Cambridge).

ORIA SEGURA, M. (1996), *Hercules en Hispania: una approximacion* (Barcelona).

ORLANDI, T. (1969), 'Un frammento copto di Teofilo di Alessandria', *Rivista degli Studi Orientali* 44, 23–26.

ORLANDOS, A. (1977), 'Epidauros: Hieron Apollonos Maleata,' *Ergon Archaiologikes Hetaireias*: 98–105.

ORSELLI, A. M. (1999), 'L'idée chrétienne de la ville: Quelques suggestions pour l'antiquité tardive et le haut moyen âge', in Brogiolo and Ward-Perkins (1999), 181–93.

OSANNA, M. (2001), 'Tra monumenti, *agalmata* e *mirabilia*: organizzazione del percorso urbano di Corinto nella *Periegesi* di Pausania', in Knoepfler and Piérart (2001), 185–201.

OSTWALD, M. (1992), 'Athens as a Cultural Centre', in *CAH* 5 (Cambridge), 306–69.

OTTO, W. F. (1965), *Dionysus, Myth and Cult* (Bloomington, Ind.).

OUSTERHOUT, R. G. (ed.) (1990), *The Blessings of Pilgrimage* (Urbana, Ill.).

PAPACHATZES, N. (1974–81), *Pausaniou Ellados Periegesis* (Athens).

PAPACHRISTODOULOU, I. (1999), 'The Rhodian Demes Within the Framework of the Function of the Rhodian State', in V. Gabrielson, *Hellenistic Rhodes: Politics, Culture and Society* (Aarhus), 27–44.

PAPACONSTANTINOU, A. (2001), *Le culte des saints en Égypte des Byzantins aux Abbassides. L'apport des sources papyrologiques et épigraphiques grecques et coptes* (Paris).

PAPADEMETRIOU, I. (1949), 'Le sanctuaire d'Apollon Maléatas', *BCH* 73, 361–83.

PARK, C. (1994), *Sacred Worlds* (London).

PARKE, H. W. (1966), *Oracles of Zeus* (Oxford).

—— (1977), *Festivals of the Athenians* (Ithaca, NY).

PARKE, H. W. (1985), *The Oracles of Apollo in Asia Minor* (London).

—— and D. E. W. WORMELL (1956), *The Delphic Oracle*, 2 vols. 1: *The History*. 2: *The Oracular Responses* (Oxford).

PARKER, R. (1983), *Miasma: Pollution and Purification in Early Greek Religion* (Oxford).

—— (1985), 'Greek States and Greek Oracles', in P. Cartledge and F. Harvey (eds.), *Crux: Essays Presented to G.E.M. de Ste Croix on his 75th Birthday*, History of Political Thought 6 (1985), 298–326. (Reprinted in Buxton (2000), 76–108.)

—— (1996), *Athenian Religion: A History* (Oxford).

PATON, W. R., and E. L. HICKS, (1891), *The Inscriptions of Cos* (Oxford).

PATLAGEAN, E. (1983), 'Ancient Byzantine Hagiography and Social History', in Stephen Wilson (ed.), *Saints and Their Cults* (Cambridge), 101–21.

PEARCE, S. M. (1995), *On Collecting: An Investigation into Collecting in the European Tradition* (London).

PEARCY, L. T. (1988), 'Theme, Dream and Narrative: Reading the *Sacred Tales* of Aelius Aristides', *TAPA* 118, 377–91.

PEEK, W. (1963), 'Fünf Wundergeschichten aus dem Asklepieion von Epidauros', *Abh. Leipzig* 56, 3–9. (Repr. (1977) with Nachtrag in Gerhard Pfohl (ed.), *Inschriften der Griechen: Epigraphische Quellen zur Geschichte der antiken Medizin* (Darmstadt), 66–78.)

PELEKIDES, C. (1962), *Histoire de l'éphébie attique des origines à 31 avant Jésus-Christ* (Paris).

PEÑA, I. (2000), *Lieux de pèlerinage en Syrie* (Milan).

PENGLASE, C. (1994), *Greek Myths and Mesopotamia: Parallels and Influence in the Homeric Hymns and Hesiod* (London).

PENSABENE, P. (1990), 'Il templo di Saturno a Dougga e tradizioni architettoniche d'origine punica', in A. Mastino (ed.) *L'Africa romana: atti del VII convegno di Studio Sassari* (Sassari), 251–93.

PERDRIZET, P., and G. LEFEBVRE (1919), *Les graffites grecs du Memnonion d'Abydos* (Nancy, Paris, and Strasbourg).

PEREZ, G. A. (1991), 'John the Baptist, Saint', *Coptic Encyclopaedia* 5, 1354–7.

PERKINS, J. (1992), 'The "Self" as Sufferer', *Harvard Theological Revue* 85, 245–72.

—— (1995), *The Suffering Self: Pain and Narrative Representation in the Early Christian Era* (London).

PERLMAN, P. (1995), 'Invocatio and imprecatio. The Hymn to the Greatest Kouros from Palaikastro and the Oath in Ancient Crete', *JHS* 115, 161–6.

—— (2000), *City and Sanctuary in Ancient Greece: The Theorodokia in the Peloponnese*. Hypomnemata 121 (Göttingen).

PERPILLOU-THOMAS, F. (1993), *Fêtes d'Egypte Ptoléma'ique et romaine d' après la documentation papyrologique grecque* (Louvain).

PERRONE, L. (1977), 'Vie eligieuse et thédogie en Palestine durant la première phase des controversés christologiques', *Proche-Orient Chrétien* 28, 212–49.

PERRONE, L. (1980), *La Chiesa di Palestina e le controversie cristologiche: Dal concilia di Efeso (431) al secondo concilia di Constantinopoli (553)* (Brescia).

—— (1995), 'Monasticism in the Holy Land: From the Beginnings to the Crusades', *Proche-Orient Chrétien* 45, 31–63.

—— (1998), 'Monasticism as a Factor of Religious Interaction', in Kofsky and Stroumsa 1998, 67–95.

PETER, H. W. G. (1870), *Historicorum Romanorum reliquiae* (Leipzig).

PETERSON, I. V. (1989), *Poems to Śiva: The Hymns of the Tamil Saints* (Princeton).

PETSALIS-DIOMIDIS, A. (2001), ' "Truly beyond miracles": the Body and Healing Pilgrimage in the Eastern Roman Empire in the Second Century AD', doctoral dissertation at the The Courtauld Institute of Art, University of London.

PETZL, G. (1995), 'Ländliche Religiosität in Kleinasien', in H. von Hesberg (ed.), *Was ist eingentlich Provinz. Zur Beschreibung eines Bewusstseins* (Cologne), 173–84.

PFAFFENBERGER, B. (1979), 'The Kataragama Pilgrimage: Hindu-Buddhist Interaction and its Significance in Sri Lanka's Polyethnic Social System', *Journal of Asian Studies* 38(2), 253–70.

PFISTER, F. (1951), *Die Reisebilder des Herakleides. Einleitung, Text* (Vienna).

PHAN, P. C. (1988), *Grace and the Human Condition* (Wilmington, Del.).

PHILIPP, H. (1994), 'Olympia, die Peloponnese und die Westgriechen', *JdI* 109, 77–92.

PHILLIPS, E. D. (1952), 'A Hypochondriac and his God', *G&R* 21, 23–36.

PICCIRILLI, L. (ed.) (1973). *Gli arbitrati interstatali greci. Dalle originial 338 a.C.* (Pisa).

PINCH, G. (1993), *Votive Offerings to Hathor* (Oxford).

PIRENNE-DELFORGE, V. (ed.), (1998*a*), *Les Panthéons des cités: des origines à la Périégèse de Pausanias. Kernos* Suppl. 8 (Liege).

—— (1988*b*), 'La notion de "panthéon" dans la *Périégèse* de Pausanias', in Pirenne-Delforge (1998*a*), 129–48.

POLANSKI, T. (1998*a*), *Oriental Art in Greek Imperial Literature* (Trier).

—— (1998*b*), 'Is it or is it not Lucian's? An Art Historian's Supplement to the Controversy over the Authorship of the "Syrian Goddess" ', *Polska Akademia Umiejętności: Prace Komisji Filologii Klasycznej* 27, 161–84

POLLACK-ELTZ, A. (1991), 'Pilgrimages to Sorte in the Cult of María Lioniza in Venezuela', in Crumrine and Morinis (1991), 205–15.

POMTOW, H. (1899), 'Delphische Inschriften', *Philologus* 58, 52–76.

Popko, M. (1994), *Zippalanda: ein Kultzentrum im hethitischen Kleinasien. TH* 21 (Heidelberg).

—— (1999), 'Berg als Ritualschauplatz. Ein Beitrag zur Kenntnis der hethitischen Religion', *Hethitica* 14, 97–108.

Pouilloux, J. (1952), 'Promanties collectives et protocole Delphique', *BCH* 76, 484–513.

—— (1974), 'Les décrets Delphiques pour Matrophanes de Sardes', *BCH* 98, 159–69.

Prandi, L. (1989). 'La rifondazione del "Panionion" e la catastrofe di Elice (373 a. C.)', in M. Sordi, (ed.) *Fenomeni naturali e avvenimenti storici nell' antichità.* Contributi dell' Istituto di storia antica 15. Università Cattolica del Sacro Cuore Scienze storiche. 44 (Milan), 43–59.

Pratt, M. L. (1992), *Imperial Eyes: Travel Writing and Transculturation* (London).

Preston, J. J. (1992), 'Spiritual Magnetism: An Organizing Principle for the Study of Pilgrimage', in Morinis (1992), 31–46.

Price, S. R. F. (1999), *Religions of the Ancient Greeks* (Cambridge).

Pritchard, J. B. (ed.) (1955), *Ancient Near Eastern Texts Relating to the Old Testament,* 2 vols., 2nd edn. (Princeton).

Pritchett, W. K. (1998), *Pausanias Periegetes I* (Amsterdam).

—— (1999), *Pausanias Periegetes II* (Amsterdam).

Prost, F. (2001), 'Sparte et les Cyclades au Ve siècle: à propos d' ID 87', *REA* 103, 241–60.

Pryor, J. H. (1988), *Geography, technology, and war: studies in the maritime history of the Mediterranean, 649–1571* (Cambridge).

Pullan, W. (1993), 'Mapping Time and Salvation: Early Christian Pilgrimage to Jerusalem', in G. D. Flood (ed.), *Mapping Invisible Worlds* (Edinburgh), 23–40.

—— (1997–8), 'Jerusalem from Alpha to Omega in the Santa Pudenziana Mosaic', in *The Real and Ideal Jerusalem in Jewish, Christian and Islamic Art. Jewish Art* 23/4, 405–17.

—— (2000), ' "Ascent and Descent" in the Constantinian Church of the Nativity in Bethlehem', in S. G. Wilson and M. Desjardins (eds.), *Text and Artifact in the Religions of Mediterranean Antiquity. Essays in Honour of Peter Richardson* (Waterloo), 308–21.

Puttkammer, F. (1912), *Quo modo Graeci victimarum carnes distribuerint* (Diss. Königsberg).

Quet, M.-H. (1993), 'Parler de soi pour louer son dieu: le cas d'Aelius Aristide (du journal intime de ses nuits aux *Discours Sacrés* en l' honneur du dieu Asklépios)' in M.-F. Baslez, Ph. Hoffmann, and L. Pernot (eds.), *L'invention de l'autobiographie d'Hésiode à saint Augustin* (Paris), 211–51.

RAAFLAUB, K. (1986), 'Grundzüge, Ziele und Ideen der Opposition gegen die Kaiser im 1. Jh. n. Chr.', *Opposition et Résistances à l'émpire d'Auguste à Trajan* 33, 1–55.

RADT, W. (1988), *Pergamon: Geschichte und Bauten, Funde und Erforschung einer antiken Metropole* (Cologne).

—— (1999). *Pergamon: Geschichte und Bauten einer Antiken Metropole* (Darmstadt).

RAGONE, G. (1986), 'La guerra meliaca e la struttura originaria della lega ionica in Vitruvio 4, 1, 3–6', *RFIC* 104, 173–205.

—— (1996), 'La Ionia, Asia Minore, Cipro', in S. Settis (ed.), *I Greci. Storia, cultura, arte, societa. I. Una storia greca. 1. Formazione* (Torino), 903–43.

RAHNER, K. (1990), 'Grace as the Heart of Human Existence', in P. Imhof and H. Biallowans (eds.), *Faith in a Wintry Season*, (New York).

RAPHAËL, F. et al. (1973), *Les pèlerinages de l'antiquité biblique et classique à l'occident médiéval*. Etudes d'Histoire des Religions 1 (Paris), 33–53.

RAUBITSCHEK, A. E. (1946), 'Octavia's Deification at Athens', *TAPA* 77, 146–50.

RAUSCH, H. (1982), *Theōria: Von ihrer sakralen zur philosophischen Bedeutung* (Munich).

RAY, J. D. (1976), *The Archive of Hor* (London).

REARDON, B. P. (1971), *Courants littéraires grecs des IIe et IIIe siêcles après J.-C* (Paris).

REDFIELD, J. (2003), *The Locrian Maidens: Love and Death in Greek Italy* (Princeton).

REGENBOGEN, O. (1956), 'Pausanias', *RE* Suppl. 8 (Stuttgart), 1008–97.

REHM, A. (1940), '$MNH\Sigma\Theta H$', *Philologus* 94, 1 ff.

REMUS, H. (1983), *Pagan–Christian Conflict over Miracle in the Second Century* (Cambridge, Mass.).

—— (1996), 'Voluntary Association and Networks. Aelius Aristides at the Asclepieion in Pergamum', in J. S. Kloppenborg and S. G. Wilson (eds.), *Voluntary Associations in the Graeco-Roman World* (London), 146–75.

RENOUX, A. (1961), 'Un manuscrit du lectionnaire arménien de Jérusalem (cod. Jérus. arm. 121)', *Le Muséon* 74, 361–85.

—— (1963), 'Liturgie de Jérusalem et lectionnaires arméniens. Vigiles et année liturgique', in Mgr. Cassien and B. Botte (eds.), *La prière des heures*. Lex Orandi 35 (Paris), 167–200.

—— (1969, 1971), *Le codex arménien Jérusalem 121*, 2 vols., Patrologia Orientalis 35 and 36 (Turnhout).

RENOUX, C. (1977), 'Les ministres du culte à Jérusalem au IVe et au Ve siécles', in *L'assemblée liturgique et diffoérents rôles dans l'assemblée*. Conférences Saint-Serge, 1976 (Rome), 253–67.

RENOUX, C. (1984), 'La lecture biblique dans la liturgie de Jérusalem', in C. Mondésert (ed.), *Le monde grec ancien et la Bible* (Paris), 399–420.

REY-COQUAIS, J.-P. (1974), *Arados et sa pérée aux époques grecque, romaine et byzantine: recueil des témoignages littéraires anciens, suivi de recherches sur les sites, l'histoire, la civilisation* (Paris).

REYMOND, E. A. E., and J. W. B. BARNS, (1973), *Four Martyrdoms from the Pierpont Morgan Coptic Codices* (Oxford).

RIEDWEG, C. (1987), *Mysterienterminologie bei Platon, Philo, und Klemens von Alexandria* (Berlin).

RIGSBY, K. J. (1996), *Asylia. Territorial Inviolability in the Hellenistic World* (California).

ROBB, K. (1994), *Literacy and Paideia in Ancient Greece* (Oxford).

ROBERT, C. (1909), *Pausanias als Schriftsteller* (Berlin).

ROBERT, J., and L. ROBERT (1964), 'Bulletin épigraphique', *REG* 77, 127–259.

ROBERT, L. (1937), *Études Anatoliennes* (Paris).

ROBERTSON SMITH, W. (1927), *Lectures on the Religion of the Semites*, 3rd edn. (London).

ROEBUCK, C. (1955), 'The Early Ionian League', *CPh* 50, 26–40.

ROGERS, G. (1991), *The Sacred Identity of Ephesus* (London).

ROLLER, L. E. (1999), *In Search of God the Mother: The Cult of Anatolian Cybele* (Berkeley).

ROMANO, D. G. (1993), 'Post 146 B.C. Land Use in Corinth, and Planning of the Roman Colony of 44 B.C.', in T. E. Gregory (ed.), *The Corinthia in the Roman Period*. JRA Suppl. 8 (Ann Arbor), 9–30.

ROMM, J. S. (1992), *The Edges of the Earth in Ancient Thought* (Princeton).

ROSE, G. (1993), *Feminism and Geography: The Limits of Geographical Knowledge* (Minneapolis).

ROUSSEL, P. *Les cultes égyptiens à Délos du IIIe au Ier siècle av. J.-C.* (Nancy, 1916).

ROUX, G. (1958), *Pausanias en Corinthie (Livre II, 1 à 15): texte, traduction, commentaire archéologique et topographique* (Paris).

—— (1979), *L'Amphictionie, Delphes et le temple d'Apollon au IVe siècle* (Lyons).

—— (1990), 'Une querelle de préséance à Delphes: les promanties des Tarentins et des Thouriens', *ZPE* 80, 23–9.

ROWE, A. (1957), 'The Great Serapeum of Alexandria, Part 1: The Archaeological Evidence', *Bulletin of the John Rylands Library* 39(2), 485–521.

ROWE, C. J., (1993), *Plato* Phaedo (Cambridge).

ROWLAND, C. (1982), *The Open Heaven* (London).

—— (1985), *Christian Origins* (London).

RUBENSOHN, O. (1892), *Die Mysterienheiligtümer in Eleusis und Samothrake* (Berlin)

RUBENSON, S. (1995) 'The Egyptian Relations of Early Palestinian Monasticism' in O'Mahoney (1995) 35–46.

RUBIN, Z. (1998), 'Porphyrius of Gaza and the Conflict between Christianity and Paganism in Southern Palestine', in Kofsky and Stroumsa (1998), 31–66.

—— (1999), 'The Cult of the Holy Places and Christian Politics in Byzantine Jerusalem' in Levine 1999, 151–62.

RUNCIMAN, S. (1951), *A History of the Crusades* (Cambridge).

RUSSELL, D. A. (1990), 'Aelius Aristides and the Prose Hymn', in D. A. Russell (ed.), *Antonine Literature* (Oxford), 199–221

RUTGERS, L. V. (1995), *The Jews of Late Ancient Rome* (Leiden).

RUTHERFORD, I. C. (1995), 'Theoric Crisis. The Dangers of Pilgrimage in Greek Religion and Society', *SMSR* 61, 176–192.

—— (1998*a*), *Canons of Style in the Antonine Age: Idea-Theory in its Literary Context* (Oxford).

—— (1998*b*), 'Theoria as Theatre: The Pilgrimage Theme in Greek Drama', *PLLS* 10, 131–56.

—— (1998*c*), 'The Island at the Edge. Space, Language and Power in the Pilgrimages Traditions of Philai' in Frankfurter (1998*b*), 229–56.

—— (1999), '*To the land of Zeus* . . . : Patterns of pilgrimage in Aelius Aristides', *Aevum Antiquum* 12, 133–48.

—— (2000*a*), 'Theoria and Darśan: Pilgrimage and Vision in Greece and India', *CQ* 50, 133–46.

—— (2000*b*), 'Pilgerschaft', in *DNP* 9, 1014–19.

—— (2001*a*), 'Tourism and the Sacred: Pausanias and the Traditions of Greek Pilgrimage', in Alcock et al. 2001, 40–52.

—— (2001*b*), *Pindar's Paeans* (Oxford).

—— (2002), 'Theoria', in *DNP* 12/1, 398–99.

—— (2003), 'Pilgrimage in Greco-Roman Egypt: New Perspectives on Graffiti from the Memnonion at Abydos', in R. Matthews and C. Roemer (eds.), *Ancient Perspectives on Egypt* (London), 171–90.

—— (2004*a*), ' "Χορὸς εἰς ἐκ τῆσδε τῆς πόλεως" (Xen. *Mem.* 3.3.12): Song-Dance and State-Pilgrimage at Athens', in Wilson and Murray (2004), 67–90.

—— (2004*b*), 'Theoria and the Olympic Games. A Neglected Aspect if Ancient Athletics', in M. A. Kaila, G. Thill, H. Theodoropoulou, and Y. Xanthacou (eds.), *Hue Kue. Oi Olumpakoi Agones sten Arkhaioteta. The Olympic Games in Antiquity. Bring Forth Rain and Bear Fruit* (Athens 2004), 171–83.

—— (2005) 'In a Virtual Wild Space. Pilgrimage and Rite de Passage from Delphi to Sabarimalai', in D. Yatromanolakis and P. Roilos (eds.) *Ritual Poetics* (Cambridge, Mass.).

RUTHERFORD, I. C. (2006), 'Black Sails to Achilles...', in J. Elsner and E. Bowie (eds.), *Philostratus* (Cambridge).

—— (forthcoming *a*), 'The Dance of Wolfmen of Aukuwa. Networks, Amphlictionies, and Pilgrimage in Hittite Religion', Proceedings of the 5th Hittite International Congress

—— (forthcoming *b*), 'An Ancient Symbol for Pilgrimage: The Palm Sign and its Meaning', forthcoming in Proceedings of the Conference: 'Pilgrimage. Jerusalem, Rome, San Diego', Cork, July 2000.

SADEK, A. I. (1987), *Popular Religion in Egypt during the New Kingdom*. Hildesheimer Ägyptologische Beiträge 27 (Hildesheim).

SAGHY, M. (2000), ' "Scinditur in partes populus": Pope Damasus and the Martyrs of Rome', *Early Medieval Europe* 9, 273–87.

SAID, S. (ed.) (1991), *Ellenismos. Quelques jalons pour une histoire de l'identité grecque. Acts du colloque de Strasbourg 25.27 octobre 1989* (Leiden).

SAKELLARIOU, M. B. (1958), *La migration grecque en Ionie. Centre d'études d'Asie Mineure* [Collection] 10 Ionie, 1 (Athens).

Samothrace. Excavations Conducted by the Institute of Fine Arts of New York University, 1 (Princeton) 1958– .

SALLNOW, M. J. (1981), '*Communitas* Revisited: The Sociology of Andean Pilgrimage', *Man* 16, 163–182.

—— (1987), *Pilgrims of the Andes: Regional Cults in Cusco* (Washington, DC).

SALOMON, R. (ed. and tr.) (1985), *The Bridge to the Three Holy Cities: The* Sāmānya-praghaṭṭaka *of Nārāyaṇa Bhaṭṭa's* Tristhalīsetu (Delhi).

SÀNCHEZ, P. (2001), *L'Amphictionie des Pyles et de Delphes. Recherches sur son rôle historique, des origines au IIe siècle de notre ère*. Historia Einzelschrift 148 (Stuttgart).

SANSONE, D. (1988), *Greek Athletics and the Genesis of Sport* (London).

SANTANIELLO, C. (1996), 'Aspetti della demonologia plutarchea: Tra il "De defectu oraculorum" e altri scritti del corpus', in Gallo 1996, 357–71.

SATRAN, D. (1995), *Biblical Prophets in Byzantine Palestine: Reassessing the* Lives of the Prophets. SVTP 11 (Leiden).

SAUNERON, S. (1962), *Les fêtes religieuses d' Esna aux derniers siècles du paganisme* (Cairon).

—— (1964), 'Villes et légendes d' Égypte', *BIFAO* 62, 33–57

SAYED, R. (1982), *La diesse Neith de Sais*. Bibliothèque d'Étude 86 (Cairo).

SCHACHTER A. (1981–), *Cults of Boeotia*. BICS Suppl. 38 (London).

SCHEID, J. (2000), 'Réflexions sur la notion de lieue de culte dans les Gaules romaines' in W. van Andringa (ed.), *Archéologie des sanctuaires en Gaule romaine* (Saint-Étienne), 19–26.

SCHEPEN, G., and K. DELCROIX (1996), 'Ancient Paradoxography: Origins, Evolution, Production and Reception', in O. Pecere and A. Stramaglia (eds.),

La letteratura di consumo nel mondo greco-latino : atti del convegno internazionale, Cassino, 14–17 settembre 1994 (Cassino), 373–460.

SCHLATTER, F. (1992), 'Interpreting the Mosaics of Sta Pudenziana', *Vigiliae Christianae* 46, 276–95.

SCHMITZ, T. (1997), *Bildung und Macht. Zur sozialen und politischen Funktion der Zweiten Sophistik in der griechischen Welt der Kaiserzeit* (Munich).

SCHNEIDER, W. (1997), 'Ein kryptisches Denkmal im Zentrum der Pausanias-Perihegese', *Hermes* 125, 492–505.

SCHOLTEN, J. B. (2000), *The Politics of Plunder: Aitolians and their Koinon in the Early Hellenistic Era, 279–217 B.C.* (Berkeley).

SCHRÖDER, S. (1999), *Geschichte und Theorie der Gattung Paian. Beiträge zur Altertumskunde* (Stuttgart and Leipzig).

SCHULTEN, A. (1984), *Tartessos*, 3rd edn. (Madrid).

SCOTT, K. (1928), 'The Deification of Demetrius Poliorcetes', *AJP* 49, 137–66, 217–39

SCRANTON, R. L. (1951), *Corinth I.iii: Monuments in the Lower Agora and North of the Archaic Temple* (Princeton).

SCULLION, S. (2001), 'Three Notes on Inscriptions', *ZPE* 134, 116–20.

SELDEN, D. (1998), 'Alibis', *Classical Antiquity* 17, 289–412.

SEYRIG, H. (1971), 'Le monnayage de Hiérapolis de Syrie à l'époque d'Alexandre', *RN* 13, 11–21.

SFAMENI GASPARRO, G. (1996), 'Plutarco e la religione delfica: il dio "filosofo" e il suo esegeta', in Gallo (1996), 157–88.

—— (1998), 'Elio Aristide e Asclepio, un retore e il suo dio: salute del corpo e direzione spirituale', in E. Dal Covolo and I. Giannetto (eds.), *Cultura e promozione umana. La cura del corpo e dello spirito nell'antichità classica e nei primi secoli cristiani. Un magistero ancora attuale? Convegno internazionale di studi Oasi 'Maria Santissima' di Troina, 29 ott.–1 nov. 1997* (Troina EN), 123–43.

SHAHID, I. (1998), 'Arab Christian Pilgrimages in the Proto-Byzantine Period', in Frankfurter (1998*b*), 373–89.

SHIPLEY, G. (1987), *A History of Samos, 800–188 BC* (Oxford).

—— and JOHN SALMON, (eds.) (1996), *Human Landscapes in Classical Antiquity: Environment and Culture* (London).

SHIRANE, H. (1998), *Traces of Dreams: Landscape, Cultural Memory, and the Poetry* (Stanford).

SIDEBOTHAM, S. (1986), *Roman Economic Policy in the Erythra Thalassa 30 BC–AD 217* (Leiden).

SIDWELL, K. (1996), 'Purification and Pollution in Aeschylus' *Eumenides*', *CQ* 46, 44–57.

SIEBERT, G. (1973), 'La Grèce antique', in F. Raphaël et al. 1973, 33–53.

SIEGEL, J. P. (1975), *The Severus Scroll and 1QIsa* (Missoula, Mont.).

SIIKALA, A.-L. (1987), 'Siberian and Inner-Asian Shamanism', *Encyclopedia of Religion* 13, 208–15.

SIMON, M. (1973), 'Les pèlerinages dans l'antiqité chrétienne', in Raphael et al. 1973, 95–115.

SINGH, R. L., and R. P. B. SINGH (eds.) (1987), *Trends in the Geography of Pilgrimages: Homage to David E. Sopher* (Varanasi).

SINN, U. (1993), 'Greek Sanctuaries as Places of Refuge', in N. Marinatos and R. Hägg (eds.), *Greek Sanctuaries: New Approaches* (London), 88–109. (Repr. in Buxton 2000, 155–79.)

SIVAN, H. (1988*a*), 'Holy Land Pilgrimage and Western Audiences: Some Reflections on Egeria and her Circle', *CQ* 38, 528–35.

—— (1988*b*), 'Who Was Egeria? Piety and Pilgrimage in the Age of Gratian', *HThR* 81, 59–72.

SLATER, C. (1991), 'The Literature of Pilgrimage: Present-Day Miracle Stories from Northeast Brazil', in Crumrine and Morinis 1991, 175–205.

SMITH, J. A. (1999), 'Sacred Journeyings: Women's Correspondence and Pilgrimage in the Fourth and Eighth Centuries', in J. Stopford (ed.) *Pilgrimage Explored* (Woodbridge), 41–56.

SMITH, R. R. R. (1998), 'Cultural Choice and Political Identity in Honorific Portrait Statues from the Greek East in the second century A.D.', *JRS* 88, 56–93.

SMITH, J. Z. (1987), *To Take Place: Toward Theory in Ritual* (Chicago).

—— (1990), *Drudgery Divine* (London).

SNODGRASS, A. M. (1986), 'Interaction by Design: the Greek City State', in C. Renfrew and J. Cherry (eds.), *Peer Polity Interaction and Sociopolitical Change* (Cambridge), 47–58.

—— (2001) 'Pausanias and the Chest of Kypselos', in Alcock et al. 2001, 127–41.

SNYDER, G. F. (1985), *Ante Pacem* (Macon).

SOKOLOWSKI, F. (1965), 'A New testimony of the Cult of Artemis at Ephesus', *HThR* 58, 427 ff.

—— (1969), *Lois sacrées des cités grecques* (Paris).

—— (1970), 'Réglement relatif à la célébration des Panionia', *BCH* 94, 109–112.

—— (1974), 'Propagation of the Cult of Sarapis and Isis in Greece', *GRBS* 15, 441–8.

SOLIGNAC, A. A. (1983), 'Pèlerinages', *Dictionnaire de Spiritualité*, 12/1, (Paris), cols. 888–940.

SOLIN, H. (1983), 'Juden und Syrer im westlichen Teil der römischen Welt', *ANRW* II.29.2, 587–789.

SOMMERSTEIN, A. H. (1985), *Aristophanes' Peace*. Ed. with tr. and notes (Warminster).

SONTAG, S. (1991), *Illness as Metaphor* and *Aids and Its Metaphors* (London).

SOPHER, D. E. (1968), 'Pilgrim Circulation in Gujarat', *Geographical Review* 58, 392–425.

SOSKICE, J. M. (1989), *Metaphor and Religious Language* (Oxford).

SOURDILLE, C. (1910), *Hérodote et la religion d'Égypte* (Paris).

SOURVINOU-INWOOD, C. (1990), 'What is *Polis* Religion?' in O. Murray and S. Price (eds.), *The Greek City from Homer to Alexander* (Oxford), 295–322. (Repr. in Buxton 2000, 13–37.)

—— (1995), *Reading Greek Death: To the End of the Classical Period* (Oxford).

SPAWFORTH, A. (1999), 'The Panhellenion Again', *Chiron* 29, 339–52.

—— and S. WALKER, (1985), 'The World of the Panhellenion I. Athens and Eleusis', *JRS* 75, 78–104.

—— —— (1986), 'The World of the Panhellenion II: three Dorian cities', *JRS* 76, 88–105.

STEINSAPIR, A. I. (1999), 'Landscape and the Sacred: The Sanctuary dedicated to Holy, Heavenly Zeus Baetocaece', *Near Eastern Archaeology* 62(3): 182–94.

STEPHENS, S. (1998), 'Callimachus at Court', in M. A. Harder, R. F. Regtuit, and G. C. Wakker (eds.), *Genre in Hellenistic Poetry* (Groningen), 167–85.

STILLWELL, R., R. L. SCRANTON, and S. E. FREEMAN (1941), *Corinth I.ii: Architecture*. (Cambridge, Mass.).

STODDARD, R., and A. MORINIS (eds.) (1997), *Sacred Places, Sacred Spaces: The Geography of Pilgrimage* (Baton Rouge, La.).

STRACK, P. L. (1931), *Untersuchungen zur römischen Reichsprägung des 2 Jahrhundrets*, 2 vols. (Stuttgart).

SWAIN, S. (1996), *Hellenism and Empire: Language, Classicism, and Power in the Greek World*, AD 50–250 (Oxford).

—— (1999), 'Defending Hellenism: Philostratus, *In Honour of Apollonius*', in Edwards, Goodman, and Price 1999, 157–96.

SYME, R. (1958), *Tacitus* (Oxford).

—— (1969), 'Pliny the Procurator', *Harvard Studies in Classical Philology*, 73, 201–36.

—— (1977), 'The March of Mucianus', *Antichthon* 11 (1977) 78–92.

SZLEZÁK, T. A. (1999), *Reading Plato* (London).

TACHEVA-HITOVA, M. (1983), *Eastern Cults in Moesia Inferior and Thrace* (Leiden).

TAKÁCS, S. A. (1994), 'The Magic of Isis Replaced or Cyril of Alexandria's Attempt to Redirect Religious Devotion', Varia 5 *Poikila Byzantina* 13, 491–507.

TAKÁCS, S. A. (1995), *Isis and Sarapis in the Roman World* (Leiden).

TALBOT, A. M. (2002), 'Pilgrimage to Healing Shrines: The Evidence of Miracle Accounts', *DOP* 56, 153–73.

TAMBIAH, S. (1981), *A Performative Approach to Ritual*. Radcliffe Brown Lectures in Social Anthropology (Oxford).

TAM TINH, T. (1990), 'Isis', *LIMC* 5.1 (Zurich and Munich), 761–96.

TAUSEND, K. (1992), *Amphiktyonie und Symmachie. Formen zwischenstaatlicher Beziehungen im archaischen Griechenland*. Historia, Einzelschriften 73 (Stuttgart).

TAYLOR, J. E. (1993), *Christians and the Holy Places* (Oxford).

TELFER, W. (1957), 'Constantine's Holy Land Plan', *Studia Patristica* 1, 696–700.

THEILER, W. (1982), *Poseidonios: die Fragmente*. Texte und Kommentare 10 (Berlin and New York).

THEISSEN, G., and J. RICHES, (1983), *The Miracle Stories of the Early Christian Tradition* (Edinburgh).

THELAMON, F. (1981), *Païens et chrétiens au IVe siècle: L'apport de l''Histoire ecclésiastique' de Rufin d'Aquilée* (Paris).

THOMAS, R. (1992), *Literacy and Orality in Ancient Greece* (Cambridge).

—— (2000), *Herodotus in Context: Ethnography, Science, and the Art of Persuasion* (Cambridge).

THOMPSON, D. J. (1988), *Memphis under the Ptolemies* (Princeton).

THOMPSON H. A., and R. E. WYCHERLEY (1972) *The Athenian Agora XIV: The Agora of Athens: The History, Shape and Uses of an Ancient City Center* (Princeton).

THOMSON, R. W. (1985), 'Jerusalem and Armenia', *Studia Patristica* 18, 77–91.

THOUVENOT, R. (1940), *L'Essai sur la province de Bétique* (Paris).

TIMBIE, J. (1998), 'A Liturgical Procession in the Desert of Apa Shenoute', in Frankfurter 1998*b*, 415–41.

TKACZ, C. (2002), *The Key to the Brescia Casket* (Notre Dame, Ind.).

TOBIN, J. (1997), *Herodes Attikos and the City of Athens. Patronage and Conflict under the Antonines* (Amsterdam).

TÖRÖK, L. (1978), 'Two Meroitic Studies. The Meroitic Chamber in Philae and the Administration of Nubia in the 1st–3rd Centuries AD', *Oikoumene* 2, 217–37.

TOLMAN, E. C. (1948), 'Cognitive Maps in Rats and Men', *Psychological Review* 55, 189–208.

TOMLINSON, R. A. (1976), *Greek Sanctuaries* (London).

TORELLI, M. (2001), 'Pausania a Corinto. Un intelletuale greco del secondo secolo e la propaganda imperiale romana', in Knoepfler and Piérart 2001, 135–84.

Totti, M. (1985), *Ausgewählte Texte der Isis-und Sarapis-Religion* (Hildesheim).

Toutain, J. (1917), *Les cultes païens dans l'empire romain* (Paris).

Traiana, G. (1987), 'Il mondo di C. Licinio Muciano', *Athenaeum* 65, 379–406.

Travlos, J. (1988), *Bildlexikon zur Topographie des antiken Attika* (Tübingen).

Tréhaux, J. (1951–3), 'La réalité historique des offrandes hyperboréennes', in *Studies Presented to David Moore Robinson* on *his Seventieth Birthday* (Saint Louis), 2. 758–74.

Tsirkin, J. (1981), 'The Labours, Death, and Resurrection of Melqart as depicted on the gates of the Gades Herakleion', *Rivista di studi fenici* 9, 21–7.

Turcan, R. (1996), *The Cults of the Roman Empire* (Oxford).

Turner, V. (1969), *The Ritual Process: Structure and anti-Structure* (London).

—— (1973), 'The Center Out There: Pilgrim's Goal', *History of Religions* 12, 191–230.

—— (1974*a*), 'Pilgrimage and Communitas', *Studia Missionalia* 23, 305–27.

—— (1974*b*), *Dramas, Fields and Metaphors: symbolic action in human society* (Ithaca-London).

—— (1974*c*). 'Pilgrimage and Social Processes', in id. 1974*b*, 166–230.

—— (1982). *From Ritual to Theatre: The Human Seriousness of Play.* Performance studies series 1 (New York).

—— and E. Turner, (1978), *Image and Pilgrimage in Christian Culture: Anthropological Perspectives* (New York).

Tweed, T. (1997), *Our Lady of the Exile: Diasporic Religion at a Cuban Catholic Shrine in Miami* (New York).

Vallois, R. (1931), 'Les strophes mutilées du péan de Philodamos,' *BCH* 55, 241–365.

Vandebeek, G. (1946), *De Interpretatio Graeca van de Isisfiguur.* Studia Hellenistica 4 (Löwen).

Van den Hout, T. P. J. (1991), 'A Tale of Tissaruli(ya): A Dramatic Interlude in the Hittite KI.LAM Festival', *Journal of Near Eastern Studies* 50, 193–202.

Van Dam, R. (1985), *Leadership and Community in Late Antique Gaul* (Berkeley).

Van der Vliet, J. (1991), 'Varia magica coptica', *Aegyptus* 71, 217–42.

Vandoni, M. (1964), *Feste pubbliche e private nei documenti greci* (Milan).

Van Esbroeck, M. (1991), 'Three Hebrews in the Furnace', *Coptic Encyclopaedia* 7, 2257–9.

Van Loon, G. J. M. (1999), *The Gate of Heaven: Wall Paintings with Old Testament Scenes in the Altar Room with the Hurus of Coptic Churches* (Istanbul).

Van Oort, J. (1991), *Jerusalem and Babylon: A Study of Augustine's* City of God *and the Sources of his Doctrine of Two Cities* (Leiden).

Van Straten, F. (1992), 'Votives and Votaries in Greek Sanctuaries', in J. Bingen and A. Schachter (eds.), *Le sanctuaire Grec*. Entretiens sur l'Antiquité classique 37 (Geneva) 247–85.

Vernant, J.-P. (1991*a*), *Mortals and Immortals* (Princeton).

—— (1991*b*), 'Psuche: Similacrum of the Body or Image of the Divine?' in Vernant (1991*a*), 186–92.

Veyne, P. (1988), *Did the Greeks Believe in their Myths?* (Chicago).

—— (1990), *Bread and Circuses: Historical Sociology and Political Pluralism* (London).

Vidman, L. (1969), *Sylloge Inscriptionum Religionis Isiacae et Sarapiacae*. RGVV 28 (Berlin).

Vikan, G. (1982), *Byzantine Pilgrimage Art* (Washington, DC).

—— (1984), 'Art, Medicine and Magic in Early Byzantium', *DOP* 38, 65–86.

—— (1990), 'Pilgrims in Magi's Clothing: The Impact of Mimesis on Early Byzantine Pilgrimage Art' in Ousterhout 1990, 97–107.

—— (2003), *Sacred Images and Sacred Power in Byzantium* (Aldershot).

Vollgraff, G. (1927), 'Le péan delphique à Dionysos,' *BCH* 51, 423–66.

Volokhine, Y. (1998), 'Les déplacements pieux en Égypte pharaonique. Sites et pratiques cultuelles', in Frankfurter 1998*b*, 51–97.

Vreeland, J. (1991), 'A Pilgrimage Fiesta: Easter Week Ritual at Catacaos, Piura, Peru', in Crumrine and Morinis 1991, 229–56.

Wagner, G. (1983), 'Une nouvelle dédicace à Bubastis', *ASAE* 69, 247–252.

—— (1996), 'Les inscriptions grecques d'Aïn Labakha (steles—graffites—depinti)', *ZPE* 111, 97–114.

Walbank, M. (1989), 'Pausanias, Octavia and Temple E at Corinth', *BSA* 84, 361–94.

—— (1996), 'Evidence for the Imperial Cult in Julio-Claudian Corinth', in A. M. Small (ed.), *Subject and Ruler: The Cult of the Ruling Power in Antiquity*. JRA suppl. 17 (Ann Arbor), 201–12.

—— (1997), 'The Foundation and Planning of Early Roman Corinth', *JRA* 10, 95–130.

Walker, P. W. L. (1990), *Holy City, Holy Places? Christian Attitudes to Jerusalem and the Holy Land in the Fourth Century* (Oxford).

Walker, S., and A. Cameron, (eds.) (1989), *The Greek Renaissance in the Roman Empire* (London).

Wallace, R. W. (1997), 'Poet, Public, and "Theatrocracy": Audience Performance in Classical Athens', in L. Edmunds and R. W. Wallace (eds.), *Poet, Public, and Performance in Ancient Greece* (Baltimore), 97–111.

Walters, C. C. (1974), *Monastic Archaeology in Egypt* (Warminster).

WARD-PERKINS, J. B. (1994), *Roman Imperial Architecture* (New Haven).

WATKINS, C. (1995), *How to Kill a Dragon* (Oxford).

WEBER, M. (1925), *Wirtschaft und Gesellschaft* (Tübingen).

WEBSTER, J., and N. J. COOPER, (eds.) (1996), *Roman Imperialism: Post-colonial Perspectives* (Leicester).

WEINREICH, O. (1909), *Antike Heilungswunder: Untersuchungen zum Wunderglauben der Griechen und Römer*. Religions-geschichtliche Versuche und Vorarbeiten 8.1 (Giessen).

WEISEMAN, Z. (1992), 'Israel's Ancient Amphictiony—History or Utopia', *Bulletin of the Middle Eastern Culture Center in Japan* 6, 105–120.

WEISS, C. (1998), 'Literary Turns: the Representation of Conversion in Aelius Aristides' *Hieroi Logoi* and in Apuleius' *Metamorphoses*' (Yale University, Ph.D. 1998).

WEITZMANN, K. (1974), 'Loca Sancta and the Representational Arts of Palestine', *DOP* 28, 33–55.

—— (1976), *The Monastery of St Catherine at Mount Sinai: The Icons*. vol. 1 (Princeton).

WELLES, C. B. (1934). *Royal Correspondence in the Hellenistic Period* (New Haven).

WELLESLEY, K. (1975), *Long Year: A.D. 69* (London).

WELLHAUSEN, J. (1897), *Reste arabischen Heidentums*, 2nd edn. (Berlin).

WEST, M. L. (1965). 'The Dictaean hymn to the Kouros', *JHS* 85, 149–59.

—— (1997), *The East Face of Helicon: West Asiatic Elements in Greek Poetry and Myth* (Oxford).

WESTENHOLZ, J. (ed.) (1995), *The Jewish Presence in Ancient Rome* (Jerusalem).

WESTERMANN, A. et al. (1963), Aristotle, Antigonus, Apollonius, Phlegon o. T. and Psellus, M. (*Paradoxographoi [romanized]* = *Scriptores rerum mirabilium Graeci: insunt (Aristotelis) Mirabiles auscultationes, Antigoni, Apollonii, Phlegontis Historiae mirabiles, Michaelis Pselli Lectiones mirabiles, reliquorum eiusdem generis scriptorum deperditorum fragmenta: accedunt Phlegontis Macrobii et Olympiadum reliquiae et anonymi Tractatus de mulieribus, etc.* (Amsterdam).

WESTRA, H. J. (1995), 'The Pilgrim Egeria's Concept of Place', *Mittellateinisches Jahrbuch*. 30, 93–100.

WESTREM, S. D. (ed.) (1991), *Discovering New Worlds: Essays on Medieval Exploration and Imagination* (New York).

WHITE, L. M. (1992), *Building God's House in the Roman World Architectural Adaptation among Pagans, Jews, and Christians* (Baltimore and London).

WHITMARSH, T. (2001), *Greek Literature and the Roman Empire: The Politics of Imitation* (Oxford).

WILAMOVITZ -MOELLENDORF, U. v. (1886), *Isyllos von Epidauros* (Berlin).

—— (1906/1937). 'Panionium', Sitzungsberichte der Königlich Preussischen Akademie der Wissenschaften, 3 (1906). Sitzung der philosophisch-historischen Classe vom 18. Januar, 38–57; Repr. in Kleine Schriften V.1 (1937), 128–51.

—— (1921), *Griechische Verskunst* (Berlin).

WILCKEN, U. (1927), *Urkunden der Ptolemäerzeit (Altere Funde). 1. Papyri aus Unterägypten* (Berlin).

WILD, R. A. (1981), *Water in the Cultic Worship of Isis and Sarapis. EPRO* 87 (Leiden).

WILFONG, T. G. (1998), 'The Non-Muslim Communities: Christian Communities', in Carl F. Petry (ed.), *Cambridge History of Egypt* (Cambridge) 1.175–97.

WILKEN, R. L. (1992), *The Land Called Holy: Palestine in Christian History and Thought* (New Haven and London).

WILKINSON, J. (1971), *Egeria's Travels* (London).

—— (1976), 'Christian Pilgrims in Jerusalem during the Byzantine Period', *Palestine Exploration Quarterly*, 108, 75–101.

—— (1977), *Jerusalem Pilgrims Before the Crusades* (Jerusalem and Warminster).

—— (1981), *Egeria's Travels* (Jerusalem and Warminster; 2nd edn. 1999).

—— (1990), 'Jewish Holy Places and the Origins of Christian Pilgrimage', in Ousterhout 1990, 41–53.

WILLERS, D. (1990), *Hadrians panhellenisches Programm. Archäologische Beiträge zur Neugestaltung Athens durch Hadrian* (Basel).

WILLIAMS, C. K. (1969), 'Excavations at Corinth, 1968', *Hesperia* 38, 36–63.

—— (1987), 'The Refounding of Corinth: Some Roman Religious Attitudes', in Macready and Thompson 1987, 26–37.

—— (1989), 'A Re-evaluation of Temple E and the West End of the Forum of Corinth', in Walker and Cameron 1989, 156–62.

—— J.MacINTOSH, and J. E. FISHER (1974), 'Excavations at Corinth, 1973', *Hesperia* 43, 1–76.

—— and J. E. FISHER (1975), 'Corinth, 1974: Forum Southwest', *Hesperia* 44, 1–50.

—— and ZERVOS, O. (1984), 'Corinth 1983. The Route to Sicyon', *Hesperia* 53, 83–122.

—— —— (1990), 'Excavations at Corinth, 1989: The Temenos of Temple E', *Hesperia* 59, 325–69.

WILLIAMS, W. (1998), *Pilgrimage and Narrative in the French Renaissance* (Oxford).

—— (1999), ' "Rubbing Up Against Others": Montaigne on Pilgrimage' in Elsner and Rubiés 1999, 101–23.

WILSON, P., and P. MURRAY (2004), *Music & the Muse* (Oxford).

WIPSZYCKA, E. (1992), 'Le nationalisme a-t-il existé dans l' Égypte byzantine?' *Journal of Juristic Papyrology* 22, 83–128.

WISEMAN, J. (1979), 'Corinth and Rome I: 228 BC–AD 267.' *ANRW* 2.7.1, 438–548.

WOODS, D. (1991), 'The Date of the Translation of the Relics of SS. Andrew and Luke to Constantinople', *VChr* 45, 286–92.

WOOLF, G. (1994), 'Becoming Roman, Staying Greek: Culture, Identity and the Civilizing Process in the Roman East', *PCPhS* 40, 116–43.

—— (1997), 'The Roman Urbanization of the East', in S. Alcock (ed.), *The Early Roman Empire in the East* (Oxford), 1–14.

WÖRRLE, M. (1969), 'Die Lex Sacra von der Hallenstrasse (Inv. 1965, 20)', in Habicht (1969), 167–90.

YEGÜL, F. K. (1991), 'Roman Architecture in the Greek World' (Review of MacReady and Thompson 1987) *JRA* 4, 345–55.

YOYOTTE, J. (1960), 'Les pèlerinages dans l' Égypte ancienne', in *Sources orientale. 3: Pèlerinages* (Paris), 18 ff.

—— (1962), 'Études géographiques II. Les localités méridionales', *Revue d'Égyptologie* 104, 75–111.

ZACHER, C. (1976), *Curiosity and Pilgrimage* (Baltimore).

ZANKER, P. (1995), *Die Maske des Sokrates. Das Bild des Intellektuellen in der antiken Kunst* (Munich).

ZIEGENAUS, O. (1981), *Das Asklepieion. Teil 3: Die Kultbauten aus römischer Zeit an der Ostseite des heiligen Bezirks Altertümer von Pergamon XI, 3* (Berlin).

—— and G. DE LUCA (1968), *Das Asklepieion. Teil 1: Der südliche Temenosbezirk in hellenistischer und frührömischer Zeit Altertümer von Pergamon XI, 1* (Berlin).

—— —— (1975), *Das Asklepieion. Teil 2: Der nördliche Temenosbezirk und angrenzende Anlagen in hellenistischer und frührömischer Zeit Altertümer von Pergamon XI, 2* (Berlin).

Index